Microsoft® Official Academic Course

Microsoft Office: 2013 Edition

WILEY

EDITOR	Bryan Gambrel
PUBLISHER	Don Fowley
DIRECTOR OF SALES	Mitchell Beaton
EXECUTIVE MARKETING MANAGER	Chris Ruel
ASSISTANT MARKETING MANAGER	Debbie Martin
MICROSOFT STRATEGIC RELATIONSHIPS MANAGER	Gene Longo of Microsoft Learning eXperience
EDITORIAL PROGRAM ASSISTANT	Allison Winkle
SENIOR CONTENT MANAGER	Kevin Holm
SENIOR PRODUCTION EDITOR	Jill Spikereit
CREATIVE DIRECTOR	Harry Nolan
COVER DESIGNER	Tom Nery
TECHNOLOGY AND MEDIA	Wendy Ashenberg; Jennifer Welter
WRITERS	Walter Holland; Jennifer Smith, Microsoft MVP
EDITOR	Christopher Smith
TECHNICAL EDITORS	Lauren Mickol; Cathy Auclair
PROJECT MANAGER	Cheri White
PRODUCTION	American Graphics Institute; Avlade

This book was set in Adobe Garamond Pro and printed and bound by Courier/Kendallville. The covers were printed by Courier/Kendallville.

ISBN 978-0-470-13306-4

Printed in the United States of America

10 9 8 7 6 5 4 3 2 1

Foreword from the Publisher

Wiley's publishing vision for the Microsoft Official Academic Course series is to provide students and instructors with the skills and knowledge they need to use Microsoft technology effectively in all aspects of their personal and professional lives. Quality instruction is required to help both educators and students get the most from Microsoft's software tools and to become more productive. Thus our mission is to make our instructional programs trusted educational companions for life.

To accomplish this mission, Wiley and Microsoft have partnered to develop the highest quality educational programs for Information Workers, IT Professionals, and Developers. Materials created by this partnership carry the brand name "Microsoft Official Academic Course," assuring instructors and students alike that the content of these textbooks is fully endorsed by Microsoft, and that they provide the highest quality information and instruction on Microsoft products. The Microsoft Official Academic Course textbooks are "Official" in still one more way—they are the officially sanctioned courseware for Microsoft IT Academy members.

The Microsoft Official Academic Course series focuses on workforce development. These programs are aimed at those students seeking to enter the workforce, change jobs, or embark on new careers as information workers, IT professionals, and developers. Microsoft Official Academic Course programs address their needs by emphasizing authentic workplace scenarios with an abundance of projects, exercises, cases, and assessments.

The Microsoft Official Academic Courses are mapped to Microsoft's extensive research and job-task analysis, the same research and analysis used to create the Microsoft Office Specialist (MOS) exams. The textbooks focus on real skills for real jobs. As students work through the projects and exercises in the textbooks they enhance their level of knowledge and their ability to apply the latest Microsoft technology to everyday tasks. These students also gain resume-building credentials that can assist them in finding a job, keeping their current job, or in furthering their education.

The concept of life-long learning is today an utmost necessity. Job roles, and even whole job categories, are changing so quickly that none of us can stay competitive and productive without continuously updating our skills and capabilities. The Microsoft Official Academic Course offerings, and their focus on Microsoft certification exam preparation, provide a means for people to acquire and effectively update their skills and knowledge. Wiley supports students in this endeavor through the development and distribution of these courses as Microsoft's official academic publisher.

Joe Heider
General Manager and Senior Vice President

Preface

Welcome to the Microsoft Official Academic Course (MOAC) program for Microsoft Office 2013. MOAC represents the collaboration between Microsoft Learning and John Wiley & Sons, Inc. publishing company. Microsoft and Wiley teamed up to produce a series of textbooks that deliver compelling and innovative teaching solutions to instructors and superior learning experiences for students. Infused and informed by in-depth knowledge from the creators of Microsoft Office and Windows, and crafted by a publisher known worldwide for the pedagogical quality of its products, these textbooks maximize skills transfer in minimum time. Students are challenged to reach their potential by using their new technical skills as highly productive members of the workforce.

Because this knowledgebase comes directly from Microsoft, architect of the Office 2013 system and creator of the Microsoft Office Specialist (MOS) exams (www.microsoft.com/learning/mcp/mcts), you are sure to receive the topical coverage that is most relevant to students' personal and professional success. Microsoft's direct participation not only assures you that MOAC textbook content is accurate and current; it also means that students will receive the best instruction possible to enable their success on certification exams and in the workplace.

THE MICROSOFT OFFICIAL ACADEMIC COURSE PROGRAM

The *Microsoft Official Academic Course* series is a complete program for instructors and institutions to prepare and deliver great courses on Microsoft software technologies. With MOAC, we recognize that, because of the rapid pace of change in the technology and curriculum developed by Microsoft, there is an ongoing set of needs beyond classroom instruction tools for an instructor to be ready to teach the course. The MOAC program endeavors to provide solutions for all these needs in a systematic manner in order to ensure a successful and rewarding course experience for both instructor and student—technical and curriculum training for instructor readiness with new software releases; the software itself for student use at home for building hands-on skills, assessment, and validation of skill development; and a great set of tools for delivering instruction in the classroom and lab. All are important to the smooth delivery of an interesting course on Microsoft software, and all are provided with the MOAC program. We think about the model below as a gauge for ensuring that we completely support you in your goal of teaching a great course. As you evaluate your instructional materials options, you may wish to use the model for comparison purposes with available products.

Illustrated Book Tour

PEDAGOGICAL FEATURES

The MOAC courseware for Microsoft Office 2013 system are designed to cover all the learning objectives. Many pedagogical features have been developed specifically for Microsoft Official Academic Course programs. Unique features of our task-based approach include a Lesson Skills Matrix that correlates skills taught in each lesson to real-world business application, business case scenarios, and three levels of increasingly rigorous lesson-ending activities: Competency, Proficiency, and Mastery Assessment.

Presenting the extensive procedural information and technical concepts woven throughout the textbook raises challenges for the student and instructor alike. The Illustrated Book Tour that follows provides a guide to the rich features contributing to Microsoft Official Academic Course program's pedagogical plan. Following is a list of key features in each lesson designed to prepare students for success on the certification exams and in the workplace:

- Each lesson begins with a **Lesson Skill Matrix**. More than a standard list of learning objectives, the skill matrix correlates each software skill covered in the lesson to real-world application.

- Each lesson features a real-world **Business Case** scenario that places the software skills and knowledge to be acquired in a real-world setting.

- Every lesson opens with a **Software Orientation**. This feature provides an overview of the software features students will be working with in the lesson. The orientation will detail the general properties of the software or specific features, such as a ribbon or dialog box; and it includes a large, labeled screen image.

- Concise and frequent **Step-by-Step** instructions teach students new features and provide an opportunity for hands-on practice. Numbered steps give detailed, step-by-step instructions to help students learn software skills. The steps also show results and screen images to match what students should see on their computer screens.

- Illustrations: Screen images provide visual feedback as students work through the exercises. The images reinforce key concepts, provide visual clues about the steps, and allow students to check their progress.

- Key **Terms:** Important technical vocabulary is listed at the beginning of the lesson. When these terms are used later in the lesson, they appear in bold italic type with yellow highlighter and are defined. The Glossary contains all of the key terms and their definitions.

- Engaging point-of-use **Reader aids**, located throughout the lessons, tell students why this topic is relevant (*The Bottom Line*), provide students with helpful hints (*Take Note*), or show alternate ways to accomplish tasks (*Another Way*), or point out things to watch out for or avoid (*Troubleshooting*). Reader aids also provide additional relevant or background information that adds value to the lesson.

- **Workplace Ready.** These new features preview how the Microsoft Office 2013 system applications are used in real-world situations.

- Each lesson ends with a **Skill Summary** recapping the topics covered in the lesson.

- Knowledge **Assessment:** Provides a total of 20 questions from a mix of True/False, Fill-in-the-Blank, Matching or Multiple Choice testing students on concepts learned in the lesson.

- Competency, **Proficiency, and Mastery Assessment:** provide three progressively more challenging lesson-ending activities.

Online files: The student companion website contains the data files needed for each lesson. These files are indicated by the file download icon in the margin of the textbook.

LESSON FEATURES

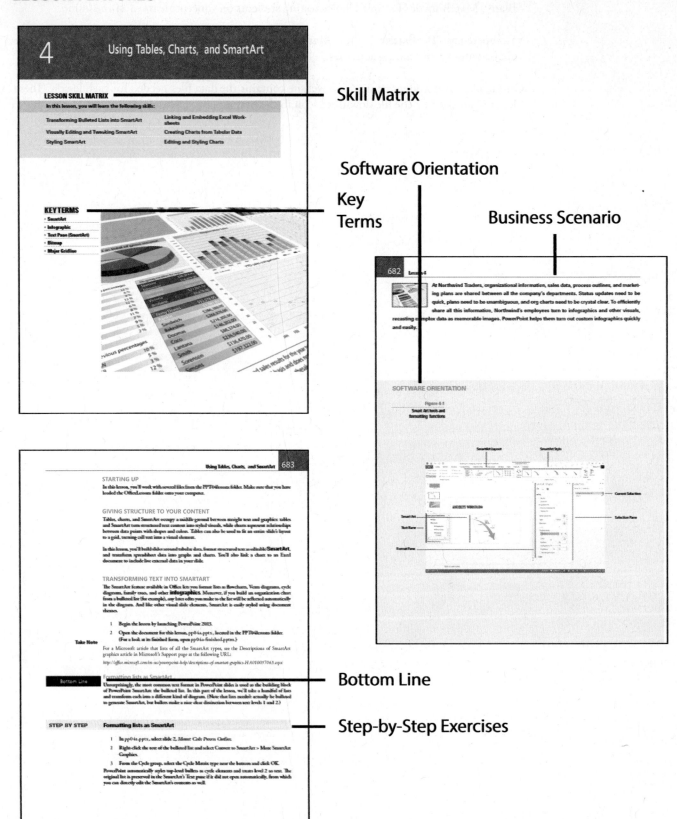

Skill Matrix

Software Orientation

Key Terms

Business Scenario

Bottom Line

Step-by-Step Exercises

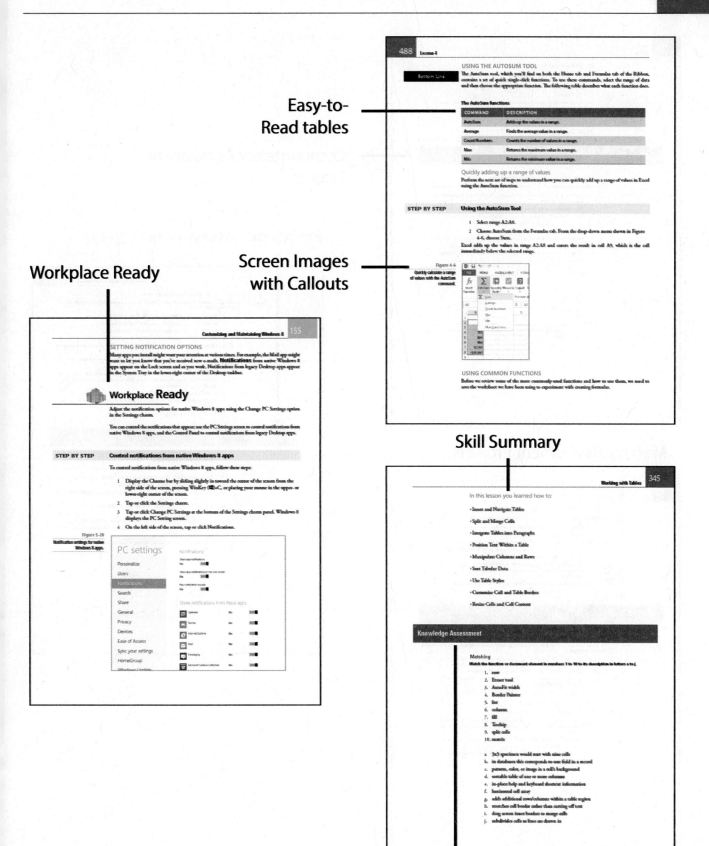

Easy-to-
Read tables

Screen Images
with Callouts

Workplace Ready

Skill Summary

Knowledge Assessment Questions

X

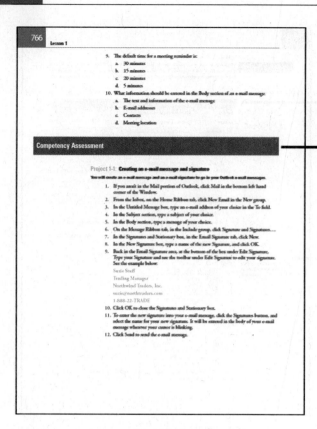

Compentency Assessment Projects

Proficiency Assessment Projects

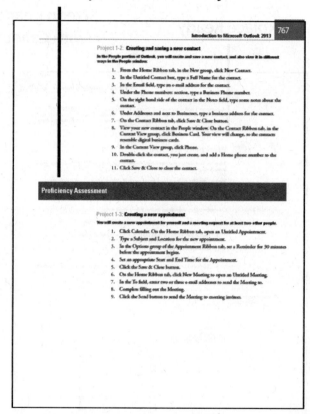

Mastery Assessment Projects

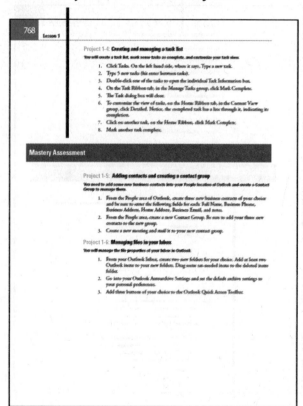

Conventions and Features Used in This Book

This book uses particular fonts, symbols, and heading conventions to highlight important information or to call your attention to special steps. For more information about the features in each lesson, refer to the Illustrated Book Tour section.

Bottom Line	This feature provides a brief summary of the material to be covered in the section that follows.
Take Note	Reader aids appear in shaded boxes found in your text. Take Note provides helpful hints related to particular tasks or topics.
ALT+TAB	A plus sign (+) between two key names means that you must press both keys at the same time. Keys that you are instructed to press in an exercise will appear in the font shown here.
Key Term	Key terms appear in bold italic.
Type My Name is	Any text you are asked to key appears in color.
Click OK	Any button on the screen you are supposed to click on or select will also appear in color.
BudgetWorksheet1	The names of data files will appear in bold and red for easy identification. These data files are available for download from the Student Companion Site (www.Wiley.com/college/Microsoft)

Instructor Support Program

The *Microsoft Official Academic Course* programs are accompanied by a rich array of resources that incorporate the extensive textbook visuals to form a pedagogically cohesive package. These resources provide all the materials instructors need to deploy and deliver their courses. Resources available online for download include:

• The **Instructor's Guide** contains Solutions to all the textbook exercises as well as chapter summaries and lecture notes. The Instructor's Guide and Syllabi for various term lengths are available from the Instructor's Book Companion site (www.wiley.com/college/microsoft).

• The **Solution Files** for all the projects in the book are available online from our Instructor's Book Companion site (www.wiley.com/college/microsoft).

• The **Test Bank** contains hundreds of questions organized by lesson in multiple-choice, true-false, short answer, and essay formats and is available to download from the Instructor's Book Companion site (www.wiley.com/college/microsoft). A complete answer key is provided.

• This title's test bank is available for use in Respondus' easy-to-use software. You can download the test bank for free using your Respondus, Respondus LE, or StudyMate Author software.

• Respondus is a powerful tool for creating and managing exams that can be printed to paper or published directly to Blackboard, WebCT, Desire2Learn, eCollege, ANGEL and other eLearning systems.

• **Comprehensive Projects:** Two comprehensive projects are provided on the Instructor's Book Companion Site for the Word, Excel, PowerPoint and Access units These projects cover topics from all lessons in the book up to that point. Solution files suitable for grading with OfficeGrader are also provided.

• PowerPoint **Presentations and Images**. A complete set of PowerPoint presentations is available on the Instructor's Book Companion site (www.wiley.com/college/microsoft) to enhance classroom presentations. Tailored to the text's topical coverage and Skills Matrix, these presentations are designed to convey key Microsoft Office concepts addressed in the text.

• All figures from the text are on the Instructor's Book Companion site (www.wiley.com/ college/ microsoft). You can incorporate them into your PowerPoint presentations, or create your own overhead transparencies and handouts.

• By using these visuals in class discussions, you can help focus students' attention on key elements of Windows Server and help them understand how to use it effectively in the workplace.

• **Wiley OfficeGrader** automated grading system allows you to easily grade student data files in Word, Excel, PowerPoint or Access format, against solution files. Save tens or hundreds of hours each semester with automated grading. More information on Wiley OfficeGrader is available from the Instructor's Book Companion site (www.wiley.com/college/microsoft).

• The **Student Data Files** are available online on both the Instructor's Book Companion Site and for students on the Student Book Companion Site.

- **Wiley Faculty Network:** When it comes to improving the classroom experience, there is no better source of ideas and inspiration than your fellow colleagues. The Wiley Faculty Network connects teachers with technology, facilitates the exchange of best practices, and helps to enhance instructional efficiency and effectiveness. Faculty Network activities include technology training and tutorials, virtual seminars, peer-to-peer exchanges of experiences and ideas, personal consulting, and sharing of resources. For details visit www.WhereFacultyConnect.com.

DREAMSPARK PREMIUM

FREE 3-YEAR MEMBERSHIP AVAILABLE TO QUALIFIED ADOPTERS!

DreamSpark Premium is designed to provide the easiest and most inexpensive way for schools to make the latest Microsoft developer tools, products, and technologies available in labs, classrooms, and on student PCs. DreamSpark Premium is an annual membership program for departments teaching Science, Technology, Engineering, and Mathematics (STEM) courses. The membership provides a complete solution to keep academic labs, faculty, and students on the leading edge of technology.

Software available through the DreamSpark Premium program is provided at no charge to adopting departments through the Wiley and Microsoft publishing partnership.

Contact your Wiley rep for details.

For more information about the DreamSpark Premium program, go to Microsoft's DreamSpark website

IMPORTANT WEB ADDRESSES AND PHONE NUMBERS

To locate the Wiley Higher Education Rep in your area, go to the following Web address and click on the "Contact Us " link at the top of the page.

www.wiley.com/college

Or Call the MOAC Toll Free Number: 1 + (888) 764-7001 (U.S. & Canada only).

To learn more about becoming a Microsoft Certified Professional and exam availability, visit www.microsoft.com/learning/mcp.

Student Support Program

STUDENT DATA FILES

All of the practice files that you will use as you perform the exercises in the book are available for download on our student companion site. By using the practice files, you will not waste time creating the samples used in the lessons, and you can concentrate on learning how to use Microsoft Office 2013. With the files and the step-by-step instructions in the lessons, you will learn by doing, which is an easy and effective way to acquire and remember new skills.

COPYING THE PRACTICE FILES

Your instructor might already have copied the practice files before you arrive in class. However, your instructor might ask you to copy the practice files on your own at the start of class. Also, if you want to work through any of the exercises in this book on your own at home or at your place of business after class, you may want to copy the practice files.

STEP BY STEP   **Copying the Practice Files**

OPEN Internet Explorer.

1. In Internet Explorer, go to the student companion site: www.wiley.com
2. Search for your book title in the upper right hand corner.
3. On the Search Results page, locate your book and click on the Visit the Companion Sites link.
4. Select Student Companion Site from the pop-up box.
5. From the menu, select the arrow next to Browse By Resource and select Student Data Files from the menu.
6. A new screen will appear.
7. On the File Download dialog box, select Save As to save the data files to your external drive (often called a ZIP drive or a USB drive or a thumb drive) or a local drive.
8. In the Save As dialog box, select a local drive in the left-hand panel that you'd like to save your files to; again, this should be an external drive or a local drive. Remember the drive name that you saved it to.

Acknowledgments

We'd like to thank the many instructors and reviewers who pored over the Microsoft Official Academic Course series design, outlines and manuscript, providing invaluable feedback in the service of quality instructional materials.

Erik Amerikaner, Oak Park Unified

Sue Bajt, Harper College

Gregory Ballinger, Miami-Dade College

Catherine Bradfield, DeVry University

DeAnnia Clements, Wiregrass Georgia Technical College

Mary Corcoran, Bellevue College

Andrea Cluff, Freemont High School

Caroline de Gruchy, Conestoga College

Janis DeHaven, Central Community College

Rob Durrance, East Lee County High School

Janet Flusche, Frenship High School

Greg Gardiner, SIAST

Debi Griggs, Bellevue College

Phil Hanney, Orem Junior High School

Dee Hobson, Richland College

Terri Holly, Indian River State College

Kim Hopkins, Weatherford College

Sandra Jolley, Tarrant County College

Joe LaMontagne, Davenport University

Tanya MacNeil, American InterContinental University

Donna Madsen, Kirkwood Community College

Lynn Mancini, Delaware Technical Community College

Edward Martin, Kingsborough Community College-City University of New York

Lisa Mears, Palm Beach State College

Denise Merrell, Jefferson Community and Technical College

Diane Mickey, Northern Virginia Community College

Robert Mike, Alaska Career College

Cynthia Miller, Harper College

Sandra Miller, Wenatchee Valley College

Mustafa Muflehi, The Sheffield College

Aditi Mukherjee, University of Florida—Gainesville

Linda Nutter, Peninsula College

Diana Pack, Big Sandy Community & Technical College

Bettye Parham, Daytona State College

Tatyana Pashnyak, Bainbridge State College

Kari Phillips, Davis Applied Technical College

Michelle Poertner, Northwestern Michigan College

Barbara Purvis, Centura College

Dave Rotherham, Sheffield Hallam University

Theresa Savarese, San Diego City College

Janet Sebesy, Cuyahoga Community College-Western

Lourdes Sevilla, Southwestern College

Elizabeth Snow, Southwest Florida College

Amy Stolte, Lincoln Land Community College

Dorothy Weiner, Manchester Community College

We would also like to thank the team at Microsoft Learning Xperiences (LeX), including Alison Cunard, Tim Sneath, Zubair Murtaza, Keith Loeber, Rob Linsky, Anne Hamilton, Wendy Johnson, Gene Longo, Julia Stasio, and Josh Barnhill for their encouragement and support in making the Microsoft Official Academic Course programs the finest academic materials for mastering the newest Microsoft technologies for both students and instructors.

Author Credits

JENNIFER SMITH

Thanks to James Senior, Chris Mayo, and the many Windows product managers for their useful assistance in gathering the information required for the Windows 8 section of this book. Thanks also to the teams at Avlade and at American Graphics Institute for their many contributions to this book.

Contents

PART IX: Microsoft® Publisher® 2013

Contents

PART I: MICROSOFT® WINDOWS® 8

PART II: INTERNET EXPLORER AND THE WEB

1 Surfing the Web 175

2   Sharing Device Settings and Content   211

PART III: MICROSOFT® WORD® 2013

1   Microsoft Word 2013 Jumpstart   253

2   Getting Started with Word 2013   271

5 Working with Tables 327

PART IV: MICROSOFT® EXCEL® 2013

1 Creating a Worksheet in Excel 2013 413

3   Using Formulas in Excel 2013   479

4   Working with Charts   509

5 Working with Data   539

PART V: MICROSOFT® POWERPOINT® 2013

2 Getting Started with PowerPoint 2013   645

3 Designing a Presentation   663

4   Using Tables, Charts, and SmartArt   681

PART VI: MICROSOFT® OUTLOOK® 2013

2 Getting Started with Microsoft Outlook 2013

PART VII: MICROSOFT® ONENOTE® 2013

1   Microsoft OneNote 2013 Jumpstart   797

PART VIII: MICROSOFT® ACCESS® 2013

1 Introduction to Microsoft Access 2013   837

2   Getting Started with Microsoft Access 2013   861

Contents

Microsoft Windows 8

LESSON SKILL MATRIX

In this lesson, you will learn the following skills:

How to sign into Windows

About Microsoft accounts and local accounts

How to use Windows 8 with a Mouse and Keyboard

How to find help when troubleshooting

How to shut down Windows 8

KEY TERMS

- **Lock Screen**
- **Sign in screen**
- **Start Screen**
- **Local accounts**
- **Hotspots**
- **WinKey**
- **Charms bar**
- **Desktop app**
- **Quick Link menu**
- **Sleep mode**
- **Hibernate mode**
- **Restart command**
- **Shut Down**

 Elaine recently purchased a new laptop running Windows 8. She needs to learn how to sign into a new account on her laptop and use the mouse and keyboard on the new operating system before she starts a new accounting position at Fabrikam.

SOFTWARE ORIENTATION

To use your Windows personal computer or tablet, you must be able to use Windows 8. Windows 8 is an operating system, which controls the way in which applications, also known as apps, interact with you, the user, and with other parts of the computer such as the display and keyboard, and with other connected devices, such as printers. After you log-in to Windows 8, you can access and manage your device.

Figure 1-1

Windows 8 Charms

SIGNING IN TO WINDOWS

When you start Windows 8, the default appearance is for it to display a **lock screen**. You'll need to sign-in to Windows in order to perform any tasks such as checking email or writing a document.

The sign-in process involves moving past the lock screen, selecting an account to use, and entering the password for that account.

Take Note While it's possible to avoid the sign-in process and jump directly to the Start screen if you set up a local account, this option is not advisable for most users. The sign-in process requires you to enter your password, and keeps unauthorized users from accessing your account. For this reason, it's advisable to always use the sign-in process.

Figure 1-2

The Windows Lock screen appears when you first start your computer.

Image used with permission of Microsoft

To sign-in to your computer and start using Windows 8, do any of the following from the Lock screen.

• **Use** your finger to swipe up the screen.

• **Click** your mouse anywhere on the screen.

• **Press** any key on your keyboard.

The **Sign In screen** appears; it will look like the one below and display an e-mail address below your name if you are signing in using a Microsoft account.

Figure 1-3

The Windows 8 sign in screen.

Diane Prescott
dprescott@agitraining.com

Image used with permission of Microsoft

Type your password and tap or click the arrow beside the password box to display the Windows 8 Start screen.

Take Note   If you're using a touch device, the on-screen touch keypad automatically appears so that you can type your password

UNDERSTANDING MICROSOFT ACCOUNTS AND LOCAL ACCOUNTS

Your account contains information about how you prefer your computer to operate, its appearance, along with the documents and applications you use. There are two types of accounts available with Windows 8. One option allows you to have your information shared between various computers you use with data backed-up over the Internet, the other is suitable if you only use computer and don't wish to have your data stored for you.

Microsoft accounts

 Workplace Ready

Use a Microsoft account to share your settings and important files in the cloud when you work on multiple devices.

Use a Microsoft account to share your settings and important files in the cloud when you work on multiple devices. Microsoft accounts are made up of an e-mail address registered with Microsoft and a required password. Microsoft accounts don't need to be from a Microsoft operated service. You can use your company email address or a personal email address from any provider. Yet all *hotmail.com*, *live.com*, and *outlook.com* e-mail addresses are automatically Microsoft accounts because Microsoft owns and manages these domains and e-mail addresses.

Take Note   You don't need a *hotmail.com*, *live.com*, or *outlook.com* e-mail address to have a Microsoft account. You can register any e-mail address as a Microsoft account.

When you sign in to Windows 8 using a Microsoft account, you are connecting your computer to Microsoft's computers in *the cloud*. These computers are operated by Microsoft for the purpose of backing up your data and sharing your data between different computers you might own. If you sign into Windows 8 on your desktop PC, Windows automatically synchronizes some settings, such as your picture, backgrounds, Internet Explorer history and favorites to and from the cloud. If you sign in to Windows 8 on another device, such as a tablet PC, using the same Microsoft account, the synchronized settings from your desktop computer appear on your tablet PC. Many Windows 8 native apps require that you sign in to Windows using a Microsoft account.

Local accounts

Local accounts are made up of a name rather than an e-mail address and a password, which is optional. There are two types of local accounts: administrator and standard. As you start working with Windows 8, the key concept for you to understand is that when you sign in to Windows 8 using a local account, you are signing in to just your PC, not the cloud. No synchronization happens when you sign in using a local account. Windows 8 remembers your computer's settings just like previous versions of Windows did, and these settings are connected to one specific computer.

If you use multiple Windows 8 devices and want your settings to travel with you between devices and you also want to use the Windows 8 native apps, use a Microsoft account.

Take Note   You can control the settings that Windows 8 synchronizes when you sign in using a Microsoft account.

STEP BY STEP   **Registering an existing e-mail address as a Microsoft account**

If you have a **hotmail.com, live.com**, or **outlook.com** e-mail address, you already have a registered Microsoft account and can jump ahead to the next section. If you don't have one of these e-mail addresses and you will want to register an existing e-mail address as a Microsoft account using the following steps:

1   Open a web browser such as Internet Explorer. Right-click or swipe up or down the page to make the address bar visible.

2   Type signup.live.com in the address bar and press Enter to display the Microsoft account signup form.

Figure 1-4

The form you complete to register an e-mail address as a Microsoft account.

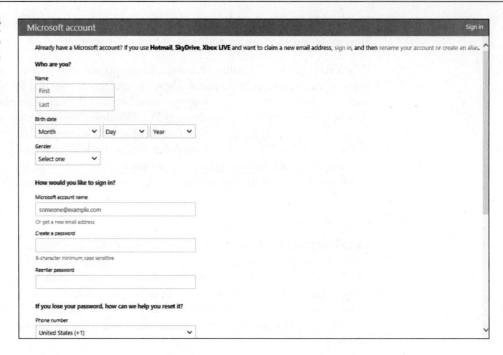

Figure 1-4

The form you complete to register an e-mail address as a Microsoft account.

3 Complete the form, supplying the e-mail address you want to use as your Microsoft account in the Microsoft account name text field.

Take Note Do not supply the password associated with the e-mail address; instead, make up a new password that you want to use to sign in to Windows 8 or any website where you will use your Microsoft account.

4 At the bottom of the form, tap or click the I accept button.

USING WINDOWS 8 WITH A MOUSE AND KEYBOARD

Windows 8 works well, regardless of whether you are using a touchscreen device or traditional keyboard, mouse or trackpad.

If you are using Windows 8 with a traditional mouse and keyboard, there are hundreds of mouse and keyboard shortcuts that can help you work more efficiently; you can find a complete list at *http://windows.microsoft.com/en-US/windows-8/keyboard-shortcuts*.

Workplace **Ready**

Use keyboard shortcuts to help you work more efficiently with tasks you perform the most often.

In this section, you'll learn about the shortcuts you are likely to use most often.

Understanding Corner Navigation

Microsoft has built "hotspots" into each of the corners of the Windows 8 Start screen that aid both mouse and touch users. To take advantage of the corner **"hotspots,"** you need to move the mouse to the corner of the screen, so the mouse pointer appears almost outside the screen edge. A portion of the pointer may disappear.

Getting back to the Start screen

To get back to the Start screen, open any app—from the Windows 8 Start screen. After you open an app, you can redisplay the Start screen by:

• Pressing the Windows logo key (■), also known as the **WinKey**.

• Pointing the mouse at the lower-left corner of the screen until a small image of the Start screen appears, and then click it.

Figure 1-5

Click the image of the Start screen in the lower-left corner of your monitor to redisplay the Start screen.

Image used with permission of Microsoft

You also can display the Start screen from the Charms bar which appears along the right side of your display. You can display the Charms bar along the right side of the screen by dragging your mouse down or swiping across the right edge of the screen then click Start to return to the Start screen.

Take Note If you are viewing the Start screen when you use any of these shortcuts, you can switch back to the last app you were viewing. Pressing the WinKey (■) switches you back and forth between the Start screen and the last app you viewed.

Your touch device may also have a Windows logo key (■) that you can press to redisplay the Start screen.

Displaying the Charms bar

You can use the Charms bar to perform a search on your computer, to share information between Windows 8 native apps, to display the Start screen, to connect hardware on your computer to Windows 8 native apps, or to display settings available for Windows 8 native apps or settings available for Desktop apps.

To display the **Charms bar**, shown in the figure, do one of the following:

Figure 1-6

The Charms bar appears on the right side of your screen.

- Press WinKey (▦)+C

- Point the mouse in the lower-right or upper-right corner of the screen. Remember that you need to move the mouse to the corner of the screen, so the mouse pointer appears outside the screen edge.

You can then point the mouse at each charm on the Charms bar and click to select the appropriate charm.

You also can use the following keyboard shortcuts to directly open a Charm:

Workplace Ready

Use shortcuts to efficiently access useful functionality in Windows 8, which you can use to change settings, connect devices, share information, or search.

- WinKey (▦)+I opens the Settings charm

- WinKey (▦)+K opens the Devices charm

- WinKey (▦)+H opens the Share charm

- WinKey (▦)+Q opens the Search pane

SWITCHING AMONG OPEN APPS

The Desktop is an app

In earlier editions of Windows, the Desktop represented the operating system, and users did all their work from the Desktop. All programs (apps) required the Desktop to function.

Windows 8 introduces a new kind of app that doesn't need the Desktop to run. These Windows 8 native apps function in much the same way other computer programs function, each with their own set of commands you use to accomplish what you want. The Windows 8 native apps don't need the traditional Desktop you used in earlier editions of Windows.

Once you understand that Windows 8 supports two kinds of apps (those that need the Desktop and those that don't), you'll find it easy to visualize the Desktop as an app, with its own set of commands that you use to control it. The Desktop has the distinction of being the only app that can run other apps. You can open multiple programs on the Desktop, just as users have done in earlier editions of Windows. But, because the Desktop is an app, you must use the Desktop techniques described in Lesson 3, "Working with Desktop Apps" to switch among open Desktop apps. You cannot use the techniques described in this section. When you switch among open apps as described in this section, the Desktop is a single app that you can display, even if multiple Desktop programs are running.

To switch among open Windows 8 apps, including the **Desktop app** , do one of the following from any running app:

- Press WinKey ()+Tab

- Slide the mouse pointer to the upper-left corner of the screen; the last app you viewed appears. Slide the mouse down the left side of the screen to display the Running Apps bar.

Take Note   No official name seems to exist for the bar that appears down the left side of your screen when you perform any of the actions listed above. Since it displays a list of apps currently running on your computer, in this lesson, we'll refer to it as the Running Apps bar.

Once the Running Apps bar appears, click the app you want to display.

Figure 1-7

The Running Apps bar appears on the left side of the screen.

Photos used with permission from Microsoft Images and clip art used with permission of Microsoft.

Take Note   Alt+Tab works as it did in earlier editions of Windows. You can press and hold Alt as you press Tab to cycle through all the running apps. Release Alt when you see the app you want to switch to.

The **Quick Link menu** displays a wide range of useful commands, especially for power users. With it, you can switch to the Desktop or open Desktop apps such as the Device Manager, Control Panel, Disk Manager, Computer Management Console, Task Manager, File Explorer, etc.

Workplace **Ready**

Quickly switch to the Desktop or Desktop apps that you can use to manage your computer or explore files on your hard drive.

Figure 1-8

A useful context menu to help you quickly navigate to commonly used applications.

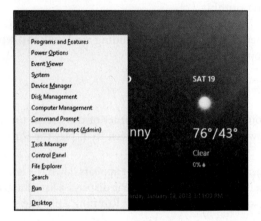

You can easily display the Quick Link menu by pressing WinKey (⊞)+X. To display it using your mouse, follow these steps:

1   From any app or on the Start screen, slide the mouse to the lower-left corner of your screen.

2   When the image of the last app you used appears, right-click it.

Closing an app

Closing a Windows 8 native app is not as obvious as closing a program that runs on the Desktop. You won't find a red X in the upper-right corner of Windows 8 native apps. While you don't have to close Windows 8 native apps most users, through force of habit, want to close them. These apps run in the background on your computer and don't take up as much memory as legacy programs do. You can do any of the following to close an app:

• On your keyboard, press Alt+F4.

• Using your mouse, do one of the following:

• Display the Running Apps bar on the Start screen as described in the section "Switching among open apps," then tap and hold, right-click a tile and tap, or click Close.

Figure 1-9

Display the Running Apps bar and tap and hold or right-click an app to close it.

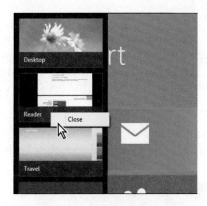

Photos used with permission from Microsoft
Images and clip art used with permission of Microsoft.

• While viewing the app, move the mouse pointer to the top of the screen until it changes to a hand. Then, click and drag down to the bottom of your screen. The app will minimize as you drag; when you drag it off the bottom of screen, the app closes.

Figure 1-10

Drag from the top of the app to the bottom to close it.

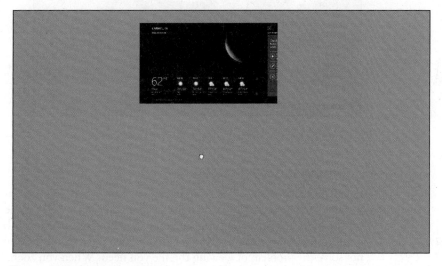

Photos used with permission from Microsoft

Take Note As mentioned previously, the Desktop app is in a category of its own. You can use either mouse technique to close the Desktop app, but the keyboard shortcut prompts you to shut down your computer. You will learn about shutting down your computer later in this lesson.

Displaying the Desktop

While the Windows 8 Desktop app is different from the desktop in earlier editions of Windows, the Windows 8 Desktop will be more familiar to Windows users than the Start Screen.

To display the Desktop app, you can:

• Press WinKey (⊞)+D.

• Click the Desktop tile on the Start screen.

Locking your computer

If you want to walk away from your computer, yet you don't want to shut it down, you can lock it. Locking the computer displays the lock screen shown at the beginning of this lesson and leads you to the sign in screen, where you must re-enter your password to sign in to your computer. You can lock your computer using either of the following methods:

● Press WinKey (⊞)+L.

● Click your name or picture on the Start screen and then click Lock.

Photos used with permission from Microsoft

Zooming the Start screen

If you're not working on a wide-screen monitor, or if you are and you have lots of programs installed on your computer, you'll notice that you can't see all the tiles representing your programs on the Start screen, unless you swipe or use the scroll bar at the bottom of the Start screen to scroll to the right. Although you can reorganize the tiles on the Start screen, reorganizing might not solve the problem of viewing the tile you need. When you zoom out, the Start screen displays many small tiles. You can click an area of the screen to zoom in to that area so that you can click a tile and launch an app.

Figure 1-12

The Start screen when zoomed out.

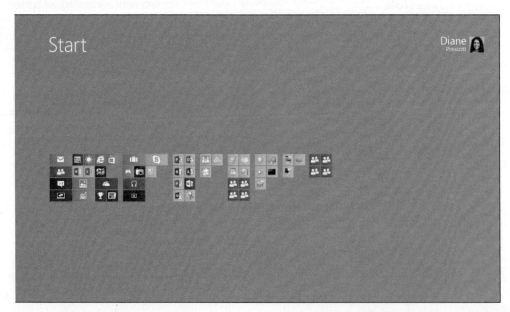

You can zoom out or in the Start screen using any of the following techniques:

- Press Ctrl+minus (-) to zoom out and view a larger number of smaller tiles or Ctrl+plus (+) to view a smaller number of larger tiles.

- Press and hold Ctrl as you use the scroll wheel on your mouse.

- Click the Zoom button in the lower-right corner of the Start screen.

Figure 1-13

You can click the Zoom button to zoom out and view many small tiles on the Windows Start screen.

STEP BY STEP   **Getting Help**

If you run into a problem using Windows 8, you can use web-based help or you can search the Desktop Windows Help and Support app using a search word or phrase to view a list of links to related Help articles.

To use web-based support:

1   Display the Charms bar.

2   Choose the Settings charm.

3   At the top of the pane, choose Help.

4   Select a topic, and the Windows 8 native app for Internet Explorer opens the Help page.

Figure 1-14

Web-based topics
you can read using
Windows 8 native help.

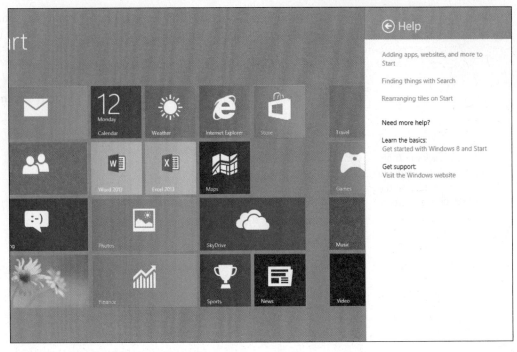

Images and clip art used with permission of Microsoft.

Using the Desktop Windows Help and Support app, you can control the search by supplying a search keyword or phrase. For example, you can search for help in using the built-in Windows word processing program, WordPad.

Take Note   The fewer words you supply as your search criteria, the more results Help and Support will display.

STEP BY STEP   **Getting Help and Support**

The Windows Help and Support app runs as a Desktop program, but you launch it from the Start screen:

1   Display the Start screen.

2   Type **Help** to display a list of help sources.

Figure 1-15

Any apps, settings, or file
names containing the word
"help" appear in a list.

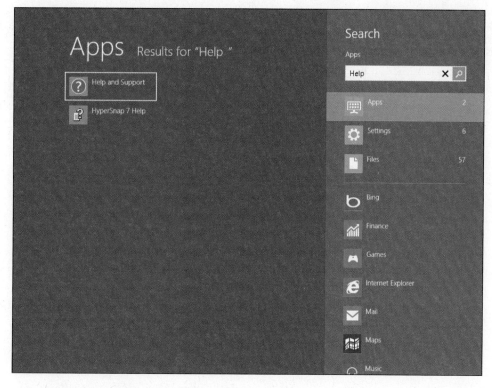

3   Tap or click **Help and Support**.

4   Type **word processing**, in the text field at the top of the window and press **Enter**, or tap or click the **magnifying glass** button Windows Help and Support displays a list of links to articles that relate to the phrase you typed.

Figure 1-16

Type a keyword or phrase for
which you want to search in
the text field at the top of the
Help and Support window.

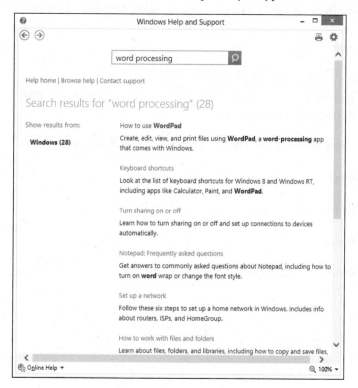

1   Click or tap a link that seems relevant to display the article.

Figure 1-17

A typical article in the Windows Help and Support app.

Take Note   You can also browse Help topics without searching. Tap or click the Browse Help link just below the Search text field to display the Help table of contents, which contains a series of topic links. Tap or click a link to see additional links related to that topic. As you click each link, your search narrows. Eventually, Windows Help and Support displays an article.

Keep in mind that if you are using Windows 8.1 you can access Help directly from the Search Charm.

SHUTTING DOWN WINDOWS 8

Windows 8's default shut down and start up processes are different from those of all previous editions of Windows.

When you shut down a desktop computer, you'll see three choices:

• Sleep

• Shut Down

• Restart

Laptop and tablet computers may also display a "hibernate" option.

What's the difference between sleep, hibernate, restart, and shut down?

Sleep mode is a power-saving state. In Sleep mode, also called Standby mode, power is withheld from non-essential components. A computer can quickly resume operation, typically in seconds, when you wake it from Sleep mode, usually by moving your mouse or possibly by touching the power button on the computer. Once it awakens, you'll find everything exactly as it was when you put the computer to sleep—all open programs and running apps will be just where they were. You can think of a computer in Sleep mode in the same way you think of a DVD player that you have paused: both devices immediately stop what they are doing and start almost immediately when you tell them to start. The one danger you face from using Sleep mode on your computer comes from the potential for an external power failure. If power is cut off from your computer, the sleep state is lost. You won't be able to wake your computer; instead, you'll need to restart it. Because of the potential for power failure, you should save data in open programs before you put your computer to sleep. That way, you won't lose any information due to a power failure.

Hibernate mode is also a power-saving state, designed primarily for laptop computers. Sleep mode puts your computer's state (open programs, settings, etc.) in memory, while Hibernate mode saves your computer's state to a file on your hard disk, and then turns off your computer. Hibernate mode uses less power than sleep mode and restores your computer to an awake state fairly quickly, typically when you touch the Power button on the computer; when your computer wakes up, things will be just the way they were when you put the computer in Hibernate mode.

The **Restart command** does not attempt to save your computer's state; instead, it closes all open programs then temporarily powers off the machine and immediately powers it on again. The Restart process essentially clears everything out of your computer's memory and does not attempt to save your computer's state to your hard drive. Restarting your computer can be a useful problem-solving technique if your computer starts misbehaving

When you use the **Shut Down command**, you essentially turn off the computer so that it uses no electricity. Windows does not try to retain any record of open programs or files in memory or on your hard drive. Instead, Windows assumes that you will close all your programs and save all your work before you shut down the computer. If you don't, the Shut Down command closes your programs for you, without saving your work. Since shutting down a computer essentially eliminates the computer's use of power, a power failure has no effect on the computer, and you won't lose any work. At the same time, when you turn your computer back on, it will need to go through its startup process, which takes more time than awakening a computer from either Sleep or Hibernate mode.

Windows 8's Shut Down command performs the same function that hibernating performed in previous editions. Windows Help and Support refers to this behavior as "fast startup" and describes fast startup as follows:

"Fast startup is a setting that helps your PC start up faster after shutdown. Windows does this by saving system info to a file upon shutdown. When you start your PC again, Windows uses that system info to resume your PC instead of restarting it."

Essentially, when you shut down a Windows 8 computer, the operating system performs a hybrid shutdown, closing all user sessions, then copying anything that is still running in RAM (primarily, the core of the operating system) onto the hard drive, and finally turning off the system hardware. When Windows 8 starts up after a hybrid shutdown, it performs an abbreviated startup. After starting the computer's hardware, Windows 8 reloads its core from the hard drive, picking up right from where it left off. Starting a powered-off computer that uses Windows 8 is typically much faster than starting a powered-off computer using earlier editions of Windows.

Take Note   Since Windows 8 uses the Shut Down command differently than earlier editions of Windows, you might run into trouble trying to get into your computer's BIOS using traditional techniques such as tapping F2 while the computer starts up. You might need to contact your computer's manufacturer to find out how to bypass the Windows 8 startup process to get into the BIOS.

To shut down or restart your computer, or to put it to sleep, you can start the Desktop app and then press Alt+F4 to display this dialog box and choose an option from the list.

Figure 1-18

Select an option to shut down or restart your computer or put it to sleep.

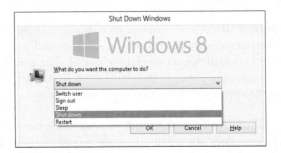

STEP BY STEP   **Shut down, restart, or put your computer to sleep**

Follow these step to shut down, restart, or put your computer to sleep:

1   Press **WinKey** (■)+**C** to display the Charms bar.

2   Click or use the arrows keys on the keyboard to highlight and then select the **Settings** charm.

Take Note   To directly display the Settings charm, press WinKey (■)+I.

3   Click the **Power** button.

4   Click a choice.

Figure 1-19

Select an option from the
Power button, available on the
Settings charm.

What you learned in this lesson

- How to sign into Windows

- About Microsoft accounts and local accounts

- How to use Windows 8 with a Mouse and Keyboard

- How to find help when troubleshooting

- How to shut down Windows 8

Bottom Line

This chapter showed you how to set up accounts, lock and shut down your computer, and access fundamental controls such as settings, help, and use connected devices.

Knowledge Assessment

True / False

Circle T if the statement is true or F if the statement is false.

T F 1. You need to have a Microsoft operated email account to register a new account with Windows 8

T F 2. A Microsoft account lets you sync your files and settings between devices.

T F 3. A Local account can be shared between devices, as long as you use the same username and password combination.

T F 4. A desktop app and a native app are functionally the same.

T F 5. You can use the Quick Link menu to open Desktop apps.

T F 6. You need to close native apps because they consume too much memory.

T F 7. You cannot zoom the Start screen in or out, you can only scroll left and right.

T F 8. There is no difference between putting your computer into sleep and hibernate mode, sleep mode is for a desktop and hibernate is for a laptop.

T F 9. Locking your computer powers your computer off so no one else can use it.

T F 10. You can shut down your computer from the Charms bar.

Multiple Choice

Select the best response for the following statements.

1. What are the two kinds of apps that Windows 8 can run?
   a. Desktop apps and Charm apps.
   b. Native apps and Desktop apps.
   c. Native apps and Windows apps.

2. What is a unique feature of the desktop app?
   a. The desktop is the only app that can run other apps.
   b. The desktop app can only run native apps.
   c. The desktop app can only run desktop apps.
   d. The desktop is the only location where you can access Clippy, a virtual assistant.

3. How do you display the Charms bar?
   a. Point the mouse in the lower-left corner of the screen.
   b. Press WinKey+B
   c. Press WinKey+C

4. Name two of the Charms on the Charms bar.
   a. Settings and Devices
   b. Share and Save
   c. Search and Launch
   d. Save and Search

5. Name one way to cycle through Windows 8 apps.
   a. Press WinKey+Spacebar
   b. Press Alt+Tab
   c. Press WinKey+Shift
   d. Slide the mouse pointer to the lower-left corner of the screen.

6. How do you display the Start screen only using the keyboard?
   a. Press Ctrl+W
   b. Press WinKey+Shift
   c. Press WinKey

7. How can you display the Quick Link menu using your mouse or a shortcut?
   a. WinKey+Q
   b. Slide the mouse to the lower-right corner of your screen and right-click the image of the app
   c. WinKey+X
   d. Slide the mouse to the center of the screen, and click WinKey+Q

8. How can you close an app using the keyboard?
   a. Press Ctrl+F2
   b. Press Alt+F4
   c. Press WinKey+C

9. How do you lock your computer?
   a. Press WinKey+M
   b. Click your name or picture on the Start screen and click Lock.
   c. Hold the WinKey and right-click, then click the Lock icon.

10. How do you launch the Help and Support application?
    a. Return to the desktop and press WinKey+C to launch Clippy, a virtual assistant.
    b. From the Start Screen, type Help and choose Help and Support then enter a query.
    c. From the Charms bar, select the Help icon and then enter a query.

Competency Assessment

Project 1-1: Help and Support

1. Access the Start screen, and then type Help and choose Help and Support.
2. Search for Help on Signing In.
3. Search for or locate information on creating a strong password.

Project 1-2: Hibernate Mode

1. Open the desktop app.
2. Press Alt+F4 to display the Shut Down options dialog box.
3. Sleep or Hibernate your computer.
4. After your computer is in sleep or hibernate mode, wake your computer and log in.

Proficiency Assessment

Project 1-3: Changing the Password

1. Change the password of your main user account.
2. Lock your computer, and then sign in using your new password.

Project 1-4: Switch between running apps

1. Switch between running apps in two different ways: Use WinKey+Tab to access and then switch to another running app.
2. After you have switched apps, use Alt+Tab to cycle through your other running apps.

Mastery Assessment

Project 1-5: Access Quick Link

1. Access the Quick Link menu and open the Control Panel.
2. Change your desktop background to an image, and change your screen resolution.

Project 1-6: Create more then one user

1. Create a second and third user account on your computer; one that is a local account and a second that is a Microsoft account with admin privileges.
2. Logout and then sign as each user
3. Sign into your main user account again.

LESSON SKILL MATRIX

In this lesson, you will learn the following skills:

Navigate on the Start screen

Work with tiles

Search your computer

Reorganize the Start Screen

Work with the Charms bar

KEY TERMS

- **Panning**
- **Hot spots**
- **Tiles**
- **Live tiles**
- **Windows legacy apps**
- **Pinning**
- **Unpinning**

Simon recently upgraded his laptop to Windows 8, while working on a major project at Fabrikam, Inc., a real estate agency. He needs to learn how to search his computer to locate all of his existing project files, and reorganize the Start Screen so he can manage the project efficiently.

SOFTWARE ORIENTATION

The Windows 8 start screen is your starting point for working with apps and your device.

Figure 2-1

Windows 8
Start Screen

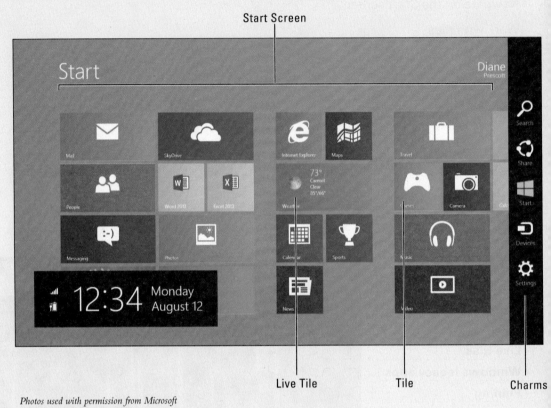

Photos used with permission from Microsoft

STARTING UP

You will not need to work with any files for this lesson.

REVIEWING NAVIGATION

The Start screen was designed to accommodate users of touch devices, but those who are using a mouse and keyboard can still find their way around the Start screen. For common mouse and keyboard shortcuts you can use with Windows 8, refer to Lesson 1, "Getting Started with Windows 8."

In this lesson, we'll begin with a short review of navigation techniques. The following table lists some common actions you'll take while using Windows 8, along with their mouse, keyboard, and touch equivalents.

Take Note   Blank boxes in the table below indicate that an equivalent action could not be found.

Action	Mouse	Keyboard	Touch
Choosing	Click	Press Enter	Tap when using the Start screen or a Windows 8 native app; double-tap when using the Desktop app
Open any app (including the Desktop)	From the Windows Start screen, click the app		From the Windows Start screen, tap the app
Display the App bar, which contains commands and options for a Windows 8 native app	Right-click anywhere on the screen	Press WinKey (⊞)+Z	Drag up slightly from the bottom of the screen
Display the Start screen while working in an app (including the Desktop app)	Slide the mouse into the upper- or lower-right corner to display the Charms bar, and then click Start	Press WinKey (⊞)	From the right edge of the screen, swipe to the left slightly to display the Charms bar; then tap the Start button
Display a list of all apps installed on the computer	From the Start screen, right-click to display the Apps bar at the bottom of the screen; then click All Apps	From the Start screen, press WinKey (⊞)+Z and then press Enter	Drag up slightly from the bottom of the screen and then tap All Apps
Scroll horizontally (also called **panning**) from one side of the Start screen to the other	Use your mouse's scroll wheel	Click the arrow keys or drag the scroll box at the bottom of the screen	Slide your finger from left to right or from right to left
Scroll vertically in legacy apps	Use your mouse's scroll wheel	Use the arrow keys to scroll one line at a time or the Page Up or Page Down keys to scroll one screen at a time	Slide your finger up the page to scroll down and down the page to scroll up
Display the Charms bar	Slide your mouse to the top- or bottom-right corner of your screen	Press WinKey (⊞)+C	Swipe in from the right edge of the screen
Switch apps	Slide the mouse pointer to the upper-left corner of the screen. When the last app you viewed appears, slide the mouse down the left side of the screen to display the Running Apps bar shown in the figure	Press WinKey (⊞)+Tab	From the left edge of the screen, swipe your finger to the right slightly and then back again to the edge to display the Running Apps bar, making a loop with your finger

Action	Mouse	Keyboard	Touch
Zoom the Start screen	Click the Zoom box in the lower-right corner of the Start screen	Press Ctrl+Plus sign to zoom in, or Ctrl+Minus sign to zoom out	Pinch your fingers together to zoom out; pinch them out to zoom in
Display the Quick Link menu	From any app or on the Start screen, slide the mouse to the lower left corner of your screen. When the image of the last app you used appears, right-click	Press WinKey (⊞)+X	
Using the Desktop app or a legacy program, display a shortcut menu	Right-click	Press Shift+F10	Tap and hold
Close a Windows 8 native app	Drag the mouse pointer down from the top of the screen to the bottom	Press Alt+F4*	Drag your finger down from the top of the screen to the bottom
Shut down your computer	Place the mouse pointer in the upper- or lower-right corner of the screen to display the Charms bar. Click the Settings charm, click the Power button, and then click an option	Display the Desktop App Using Alt+D. Then, Press Alt+F4 while viewing the Desktop App. From the Start Screen, press the Windows Logo Key (Windows Key Image)+I to display the Settings Charm; then press tab and the Arrow Keys until you highlight power. Then, press Enter to choose an option	Swipe in from the right edge of the screen to display the Charms bar. Tap the Settings charm, tap the Power button, and then tap an option

* The keyboard shortcut works for all apps, except the Desktop app; if you use the keyboard shortcut Alt+F4 while viewing the Desktop app, Windows 8 will prompt you to shut down your computer.

Take Note   Microsoft has encouraged hardware manufacturers to introduce their own touch gestures; to find out whether your device supports additional gestures, go to your device manufacturer's website.

Corner navigation

The Windows 8 Start screen uses the corners of the display as "**hot spots**" for your finger or your mouse, with keyboard shortcuts available for each corner. Each corner has a function; remembering the function will help you immeasurably when navigating in Windows 8.

- The upper- or lower-right corner displays the Charms bar.

- The upper-left corner controls the display of the Running Apps bar.

- The lower-left corner controls the display of a handy context menu.

Take Note   Be aware that the corner hot spots are very close to the edge of your screen. To access a hot spot with your mouse, you might need to move the pointer almost outside the screen.

Redisplaying the Start screen

Although we explained how to redisplay the Start screen in the table shown in the preceding section, it bears repeating, since you tend to start everything from the Start screen. If you're using a keyboard and mouse to navigate Windows 8, you can most quickly redisplay the Start screen by pressing the WinKey (⊞) on the keyboard. If you're using a touch device, swipe left from the right edge of the screen to display the Charms bar, then tap the Start button.

Take Note   Repeatedly pressing WinKey (⊞) cycles between the Start screen and the last app you were viewing.

SEARCHING

You can easily perform searches on your computer in Windows 8 in a couple of different ways. First, you can start typing while viewing the Start screen. For example, if you've installed Microsoft Office and you would like to run Microsoft Excel. While viewing the Start screen, start typing Excel. As you type, Windows displays the Search bar on the right side of the screen, and programs that match your search criteria on the left side of the screen. To run a program that appears in the search results list, tap, click it, or use the arrow keys on the keyboard to highlight it and press Enter.

Figure 2-2

To find a program you want to run, start typing its name while viewing the Start screen.

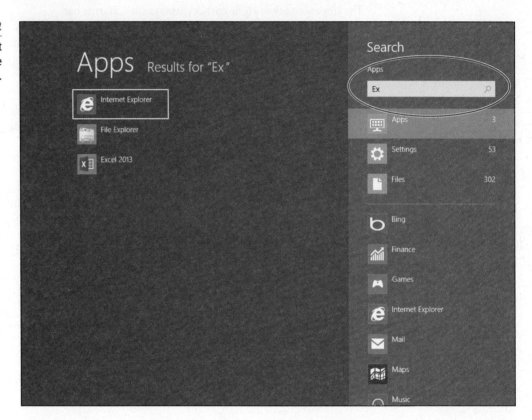

By default, when you type on the Start screen, Windows searches for apps. But the Search charm helps you narrow your search by enabling you to search for apps, settings, or files. These choices appear in the Search charm's Search bar on the right side of the screen. You can start typing, let Windows 8 search for an app, and when the Search bar appears, click Settings or Files to change the type of search.

Figure 2-3

Using the Search bar, you can narrow your search.

Using touch gestures or a mouse, you can select a search category if you display the Charms bar and select the Search charm, then select the search category from the Search bar. You can also use any of the following three keyboard shortcuts to specify a search category:

- WinKey (⊞)+Q searches for apps

- WinKey (⊞)+W searches for settings

- WinKey (⊞)+F searches for files

STEP BY STEP   To use the Search charm and search for files

1   Display the Search bar for files by pressing **WinKey** (⊞)+**F** or by selecting the **Search** charm from the Charms bar and then tapping or clicking **Files** at the top of the Search bar.

2   In the Search box at the top of the Search bar, type the first few letters of the file for which you want to search. Possible files appear below the search box.

3   If the file you want to open doesn't appear in the list, type a few more letters.

4   When the file appears, tap or click it to open it.

Figure 2-4

Using the File search charm, search results appear below the Search box.

STEP BY STEP   **Typing on the Start screen**

Do you have to specify the type of search you want if you are searching for something other than an app? Well, yes and no. Although Windows searches for apps by default, you can type on the Start screen and then change the type of search after Windows displays the Search bar.

   1   While viewing the Start screen, type a couple letters of the file name (such as "Ge" of Gettysburg Address, in this example).

   2   When the Search bar appears, select the type of search you really meant—Settings or Files. Windows 8 searches again, this time showing names that contain the letters you typed and match the type of search you selected.

   3   If the file doesn't appear, type a few more letters.

   4   Results appear on the left side of the screen. Tap or click one to open it.

Figure 2-5

You can type a search string on the Start screen and then specify the type of search without using the Charms bar.

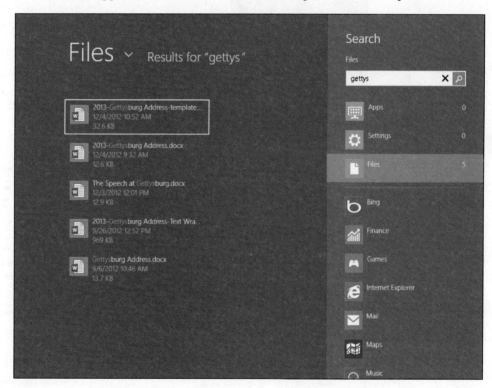

If you are using Windows 8.1 you have additional search options. You can select the type of file you are looking for directly beneath the Search heading, as well as the ability to click on the magnifying glass icon to see a full search result page.

Figure 2-6

In Windows 8.1 you have additional search options.

Figure 2-7

Click on the Magnifying Glass to see a full result page in Windows 8.1

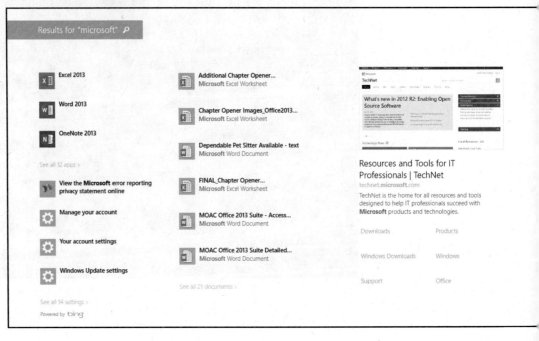

WORKING WITH TILES

The Start screen contains **tiles** that represent the apps you run. You can think of tiles as the desktop icons you used in earlier editions of Windows to run programs. If you were concerned with icon organization in earlier editions of Windows, you could drag your icons around to place them where you wanted, pin them to the Windows task bar or the top of the Start menu, and even place them in folders on the Windows Start menu.

In Windows 8, you can also control and organize tiles. The tiles that represent Windows 8 native apps also display updated information on the Start screen—a phenomenon called **live tile**. Now, you have several ways that you can control tile behavior and the appearance of the Windows 8 Start screen to make it reflect the way you work.

Customize how your Start Screen looks in order to work most efficiently. Organize the apps you use the most at the center of the screen, and move apps you use less frequently off to the side.

Setting tile options

Change options for tiles you use the most and least. Unpin apps you rarely use, and make pins you use frequently a larger size.

To set the options for a tile, display the options by right-clicking the tile or, on touch devices, you can display a tile's options by dragging the tile down slightly until a checkmark appears above the upper-right corner of the tile, then release the tile. The options appear at the bottom of the Start screen, and a checkmark appears in the tile you selected. In addition, the options you see depend on whether you select a Windows 8 native app tile or a legacy program tile.

Take Note   You can hide tile options by right-clicking the tile or dragging the tile down slightly (swiping) so that the checkmark disappears and then release the app.

For Windows 8 native apps, you can select any of the options shown in the following list.

Option	Function
Unpin from the Start screen	The app remains on your computer and you can still run it; you simply won't see a tile for it on the Start screen. For details on running an app that doesn't appear on the Start screen, see the next section.
Uninstall the app	This option removes the app from your computer and from the Start screen.
Control the size of the tile on the Start screen	This option allows you to resize your apps depending on organization or importance.
Tap or click the Turn Live Tile Off option	For tiles that can display updated information, this option makes the tile stop displaying that information.

 ## Workplace **Ready**

Turn off Live Tiles that could contain sensitive information that you do not want your co-workers to see, particularly if you regularly share your screen. Live tiles can display images from your connected accounts, such as photos and the contents of Facebook messages.

Figure 2-8

The options you can set for a Windows 8 native app. This Start screen shows some of the new tile size options available for Windows 8.1

Photos used with permission from Microsoft

For legacy apps, the ones that run on the Desktop app, you can select any of the options listed in the following table.

Option	Function
Unpin from Start	The app remains on your computer and you can still run it; you simply won't see a tile for it on the Start screen. For details on running an app that doesn't appear on the Start screen, see the next section.
Pin to taskbar	Pin an icon for this app to the Desktop taskbar so that you can run the app directly from the Desktop.
Open a new window	This option enables you to run a second instance of a program that's already running.
Run as administrator	This option enables a user logged in using a standard local account to run a program using administrator level privileges.
Open file location	This option switches to the Desktop and launches File Explorer, displaying the folder containing the file used to run the program.

Workplace **Ready**

Some application functionality, such as installing a new app, may require you to run the program as an administrator.

Figure 2-9

The tile options available for a legacy app.

Photos used with permission from Microsoft Images and clip art used with permission of Microsoft.

Take Note If you change your mind and don't want to change an app's options, drag up slightly from the bottom of the screen or right-click the bar displaying the options.

Displaying tiles in list format

By default, when you first install Windows, the only apps that appear on the Windows 8 Start screen are the Windows 8 native apps. **Windows legacy apps**, such as WordPad, the Calculator, and Paint are installed, but are not pinned to the Start screen.

Take Note   If you bought Windows 8 pre-installed on a computer, the manufacturer may have added apps to the Start screen, including some of the legacy apps.

You can quickly and easily display all the apps installed on your computer in list format by dragging your finger up slightly from the bottom of the screen or by right-clicking anywhere on the Start screen. When a bar appears at the bottom of the Start screen, tap or click All Apps at the right edge of the bar.

Figure 2-10

Display apps in list format on the Start screen.

The Windows 8 native apps appear, by default, at the beginning of the list, and as you scroll to the right, legacy apps appear. You can think of the groups in which the legacy apps appear as the folders that appeared on the Start menu in earlier editions of Windows.

Figure 2-11

Legacy apps are organized into groups.

In Windows 8.1 you can see your app list by clicking on the arrow in the lower-left corner of the Start Screen.

Figure 2-12

Click on the arrow in the lower-left of the Start screen in Windows 8.1 to quickly show all applicationss.

Photos used with permission from Microsoft

Pinning and unpinning tiles

Most programs you install automatically create tiles for themselves on the Windows 8 Start screen. In addition, most of them place tiles into groups on the Start screen. But you can control the programs that appear on the Start screen.

STEP BY STEP   Pinning to the Start screen

For example, if you want tiles for certain Windows Accessories to appear on the Start screen, you can easily add tiles for these apps to the Start screen by **pinning**:

Take Note   Pinning is the term used to describe adding a tile to the Start screen or the Desktop task bar; **unpinning** is the term used to describe removing a tile from either location. Note that unpinning is not the same as uninstalling, which completely removes the app from your computer.

1   Drag your finger up slightly from the bottom of the screen or right-click anywhere on the Start screen to display the options bar at the bottom of the screen.

2   Choose All Apps.

3   Find the app for which you want to create a tile on the Start screen.

4   Right-click the app or drag the app down slightly. When a checkmark appears above the upper-right corner of the app, release it to display the bar at the bottom of the Start screen.

Figure 2-13

Display the options for the app.

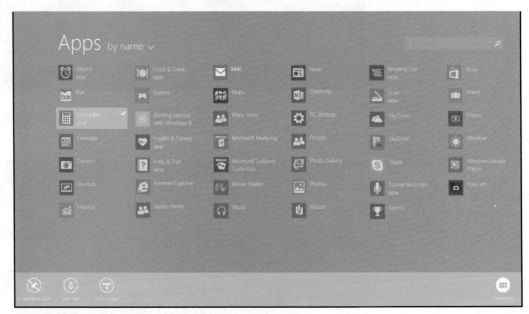

5   Tap or click Pin to Start.

When you redisplay the Start screen in its default view and you scroll to the right, you'll find a tile for the app you selected at the end of the Start screen.

Figure 2-14

A tile for the app now appears on the Start screen.

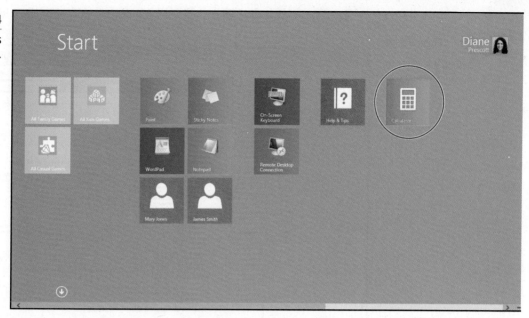

To remove a tile from the Start screen, repeat the steps, choosing Unpin from Start in Step 4. Remember, unpinning is not the same as uninstalling. Even though no tile appears for the app on the Start screen, you can still run it by tapping or clicking it while viewing all apps.

STEP BY STEP   **Pin web pages to the Start screen**

Workplace **Ready**

Pin the pages you visit every day to the Start screen to quickly access them while you work. For example, you might pin your company's intranet dashboard to your Start screen.

You can also pin web pages to the Start screen; if you visit a site frequently, you might find pinning it to the Start screen useful. The following example uses the legacy Internet Explorer on the Desktop to find a website and then pin it to the Start screen. After the steps, you'll find a tip that tells you how to use the Windows 8 native Internet Explorer to pin a page to the Start screen.

    1   Display the page in Internet Explorer.

2   Tap or click the Gear tool in the upper-right corner of the window.

Figure 2-15

Adding a website to
the Start screen.

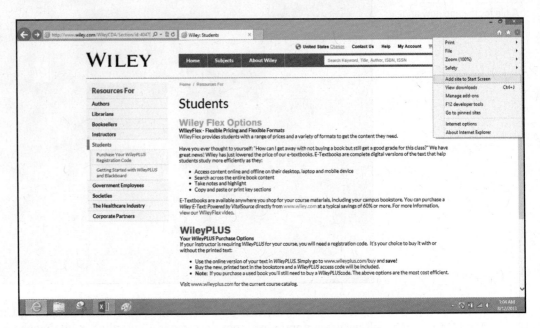

3   Choose Add Site to Start Screen. Internet Explorer displays a dialog box showing the web site title and address.

4   Tap or click Add. Windows adds a tile for the website to the end of the Start screen.

Take Note   The steps above work in both the legacy version and the Windows 8 native version of Internet Explorer. In the native version, for Step 2, tap or click the Pin icon at the bottom of the window and then tap or click Pin to Start. In the window that appears—the equivalent of Step 3 above—tap or click Pin to Start again.

Rearranging tiles

By now, you've noticed that you can easily launch programs that have tiles on the left side of the Start screen, but it's not quite as easy to launch a program that has a tile on the right side of the screen. You have to scroll to find it, or you need to type a few letters of its name.

The default order of the Start screen is not set in stone, you can move tiles around to suit your needs. For example, if you don't use a Windows native app, move it to the right or unpin it from the Start screen. If you use a legacy app regularly, move it to the left side of the screen.

How do you move a tile? Tap and hold the tile, then move it either up or down, and then drag it to a new position. Using a mouse, drag the tile in any direction to the new position.

To quickly move a tile a long distance, i.e., from one end of the Start screen to the other, drag the tile down to the bottom of the screen. Windows 8 zooms the Start screen to display all the tiles at once. You can then drag and drop the tile where you want it.

Figure 2-16

Moving a tile a long distance.

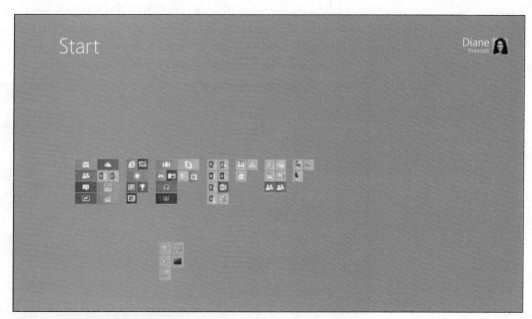

Photos used with permission from Microsoft

Before you dive into moving all your tiles around, consider creating groups for them and then move the entire group at once.

STEP BY STEP   **Creating and managing tile groups**

Workplace **Ready**

Group apps that you use daily for your work into a single group to work more efficiently. If you use a lot of apps each day, group apps that you use for particular tasks into task-related groups such as a group for Scheduling and another for Communication.

For an even cleaner Start screen, you can organize tiles into groups. For example, if you added Movie Maker and Photo Gallery to your computer from the available Windows Essentials tools (formerly called Windows Live tools) along with some of the standard accessories that you use frequently, such as the Calculator, Notepad, and the Snipping tool. Storing these apps in a group and naming it "My Windows Tools" will enable you to use that screen space for other essential apps. You can begin by creating a new group.

1   Use the mouse to drag one of the tiles that should be part of the group to an open space until you see a vertical gray bar. Using a touch device, you can drag the tile down slightly until a checkmark appears above the upper-right corner of the tile, then drag the tile to an open space until the vertical gray bar appears.

Figure 2-17

Creating a new group.

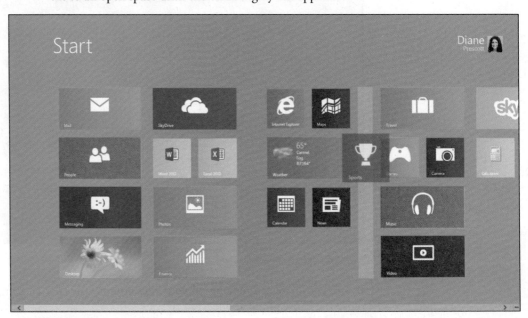

Images and clip art used with permission of Microsoft.

2   Release the tile. Windows 8 creates a new group and places the tile in that group.

Images and clip art used with permission of Microsoft.

3   Using the technique described in Step 1, drag more tiles next to the first tile.

4   Repeat Step 3 until all appropriate tiles appear in the group.

STEP BY STEP   **Naming tile groups in Windows 8**

Naming groups helps you organize your start screen and make apps easier to locate efficiently.

To name the group in Windows 8, follow these steps:

1   View all the tiles, or zoom out, by pinching your fingers together on the Start screen or clicking the Zoom button in the lower-right corner of the Start screen.

2   Select the group you want to name. Using a mouse, you can right-click the group to select it and display a bar at the bottom of the screen. To select a group on a touch device, drag the group down slightly until a checkmark appears. When you release the group, Windows displays the bar at the bottom of the screen.

Figure 2-19

A. Name group button.
B. Name group dialog box.
C. Selected group.

Photos used with permission from Microsoft

3   Tap or click the Name group from the bar at the bottom of the screen.

4   Enter My Windows Tools.

5   Tap or click Name. When you redisplay the Start screen in its default form, the group name you assigned appears above the group.

Figure 2-20

A named group on the Start screen.

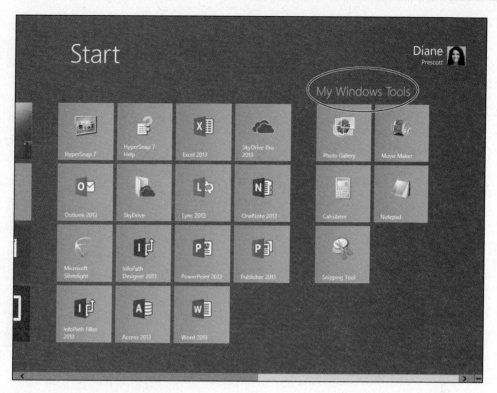

Photos used with permission from Microsoft

Take Note You can move an entire group to a new position on the Start screen: complete Step 1 above; then select the group (if you select using touch techniques, don't release the group) and drag it to its new position on the Start screen.

To name your group in Windows 8.1 do the following

STEP BY STEP   **Naming a group in Windows 8.1**

1   Right-click, or swipe down on any tile within a group.

2   Click inside the group name that is displayed above the group.

3 Press **Enter** when you have entered a group name.

Figure 2-21

In Windows 8.1 you can name the group after swiping any tile the Start screen.

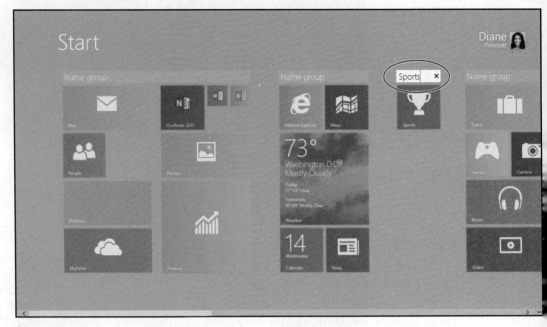

Photos used with permission from Microsoft

WORKING WITH THE CHARMS BAR

The Charms bar is a multi-purpose bar that appears on the right side of the screen. If you display it from the Start screen, it can help you to:

• Perform searches on your computer

• Share information between Windows 8 native apps

• Display the Start screen or the last app you viewed

• Connect hardware on your computer to Windows 8 native apps

• Display settings available for Windows 8 native apps

Figure 2-22

The Charms bar appears on the right side of your screen.

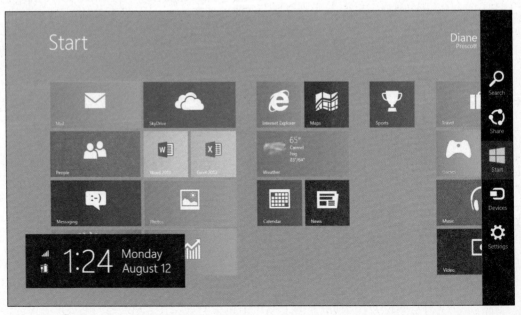

Photos used with permission from Microsoft

Be aware that things look a little different if you display the Charms bar from the Desktop app. The Share and Devices charms function only for Windows 8 native apps; on the Desktop app, you won't see any available options for these two charms. You will, however, see options for the Settings charm that are specific to Desktop apps.

To display the Charms bar, do one of the following:

• Press WinKey (⊞)+C

• Point the mouse in the lower-right or upper-right corner of the screen

• Swipe in from the right side of the screen

Using keyboard shortcuts, you can open a Charm directly, as indicated in the following table.

Shortcut key combination	Result
WinKey (⊞)+Q	Opens the Search pane to search for apps
WinKey (⊞)+F	Opens the Search pane to search for files
WinKey (⊞)+W	Opens the Search pane to search for settings
WinKey (⊞)	Displays the Start screen or the last app you viewed
WinKey (⊞)+I	Opens the Settings charm
WinKey (⊞)+K	Opens the Devices charm
WinKey (⊞)+H	Opens the Share charm

We covered the Search charm and its associated pane earlier in this lesson. The Start charm simply displays the Start screen if you're viewing an app. If you're viewing the Start screen and select the Start charm, Windows 8 displays the last app you viewed. When using a keyboard and mouse, you can bypass the Start charm and press WinKey (⊞) to display the Start screen or toggle between the Start screen and the last app you viewed.

STEP BY STEP   **Working with the Charms Bar**

In this example, you will use the Devices charm while working in a Windows 8 native app to print a web page from the Windows 8 native version of Internet Explorer.

1   Open Internet Explorer from the Start screen and navigate to a web page.

2 Open the Charms bar and tap or click the Devices option. The Devices charm lists all devices—both wired and wireless—attached to your computer.

Figure 2-23

The Devices charm and the Windows 8 native app for Internet Explorer.

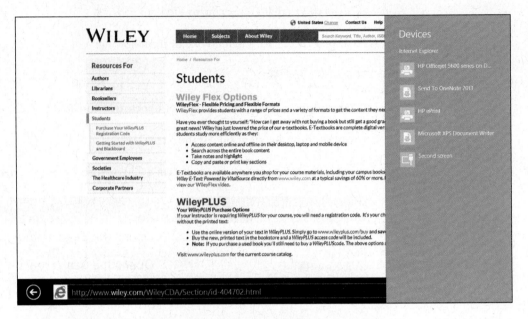

3 Choose a printer to use to print the page.

The Share charm is the Windows 8 native app equivalent to the Windows legacy app, Clipboard, that runs in the Desktop app. The Windows Clipboard is used to share information between legacy apps on the Desktop. The Share charm enables you to share information between Windows 8 native apps.

Quickly move information between native apps using the Share charm. When you have a file open, activate the charm to send the information to another app and continue your work.

STEP BY STEP   **Attaching a picture to an e-mail**

In this example, you will attach a picture to an e-mail.

1 From the Start screen, choose the Photos app. From the library options, tap or click one of the options: Pictures, SkyDrive, Flickr, Facebook, or an external device. You must have at least one photo in one of the libraries for this example.

2 Choose a photo from your chosen library.

3   Open the Charms bar, and tap or click the Share option. Windows 8 displays a list of native apps with which you can share the picture.

Figure 2-24

Figure 2-24

Display the Share charm while working in a Windows 8 native app, and you'll see other native apps with which you can share information.

Images and clip art used with permission of Microsoft.

4   From the list, select the Mail app. The Windows 8 native Mail app opens and an e-mail message is started for you with the photo embedded.

Figure 2-25

Sharing information between two Windows 8 native apps.

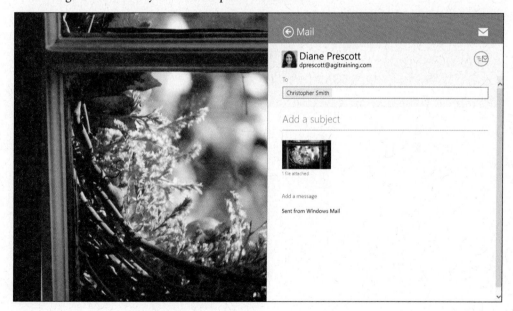

Images and clip art used with permission of Microsoft.

From the Start screen, you can control settings for tiles and also get Help. You can also access settings for your network, speaker volume, display brightness, display notifications, and change PC settings; shut down your computer, enable Sleep mode, or restart. From a touch device, you can display the on-screen keyboard.

Figure 2-26

The Settings charm as it appears from the Start screen.

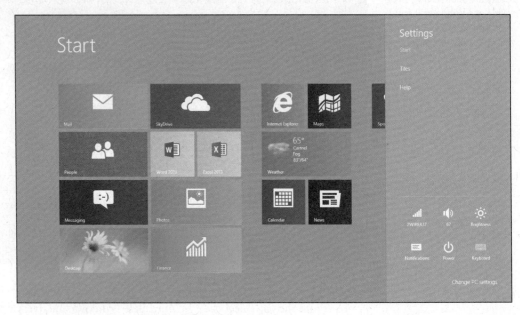

Images and clip art used with permission of Microsoft.

Take Note   If you open the Settings charm while working in a Windows 8 native app, options you can use to control the settings of that app are displayed.

There are different options available when you display the Settings charm from the Desktop. The options at the bottom of the Settings charm pane are the same as the ones you see when you display the Settings charm from the Start screen. But at the top of the Settings charm pane, you find options to display the Desktop Control Panel, the Desktop Personalization window, your PC's information, and the Desktop Windows Help and Support app.

Figure 2-27

The Settings charm as it appears while using the Desktop app.

In this lesson you learned how to:

• Navigate on the Start screen

• Work with tiles

• Search your computer

• Reorganize the Start Screen

• Work with the Charms bar

Bottom Line

This chapter shows you how to organize the Start Screen in order to quickly and easily locate the apps you work with on a daily basis. You also learn how to use the Charms bar to share files and access your hardware devices.

True/False

Circle T if the statement is true or F if the statement is false.

T F   1. The corners of the display can be used to navigate to special functionality.

T F   2. Pressing the WinKey repeatedly can be used to cycle between open documents.

T F   3. You can launch applications from the Search bar.

T F   4. Use WinKey+A to search for apps.

T F   5. You can only change the size of tiles on the Start screen by zooming in and out from the Start screen.

T F   6. You can display tiles in a list format in addition to tile format.

T F   7. When you unpin an application, you are removing it from your computer.

T F   8. You can only move single tiles on the Start Screen.

T F   9. You can enter an email address to send an image to using the Share charm, but you cannot customize the message.

T F 10. You can enable and disable notifications from the Settings charm.

Multiple Choice

Select the best response for the following statements.

1. What happens when you press Alt+F4 when using the Desktop app?
   a. The computer locks.
   b. You open the Settings window.
   c. The computer shuts down.
   d. You start a new search.

2. What is one way to open tile settings?
   a. Right-click the tile.
   b. Option-click the tile.
   c. Ctrl-click the tile.
   d. Press WinKey+S, and choose Settings.

3. What are two tile settings you can change by right-clicking the tile?
   a. Uninstall the application.
   b. Unpin the application from the Start screen.
   c. Stop displaying updated information.
   d. B and C
   e. All of the above.

4. What are some of the additional settings you can control for legacy applications (ones that run on the Desktop app)?
   a. Stop the app from running.
   b. Open a new window.
   c. Open file location
   d. B and C.
   e. All of the above.

5. How do you show all installed applications on the Start Screen?

   a. Right-click and choose All apps from the right-edge of the bar that appears.

   b. Right-click and choose All apps from a context menu.

   c. Ctrl-click and choose All apps from the right-edge of the bar that appears.

   d. Move the mouse to the bottom of the screen, and choose All apps from the Charms bar.

6. What does pinning an app refer to?

   a. Installing an application onto the Start Screen.

   b. Launching a pinned application.

   c. Opening the app from the Start screen.

   d. Adding a tile to the Start screen or Desktop task bar that represents an application.

7. What is one way to create a tile group?

   a. Right-click a tile and select New Group option at the bottom of the screen and then be drag more tiles to the first tile.

   b. Select the New Group charm, and drop apps on a grey bar that appears.

   c. Drag a tile to an open space, and drop it on a grey bar that appears and then drag more tiles to the first tile.

   d. B and C.

8. How do you move a group of tiles to a new location on the Start Screen?

   a. Select the group, and while pressing WinKey+M drag it to a new position.

   b. Select the group, press WinKey+M, and then click a new location on the Start Screen.

   c. Drag or swipe around the group of tiles and then click a new location on the Start screen.

   d. Select the group and drag it to a new position.

9. What option or device would you use to share a picture from an external hard drive?

   a. Select the image file and choose WinKey+S.

   b. Bluetooth.

   c. The Share charm.

   d. None of the above.

10. How do you name a group of tiles in Windows 8.0?

   a. With all tiles visible, right-click a tile group and enter the new name into the box that appears in the Charms bar.

   b. With all tiles visible, right-click the tile group and enter a new name into the bar at the bottom of the screen.

   c. Shift-click on all tiles in a group and then press Ctrl+G and enter the group name into the Group dialog box.

   d. Swipe down on the group name. When the Group Name text field becomes active, enter a new name for the group.

Competency Assessment

Project 2-1: Pin web pages to your start screen

1. Open the page in Internet Explorer
2. Tap the Gear, tool in the upper-right corner of the window, and select Add Site to Start Screen.
3. Click the Add button to add a tile to the Start screen representing that web page.

Project 2-2: Print an email

1. Open an email message.
2. Open the Charms bar and click the Devices option.
3. Choose a printer to print the email message.

Proficiency Assessment

Project 2-3: Organize your Start Screen

1. Group your apps into at least three groups: Tools, Workplace apps, and Web/Sharing.
2. Name each of the groups to accurately represent your apps.

Project 2-4: Use the Charms bar.

1. Use Charms in the Charms bar to copy a picture from a web page into an email.
2. Print the message.

Mastery Assessment

Project 2-5: Pin to the Start page

1. Find five apps that are installed on your computer but not pinned to your Start page.
2. Pin them to your Start page, and then group them into a tile group.
3. Install one new app, and group it with that new tile group.
4.. After you have grouped the six apps, name the tile group and finally display all tiles in list format.

Project 2-6: Pin a Legacy app to your taskbar

1. Pin a legacy app to your taskbar, and run the app as administrator.
2. After the app is running, open it in a new window so two instances of the program are running.

LESSON SKILL MATRIX

In this lesson, you will learn the following skills:

Examine the Desktop

Pin and unpin apps

Work with the Recycle Bin

Manage app windows

Work with Desktop tools

KEY TERMS

- **Recycle Bin**
- **Taskbar Tiles**
- **Internet Explorer**
- **File Explorer**
- **System Tray**
- **Notification Area**
- **Action Center**
- **desktop shortcut**
- **Folders**
- **Navigation pane**
- **Title bar**
- **App control menu**
- **Minimize button**
- **Restore button**
- **Ribbon**
- **Quick Access Toolbar**

Julene is working with a major new vendor, who recently started performing contract work for Northwind Traders an outdoor apparel company. The vendor is delivering files created in Microsoft Office on Windows 7, which run on the Desktop app in Junlene's copy of Windows 8. She needs to learn how to work efficiently on the Desktop in order to review and augment the vendor's files.

SOFTWARE ORIENTATION

Some apps operate in an environment known as the desktop. These desktop apps are often those created for older versions of Windows, or apps that function more appropriately with a more traditional computer interface.

Figure 3-1

The Windows 8 Desktop

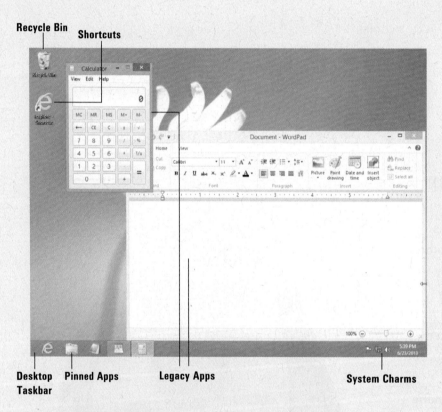

Recycle Bin   Shortcuts

Desktop Taskbar   Pinned Apps   Legacy Apps   System Charms

Image used with permission from Microsoft. Photos used with permission from Microsoft

STARTING UP

In this lesson, you will work with several files from the lessons that accompany this book. Make sure that you have loaded the files onto your computer before starting this lesson.

RUNNING DESKTOP APPS

Although Windows 8 introduces a new type of app, you can still run most legacy apps—"legacy" refers to the type of application that has been around for 20 years or more. If your legacy app could run under Windows Vista or Windows 7, you can run it under Windows 8. You might even be able to run some apps dating back to Windows XP, but if those apps didn't work under Windows Vista and Windows 7, they won't work under Windows 8, either.

Take Note   If you used "XP Mode" in Windows 7 to run programs that were written for Windows XP and didn't work properly in Windows 7, you'll need Windows 8 Pro. Using it and a licensed copy of Windows XP, you can set up and run a Hyper-V virtual computer that will let you run your old XP programs from inside Windows 8.

Run a Desktop app the same way you run Windows 8 native apps: from the Start screen, tap or click the tile of the app you want to run. The Desktop app opens, followed by your legacy app.

Figure 3-2

Opening a legacy app from the Start screen, opens the app on the Desktop.

You can open the Desktop app itself by tapping or clicking its tile on the Start screen or by pressing WinKey (⊞)+D.

GETTING TO KNOW THE DESKTOP APP

From the Desktop app, you can run legacy programs that come with Windows, such as Internet Explorer, File Explorer, Windows Media Player, Paint, WordPad, and the Calculator, as well as legacy programs that you add to your computer, such as Microsoft Office and Intuit Quicken. As you will read in the "Pinning and Unpinning Desktop Apps" section later in this lesson, you can launch legacy apps from the Desktop and from the Start screen.

Understanding the Desktop workspace will help you accomplish tasks quickly and easily.

Figure 3-3

A. Pinned apps: Internet Explorer, Windows Media Player, and File Explorer.
B. Taskbar.
C. Recycle Bin.
D. System Tray.
E. Notification Area.
F. Action Center.
G. Network Access Indicator.
H. Speaker Volume Control.
I. Date & Time.

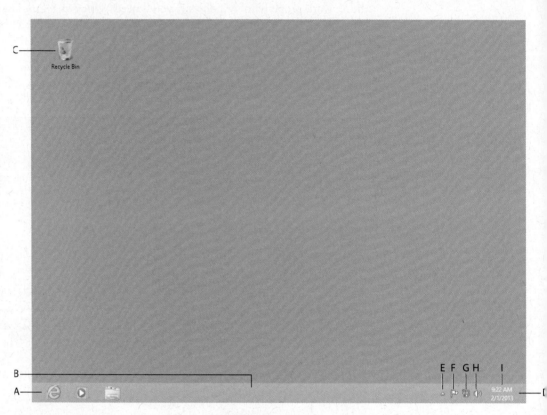

You'll find the following elements available by default when you use the Desktop app:

• The Recycle Bin

• The Taskbar

• Pinned apps

• The System Tray

The Recycle Bin

When you delete a file from your computer, Windows doesn't delete it immediately. Instead, Windows typically moves it to the Recycle Bin, a temporary holding area for things you intend to delete. If you find you have mistakenly deleted a file, you can, in all likelihood, find it in the Recycle Bin and restore it. To permanently delete files, you empty the Recycle Bin. You can read more about the Recycle Bin later in this lesson.

The Taskbar

The **taskbar** displays buttons that represent apps you can open—pinned apps—and apps you have opened. You can tap or click a button on the taskbar to run an app pinned to the taskbar, and you can use the taskbar to switch between open apps, as described later in this lesson.

Pinned apps

By default, Windows pins two apps to the taskbar:

- **Internet Explorer** is the legacy version of the Microsoft web browser; you'll also find the Windows 8 native version of Internet Explorer on the Start screen. Both versions do the same thing: they let you visit websites of your choice.

- **File Explorer** is the program you use to work with files on your computer, viewing them, organizing them by creating folders for them, moving or copying them, renaming them, and deleting them.

The System Tray

The **System Tray** consists, by default, of five elements that provide information about your computer.

Figure 3-4

The System Tray.

The **Notification Area** periodically displays messages pertinent at the time they appear. You can tap or click the arrow in the Notification Area to display icons for system and program features that have no presence on the desktop. In this example, the icon shown appears whenever an external hardware device, such as a USB thumb drive (also called a *flash drive*), is attached to the computer.

Figure 3-5

The Notification Area temporarily displays pertinent messages and icons for features that don't appear on the Desktop.

The flag in the System Tray represents the **Action Center**. When you need to take an action, a message will appear and the flag will contain a red X. If you tap or click the flag, the Action Center window opens, displaying a message about the action you need to take. You can tap or click the message in the middle of the window to address the problem. Once you resolve the problem, the red X disappears from the flag.

Figure 3-6

The Action Center window.

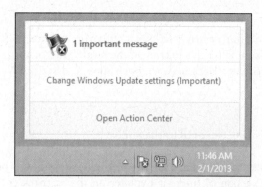

The appearance of the **network access indicator** depends on the type of connection your device uses. If your device uses a wired connection, the network access indicator resembles a monitor. If your device uses a wireless connection, the network access indicator displays bars that indicate the signal strength, with five bars being the strongest possible signal.

Figure 3-7

The network access indicator on a device using a wired connection.

Figure 3-8

The network access indicator on a device using a wireless connection.

You can tap the network access indicator to determine your current connection status and to find available networks to which a wireless device can connect.

You can tap or click the speaker volume control button to increase or decrease the volume of speakers connected to your device. If you use external speakers on a desktop computer, they typically have a volume control knob; you can control their volume using the volume control knob or using the button in the system tray. However, the speaker volume control button is most useful on portable devices that use internal speakers.

Figure 3-9

The speaker volume control button.

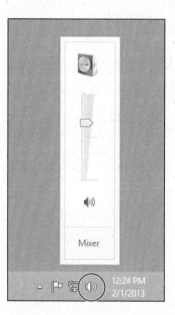

Besides displaying the current date and time in the System Tray, this area provides some additional functionality. If you point the mouse at the area, a tool tip displays the day as well as the date.

If you click the date and time, the current month's calendar appears, with today highlighted. Today's date appears above the calendar, and the time appears on an analog clock.

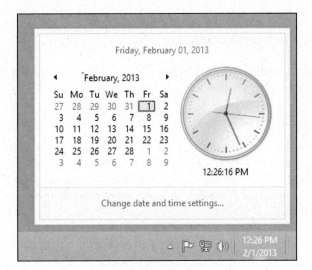

PINNING AND UNPINNING DESKTOP APPS

The tiles on the Start screen are the primary tools to use to start apps. But if you regularly use a legacy app that doesn't have a tile on the Start screen by default. You can pin the app to the Start screen.

If you work predominantly on the Desktop, you might find it more convenient to start legacy apps from the Desktop instead of from the Start screen. As you saw in the preceding section, Windows automatically pins Internet Explorer and File Explorer to the taskbar. You're not limited to just these apps appearing on the taskbar; you can pin any legacy app to the taskbar.

The Desktop app will also allow you to create shortcuts for legacy apps on the Desktop.

STEP BY STEP   **Pinning to the Start screen**

By default, the Calculator doesn't have a tile on the Start screen; but you can always add a tile for the Calculator to the Start screen.

1   Display the Start screen.

Take Note   To display the Start screen, slide the mouse into the upper- or lower-right corner to display the Charms bar and then click Start; press WinKey (⊞); or, from the right edge of the screen, swipe to the left slightly to display the Charms bar, and then tap the Start button. In Windows 8.1 you can position your finder (for touch devices) or your cursor in the lower-left corner to access the Start screen.

2   Use a physical keyboard or the touch keyboard to type the first few letters of "Calculator" to locate the Calculator app.

3   Display the App bar by right-clicking the app tile or dragging the app tile down slightly until a checkmark appears above the tile, and then releasing the tile.

Figure 3-12

Display the App bar.

4   Tap or click **Pin to Start**.

Windows 8 adds a tile for the app to the right side of the Start screen.

If you change your mind and no longer want the tile on the Start screen, right-click or drag the app's tile down slightly until a checkmark appears above the tile and then release the tile. From the App bar, tap or click Unpin from Start.

Pinning to the taskbar

You can pin an app to the Desktop taskbar and then run the app by tapping or clicking the app's taskbar button. If you work on the Desktop a lot, you might find having a taskbar button for the app more convenient than having a tile for the app on the Start screen.

Take Note   Start screen tiles and taskbar buttons are not mutually exclusive; you can have both for any app. Just follow the steps in the preceding section and in this section.

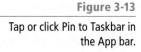

STEP BY STEP   **Pin an app to the Desktop taskbar**

To pin an app to the Desktop taskbar, follow these steps:

1   Display the Start screen.

2   Use a physical keyboard or the touch keyboard to type the first few letters of "Calculator" to locate the Calculator app.

3   Display the App bar by right-clicking the app tile or dragging the app tile down slightly until a checkmark appears above the tile, and then releasing the tile.

4   Tap or click Pin to Taskbar.

Figure 3-13

Tap or click Pin to Taskbar in the App bar.

Nothing appears to happen on the screen, but if you launch the Desktop app, you'll find a button on the taskbar for the app.

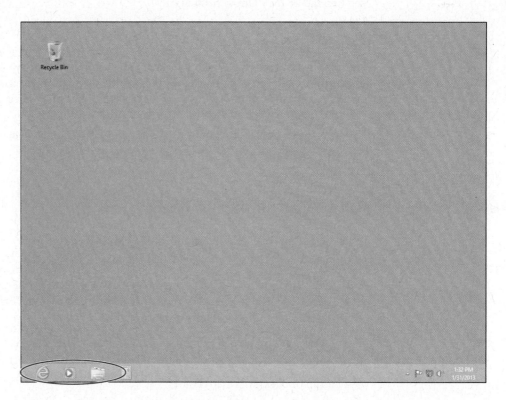

To run an app that you've pinned to the Desktop taskbar, you can tap or click that button, or you can press WinKey (⊞)+a number that corresponds to the app's position on the taskbar. In the figure, Internet Explorer is in the first position, File Explorer is in the second position, and the Calculator is in the third position on the taskbar. You can open the Calculator if you press WinKey (⊞)+3. Similarly, you can open File Explorer if you press WinKey (⊞)+2, and Internet Explorer if you press WinKey (⊞)+1.

If you change your mind and no longer want a program pinned to the taskbar, you can remove it by doing one of the following:

• From the Start menu, follow the steps presented earlier in this section, but in Step 4, tap or click Unpin from Taskbar.

• From the Desktop app, right-click or tap and hold the shortcut on the Desktop taskbar; from the shortcut menu that appears, tap or click Unpin this Program from the Taskbar.

Figure 3-15

Unpinning the calculator from the Desktop taskbar.

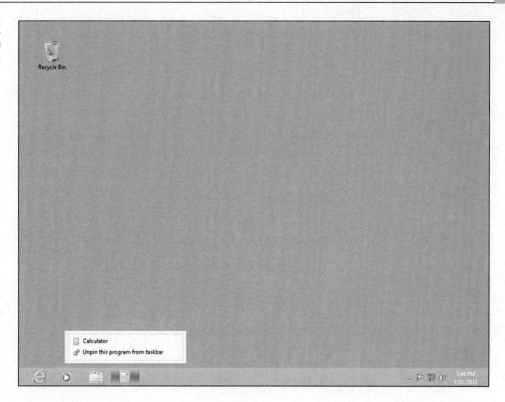

To the Desktop

Workplace **Ready**

If you commonly use the desktop and legacy apps, adding shortcuts for all of your commonly used apps can save you from hunting through lists of every installed app. Group your most used shortcuts together on the desktop.

If you've used earlier editions of Windows, you should be familiar with shortcuts on the Desktop that run programs. You can still create shortcuts on the Desktop for any legacy program. Let's create a **Desktop shortcut** for the Calculator.

STEP BY STEP   **Create a Desktop shortcut for the Calculator**

1   Display the Start screen.

2   Use a physical keyboard or the touch keyboard to type the first few letters of "Calculator" to locate the Calculator app.

3   Display the App bar by right-clicking the app tile or dragging the app tile down slightly until a checkmark appears above the tile, and then releasing the tile.

4   Tap or click Open File Location. File Explorer opens to the folder that stores the program.

5   Right-click or tap and hold the program to view a shortcut menu.

6   From the shortcut menu, tap or click Send To.

7   Tap or click Desktop (Create Shortcut).

Figure 3-16

Creating a Desktop shortcut for the Calculator legacy app.

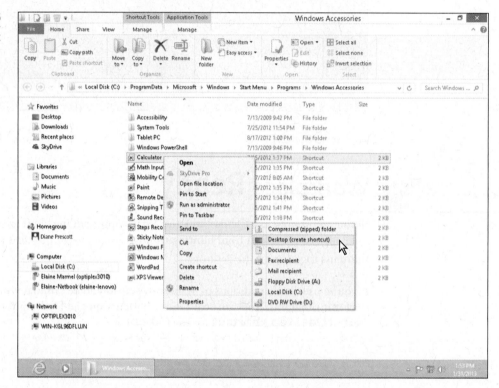

8   Tap or click the X in the upper-right corner of File Explorer to close it and view the Desktop, which now contains a shortcut to the Calculator app.

Figure 3-17

A shortcut for the Calculator
app appears on the Desktop.

To run the Calculator using the shortcut, double-tap or double-click the shortcut.

If you change your mind and no longer want the Desktop shortcut, drag it into the Recycle Bin.

VIEWING THE CONTENTS OF YOUR COMPUTER

Information you create from various apps is stored in files. Windows helps you organize that information using **folders** in which you can place related files. *Related files* is a relative term—one that you define. By default, Windows creates four folders for you to use: Documents, Music, Pictures, and Videos. You can store all information inside any of these folders, but finding things later will be easier if you create folders inside folders. For example, you can separate pictures from various vacations into folders named for the vacation. You use File Explorer—called Windows Explorer in earlier editions of Windows—to help manage your files.

The left side of the File Explorer screen is called the **Navigation pane** and displays common locations on your computer that you might need to review. The content of whatever you click on the left side of the screen appears on the right side of the screen. File Explorer opens by default to the Libraries folder (selected in the Navigation pane), and the right side of the screen shows that the Libraries folder contains four folders: Documents, Music, Pictures, and Videos.

Figure 3-18

File Explorer as it appears when it opens.

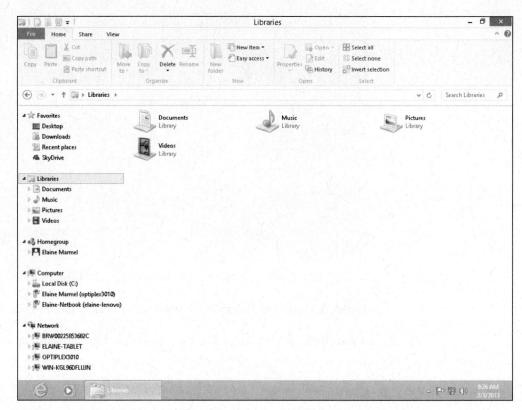

At the top of the screen, you see File Explorer's toolbar and Ribbon interface

File Explorer can also show you information about storage media attached to your computer, including the computer's hard drive and any external hard drives, USB drives, and CD or DVD drives. To view the contents of your computer, follow these steps:

Viewing the contents of your computer

1   On the Desktop, tap or click the File Explorer button on the taskbar to display File Explorer.

2   In the Navigation pane, tap or click Computer. The right side of the screen displays devices connected to your computer; in the case of storage devices, such as your hard drive and external hard drives, you also see information about space usage.

Figure 3-19

You can view the devices attached to your computer by tapping or clicking Computer in the Navigation pane.

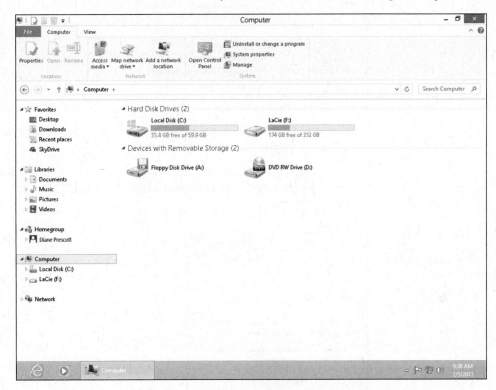

3   Tap and hold or right-click Computer in the Navigation pane.

4   From the shortcut menu that appears, tap or click Properties to display your computer's information in the Desktop Control Panel.

Figure 3-20

From the Desktop Control
Panel, you can view
information about your
computer, including the
version of Windows 8 you're
using and the amount of
memory contained in your
computer.

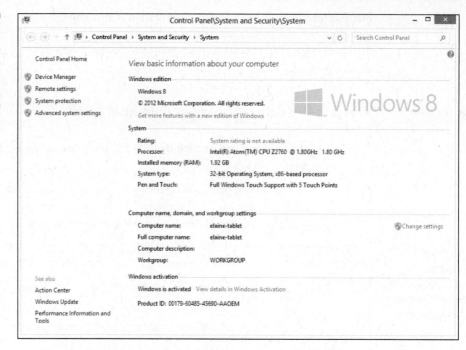

5   Tap or click the X in the upper-right corner of the window to close the Control Panel
    and redisplay File Explorer.

6   To view more details about a storage device, such as your Local Disk C, tap and hold or
    right-click the device to display a shortcut menu.

7   Tap or click Properties to display the Properties box for that storage device.

Figure 3-21

From a storage device's
Properties box, you can view
a pie chart depicting used and
free space.

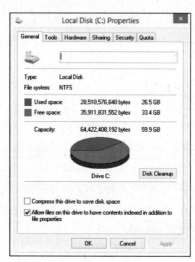

8   Tap or click OK to close the Properties box.

WORKING WITH THE RECYCLE BIN

The Recycle Bin's sole purpose is to serve as a holding tank for things you delete from your computer. That is, when you opt to delete something—a file you created, a shortcut to a program, etc.—Windows doesn't really delete the item. Instead, Windows places the item in the Recycle Bin. That way, if you accidentally delete something you meant to keep, you can open the Recycle Bin, find the item, and restore it.

Take Note   As a general rule, don't delete files that you don't recognize just because you don't recognize them. For example, a file you don't recognize might be part of an app, and without that file, the app can't run. If you can't confirm a file's content, don't delete it.

Deleting a file

You can delete shortcuts on your Desktop or files you see in File Explorer. In fact, you can view items on the Desktop from File Explorer by tapping or clicking Desktop in File Explorer's Navigation pane. For this example, if you previously created a Desktop shortcut for the Calculator that you now feel you don't need. To delete it, do any of the following:

• Drag the shortcut on top of the Recycle Bin. When a tip appears, suggesting that you move the item to the Recycle Bin, lift your finger or release the mouse button.

Figure 3-22

Dragging an item to the Recycle Bin.

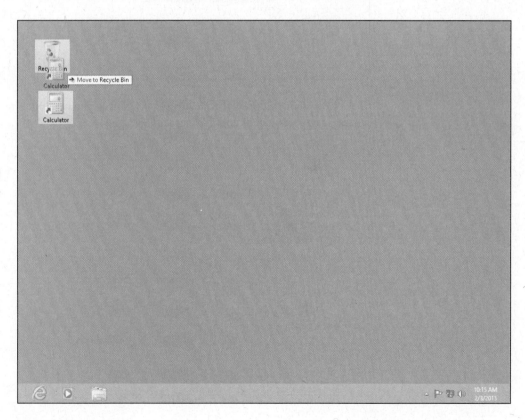

• Tap and hold or right-click the item to display a shortcut menu. Then, tap or click Delete. When confirmation message appears, tap or click Yes.

Figure 3-23

Tap or click Delete from the
shortcut menu.

Figure 3-24

To move the item into the
Recycle Bin, tap or click Yes.

- Select the item and press the Delete key on your keyboard. Once again, when the confirmation
message appears, tap or click Yes.

STEP BY STEP   **Restoring a file from the Recycle Bin**

If you accidentally deleted a file, follow these steps to open the Recycle Bin and restore the file.

Workplace **Ready**

If you send files to the Recycle Bin, they are not immediately deleted. Leave them in the Recycle Bin until you are sure you want or need to delete the file.

1   On the Desktop, double-tap or double-click the Recycle Bin. File Explorer opens. Although you don't see the Recycle Bin in the Navigation pane, the address bar below the Ribbon and above the main part of the File Explorer window confirms that you're viewing the contents of the Recycle Bin.

Take Note   If you prefer to use shortcut menus, you can tap and hold or right-click the Recycle Bin and choose Open from the shortcut menu that appears.

Figure 3-25

The address bar confirms that you are viewing the contents of the Recycle Bin.

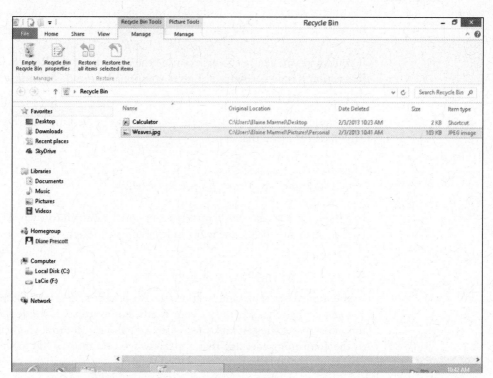

2   Tap or click the item you accidentally deleted.

3   On the Ribbon, tap or click Restore the Selected Items. Windows removes the item from the Recycle Bin and replaces it in its original location.

Emptying the Recycle Bin

To truly delete a file from your computer, you must empty the Recycle Bin. You can tell when the Recycle Bin contains files waiting for deletion by its appearance on your Desktop. When the Recycle Bin is empty, it appears to contain no trash. When the Recycle Bin contains items, it appears to contain trash.

Figure 3-26

L. The image of the Recycle Bin when it's empty. R. The image of the Recycle Bin when it contains files waiting for deletion.

Take Note   The Recycle Bin is a special file on your computer that has a fixed size. If you never empty it, eventually Windows won't be able to store things you delete in the Recycle Bin because the Recycle Bin will be unable to hold additional items. In this case, when you delete, you delete permanently.

If you want, you can open and examine the contents of the Recycle Bin before you empty it, but that action is only necessary if it gives you peace of mind. To empty the Recycle Bin, do either of the following:

• Tap and hold or right-click the Recycle Bin on the Desktop and choose Empty Recycle Bin from the shortcut menu that appears.

• Double-tap or double-click the Recycle Bin to display it in File Explorer; then, on the File Explorer Ribbon, tap or click Empty Recycle Bin.

In either case, a confirmation message asks you to confirm that you want to empty the Recycle Bin (and permanently delete the items in it). Tap or click Yes.

Customizing the Recycle Bin

As mentioned in the previous section, the Recycle Bin is a special file and has a fixed size. However, you can change that size to suit your needs. For example, if you feel the Recycle Bin is taking up too much space, you can make it smaller. You also can control whether you must view and respond to the confirming message that appears when you move a file to the Recycle Bin, and if you're confident that you don't ever accidentally delete files, you can opt not to use the Recycle Bin at all.

Take Note   Each drive attached to your computer has its own Recycle Bin used by Windows to manage files you delete on that particular drive.

To customize the Recycle Bin, first do one of the following to display the Recycle Bin Properties box:

• Tap and hold or right-click the Recycle Bin on the Desktop and tap or click Properties on the shortcut menu that appears.

• Double-tap or double-click the Recycle Bin to open it in File Explorer, and then tap or click the Recycle Bin Properties button on File Explorer's Ribbon.

STEP BY STEP **Customizing the Recycle Bin**

Once the Recycle Bin Properties box appears, you can continue with the following steps:

Figure 3-27

Use this dialog box to customize the behavior of the Recycle Bin.

1   Select the drive containing the Recycle Bin you want to customize.

2   In the Settings section, tap or click an option. You can change the size of the Recycle Bin or opt not to use it.

3   To avoid viewing the confirmation message each time you place a file in the Recycle Bin, remove the check from the Display Delete Confirmation Dialog check box. Note that unchecking this box stops the confirmation message from appearing when you place a file in the Recycle Bin, but Windows continues to prompt you to confirm your action when you empty the recycle Bin.

4   Tap or click OK to save your settings.

MANAGING DESKTOP APP WINDOWS

Every Desktop app appears in its own window. You can display multiple windows simultaneously, and in this section, you learn about managing open windows. To make your Desktop workspace more functional, you can:

• Resize a window,

• Move a window,

• Show windows side by side

• Switch between app windows

Exploring a Desktop app window

Although app windows may look different, each app shares some common elements with every other app. Learning to use these common elements can help you be more efficient while working on the Desktop.

Figure 3-28

A. App control menu.
B. Title bar.
C. Minimize.
D. Restore.
E. Close.

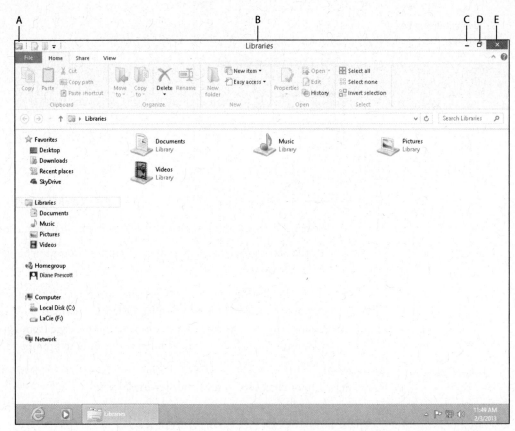

Every app has a **title bar**, which typically—but not always—displays the app's name and the name of the document that is currently open. File Explorer doesn't display its app name, but instead displays the name of the folder currently selected in the Navigation pane.

The **app control menu** contains commands that help you control the size and appearance of the app window as well as close the window.

The three buttons in the upper-right corner provide you with shortcuts to the commands that appear on the app control menu. Tap or click the **Minimize button** to reduce the app window to a button on the taskbar. Tap or click the taskbar button to once again view the app.

Figure 3-29

When you minimize a
running app on the Desktop,
it appears as a highlighted
button on the taskbar.

The **Restore button** appears only when an app window is maximized to fill the entire computer screen. If you tap or click the Restore button, Windows redisplays the window in a size somewhere between minimized and maximized. Displaying an app at a size between Minimize and Maximize is particularly useful when you want to view multiple windows simultaneously.

Figure 3-30

A window that is not maximized or minimized.

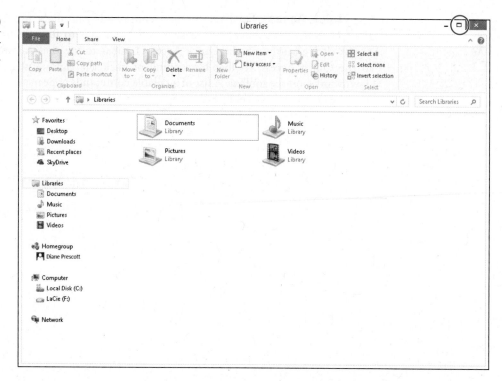

When you display a window in a size between Maximize and Minimize, the Maximize button becomes available; click it to make the window fill the screen.

Many legacy apps that work in the Desktop app use the **Ribbon interface** that Microsoft introduced with its Office 2007 apps. These apps contain a Ribbon and a Quick Access toolbar; both of these elements contain commands that pertain, for the most part, specifically to the app you're viewing, with a few exceptions. The exceptions apply in particular to commands that are common to all Desktop apps and are not really controlled by the legacy app, but rather by the Desktop. These exception commands are the Cut, Copy, Paste, and Print commands you'll read about later in this lesson.

A   B

Figure 3-31

A. Quick Access Toolbar.
B. A Ribbon.

The Ribbon contains tabs of related commands. File Explorer's tabs are Home, Share, and View. Each tab further organizes commands into groups, and group names appear below each group; the Home tab contains the Clipboard, Organize, New, Open, and Select groups. You can tap or click a tab to view the commands available on it, and you can tap or click a command to use it.

Take Note   In some apps, you might want to get the Ribbon out of the way while you work; you can minimize the Ribbon to display only the tab names by tapping or clicking the upward-pointing caret at the right edge of the Ribbon, just below the Close button. To use a command on the Ribbon, tap or click the tab containing the command, and the Ribbon appears until you select a command; then it minimizes again. To expand the Ribbon to its full size (so that it no longer minimizes), tap or click the downward pointing caret at the right edge of the Ribbon, just below the Close button.

Minimize the ribbon while you work to maximize the available working space in the window. Click the upward-facing caret at the right-edge of the window to control the display.

The **Quick Access Toolbar** contains commands you might use frequently when working in the app so that you don't need to switch Ribbon tabs to find frequently-used commands: you tap or click a button on the Quick Access Toolbar to use that command. You can add buttons to the Quick Access Toolbar by tapping or click the right-most button—the arrow pointing downward—on the toolbar. A list of available commands appears; tap or click a command to add it to the Quick Access Toolbar.

Adding buttons to this toolbar help you work without needing the Ribbon open all of the time. Customize this toolbar with commonly used commands so you can close the Ribbon and still work efficiently.

Figure 3-32

Select a command from this menu to add it to the Quick Access Toolbar.

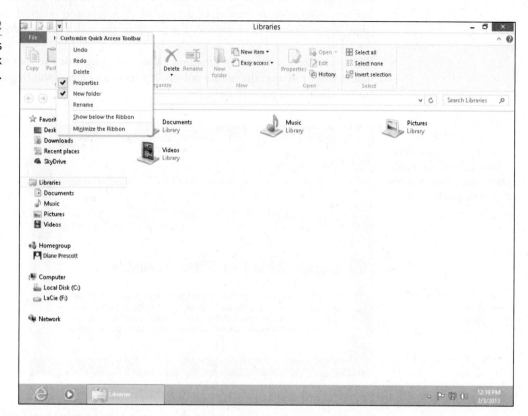

Finally, most legacy apps that use the Ribbon interface have a special menu at the left edge of the Ribbon; typically, the File menu. When you tap or click that menu, you find commands common to most apps that enable you to, for example, open a document, close, or exit the program.

Resizing Desktop app windows

As long as an app's window is neither maximized nor minimized, you can control its size by dragging one of its edges. If you drag any corner of a window, you can maintain its proportionate size when you drag, increasing or decreasing its height and width simultaneously. If you drag an edge, you increase or decrease only the height or the width of a window.

You can resize a window by dragging either your finger or the mouse pointer. When you use a mouse while resizing, the mouse pointer changes to a pair of pointing arrows; if you resize using a corner, the arrows point diagonally.

Figure 3-33

When you resize a window from a corner, the mouse pointer appears as a pair of diagonally pointing arrows.

Moving a Desktop app window

As you saw in the previous section, when a window is neither maximized nor minimized, you can resize the window. In addition, when a window is neither maximized nor minimized, you can move the window to a new position on the screen by dragging the app's title bar.

Figure 3-34

Move a window by dragging its title bar.

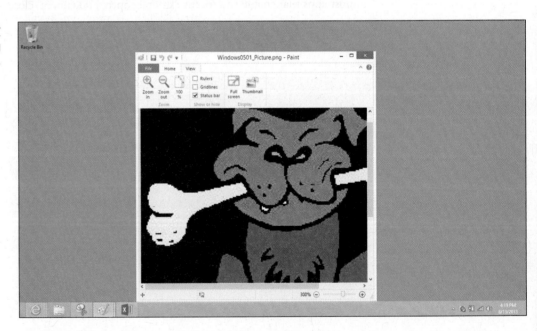

Clip art used with permission from Microsoft.

Showing windows side by side

Displaying windows side by side in the Desktop app is the equivalent of snapping Windows 8 native apps. The most major distinction between the two techniques, however, is that legacy apps can share information across windows, as you'll see later in this lesson, but Windows 8 native apps cannot.

Many people copy files from one storage device to another, often to create a second copy—a backup—of an important document. It's easiest to copy a file from one drive to another if you open two File Explorer windows and place them side by side. Then, display the drive containing the file (the source drive) in one window and the drive where you will store the copy (the target drive) in the other window. You can then drag the file from the source drive to the target drive.

Take Note   You can display two File Explorer windows or the windows of two different legacy apps side by side; for example, you can display the legacy apps Paint and WordPad side by side.

For this example, you need to open two windows of File Explorer. To open the first File Explorer window, tap or click the File Explorer button on the Desktop taskbar or press WinKey (⊞)+E. To open another File Explorer window, do one of the following:

- Tap and hold or right-click the File Explorer button on the taskbar. When the menu appears, tap or click File Explorer.

- Press WinKey (⊞)+E again.

- To display the two windows side by side, do any of the following:

- Click one window and press WinKey (⊞)+Right Arrow to place that window on the right side of the screen. Then, click the other window and press WinKey (⊞)+Left Arrow to place that window on the left side of the screen.

- Using your finger or your mouse, drag the title bar of one window toward one edge of the screen. When your finger or the mouse pointer reaches the edge of the screen, a window outline appears; lift your finger or release the mouse button. Repeat for the other window, dragging to the opposite side of the screen.

Figure 3-35

Dragging to place windows side by side.

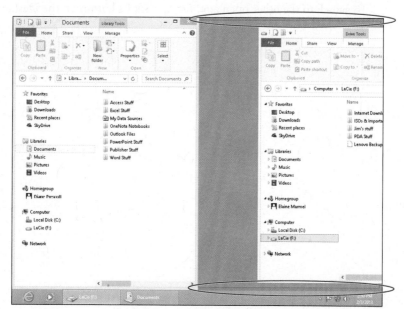

Figure 3-36

Two File Explorer windows, side by side.

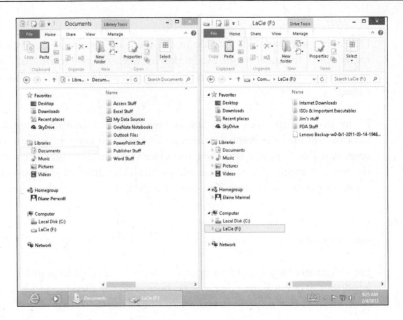

The two windows operate independently; you can select one folder or device in the left window and a different one in the right window.

Switching between Desktop app windows

In this next section, you will use WordPad to create a flyer advertising a pet sitting service. You will also use the legacy app, Paint, to review all your available pictures to add to your flyer. Open both apps from the Windows Start screen.

In this example, you want to maximize the windows of both apps so that each app fills your screen. You can maximize both windows and then switch between the two apps using the Desktop taskbar.

Remember that an app's window is maximized when you see the Restore button in the upper-right corner. If you see the Maximize button in the upper-right corner, tap or click it to maximize the window.

To switch to the other open app, tap or click its button on the Desktop taskbar.

Take Note If you use a mouse, you can display a thumbnail of each running legacy app by pointing the mouse at the app's button on the taskbar.

Figure 3-37

Tap a button on the taskbar to switch to a different legacy app.

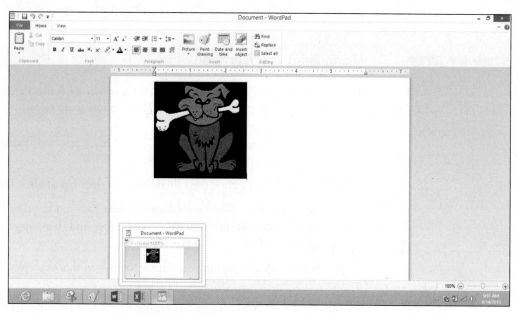

Clip art used with permission from Microsoft.

USING UNIVERSAL DESKTOP TOOLS

Although you can run a myriad of legacy apps on the Desktop, some of the tools you use while working in those apps are actually controlled by the Desktop app itself. And those tools are quite powerful.

• You can share information between legacy apps using the Desktop Cut, Copy, and Paste tools.

• The Desktop app manages printing for all legacy apps, eliminating the need for you to describe your printer to each app.

Cut, copy, and paste

One of the most useful features available for Desktop apps is the ability to share information.

Copying information leaves the information you copy in the original document. If you want to move information, you "cut" it instead of copying it. Cutting information removes it from the original app.

STEP BY STEP **To view the final product**

To view the final product, follow these steps:

1 Open WordPad.

Take Note You might find the WordPad app most easily by typing its name on the Windows 8 Start screen.

2 Tap or click the File menu, and then tap or click Open.

3 Navigate to the Windows03lessons folder that you saved to your hard drive.

4 Tap or click the file called **Windows0501_done.rtf**.

5   Tap or click Open. The flyer appears in WordPad.

6   Now that you've seen the final product, tap or click the X in the upper-right corner of the WordPad window. If you are prompted to save, click Don't Save.

STEP BY STEP   Using Paint and Wordpad

To copy information from one program to another, we'll use Paint and WordPad and two files stored in the Windows03lessons folder. Then, follow these steps:

1   Using the Search charm in the Charms bar, open both Paint and WordPad, and if necessary, maximize their screens.

2   In Paint, tap or click the File menu, and then tap or click Open.

3   Navigate to the Windows03lessons folder that you saved to your hard drive, tap or click the file called **Windows0501_Picture.jpg**, and then tap or click Open. The image appears in Paint.

4   Select the information you want to copy—in this example, the picture.

Take Note   To select information in Paint, tap or click the Select tool on the Home tab and then drag over the information from the upper-left corner to the lower-right corner. Paint displays a dotted line around the selected area.

5   On the Ribbon, tap or click the Copy button.

Figure 3-38

A. Copy Button.
B. Paint's Selection tool.
C. Two open apps.
D. Paint's dotted selection line.

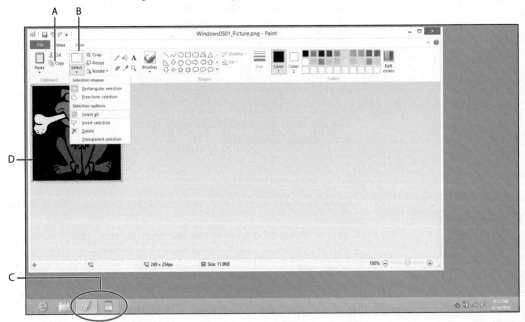

Clip art used with permission from Microsoft.

6   On the Desktop taskbar, tap or click WordPad to display it.

7   Tap or click the File menu, and then tap or click Open.

8   Navigate to the Windows03lessons folder that you saved to your hard drive, tap or click the file called **Windows0501_Text.rtf**, and then tap or click Open. The text for the flyer appears in WordPad.

9   Tap or click at the location where you want the information to appear—in this example, tap or click below all the text in the document.

10 Tap or click the Paste button. The information you copied (in this example, the picture from Paint) appears in the app you're currently viewing (in this example, WordPad). It also continues to appear in the original app you selected in Step 2.

Figure 3-39

Paste the image, and the image appears in your WordPad document.

Clip art used with permission from Microsoft.

Take Note   If you had tapped or clicked Cut in Step 5, the information you selected in Step 4 would no longer appear in the app you selected in Step 2 (in our example, the picture would disappear from Paint).

11 In WordPad, tap or click the File menu and then tap or click Save As. In the dialog box that appears, provide a new name for the flyer and tap or click Save.

12 Click the X in the upper-right corner of WordPad and then Paint to close the apps. If you are prompted to save, click Don't Save.

Printing

Windows has managed printing for all apps basically since its inception. Nothing has changed in that regard in Windows 8: essentially, whenever you work in an app and decide to print, you issue a print command to the app—typically by tapping or clicking the File menu and then tapping or clicking Print—and the app passes that command along to Windows. Using this approach, you only need to set up your printer once; it is then available to all apps on your computer.

The method used to set up a printer can vary, depending on the make and model of your printer. But one thing remains constant: once you set up the printer, you won't need to configure it again. You can work on any app as you normally would, and when you need to print, you use the app's Print command, which usually appears on the app's File menu (the left-most tab on the Ribbon for legacy apps that use a Ribbon). The app forwards your message to the operating system, which manages the rest of what needs to be done for you.

Use the Devices and Printers page of the Desktop's Control Panel to see images of installed printers.

Figure 3-40

Printers available on your computer appear in the Printers section of the Devices and Printers page, which is part of the Desktop's Control Panel.

Clip art used with permission from Microsoft.

To display the Devices and Printers page

To display the Devices and Printers page, follow these steps:

1 Press **WinKey** (⊞)**+X** and then click **Control Panel**, or on the Start screen, type **Control Panel** and press **Enter**.

2 In the Control Panel window that appears, tap or click **Hardware and Sound**.

3 In the Hardware and Sound window, tap or click **Devices and Printers**.

4 After you've reviewed available printers, you can tap or click the **X** in the upper-right corner to close the Devices and Printers window.

THE DEFAULT PRINTER

Selecting a default printer

In the Devices and Printers window, the printer that contains the green checkmark is the default printer that Windows will use when you print from a legacy app. You can select a different default printer.

1 Tap and hold or right-click the printer that you want to set as the default printer.

2 Tap or click **Set As Default Printer**. The green checkmark moves to the printer you selected.

3 Tap or click the **X** in the upper-right corner to close the Devices and Printers window.

In this chapter, you learned how to:
- Examine the Desktop

- Pin and unpin apps

- Work with the Recycle Bin

- Manage app windows

- Work with Desktop tools

Bottom Line

This chapter shows you how to work with apps running in the Desktop app, such as pinning and unpinning from the task bar and moving and adjusting windows. You also learn how to work with the Recycle Bin, restore and delete files, and work with desktop tools such as the Ribbon and Quick Access toolbar.

Knowledge Assessment

True/False

Circle T if the statement is true or F if the statement is false.

T F **1.** The taskbar only contains apps that are actively running.

T F **2.** You can use the System tray to access the Action Center.

T F **3.** The Notification area notifies you about new email messages to read.

T F **4.** You can only pin legacy apps to the Desktop taskbar.

T F **5.** You can launch the Desktop Control Panel from the File Explorer to view information about your computer.

T F **6.** When you right-click a file and choose Delete from the content menu, that file is always permanently deleted.

T F **7.** The Recycle Bin changes its appearance depending on the state of the folder.

T F **8.** The Ribbon contains tabs of commands related to the current window.

T F **9.** You can display two windows side by side by using WinKey+Right Arrow with the first window selected, and WinKey+Left Arrow with the other selected.

T F **10.** If you cut a piece of information, it is the same as deleting it from the computer.

Multiple Choice

Select the best response for the following statements.

1. What is the Recycle Bin used for?
   a. To hold files you want to move to a new location.
   b. To transfer files between the Start screen and Desktop app.
   c. To temporarily hold things you intend to delete, and then for either restoring the files or deleting them permanently.
   d. To restore files that have been permanently deleted.

2. What are the two apps that are pinned by default to the Desktop taskbar?
   a. File Explorer and Mail
   b. Internet Explorer and Mail
   c. Calculator and File Explorer
   d. Internet Explorer and File Explorer

3. The network access indicator displays information about what kind of network?
   a. Your wired connection.
   b. Your internet connection.
   c. Your wireless connection.
   d. A and C.
   e. B and C.

4. What does the Navigation pane in the File Explorer contain?
   a. Your local computer network.
   b. A compact web browser for navigating websites.
   c. Common locations on your computer.
   d. Connected storage media connected to your computer, such as external hard drives and USB thumb drives.

5. How do you move a shortcut from the desktop to the Recycle Bin?
   a. Right-click the file and choose Delete.
   b. Drag it over the Recycle Bin on the desktop.
   c. Drag it to the System Tray, and then choose Move to Recycle Bin from a menu that opens.
   d. A and B.
   e. B and C.

6. How do you restore a file that has been moved to the recycle bin?
   a. Drag the file from the Recycle Bin to another folder, such as Documents.
   b. From the Recycle bin, click the file and choose Restore the Selected Items from the Ribbon.
   c. From the Recycle bin, right-click the file and choose Restore.
   d. All of the above.
   e. B and C.

7. What functionality exists in the upper-right corner of a Desktop app window?
   a. A control used to switch between app windows and show the windows side-by-side.
   b. Buttons to resize the dimensions of the window.
   c. The App control menu.
   d. Buttons to minimize, restore, and close the window.

8. How do you add buttons to the Quick Access Toolbar?
   a. Click the Add button, and drag the buttons that appear in a menu to the toolbar.
   b. Click the button on the right of the toolbar, a downward arrow, and choose from the list of available commands.
   c. Click the Gear icon on the right of the toolbar, and choose from a menu of available commands.

9. What page do you view available printers on your computer?
   a. Devices and Printers page from the Desktop's Control Panel.
   b. Devices and Printers page from the System Tray.
   c. Print command from the Ribbon.

10. What printer is considered the default when viewing available devices?
   a. The printer that is highlighted with a blue box.
   b. The printer in the Default section.
   c. The printer with a green checkmark.
   d. The printer with the largest icon.

Competency Assessment

Project 3-1: Pinning and shortcuts.

1. Install a new legacy app.
2. Pin this app to the Desktop taskbar, Start screen, and also create a Desktop shortcut for the app.

Project 3-2: **Devices**

1. Use the Navigation pane to locate the default Documents, Music, Pictures, and Video files and Computer.

2. Use the Navigation pane to locate the item that provides information about devices connected to your computer.

Proficiency Assessment

Project 3-4: **Quick Access Toolbar**

1. Open WordPad, and maximize the Ribbon if it isn't already maximized.

2. Customize the Quick Access Toolbar so it only contains Save, Send in email, and Print Preview.

3. After you finish, minimize the Ribbon.

Project 3-5: **Recycle Bin**

1. Create a new document you do not need to keep, or duplicate an existing one.

2. Send the file to the Recycle Bin, then restore it, and then delete the file permanently.

Mastery Assessment

Project 3-6: **Recycle Bin**

1. Adjust the fixed size of the Recycle Bin for your main computer, and that of any external drives connected to your computer.

Project 3-7: **Copying and Pasting**

1. Copy images, text, and hyperlinks from a web page, and paste them into a WordPad document.

2. Then, cut and paste the content between two WordPad documents.

LESSON SKILL MATRIX

In this lesson, you will learn the following skills:

Navigate files and folders

Manage files and folders with File Explorer

Work with libraries

Search for files in the File Explorer

KEY TERMS

- **Subfolders**
- **Preview pane**
- **Compressed file**
- **Libraries**

 Rob at Contoso is a program manager for three teams: accounting, marketing and engineering. Rob manages hundreds of files and folders of many file types, and needs to use the File Explorer efficiently in order to appropriately manage the large number of documents he handles every day.

SOFTWARE ORIENTATION

Items you create and apps you install on your device are stored in locations you specify. You need to be able to indicate where things are stored and know how to locate your apps or documents the next time you need them.

Figure 4-1

A. Quick Access Toolbar.
B. File Explorer
C. Search box.
D. Ribbon tabs.
E. Ribbon.
F. Navigation pane.
G. Selected Folder.
H. Folder Contents (currently containing Library folders)

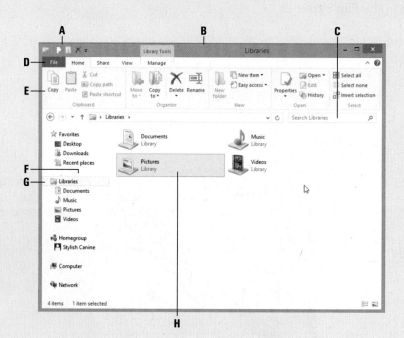

STARTING UP

In this lesson, you will work with several files from the lessons that accompany this book. Make sure that you have loaded the files onto your computer before starting this lesson.

NAVIGATING IN FILE EXPLORER

File Explorer, a legacy Desktop app that comes with Windows, is an organizational tool you can use to manage the files on your computer's hard drive. As you'll see in this lesson, you can create folders and place your files in them, delete files and folders, and copy and move files and folders. Before you begin the exercises in this lesson, you need to become familiar with File Explorer's interface.

STEP BY STEP   **Opening File Explorer**

1   Open the Desktop app (tap or click it on the Start screen or press WinKey (⊞)+D).

2   Tap or click the File Explorer button on the Desktop taskbar.

Figure 4-2

A. Quick Access Toolbar.
B. Ribbon tabs.
C. Ribbon.
D. Address bar.
E. Search box.
F. Contents of the currently selected folder.
G. Currently selected folder.
H. Navigation page.
I. Tap or click here to open File Explorer.

In the File Explorer window, you'll find:

- The Quick Access Toolbar: you can use this toolbar to quickly perform common activities in File Explorer, such as creating a new folder or viewing the properties of a file or folder.

- The Ribbon: the Ribbon contains commands you can use while you work in File Explorer. The commands are organized using tabs, and each tab contains groups; group names appear below the commands on the Ribbon. For example, the Home tab, shown in the figure, contains the Clipboard, Organize, New, Open, and Select groups.

- The Navigation pane: appearing along the left side of the File Explorer window, use this pane to navigate to folders and files you want to use.

- The currently selected folder: in the Navigation pane, the highlighted folder represents the currently selected folder. File Explorer opens, by default, to the Libraries folder.

Take Note   You will learn more about the Libraries folder later in this lesson.

The contents of the currently selected folder: once you select a folder in the Navigation pane, File Explorer displays the contents of that folder in the right pane. Folders can contain other folders as well as files. Since this pane has no official name, this lesson will refer to it as the "right-hand contents pane."

• The address bar: the address bar identifies the path name of the currently-selected folder and contains a Forward and Back button that you can use to navigate upward or downward through folders.

• The Search box: you can use this box to search for files or folders on your computer. Read more about the Search box later in this lesson.

Understanding Path and File names

All files typically are named using two parts that are separated by a period (.); although it is possible for a filename to contain several parts, all separated by periods. In all cases, the part to the right of the last period is called the extension and the part to the left—including any other periods—is called the filename. Filenames can be as long as you want, and typically consist of letters and numbers. Extensions are supplied by the program used to create the file and are typically either three or four characters long. By default, File Explorer doesn't display extensions, but displaying them can be most helpful when you work with files. (For more information, see the section, "Understanding and Viewing File Formats" later in this lesson.)

Folder names typically don't have an extension, but you can supply an extension when you name a folder.

A path name identifies the exact placement of a file or folder on your computer. For example, if your hard drive is drive C, the path name of any file or folder located on your hard drive begins with C. Traditionally, when you write out a path name, it includes the drive name, a colon, and a back slash (\), followed by folder names separated by back slashes, with the last entry in the path name being either a folder or a filename. A typical path name might be: C:\Users*username*\My Documents\Windows0401_01.jpg, where *username* is the name of the account being used on the computer—often your name.

When a folder contains additional folders, a small caret appears to the left of that folder in the Navigation pane. The direction of the caret visually indicates whether the folder is open or closed. A black, downward-pointing caret identifies an open folder, while a white, sideways-pointing caret identifies a closed folder. You can tap or click the caret to open or close the folder. Folders inside other folders appear indented in the Navigation pane.

Take Note   Tapping or clicking a caret beside a folder opens the folder in the Navigation pane but does not display the folder's contents. You must tap or click the folder image or the folder name to view its contents in the right-hand contents pane

Figure 4-3

You can open folders to see their contents or close them to hide their contents.

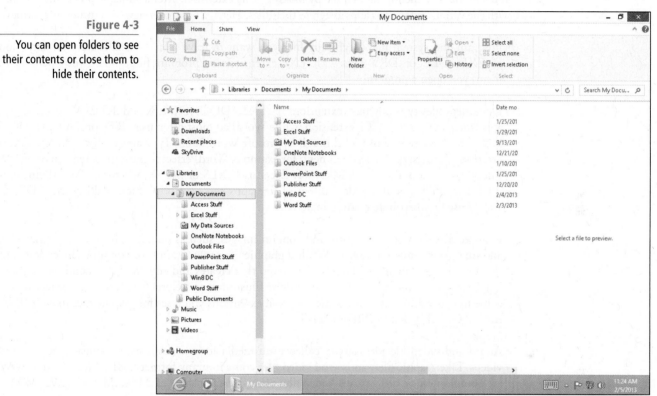

Some folders have no caret beside them; these folders might contain files, but they don't contain any additional folders; the missing caret provides you with a visual indicator that a folder contains no additional folders.

Take Note   Folders inside other folders are typically referred to as **subfolders**. A folder that contains subfolders is typically referred to as a parent folder.

MANAGING FILES AND FOLDERS

Using File Explorer, you can manage the files on your computer's hard drive as if the hard drive were a digital filing cabinet. Windows creates some folders for you, and you can create additional folders as you need them. For example, you could drop all your vacation pictures into the Pictures folder, but you might prefer to organize them into folders that match the place you visited so you can find a picture more easily.

Understanding and viewing file formats

You can identify the format of a file by looking at its extension; after a while, you become familiar with the various extensions apps assign to their files. Here's a basic overview of common file formats:

- Program and system files—typically files you want to leave alone—usually have an extension of .EXE, .DLL, or .DRV. Files with .EXE extensions are program files; should you open one of them, you open a program.

- Document files typically have extensions of .TXT, .DOC, .DOCX, and .RTF. Windows legacy app Notepad uses the .TXT extension, while WordPad most often uses .RTF or .DOCX. .DOC is used by Microsoft Word 97 through Microsoft Word 2003. Typically, each vendor creates an extension for each product's document; for example, WordPerfect files use an extension of .WPD, Adobe Photoshop uses .PSD, Microsoft Excel uses .XLS or .XLSX, Microsoft PowerPoint uses .PPT and .PPTX, and a wide number of free apps can read .PDF files, making the .PDF file widely used to distribute reading material.

- Graphic files are visual in nature and contain images, such as photographs, pictures, drawings, and images of computer screens. While a graphic file can contain text, you typically cannot edit the text in a graphic file without using an app that creates and edits files that combine text and graphics, such as the legacy app Paint, Adobe Illustrator, and Corel Paint Shop Pro. Graphic files come in many different types; some common extensions you'll see for graphic files include .JPG, .BMP, .GIF, .PNG, and .TIF (or .TIFF).

- Audio and video file formats are called multimedia formats and include music, movies, and videos. Like graphic files, audio and video files come in many formats .MP3, .WMA, and .WAV are common music file formats. Video files often use extensions of .MP4, .MPEG, .AVI, .WMV, and .MOV.

STEP BY STEP   **Viewing file format extensions**

File Explorer doesn't display file extensions by default, but you can change your settings to help you identify a file's type. Follow these steps:

1 Tap or click the View tab in File Explorer.

2 Tap or click the Options button to display the Folder Options dialog box.

Figure 4-4

Use the View tab of the Folder Options dialog box to control the way filenames appear on your computer.

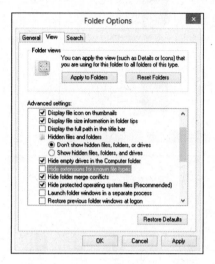

3 Tap or click the View tab.

4 Remove the checkmark from the Hide Extensions for Known File Types checkbox.

5 Tap or click OK.

Changing views

You can control the way files appear in the right-hand contents pane using any of eight views; each view provides you with different information.

Change the way files appear depending on the type of files you are working with. You might need more data about a file if you have many similarly named files, or if you are working with images you may want to display an image preview.

Switch views by tapping or clicking the View tab, and then selecting a view from the Layout group.

Figure 4-5

The Extra Large Icons view.

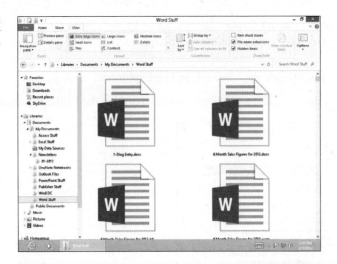

Figure 4-6

The Large Icons view.

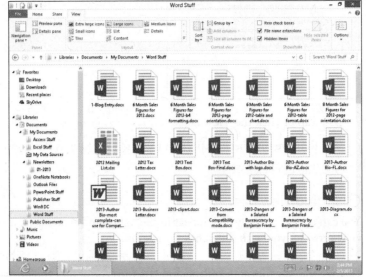

Figure 4-7

The Medium Icons view.

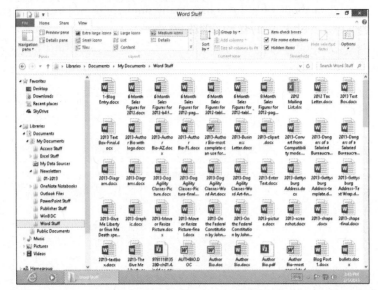

Figure 4-8

The Small Icons view.

Figure 4-9

The List view.

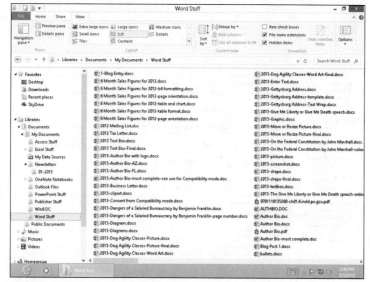

Figure 4-10

The Details view.

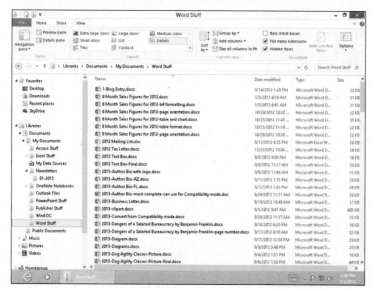

Figure 4-11

The Tiles view.

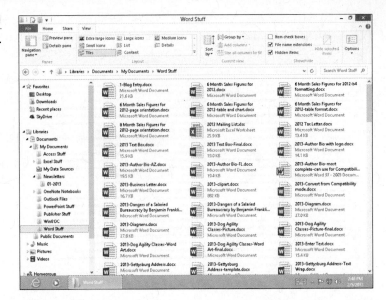

Figure 4-12

The Content view.

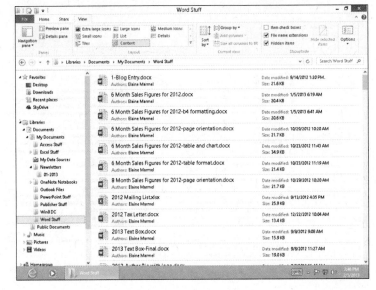

When you view pictures, you might find the **Preview pane** handy. For example, in the right-hand contents pane, you can view your pictures in List view, Details view, Small Icons, Medium Icons, or any other view; to see a larger view of one of your pictures in the Preview pane, tap or click the image file in the right-hand contents pane.

Figure 4-13

Viewing a picture in the Preview pane.

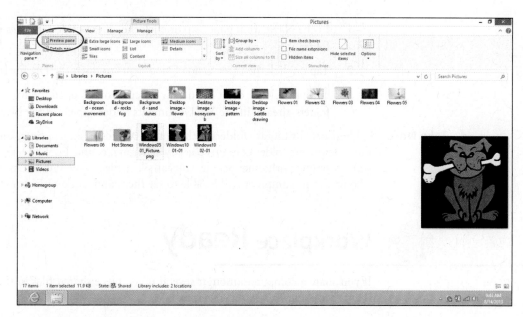

Images and clip art used with permission from Microsoft.

To display the Preview pane, tap or click the View tab, and in the Panes group, tap or click Preview Pane.

Creating a new folder

The most commonly used folder on a computer that uses Windows is the My Documents folder. You can store all documents in the My Documents folder, but that would be the equivalent of putting all the papers in your office in one file cabinet that had only one drawer. You'd have a better time finding things if you organized your papers into folders and established an organizational scheme for the folders within the file cabinet drawers—for example, many people organize file folders alphabetically.

You can think of your computer's hard drive as a digital file cabinet, but your digital file cabinet has one advantage over a physical file cabinet: it has, essentially, no limit on the number of folders it can hold.

Take Note   Most files take up very little space, with graphic files taking up more space than document files. But the size of today's hard drives is so large that you'd have to work very hard to fill up your hard drive, even if you store many years' worth of pictures on it from annual vacations. For the most part, you have an almost limitless amount of space in which to store information.

STEP BY STEP   **Create a set of folders for a newsletter project**

When you create a new folder, you first select the parent folder in which you want to place the new folder. Follow these steps to create a set of folders for a newsletter project.

1   In the Navigation pane, tap or click the caret beside Libraries to open the Libraries folder.

2   Tap or click the caret beside Documents to open the Documents folder.

3   Tap or click the caret beside My Documents to open the My Documents folder. Any folders already in the My Documents folder appear in the Navigation pane.

Take Note   All four default Library folders each contain two folders: one private and one public. For example, the Documents folder contains the My Documents and Public Documents folders. If you share your computer with other people, you can place files in the Public Documents folder and everyone who uses your computer will be able to see them and work with them.

Workplace **Ready**

If you share a computer amongst several users, place shared files in the Public Documents folder that is accessible to all user accounts.

1   Tap or click the words "My Documents" in the Navigation pane. Any folders already in the My Documents folder appear on the right side of the File Explorer screen.

2   Tap or click the Home tab on the Ribbon.

3   Tap or click the New Folder button. A new folder appears in the right-hand contents pane of File Explorer; the words "New folder" appear highlighted in blue, waiting for you to replace them with a folder name.

Figure 4-14

Creating a new folder in the My Documents folder.

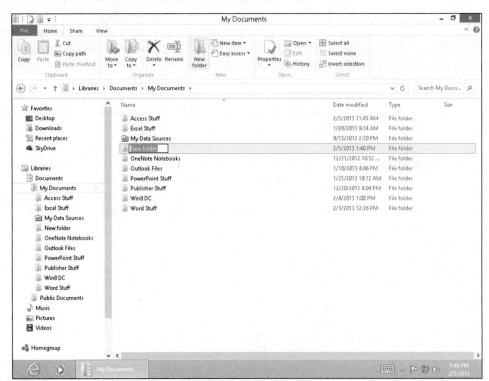

4 Type Newsletters and press, tap, or click Enter.

Figure 4-15

The newly created folder
appears in the Navigation
pane and in the right-hand
contents pane.

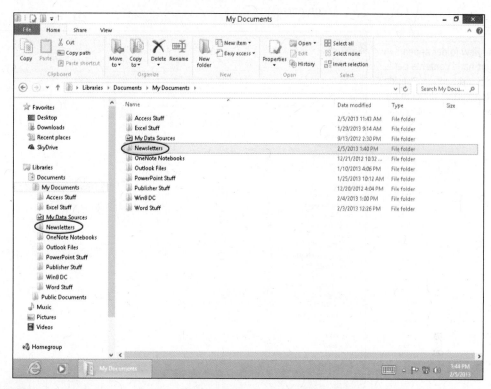

STEP BY STEP   **Create a folder within the Newsletters folder**

To create a folder within the Newsletters folder follow these steps:

1 In the Navigation pane, tap or click the Newsletters folder.

2 Tap or click the Home tab on the Ribbon.

3 Tap or click the New Folder button. A new folder appears in the right-hand pane of File Explorer; the words "New folder" appear highlighted in blue, waiting for you to replace them with a folder name.

4   Type **01-2013** and press, tap, or click **Enter**. The new folder appears in the right-hand contents pane.

Figure 4-16

The new folder appears in the right-hand contents pane, and a caret appears beside the Newsletters folder in the Navigation pane.

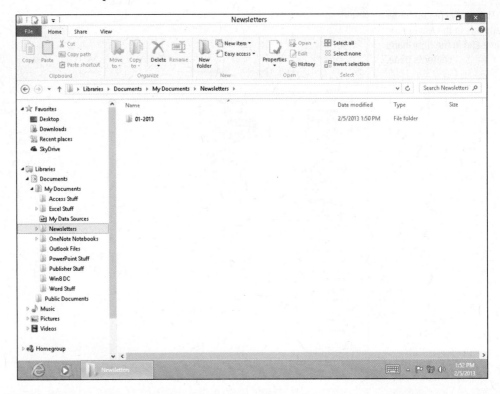

Take Note   In the Navigation pane, File Explorer organizes folders inside of other folders in alphabetical order by default, and digits, from 0–9, come before letters. In our example, the newsletter will have monthly issues; naming the folders using numbers for each month ensures that the monthly folders appear in order from January to December for the year.

Selecting and deselecting files

Whenever you want to rename, copy, move, or delete a file or folder, you must first select the file or folder. Although you can select folders in the Navigation pane, most people prefer to focus on selecting files or folders in the right-hand contents pane. Consequently, most people prefer to tap or click in the Navigation pane primarily to make the information they want to work on appear in the right-hand contents pane.

Typically, a user might choose to work in the Details view because this view provides the most information about a file on a single line.

To select a single file, tap or click that file in the right-hand contents pane. File Explorer highlights the selected file in blue.

Figure 4-17

A single file selected in Details view.

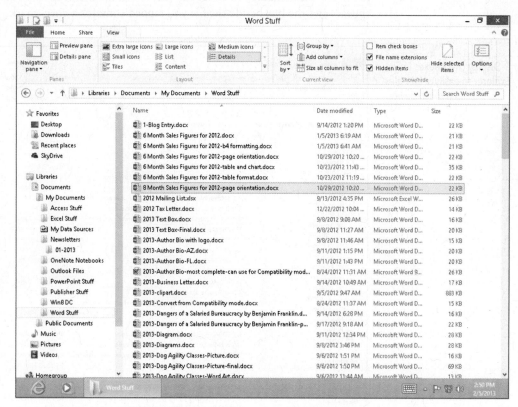

To cancel a selection, tap or click anywhere outside the selection; for example, you could tap or click a different folder in the Navigation pane.

To select multiple files using a touch device, display item checkboxes beside each filename. On File Explorer's View tab, in the Show/Hide group, tap Item Check Boxes. A blank column appears to the left of the filename. To select any file, tap in the blank space beside that filename; a checkbox appears and the box beside the file you tapped contains a checkmark.

Figure 4-18

Display checkboxes in File Explorer to easily select files on a touch device.

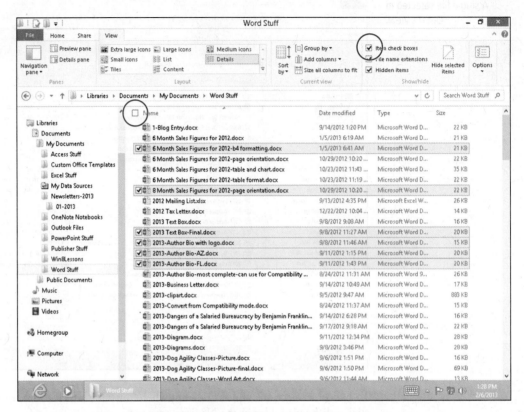

Take Note   You can quickly select all the files in a folder by tapping the checkbox that appears above the column and beside the Name column heading.

To use a keyboard to select multiple files simultaneously, use either of the following two techniques.

Selecting multiple contiguous files

1   If necessary, switch to Details view.

2   Tap or click the first file.

3   Press and hold the Shift key.

4   Tap or click the last file you want to select. All selected files appear highlighted in blue.

Figure 4-19

Selecting multiple contiguous files.

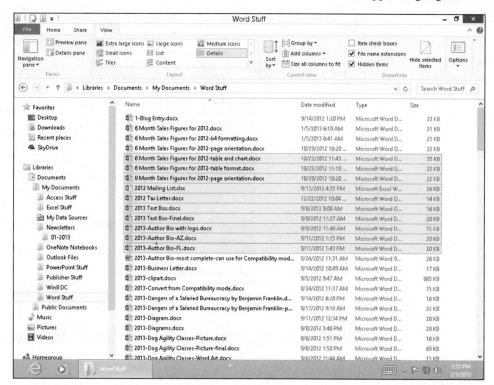

STEP BY STEP   Selecting multiple files that do not appear contiguously in Details view

1   Tap or click the first file you want to select.

2   Press and hold the **Ctrl** key.

3   Tap or click the next file you want to select.

4   Repeat Steps 2 and 3 for each file you want to select. All selected files appear highlighted in blue.

Figure 4-20

Selecting multiple non-contiguous files.

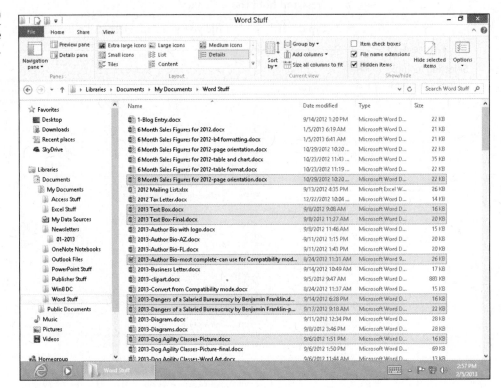

Renaming files and folders

You may find that you want to change the name of a file or folder to keep things organized or, perhaps, there was a mistake in the filename. In such cases, you can easily rename files or folders using File Explorer; the technique used is applicable to both files and folders.

Take Note   If you rename a file, only rename the filename portion; don't change the extension, or the app that created the file won't be able to recognize and open it

---

STEP BY STEP   **Renaming folders**

In the next exercise, you will rename the folders you created for your newsletter project. Follow these steps:

1   Tap or click **My Documents** in the Navigation pane.

Take Note   Tap or click the caret beside the folder you select in Step 1 so that any folders inside the selected folder are visible in the Navigation pane. That way, you can more easily see the effects of renaming the folder.

2   In the right-hand contents pane, tap or click the **Newsletter** folder.

3   Press **F2** on the keyboard or, on the Home tab, tap or click the **Rename** button in the Organize group. The folder name appears in the right-hand contents pane highlighted in bright blue.

Figure 4-21

A folder being renamed.

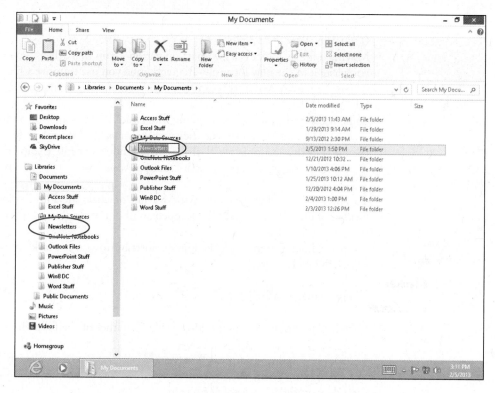

4   Type **Newsletter-2013** for the new name of the folder and press, tap, or click **Enter**. The folder appears in both the Navigation pane and the right-hand contents pane with its new name.

Figure 4-22

The folder after renaming.

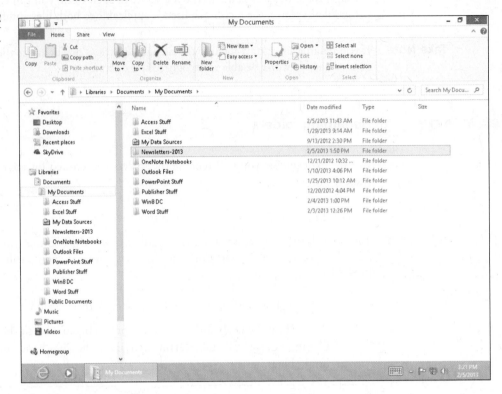

Moving files and folders

Moving a file or folder is a two-part operation—you first select and cut the file or folder and then you paste it in the new location. The technique you use to move a file is the same as the technique you use to move a folder; this example demonstrates how to move a file from one folder to another.

Some users find moving and copying files easier if they can view two folders simultaneously: the source folder containing the file they want to move and the target folder where they want to move the file. For this example, we'll display two windows of File Explorer side-by-side, as described in the previous lesson, "Working with Desktop Apps."

To open the first File Explorer window, tap or click the File Explorer button on the Desktop taskbar or press WinKey (■)+E. To open another File Explorer window, do either of the following:

• Tap and hold or right-click the File Explorer button on the taskbar. When the menu appears, tap or click File Explorer.

• Press WinKey (■)+E again.

• To display the two windows side by side, do either of the following:

• Click one window and press WinKey (■)+Right Arrow to place that window on the right side of the screen. Then, click the other window and press WinKey (■)+Left Arrow to place that window on the left side of the screen.

• Using your finger or your mouse, drag the title bar of one window toward one edge of the screen. When your finger or the mouse pointer reaches the edge of the screen, a window outline appears; lift your finger or release the mouse button. Repeat for the other window, dragging to the opposite side of the screen.

STEP BY STEP   **Moving files**

Now we'll move a file from the Win8Lessons folder for this chapter to the Newsletters-2013\01-2013 folder.

1 In File Explorer on the left side of your screen, use the Navigation pane to navigate to and select the Windows04lessons folder that you saved to your hard drive.

2 In File Explorer on the right side of your screen, use the Navigation pane to navigate and select to the folder in which you want to place the file.

Take Note You can identify which File Explorer window is active by the on-screen colors. By default, selected files appear light blue in the active window.

3 In File Explorer on the left, tap or click the file called **Windows0401_test.rtf**. File Explorer selects the file.

4 On the Home tab of the Ribbon, tap or click the Cut button.

Figure 4-23

Moving a file from the selected folder on the left to the se- lected folder on the right.

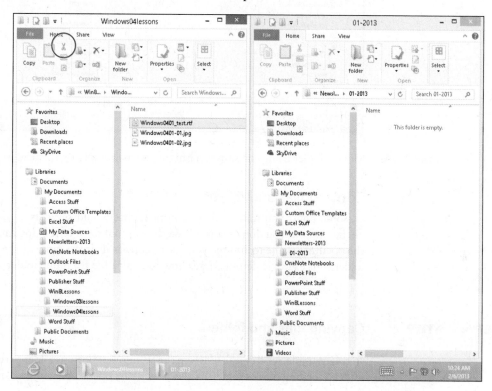

5 Tap or click the title bar of File Explorer on the right side of your screen.

Take Note When windows are set side by side, File Explorer remembers the last folder you selected in both windows. You don't need to reselect the folder on the right; you can simply tap or click the title bar on the File Explorer window on the right

6   On the Ribbon, tap or click the **Paste** button. The file you selected in Step 3 appears in the folder you selected in Step 2 and disappears from the folder you selected in Step 1.

Figure 4-24

When you move a file, it disappears from its original location.

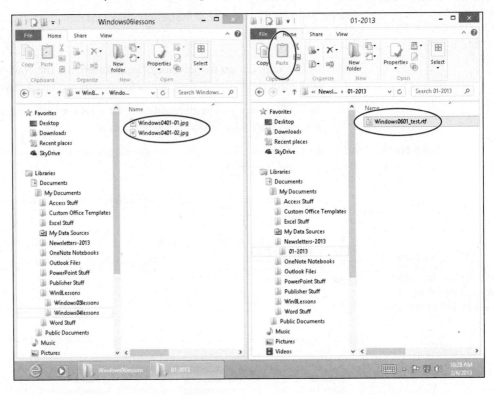

Take Note   Move a folder using the same technique, but select a folder instead of a file in Step 3.

Copying files and folders

At some point you may have a document that would serve as a good starting point for a new document, but you don't want to lose the original form of the document. You can make a copy of the document. The technique you use to copy a file is the same as the technique you use to copy a folder; this example demonstrates how to copy a file from one folder to another.

STEP BY STEP   **Copying files and folders**

In this example, we'll copy a file from the Windows04lessons folder to the Newsletters-2013\01-2013 folder. Copying files or folders is also a two-part operation: you first select and copy a file or folder, and then you paste it.

1   In File Explorer, use the Navigation pane to navigate to the Windows04lessons folder that you saved to your hard drive.

2   Tap or click the file called **Windows0401_test.rtf**. File Explorer selects the file.

3 On the Home tab of the Ribbon, tap or click the Copy button.

Figure 4-25

Select the file you want to copy and tap or click the Copy button on the Ribbon.

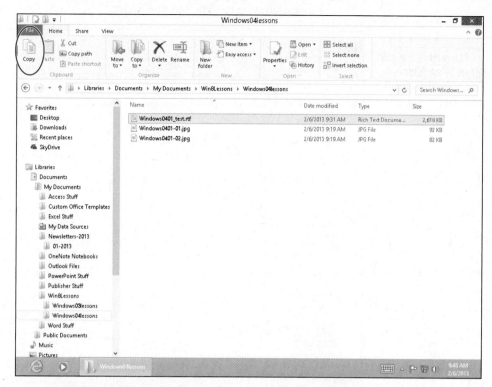

4 In the Navigation pane, tap or click the folder in which you want to place the file.

5 Tap or click the Paste button on the Ribbon. A copy of the file appears in the folder you selected in Step 4.

Figure 4-26

A copy of the file appears in the folder selected in the Navigation pane.

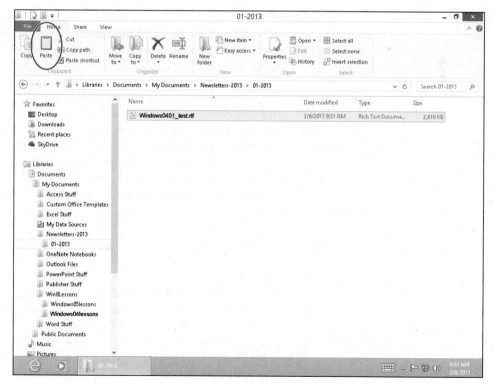

6   To verify that the original still appears in the folder you selected in Step 1, use the Navigation pane to redisplay that folder.

Figure 4-27

The original file still appears in the folder you selected in Step 1.

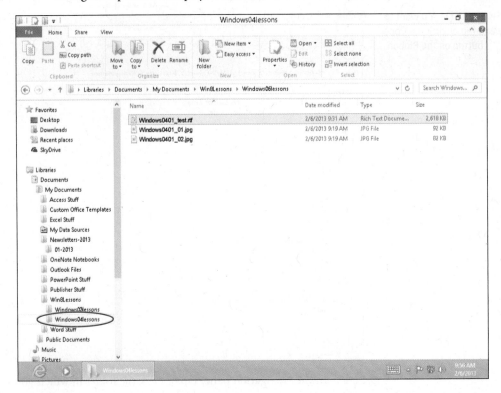

Take Note   Copy a folder using the same technique, but select a folder instead of a file in Step 2.

Copying files and CDs

You can copy files to CDs using the steps presented in this section with a few modifications. Before you choose to store files on a CD, be aware that CDs can fail without warning.

To copy files to a CD, place a blank CD into the CD/DVD drive. In the Navigation pane, tap or click the CD/DVD drive, and File Explorer displays the Burn a Disc wizard. Optionally, supply a disc title, and then tap or click Like a USB Flash Drive to create a CD to which you can add files to the disc at a later date. Tap or click Next. File Explorer formats the disc in the CD/DVD drive and then displays a File Explorer window with the CD/DVD drive selected in the Navigation pane and a message in the right-hand pane that tells you to drag files to the folder to add them to the disc. You can drag and drop files on the disc, or you can copy and paste files using the buttons on Home tab of the Ribbon, the same way you'd copy and paste any file or folder. When you Paste, select the CD/DVD drive as the target location.

Zipping and unzipping compressed files

At times, you might receive an e-mail attachment or download a file from the Internet that arrives in *compressed* form; the **compressed file** actually contains one or more files that were compressed to save space, making the e-mail or download delivery time shorter. To use those files, you need to extract the files from the compressed file.

Because a compressed file actually contains multiple files, File Explorer treats the compressed file like a special type of folder. You'll hear these special files called *compressed folders*, *zipped folders*, *zipped files*, or *ZIP archive files*.

You also can create compressed folders to send large files, such as pictures, via e-mail.

STEP BY STEP **Zipping and unzipping compressed files**

In this example, we'll create a compressed folder using some of the files in the Windows04lessons folder.

1   In File Explorer, use the Navigation pane to navigate to the Windows04lessons folder

2   Select the two files named **Windows0401-01.jpg** and **Windows0401-02.jpg**.

Take Note   Remember: to select both files using the keyboard and mouse, click the first file and then press and hold Ctrl as you click the second file. To select both files using a touch device, display Item Check Boxes using the View tab on the Ribbon; then, tap each file to check the boxes beside the filenames.

3   Tap and hold or right-click the selected files to display a shortcut menu.

Figure 4-28

Creating a compressed folder.

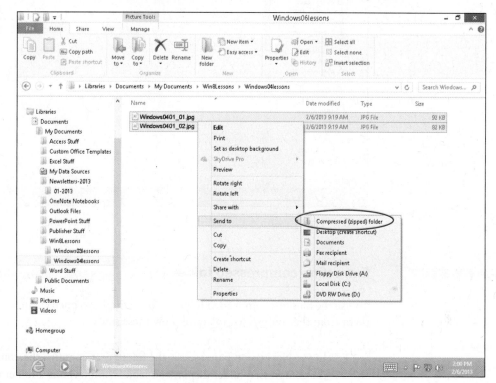

4   From the shortcut menu, tap or click Send To.

5   Tap or click Compressed (zipped) folder. File Explorer zips your files into a new compressed file and suggests, for the file name, the name of the last file you selected to zip. File Explorer presents the name highlighted so you can change it.

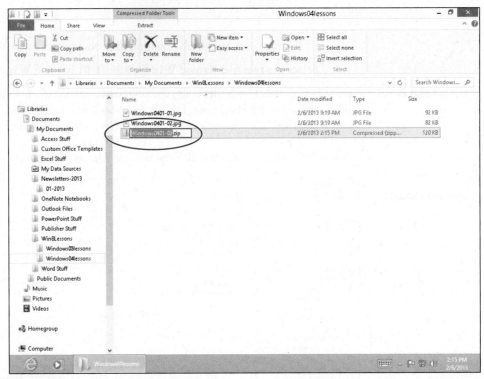

Figure 4-29

A new compressed file appears ready to be renamed.

6   Type Lesson 4 Pictures and press Enter or tap or click an empty spot in the window.

STEP BY STEP   Extracting compressed folders

To use the files in a compressed folder—for example, to open them in an app—you should extract them from the compressed folder. Follow these steps:

1   In the Navigation pane, select the folder that contains the compressed folder. On its left, the compressed folder displays an icon that looks like a folder containing a zipper.

2   Tap or click the compressed folder to select it.

3   Tap or click the Extract tab on the Ribbon.

4   Tap or click the Extract All button. File Explorer displays the Extract Compressed (Zipped) Folders window and suggests a destination folder in which to place the file it extracts. By default, the folder name is the name of the compressed file and will appear inside the same folder that contains the compressed file. In this example, File Explorer will place the unzipped files in a folder call Lesson 4 Pictures, and that folder will appear inside the Windows04lessons folder.

Figure 4-30

File Explorer suggests using the name of the compressed folder for the name of the folder where the unzipped files will appear.

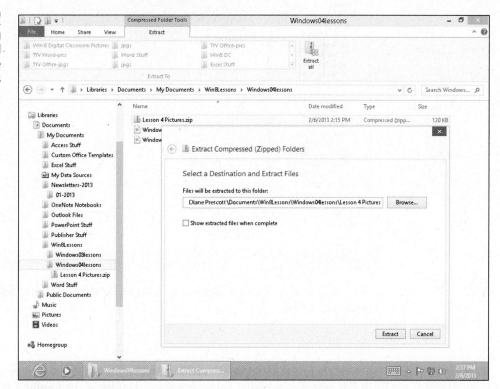

5   Tap or click the Show Extracted Files When Complete checkbox to deselect it.

Take Note   If you leave the box selected, File Explorer will not only extract the files, but also open another File Explorer window to display the files. To avoid this distraction, uncheck the box.

6   Tap or click the Extract button. File Explorer extracts the files to the new folder, which appears along with the original zip file.

Figure 4-31

The compressed file and the folder containing the extracted files both appear in the same folder.

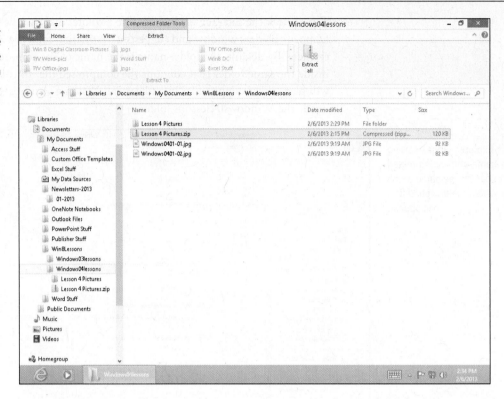

You can now select the new folder just as you would select any other folder and work with the files in the new folder.

Deleting files and folders

You might find that you don't need a particular file or folder anymore, so you can choose to delete it. For example, now that you've extracted the files in the Lesson 4 Pictures.zip compressed file, you can delete the file.

Take Note   Only delete documents you have created or documents that someone else has given to you. Do not delete any files associated with Windows 8 or any of your programs; if you do, a program or your computer might no longer work. As a rule of thumb, don't delete anything unless you can confirm its content and know it is something you don't need.

To delete a file, select it by tapping or clicking it. You can select multiple files to delete at the same time. Then, press the Delete key on your keyboard or tap the Home tab on the Ribbon and tap the Delete button.

Figure 4-32

Tap or click the Delete button to delete the selected file(s) or folder(s).

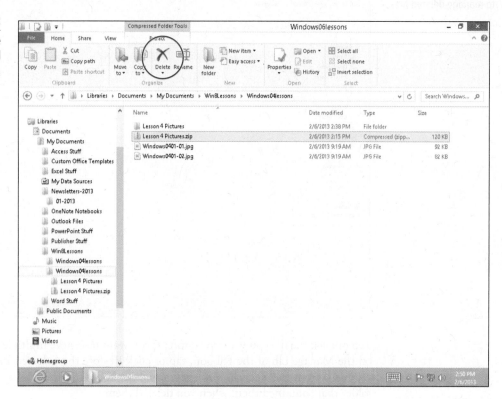

When you delete a file or folder, it typically moves to the Recycle Bin. If you accidentally delete a file, you can restore it from the Recycle Bin. On the Desktop, double-tap or double-click the Recycle Bin; the contents of the Recycle Bin appears in a File Explorer window.

Take Note   A file might not appear in the Recycle Bin if there is no room in the Recycle Bin for the file. File Explorer will warn you before you delete a file that won't fit in the Recycle Bin.

Figure 4-33

The Recycle Bin window in File Explorer contains special tools to manage deleted files.

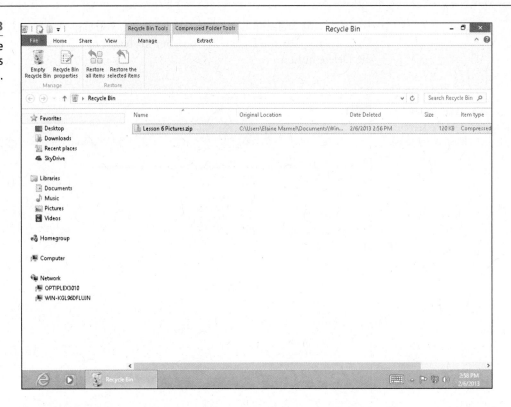

Tap or click the file you want to restore; if you want to restore multiple files, select them all. Then, on the Manage tab of the Ribbon, tap or click Restore the Selected Items. File Explorer removes the file(s) from the Recycle Bin (they no longer appear in the window) and returns them to the folder that contained them when you deleted them.

Emptying the Recycle Bin

The Recycle Bin is a special file on your computer that has a fixed size. If you never empty it, eventually Windows won't be able to store things you delete in the Recycle Bin because the Recycle Bin will be unable to hold additional items. In this case, when you delete, you delete permanently. We strongly suggest that you periodically empty the Recycle Bin.

For your peace of mind, you can choose to open and examine the contents of the Recycle Bin, but it's not necessary. To empty the Recycle Bin, do either of the following:

- Tap and hold or right-click the Recycle Bin on the Desktop and choose Empty Recycle Bin from the shortcut menu that appears.

- Double-tap or double-click the Recycle Bin to display it in File Explorer; then, on the File Explorer Ribbon, tap or click Empty Recycle Bin.

In either case, a confirmation message asks you to confirm that you want to empty the Recycle Bin (and permanently delete the items in it); tap or click Yes.

WORKING WITH LIBRARIES

Libraries are another type of special folder that you can use to help you organize your files. Windows comes with four libraries already created for you—Documents, Music, Pictures, and Videos, each of which contains a public and private folder—but you can create your own libraries to support the way you work.

For example, imagine you've transferred vacation pictures to your hard drive and to your external hard drive, with each vacation's pictures stored in its own folder. Now, you want to assemble an album using photos from many different folders stored on separate hard drives. Your first step would be to create a library.

Another example is if you create a monthly newsletter that contains pictures to go along with the text. Although you can keep everything in one folder, the large number of files in one folder might make things difficult when you start to work. On the other hand, if you use separate folders for text and pictures, your information is spread out and can be much more difficult to track and use. Your best solution is to keep your information organized in separate folders and use a library to collect the folders you need to use simultaneously.

Libraries are *virtual folders*. Libraries don't actually store your files; instead, they are shortcuts to the folders that store your files. Using a library enables you to gather and work with files that are stored in several folders in different places—even on separate hard drives. If you delete a file in the folder, the library updates to reflect the change. Similarly, if you delete a file in the library, the folder updates to reflect the deletion.

 # Workplace **Ready**

Use Libraries to gather files that are stored in different locations. This is useful if you use a set of files for a single purpose that need to be stored in their respective project folders. For example, all of your scheduling files from different projects could be stored in a single library.

The default libraries display physical folders that you can find if you use File Explorer's Navigation pane to display C:\Users*username*\\, where *username* is the name of the account you're using when you sign in to your computer. If you examine the contents of the My Documents, My Music, My Pictures, and My Videos folders, you'll find it matches exactly to the content that appears when you display these folders under Libraries in the Navigation pane.

Figure 4-34

View your account in File Explorer's Navigation pane to see folders for My Documents, My Music, My Pictures, and My Videos, all of which appear in the default libraries.

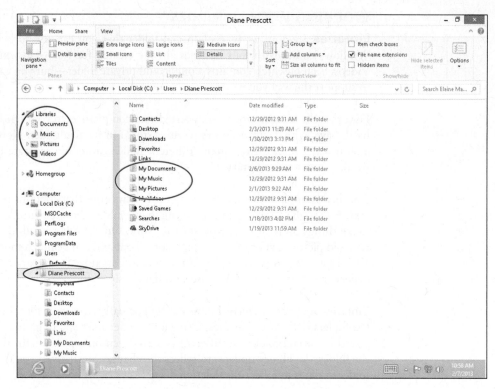

Creating a library

You can easily create your own libraries; each library you create can include up to 50 folders.

STEP BY STEP   **Creating a library**

To illustrate how to create libraries, follow this exercise to create a library for your monthly newsletters:

1   Tap or click **Libraries** in the Navigation pane.

2   On the Home tab, tap or click the New Item button in the New group.

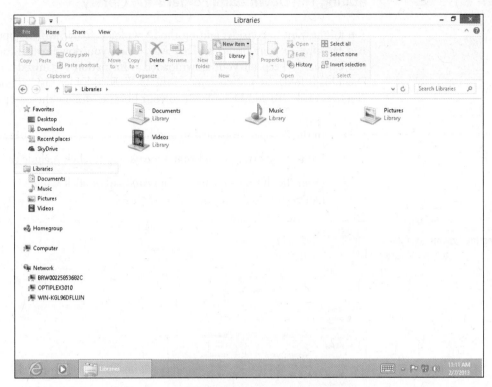

Figure 4-35

Creating a new library.

3   Tap or click Library. A new folder appears in the right-hand contents pane, with the name New Library highlighted in blue, waiting for you to provide a name.

4   Type Newsletters. The new library is empty; you need to include folders in it.

5   In the Navigation pane, tap or click the new library you just created. The right-hand contents pane indicates that your library contains no folders. Read on to learn how to include folders in your library.

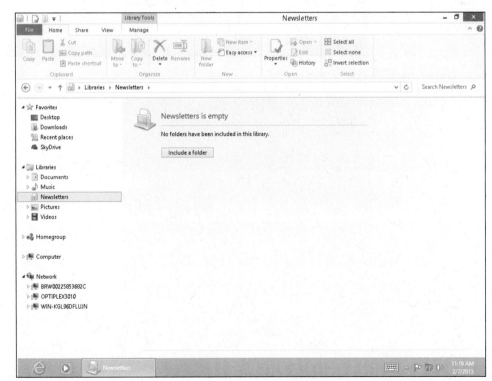

Figure 4-36

An empty library.

STEP BY STEP   **Adding The Downloads Folder As A Library**

You might want to consider adding the Downloads folder, which appears in the Navigation pane as a favorite, to your libraries. That way, when you download information from the Internet, you can easily keep all your downloaded information organized in one place. Setting up the Downloads folder as a library makes the Download folder easy to find since you can navigate to Libraries easily. To add Downloads to your libraries, follow these steps:

1   In the Navigation pane, tap and hold or right-click Downloads.

2   From the shortcut menu that appears, tap or click include in library.

3   From the shortcut menu that appears, tap or click Create New Library to add the Downloads folder to the Libraries folder.

Figure 4-37

Adding the Downloads folder to your library.

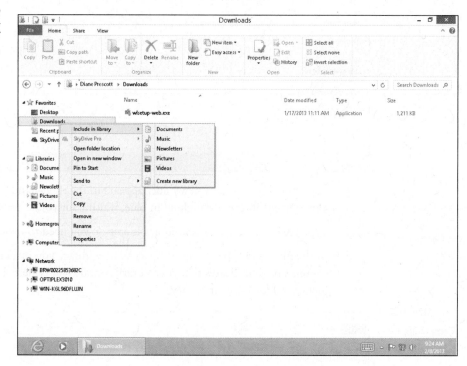

STEP BY STEP   **Adding folders to a library**

To make use of the library, you need to add folders to it. When you add a folder, remember that you aren't moving or copying files; instead, you are creating a link from the library location to a folder's physical location to help you use the information in that folder more easily.

1   In the right-hand contents pane, tap or click Include a Folder. The Include Folder in **library name** dialog box appears (where **library name** is the name of the library you created in the previous exercise); use this dialog box to include folders in your library. For this example, we will add the Newsletter-2013 folder in the My Documents folder and the Newsletter folder in the My Pictures folder.

Figure 4-38

Use this dialog box to select a folder to include in your library.

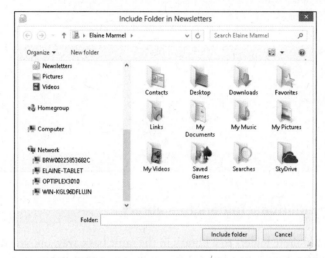

2   Double-tap or double-click My Documents.

3   Select the **Newsletters-2013** folder to include in the library.

Figure 4-39

Adding a folder to the library.

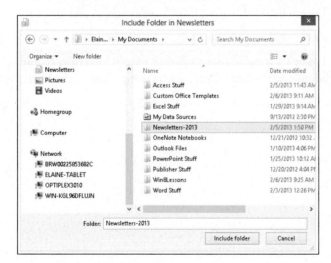

4   Tap or click the Include Folder button. File Explorer redisplays the new library and shows that it contains one folder.

Figure 4-39
The selected folder
and its contents appear
in the new library.

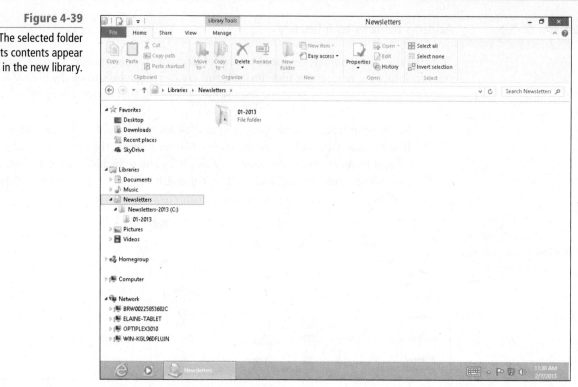

Figure 4-39
The selected folder and its contents appear in the new library.

STEP BY STEP   Adding additional folders to a library

You can add more folders to a library in the same basic way, but you'd start from a different place because there'd no longer be an Include Folder button in the right-hand contents pane for the library. To add another folder to a library, follow these steps:

1 Tap or click the library to which you want to add a folder.

2 Tap or click the Manage tab on the Ribbon.

3 Tap or click the Manage Library button. The **library name** Library Locations dialog box appears, where **library name** is the name of the library you selected in Step 1.

Figure 4-40

Adding more folders to
a library.

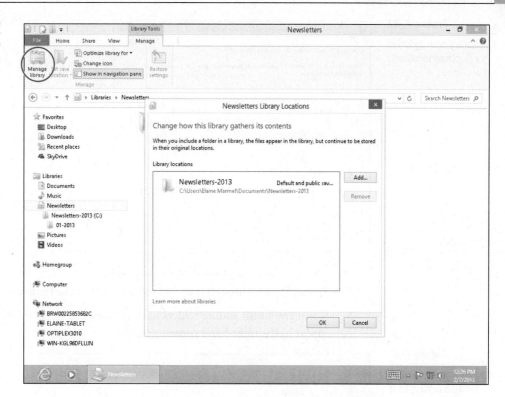

4   Tap or click the Add button to redisplay the Include Folder in **library name** you saw in
    the preceding set of steps.

5   Navigate to the folder you want to include.

Figure 4-41

Navigating to include another
folder in the library.

6   Tap or click **Include Folder**. File Explorer updates the included locations for the library.

Figure 4-42

The library now includes
two locations.

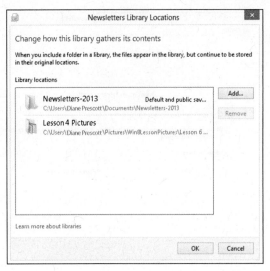

7   Repeat Steps 4 through 6 to add more folders to the library.

8   When you finish adding folders to the library, tap or click OK. The library's contents
appear in the right-hand contents pane.

Figure 4-43

The new library after adding
two folders to it.

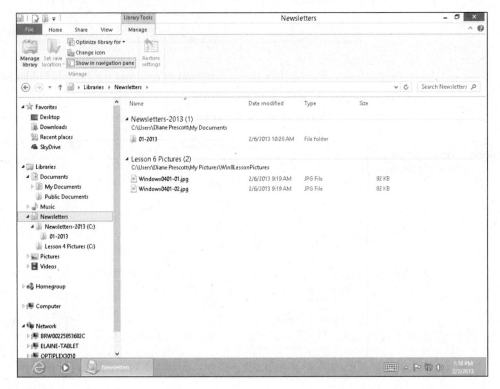

Libraries and deletions

It's important to understand how your actions can affect files and folders in a library.

First, if you delete a library, File Explorer moves the library to the Recycle Bin—but that action doesn't affect the files and folders in the library, because they are accessible elsewhere on your hard drive. Deleting a library does not delete any files or folders included in the library.

Take Note   If you accidentally delete one of the four default libraries—Documents, Music, Pictures, or Videos—you can restore it. Tap and hold or right-click Libraries in the Navigation pane, and from the shortcut menu that appears, tap or click Restore default libraries.

Deleting files or folders that you included in a library has a different effect. If you delete files or folders while working in a library, File Explorer also deletes them from their original locations. Similarly, if you include a folder in a library and then delete the folder from its original location, the folder disappears from both the original location and the library. This occurs because the library entry is really a link to the original location.

If you want to eliminate a folder from a library but keep it in its original location, you should remove the folder containing the item from the library. Removing a folder from a library eliminates the folder from the library but doesn't delete any items in the folder.

STEP BY STEP   **Removing folders from a library**

1   Tap or click the library from which you want to remove a folder.

2   Tap or click the Manage folder on the Ribbon.

3   Tap or click the Manage Library button. The **library name** Library Locations dialog box appears, where **library name** is the name of the library you selected in Step 1.

4   Tap or click the folder you want to remove from the library.

5   Tap or click the Remove button. File Explorer removes the folder from the library.

Take Note   Remember, removing a folder from a library does not affect the folder's contents; the action simply disconnects the folder from the library.

6   Repeat Steps 4 and 5 for each folder you want to remove from the library.

7   Click OK.

SEARCHING FOR FILES IN FILE EXPLORER

You can use the Search box in the upper-right corner of File Explorer to help you locate a file on which you need to work.

Take Note   You can open a file in File Explorer by double-tapping or double-clicking it. The program used to create the file opens, along with the file.

You can limit a search and get the best and most reliable results if you tap or click the folder in the Navigation pane that you think contains the file. For example, if you search from the Newsletters library for filenames containing the word Windows, File Explorer displays results using those files found in the folders included in the Newsletters library.

Figure 4-44

Start a search by selecting, in the Navigation pane, the folder most likely to contain the file.

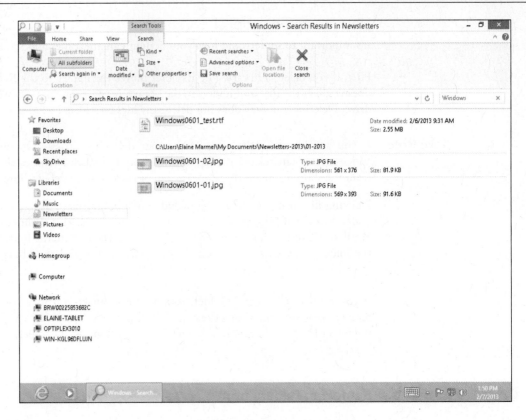

If your search returns many possible files, try narrowing your search further by first selecting a folder further down the path. In this example, you can narrow the search further by selecting a folder in the Newsletters library and then searching.

Figure 4-45

Selecting a folder inside the Newsletters library narrows the search to just that folder.

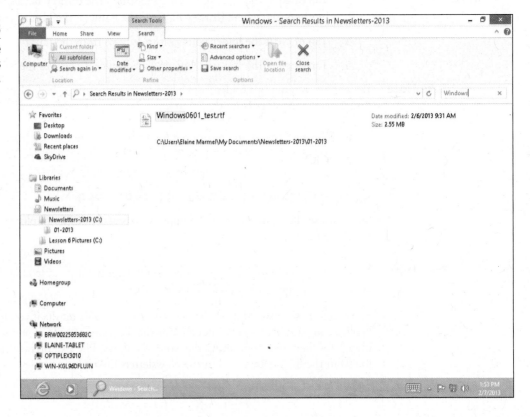

In this chapter you learned how to:

- Navigate files and folders

- Manage files and folders with File Explorer

- Work with libraries

- Search for files in the File Explorer

Bottom Line

This chapter showed you how to use the File Explorer to locate files and folders, and create new types of folders such as compressed archive folders and libraries.

Knowledge Assessment

True/False

Circle T if the statement is true or F if the statement is false.

T F 1. The File Explorer is a search bar that you use to run a search command for files on your computer.

T F 2. Use the View tab in the File Explorer to control the way files appear in the contents pane.

T F 3. You can select non contiguous files in a holder while pressing the Ctrl key.

T F 4. When renaming a file, you should rename the filename and the extension.

T F 5. You can rename a file by selecting the name, and then typing a new name once editable.

T F 6. To move a file from one folder to another, you hold the WinKey and then drag the file between the two windows.

T F 7. You can copy a file and a folder in the same way.

T F 8. To compress selected files, right-click and choose Send to > Compressed (zipped) folder.

T F 9. You should periodically empty the Recycle Bin because if it completely fills, your computer will not function until you empty it.

T F 10. You can create a Library in the Navigation page of the File Explorer.

Multiple Choice

Select the best response for the following statements.

1. You can use the Quick Access Toolbar in the File Explorer for what task?
   a. Create a Folder.
   b. Move a file to the Recycle Bin.
   c. View Folder properties.
   d. All of the above.
   e. A and C.

2. What is another name for a folder that contains subfolders?
    a. Master folder.
    b. Mega folder.
    c. Parent folder.
    d. Child folder.

3. If file extensions are hidden on your computer, you can turn them on using which dialog box?
    a. File Manager.
    b. Folder Options.
    c. File Options.
    d. Extensions manager.

4. In a folder with many files, how do you select all files using a single step?
    a. Select a checkbox above the first row next to the Name column.
    b. Choose Select all Checkboxes in the Ribbon.
    c. Select each item, one-by-one.
    d. All of the above.

5. How do you determine that a file is selected?
    a. The filename is underlined.
    b. The filename has an outline.
    c. The filename is highlighted.
    d. The filename is bold.

6. What is a compressed file?
    a. A file that was corrupted.
    b. A file that contains multiple files.
    c. A single file that was made smaller using an app.
    d. A file that you moved into a special folder that compresses files.

7. How do you decompress a file?
    a. Select the file and choose Decompress from the shortcut menu to open a window to perform the operation.
    b. Select the file and choose Extract All from the shortcut menu to open a window to perform the operation.
    c. Select the Decompress tab from the Ribbon, then choose Decompress All.
    d. None of the above.

8. You select a file and click the Delete button, but the Recycle Bin is full. What happens?
    a. Nothing happens.
    b. The file is permanently deleted.
    c. A warning appears and the file moves to the Recycle Bin.
    d. A warning appears allowing you to confirm permanent deletion or cancel the operation.

9. When should you use a Library folder?
    a. When you want to collect documents to archive.
    b. When you want to gather shortcuts to files in various locations within a single virtual folder.
    c. When you need to place documents in a location they cannot be deleted.
    d. When you need to share documents with public user accounts.

10. Deleting a library from your computer has what effect on the files?
    a. You cannot delete a library after it has been created.
    b. It deletes all of the files and folders from your computer.
    c. It creates virtual copies of all files and folders in a new location.
    d. It moves all of the files to the Recycle Bin.
    e. It does not affect the files and folders, which remain in their original location.

Competency Assessment

Project 4-1: Compressing files

1. Select three files within a folder and create a compressed folder containing them.

Project 4-2: Using File Explorer

1. Search for three files and two folders on your hard drive using the File Explorer.

Proficiency Assessment

Project 4-3: Create a new folder and subfolder

1. Create a new folder within My Documents, and then a subfolder within that folder.
2. Navigate within the subfolder, create a new folder in that directory, and then navigate back to My Documents.

Project 4-3: File search

1. Limit a new file search to a single folder on your hard drive.

Mastery Assessment

Project 4-4: Moving select files and folders

1. Move a selection of files and folders to a new location in three different ways: cut and paste, copy and paste, and dragging between two folders.

Project 4-5: Create a new library

1. Create a new library that includes files and folders from several different locations on your hard drive.
2. Create a new file that you do not need to keep in My Documents, and include it within the new library.
3. Delete the new file, then locate it on your hard drive. Now delete the library, and locate the other files you included.

Customizing and Maintaining Windows 8 5

LESSON SKILL MATRIX

In this lesson, you will learn the following skills:

Understand how to change settings in Windows 8

Personalize Windows

Change date and time settings

Update Windows 8

Set notification options

End misbehaving programs

Uninstall programs

Back up files

Set system recovery options

KEY TERMS

- Control Panel
- Lock screen
- Account picture
- Theme
- Windows Update
- Notifications
- Task Manager
- File History
- Refresh
- Reset

Julene received a new laptop from the IT department at Northwind Traders and needs to configure her machine to run automatic updates on a regular basis to make sure she receives the latest security fixes on a regular basis. She also wants to set up File History to make sure her important data files get backed up to an external hard drive or a network hard drive..

SOFTWARE ORIENTATION

Customizing Windows 8 to your needs and the way you work helps you to use your devices more easily and work more efficiently.

Figure 5-1

A. Personalize Lock screen settings.
B. Personalize Start screen settings.
C. Upload/Create an account picture settings.
D. Current Lock screen image.
E. Available Lock screen background images.
F. Browse for new Lock screen background images.
G. Specify which apps will display notifications while computer is locked.

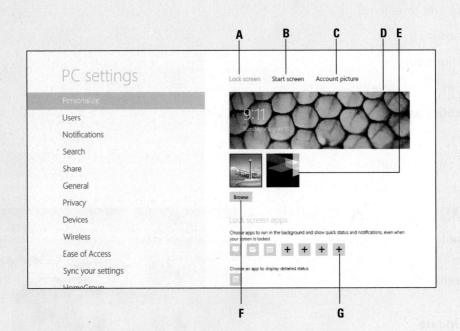

Images used with permission from Microsoft.

STARTING UP

You will not need to work with any files for this lesson.

UNDERSTANDING HOW TO CHANGE SETTINGS IN WINDOWS 8

The Windows 8 operating system introduces an entirely new type of Windows to the world: a two-layered edition of Windows. In the simplest possible terms, users of past editions of Windows saw the Desktop when they started their computers, and they customized and maintained the Desktop using the **Control Panel**. Windows 8 continues to support the Desktop environment along with the apps that run on it, and Windows 8 users can customize and maintain the Desktop using the Control Panel.

But Windows 8 also introduces a new environment under which a new type of app can run, referred to as the "native Windows 8." It shouldn't be surprising that the new environment has its own tool for customization and maintenance: the PC Settings screen.

To summarize, you customize and maintain Windows 8 in two different ways:

• When you want to affect the native Windows 8 apps, work in the PC Settings screen.

• When you want to affect apps that run on the legacy Desktop, or the legacy Desktop app itself, use the Control Panel.

If you've used previous editions of Windows and are somewhat familiar with the Control Panel, we suggest that you think of Windows 8 as having two control panels: one that controls the native Windows 8 apps and the Start screen, and one that controls the Desktop and apps that run on it. If you visualize two control panels, we believe you'll find it easier to understand where to go when you want to make a change.

PERSONALIZING WINDOWS

You can personalize the two environments of Windows 8:

• For native Windows 8: the environment's Start screen, Lock screen, and account picture.

• For the Desktop app: the app's appearance.

STEP BY STEP   **Personalizing the Start screen**

Personalize your start screen's colors and background patterns using the PC settings in the Charms bar.

The Start screen is an element of the native Windows 8 environment; use the PC Settings screen to personalize it. You can personalize the Start screen by selecting a background color scheme and pattern for it.

1   Display the Charms bar by sliding slightly in toward the center of the screen from the right side of the screen, pressing WinKey (⊞)+C, or placing your mouse in the upper- or lower-right corner of the screen.

2   Tap or click the Settings charm.

Figure 5-2

Select the Settings charm.

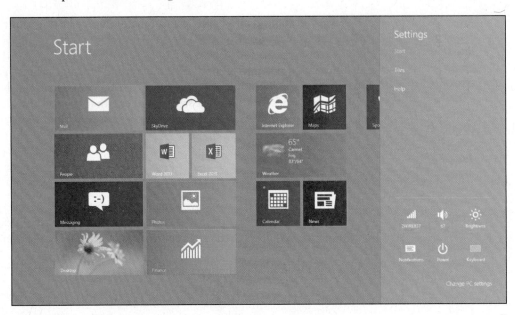

Images and templates used with permission of Microsoft

3   Tap or click Change PC Settings at the bottom of the Settings charm panel. Windows 8 displays the PC Setting screen.

4   On the left side of the screen, tap or click Personalize.

5   At the top of the right side of the screen, tap or click Start screen.

Figure 5-3

Use this screen to select a background color scheme and pattern for the Windows 8 Start screen.

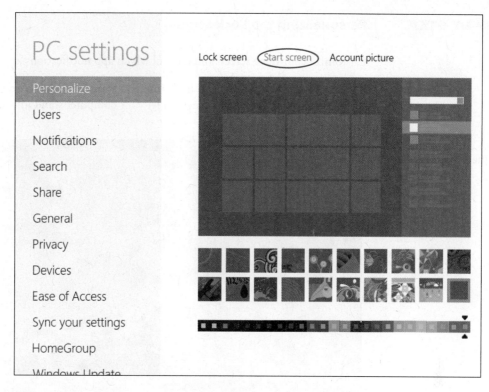

Images and templates used with permission of Microsoft

6   Tap or click a color scheme from the bottom band of color schemes; Windows displays a preview of the color scheme.

7   Using the two rows above the color schemes, select a background pattern; Windows displays a preview of the background pattern.

8   When you're done, redisplay the Start screen to see the effects of your changes.

Figure 5-4

The Start screen changes to match your selections.

Images and templates used with permission of Microsoft

STEP BY STEP   **Personalizing the Lock screen**

Customize your Lock screen and control which app notifications appear in your Lock screen.

The **Lock screen** appears the first time you start Windows 8 and each time you restart your computer. It also appears any time you let your computer stand idle or if you lock your computer.

Figure 5-5

The default Lock screen.

Image used with permission of Microsoft.

Using the PC Setting screen, you can select your own image to appear on the Lock screen.

1   Display the Charms bar by sliding slightly in toward the center of the screen from the right side of the screen, pressing WinKey (⊞)+C, or placing your mouse in the upper- or lower-right corner of the screen.

2   Tap or click the Settings charm.

3   Tap or click Change PC Settings at the bottom of the Settings charm panel. Windows 8 displays the PC Setting screen.

4   On the left side of the screen, tap or click Personalize.

5   At the top of the right side of the screen, tap or click the Lock screen.

Figure 5-6

Select a different image for the
Windows 8 Lock screen.

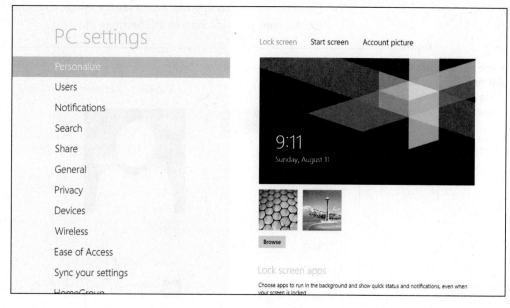

Images used with permission from Microsoft.

6   Tap or click one of the five default images below the preview.

Take Note   To use a photo stored in your Pictures library, tap or click the Browse button.

Workplace **Ready**

Customize your Lock screen by using a custom background image on your computer.

Once you select an image, Windows 8 uses that image whenever it displays the Lock screen.

STEP BY STEP   ## Setting an account picture

By default, Windows 8 uses a generic icon to represent your account, but you can change it. Since the icon represents an **account picture**, many people use a picture of themselves, but you can use any picture you want.

Customize your account picture to a personal photo from your hard drive, or by taking a picture if your device contains a camera or webcam.

1   Tap or click your name on the Windows Start screen.

2 From the menu that appears, tap or click **Change Account Picture**. Windows 8 displays the Account picture screen in PC Settings.

Figure 5-6

Use this screen to select a different image for the Windows 8 account picture that appears on the Start screen.

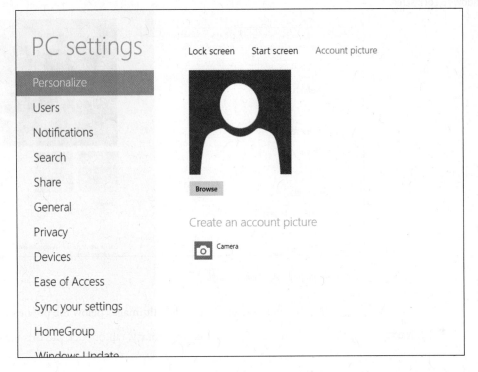

3 Tap or click the **Browse** button to select an image from your Pictures library.

Take Note If you're working on a device that contains a camera, you can tap or click the Camera button to take a picture to use.

 • The picture you select appears on the Start screen and the log in screen, if you log into your computer using a password.

Take Note If you log in to your computer using a Microsoft account, supply the password associated with that account.

STEP BY STEP   **Personalizing the Desktop**

Workplace **Ready**

Personalize your desktop by changing the default theme to a theme you downloaded from the Internet.

Most people choose to use a **theme**, which is a predefined set of background images, colors, sounds, and screen savers, to personalize the Desktop. Although you can set these features individually, this section focuses on selecting and changing a theme's slideshow of background images. You also learn where to get more themes.

1   From the Start screen, tap or click the Desktop app.

2   Tap and hold or right-click a blank spot on the Desktop.

3   From the shortcut menu that appears, tap or click Personalize to open the Control Panel's Personalization window.

Figure 5-7

A. A personalized saved theme.
B. Get more themes online link.
C. Windows Default Themes.
D. Desktop Background options link.

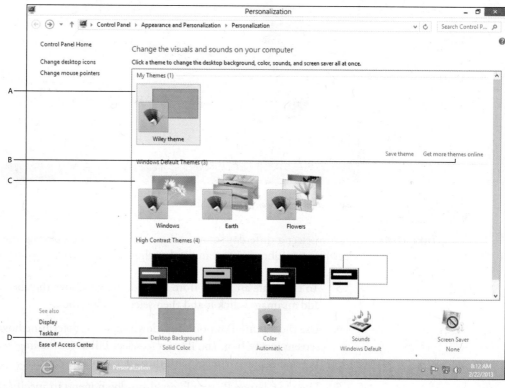

Images used with permission from Microsoft.

• You can select a theme from the default themes provided and close the Control Panel if you're satisfied with the selection. You also can customize the theme. For example, instead of using one background image, many themes, including the default Earth and Flowers themes, provide a slideshow of background images. You can control that slideshow by changing the timing between the image changes and even the images included in the slideshow. You also can control:

• The colors of the taskbar and window borders

• The sounds you hear when actions, such as errors, occur

• Whether a screen saver appears if you leave your computer idle for a specified time

STEP BY STEP   **Customize a theme's Desktop Background slideshow**

Use the following steps to customize a theme's Desktop Background slideshow:

1   Tap or click the Earth theme.

2   Tap or click the Desktop Background link to display the options for changing your Desktop background.

Figure 5-8

Customize the behavior of the Desktop Background images for the Earth theme.

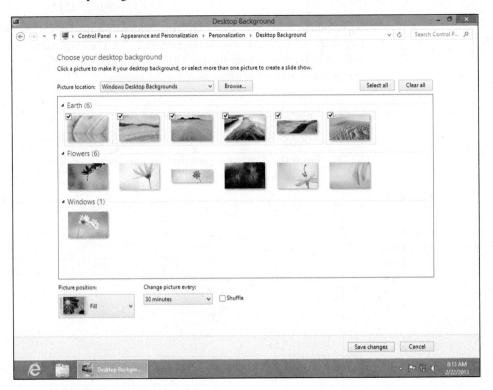

Images used with permission from Microsoft.

Take Note   You can select a different set of background images by opening the Picture Location list. If you select Pictures Library, you can display photos from the library on your Desktop.

3   To eliminate an image from the slideshow, remove the checkmark from its checkbox. To add an image, click it and then select its checkbox.

4   Use the Picture Position drop-down menu to determine how the image appears on your screen; most often, you'll want to select Fill to let the image cover the entire Desktop, but you can experiment with the other available choices.

5   Use the Change Picture Every drop-down menu to specify the amount of elapsed time between slideshow images. Use the Shuffle checkbox to make Windows mix up the images instead of displaying them in a specific order.

6   When you finish customizing the Desktop background slideshow, tap or click the
Save Changes button at the bottom of the window to redisplay the Control Panel's
Personalization window. A new entry appears in the My Themes section, and that entry
represents the theme you modified.

Figure 5-9

The Personalization
window reappears.

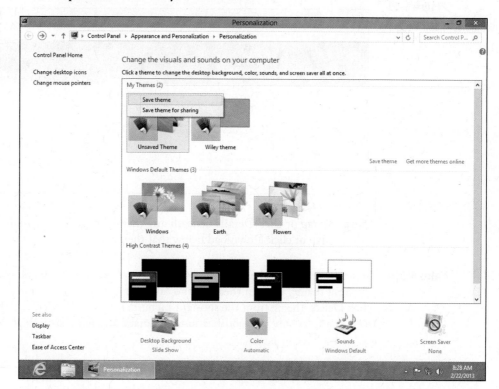

Images used with permission from Microsoft.

7   Tap and hold or right-click the Unsaved Theme and tap or click Save Theme.

8   In the dialog box that appears, type a name that identifies the theme.

• If you aren't satisfied with the default themes that come with Windows, you can find more themes online; most themes are free. Tap or click the Get More Themes Online link at the right edge of the My Themes section. Internet Explorer opens and displays the Themes page.

Figure 5-10

The Windows Themes page.

• **You** can tap or click Details beneath any theme image to read more about the theme. To use a theme, tap or click Download below that theme.

Take Note   You cannot delete a theme in the My Themes section while you are using it, but if you switch to a different theme, you can then tap and hold or right-click the theme you want to delete and tap or click Delete Theme from the shortcut menu that appears. Deleting a theme from the My Themes section affects only the modifications you made and not the original theme.

DATE AND TIME SETTINGS

Verify that your computer is set up to adjust it's clock for daylight savings time automatically.

STEP BY STEP   **Set-up to adjust clock for daylight savings time**

From the PC Settings screen, you can control your time zone and whether your computer automatically adjusts the time to accommodate daylight savings time.

1   Display the Charms bar by sliding slightly in toward the center of the screen from the right side of the screen, pressing **WinKey** (⊞)+**C**, or placing your mouse in the upper- or lower-right corner of the screen.

2 Tap or click the Settings charm.

3 Tap or click Change PC Settings at the bottom of the Settings charm panel. Windows 8 displays the PC Setting screen.

4 On the left side of the screen, tap or click General.

Figure 5-11

From the General tab of the PC Settings screen, you can adjust the time zone and daylight saving time settings.

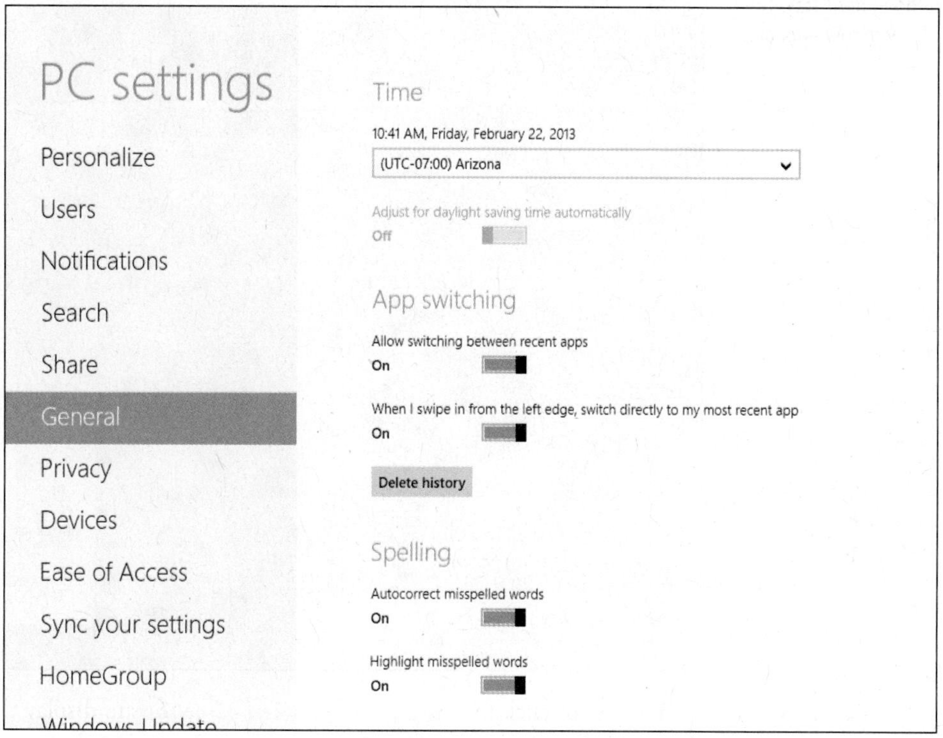

- From the legacy Desktop, today's date and time appear in the System Tray at the right edge of the taskbar. Using legacy Desktop tools, you can:

- Select a time zone

- Change the date and time

- Display additional clocks for time zones you select

Use the legacy Desktop tools to display additional clocks for additional time zones in your system tray.

- Control the way your computer synchronizes its clock with Internet time

STEP BY STEP | **Display legacy Desktop date and time tools**

To display legacy Desktop date and time tools, follow these steps:

1 Display the Desktop app.

2   In the lower-right corner of the screen, at the right edge of the taskbar, tap or click the displayed date and time. The Desktop app displays this month's calendar, highlighting today's date, and an analog clock displaying the current time.

Figure 5-12

When you click the date and time in the System Tray, this window appears.

3   Tap or click Change Date And Time Settings to display the Date and Time dialog box.

From the Date and Time tab, you can change the date and time as well as the time zone. From the Internet Time tab, you can change the website Windows uses to synchronize your computer's clock; the default website is time.windows.com. Using the Additional Clocks tab, you can display two additional clocks each time you tap or click the date and time information in the System Tray.

STEP BY STEP   **Add clocks to the date and time display**

To add clocks to the date and time display, follow these steps:

1   Tap or click the Additional Clocks tab.

2   Tap or click the first Show This Clock checkbox to select it.

3   Use the Select Time Zone drop-down menu to select a time zone for the clock.

4   In the Enter Display Name box, type a name for the clock, such as the time zone you selected.

5   Repeat Steps 3 to 5 for the second Show This Clock checkbox.

Figure 5-13

Set up clocks for two
additional time zones.

6   Click OK.

When you tap or click the date in the System Tray, the legacy Desktop displays this month's
calendar and clocks for three time zones.

Figure 5-14

You can keep track of the time
in up to three time zones.

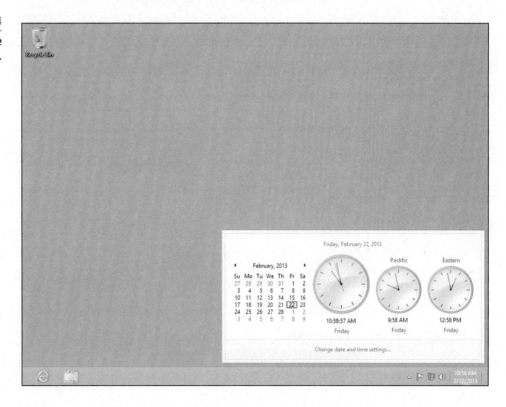

UPDATING WINDOWS 8

From time to time, Microsoft releases patches to its operating systems and other programs, such as Microsoft Office. These patches are free, and generally, they modify the operating system to make it more usable and more secure. You can obtain the patches via the **Windows Update** utility that comes with Windows 8.

STEP BY STEP	Manually check for Windows update

By default, Windows 8 automatically checks for and installs any updates designated as "important." You can view the status of updates and even manually check for updates from the PC Settings screen:

1   Display the Charms bar by sliding slightly in toward the center of the screen from the right side of the screen, pressing WinKey (⊞)+C, or placing your mouse in the upper- or lower-right corner of the screen.

2   Tap or click the Settings charm.

3   Tap or click Change PC Settings at the bottom of the Settings charm panel. Windows 8 displays the PC Setting screen.

4   On the left side of the screen, tap or click Windows Update.

Figure 5-15

You can manually check for updates.

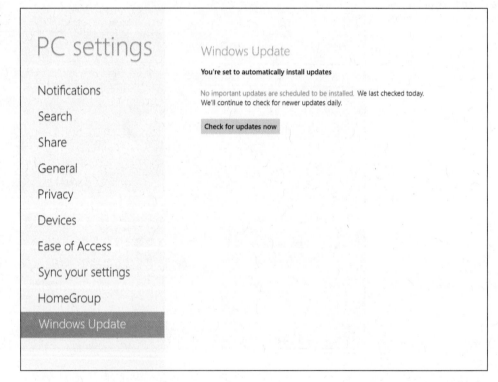

5   To manually check for updates, tap or click the Check For Updates Now button.

STEP BY STEP   **Control the behavior of the Windows Update utility**

If you want to control the behavior of the Windows Update utility, use the Desktop Control Panel.

Customize the behavior of the Windows Update utility using the Desktop Control Panel.

1   Display the Start screen.

2   Type **Control Panel**.

3   When the Control Panel entry appears, tap or click it.

4   In the Search box in the upper-right corner of the Control Panel, type **Windows Update** and tap or click the **magnifying glass** or press **Enter**.

Figure 5-15

Tap or click Windows Update.

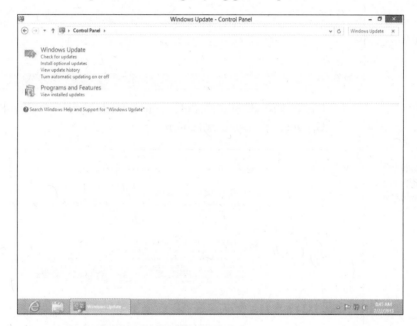

5   Tap or click the **Windows Update** entry in the list that appears to display the Windows Update window.

Figure 5-17

The Windows Update
utility window.

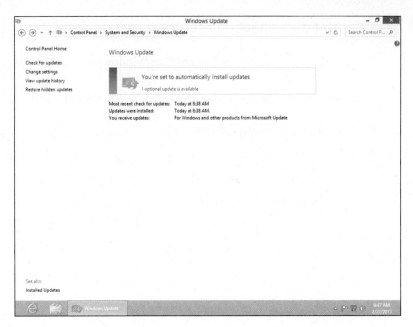

6 On the left side of the window, tap or click Change Settings to display the Windows Update settings you can control.

Figure 5-18

You can change the
legacy Windows Update
settings to manual using the
Control Panel.

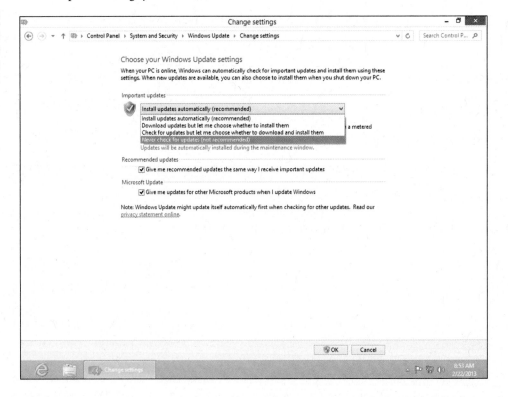

The Important Updates section displays the way Windows handles updates; you can use the drop-down menu to change the method. You can opt not to receive recommended updates or updates for other Microsoft products by removing the checkmarks from those checkboxes. When you finish, tap or click OK.

SETTING NOTIFICATION OPTIONS

Many apps you install might want your attention at various times. For example, the Mail app might want to let you know that you've received new e-mails. **Notifications** from native Windows 8 apps appear on the Lock screen and as you work. Notifications from legacy Desktop apps appear in the System Tray in the lower-right corner of the Desktop taskbar.

Workplace **Ready**

Adjust the notification options for native Windows 8 apps using the Change PC Settings option in the Settings charm.

You can control the notifications that appear; use the PC Settings screen to control notifications from native Windows 8 apps, and the Control Panel to control notifications from legacy Desktop apps.

STEP BY STEP | **Control notifications from native Windows 8 apps**

To control notifications from native Windows 8 apps, follow these steps:

1   Display the Charms bar by sliding slightly in toward the center of the screen from the right side of the screen, pressing WinKey (⊞)+C, or placing your mouse in the upper- or lower-right corner of the screen.

2   Tap or click the Settings charm.

3   Tap or click Change PC Settings at the bottom of the Settings charm panel. Windows 8 displays the PC Setting screen.

4   On the left side of the screen, tap or click Notifications.

Figure 5-19

Notification settings for native Windows 8 apps.

PC settings

Personalize
Users
Notifications
Search
Share
General
Privacy
Devices
Ease of Access
Sync your settings
HomeGroup
Windows Update

Notifications

Show app notifications
On

Show app notifications on the lock screen
On

Play notification sounds
On

Show notifications from these apps

	Calendar	On
	Games	On
	Internet Explorer	On
	Mail	On
	Messaging	On
	Microsoft Solitaire Collection	On

5   To turn off all notifications, tap or click the Show App Notifications button so it changes from On to Off.

6   To hide notifications on the Lock Screen, tap or click the Show App Notifications On The Lock Screen button so it changes from On to Off.

7   To eliminate sounds when Windows notifies you, tap or click the Play Notification Sounds button so it changes from On to Off.

8   Use the list below these buttons to control which apps can notify you.

STEP BY STEP   **Customize the notifications from Legacy Desktop**

Notifications from legacy Desktop apps appear in the legacy Desktop app's System Tray at the right edge of the taskbar. In addition, the taskbar displays icons for some programs. You can hide the icons of programs that you don't need to see (typically, you won't need to see a program icon if you don't use that icon for anything) and you can control the notifications issued by legacy Desktop apps.

Customize the notifications from legacy Desktop apps (such as volume, power settings, network settings, etc).

1   Display the Start screen.

2   Type Control Panel.

3   When you see the Control Panel entry appear, tap or click it.

4   In the Search box in the upper-right corner of the Control Panel, type Notifications and tap or click the magnifying glass or press Enter.

5   Tap or click Notification Area Icons to display the Notification Area Icons window.

Figure 5-20

Change the Notification Area Icon behavior to control the messages and icons that appear in the System Tray at the right edge of the Desktop taskbar.

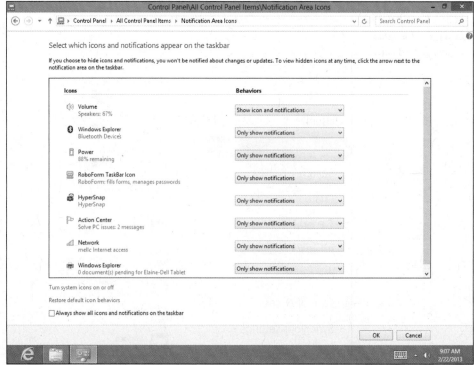

6   Tap or click a drop-down menu in the Behaviors list for the icon you want to control and choose a behavior.

7   When you finish, tap or click **OK**.

MANAGING DEVICES

You can view devices connected to your computer and add or remove a device from the PC Settings screen; from the Desktop, you can view information about a particular device and troubleshoot it if it isn't behaving properly.

Take Note   You rarely need to add or remove a device from the PC Settings screen. If you detach a device that's connected to your computer using a wireless connection or a physical one, Windows typically removes the device from the list automatically. If you attach a new device wirelessly or with a physical connection, Windows typically recognizes the device automatically. If Windows doesn't recognize the device, you should follow the manufacturer's instructions for adding the device to your system setup.

STEP BY STEP   **Managing devices**

To use the PC Settings screen to view devices connected to your computer, follow these steps:

1   Display the Charms bar by sliding slightly in toward the center of the screen from the right side of the screen, pressing **WinKey** ()**+C**, or placing your mouse in the upper- or lower-right corner of the screen.

2   Tap or click the **Settings** charm.

3   Tap or click **Change PC Settings** at the bottom of the Settings charm panel. Windows 8 displays the PC Setting screen.

4   On the left side of the screen, tap or click **Devices** to display the list of devices connected to your computer.

Figure 5-21

The PC Settings window displays the devices attached to your computer.

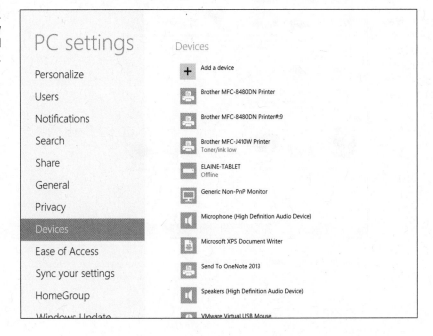

On the Desktop, you can view a complete list of all devices attached to your computer from the Device Manager. Typically, you only need the Device Manager if something isn't working properly. To view the Device Manager, search for Device Manager from within the Control Panel while in the Desktop app.

Figure 5-22

The Device Manager window.

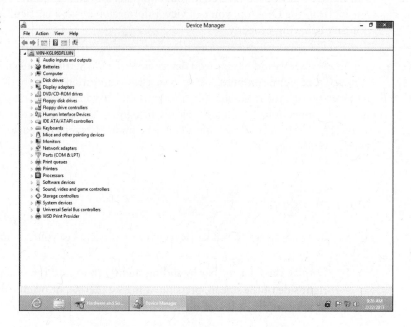

You can view devices and printers attached to your computer in the Devices and Printers window.

Figure 5-23

The Devices and Printers window.

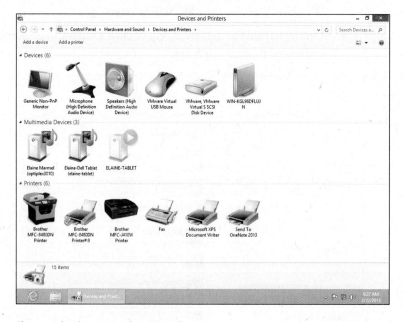

Clip art used with permission from Microsoft.

STEP BY STEP   **Viewing properties of your hard drive**

You can tap and hold or right-click any device and then tap or click Properties to view information about that device. For example, follow these steps to see the properties of your hard drive:

1   Open File Explorer.

2   In the Navigation pane on the left, tap or click the **Computer** entry.

3   In the contents pane that's on the right side of the screen, tap and hold or right-click the entry for your hard disk.

4   From the shortcut menu that appears, tap or click **Properties** to display the Properties box for your hard drive.

Figure 5-24

The General tab of the Properties box for a hard drive.

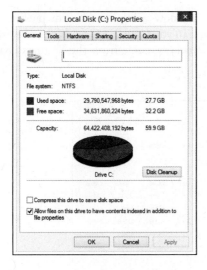

5   Tap or click the **Cancel** button after you finish viewing disk information.

• On the General tab of any drive's Properties box, you will see a pie chart depicting free and used space on the drive. You can also access Disk Cleanup tools from this dialog box; the Disk Cleanup utility helps you remove unnecessary files that are taking up space on your drive.

• The Tools tab enables you to check for errors on the disk and optimize and defragment the drive. Be aware that Windows automatically optimizes and defragments your drive on a regular basis, so you shouldn't need to take this action manually.

• The Hardware tab lists information about the disk drive, including its status, which is typically "This device is working properly."

• You can use the Sharing tab to share a drive; you only need the Sharing tab if you are not using a HomeGroup.

• Use the Security tab to establish privileges for users of the drive.

• You can use the Quota tab if your drive supports allocating limited space to various users who access the drive.

ENDING A MISBEHAVING PROGRAM

Terminate a misbehaving or non-responsive application.

Sometimes, an app you're using misbehaves. It might freeze or become unresponsive in other ways. In these situations, ending the program often solves the problem.

Take Note   You might also need to restart your computer; if that doesn't help your program stop misbehaving, you might need to take additional troubleshooting measures. For example, contact the vendor of the program for help.

End a misbehaving native Windows 8 app by closing it. Press Alt+F4, or using your mouse or your finger, drag down the center of your screen from top to bottom. You also can close it from the **Task Manager**, which is the tool you use to end a misbehaving legacy Desktop app.

To display the Task Manager window using a keyboard, press Ctrl+Shift+Esc. If you haven't connected a keyboard and mouse to your touch device, display the Start screen and use the Touch Keyboard And Handwriting Panel, available from the Settings charm, to type Task Manager. When the entry appears, tap it.

Figure 5-25

The Task Manager.

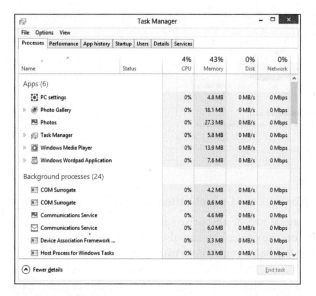

The Windows 8 Task Manager is much improved over the Task Manager of earlier editions of Windows. On the Processes tab, you see each app that's running; close a misbehaving app by tapping or clicking it and then tapping or clicking the End Task button in the lower- right corner of the window.

Take Note   You also can end background processes from the Processes tab, but be aware that ending a process can make your computer unstable and you might then need to restart it.

You can use the Performance tab in the Task Manager window to monitor CPU, Memory, Disk, and Ethernet performance.

The App History tab shows resource usage by app for the past 30 days.

Using the Startup tab, you can identify programs that start whenever Windows starts; if you don't need a particular program to start every time Windows starts, you can tap or click it and then tap or click the Disable button. That way, the program won't take up resources when you don't need it and you can start it when you do need it.

The Users tab displays users connected to your computer; if necessary, you can tap or click a user and then tap or click the Disconnect button to disconnect that user from your computer.

The Details tab displays detailed information for each running process, and the Services tab displays detailed information for each running service.

UNINSTALLING A PROGRAM

Installing programs is easy. To install a native Windows 8 app, look for it in the Windows Store, buy it if necessary, and Windows installs it for you. Installing a legacy Desktop app is almost as easy. Typically, you download the installation file or insert a CD or DVD into your CD/DVD drive and then follow the on-screen instructions.

There will come a time when you determine that you no longer need a program that is installed on your computer. Perhaps you've replaced it with another program that better suits your needs or perhaps you've just stopped using the program.

In cases like these, you should uninstall the program so it stops taking up space on your computer. When you uninstall a native Windows 8 app, Windows also removes any apps related to it .

STEP BY STEP   **Uninstall an unwanted program from the Start screen**

1   On the Start screen, tap and hold and slide down slightly or right-click the app's tile to select it.

2   Display the App bar by swiping down slightly from the top of the screen or by right-clicking anywhere on the screen.

3   Tap or click the Uninstall button. A message appears, telling you that the app (and any related apps) will be removed from your computer.

Figure 5-26

Uninstalling a native Windows 8 app.

Images and templates used with permission of Microsoft

4   Tap or click the Uninstall button; Windows removes the app and any related apps.

• **When** well-behaved legacy Desktop apps install, they also include an uninstall routine, and they place a link to that routine in the Programs and Features window of the Control Panel.

Take Note   If you don't see an entry in the Programs and Features window for the program you want to uninstall, try checking for an entry in the All Apps list (while viewing the Start screen, display the App bar by swiping down slightly from the top of the screen or by right-clicking anywhere on the screen. Then, tap or click the All Apps button). If you don't find an entry there, you're probably dealing with an ill-behaved program that won't easily uninstall. Try searching the Internet for the program name and include the word "uninstall" to find help.

STEP BY STEP   **Uninstall a legacy Desktop app**

To uninstall a legacy Desktop app, follow these steps:

1   Display the Start screen.

2   Type **Control Panel**.

3   When you see the Control Panel entry appear, tap or click it.

4   On the Control Panel home page, tap or click the **Uninstall A Program** link that appears under the Programs link. The Programs and Features window appears, displaying a list of well-behaved, installed legacy apps.

Figure 5-27

Use this window to uninstall a program.

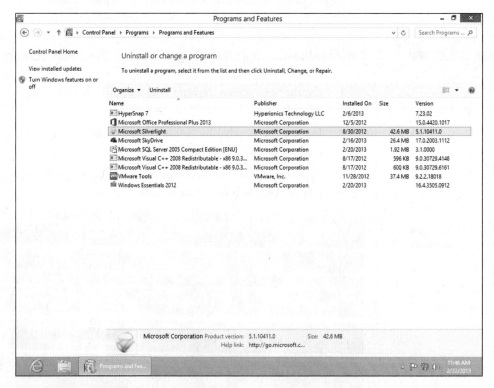

5   Tap or click the program you want to remove.

6   Tap or click the **Uninstall** button above the list of installed apps.

7   Follow the directions that appear on the screen.

Each legacy app has its own uninstall process, so the steps vary from program to program. For example, some programs might suggest that you restart your computer to complete the uninstall process.

BACKING UP YOUR FILES

If you're using Windows 8 Pro or higher and you have an external hard drive, a second hard drive, or a network hard drive, you can take advantage of **File History** to back up your data files. Once an hour, File History takes a snapshot of all the files in all libraries and on your Desktop, along with your Internet Explorer favorites, SkyDrive, and your Contacts data. File History continues to take snapshots until the drive where you're storing the history fills up. Over time, File History can store many copies of your data files; File History will notify you when you're getting close to running out of space so you can get another external hard drive.

You can disconnect the drive that File History uses for backups. While the drive is disconnected, File History continues to take snapshots of your data and stores them in a reserved space on the local hard drive, using up to 5% of your hard drive space. When you reconnect the drive, File History writes the files to the drive.

Take Note   You can change the settings File History uses, as you will see in an upcoming section in this lesson.

Turning on File History

Workplace **Ready**

Use File History to make sure your critical files are backed up to a secondary hard drive regularly.

The first time you use File History will take a very long time, even many hours. We suggest that you wait to use File History the first time until a time when you plan to walk away from your computer.

STEP BY STEP   **Setting up and running File History**

To set up and run File History, follow these steps:

1   Display the Start screen.

2   Type **Control Panel**.

3   When the Control Panel entry appears, tap or click it.

4   In the Search box in the upper-right corner of the Control Panel, type **File History** and tap or click the **magnifying glass** or press **Enter**.

5   Tap or click the **File History** entry in the list that appears to display the File History window.

6   Make sure the drive you want to use for your backup is attached to your computer.

7   Tap or click the Turn On button. A message box appears, asking if you want other members of your HomeGroup to use this drive to back up their files.

Figure 5-28

Turning on File History.

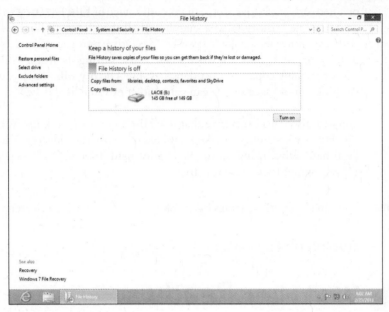

8   Click Yes or No, as appropriate in your situation. File History begins its backup; in the middle of the File History window, you'll see a message confirming that File History is running.

Figure 5-29

The File History window during a backup.

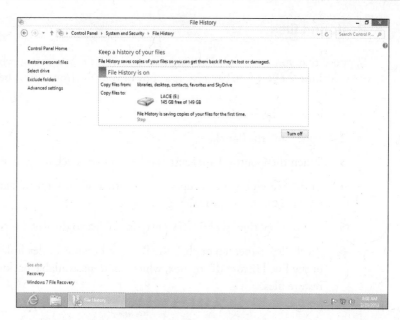

At this point, you need to wait for File History to complete the first backup. When the backup finishes, the Stop link in the File History window will be replaced by a Run Now link and the last date and time that File History copied your files. You can use the Run Now link to manually start a File History backup. Remember, though, that File History will automatically run every hour.

Figure 5-30

When File History finishes its first backup, the Run Now link appears.

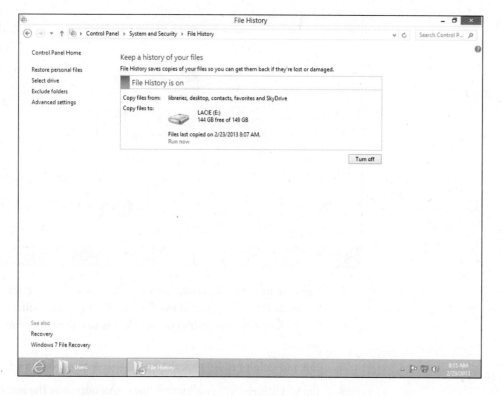

Take Note   You can view the backed up files using File Explorer. Just navigate to the drive where you stored the backup and you'll find a folder called FileHistory. You can navigate its contents to see what File History backed up.

STEP BY STEP   Restoring files

Suppose that you discover, after long hours of work, that a change you made three days ago just isn't working for you. You can restore a copy of your file from a time before you made that change.

1   Display the Start screen.

2   Type **Control Panel**.

3   When the Control Panel entry appears, tap or click it.

4   In the Search box in the upper-right corner of the Control Panel, type **File History** and tap or click the **magnifying glass** or press **Enter**.

5   Tap or click the **File History** entry in the list to display the File History window.

6   In the left pane, tap or click the **Restore Personal Files** link to display the Home level of the File History dialog box, which contains available backups from which you can restore files.

Figure 5-31

Use the File History dialog box to find a file to restore.

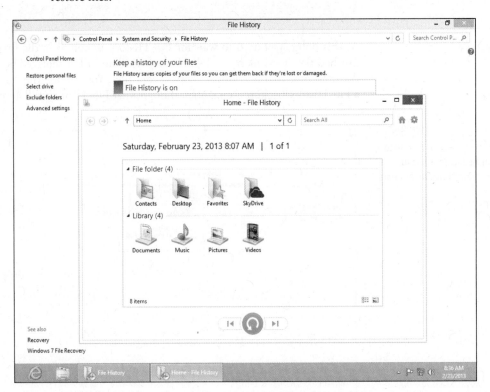

7   Navigate to the folder containing the file you want to restore. The time and date of the backed-up file appear above the file. If you want a different version of the file, use the Back or Forward arrows in the address bar above the date to navigate to a different backup.

8   Tap and hold or right-click the file you want to restore to select it.

9   Tap or click the **Restore** button (the green button at the bottom of the window). File History displays a Message box that offers you options concerning overwriting existing files.

Take Note   If you tap or click the Restore button while viewing the Home level of the File History dialog box, File History assumes you want to restore all files in a backup. You can restore all items in a folder by tapping or clicking that folder.

Figure 5-32

Choose File History's behavior concerning overwriting existing files.

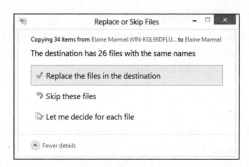

10 Select an option; File History begins the restoration process.

STEP BY STEP   **Changing File History settings**

Workplace Ready

Change the default File History settings to control how often files get backed up, or which files or folders should be excluded from the backup.

You can make changes to File History's default settings. For example, you can exclude files or folders from the backup, make backups more or less frequently, or change the amount of space File History uses on your local drive when your external hard drive isn't connected.

1 Display the Start screen.

2 Type **Control Panel**.

3 When the Control Panel entry appears, tap or click it.

4 In the Search box in the upper-right corner of the Control Panel, type **File History** and tap or click the **magnifying glass** or press **Enter**.

5 Tap or click the **File History** entry that appears to display the File History window.

6 If you click the **Exclude Folders** on the left, you can identify folders you don't want File History to back up. Tap or click the **Add** button and then navigate to the folder you want to exclude, tap or click it, and then tap or click the **Select Folder** button. Once you finish selecting folders to exclude from a backup, tap or click the **Save Changes** button to redisplay the File History window.

7 If you tap or click the **Advanced Settings** link on the left, you can change the frequency File History uses to make backups, the amount of space used on your local drive to store backups when your backup drive is disconnected, or the amount of time File History saves backups (the default is "Forever").

8 When you finish making changes, tap or click the **Save Changes** button to redisplay the File History window.

SYSTEM RECOVERY OPTIONS

Windows 8 contains two options you can use if Windows begins to consistently misbehave: **Refresh** and **Reset**. These actions are drastic, and you should consider using them only if all other attempts to fix your computer have failed.

Refreshing

Comparatively, Refreshing is the lesser drastic approach to system recovery, but you still run the risk of losing data if you don't back up properly. When you refresh, Windows will clear all the legacy settings and apps, and anything not within Windows users folders; it then reinstalls Windows and places a list of what was eliminated on the Desktop for your review.

In particular, the refresh process keeps the following:

- Accounts, passwords, backgrounds, Internet Explorer favorites, wireless network connections and settings, drive letter assignments, BitLocker settings and passwords if your version of Windows supports BitLocker, and your Windows installation key.

- All files in the User folder, which includes every user's libraries (Documents, Pictures, Music, Videos, and Downloads).

- Any folders you might have added to the C:\ drive.

- File History versions.

- Anything stored in partitions that don't contain Windows.

- Apps from the Windows Store.

- The refresh process destroys the following:

- Display settings, firewall customizations, and file type associations.

- Files not stored in the User folder, unless you stored them in folders directly off the C:\ drive as noted above.

- All legacy Desktop apps and their settings, installation keys, and passwords.

Resetting

Resetting is the most drastic system recovery tool available; it wipes your hard drive and reinstalls Windows. You lose all your personal data, all your settings, and programs you installed, including their settings, product keys, and passwords.

Using system recovery options

Obviously, these choices are drastic actions, so use them at your own risk. Both options use the Windows Recovery Environment to do their work, and if Windows can't boot normally, you may find yourself in the Windows Recovery Environment automatically. Should you deliberately choose to either reset or refresh your computer, you can launch these options and boot into the Windows Recovery Environment from the PC Settings screen.

1   Display the Charms bar by sliding slightly in toward the center of the screen from the right side of the screen, pressing **WinKey** (⊞)**+C**, or placing your mouse in the upper- or lower-right corner of the screen.

2   Tap or click **Change PC Settings** at the bottom of the Settings charm panel. Windows 8 displays the PC Setting screen.

3   On the left side of the screen, tap or click **General**.

4   Scroll down the right side to see the Refresh and Reset options; the Reset option heading is "Remove Everything and Reinstall Windows."

Figure 5-33

The system recovery options available from the PC Settings screen.

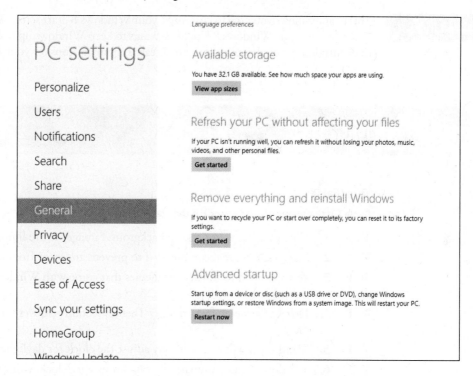

In this chapter, you learned:

- Understand how to change settings in Windows 8

- Personalize Windows

- Change date and time settings

- Update Windows 8

- Set notification options

- End misbehaving programs

- Uninstall programs

- Back up files

- Set system recovery options

Bottom Line

This chapter shows you how to customize your Windows 8 Start screen and Desktop. We also learnt how to change our Windows 8 Update settings to keep Windows up to date. Finally, we learnt how to uninstall unwanted applications and create system backups for your important data files.

Knowledge Assessment

True/False

Circle T if the statement is true or F if the statement is false.

T   F   1. When setting your desktop background image, you're limited to a single, static image.

T   F   2. Screen savers are recommended to prevent an image from burning into your monitor.

T   F   3. You're limited to the default themes that come with Windows 8 or creating your own themes.

T   F   4. Deleting a theme from the My Themes section removes the theme from your hard drive.

T   F   5. Windows 8 will automatically adjust the clock for daylight savings time.

T   F   6. Windows 8 can automatically synchronize it's clock with an Internet time server.

T   F   7. You can display up to three clocks in Windows 8.

T   F   8. By default, Windows 8 will automatically install system updates.

T   F   9. To disable application notifications, you must turn off notifications for each app separately.

T   F   10. Backing up files in Windows 8 requires special software.

Multiple Choice

Select the best response for the following statements.

1. A theme contains which of the following items?
    a. Background images
    b. Colors
    c. Sounds
    d. Screen savers
    e. All of the above

2. Native Windows 8 apps can be customized in which of the following ways?
    a. The PC Settings screen
    b. Legacy Desktop app
    c. All of the above

3. The Windows 8 lock screen appears in which of the following situations?
    a. The first time you start Windows.
    b. Whenever you reboot your computer.
    c. Your computer sits idle.
    d. All of the above.

4. Where can you find new themes for Windows 8?
    a. Windows 8 comes with default themes.
    b. You can create your own custom themes.
    c. You can download new themes from the Internet.
    d. All of the above.

5. A theme can contain which of the following customizations?
    a. The colors of the taskbar and window borders.
    b. The sounds you hear when actions, such as errors, occur.
    c. Whether a screen saver appears if you leave your computer idle for a specified time.
    d. All of the above.

6. Which of the following date and time settings can be set from the PC Settings screen?
    a. Time zone
    b. Adjust for daylight savings time automatically
    c. Display additional clocks for time zones you select
    d. Both A and C
    e. Both A and B

7. Windows Update settings can be changed from which of the following locations?
    a. PC Settings
    b. Desktop Control Panel
    c. All of the above.

8. Where to notifications appear for legacy Desktop apps?
    a. Lock screen
    b. Desktop
    c. System tray
    d. All of the above

9. Misbehaving apps can be quit using which of the following methods?
    a. Alt+F4
    b. Task Manager
    c. Rebooting
    d. All of the above.
10. File History takes a snapshot of which of the following files?
    a. files on your Desktop
    b. Internet Explorer favorites
    c. SkyDrive
    d. Applications
    e. All of the above
    f   A, B, and C.

Competency Assessment

Project 5-1: Personalize the Start screen

1. Personalize the Start screen and change the color scheme and background pattern.

Project 5-2: Personalize the Desktop

1. Personalize the Desktop and change the Desktop Background image and screen saver options.

Proficiency Assessment

Project 5-3: Change notification settings

1. Change notification settings to disable notifications from the Mail app.

Project 5-4: Using Task Manager

1. Use the Windows 8 Task Manager to quit a misbehaving native Windows 8 app.

Mastery Assessment

Project 5-5: Uninstallign a native Windows 8 application

1. Uninstall a native Windows 8 app.

Project 5-6: Creating a system backup

1   Create a system backup of your files.

Internet Explorer and the Web

1 Surfing the Web

LESSON SKILL

In this lesson, you will learn the following skills:

Understanding the World Wide Web

Managing settings

Using the two versions of Internet Explorer that ship with Windows 8

Using the Windows 8 native version of Internet Explorer

Using the Desktop version of Internet Explorer

KEY TERMS

- **World Wide Web**
- **The Web**
- **The Internet**
- **Internet Service Provider (ISP)**
- **Web Browser**
- **Web Pages**
- **Web Address**
- **Websites**
- **Links**
- **Extensions**
- **App Bar**
- **Cookies**
- **History**

Julene at Northwind Traders wants to learn how to browse websites privately in Internet Explorer so that cookies, temporary Internet files, history, and other data is not stored on her computer.

SOFTWARE ORIENTATION

An understanding of the apps and tools available on your device that enable you to access the Internet and sites connected to the World WIde Web helps you work more efficiently and securely

Figure 1-1

Internet Explorer workspace

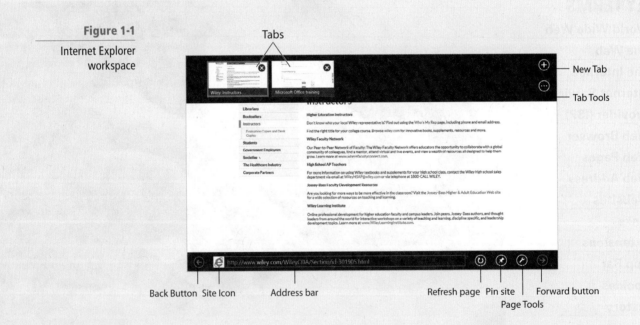

STARTING UP

You will not need to work with any files for this lesson.

UNDERSTANDING THE WORLD WIDE WEB

The **World Wide Web**, often referred to as **the Web** or **the Internet**, is a collection of computers called *web servers* that are located around the world and contain massive amounts of information. These web servers are powerful computers connected to each other and to a system of computers that share their information with anyone who can connect to the web. The term *web* refers to a spider web, which offers a good way to visualize the connected web servers.

Take Note You can connect to the Internet as long as your computer contains a network card and you have signed up with an **Internet Service Provider (ISP)**. Your ISP will provide you with the information you need to connect your computer to the Internet.

There are five web-related concepts to master to get the most out of using the web:

- Web browsers
- Web pages
- Web addresses
- Websites
- Links

Web browsers

You can view information from the Internet using an app called a *web browser*, or *browser*, for short. Windows 8 comes with Internet Explorer, Microsoft's browser. You also can use any number of other popular browsers, such as Firefox, Safari, or Google Chrome. Browsers are typically free and you can download them from the Internet and install them.

Web pages

Web pages present the information you view when you browse the Internet. Each web page can present its information using a combination of text, images, and sounds, including music and videos.

Web addresses

Web addresses uniquely identify each web page. A web address is also called a *URL* (pronounced using its letters), and URL stands for *Uniform Resource Locator*. A typical web address might look like *http://www.example.com*. If you know a web page's address, you can type that address into your browser's address bar to view that page.

Websites

Websites are collections of related web pages. Typically, a website is associated with—and controlled by—a particular person, business, or government organization. You can often identify the type of owner for a site by looking at the last part of the site's address. For example, .com is usually a commercial site, while .gov is a government site, and .org usually indicates the site is controlled by a non-profit organization.

Links

You'll often find links, also called hyperlinks, on a web page. These links connect one web page to another. If you tap or click a link on a web page, your browser displays the page to which the link refers. Links can have different appearances, but they often appear underlined or in a different color than other text on the page.

Bottom Line

THE TWO VERSIONS OF INTERNET EXPLORER

Two versions of Internet Explorer ship with Windows 8: a Windows 8 native version and a legacy Desktop version. Although the two versions of Internet Explorer share settings and other technological features, the way they work feels very different to the user who has used the legacy Desktop version in the past.

Does one version of Internet Explorer have advantages over the other? That depends on circumstances and what you consider important. For example, the Windows 8 native version operates much faster than the legacy version because the Windows 8 native version doesn't allow you to use plugins or add-in programs, **extensions**, or toolbars. In particular, the native Windows 8 native version of Internet Explorer doesn't display Flash animations on websites unless Microsoft has added the site to a list of sites allowed to display Flash animations. In addition, the entire screen of the Windows 8 native version is devoted to the webpage you're viewing, with no visible address bar, tabs, or menus unless you choose to display them.

On the other hand, the legacy version of Internet Explorer keeps visible commonly-used browsing tools such as tabs, the address bar, a "favorites" navigational bar, and the capability to run add-ons, plugins, and toolbars.

Figure 1-2

The Windows 8 native version of Internet Explorer.

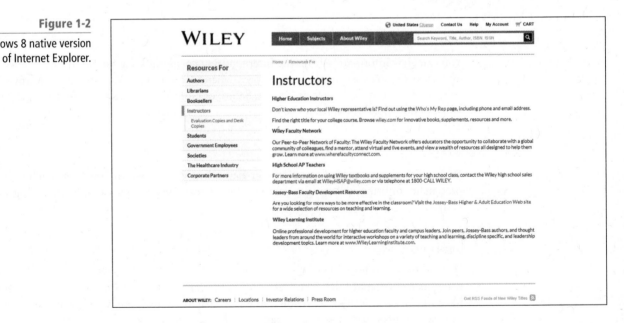

Figure 1-3

The legacy Desktop version of Internet Explorer.

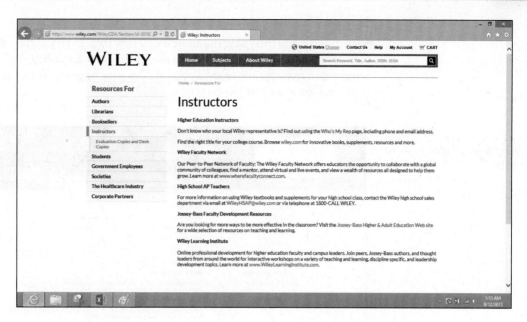

USING THE WINDOWS 8 NATIVE VERSION OF INTERNET EXPLORER

To open the Windows 8 native version of Internet Explorer, tap or click its tile on the Start screen. By default, when you open the Windows 8 native version, you see a full screen of the web page you've set as your Home page. You don't see an address bar or any toolbars at the top of the screen.

Take Note

The Home page is a web page that you can set to be the default web page that displays when you open your web browser. For information on setting a Home page, see "Managing settings" at the end of this lesson.

Navigating through web pages

Switch web pages by typing the address of a new page in the address bar. The address bar appears at the bottom of the screen when you display Internet Explorer's App bar by slightly sliding your finger down from the top of the screen, sliding your finger up from the bottom of the screen, or by right-clicking anywhere on the screen.

Figure 1-4

The address bar appears at the bottom of the screen when you display the App bar.

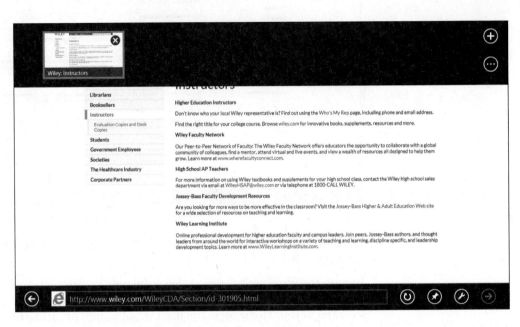

http://www.wiley.com/WileyCDA/Section/id-301905.html

Take Note   If you accidentally display the App bar, you can hide it by repeating the motion you used to display it; either slightly slide your finger down from the top of the screen or up from the bottom of the screen, or right-click anywhere outside the App bar.

The Windows 8 native version of Internet Explorer supports tabbed browsing so you can open multiple web pages and switch among them. To open a new tab and display a second web page, display the **App bar** and then tap or click the plus sign in the upper-right corner. The screen changes to display a tiled list of favorites—you can tap or click one to visit that page—and a blank address bar. You can type an address in the address bar and tap or click the Go arrow to the right of the address bar to go to that page.

Figure 1-5

Opening a new tab in Internet Explorer.

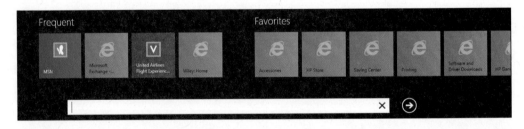

Take Note   As you type, Internet Explorer searches for website names that match what you type; if you see the one you want before you finish typing, tap or click it to display the website.

To switch among Internet Explorer tabs, display the App bar. At the top of the screen, images appear representing each open tab. Tap or click one to view that web page.

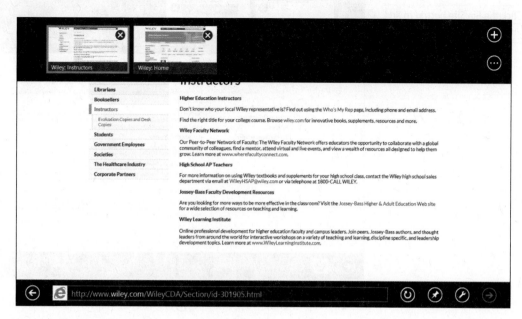

You can close a tab by tapping or clicking the X that appears in the tab image when you display open tabs on the App bar.

If you've visited several web pages using one tab, you can travel forward and backward between those pages by tapping or clicking the Forward and Back arrows on either side of the address bar.

STEP BY STEP | **Pinning a site**

If you've used any browser in the past, you've probably learned about establishing shortcuts to web pages you visit frequently. Internet Explorer calls these shortcuts "Favorites" and you can create a favorite in the Windows 8 native version of Internet Explorer using these steps:

1   Display the page you want to establish as a favorite.

2   Display the App bar.

3   At the bottom of the screen, tap or click the **Pin Site** button.

Figure 1-7

Click the Pin Site button to add the web page to your favorites.

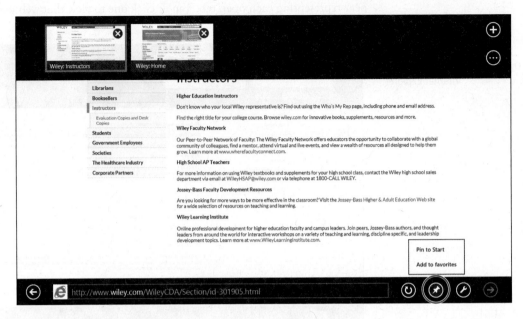

4   Tap or click **Add to Favorites**. Internet Explorer adds the site to your list of favorites.

To visit a favorite site, display the App bar. Then, tap or click in the address bar to view sites you visit frequently and Favorite sites. The newest favorite appears at the right edge of tiles. To display a favorite or frequently visited site in a new tab, tap and hold or right-click the tile, and from the shortcut menu that appears, tap or click Open in New Tab.

Figure 1-8

Favorites appear when you tap or click in the address bar.

Take Note   To remove a frequent site or a Favorite site, tap and hold or right-click the tile for the site. When the shortcut menu appears, tap or click Remove.

You might have noticed that the shortcut menu gives you the option to pin the site to the Start screen; when you select this option, a tile for the site appears on the Start screen and you can open the site directly from the Start screen.

STEP BY STEP   **Browsing privately**

By default, when you browse using Internet Explorer, it allows websites leave cookies on your computer. **Cookies** are small text files that contain pieces of relatively harmless data containing information about a user's activity on the website. In addition, Internet Explorer keeps track of the web pages you visit—known as **history**—and also stores temporary files on your computer.

If you use Internet Explorer's InPrivate mode, you can visit websites without leaving a trail of the visit. When you browse using InPrivate mode, Internet Explorer allows no cookies or temporary files to be stored on your computer and keeps no record of pages you visit.

Take Note   Cookies can be viewed as an invasion of privacy, but they can serve a valuable purpose. For example, some cookies are designed to notify a website of your activity on a prior visit, and other cookies help websites determine whether to allow you to send sensitive information.

If you want to browse the Internet privately, use **InPrivate** mode:

1   Display the App bar.

2   At the top right edge of the screen, tap or click the **Tab Tools** button.

Figure 1-9

Opening an InPrivate browsing tab.

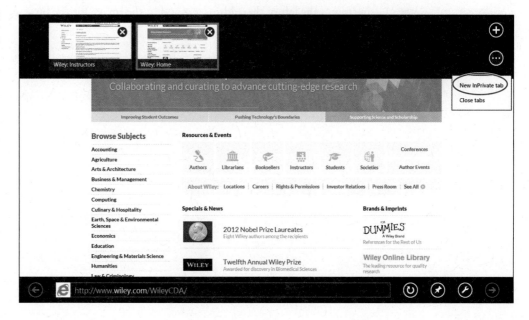

3   From the shortcut menu that appears, tap or click **New InPrivate Tab**. Internet Explorer displays a screen telling you that InPrivate mode is enabled and Internet Explorer won't store any information about your browsing session from the current tab.

Figure 1-10

Internet Explorer informs you that InPrivate mode is turned on.

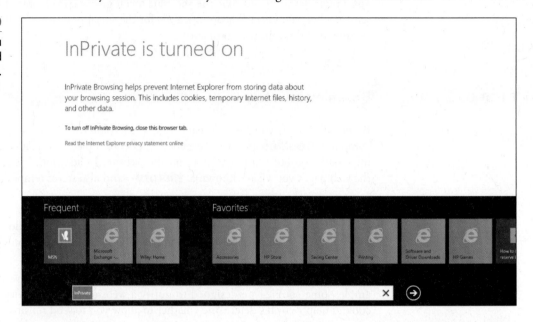

4   In the address bar, type a web address or tap or click a frequently visited or favorite site.

Remember, the private session applies only to the current tab. If you want to open a new tab but continue private browsing, repeat the preceding steps to open that new tab using InPrivate mode.

Take Note   You can always tell when you're browsing privately: display the App bar and look for the InPrivate button to the left of the address bar and in the image for the browser tab.

Searching the Internet

You've already seen how to use the Windows 8 native version of Internet Explorer to search for websites; as you start typing in the address bar, the default search engine displays tiles for websites with names that contain the letters you type. You can click one to view that page.

Figure 1-11

Internet Explorer searches for matching sites as you type in the address bar.

If you keep typing and don't supply a website ending such as .com or .org, Internet Explorer assumes you want to search for the item. The default search engine, Bing, displays a list of possible websites for you to visit.

Figure 1-12

A Bing search page.

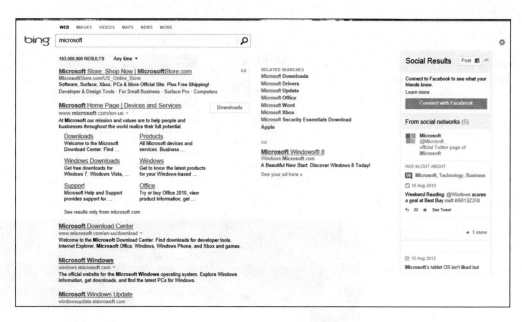

Take Note   To change the default search engine, see "Manage settings and defaults" at the end of this lesson.

STEP BY STEP   **Searching the Internet**

You also can search for information on a page:

1   Press **Ctrl+F** or display the App bar.

2   Tap or click the **Page Tools** button on the right side of the address bar (it looks like a wrench).

3 From the shortcut menu that appears, tap or click **Find on Page**. Internet Explorer replaces the address bar with a Find box, where you can type search text.

Figure 1-13

Searching for text on a web page.

Printing and sharing web pages

You can print a web page using the Devices charm. Display the page and then display the Charms bar to select the Devices charm. Select a printer and Windows 8 prints the web page.

Figure 1-14

Use the Devices charm to select a printer while viewing a web page you want to print.

To share a web page, you can use the Mail app or, if you've set up links to a social networking site, you can use the People app. Display the Charms bar and select the Share charm to select an app.

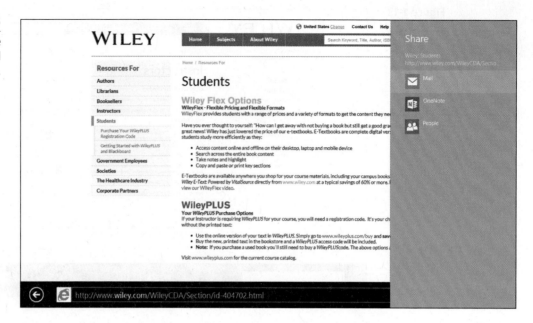

Changing your Internet settings

The Windows 8 native version of Internet Explorer uses many of the settings established for the legacy Desktop version of Internet Explorer; for example, both versions of the browser use the same Home page, but you can establish a Home page only from the legacy Desktop version of Internet Explorer. To change those settings, you need to work in the Desktop version of Internet Explorer. Later in this lesson, in the "Managing settings " section, you'll explore some of those settings.

You can, however, change the following settings from the Windows 8 native version of Internet Explorer:

• Delete browsing history.

• Turn on or off whether Internet Explorer reports your physical location to websites.

• Set the zoom level for all pages.

• Turn on or off the Flip Ahead feature.

• Manually switch the language encoding on a web page if Internet Explorer doesn't seem to correctly interpret it.

Take Note   The Flip Ahead feature is a navigation tool. While reading a multi-page article, using Flip Ahead, you can use a flipping gesture like the one you might use while reading a book to navigate ahead to a subsequent page. The Flip Ahead feature doesn't increase your browsing speed, but it does send information to Microsoft on the pages you view so that Microsoft can improve the Flip Ahead feature.

To change settings for the Windows 8 native version of Internet Explorer, follow these steps:

1 Open the Windows 8 native version of Internet Explorer.

2 Display the Charms bar.

3 Select the Settings charm.

4 Tap or click Internet Options to display and change the options listed previously.

Figure 1-16

Use the Settings charm while viewing the Windows 8 native version of Internet Explorer to change its settings.

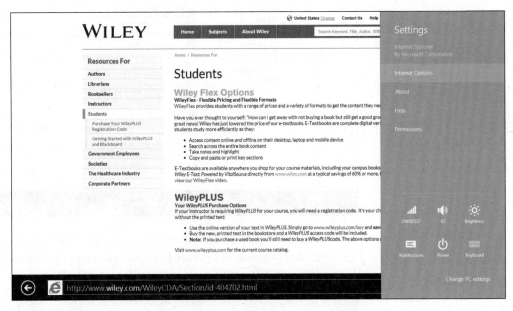

On the Settings charm panel for Internet Explorer, you also can select:

• About, which displays the version of Internet Explorer you're using.

• Help, which displays a website with answers to frequently asked questions about Internet Explorer.

• Permissions, which lets you opt to hide or display notifications from Internet Explorer on the Start screen and the Desktop.

STEP BY STEP   **Switching to the Desktop view**

When using the Windows 8 native version of Internet Explorer, you could come across a website that displays incorrectly. The most likely reason for the page not displaying correctly could be that the site is using Adobe Flash, but Microsoft hasn't included that site in the list of sites permitted to display Flash in the Windows 8 native version of Internet Explorer. In such cases, you can switch to the legacy Desktop version. When you make the switch, the Desktop version of Internet Explorer automatically displays the page you were viewing in the Windows 8 native version, so you don't need to do any additional browsing.

To switch from the Windows 8 native version of Internet Explorer to the Desktop version of Internet Explorer, follow these steps:

1   On the current web page, display the App bar.

2   To the right of the address bar, tap or click the Pages Tools button (the wrench icon).

Figure 1-17

Tap or click the Page Tools button.

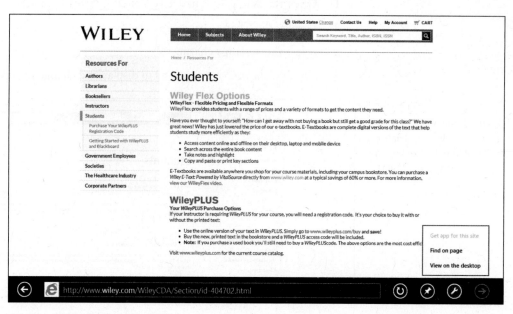

3   From the shortcut menu that appears, tap or click View On The Desktop. The legacy Desktop version of Internet Explorer opens and displays the same page you were viewing in the Windows 8 native version of Internet Explorer.

Figure 1-18

The legacy Desktop version of Internet Explorer displays the same page you were viewing in the Windows 8 native version of Internet Explorer.

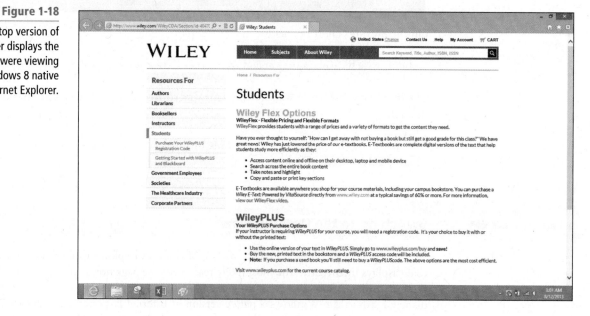

By the way, making this switch doesn't close or affect the Windows 8 native version of Internet Explorer; it's still running and you can switch back to it to continue browsing or to close it.

USING THE DESKTOP VERSION OF INTERNET EXPLORER

Bottom Line

In Windows 8, the legacy version of Internet Explorer is available from the Desktop app.

Navigating through web pages

When you open the legacy version of Internet Explorer, you see familiar toolbars and navigational aids. To work with the legacy Desktop version of Internet Explorer, tap or click the Desktop app from the Start screen or press WinKey (⊞)+D. Then, tap or click the Internet Explorer button on the Desktop taskbar.

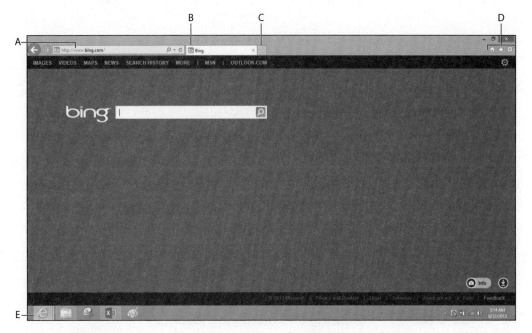

Figure 1-19

A. Address bar. B. Tab. C. Tap or click here to open a new tab. D. Browser tools. E. Tap or click here to open Internet Explorer.

You can switch web pages by typing the address of a new page in the address bar at the top of the screen. You can open additional tabs to browse multiple web pages by tapping or clicking the gray square beside the X at the right edge of the address bar. The screen changes to display a list of favorite sites you have visited. You can tap or click one to visit that page, or you can type in the blank address bar and tap or click the Go arrow to the right of the address bar to visit a page. As you type, Internet Explorer searches for website names that match what you type; if you see the website you want before you finish typing, tap or click the name to display the page.

Figure 1-20

A. Forward and Back buttons.
B. Go arrow.

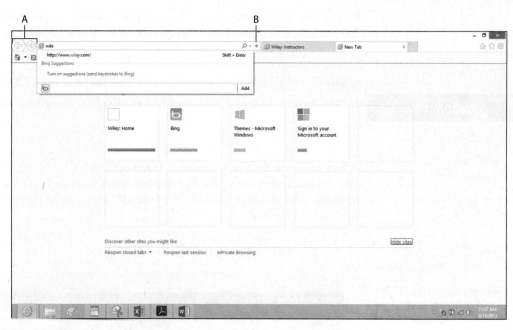

Images and templates used with permission of Microsoft

To close a tab, tap or click the X at the end of the address bar.

Take Note   If only one X appears at the end of the address bar, tapping or clicking it closes Internet Explorer. You also can close Internet Explorer by tapping or clicking the red X in the upper-right corner on the Internet Explorer window.

To switch among Internet Explorer tabs, tap or click a tab to view that web page. If you've visited several web pages using one tab, you can travel forward and backward between those pages by tapping or clicking the Forward and Back arrows on either side of the address bar.

STEP BY STEP   **Creating and managing favorites**

In the legacy Desktop version of Internet Explorer, you can also create favorites to web pages you visit frequently. Follow these steps:

1   Display the page you want to establish as a favorite.

2   Tap or click the **Favorites** button at the right edge of the address bar. (The Favorites button looks like a star.)

3 Tap or click the **Add To Favorites** button that appears just below the Favorites button. Internet Explorer adds the site to your list of favorites.

Figure 1-21

Creating a favorite.

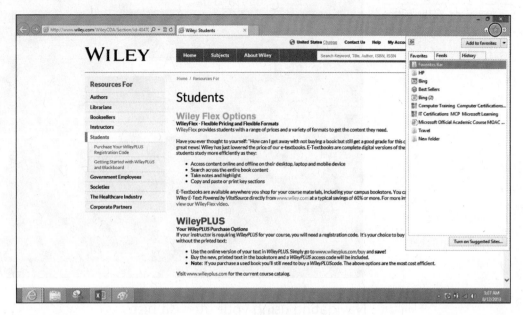

Creating a favorite.

To visit a favorite site, tap or click the Favorites button and then tap or click one of the favorites in the list. The newest favorite appears at the bottom of the list.

Take Note To remove a Favorite site, tap or click the Favorites button and then tap and hold or right-click the site in the list. When the shortcut menu appears, tap or click Delete.

You also can pin web pages to the Desktop taskbar; you can then display the site without first opening Internet Explorer and navigating to the site. Drag the icon just to the left of the web page address—called the *favicon*—to the task bar.

Figure 1-22

A. Favicon. B. This button
appears as you drag.

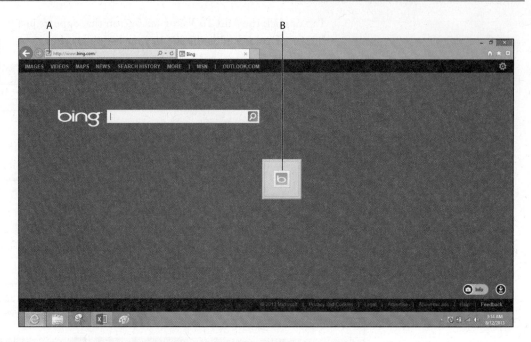

Navigating using your site visit history

Bottom Line

You can navigate to web pages you've visited using the **Forward** and **Back** buttons in Internet Explorer, or you can jump directly to a site you've recently visited using your browsing history. When you display the **Favorites list**, tap or click the **History tab**. The History tab displays the sites you've visited, which are organized, by default, by date (you can switch to view your history in alphabetical order by site name or ordered by most visited). You also can search through your site visit history by supplying a keyword.

Searching the Internet

In the legacy Desktop version of Internet Explorer, as in the Windows 8 native version, you can search for information on the Internet by typing in the address bar. As you type, Internet Explorer suggests websites that match the characters you type. If you supply a website extension, such as .com or .org, and press Enter or tap or click the Go arrow, Internet Explorer takes you to the site you typed, assuming you typed a valid web address.

If you don't supply a valid website extension, Internet Explorer assumes you want to search the Internet for the phrase you typed, and Bing, the default search engine, displays a list of potential websites for you to visit.

Take Note   You can tap or click the Search button in the address bar, but if you haven't supplied a valid website extension, Internet Explorer defaults to searching.

STEP BY STEP | **Browsing privately**

By default, when you browse using Internet Explorer, Internet Explorer allows websites to leave cookies on your computer. Cookies are small text files containing pieces of relatively harmless data containing information about a user's activity when visiting a website. In addition, Internet Explorer tracks the web pages you visit and saves them as part of your browsing history. Last, Internet Explorer stores temporary files on your computer.

When you browse privately, you visit websites without leaving a trail of the visit; Internet Explorer allows no cookies or temporary files to be stored on your computer and keeps no record of pages you visit.

If you want to browse the Internet privately, use InPrivate mode:

1 Open Internet Explorer on the Desktop.

2 At the top right edge of the screen, tap or click the Tools button (the one that looks like a gear).

3 From the shortcut menu that appears, tap or click Safety.

Figure 1-23

Opening an InPrivate browsing session.

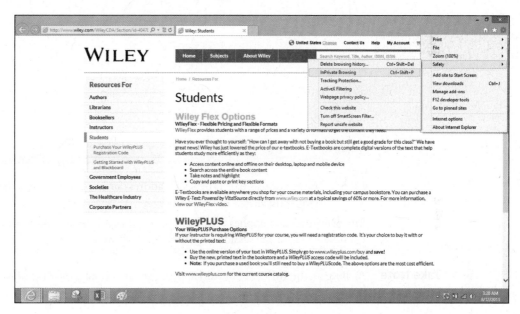

4   Tap or click **InPrivate Browsing**. Internet Explorer opens a new instance of itself—you'll see two Internet Explorer buttons on the Desktop taskbar. The window that appears contains the InPrivate button at the left edge of the address bar; a message appears explaining that InPrivate mode is enabled; and Internet Explorer doesn't store any information about your browsing session.

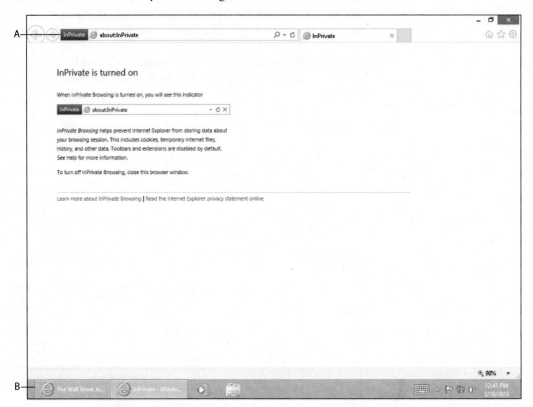

5   In the address bar, type a web address or use the Favorites button to tap or click a frequently visited or a favorite site.

The private session applies only to the current InPrivate instance of Internet Explorer, but you can open new tabs in the session as you browse privately.

Take Note   As long as the InPrivate button appears at the left edge of the address bar, you know that you're browsing privately.

MANAGING SETTINGS

Bottom Line

As you learned earlier in this lesson, you can manage some browser settings from the Settings charm when you open the Windows 8 native app version of Internet Explorer. You can control many more of Internet Explorer's settings from the legacy Desktop app.

STEP BY STEP | **Changing interface settings**

You can customize the default appearance of the legacy Internet Explorer app. For example, the legacy Internet Explorer doesn't display the Command bar or the Favorites bar, but you can add these screen elements.

1   Tap and hold or right-click the Internet Explorer title bar to display a shortcut menu.

2   Tap or click a screen element you want to add. In this example, add the Command bar; it helps you quickly print web pages, start an InPrivate browsing session, and change Internet Explorer settings, so you'll use it in the rest of this lesson.

Figure 1-25

A. Command bar. B. Screen elements you can add.

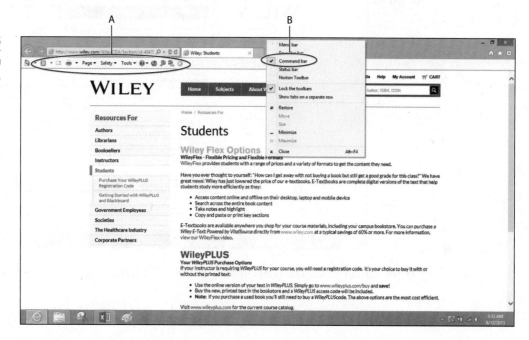

Take Note   The Favorites bar can display buttons for favorites you've established. To do so, display the Favorites bar. Then, tap or click the Favorites button to display your favorites. You'll see a folder called Favorites at the top of the list. Drag any listed favorite into that folder, and a button for it appears on the Favorites bar.

STEP BY STEP   **Setting your home page**

The home page is the web page that appears when you open Internet Explorer (or any browser). The default home page is Bing, Microsoft's search engine but, you can change the home page to any web page you want.

Take Note   Both versions of Internet Explorer use the same home page.

1   Display the web page you want to use as your home page.

2   Tap or click the Tools button to display a menu. (The Tools button looks like a gear and it's located in the upper-right corner; you can also use the Tools button on the Command bar.)

Figure 1-26

A. Home button. B. Tools button.

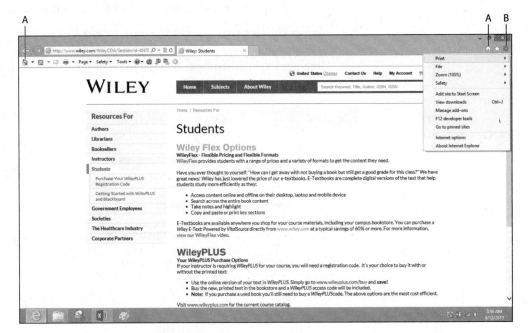

Take Note   You can tap the Home button in the upper-right corner or on the Commands bar to quickly re-display your home page at any time.

3   Tap or click Internet Options to display the Internet Options dialog box.

4   In the General tab, tap or click the Use Current button. The address for your home page changes to the address of the page you're currently viewing.

Take Note   If you don't tap or click the Use Current button and instead tap or click the Use New Tab button, Internet Explorer sets a blank tab as your home page; starting with a blank page can considerably speed up browsing.

5   Tap or click OK.

Figure 1-27

Tap or click the Use Current button to set the current web page as your home page.

Take Note   You can set Internet Explorer to open several pages (and therefore have several different home pages) by listing the page addresses in the box at the top of the General tab. After you list each page, don't tap or click the Use Current button; instead, just tap or click OK.

STEP BY STEP   **Adding a search engine**

Internet Explorer's default search engine is Bing, owned by Microsoft. If you prefer a different search engine, you can choose to set that search engine as the default engine Internet Explorer uses. When you choose a search engine, you choose it for both the Windows 8 native version and the legacy version of Internet Explorer. Follow these steps:

1   With Internet Explorer open, tap or click the down arrow beside the Search magnifying glass in the address bar. Tap or click the **Add** button in the lower-right corner of the menu that appears. Internet Explorer opens the Internet Explorer Gallery web page in a new tab.

Figure 1-28

Tap or click the down arrow to add another search engine.

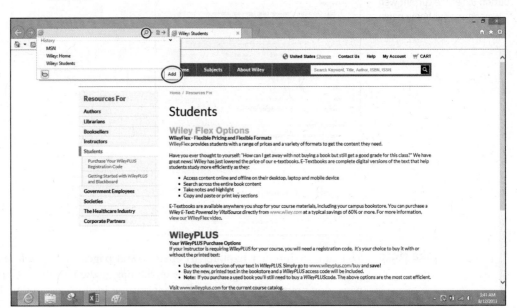

2   Scroll down, look for the search engine you want to use, and tap or click it. In this example, tap or click **Start Page** (Start Page is a search engine that protects your privacy by not keeping track of your searches). The search engine you choose appears on a new web page.

3   Tap or click **Add to Internet Explorer**. The Add Search Provider dialog box appears.

Figure 1-29

Your selected search engine appears on a new web page.

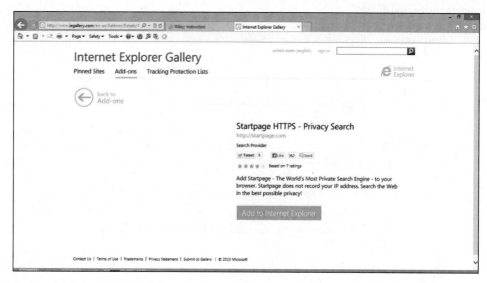

Clip art used with permission of Microsoft

4   In the Add Search Provider dialog box, tap or click the Add button. Internet Explorer adds the search engine and sets it as the default search engine. It then redisplays the web page where you added the search engine.

Figure 1-30

Use this dialog box to add a search engine, and if you want, set it as the default search engine.

Take Note   To set the new search engine as the default search engine, tap or click the Make This My Default Search Provider checkbox.

5   Tap or click the tab's X to close it.

The next time you type in the address bar, notice that two search engines appear; the one on the left is the one you selected as the default search engine.

STEP BY STEP   **Changing the default search engine**

1   On the Commands bar, tap or click Tools.

2   Tap or click Manage add-ons. The Manage Add-ons window appears.

3   On the left side, tap or click Search Providers. Your installed search providers appear; the default search engine displays "Default" in the Status column.

4   Tap or click the search engine you want to use by default.

5   In the lower-right corner, tap or click the Set as Default button.

Figure 1-31

Selecting a new default search engine

6   Tap or click the Close button.

Take Note   You also can remove a search engine you no longer need by tapping the Remove button.

Setting your default browser

Windows 8 contains two versions of Internet Explorer; the version that opens when you click a link depends on where you are in Windows 8. If you're working in a Windows 8 native app and click a link, then the Windows 8 native version of Internet Explorer opens. If you're working on the Desktop using a legacy app and you click a link, the legacy version of Internet Explorer opens.

Windows 8 allows you to change this behavior by choosing one of them to be the default browser at all times.

1   Open legacy Internet Explorer on the Desktop.

2   Tap or click the Tools button in the upper-right corner (the one that looks like a gear) or tap or click the Tools button on the Command bar.

3   Tap or click Internet Options to display the Internet Options dialog box.

4   Tap or click the Programs tab.

5   In the first section of the tab, tap or click the list box to choose how you open links. Choose Always in Internet Explorer to use the Windows 8 native version or Always in Internet Explorer on the Desktop to use the legacy version.

Figure 1-32

Decide which version of Internet Explorer opens when you tap or click a link.

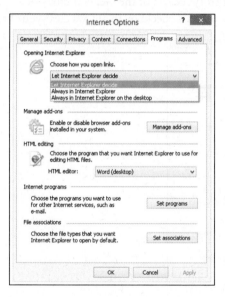

6   Tap or click OK.

Housekeeping

To ensure your browsing experience runs smoothly, you should consider deleting, from time to time, temporary files, browsing history, and cookies.

Internet Explorer stores temporary files—copies of web pages you visit—in the **Temporary Internet Files** folder on your hard drive. Internet Explorer uses those files to speed up your browsing experience; when you visit a page you've visited in the past, Internet Explorer loads the copy stored in the Temporary Internet Files folder instead of loading a new copy. This process saves lots of time, especially if you're using a slow Internet connection, but it also takes up lots of room on your hard drive—250 MB, by default.

Browsing history, on the other hand, doesn't take up much space on your hard drive. Even if you surf voraciously, your history file will probably not exceed 1 MB. But it does contain a list of every site you've visited and you might not want that list available to anyone who sits down at your computer.

Last, as mentioned previously, cookies are typically innocuous, but there are companies out there that exploit them. After a while, as you visit websites, you might start seeing advertising that seems surprisingly aware of your interests—almost as if it were targeted at you. If you find that disconcerting, you can delete your cookies. Be aware that cookies will replenish themselves as you continue browsing.

Take Note   It's also possible that your bank's website will no longer recognize you if you delete cookies—and then you'll need to go through the bank's process of re-establishing you as a valid visitor. While the process is rarely difficult, you might find it annoying.

STEP BY STEP   **Deleting stored information in Internet Explorer**

To delete information that Internet Explorer stores, follow these steps:

1   Open legacy Internet Explorer.

2   Tap or click the Tools button on the Command bar.

3   Tap or click Internet Options.

4   In the Browsing History section of the General tab, you can tap or click the Delete Browsing History on Exit checkbox to always clear your browsing history.

Figure 1-33

You can delete browsing history every time you close Internet Explorer.

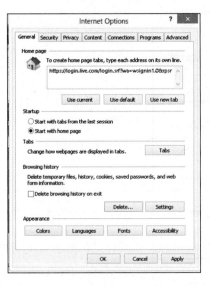

5   Tap or click the Delete button to display the Delete Browsing History dialog box.

Take Note   Once you've set your preference for deleting browsing history when you close Internet Explorer, you can skip Steps 1–5 and open the Delete Browsing History dialog box directly. Tap or click the Safety button on Internet Explorer's Command bar and then tap or click Delete Browsing History.

6   Tap or click the checkboxes beside the browsing history elements you want to delete. Read the descriptions under each item to decide if you want to delete that type of information.

In this lesson you learned how to:

- Understanding the World Wide Web

- Using the Windows 8 native version of Internet Explorer

- Managing settings

- Using the Desktop version of Internet Explorer

- Using the two versions of Internet Explorer that ship with Windows 8

Knowledge Assessment

True/False

T F 1. The legacy Desktop version of Internet Explorer 10 is faster than the Windows 8 native version of Internet Explorer 10.

T F 2. The native Windows 8 version of Internet Explorer only displays Flash animations from approved websites.Selecting a field's handle and pressing Delete clears out the data the field refers to.

T F 3. Websites can be pinned to the Start screen for easier access.

T F 4. Internet Explorer 10 uses InPrivate mode by default.

T F 5. Once the Windows 8 native version of Internet Explorer is in InPrivate mode, all future tabs will not leave cookies, track web pages, or store temporary files on your computer.

T F 6. Only the Desktop version of Internet Explorer 10 can change the browser's homepage.

T F 7. By default, Internet Explorer saves up to 25 MB of temporary Internet files.

T F 8. Deleting your browser's cookies will cause you to need to log in to various websites again.

T F 9. Both the native and legacy versions of Internet Explorer share settings.

T F 10. When you delete your browsing history, you lose login data for all your websites.

Multiple Choice

1. Which of the following statements are not true?
   a. The Windows 8 native version of Internet Explorer does not support plugins.
   b. The Windows 8 native version of Internet Explorer does not support extensions.
   c. The Windows 8 native version of Internet Explorer does not support toolbars.
   d. The Windows 8 native version of Internet Explorer does not support Flash animations.

2. Internet Explorer uses which of the following search engines by default?
   a. Google
   b. Yahoo!
   c. Bing
   d. Ask

3. Which of the following Internet settings cannot be set in the Windows 8 native version of Internet Explorer 10?

    a. Deleting the browsing history

    b. Setting the browser homepage

    c. Setting whether Internet Explorer reports your physical location to websites.

    d. Setting the zoom level for all pages.

4. Where can you find the current version number for the Windows 8 native version of Internet Explorer?

    a. The About section of the Settings charm panel

    b. The Help section of the Settings charm panel

    c. The Internet Options section of the Settings charm panel

    d. The Permissions section of the Settings charm panel

5. The History tab cannot sort results in which of the following ways?

    a. Date

    b. Site name

    c. Most visited

    d. Time spent on website

6. Which of the following versions of Internet Explorer 10 support tabbed browsing?

    a. The Windows 8 native version of Internet Explorer

    b. The legacy Desktop version of Internet Explorer

    c. All of the above

7. Which of the following statements are not true?

    a. Internet Explorer 10 can only set a single homepage.

    b. Internet Explorer 10 can use multiple search engines.

    c. Internet Explorer 10 can use a blank homepage.

8. Which of the following statements are true?

    a. Internet Explorer 10 can speed up browsing performance by saving temporary Internet files to your hard drive.

    b. By default, Internet Explorer saves a list of all the websites you visit.

    c. Website Cookies can be used to track you on the Internet.

    d. All of the above.

9. What are the best ways to keep your passwords safe in Internet Explorer?

    a. Don't allow the browser to save your logins.

    b. Use different passwords for each website you visit on the Internet.

    c. Use a password manager browser plug-in to manage your passwords.

    d. All of the above.

10. What are the benefits of using InPrivate browsing?

    a. Your browsing history is not saved to your hard-drive.

    b. Cookies are not saved to your hard-drive.

    c. Temporary Internet files are not saved to your hard-drive.

    d. All of the above.

Competency Assessment

Project 1-1: Pin a website to add it to your list of favorites

1. Launch Word and browse the template gallery. Open a variety of templates to see the range of built-in document types Word offers.

2. Search Microsoft's online template collection for calendar and select a monthly calendar template. Try editing the template and saving it as a .docx file, then as a new .dotx (template) file.

3. Select File > New (rather than pressing Ctrl+N) and find the calendar template you selected near the top of the template gallery. Click the pin icon to keep it permanently in the gallery.

4. Close any open files and leave Word open for the next exercise.

Project 1-2: Browse a website privately

Browse a website privately using Internet Explorer 10 so that cookies, temporary Internet files, and browser history are not maintained.

1. Open the project file **declaration_text** and save it in your working directory as project_1-2_formatting.

2. Click once on the word events in the first line and press Ctrl+I to apply italic formatting.

   Word will italicize the entire word, assuming from context that you didn't mean to insert italicized characters in the middle of a non-italicized word.

3. Double-click the word events to select the whole word, then click the italics symbol in the formatting popup to remove italic formatting from the word.

4. Triple click events to select the entire line (paragraph) and apply italic formatting again. Then repeat the action.

5. Click in the final paragraph on pages 3-4 and select the Intense Quote style.

6. Add the line Declaration of Independence to the top of the document, formatted with the Title style.

7. Select everything except the title, first paragraph, and final paragraph, and format it as two-column text (Page Layout > Columns > Two).

8. Save your work and leave the document open for the next exercise.

Proficiency Assessment

Project 1-3: Set a new default search engine

1. Save your document as **project_1-3_headings.**
2. Insert the line Bill of Particulars before the line "He has refused his Assent to Laws…" on page 1. Format the new line with the Heading 2 style.
3. Insert a Heading 2 line, Legal Affronts, before the "For quartering large bodies…" line on page 2.
4. Insert the Heading 2 line, Good Faith, before the In ever stage… paragraph on page 3.
5. Collapse the three new headings by mousing over them and clicking the' folding arrows that appear.

   (It is most convenient to carry out this step in order from first heading to last.)
6. Save your document and leave it open for the next exercise.

Project 1-4: Share a website

Share a specific web page via e-mail or a social networking site.

1. Save your document as **project_1-4_style_color.**
2. Expand the three headings.

   (It is most convenient to do so in reverse order, starting with the last heading and working your way back through the document.)
3. Open the Design tab.
4. Select the Lines (Distinctive) Style Set.
5. Select the Violet II color scheme.
6. Save your work and leave the document open for the next exercise.

Mastery Assessment

Project 1-5: Set your default browser

1. Save your document as **project_1-5_theme.**
2. In the Design tab, experiment with various themes.

   Note that changing the theme overrides your choice of color scheme, though not document/character formatting like columns and italics.
3. Assign the Main Event theme with the Red Orange color scheme and Lines (Stylish) Style Set.
4. Assign the List Paragraph style to the first paragraph ("When in the course of…").

   Note that the italics are overridden by the new style assignment.
5. Save your work and leave Word open for the next exercise.

Project 1-6: Deleting your History and Cookies

1. Save your document as **project_1-6_modding_styles**.
2. Select the first paragraph, *When in the course...* and assign it the same color as the Bill of Particulars heading has.
3. Select the paragraph again and update the List Paragraph style to reflect the new formatting.
4. Apply the List Paragraph style to the closing paragraph.
5. Alter all body text (Normal style) in the document to full justification rather than Align Left, by updating the style itself.

    Note that the Title style will also switch to full justification – it's a modification of the Normal style.
6. Fix the Title style by updating it to Align Left.
7. Save your work and close Excel.

2

Sharing Device Settings and Content

LESSON SKILL

In this lesson, you will learn the following skills:

Synchronize Windows 8 settings across devices	Understand basics of cloud storage
Working with Text and Fields	Use the Windows 8 native SkyDrive app
Introducing SkyDrive	Tracked Changes and Comment Threads
Browse with SkyDrive	Synchronize and fetch files using the legacy Desktop SkyDrive app

KEY TERMS

- **Microsoft account**
- **SkyDrive**
- **Local account**
- **Legacy SkyDrive app**

Julene at Northwind Traders received a new desktop computer and tablet PC and wants to convert her account to a Windows account so she can synchronize documents and settings between her laptop, desktop, and tablet PCs.

SOFTWARE ORIENTATION

Windows 8 makes it easy to share content and settings across several devices, such as a tablet, notebook, and desktop computer.

Figure 2-1

Internet Explorer workspace

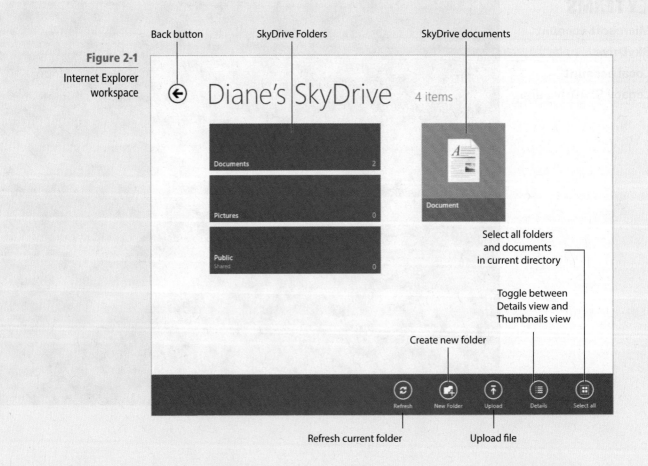

STARTING UP

In this lesson you will work with several lesson files. Make sure that you have access to the lesson files before you start the lesson.

SYNCHRONIZING WINDOWS 8 SETTINGS ACROSS DEVICES

Bottom Line

Windows 8 introduces the **Microsoft account**, a new type of log in account that you can use when you start your computer. Each time you log in to Windows 8 using a Microsoft account, you connect your computer to the cloud. By connecting to the cloud, you can use the same settings on all your Windows 8 devices to make your Windows 8 experience a familiar one.

By default, when you connect to the cloud from your desktop PC Windows 8 automatically synchronizes some settings to the cloud (for example, your pictures, your backgrounds, your Internet Explorer history and favorites, and more). If you later sign in to another device (such as to a tablet PC) using the same Microsoft account, Windows 8 synchronizes the settings from your desktop PC to your tablet PC to make your Windows 8 experience familiar on all your devices. If, while working on your tablet PC, you make any change to the settings that Windows 8 synchronizes, those new settings will appear on your desktop PC the next time you log in using your Microsoft account.

Although the default behavior for Windows 8 is to synchronize settings between devices on which you use the same Microsoft account when you sign in, you can change that default behavior and control synchronization. To make changes to the Windows 8 device synchronization settings, you need to log in to your Windows 8 device using your Microsoft account. If you've been using a **local account**, you can switch to your Microsoft account using these steps:

Take Note If you haven't established a Microsoft account, see Lesson 1, "Getting Started with Windows 8."

STEP BY STEP **Synchronizing Windows 8 settings across devices**

1 Display the Charms bar by sliding slightly in toward the center of the screen from the right side of the screen, pressing WinKey (■)+C, or placing your mouse in the upper- or lower-right corner of the screen.

2 Tap or click the Settings charm.

3 Tap or click Change PC Settings.

4   On the left side of the PC Settings screen, tap or click Users.

Figure 2-2

Switching to a Microsoft
account.

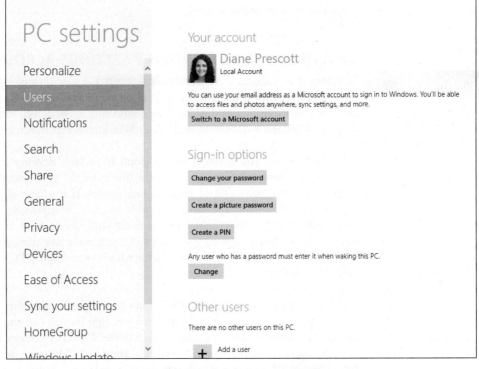

Images and clip art used with permission of Microsoft.

5   Tap or click the Switch to a Microsoft account button.

6   Provide the password for your local account and tap or click Next.

Figure 2-3

Provide the password for your
local account.

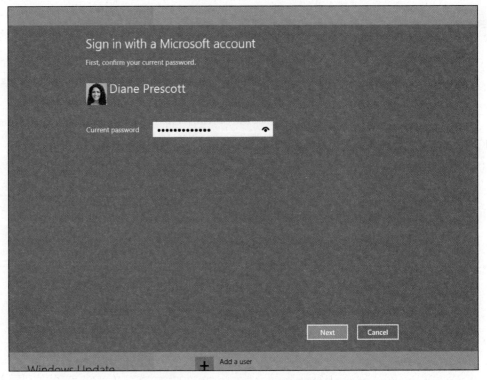

Images and clip art used with permission of Microsoft.

7   Supply your Microsoft account e-mail address and tap or click Next.

8 Supply the password to your Microsoft account. Remember, this password is not necessarily the same as the password you use to collect e-mail for this address.

Figure 2-4

Supply your Microsoft account e-mail address and password.

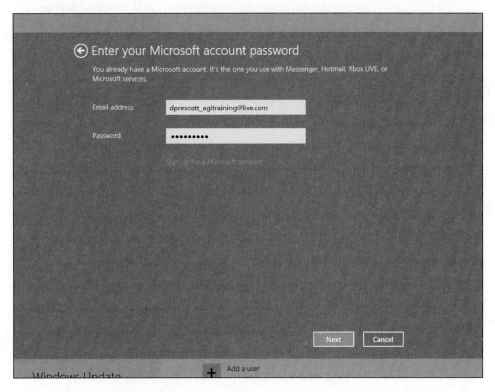

9 Tap or click Next to display the last screen of the wizard that switches you to your Microsoft account.

Take Note You might be prompted to supply security information at this point. If so, provide the information and tap or click Next.

Figure 2-5

The final screen for switching to your Microsoft account.

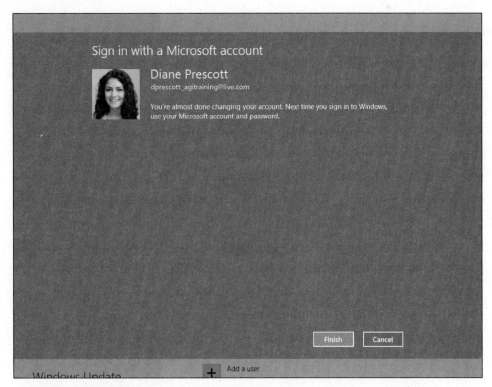

Photos used with permission from Microsoft

10 Tap or click Finish.

Windows 8 switches to your Microsoft account and redisplays the PC Settings screen. Notice that you now have the option to switch to a local account; after you set synchronization settings, you can repeat the preceding steps to switch back to a local account.

Figure 2-6

When you're logged in to Windows 8 using a Microsoft account, you can switch to a local account using the preceding steps.

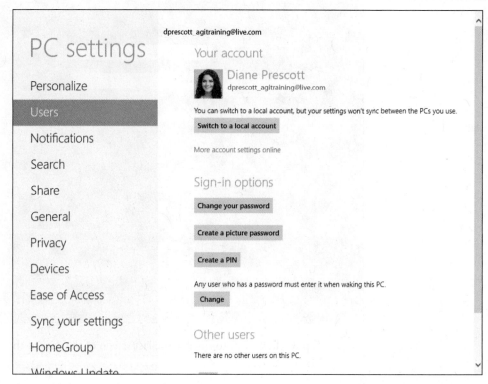

Photos used with permission from Microsoft

STEP BY STEP   **Changing your synchronization settings**

Next, review and make changes to your Windows 8 synchronization settings. Follow these steps:

1   Scroll down the left side of the PC Settings screen and tap or click **Sync Your Settings**. The settings you can synchronize appear.

Figure 2-7

The settings you can synchronize.

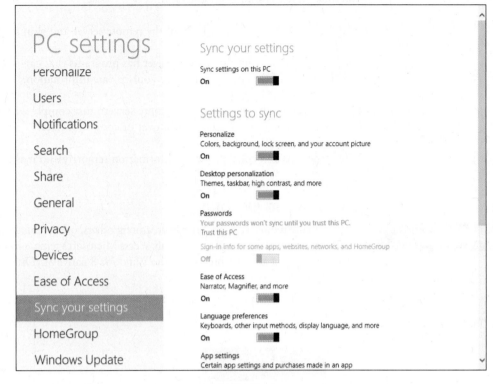

2   Tap or click a setting to turn it off.

Take Note   To turn off all synchronization, tap or click the first option.

3   Scroll down the right side of the screen to view additional synchronization settings you can control and make changes to them as needed.

4   Close PC Settings by pressing **Alt+F4** or by dragging your finger or the mouse down from the top of the screen to the bottom of the screen.

THE BASICS OF CLOUD STORAGE

Bottom Line   Storing your files in the cloud (that is, on a remote server operated by a company you typically pay for the storage space) has both advantages and disadvantages. Among the advantages:

• You can access files at any time, from anywhere, using any computer.

• You can easily share files you select with remote users.

• If you store important information remotely, it will still be available to you if your home or office is robbed or burns down.

• Most companies that offer remote storage provide a free amount of storage, so you might not need to pay for your remote storage.

- Among the disadvantages:

- You must have a working Internet connection to use your remotely stored files.

- A hacker could breach the security of the remote server and gain access to your private files.

- The company operating the remote server has programs that can scan your private information, and employees of the company can see your private information.

- By law, the company operating the remote server must comply with any court orders it receives from law enforcement officials to turn over or copy your data.

- Weigh the pros and cons of storing information remotely and make your own decision.

INTRODUCING SKYDRIVE

Bottom Line

If you opt to use remote storage, Microsoft, among others, offers remote storage and provides you with up to 7 GB of storage for free. You can easily access Microsoft's remote storage, called **SkyDrive**, using a Microsoft account and any browser or the Windows 8 native SkyDrive app.

Figure 2-8

The Windows 8 native SkyDrive app.

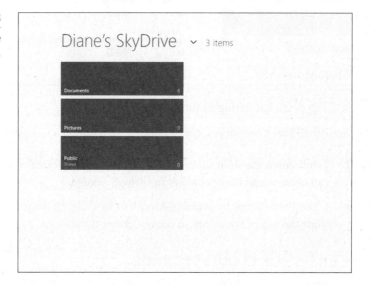

Figure 2-9

The browser version of SkyDrive shown in the legacy Desktop app Internet Explorer.

Take Note   There is a legacy Desktop SkyDrive app that you can install; it gives you the most powerful of all cloud features: the ability to remotely download a document that you haven't uploaded to your SkyDrive. See the section, "Using the legacy Desktop SkyDrive app" later in this lesson.

SkyDrive is more than just online storage. In addition to uploading and downloading documents, you can open and edit documents. If you use the Windows 8 native version of SkyDrive, you will be able to open documents using a locally installed app. For example, if you open a word-processing document, SkyDrive will open the document in WordPad or Microsoft Word, if you have installed Microsoft Word.

If you use the browser version of SkyDrive and you open a document, SkyDrive attempts to use one of the Office Web Apps: Word, Excel, PowerPoint, or OneNote.

The browser version of SkyDrive has more capabilities than the Windows 8 native version of SkyDrive. For example, you can create documents in the browser version of SkyDrive, and you can then download them to your hard drive.

Although you can't create documents in the Windows 8 native SkyDrive app, you can accomplish a lot using it.

USING THE WINDOWS 8 NATIVE SKYDRIVE APP

Bottom Line   You don't need to be signed in to Windows 8 using a Microsoft account to use the Windows 8 native SkyDrive app. If you're signed into Windows using a local account and you tap or click the SkyDrive app on the Start screen, you're prompted to provide your Microsoft account information. Once you fill in this information, the SkyDrive app saves it. Then, all you need is a working Internet connection to use the SkyDrive app.

Figure 2-10

If you try to launch the SkyDrive app while signed in to Windows 8 under a local account, this screen appears.

Photos used with permission from Microsoft

When the Windows 8 native SkyDrive app appears, some see three folders by default, and these folders are represented by tiles: Documents, Pictures, and Public.

Take Note   The folders shown are an example of what you might see; your SkyDrive might show different folders.

Figure 2-11

The default screen for the Windows 8 native SkyDrive app.

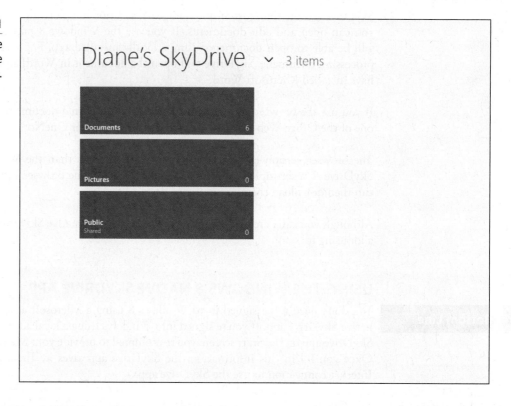

STEP BY STEP   **Adding a folder**

You aren't limited to these three folders, but you might prefer to add folders inside the default folders. For example, in the Documents folder, you might want to create folders for the different types of documents you create, and then tap or click the folder to access a file.

Initially, your SkyDrive default folders won't contain any folders. To add a folder, follow these steps:

1   From the location where you want to add the folder (either the opening SkyDrive screen or inside one of the default folders), display the App bar by swiping down slightly from the top of the screen or by right-clicking anywhere on the screen.

2   Tap or click the New Folder button.

3   In the window that appears, type the name of the new folder.

4   Tap or click the **Create Folder** button.

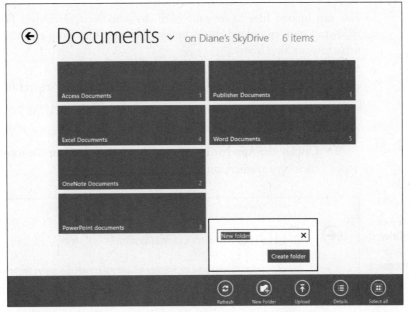

As mentioned, you open a folder by tapping or clicking it. After you've added folders inside folders and you've drilled down into a folder, you navigate up to a higher folder level using the Back button.

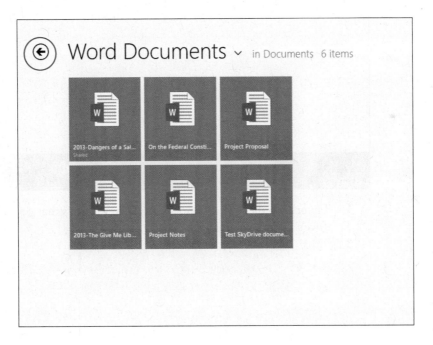

Uploading files

You can upload files from your hard drive to your SkyDrive. For this example, you use the following steps to upload the Windows10lessons files from the My Pictures folder on your hard drive to your SkyDrive:

1   Place the lesson files for this lesson into your my Pictures folder.

2   In the native Windows 8 SkyDrive app, tap or click the **Public** folder (or other preferred folder).

2   Display the App bar by swiping down slightly from the top of the screen or by right-clicking anywhere on the screen.

Figure 2-14

To upload a file from your hard drive to your SkyDrive, navigate to the SkyDrive folder where the file should appear.

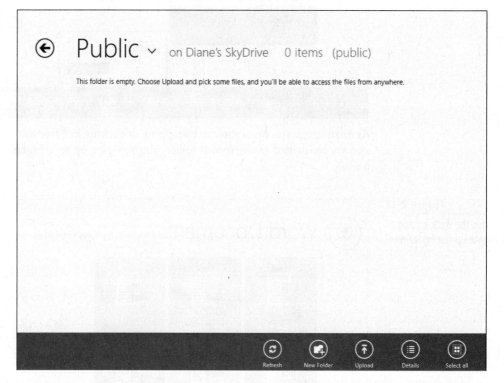

3   Tap or click the **Upload** button. SkyDrive suggests that you select files from your hard drive's Documents folder.

4 To select a different folder, tap or click **Files** to display a list of locations on your hard drive that you can search for files to upload to your SkyDrive.

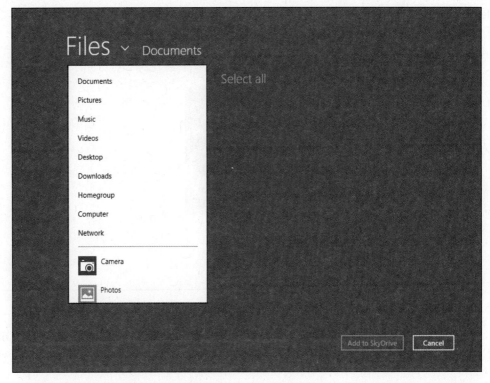

Figure 2-15

Select the location on your hard drive containing the files you want to upload to your SkyDrive.

5 For this example, tap or click **Pictures** to display the contents of the Pictures folder.

6 For this example, tap or click **Windows1001-01.jpg**. A checkmark appears beside the selected file.

Figure 2-16

Selecting a file to upload to your SkyDrive.

Images and templates used with permission of Microsoft

7   Tap or click the Add to SkyDrive button. The SkyDrive app uploads **Windows1001-01.jpg** to the Public folder.

Figure 2-17

File uploaded to SkyDrive.

Images and templates used with permission of Microsoft

When you redisplay the main screen of the Windows 8 native SkyDrive app, the number of files in the folder you selected in Step 1 above updates to reflect the new addition.

STEP BY STEP   **Downloading files**

You can download files from your SkyDrive to your hard drive. For this example, you'll download the **Windows1001-01.jpg** file you just uploaded since it's the only file you have available on your SkyDrive. Follow these steps:

1   In the native Windows 8 SkyDrive app, tap or click the **Public** folder (or the folder chosen in Step 1 of the previous exercise).

2   Select the **Windows1001-01.jpg** file you want to download by tapping and holding and dragging down slightly or right-clicking. A checkmark appears beside the file.

3   Display the App bar by swiping down slightly from the top of the screen or by right-clicking anywhere on-screen.

Figure 2-18

Select the file you want to download and display the App bar.

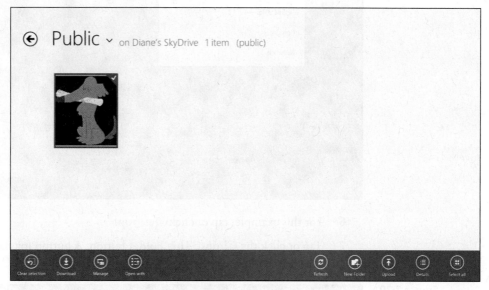

Images and templates used with permission of Microsoft

4   Tap or click the **Download** button. SkyDrive suggests that you download the file to your hard drive's Documents folder.

5   To select a different folder, tap or click **Files** to display a list of locations on your hard drive where you can download files from your SkyDrive.

Figure 2-19

Select the location on your hard drive where you want to place the files you download from your SkyDrive.

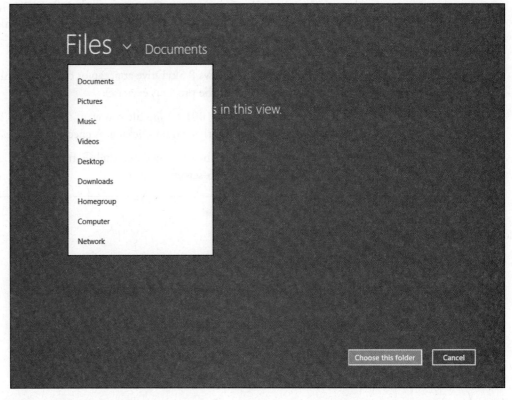

6   For this example, tap or click **Desktop**.

7   Tap or click the **Choose This Folder** button. A button for the Desktop folder appears at the bottom of the screen.

Figure 2-20

Selecting the Desktop as the download location.

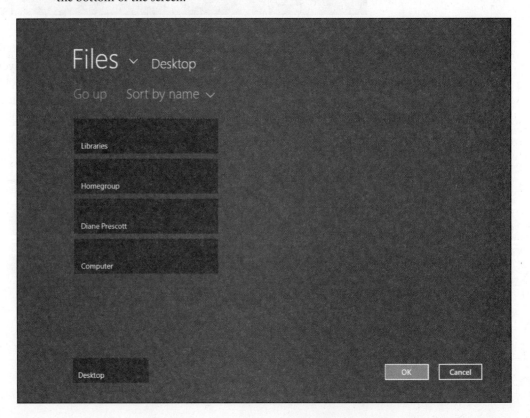

8 Tap or click **OK**. The SkyDrive app downloads the **Windows1001-01.jpg** file to the Desktop and displays its progress in the upper-right corner of the SkyDrive app screen.

Figure 2-21

Downloading a file from SkyDrive.

Images and templates used with permission of Microsoft

9 Display the Desktop app, and you'll find **Windows1001-01.jpg** on the Desktop.

Figure 2-22

The file you downloaded from your SkyDrive now appears on your Desktop.

Images and templates used with permission of Microsoft

Signing out of SkyDrive

There is no formal sign out procedure in the Windows 8 native SkyDrive app. Close the app by pressing Alt+F4 or by dragging your finger or the mouse down the screen from the top of the screen to the bottom.

BROWSING WITH SKYDRIVE

Bottom Line

You can also work with your SkyDrive space using any Internet browser. The browser version of SkyDrive is more powerful than the Windows 8 native SkyDrive app. For example, using the browser version of SkyDrive, you can create documents and folders.

In this example, we'll use the Windows 8 native version of Internet Explorer to run the browser version of SkyDrive. Open the Windows 8 native version of Internet Explorer and navigate to *www.skydrive.com*. On the sign-in screen, supply your Microsoft account user name and password.

Figure 2-23

Signing in to SkyDrive using a browser.

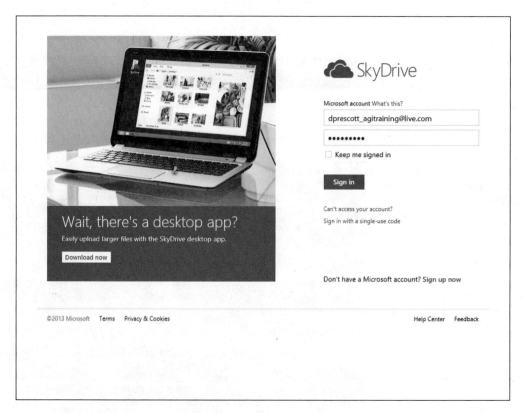

Images and templates used with permission of Microsoft

When you tap or click the Sign In button, the browser version of SkyDrive appears. Navigate this interface by using the links along the left side of the screen. To search for a file on your SkyDrive, tap or click in the Search SkyDrive box above the links in the left column. If you know the folder that contains the file you want, you can tap that folder.

Figure 2-24

The browser version of Sky-Drive.

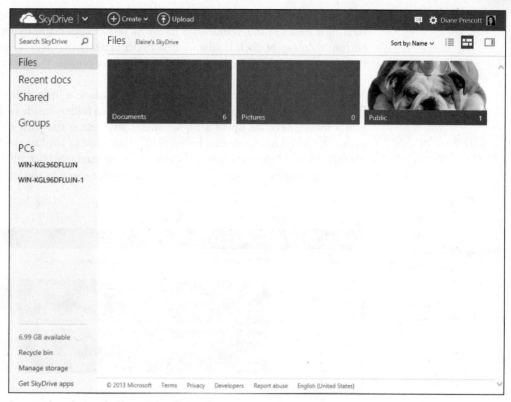

Images and templates used with permission of Microsoft

Creating folders and documents

Using the browser version of SkyDrive, you can create folders as well as Word, Excel, PowerPoint, and OneNote documents using the Web App versions of these programs. To see your choices, tap or click the Create button at the top of the screen.

Figure 2-25

In the browser version of SkyDrive, you can create documents and folders.

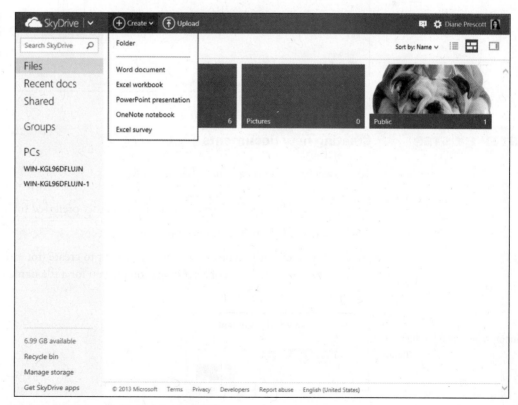

Images and templates used with permission of Microsoft

Creating a new a folder in the browser version of SkyDrive is done in much the same way as creating a folder in the Windows 8 native SkyDrive app: begin by tapping or clicking the Create button; then tap or click Folder. A new folder appears that will let you type a name for it. After typing a name, press Enter or tap or click anywhere outside the folder to save the name.

Navigating in the browser version of SkyDrive is done a little differently than navigating in the Windows 8 native SkyDrive app. After you've added folders inside folders and you've drilled down into a folder, navigate up to a higher folder level using the path that appears beside the folder name; the folder name appears below the Create button. The last entry in the folder path matches the folder name below the Create button. You can navigate back up the folder tree one folder at a time by tapping or clicking the portion of the folder name to the left of the caret (>).

Figure 2-26

A. Folder name. B. Tap to navigate up the folder tree. C. Folder path.

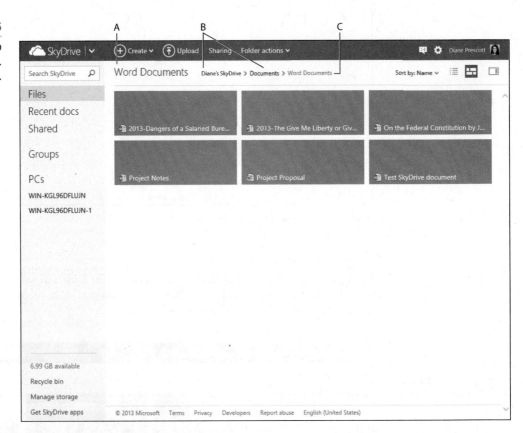

STEP BY STEP   **Creating new documents**

To create a new document, follow these steps:

1   Tap or click the Documents folder (or another preferred folder.)

2   Tap or click the Create button.

3   Tap or click the type of document you want to create (for example, Word document). The browser version of SkyDrive prompts you for a file name.

Figure 2-27

Supply a file name for the new document.

New Microsoft Word document

Test SkyDrive document   ✕ .docx

Create

4 Tap or click the Create button. The browser version of SkyDrive opens the appropriate Office Web App.

Figure 2-28

A. Save button. B. The document you are creating. C. Working in a web app. D. Close button.

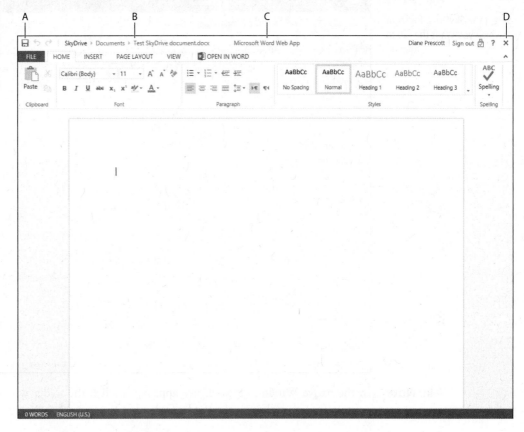

5 Create your document.

6 To save your document, tap or click the Save button.

7 To close the Web App, tap or click the Close button.

STEP BY STEP   **Uploading files**

You can upload files stored on your hard drive to SkyDrive using the browser version of SkyDrive. In this example, make sure that **Windows1002-01.jpg** is loaded onto your hard drive in the Pictures folder. Then, follow these steps:

1   From the main SkyDrive screen, tap or click the Pictures folder.

Figure 2-29

Select the SkyDrive folder in
which you want the file to
appear.

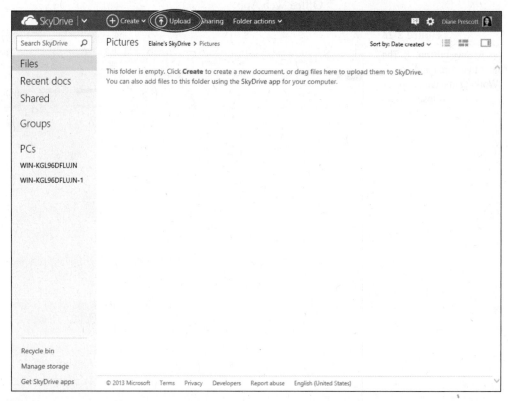

Take Note   In the native Windows 8 SkyDrive app, tap or click the folder where you want the pictures to appear. This example uses the Public folder, but you can select any folder.

2   Tap or click the Upload button at the top of the screen. The SkyDrive app suggests that you upload a file from your hard drive's Documents folder.

3   Tap or click Files to display a list of folders you can use to upload a file.

Figure 2-30

Select the folder containing
the file you want to upload.

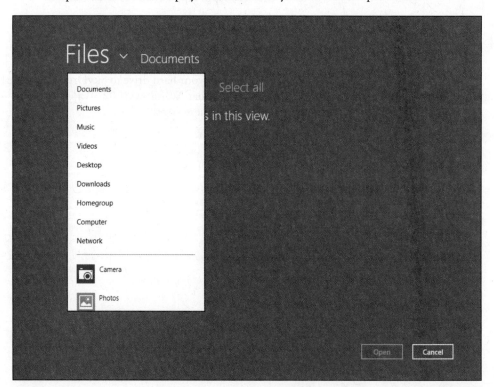

4   Tap or click **Pictures**.

5   Tap or click **Windows1002-01.jpg**. A checkmark appears beside the selected file.

Figure 2-31

Selecting a file to upload.

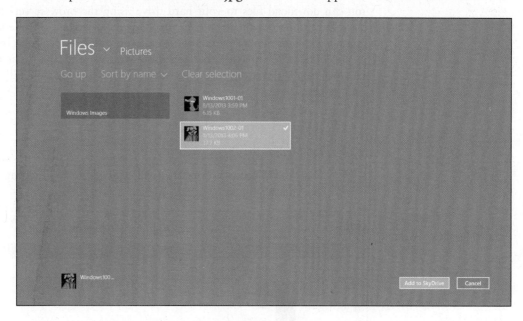

Images and templates used with permission of Microsoft

6   Tap or click the **Open** button. The browser version of SkyDrive uploads the file.

Figure 2-32

Uploading a file to SkyDrive.

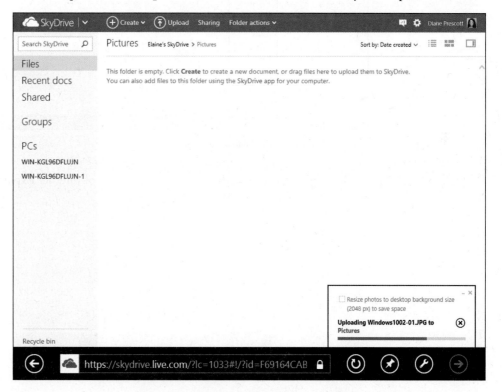

Take Note   For photos, the browser version of SkyDrive offers to resize the file to save space on your SkyDrive. You can tap or click the box to resize the file.

STEP BY STEP   Downloading a file

You can download files to your hard drive using the browser version of SkyDrive. By default, Internet Explorer downloads files to your Downloads folder, and the Windows 8 native version of Internet Explorer doesn't permit you to select a different location. To control where the browser version of SkyDrive places a file you download, use the legacy Internet Explorer app. For this example, you'll download the **Windows1002-01.jpg** file you just uploaded to the Desktop. Follow these steps:

1   In legacy Internet Explorer, log in to SkyDrive.

2   Tap or click the Pictures folder.

3   Select the **Windows1002-01.jpg** file by tapping and holding or right-clicking. A checkmark appears beside the file and a menu appears.

Figure 2-33

Select the file you want to download.

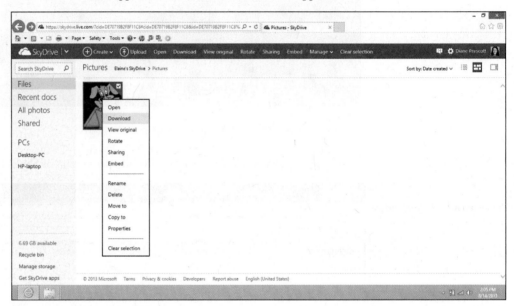

Images and clip art used with permission of Microsoft.

4   Tap or click Download. The legacy version of Internet Explorer displays a box at the bottom of the screen.

5   Tap or click the down arrow beside the Save button.

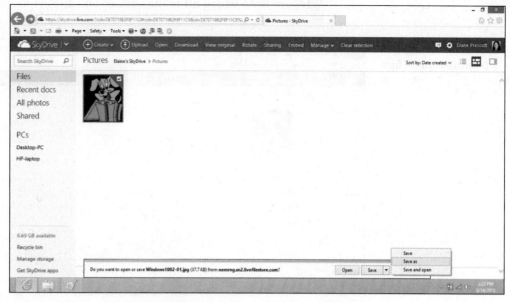

Images and clip art used with permission of Microsoft.

6   Tap or click Save As to display the Save As dialog box.

7   In the Navigation pane on the left, tap or click Desktop.

Images and clip art used with permission of Microsoft.

8   Tap or click the Save button. The browser version of SkyDrive downloads the **Windows1002-01.jpg** file to the Desktop and displays its progress in the box at the bottom of the screen.

Figure 2-36

Downloading a file from SkyDrive.

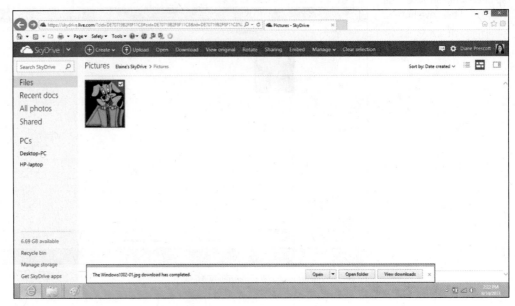

Images and clip art used with permission of Microsoft.

Tap or click Open folder to display the Desktop in File Explorer. Or switch to the Desktop. In both places, you'll see **Windows1002-01.jpg**.

Figure 2-37

The file you downloaded from your SkyDrive now appears on your Desktop.

Images and clip art used with permission of Microsoft.

Sharing files

Using the browser version of SkyDrive, you can easily share files stored on your SkyDrive with other users through any of the following methods:

- By sending an e-mail containing a link to the shared document. This is the default method suggested by SkyDrive.

- By creating a link for the document and distributing the link as necessary.

- By posting the document to Facebook, Twitter, or LinkedIn.

In this section, you learn how to use the default e-mail sharing method.

When you use the default e-mail sharing method, you provide the recipient's e-mail address and write an optional personal message. SkyDrive sends the message, which contains a link to a web page. When the recipient clicks the link in the e-mail, the web page opens, displaying the file you shared. As you create the link, you have the option of allowing the recipient to edit the shared document. You also can opt to have the recipient sign in to a Microsoft account that matches the e-mail address to which you sent the message before he or she can view the shared document.

STEP BY STEP | **Sharing files**

1 Navigate to the file you want to share.

2 Tap and hold or right-click the file.

Figure 2-38

Select a file to share.

Images and clip art used with permission of Microsoft.

3   From the menu that appears, tap or click Sharing. SkyDrive displays the window where you set up the e-mail message for the shared file.

Figure 2-39

Set up the e-mail message you want the recipient to see.

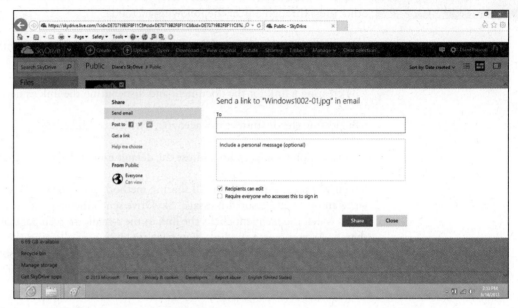

Images and clip art used with permission of Microsoft.

4   Supply the recipient's e-mail address and write a message. If you don't want to offer editing privileges, deselect the Recipient Can Edit checkbox. If you want the recipient to sign in to the Microsoft account associated with the e-mail address you supply, select the Require Everyone Who Accesses This To Sign In checkbox.

5   Tap or click the Share button.

SkyDrive sends a message to the recipient containing a link to the file. When you're finished sharing the document, you can stop sharing it using these steps:

1   Navigate to the file you want to stop sharing.

2   Tap and hold or right-click the file. SkyDrive displays the window where you set up the e-mail message for the shared file. At the bottom of the window on the left side, you'll find a list of those with whom you have shared the file.

3   Tap or click a name in the Permissions list.

Images and templates used with permission of Microsoft

4   Tap or click the Remove Permissions button. SkyDrive removes the sharing privileges.

5   Tap or click the Done button to return to SkyDrive.

Synchronizing and fetching files using the legacy Desktop SkyDrive app

Bottom Line

In addition to being able to access your SkyDrive using the Windows 8 native SkyDrive app and any browser, you can install the **legacy SkyDrive app** that works with File Explorer on the Desktop. The legacy SkyDrive app gives you two additional features that you don't have using the Windows 8 native SkyDrive app or a browser:

- **You** can synchronize files across multiple computers.

- **You** can use the "fetch" feature to remotely access files that you didn't upload to SkyDrive. This feature works as long as the computer on which the files reside is running using your Microsoft account.

The legacy SkyDrive app isn't a typical app in the sense that you don't need to run it once you install it. Installing the legacy SkyDrive app places a new folder on your computer: the SkyDrive folder. It appears in File Explorer and you work with it in File Explorer just as you work with any other folder on your computer:

- Placing a file in the SkyDrive folder automatically uploads it to your cloud SkyDrive.

- Deleting a file from your SkyDrive folder automatically deletes it from your cloud SkyDrive.

- You can add, delete, or remove folders inside the SkyDrive folder; doing so adds, deletes, and removes the same folders in your cloud SkyDrive.

• **You** can copy and move files among your SkyDrive folders and the results also appear in your cloud SkyDrive.

Figure 2-41

The SkyDrive folder in File Explorer.

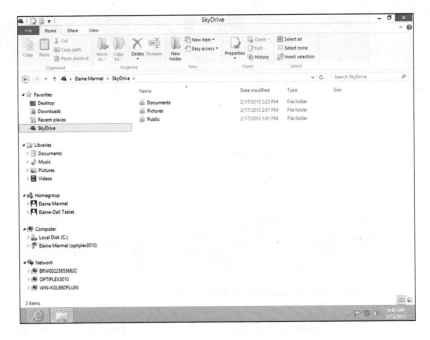

STEP BY STEP   **Installing the legacy SkyDrive app**

1   Log into your SkyDrive using a browser.

2   At the bottom of the left pane, tap or click the Get SkyDrive Apps link. SkyDrive apps for available platforms appear.

Figure 2-42

SkyDrive apps for available platforms.

3 In the left pane, tap or click Windows Desktop.

4 In the right pane, tap or click the Download Now link. A message appears at the bottom of the screen, asking if you want to run or save.

5 Tap or click the Run button. The legacy SkyDrive app installs itself and prepares for its first use.

6 In the Welcome to SkyDrive dialog box that appears, tap or click the Get Started button.

7 In the Sign In dialog box, provide your Microsoft account e-mail address and password and tap or click the Sign In button.

Figure 2-43

Provide your Microsoft account sign in information.

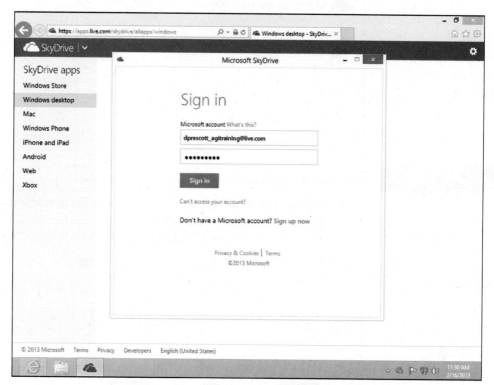

8 A message appears, showing you the location of your local SkyDrive folder. You can change the folder; for this example, tap or click the Next button.

9   The legacy SkyDrive app asks you to identify the cloud SkyDrive folders that you want to synchronize to your PC. For this example, tap or click All Files And Folders On My SkyDrive and tap or click the Next button.

Figure 2-44

Choose the SkyDrive files and folders to synchronize to your desktop computer.

Bottom Line

10   The legacy SkyDrive app lets you decide whether to enable the "fetch" feature. For this example, make sure a checkmark appears in the Let Me Use SkyDrive To Fetch Any Of My Files On This PC checkbox.

Figure 2-45

Choose to enable the "fetch" feature.

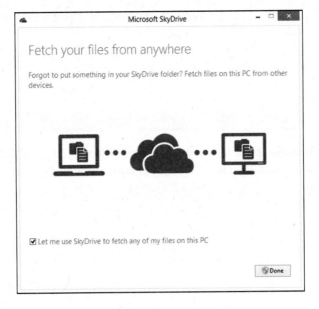

11 Tap or click the **Done** button. The SkyDrive legacy app opens File Explorer, shows you your SkyDrive folder, and displays an explanatory message.

Figure 2-46

Signing out of the browser version of SkyDrive.

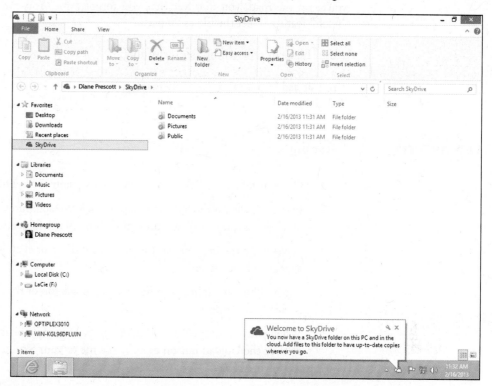

To synchronize files between your computer and your SkyDrive cloud storage, place the files into your SkyDrive folder. When you make a change locally to the file, the legacy SkyDrive app automatically uploads the changed file to your cloud SkyDrive. If you make a change to the document from the cloud SkyDrive, the legacy SkyDrive app automatically downloads the changed file to your SkyDrive folder on your computer.

For example, if you're planning to travel out of town and use a tablet PC while you're away from home or the office. Before you leave, you upload files you expect to need to your SkyDrive. Once you're on the road, you discover that you forgot a file. You can use the legacy SkyDrive app's "fetch" feature to get the file as long as:

• Your home or office computer is running.

• You signed into it using your Microsoft account.

STEP BY STEP	Fetching a file

1   On your tablet PC, log into the browser version of SkyDrive.

2   In the PCs list in the left pane, tap or click the computer to which you want to connect. SkyDrive displays a tiled representation of all the folders and libraries on your computer.

3   Navigate to the file you want to retrieve and tap or click it. A representation of the file appears on the screen.

4   Tap and hold or right-click the file, and at the top of the screen, tap or click the Upload to SkyDrive button.

5   When you're prompted for a folder on SkyDrive for the file, select a folder and then tap or click the Upload button to copy the file to your SkyDrive. You can then download the file to your tablet PC.

Signing out of SkyDrive

When you're done using the browser version of SkyDrive, you can sign out of your SkyDrive account. Tap or click your name in the upper-right corner of the screen to display a menu. At the bottom of the menu, tap or click Sign Out.

Figure 2-47

The legacy SkyDrive app shows you your SkyDrive folder.

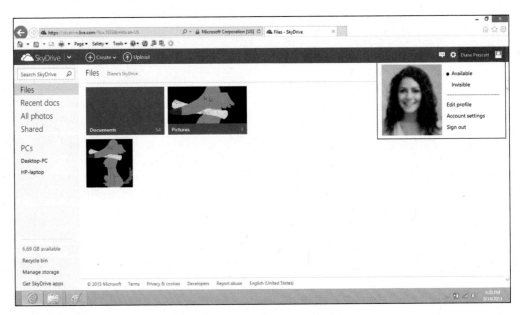

Images and clip art used with permission of Microsoft.

What you learned in this lesson:

* Synchronize Windows 8 settings across devices

* Understand basics of cloud storage

* Working with Text and Fields

* Use the Windows 8 native SkyDrive app

* Introducing SkyDrive

* Tracked Changes and Comment Threads

* Browse with SkyDrive

* Synchronize and fetch files using the legacy Desktop SkyDrive app

Knowledge Assessment

True/False

T F **1.** Signing in with a Windows account will sync your applications across computers.

T F **2.** If using a Microsoft account, changes made on a tablet PC are synchronized to your desktop PC.

T F **3.** By default, when using a Microsoft account, changes are synchronized between machines only after logging in to your computer.

T F **4.** If you change your login to a Windows account, you cannot change it back to a local account.

T F **5.** You can only use a Windows account with an Outlook.com email address.

T F **6.** Your Windows account password requires the same password you use to collect e-mail for this address.

T F **7.** You must be signed in to Windows 8 using a Microsoft account to use the Windows 8 native SkyDrive app.

T F **8.** The Windows 8 native version of Internet Explorer only allows you to download files to your Documents folder.

T F **9.** SkyDrive only allows you to share files with people in your Contact list.

T F **10.** Only the legacy SkyDrive app lets you synchronize files across multiple computers.

Multiple Choice

Select the best response for the following statements.

1. Which of the following items cannot be synchronized using a Windows account?
   a. Documents
   b. Applications
   c. Internet Explorer history
   d. Internet Explorer favorites

2. Which version of SkyDrive offers the most functionality?
   a. The browser version of SkyDrive.
   b. The Windows 8 native SkyDrive app.
   c. The legacy Desktop Skydrive app.
   d. Both A and B provide the same functionality.

3. Which of the following are advantages of using cloud storage?
   a. You can access files at any time, from anywhere, using any computer.
   b. You can easily share files you select with remote users.
   c. If you store important information remotely, it will still be available to you if your home or office is robbed or burns down.
   d. All of the above.

4. You can toggle your account between a local account and Microsoft account using the following settings section:
   a. Users
   b. General
   c. Privacy
   d. Sync your settings

5. SkyDrive documents can be shared to which of the following networks?
   a. Twitter
   b. Tumblr
   c. Facebook
   d. Both Twitter and Facebook

6. Which of the following versions of SkyDrive allows you to upload files to your SkyDrive account using the Windows File Explorer?
   a. The browser version of SkyDrive.
   b. The Windows 8 native SkyDrive app.
   c. The legacy Desktop Skydrive app.
   d. All of the above.

7. Which of the following versions of SkyDrive allows you to edit files using a locally installed app?
   a. The browser version of SkyDrive.
   b. The Windows 8 native SkyDrive app.
   c. The legacy Desktop Skydrive app.
   d. Both the native and legacy versions of the SkyDrive app.

8. Which of the following versions of SkyDrive allows you to quickly resize an image file to save space on your SkyDrive?
   a. The browser version of SkyDrive.
   b. The Windows 8 native SkyDrive app.
   c. The legacy Desktop Skydrive app.
   d. Both the native and legacy versions of the SkyDrive app.

9. Which versions of SkyDrive can you log out of?

    a. The browser version of SkyDrive.

    b. The Windows 8 native SkyDrive app.

    c. The legacy Desktop Skydrive app.

    d. Both the browser and native versions of the SkyDrive app.

10. Which of the following permissions can you assign a recipient when sharing a file via e-mail?

    a. View

    b. Edit

    c. Delete

    d. A and B

Competency Assessment

Project 1-1: Edit a SkyDrive document

Use the browser version of SkyDrive to edit a document online.

1. Launch Word and browse the template gallery. Open a variety of templates to see the range of built-in document types Word offers.

2. Search Microsoft's online template collection for calendar and select a monthly calendar template. Try editing the template and saving it as a .docx file, then as a new .dotx (template) file.

3. Select File > New (rather than pressing Ctrl+N) and find the calendar template you selected near the top of the template gallery. Click the pin icon to keep it permanently in the gallery.

4. Close any open files and leave Word open for the next exercise.

Project 1-2: Upload a file

Use the native Windows 8 SkyDrive app to upload a file.

1. Open the project file **declaration_text** and save it in your working directory as **project_1-2_formatting**.

2. Click once on the word events in the first line and press Ctrl+I to apply italic formatting.

   Word will italicize the entire word, assuming from context that you didn't mean to insert italicized characters in the middle of a non-italicized word.

3. Double-click the word events to select the whole word, then click the italics symbol in the formatting popup to remove italic formatting from the word.

4. Triple click events to select the entire line (paragraph) and apply italic formatting again. Then repeat the action.

5. Click in the final paragraph on pages 3-4 and select the Intense Quote style.

6. Add the line Declaration of Independence to the top of the document, formatted with the Title style.

7. Select everything except the title, first paragraph, and final paragraph, and format it as two-column text (Page Layout > Columns > Two).

8. Save your work and leave the document open for the next exercise.

Proficiency Assessment

Project 1-3: **Converting your account**

Convert your local user account to a Microsoft account.

1. Save your document as **project_1-3_headings**.
2. Insert the line Bill of Particulars before the line "He has refused his Assent to Laws..." on page 1. Format the new line with the Heading 2 style.
3. Insert a Heading 2 line, Legal Affronts, before the "For quartering large bodies..." line on page 2.
4. Insert the Heading 2 line, Good Faith, before the "In every stage..." paragraph on page 3.
5. Collapse the three new headings by mousing over them and clicking the folding arrows that appear.

    (It is most convenient to carry out this step in order from first heading to last.)
6. Save your document and leave it open for the next exercise.

Project 1-4: **Modify your sync settings**

Modify your Microsoft account sync settings.

1. Save your document as **project_1-4_style_color**.
2. Expand the three headings.

    (It is most convenient to do so in reverse order, starting with the last heading and working your way back through the document.)
3. Open the Design tab.
4. Select the Lines (Distinctive) Style Set.
5. Select the Violet II color scheme.
6. Save your work and leave the document open for the next exercise.

Mastery Assessment

Project 1-5: **Syncronizing and fetching files**

Synchronize and fetch files using the legacy Desktop SkyDrive app.

1. Save your document as **project_1-5_theme**.
2. In the Design tab, experiment with various themes.

    Note that changing the theme overrides your choice of color scheme, though not document/character formatting like columns and italics.
3. Assign the Main Event theme with the Red Orange color scheme and Lines (Stylish) Style Set.
4. Assign the List Paragraph style to the first paragraph ("When in the course of...").

    Note that the italics are overridden by the new style assignment.
5. Save your work and leave Word open for the next exercise.

Project 1-6: **Share a document**

Share a document on Twitter, Facebook, or e-mail using the browser version of SkyDrive.

1. Save your document as **project_1-6_modding_styles**.

2. Select the first paragraph, When in the course... and assign it the same color as the Bill of Particulars heading has.

3. Select the paragraph again and update the List Paragraph style to reflect the new formatting.

4. Apply the List Paragraph style to the closing paragraph.

5. Alter all body text (Normal style) in the document to full justification rather than Align Left, by updating the style itself.

   Note that the Title style will also switch to full justification – it's a modification of the Normal style.

6. Fix the Title style by updating it to Align Left.

7. Save your work and close Excel.

Microsoft Word 2013

LESSON SKILL MATRIX

In this lesson, you will learn the following skills:

Interface Conventions	Document Viewing Modes
Working with Text and Fields	Working with Document Windows
Applying Styles to Text	Tracked Changes and Comment Threads
Working with Themes, Style Sets, Color Schemes	
Working with Images and Video	
Styling Images	
Using Online Images and Videos	

KEY TERMS

- **Launch Screen**
- **Placeholder Text**
- **Backstage Area**
- **Field**
- **Text Style**
- **Design Tab**
- **Theme Colors**
- **Word-wrap**
- **Gallery**
- **Heading**
- **Read Mode**
- **Print Layout**
- **Web Layout**
- **Draft View**
- **Markup**

The annual Northwind Traders Catalog is a large-scale, two-month print design job calling for a heavyweight layout program, but Northwind's sales flyers, which go out several times a week, are produced in-house using Word 2013. Word's large library of templates, reusable themes, and parallel digital/print outputs let the sales team try out a variety of designs for their weekly content without fiddling with layout at the pixel level, trading a little power for a huge efficiency boost.

SOFTWARE ORIENTATION

The Microsoft Word 2013 workspace provides access to powerful tools for creating, editing, managing, and sharing documents. Many of the tools you use while working in Word are located on the ribbon, running across the top of the window. The ribbon is organized into task-oriented command tabs. Each tab is divided into task-specific command groups appropriate for the type of work you may need to perform. Because you can customize the ribbon, the tabs and display may include different options than shown in Figure 1-1.

Figure 1-1

Microsoft Word 2013 workspace

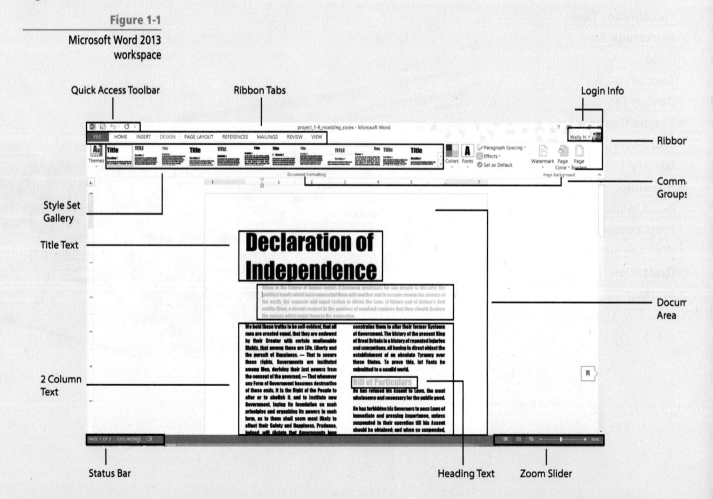

STARTING UP

In this lesson, you'll work with several files from the Word01lessons folder along with the ready-made templates available for Word 2013 from Microsoft. Make sure that you have loaded the OfficeLessons folder onto your computer. Keep in mind that Microsoft might alter the default online Word 2013 templates, and they may appear to be different from the ones used in this book. if you find that to be the case, choose a comparable Word document to follow along.

The project

Bottom Line

You'll begin this lesson by opening a document that shows several key features of Word 2013; you will then edit the document's content and layout. Note that this lesson requires you to be connected to the Internet.

STEP BY STEP | **Opening a document**

1   Launch Word 2013. Note that the new **launch screen** (see Figure 1-2) looks much like the File tab in Word 2013; file-management operations are handled in this separate area of the application, rather than in dialog boxes and pop-up menus.

Figure 1-2

Word displays a simplified version of Backstage view upon launch.

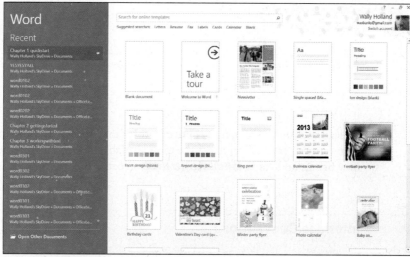

Images and templates used with permission of Microsoft

2   At the launch screen, a gallery of templates provided by Microsoft will appear. The gallery is initially populated with templates stored on your hard drive. In the search box, type hip newsletter and press Enter to search for one of Microsoft's online templates. Click the icon that appears in the list. A preview pane (see Figure 1-3) will appear with information about the template. Click Create to create a new newsletter document.

The resulting document contains **placeholder text** that serves as a useful introduction to the formatting, style, and layout tools available in Word 2013. We highly recommend that you read it.

Figure 1-3

The template you select will automatically download from office.com.

© Hill Street Studios/Blend Images/Getty Images; © Image Source/Getty Images; © Westend61/Getty Images

Interface conventions

Instead of drop-down menus, Office features task-specific toolbars in its Ribbon; click any menu item (or tab), except File, to see the tools available in Word 2013. The File tab works differently: it now brings up Word's **Backstage area** screen.

STEP BY STEP   **Interface Conventions**

1   In the upper left corner of the screen is the Quick Access Toolbar, a customizable dock for frequently-used commands. By default, it contains icons for the Save, Undo, and Redo commands, as well as the application menu and a drop-down menu for customizing the toolbar.

2　Click the image of the student at the top left of the newsletter. Note that a small icon of text wrapping around an image appears to the right of the image, as in Figure 1-4. You can click this handle for quick access to the image layout tools.

Figure 1-4

Click the Layout Options button to choose from common word-wrap settings.

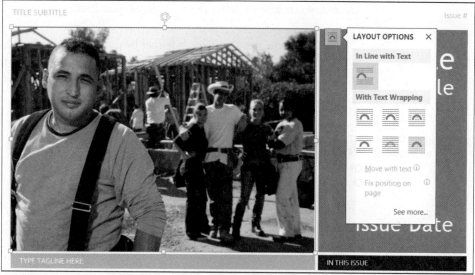

© *Hill Street Studios/Blend Images/Getty Images*

Note that three new **context tabs** appear above the ribbon: Design and Layout (under the heading Table Tools), and Format (under the heading Picture Tools). The tools for adjusting, styling, and laying out images and tables reside in these tabs.

3　Click the Layout tab and select View Gridlines from the Table group (at the left side of the ribbon). Doing so reveals that the image and surrounding colored panes are laid out as a table with six cells in two columns; the right-hand column is four cells high.

4　Now right-click the image. Note that the context menu includes commands to style and lay out the image, but does *not* provide any table-layout commands.

Working with words

Fields are like placeholder codes, which get replaced by the information they point to. Word handles fields a little differently from regular text; using fields to keep text flexible and up-to-date is a crucial step from beginner to intermediate Office user.

STEP BY STEP	Text and Fields

1　Click the word Title in the large orange cell on the upper-right area of the first page and replace it with the word Frustrum. Note the handle that appears above the text, it's labeled Title: this indicates that you're editing the content of the document's Title field. **Fields** allow you to reuse data throughout your document.

2　Click anywhere else in the document and observe that the header on each page updates to reflect the changed newsletter title.

You can change the newsletter's subtitle and tagline in the same manner: select and replace the field you want to change, and then deselect the text to see the updated subtitle in the header (and anywhere else that the Subtitle field appears in the document). Note that when you edit the Subtitle text, you're changing the stored value of the Subtitle field, but if you select the handle instead, you're able to delete the field placeholder itself.

3   Select the word **Frustrum** (either by double-clicking it or by clicking-and-dragging) and note that Word 2013 immediately offers a pop-up menu with oft-used commands for text editing: font (see Figure 1-5), size, emphasis, bullet level, and so forth.

Figure 1-5

Choosing a font in the formatting minibar.

© Hill Street Studios/Blend Images/Getty Images; © Image Source/Getty Images

Applying styles to text

Text Styles in Word 2013 serve two purposes: they let you control the appearance of your text, and they help Word structure your document. We'll focus on visuals in this chapter; document structure is the focus of Lesson 4, "Structuring Complex Documents." First, we'll style some text and use the Live Preview feature of Word 2013.

Styling text

1   Triple-click the How to Use This Template headline—the text itself, not the field handle. Triple-clicking selects an entire paragraph; in this case, this is just a single line.

2   Open the Home tab; in the Styles group, note that the Heading 1 style is highlighted, indicating the current style of the selected text.

3   Mouse over the other styles in the Styles group without selecting one. Note that the text changes appearance as you do so; when you move the mouse away from the Styles group without selecting a new style, your text reverts to its original appearance. This feature is called Live Preview.

4   Select the Subtitle style to restyle the headline.

As you can see, the headline is now invisible (white on white) and right-justified rather than left-justified. You can change the color and alignment of a single piece of text to make the headline visible again, but it's also easy to modify the styles themselves.

5   Without deselecting the headline text, click Home > Font > Font Color. The text of the How to Use This Template headline turns red.

6   Right-click Home > Styles > Subtitle. Select Update Subtitle to Match Selection from the context menu.

When you update the Subtitle style in this fashion, any text that uses the Subtitle style in the current document changes to reflect the new style: in this case, the actual newsletter subtitle, next to the front page image of the student, turns red.

7   Finally, double-click the headline below the image of the student, and then click Home > Paragraph > Align Left (or press Ctrl+L). The headline should be flush against the left margin again.

Note that your new color selection is applied to all the text that uses the Subtitle style, but the alignment change is restricted to just the currently selected text. Reformatting a single piece of text doesn't affect the definition of the Subtitle style itself.

YOUR DOCUMENT'S LOOK AND FEEL

Working with themes, style sets, and color schemes

Bottom Line

Word 2013 gives you a variety of tools for altering the overall look and feel of your document. To see these tools, click the **Design tab**, newly designed for Word 2013. In the Design tab, you'll find a drop-down menu containing the built-in Themes available for Word 2013, a gallery of Style Sets, drop-down menus for selecting color and font schemes, and a handful of other document-level tools.

Now you'll make some changes to your document and start to see how Themes, Styles, and Colors interact. A Theme is basically a bundle of Colors, Fonts, and Effects; something like a visual identity for a set of documents. A Style Set is a collection of styles meant to work well together on the page or on the screen. Style Sets may or may not specify colors and fonts. The document's color scheme and font set can be switched without changing the Theme or Style definitions.

    Working with themes, style sets, and color schemes

Let's make some changes to show how these design tools work. In particular, we'll change various aspects of this elegant pre-built template, rendering it an unreadable mess, to see how different features of a document depend on one another.

1 In the Design tab, click the Themes drop-down menu. Note the option to Reset to Theme from Newsletter Template, indicating that the document template itself includes a built-in theme.

2 Mouse over several themes. Note which aspects of the document change and which do not; for instance, the colored panes at the top of the newsletter switch to the new **Theme Colors**, but the background color for the In This Issue column remains unchanged, indicating that its background color is defined in absolute terms.

Restricting your color choices to your current Theme Colors is a good way to maintain a consistent look-and-feel for your document, and it ensures that, if you change themes, you won't leave orphaned colors, as in the In This Issue sidebar.

Figure 1-6

Switching the theme sets font, color, style, layout, and effects options with a single click.

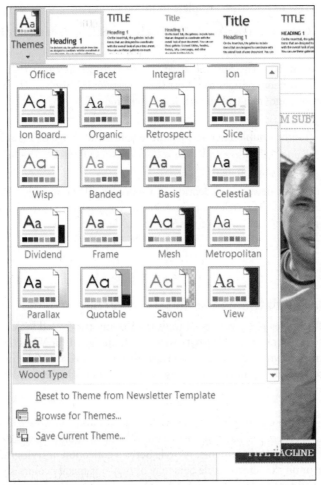

© *Hill Street Studios/Blend Images/Getty Images*

3 Choose the Wood Type theme (see Figure 1-6.) Scroll down through your document to see the changes this new theme has made.

As you can see, the careful multiple-column format is now broken: the tight fit of the text came from matching each article's length, layout, and font choice, and the new mix of styles and fonts breaks that arrangement.

Changing the document theme also reveals the difference between absolute and relative placement of images. Several images in the document retain their absolute positioning on the page and can be orphaned when you change the text; but the smaller single-column images are all placed in line with the paragraphs and have avoided being similarly orphaned. When laying out a document in Word, it's important to keep in mind the relationship between images and the text that surrounds them.

Now let's see how Themes, Style Sets, and Color Schemes relate.

4   Choose another theme and keep an eye on the Document Formatting group of the Design tab. Note that when you change themes, the gallery refreshes: the fonts and colors of each Style Set change.

Themes give overall visual guidelines; Style Sets define the relationships between styles within those guidelines.

5   Finally, choose another theme and note that the Color Scheme changes. Remember that you can still choose from all available color schemes, shown in Figure 1-7.

Figure 1-7

Color Schemes let you choose an overall palette without having to carefully match individual shades.

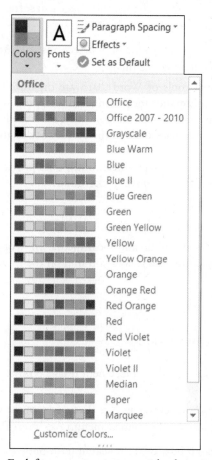

Feel free to experiment with changing colors, styles, or the document theme, noting the way changes propagate from one part of the document to another. Go ahead and edit any text you want in the document; text entry is very basic functionality, so we won't spend time on it in this Quick Start lesson. You can also experiment with changing the column layout of the article text; in particular, take note of the way the template's author makes use of hard column breaks to lay out sidebars, thus avoiding the use of floating text boxes.

Working with images and video

Bottom Line

Like the new Windows 8 and Windows RT operating systems, Office 2013 is designed to take advantage of touch interfaces, such as the Microsoft Surface; Office 2013 also treats always-on

Internet and online (vs. local hard drive) storage as standard. The way Word 2013 handles visual media reflects these assumptions. Now we'll make some changes to the visuals in our newsletter to illustrate how Word 2013 handles images and video.

STEP BY STEP   Styling an image

First we'll tour Word's layout, format, and retouching tools. Feel free to make drastic changes to the image in this section; you'll replace it afterward.

1. Click the image of the five smiling interns in the right-hand column of page 1. A horseshoe-shaped handle appears to the side; click it. The image-layout menu in Word 2013 appears. Experiment with changing the **word-wrap** mode to see how text flows around, behind, and in front of the image.

2. Make sure the image is still selected so the Format tab is available. Open the Format tab. Experiment with choosing different Picture Styles from the visual gallery in the Format tab. Note that the Picture Styles change the image's size, framing, and orientation, but leave its content unchanged.

3. Finally, use the Format > Adjust > Color, Corrections, and Artistic Effects **galleries** to make changes to the content of the image.

Note the way the image-related tools of Word 2013 are organized. The image layout context menu contains the most-used commands for placing and wrapping an image; these same tools are available from the Format > Arrange group. Image editing tools are found in the Format > Adjust group. The image's border is edited with tools in the Picture Styles group.

Word 2013 isn't really a full-featured image editor, but it does provide some tools for basic image manipulation, for example, Format > Remove Background.

Working with online images and videos

Bottom Line

Office 2013 blurs the line between online and local media. In Word, you can still embed local images, and you can drop in pictures and videos you find on the Internet, without ever switching applications.

STEP BY STEP   Inserting online images and video

Now let's get rid of the interns and find a replacement image online.

1. Right-click the image and choose Change Picture from the context menu. (In Windows RT, tap and hold to bring up the context menu.) An Insert Pictures dialog box appears.

2. In the Bing Image Search box, type the search term happy toad, and choose a replacement image from the gallery. Note that all the images in the gallery, shown in Figure 1-8. carry a Creative Commons license. When you find the one you like, click Insert.

Take Note In general, images with a Creative Commons license (there are several different CC licenses) can be reused for noncommercial purposes, as long as you credit their creators. For the purposes of this lesson, we don't need to worry about sourcing the images.

The same dialog box lets you search for local files and royalty free clip-art from Microsoft; we'll explore this tool more in a later lesson.

Figure 1-8

The image you select from your Bing Image Search will embed in your Word document, just like a local image would.

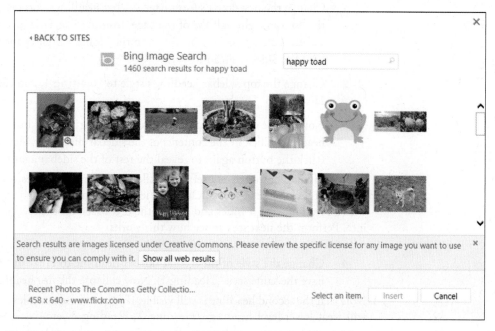

Images and templates used with permission of Microsoft

Any changes you make to an image using the Adjustments tools are lost when you replace the image, but the picture style and arrangement are preserved.

Now let's embed some online video into our otherwise conventionally static document.

3   Scroll to the bottom of your document and place your cursor. Click Insert > Online Video.

4   In the Search YouTube box, type cute toddler. Select a video from the gallery and click Insert.

A video object will insert into your document; Word 2013 handles online videos exactly like still images, except that you can click an embedded video to launch a built-in video player.

5   Select the video object, and then click Format > Adjust > Color or Artistic Effects to change the look of the embedded video.

Note that the Format tools affect the way the video appears on the page (the preview image) but leave the video itself untouched. If you print a Word 2013 document with an embedded video, only the (modified) preview image makes it to the printed page, but exporting the document as a PDF preserves the video link as a hyperlinked image.

DIFFERENT VIEWS OF YOUR DOCUMENT

Bottom Line

Word 2013 provides several tools and editing modes to let you work more efficiently with your document, without unnecessary visual clutter and distraction. When you're comfortable with these tools, you'll spend less time trying to figure out Word 2013's interface, and more time improving your work.

Collapsing document sections

Word treats headings as document divisions, and lets you collapse whole sections of your document into a **heading**; cleaning up your workspace with a single click.

STEP BY STEP **Collapsing document sections**

1   Change the newsletter's front page sidebar headlines, located just below the images on the bottom-right half the of the page, from Article Title to Column Break and View Formatting Breaks, respectively. In the Home > Styles gallery, note that these headlines have the Sidebar Heading style.

2   Change the top sidebar headline's style to Heading 1, and the bottom headline's style to Heading 2.

3   Now mouse over the top sidebar headline. A triangular button appears to the left of the headline. Click it; the contents of the sidebar disappear, leaving only the top headline. Click the button again to reveal the rest of the sidebar again.

This triangular button is a useful workflow tool that collapses and expands a section of the document, much like in the old Outline View. Word thinks of each document section as beginning with a Heading, and it hides and reveals the text based on the level of the Heading you're folding into. Perform the next step to see how this works.

4   Change the style of the second sidebar headline to Heading 1. Both sidebar headlines have the same style (Heading 1). Now collapse the *first* headline.

Note that the second headline is still visible: if you collapse a top-level heading (Heading 1), Word will treat lower-level headings (Heading 2, Heading 3, etc.) as subsections and assume you're not currently working with them. Word will then hide text and images until it reaches the next Heading 1 text. When working with complex documents, you're encouraged to use the built-in heading styles to take advantage of Word's document-structure features. We'll cover document structure in detail in Word Lesson 4, "Structuring Complex Documents."

Working with Word's windows

Bottom Line

Word 2013 includes a number of features, old and new, to grant you multiple perspectives on a document and foreground your work rather than your workspace. You'll customize your work environment in later lessons; in this Quick Start you'll just survey the basic tools.

STEP BY STEP **Working with Word's views**

1   Click the View > Views > Read Mode icon to view your document without any onscreen editing interface. Use the arrow keys to scroll through the document; press Escape to return to your editing window.

Read Mode is optimized for touch; in Windows RT, you can swipe left and right to move through the document. Remember that it's just a quick overview of the flow and proportions of the document, not a preview of the final print/Web output.

2   Switch between **Print Layout** (View > Views > Print Layout) and **Web Layout** to see the different print/Web outputs of the same document. In particular, note that multi-column layouts are preserved in the source file, but will not render properly when you translate your document to HTML.

3   Switch to **Draft** view to see only the text in your document; note that headers, footers, images, and multi-column layouts do not display in Draft view.

4   Collapse the Ribbon by clicking the caret (^) at its bottom-right corner. To reveal again, open one of the Tabs at the top of the screen. To make the Ribbon permanently visible, click the push pin icon at the far right, where the caret was.

5   Finally, click View > Window > Split to look at two sections of your document simultaneously. Spend a few moments becoming familiar with the screen layout. Click Remove Split to switch back to one-window mode.

A split screen is helpful when you need to move content between parts of your document, or to see one section while you edit another.

Collaboration and tracking changes

Word 2013 includes a variety of collaboration and simple version control features in the Review tab. These tools let you track a document's state through multiple rounds of revision and editing, and let you communicate with collaborators inside the Word document itself.

STEP BY STEP   **Tracking changes**

---

1   Click Review > Tracking > Track Changes. The icon turns blue. Word 2013 will now preserve your edits, allowing you to make changes without losing track of your original data.

2   Select Tracking > All Markup from the uppermost drop-down menu.

3   Now make some edits to your document; delete and insert text, tables, and images, or restyle document elements.

Word indicates each edit with a subtle colored bar down the left margin of the document, thus marking its location, and either an information bubble (for formatting changes) or inline markings (for text insertions/deletions).

Note that if you delete an image with All Markup selected, the image will seem to stubbornly remain in the document. That's not the case; Word is simply indicating where the image was, but it's not actually in the layout anymore, as the next step reveals.

4   Select Tracking > Simple Markup from the uppermost drop-down menu. This is a new feature in Word 2013. Note that the colored bars that indicate the presence of edits remain, but Word hides the details.

5   Re-select All Markup and experiment with the options under Tracking > Show Markup.

At each stage of document revision, tailor these Markup options to your needs; for instance, if you add a large piece of new text late in a project, considering unmarking Insertions/Deletions to keep your editing window orderly.

Bottom Line   Communicating with colleagues in comments

Word also lets you embed comments in a document, and preserve conversations with collaborators using the comments feature.

STEP BY STEP   **Communicating with collegues in comments**

---

1   Make sure Review > Comments > Show Comments (or Tracking > All Markup) is enabled. Select a piece of text and click Review > Comments > New Comment. In the speech bubble that appears, type Could you suggest better wording here? and press Escape to return the cursor to the document window.

2   Now mouse over your comment and click the Reply icon that appears in the bubble. Type **Sure, get back to you shortly** and press **Escape** to return to editing your document. Note in Figure 1-9 the way Word displays inline conversations between document editors (they're just like threaded blog comments).

Figure 1-9

Threaded comments help clarify your document's editing history.

Images and template used with permission of Microsoft

3   Enable Simple Markup and deselect **Comments > Show Comments**. Word collapses each conversation into a comic book-style speech bubble.

4   Finally, select your second comment and click **Comments > Delete**. Note that the response is deleted but the conversation remains.

If you delete the first comment in a thread, the entire thread is deleted along with it.

Word 2013 is also built to support real-time and distributed collaboration: the File > Share group includes tools to post a copy of your document online, inviting colleagues to view or edit the file, or even turn your .docx file into a live presentation that distant users can view using a web browser.

Save always

To complete this Word 2013 Quick Start lesson, save your newsletter to your SkyDrive folder.

STEP BY STEP   **Saving and closing a document**

1   Click **File > Save As**.

2   In the Backstage view, select your SkyDrive folder; in the Save box, type **My Hip Newsletter**, and then click **Save**.

Note that while you initially opened the newsletter's template file (.dotx) rather than a document file (.docx), Word 2013 knows to save your document as a .docx, unless you specify otherwise. That said, when you work from a template, double-check to make sure you're saving a new Word document rather than editing the template itself.

3   Close your document (press **Ctrl+W** or click **File > Close**) and click **File > Open** (or press **Ctrl+O**).

Your newsletter will appear in the list of Recent Documents. Meanwhile, the Office Upload Center will try to upload your document to the cloud; if you're working offline, the Upload Center will upload your changes as soon as it detects an Internet connection; ideally, you'll never even notice.

What you learned in this lesson:

- Interface Conventions

- Document Viewing Modes

- Working with Text and Fields

- Working with Document Windows

- Applying Styles to Text

- Tracked Changes and Comment Threads

- Working with Themes, Style Sets, Color Schemes

- Working with Images and Video

- Styling Images

- Using Online Images and Videos

Knowledge Assessment

True/False

Circle T if the statement is true or F if the statement is false.

T F 1. Word 2013 opens, by default, on a blank document.

T F 2. Selecting a field's handle and pressing Delete clears out the data the field refers to.

T F 3. A Text Style can specify font, size, color, alignment, and spacing.

T F 4. Text alignment options include right justification, left justification, center, and full justification.

T F 5. A Style Set defines the visual look of a single kind of text (e.g., Heading 1).

T F 6. To see how a Theme will affect the look of a document you must select it from the Themes Gallery.

T F 7. Theme Colors restrict the available colors in a template.

T F 8. It's not possible to edit your document in Read Mode.

T F 9. When you select an image, contextual tabs appear at the far left of the Ribbon.

T F 10. Document-wide formatting and style tools are found in the Design tab.

Fill in the Blanks

Complete the following sentences by writing the correct word or words in the blanks provided.

1. Each image comes with a _____ pop-out menu attached, which opens a pane of formatting tools.
2. The title of a newsletter can be stored for reuse in a _____.
3. The Insert Pictures dialog lets you search Microsoft's clip art library, or do an image search on _____.
4. When you use Word's built-in heading styles, you can _____ sections of your document text into the headings to clear screen space.
5. The highest-level built-in heading style is _____.
6. When you print a document containing an embedded video, only the _____ will print in its place.
7. Color correction tools for images are found in the _____ tab.
8. You can set a default Theme, Style Set, and color scheme by saving a document as a _____.
9. In place of the old File menu, clicking the File tab takes you to Office's _____.
10. You can customize a pre-formatted calendar by searching the _____ for "calendar."

Competency Assessment

Project 1-1: Creating New Documents from Templates

In this exercise you'll create a new file using the Template Gallery.

1. Launch Word and browse the template gallery. Open a variety of templates to see the range of built-in document types Word offers.
2. Search Microsoft's online template collection for **calendar** and select a monthly calendar template. Try editing the template and saving it as a .docx file, then as a new .dotx (template) file.
3. Select File > New (rather than pressing Ctrl+N) and find the calendar template you selected near the top of the template gallery. Click the pin icon to keep it permanently in the gallery.
4. Close any open files and leave Word open for the next exercise.

Project 1-2: Formatting Text

In this exercise you'll work with character- and paragraph-level formatting tools.

1. Open the project file **declaration_text** and save it in your working directory as **project_1-2_formatting**.
2. Click once on the word events in the first line and press Ctrl+I to apply italic formatting.

   Word will italicize the entire word, assuming from context that you didn't mean to insert italicized characters in the middle of a non-italicized word.
3. Double-click the word *events* to select the whole word, then click the italics symbol in the formatting popup to remove italic formatting from the word.
4. Triple-click events to select the entire line (paragraph) and apply italic formatting again. Then repeat the action.
5. Click in the final paragraph on pages 3-4 and select the Intense Quote style.
6. Add the line Declaration of Independence to the top of the document, formatted with the Title style.

7. Select everything except the title, first paragraph, and final paragraph, and format it as two-column text (Page Layout > Columns > Two).
8. Save and close your document.

Proficiency Assessment

Project 1-3: Headings

In this exercise you'll add headings to your document.

1. Open the project file **1-3-source** and save it as **project_1-3_headings**.
2. Insert the line Bill of Particulars before the line "He has refused his Assent to Laws..." on page 1. Format the new line with the Heading 2 style.
3. Insert a Heading 2 line, Legal Affronts, before the "For quartering large bodies..." line on page 2.
4. Insert the Heading 2 line, Good Faith, before the "In every stage..." paragraph on page 3.
5. Collapse the three new headings by mousing over them and clicking the folding arrows that appear.

    (It is most convenient to carry out this step in order from first heading to last.)
6. Save and close your document.

Project 1-4: Style Sets and Color Schemes

In this exercise you'll work with Style Sets and alter a file's color scheme.

1. Open the project file **1-4-source** and save it as **project_1-4_style_color**.
2. Open the Design tab.
3. Select the Lines (Distinctive) Style Set.
4. Select the Violet II color scheme.
5. Save and close your document.

Mastery Assessment

Project 1-5: Working with Themes

In this exercise you will assign an existing file a new theme and color scheme.

1. Open the project file **1-5-source** and save it as **project_1-5_theme**.
2. In the Design tab, experiment with various themes.

    Note that changing the theme overrides your choice of color scheme, though not document/character formatting like columns and italics.
3. Assign the Main Event theme with the Red Orange color scheme and Lines (Stylish) Style Set.
4. Assign the List Paragraph style to the first paragraph ("When in the course of...").

    Note that the italics are overridden by the new style assignment.
5. Save and close your document.

Project 1-6: **Modifying Styles**

In this exercise you'll modify styles to an existing file.

1. Open the project file **1-6-source** and save it as **project_1-6_modding_styles**.

2. Select the first paragraph, *When in the course...* and assign it the same color as the *Bill of Particulars* heading has.

3. Select the paragraph again and update the List Paragraph style to reflect the new formatting.

4. Apply the List Paragraph style to the closing paragraph.

5. Alter all body text (Normal style) in the document to Justified rather than Align Left, by updating the style itself.

   Note that the Title style will also switch to full justification – it's a modification of the Normal style.

6. Fix the Title style by updating it to Align Left.

7. Save your work and close Word.

LESSON SKILL MATRIX

In this lesson, you will learn the following skills:

Navigating the Launch Screen and Template Gallery	Word's Different Viewing Modes
Opening a Document	Laying Out the Page
Using and Customizing the Ribbon	Adding Headers and Footers
Customizing the Quick Access Toolbar	Splitting Your Document View
Using the Navigation Pane	

KEY TERMS

- pane
- Save
- Save As
- SkyDrive
- SharePoint
- keyboard shortcuts
- Quick Access Toolbar
- Navigation pane
- Heading style
- margins
- Portrait Orientation
- Landscape Orientation
- header
- footer
- float
- Synchronous Scrolling

Temporary office workers at Northwind Traders need to jump right into creating, editing, and formatting documents to keep up with the heavy flow of research data through the office. Maintaining an efficient digital workspace is essential to doing well in that fast-paced environment. With document views, panes, and information displays, Word 2013 suggests (without strictly enforcing) a streamlined workflow. The more quickly Northwind's project workers learn their tools, the more useful they are to the company – and its thousand impatient clients.

SOFTWARE ORIENTATION

This lesson provides you with additional foundation information to help you efficiently create and edit documents using Microsoft Word. The Home tab is an important starting point for controlling styles, navigating, and locating content within your documents.

Figure 2-1

The Home tab contains many commonly used controls for text editing.

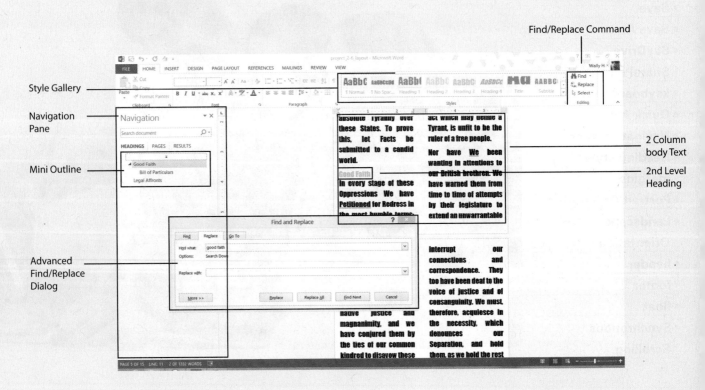

STARTING UP

In this lesson, you'll work with several files from the Word02lessons folder. Make sure that you have loaded the OfficeLessons folder onto your computer.

The Word 2013 interface

Bottom Line

Microsoft Word is a mature product; the first version of Word for Windows, in 1983, offered many computer users their first experience with a mouse. As you'd expect, Word 2013 is an incremental update rather than a revolutionary one. If you're familiar with Word 2007, 2010, or 2011, you won't find many surprises in this lesson. But Windows 8 and Windows RT, the operating systems on which Word 2013 runs, have several new features; and Word 2013 inherits its main interface features from Windows itself.

Many features of the Word 2013 work environment are common to all the apps in the Office 2013 application suite; we'll note these as we go and cover them with less detail than the unique features now available for Word.

The Start screen and template gallery

Bottom Line

When you launch Word 2013, instead of a blank document, you're greeted with a new start screen, similar to the Backstage view (which replaced the File menu). In the left-hand **pane**, a list of recent documents appears; a gallery to the right offers a collection of document templates. Note that in the Start Screen there's no obvious distinction between documents stored on your hard drive and those stored in the cloud; in fact, many of the items in the template gallery are just links to templates hosted on Microsoft's own servers.

STEP BY STEP | **The start screen and template gallery**

In the search box at the top of the gallery pane, you can search Microsoft's extensive online template database.

    1   Type **cookbook** in the search box and press **Enter**.

As of this writing, Microsoft doesn't actually offer a cookbook template, but this empty results screen does offer something useful: at the bottom of the screen is a new gallery, Search results from your other applications. If you have Publisher, Excel, and PowerPoint installed on your computer, you'll see links to templates for those programs, which you can launch directly from the Start Screen in Word 2013.

Click the back arrow in the upper-left corner. In the Recent pane, you'll see a listing of recent documents, including the hip newsletter you worked with if you completed Lesson 1. Below that list is a link to Open Other Documents, which brings up the Backstage view itself; the same as if had you clicked File > Open (or pressed Ctrl+O).

    2   At the lower left of the screen, click **Open Other Documents**.

Opening a document

Clicking File > Open brings up a three-paned window as shown in Figure 2-2. The left-hand pane should be familiar: it's the old File menu, complete with New, Open, **Save/Save As**, Print, and a handful of other commands, most of them unavailable when you launch Word 2013, because there's no document currently open. To the right of that pane is a list of Places: a customizable list of local and online storage locations. As you click each in turn, the right-hand pane provides a list of available documents in that location.

STEP BY STEP   **Opening a document**

By clicking the Add a Place button, you can add **SkyDrive** and **SharePoint** links to the Places list.

Figure 2-2

The Open command in Backstage View.

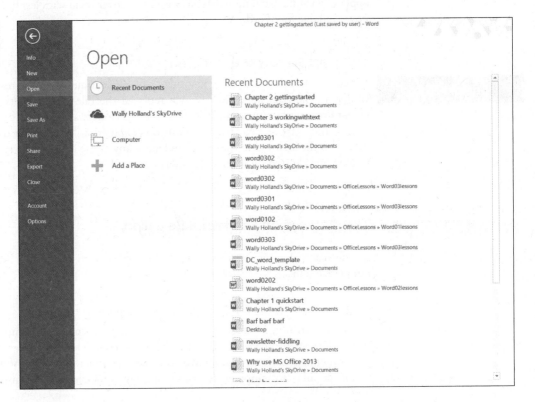

1   Choose Computer from the list and navigate to the Word02lessons folder you saved to your hard drive. Open the the file **word02a.docx**.

2   Choose File > Save As and save this document as **word02a_work**.

The Ribbon

The main visual feature of the Word 2013 workspace is the **Ribbon**, which arrived in Microsoft Office in 2007 and has spread to a variety of Windows applications. The Ribbon replaced the 20-year-old system of drop-down menus (File, Edit, and so on) with clusters of graphical icons, each located on a tab (formerly a menu) within a group (submenu). The basic idea behind the Ribbon is this: the formatting options most users need most often are in the Home tab, while context-dependent actions (such as reformatting a table, changing the dimensions of a document, or styling an image) reside in other tabs.

Take Note   For most Word tasks, **keyboard shortcuts** are faster and more precise than mouse movements. They're also easily discoverable. If you press just the Alt key in an Office application, a keyboard shortcut will appear for each tab; type one of them, and you'll get the same information for every icon within that tab. Shortcuts such as Ctrl-P (for Print) are also available for nearly every command. We've made an effort to include the most common shortcuts in the text. Of course, if you ever need help in Word (or nearly any other Windows productivity application), press F1.

Because of its size and prominence, the Ribbon sometimes gets in the way; for instance, when taking in an entire document, or drafting text with no formatting or layout. At those times, you can collapse the Ribbon into the tab bar, and only pin it back in place when necessary.

STEP BY STEP   **Expanding and collapsing the Ribbon**

1   To collapse the Ribbon, click the caret (^) on the document's far right side as displayed in Figure 2-3. Only the tab bar will remain visible at the top of the screen.

Figure 2-3

Click the caret to collapse the Ribbon

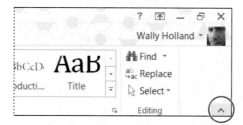

2   To expand the Ribbon, click one of the tabs. A push pin icon appears on the far right of the Ribbon as shown in Figure 2-4. To keep the Ribbon permanently visible (to pin it), click the push pin icon, which then changes back to a caret.

Figure 2-4

Click the push pin icon to expand the Ribbon.

3   Alternatively, press Ctrl-F1 to toggle Ribbon visibility.

Just as in old versions of Word, the Ribbon's commands can also be invoked with keyboard shortcuts. Alt+F works the same as clicking File; Alt+R is the equivalent to clicking Review, and so forth. Pressing the Alt key displays the keyboard equivalents for each tab (pressing Alt and then M *separately* accomplishes the same as Alt+M) and displays the Mailings tab with keyboard shortcuts for all its icons. Learning the key equivalents for your most-used tasks will increase your productivity with Word 2013 immensely.

Customizing the Ribbon

Bottom Line

Because it's so central to the user experience in Word 2013, the Ribbon can be customized in several ways. You can hide, rename, and rearrange tabs, and do the same with the groups inside them; you can even create custom tabs and groups. The latter option can streamline your workflow when performing repetitive tasks. For instance, if you are working with a table-filled document, inserting footnotes and hyperlinks into a large number of cells, and changing table formatting, you might create a temporary Ribbon tab to group together the tools you need.

STEP BY STEP   **Customizing the Ribbon**

1   Click **File** > **Options** > **Customize Ribbon** (or press **Alt+F+T**, and then click **Customize Ribbon**).

2   Click **New Tab**, then select your **New Tab (Custom)** and click **Rename**. For the name of your custom tab, type **TAAABLES**.

3   Use the arrow buttons at the right of the list (Customize the Ribbon) to move your new tab, which Word has marked Custom, to a spot between the Home and Insert tabs.

4   Click **New Group** found underneath the TAAABLES tab, then **Rename**. For the name of your custom group, type **GRUNT WORK**.

5   Make sure your GRUNT WORK group is selected in the right-hand list. From the list of Popular Commands at left, click **Hyperlink**, and then the **Add** button. Do the same with the Insert Footnote command.

6   Now select **All Tabs** from the top-left drop-down menu. The list of available commands changes to include one of the ribbon icons available in Word 2013, grouped by tab. Click through to select **Table Tools** > **Design** > **Borders** > **Borders and Shading**, and then click the **Add** button.

7   Finally, click **OK**.

Your Ribbon will update to include your custom tab and group (see Figure 2-5), which you can leave open for easy access while you work. Removing the tab works the same way.

Figure 2-5

Adding a custom group to the Ribbon.

8   Click **File** > **Options** > **Customize Ribbon**.

9   On the right-hand list, right-click your custom group and choose **Remove**. Click **OK**.

You can actually hide any of the tabs and groups in Word 2013 from the same window: simply unclick the check box next to an entry in the right-hand list to render it invisible, and then click the box again to restore the tab or group.

The Quick Access toolbar

Word 2013 also provides an always-on cluster of icons in the upper left corner of the screen called the Quick Access Toolbar. By default, this cluster of icons contains buttons to Save, Undo, and Redo, which come from the old File and Edit menus. If you click the rightmost icon in the toolbar, which resembles a tiny upside-down eject button, a drop-down menu appears with a list of available commands for the toolbar (Figure 2-6).

Figure 2-6

The Quick Access Toolbar is a customizable collection of frequently-used commands.

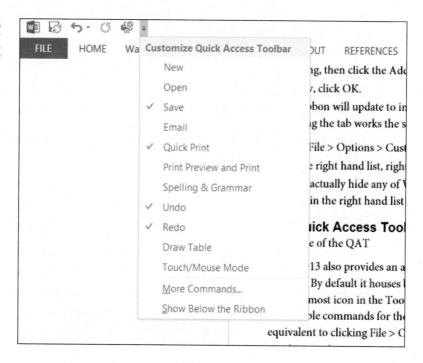

Choosing More Commands from this menu takes you to an options screen, equivalent to clicking File > Options > Quick Access Toolbar, which works just as the Customize Ribbon screen from the previous section.

You can stock your Quick Access Toolbar with the commands that you want available at all times: the Quick Print command, which was once prominent in Word's toolbar, is a popular choice; the E-mail command is also a handy option.

Take Note   Clicking File > Print (or pressing Ctrl+P) brings up the Backstage View and lets you specify a printer or digital destination, alter some document properties, and so forth. The Quick Print command bypasses that screen, and simply prints according to your default preferences. It's not available in the Ribbon by default, which is why it's in the list of recommended commands for the Quick Access Toolbar.

The Status bar

At the bottom of your Word 2013 document there is a slim status bar that doubles as an always-on info readout and a collection of buttons and toggles as shown in Figure 2-7. By default, it includes a minimal set of useful tools: the current page number, word count, a spellcheck button, zoom slider and percentage entry, and buttons to switch your document view. Clicking the page number brings up the Navigation pane; clicking the word count brings up a window with information such as character and line counts; and so forth.

Figure 2-7

The Status Bar.

You can customize the Status Bar by right-clicking anywhere along its length. The context menu lists the various options you can include on the bar. When you're finished customizing the display, press Escape to return to your document.

The Navigation pane

The Find command has undergone some changes over the last few iterations of Microsoft Word. Like as Google search, Find has gotten *fuzzier* over time: once upon a time its main use was to grab a specific piece of text; now it's to move you *near* that text. It's now part of a handy tool called the **Navigation pane**, which combines the functionality of an outline, page-thumbnail view, and the old Find command.

STEP BY STEP   **Using the Navigation pane**

1   Press Ctrl+F or click the page count display in the Status Bar to bring up the Navigation pane.

The Navigation pane lets you move quickly through your document. Let's tour the file.

2   In the Search document field, type chinatown.

3   Click Headings in the Navigation pane.

Figure 2-8

Listing Headings in the Navigation pane.

Navigation

chinatown

Result 1 of 3

HEADINGS   PAGES   RESULTS

Introduction
The San Francisco Ghost Hunt
Haunted Haight Walking Tour
Chinatown Ghost Tour
Contact Information

The Navigation pane, as shown in Figure 2-8 shows a simplified outline of the document with each level of the outline corresponding to a **Heading style** in the text: Heading 1 at the top level, and the various Heading 2 sections below. The final Heading 1 entry (Chinatown Ghost Tour) should be highlighted, indicating that the text you searched for is found within that section.

4   Click Results.

The Navigation pane shows three hits for the word *chinatown*, all in the same section of the document. You can click each result in turn to highlight its location in the editing window.

5   Click the first result in the Navigation pane, Chinatown Ghost Tour, and close the pane. You'll return to the main editing window with your cursor in the right place, ready to edit.

6   Type San Francisco Chinatown, press Ctrl+F to switch focus back to the Navigation pane, and then click Headings.

The outline dynamically updates to reflect the edit you just made; clicking any heading will place the cursor at that spot in the editing window.

Take Note   Old Fashioned outline? Word 2013 still supports the old Outline view: click View > Outline (or press Alt+W+U) to get the old bullet points and Roman numerals. The Ribbon will update to reveal the Outlining tab. To return to Print Layout view, click the Print Layout button or press Alt+W+P.

Different viewing modes

Bottom Line   There are several ways to view your document in Word 2013, all available in the View tab. Each offers a different perspective on your document, and is most useful at specific points in your workflow.

Print Layout is just what it sounds like: a WYSIWYG (What You See Is What You Get) preview of the document's final appearance on the page, with or without markup. This is the view most Word users prefer.

Web Layout is subtly different: it shows what Word will produce if you convert your document to HTML. (Switching to Web Layout mode doesn't actually do the conversion, though; you have to Save As an HTML document for that.)

Outline View is most useful early in the writing process: you build an outline for your document, and Word 2013 automatically generates the appropriate headings, providing a skeleton that you can fill in with prose, graphics, tables, and so on.

Draft View shows a pure-text view of your document, typewriter-style: no specialized fonts, no careful layout; just words on the page. Outline and Draft views let you work directly with text without worrying about layout.

Figure 2-9

The same document in Draft, Outline, and Read modes.

Anne Hotel lobby at 7 p.m. even if it's raining. Join in the fun every evening but Tuesday. This tour is not recommended for children under the age of 8.

Haunted Haight Walking Tour
Haight Ashbury is famous for its role in producing the flower child generation of the 1960's. On the Haunted Haight Walking Tour, the phantoms of the area come to life. You will hear ghoulish stories of murderers, the heads of cults and neighborhood ghosts. Your tour guide is a seasoned member of the San Francisco Ghost Society, a group that investigates paranormal happenings in the area.

Grab your jacket, because it is cool and foggy at night, and meet at Coffee to the People 1206 Masonic Avenue at 7 p.m. on the dot. You are welcome to bring a camera, but video is not allowed. This tour is wheelchair friendly and guaranteed to have no hills at all. Children under the age of 13 should not attend.

Chinatown Ghost Tour
After sundown, past and present ghosts permeate the pathways of Chinatown. During the day, this historic part of San Francisco is one of the most visited tourist attractions in the city, but at night it takes on an entirely different air. The demons from deep in Chinatown's past make themselves known just after dark. With a lamplight leading the way, discover the mystery of its ancient ghostly history. Cynthia Yee, a lifetime resident, guides you and shares the legends and folklore that she has heard since she was a small child. The walking tour lasts about 1 ½ hours and is bound to amaze you, but be sure to make a reservation.

Contact Information
(Attn: please fill in this section ASAP)

Haunted Tours of San Francisco

- Introduction
  - The City by the Bay has many attractions to amuse, amaze and entertain. None, however, are as haunting as the ghost tours after dark. Here you can encounter the specters lurking among the streets and alleyways of San Francisco. With the knowledge of area history coupled with psychic understanding, the tour guides breathe life into local legendary apparitions. Join them some evening if the spirit moves you.

- The San Francisco Ghost Hunt
  - You do not need a reservation to join in the easy-paced 3-hour San Francisco Ghost Hunt. This tour introduces you to haunted San Francisco. Who knows? You might encounter a real spirit wandering between the human and spiritual worlds. Jim Fassbinder, your tour guide, relates tales of the past based upon recorded history. You will visit streets that certain spirits do not want to vacate. You will take a walk where people report having seen the ghost of a wandering woman. Wear comfortable shoes so you can follow the path of ghostly encounters. Meet at the Queen Anne Hotel lobby at 7 p.m. even if it's raining. Join in the fun every evening but Tuesday. This tour is not recommended for children under the age of 8.

- Haunted Haight Walking Tour
  - Haight Ashbury is famous for its role in producing the flower child generation of the 1960's. On the Haunted Haight Walking Tour, the phantoms of the area come to life. You will hear ghoulish stories of

Haunted Tours of San Francisco

Introduction
The City by the Bay has many attractions to amuse, amaze and entertain. None, however, are as haunting as the ghost tours after dark. Here you can encounter the specters lurking among the streets and alleyways of San Francisco. With the knowledge of area history coupled with psychic understanding, the tour guides breathe life into local legendary apparitions. Join them some evening if the spirit moves you.

The San Francisco Ghost Hunt
You do not need a reservation to join in the easy-paced 3-hour San Francisco Ghost Hunt. This tour introduces you to haunted San Francisco. Who knows? You might encounter a real spirit wandering between the human and spiritual worlds. Jim Fassbinder, your tour guide, relates tales of the past based upon recorded history. You will visit streets that certain spirits do not want to vacate. You will take a walk where people report having seen the ghost of a wandering woman. Wear comfortable shoes so you can follow the path of ghostly encounters. Meet at the Queen Anne Hotel lobby at 7 p.m. even if it's raining. Join in the fun

every evening but Tuesday. This tour is not recommended for children under the age of 8.

Haunted Haight Walking Tour
Haight Ashbury is famous for its role in producing the flower child generation of the 1960's. On the Haunted Haight Walking Tour, the phantoms of the area come to life. You will hear ghoulish stories of murderers, the heads of cults and neighborhood ghosts. Your tour guide is a seasoned member of the San Francisco Ghost Society, a group that investigates paranormal happenings in the area.

Grab your jacket, because it is cool and foggy at night, and meet at Coffee to the People 1206 Masonic Avenue at 7 p.m. on the dot. You are welcome to bring a camera, but video is not allowed. This tour is wheelchair friendly and guaranteed to have no hills at all. Children under the age of 13 should not attend.

Chinatown Ghost Tour
After sundown, past and present ghosts permeate the pathways of Chinatown. During the day, this historic part of San Francisco is one of the most visited tourist attractions in the city, but at night it takes on an entirely different air. The demons from deep in Chinatown's past make themselves known just after dark.

The four viewing modes listed previously are holdovers from previous versions of Word. Word 2013 adds a new document view: Read Mode (Shown in Figure 2-9). Designed for tablets and touchscreens, Read Mode displays your document with no visual clutter: no Ribbon, no tool palettes, just a handful of commands. Crucially, you can't *edit* the document in Read Mode; you move through the document a page at a time, as if shuffling pieces of paper.

Read Mode is useful at the reviewing, revising, and editing stages, and when sharing documents. To switch to Read Mode, click View > Views > Read Mode, or press Alt+W+F; to return to editing, press Escape or click View > Edit Document.

LAYING OUT THE PAGE

Bottom Line

Our info sheet uses a slightly nonstandard page layout: U.S. letter paper, as usual, but with narrow 0.5″ **margins** all around. (The default for U.S. users is a 1″ margin.) Click Page Layout > Page Setup > Margins to see the standard options. For inter-office memos and book reports, it's not worth worrying about page layout, but if design matters to your document, you'll start by thinking about the size and quality of the paper (or screen) where your work will appear.

Page size, margins, and marginalia

Assume that we've laid out our flyer haphazardly for letter paper with thin margins and no page numbers. We are then told that our flyer will be included in a book of local event listings, and we need to bring our layout in line with some new artistic visual standards. Our task is to alter everything but the content of our flyer, from page size through document theme.

STEP BY STEP   **Changing the page size, margins, and orientation**

1   If it's not still open from the previous exercise, open **word02a_work.docx**.

2   Click Page Layout > Page Setup > Size > More Paper Sizes (Alt+P, SZ, A).

3   Set the page width to 6″ and its height to 9″ (the dimensions of a trade paperback book) and click OK.

Word automatically lays out the text to fit the new page size, still in **portrait** (tall and narrow) orientation, with the same 0.5″ margins. Let's change those parameters as well.

4   Select Orientation > Landscape, and then Margins > Wide (both in the Page Layout tab).

Our new layout provides tons of left and right margin space, less at the top and bottom of the page. We'll take advantage of the roomy margins and place our page numbers at left, instead of in the usual header and footer.

Take Note   The Margins > Mirrored setting sets the Inside and Outside margins, rather than Left and Right; referring directly to *print* output, in which page 1 sits alone on the right, then a spread of pages 2 (left) and 3 (right), and alternating from there. If your long document is destined for print rather than PDF or HTML, consider working with some variant of the Mirrored layout, with a generous inner margin to account for book binding; e-books don't need asymmetric layouts, nor do short documents destined for stapling.

5   Select Insert > Header & Footer > Page Number > Page Margins > Circle Left. Double-click the main document area to close the Header/Footer menu. The page number float fades, visually indicating that it's a page element unaffected by normal text entry.

Take Note   Word opens the Header/Footer design tab when you insert a page number in the margin, even though marginal page numbers are floating text boxes that have nothing to do with headers or footers; this is one area where Word's do what I mean, not what I say approach is mildly confusing. If you click directly on the marginal page number, Word offers the correct tools to format floating text boxes. We'll discuss floats in great detail in later lessons.

Headers and footers

Bottom Line

Broadly speaking, a page in Word 2013 can be separated into a **header**, **footer**, and margins (generally the same from page to page); text blocks (the main text area, different on every page); background elements such as textures and watermarks; and **floats**, which jostle for space with everything else. Most documents have empty right and left margins, but headers and footers are widely used in Office documents.

Compared to applications such as InDesign and Quark Express, Word can't easily handle complex page layout, but even its basic header/footer tools provide surprising flexibility for medium-size desktop publishing projects.

The most common use for headers and footers is to print page numbers, author info, or title and date info on every page of a document. Our paranormal event listing will be included in a Coming Events guide; after setting the right Theme and Style Set, we'll insert the guide's title into our footer on alternate pages.

Headers and footers

1   Select Design > Themes > Organic, and then select the Lines (Distinctive) Style Set.

2   Scroll to the first page of the document. Click Insert > Footer > Filigree. Place the cursor to the left of the filigree symbol and type Fun Francisco. Then place the cursor to the right of the filigree and type Thrillafornia.

3   Select Options > Different Odd & Even Pages, and then click Navigation > Next to move to the page 2 footer.

4   Double-click the center of the page 2 footer (the cursor should change to centered text) as shown in Figure 2-10.

Figure 2-10

Word 2013 correctly assumes that text placed at the center of the footer is center-aligned.

5   Type 2013 Spooktacular. Finally, double-click the main text area to close the header/footer tools.

Windows and panes: splitting your document view

Bottom Line

At times, you may need to have more than one section of your document open at once; for instance, when paraphrasing one passage elsewhere in the document, or avoiding doing so. The Window Group in Word 2013 offers some tools to help you visually manage different parts of a document; we'll use the split-screen functionality to make some edits to our flyer.

Changing the document view

1   Click View > Window > Split to divide the screen in half vertically. You can now scroll independently in each pane.

2   Click New Window to open another window on the current document.

3   Now click View Side by Side to reveal three angles on the document at once as displayed in Figure 2-11.

4   If it's not already selected, click Synchronous Scrolling.

Figure 2-11

One image, three views: Split Window and New Window.

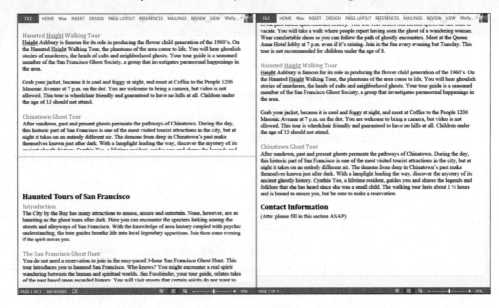

Now scroll to the very bottom of the document in one of the short windows; the tall window scrolls along with it. This feature is most useful when comparing different documents; we don't need it now.

5   Close the tall window. In one of the half-height panes, scroll to the top of the document; in the other pane, scroll to the very bottom. To switch focus between panes, just click to place the cursor as normal.

To switch focus and move the cursor between the two open panes, press F6; note that this command actually switches between the open document panes, status bar, ribbon, and Navigation pane, if open. To switch between windows within Word, press Ctrl+F6.

6   Scroll down from the top of the document to gather the names of the various tour guides. At the end of the flyer, replace the placeholder text with their contact information, styled so as to draw attention (boldface, right justified):

Jim Fassbinder (253) 555–2294

San Francisco Ghost Society (617) 22-SPOOKY

Cynthia Yee (503) 555–4YEE

7   Click View > Window > Remove Split to return to a single editing window.

8   Choose File > Save and then File > Close.

Knowledge Assessment

Fill in the Blanks

Complete the following sentences by writing the correct word or words in the blanks provided.

1. To see the keyboard shortcut for a command, _____ its icon in the Ribbon.
2. Results of the Find command are displayed in the _____.
3. The simplest view of your document, stripped of images and formatting and niceties, is the _____ View.
4. To print the page number at the bottom of every page, insert it in the _____.
5. On the third page of a document designed for print, the left margin is also known as the _____ margin.
6. Tall thin documents are laid out in _____ orientation.
7. To display two views of a document in separate windows, use the _____ command.
8. The running word count display can be added to the _____.
9. To print a document without clicking the File tab, press the _____ keyboard shortcut.
10. The Replace command appears in a Navigation Pane dropdown or the _____ tab, and can be invoked directly with the _____ shortcut.

Matching

Match the action to its associated keyboard shortcut.

1. Save As
2. Print Layout
3. Open Styles Pane
4. Italicize
5. Open File
6. Quit
7. Switch windows
8. Find/Replace
9. Close Document
10. Boldface

a. Alt+Ctrl+Shift+S
b. Ctrl+H
c. Ctrl+O
d. Ctrl+B
e. Ctrl+I
f. Ctrl+F6
g. Alt+F+A
h. Ctrl+W
i. Alt+W+P
j. Alt+F4

Competency Assessment

Project 2-1: Working with the Quick Access Toolbar

In this exercise you'll customize the Quick Access Toolbar.

1. Launch Word and create a new document.
2. Click the dropdown button on the Quick Access Toolbar and select Email.
3. Type some text in the main edit window, and then select the Email command from the Quick Access Toolbar.
4. Right click the Email command and choose Remove.
5. Select More Commands... from the dropdown. In the left hand pane, scroll down and select Styles...
6. Click the new Styles... command or press Alt+Ctrl+Shift+S to bring up the Styles task pane.

   Note the difference between this task pane and Apply Style (Ctrl+Shift+S) pane.
7. Close the pane and leave Word open for the next exercise.

Project 2-2: Customizing the Status Bar

In this exercise you'll tailor the Status Bar to your preferences.

1. Right-click in the Status Bar and select Page Number.
2. Deselect Zoom while leaving Zoom Slider selected.

   You can choose to re-enable the direct-entry zoom tool later if you'd like.
3. Dismiss the menu and click the "Page X of Y" display on the Status Bar. Dismiss the Pane.
4. Experiment with adding other Status Bar elements and finding out what commands they enact when clicked.
5. Dismiss the Customize Status Bar menu.
6. Leave Word open for the next exercise.

Proficiency Assessment

Project 2-3: Using the Navigation Pane

In this exercise you'll put the Navigation Pane to use for browsing and editing a file.

1. Open the project file called **2-3-source** and save your document as **project_2-3_headings**.
2. Open the Navigation Pane.
3. Search for king in the document and click to view all results. Click on the two results in the Navigation Pane's Results tab.

   Note that "king" is a substring – the search hits both "king" and "taking."
4. With the second search result selected, switch to the Navigation Pane's Headings tab.
5. Drag the Good Faith entry in the Headings tab to the top of the mini outline.
6. Click the Bill of Particulars heading in the Pane to switch to its page.
7. Right-click the same entry in the outline list, and select Demote.

   Note the changes to both the outline and the newly-restyled heading itself.
8. Save and close your document.

Project 2-4: Using Find/Replace

In this exercise you'll test out Word's Find/Replace tool.

1. Open the project file **2-4-source** and save it as **project_2-4_find**.
2. Press **Ctrl+F**. Open the Results tab in the Navigation Pane.
3. Type **our** in the search box, but don't press Return yet.
   Word displays search results as you type.
4. Complete the search term **ouring** and press **Return**.
5. Click the drop-down arrow on the search entry box itself and select **Replace…**
6. Replace ouring with **oring**. If prompted, continue the search from the beginning of the document, and click **OK** when all results are in.
7. Experiment with case-sensitive and case-insensitive searches in the Advanced Find dialog box, e.g., by searching for **for** with and without case-sensitive searching enabled.
8. Save and close your document.

Mastery Assessment

Project 2-5: Outline Mode

In this exercise you'll add headings and notes to a file and make use of Outline View.

1. Open the project file **2-5-source** and save it as **project_2-5_outline**.
2. Experiment with inserting a variety of headings – **Opening** and **Closing**, for instance, or a **Specific Complaints** top-level heading that includes both the Bill of Particulars and the Legal Affronts.
3. Use the Navigation Pane to quickly browse the file, using the new headings as a guide.
4. Switch to Outline View and experiment with moving and collapsing entire sections of the document.
5. Write a short note, **heading not in original**, and use Outline View to add it, as quickly as you can, to the beginning of every section of your reordered Declaration.
6. Save and close your document.

Project 2-6: Laying Out the Page

This exercise challenges you to create a page layout from scratch.

1. Open the project file **2-6-source** and save it as **project_2-6_layout**.
2. Create a new page layout for the document according to the following specifications:
   - 6" square page, **0.2"** margins on all four edges (ignore error message)
   - **40pt** title text, title alone on front page (add a Page Break)
   - **18pt** Normal text (note that Title is resized based on Normal…)
   - Page break after opening paragraph ("When in the course…")
3. Save your work and close Word.

LESSON SKILL MATRIX

In this lesson, you will learn the following skills:

Paragraph and Character Formatting

Using the Format Painter

Line and Paragraph Spacing

Formatting Multi-Column Text

Styles, Themes, and Live Preview

Adding Text Boxes and Images

Cut, Copy, and Paste

KEY TERMS

- Character
- Alignment
- Justification
- Tab Stop
- Points
- Paste Options
- Format Painter
- Absolute Placement
- Text Box
- Rotation Handle
- Grouping
- In Line with Text (object layout)

Fabrikam's clients can submit Archival Research requests through Fabrikam's website; for auditing purposes, the plain text output of these requests is reformatted as Word documents for print. Fortunately, prettying up the plain text website data dumps is easy – Word's Style system and robust options for pasting and reformatting data give Fabrikam's documentation team a set of streamlined tools for radically transforming the look of a document while keeping its information intact.

SOFTWARE ORIENTATION

Microsoft Word provides many options for controlling the appearance and position of text and objects on screen. In this lesson you'll be introduced to document formatting controls.

Figure 3-1

Formatting tools and controls

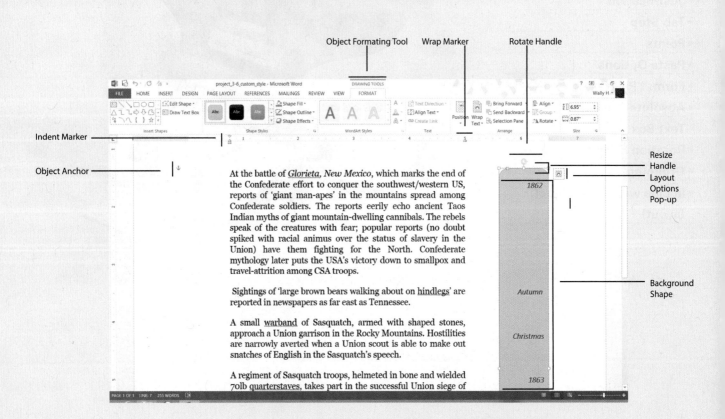

STARTING UP

In this lesson, you'll work with several files from the Word03lessons folder. Make sure that you have loaded the OfficeLessons folder onto your computer.

WORKING WITH TEXT IN WORD

Over the decades, MS Word has grown into a complex desktop publishing tool. Most of what you'll do with Word 2013 is just entering and editing text. But in a graphical application such as Word, text is as much a visual element as any image – so this lesson moves right from basic text entry and formatting to working with visual page elements.

To begin, open two files in your Word03lessons folder and look over them: **word03a.docx** and **word03b.docx**. The first is a draft info sheet on pandas; the second includes revised text from a colleague to be inserted into the info sheet. In this lesson, we'll tighten the prose in the info sheet, experiment with some layout changes, and better integrate the image and caption into the flow of the text.

Paragraph and character formatting

Bottom Line

In Word 2013, a piece of text consists of a series of **characters** (letters, numbers, symbols) that are formatted one way or another. You control every aspect of the text's appearance: font (typeface), size, spacing, emphasis (italics, bold, underline), vertical and horizontal **alignment**, **justification** (i.e., how smooth is the edge of a block of text), indentation, and more.

You can alter the formatting of an individual character, word, or line. When you select one word from a line and press Ctrl+I, you change it to italic type. The rest of the line remains as it was. In contrast, you can't double-space a single word without doing the same to its entire paragraph. Word 2013 treats italics and line spacing differently; the former is one variety of character formatting, and is handled by the controls in the Home > Font group; the latter is paragraph formatting, found in Home > Paragraph. Both sets of controls are shown in Figure 3-2.

Figure 3-2

Word's basic formatting palette.

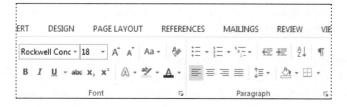

STEP BY STEP **Paragraph and character formatting**

Crucially, Word 2013 treats character and paragraph formatting commands differently in the Edit window. Let's see how:

1   Switch to **word03b.docx**. Open the Home tab.

2   Move your cursor just to the left of the word Edits, but don't select any text.

3   Click Home > Font > Underline (or press Ctrl+U).

The Underline icon is selected, but nothing happens to the text that's already on the page. You've told Word to switch to Underline text, but there's nothing selected, so the Underline command will only be applied to the text you type next.

4   Type **Important** and press the spacebar.

This is an important lesson for later: a blank space is a character just like a number, letter, punctuation mark, or symbol, and Word knows to underline blank spaces just the same. It does look foolish, but you can fix it by highlighting this space and deselecting Underline.

5   Click **Home** > **Paragraph** > **Align Right** (Ctrl+R). Move the cursor to the end of the line and type —**please update**.

6   Triple-click the word *Edits* and click **Center** (Ctrl+E).

Word applies paragraph formatting to the entire paragraph, whether you click somewhere in the line or select one or more words in it. The same applies to the rest of the formatting commands.

Indendation and Tab Stops

The ruler at the top of the main document area is toggled with the View > Show > Ruler checkbox. It both shows you the position of a page element in units of physical distance (not just points), and allows you to set the placement of text with some precision by customizing indentation and tab stops.

The hourglass symbol at the left of the ruler is actually three parts, as indicated in <<figure 3-whatever>>: the first-line indent point, the indent point for subsequent (wrapped) lines in the paragraph, and a handle to drag both indent points at once. Each indent point indicates where a line of text will begin filling in. Practice changing indent settings to see what paragraph layouts they can generate.

A fourth handle, at the far right of the ruler, indicates the rightmost border of the text block – the wrap point. Any paragraph that runs past that point will instead be wrapped to the next line.

The pictured ruler also contains several tab stops. If you don't manually add tab stops, each time you press Tab, you'll insert blank space between the current cursor position and the next 0.5" increment. (You can set the default Tab increment in Options.) Tab stops let you specify alternate destinations. In the image, you can see a center tab stop and a right-justified tab stop – tabbing to the first will insert center-justified text at that spot, and tabbing to the next will let you insert right-justified text there.

A combination of left- and right-justified tab stops lets you simulate a multi-column or tabular layout. You can add tab stops by picking the variety you want using the tab selector (left of the ruler), then clicking in the ruler itself to place it. To remove a tab stop, just drag it out of the ruler.

Feel free to experiment with adding tab stops and changing the indentation of some text.

Spacing

Word's standard text spacing is meant to be readable on-screen and in print, but if you need to adjust the amount of whitespace between lines of text, the Home > Paragraph > Line Spacing command offers a plethora of options. Clicking the icon reveals a drop-down menu; selecting Line Spacing Options from the menu brings up the Indents and Spacing tab of the Paragraph Formatting dialog box seen in Figure 3-3. The numbers in the Spacing group refer to the space between lines of a paragraph; the larger the number, the more room Word leaves between lines in a paragraph. You can mouse over the options in the menu for a Live Preview of the different settings.

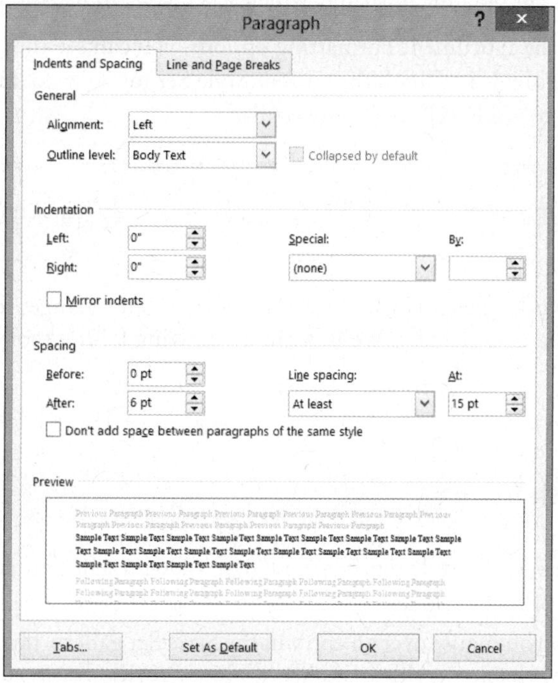

Figure 3-3

Fine-tune text block formatting in the Paragraph Settings dialog.

Take Note   The default line spacing of Normal body text is 1.0; it seems logical that double-spaced text would have a line spacing of 2.0. But that setting leaves a vast empty space between lines. For a double-spaced report or memo, use the 1.5 or even 1.15 spacing options.

Spacing between paragraphs is set with the Page Layout > Paragraph commands. The spacing is measured in **points**, just like font size; 12 point (pt.) of space atop a paragraph leaves about as much room as a line of normal text. You can also control pre and post-paragraph spacing with the Line Spacing Option screen.

The Line and Paragraph Spacing command affects a single paragraph, or every paragraph in that Style; if you want to set spacing defaults for your entire document at once, use the Design > Document Formatting > Paragraph Spacing tool.

Styles, themes, and live preview

Now take a look at **word03a.docx**. It contains several headings (Habitat, Diet, Status, and more) formatted in a different font, size, and color from the body text. Individually reformatting each heading would be a hassle; it's much easier to tell your word processor that the current text is a heading and to format this like the other headings. This is accomplished through the use of Styles—one of the most important features of Word 2013.

Styles, themes and live preview

1   Open the Home tab. A gallery of Styles appears.

2   Click several different pieces of text in your document, and their various Styles will be highlighted in the gallery: Heading 1 and Heading 2 for the top line and paragraph headings, respectively; Caption for the Figure 1 caption; Normal for the body text.

3   Open the Design tab. Click **Design > Themes** to see that Wood Type is selected—that's the current document Theme, which sets colors, fonts, and more.

4   Under the Document Formatting options, you can see that Lines (Simple) is selected (See Figure 3-4.). That's the current Style Set for your document—a collection of styles chosen to work well together visually.

Figure 3-4

A gallery of Style Sets for the current theme.

To see how to work efficiently with Styles, let's make some changes to the look of our document—both line-by-line and globally. We'll begin by drawing a little more attention to the headings in our document.

Working with Styles

1   Mouse over the style sets in the Design > Document Formatting gallery to see the names of each style set.

Note that when you mouse over an entry in the Style Set gallery, the appearance of your document changes to show the new style; this is Word's Live Preview feature at work. The new style set isn't applied until you click a gallery entry.

2   Click the paragraph heading, **Habitat**, and then select **Home > Paragraph > Align Right** (or press **Ctrl+R**). The heading is now flush with the right margin; Word treats the heading as a paragraph consisting of a single word, and then reformats the entire paragraph.

3   Double or triple-click the same heading. A mini toolbar, shown in Figure 3-5, will appear with commonly used character and paragraph-formatting commands.

Figure 3-5

The mini formatting toolbar appears by default when you select a text block

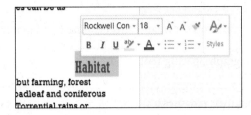

Take Note   Double-clicking selects a single word; triple-clicking selects an entire paragraph. From Word 2013's perspective, each paragraph is really a single line of characters, wrapped to fit in a single column; if your text were small enough or your page wide enough, every paragraph would fit onto its own line. But Word's formatting tools refer to paragraphs, not lines. This human-centered terminology is there to help you think about your document from a reader's perspective. Note that the word/line count in the Status Bar refers to lines in the reader sense, i.e., it counts lines on the page, not paragraphs.

4   Use the font size drop-down in the mini toolbar to set the Habitat heading to 18 pt. type.

5   Right-click the Heading 2 entry in the Home > Styles gallery and select Update Heading 2 to Match Selection.

First, we modified the heading style for one paragraph heading from Lines (Simple) Heading 2 (which sets font, color, size, and so on) to Lines (Simple) Heading 2 + right-justify + 18pt. We then instructed Word to make the same changes everywhere it finds the Heading 2 style, tweaking alignment and size, but leaving font and color the same.

To ensure that our top-level heading stands out from the paragraph headings, we'll make one more change to Heading 2 using the Modify Style tool.

6   Right-click the Heading 2 entry in the Styles gallery and chose Modify. A dialog box will appear, as in Figure 3-6.

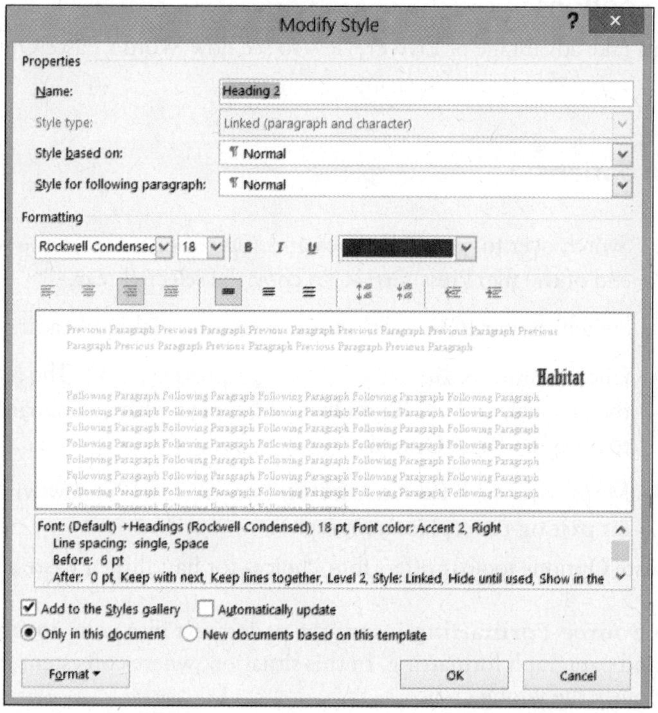

Figure 3-6

Modify Style dialog box.

7   In the drop-down color menu, select Gray-50%-Text 2 (top row, fourth from the left), and check Automatically update. Click OK.

8   Choose File > Save As. Navigate to the Word03lessons folder, and save the file as **word03a_work**.

Selecting Automatically update makes a change to all Heading 2 text in this document only. Yes, the right-justified headings look terrible atop short, wide text blocks; we'll switch to a compact two-column layout later in the lesson to make the headings more readable.

Styles in Word can be put to a wide array of uses; in Lesson 4, "Structuring Complex Documents," you'll take advantage of Word's heading styles to structure a document with many sections. In the meantime, go ahead and experiment with modifying Styles to tweak the look of your document.

Cut, copy, and paste

 # Workplace Ready

The most frequently used commands in Word are Cut, Copy, and Paste. In theory, they're very simple: select some text, duplicate it or remove it to memory, and then insert the stored text somewhere else. But remember, Word can format text at the character and paragraph levels, and when you paste Heading 3 + non-theme color text into the middle of a Caption + italics line, you have to work with the application to decide exactly how that Paste action should work.

What happens when your clipboard contains, not a string of text from a Word document, but an entire Excel spreadsheet? Or an image with a caption in a font that's not installed on your computer? In this section, we'll look at options built into Word to cover most cut/copy/paste situations.

Paste options

We can take advantage of Live Preview to see how Word's Paste Options work.

STEP BY STEP   Paste options

1   Switch over to **word03b.docx** and select the text from the word Habitat through the end of the file. Press Ctrl+C to copy the selected text.

2   Switch to **word03a_work.docx**. Select the Habitat heading and paragraph.

3   Click Home > Clipboard > Paste (or press Ctrl+V). The replacement text will overwrite the original, and a mini toolbar will appear with a clipboard icon. Click the mini toolbar to bring up Paste Options.

4   Mouse over each **Paste Option** in turn. Live Preview will show the available options for pasting the replacement text.

The Paste Options toolbar offers four choices for handling a Paste action:

Keep Source Formatting inserts the pasted text into your document as-is, preserving its character and paragraph formatting. In this situation, where consistent look and feel is important, this is obviously the wrong choice.

Merge Formatting will apply the style of the destination text to the pasted text; in this case, it chooses Heading 2 (the first style in the selected text from the info sheet) and applies that to the entire pasted selection. That makes sense for simple pastes, but not for pasting in a heading and paragraph, as we're doing.

Use Destination Styles is the default behavior for Word 2013 when pasting text from a Word document. All our source text uses the Normal style, so Word simply applies the formatting that the Normal style has in the Style Set Lines (Stylish).

Keep Text Only is useful for tasks such as converting a table to straight text. It eliminates all formatting from the source text: italics, centering, bullets, and more. In the present instance, Keep Text Only produces the same output as Merge Formatting, but that won't always be the case.

As you can see, Word has no way of knowing that our first line is a paragraph heading unless we use a heading style; the application treats our Paste as two paragraphs of Normal text. The default Paste behavior is fine; we can manually fix the heading style.

5   Press Ctrl, then S to accept Use Destination Styles paste option, then press Escape to dismiss the Paste Options minibar. Then select the lone word *Habitat* and switch its style to Heading 2.

Copying a look: Format Painter

Sometimes you want to grab, not the content of a text selection, but its formatting. This happens often enough that Word has a ready-made command for it: Home > Clipboard > **Format Painter**. To use it, select the text whose format you're grabbing, click Format Painter (or press Ctrl+Shift+C), and then click the text to which you want to apply the format (or press Ctrl+Shift+V).

Format Painter is especially valuable when you want to match to colored/resized text, but don't want to manually tweak multiple formatting options. It does not copy over the Style of the source text, just its look (so you can Paint a single sidebar to appear as a header without botching your document outline).

Word 2013 offers you refined control over the behavior of the Paste command.

STEP BY STEP   **Setting additional paste options**

1   Click Home > Clipboard > Paste > Set Default Paste.

2   In the Options screen, shown in Figure 3-7, scroll to Cut, copy, and paste.

Figure 3-7

Word's Paste feature is extremely customizable.

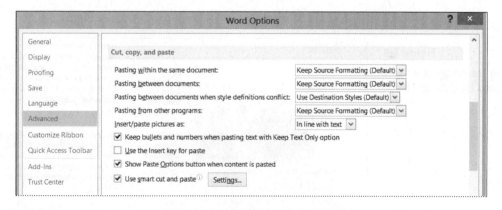

Here you can set the default behavior of Word for a variety of text-handling situations. Note the difference between *Pasting within the same document* and *Pasting between documents* when styles conflict. By default, Word assumes that when moving text around in a single document, you want to preserve its style: you wouldn't want to change the order of two paragraphs and realize you've accidentally turned one into a header. Similarly, when pasting data from another Word document, Word won't interfere with the Style Set you're working with.If the Paste Options toolbar gets in your way, you can turn it off from this same options screen. Finally, if you want to see the technical aspects of the Paste command, which invisibly adjusts word and paragraph spacing every time you move text around, click the *Use smart cut and paste settings* button. These options are meant for advanced users with specific workflow needs; there's no need for you to change these settings now, but it's helpful to know where to find them.

3   Click OK to commit changes and close the Word Options dialog box.

Working with columns

In the Page Layout tab, you'll find Word's Columns tool. By default, it provides five modes: one, two, and three-column text, and two asymmetrical two-column layouts. You can use more columns if you need to. Word uses newspaper-style multi-column layouts: text flows from left to right, and lines accumulate top to bottom within a column; the text starts on the next page only when all the columns on the current page are filled.

In other words, Word's text columns do not fill up independently of one another. For example, you wouldn't create a two-column layout with Spanish text on the left and an English translation on the right, and fill them in separately. For layouts built on parallel text streams of that sort, you'd use a specialized layout tool such as Microsoft Publisher or Adobe InDesign.

Take Note

Strictly speaking, you can make parallel columns from separate text streams in Word. If you have less than a single page of text, for instance, it's no problem: in our translation example, insert a Column Break at the end of one text stream and start the second stream. Alternatively, put each stream in one column of a tall two-column table, or do the same with text boxes, and use the Create Link command to flow text from one to the other. But there's no elegant equivalent to the newspaper-style columns in Word.

Switching to a multi-column layout dramatically changes the feel of the text on-screen and on the page; it will give our info sheet an encyclopedia look.

STEP BY STEP   **Working with columns**

1. Open **word03a_work.docx** if it is not already open. Press **Ctrl+A** to Select All, including the panda image and caption.

2. Select **Page Layout > Columns > Two**. See Figure 3-8.

Figure 3-8

Two-column layout radically alters the document's look and feel.

Pandas

Pandas have black fur on their ears, eye patches, muzzle, legs, and shoulders. The rest of its coat is white. The unusual

Figure 1: Pandas in the Wild

black and white colors puzzle scientists. Some, however, believe that the bold coloring provides camouflage in their shade-dappled snowy and rocky surroundings. The panda has a thick, wooly coat that keeps it warm in the cool forests of its habitat. Large molar teeth and strong jaw muscles are necessary for crushing tough bamboo. Although they look adorable and toy-like, these creatures can be as dangerous as any other bear.

Habitat

Pandas live in a few mountain ranges in central China. Although they once lived in lowland areas, many factors forced them to move into the mountains such as farming and forest clearing. These creatures live in forests at elevations between 5,000 and 10,000 feet with dense bamboo growing beneath the main canopy. Throughout the year, torrential rains or dense mist characterizes these forests, which are often shrouded in heavy clouds.

A wild panda's diet is almost exclusively (99 percent) bamboo. The balance consists of other grasses and occasional small rodents or musk deer fawns. In zoos, pandas eat bamboo, sugar cane, rice gruel, a special high-fiber biscuit, carrots, apples, and sweet potatoes.

Status

The panda is listed as endangered in the World Conservation Union's (IUCN's) Red List of Threatened Animals. There are about 1,600 left in the wild. Nearly 300 pandas live in zoos and breeding centers around the world, mostly in China.

Social Structure

Adult pandas are generally solitary, but they do communicate periodically through scent marks, calls, and occasional meetings. Offspring stay with their mothers from one and a half to three years. The panda has lived in bamboo forests for several million years. It is a highly specialized animal, with unique adaptations.

Conserving the Panda

Early panda conservation work included intensive field studies of wild panda ecology and behavior. Current work focuses on the following areas: Minshan Mountains in Sichuan and Gansu provinces and the Qinling Mountains in Shaanxi province.

The work includes: increasing the area of habitat under legal protection, creating green corridors to link isolated pandas, and continued research and monitoring.

© fototrav/iStockphoto

You can now use Undo (Ctrl+Z) and Redo (Ctrl+Y) to toggle back and forth between the one and two-column layouts. The line beneath the top heading stretches across the left-hand column only; there's less whitespace, yielding a denser layout; crucially, the sub-headings stand out much more in a two-column format. However, the image and caption use **absolute placement** on the page, rather than adjusting to the change in text flow, and no longer work in the new layout. Make sure the document is now set to single column.

TEXT BOXES AND IMAGES

bottom line

In previous lessons, we've encountered images, tables, and text boxes: design elements that are separate from the flow of text in a document. When text and other page elements work well together, your documents can be not just functional but beautiful. Here, we'll work with a simple **text box**, the panda caption, and see how it integrates into the flow of our document text.

Placing text boxes and images

The caption beneath the panda image is formatted as a text box. We'll make several changes to its content and appearance, use the Group tool to link it to the image and streamline our workflow, and then place the photo and caption together.

STEP BY STEP   **Place text boxes and images**

1 Click the Figure 1: Pandas in the Wild text. The outline of the text box appears, along with the Layout Options icon, several handles (small white boxes) to resize the text box, and a handle above to rotate the box.

2 Press **Ctrl+A** (Select All). Change the text to Wild Pandas.

3 Click one of the handles on the right-hand side of the box (see Figure 3-9), and then drag it to the left until it's tight with the word *Pandas*, without causing the text to wrap. This resizes the text box, which now takes up only as much space as it needs.

Figure 3-9

Resize the text box.

© *fototrav/iStockphoto*

No surprises so far: the text box can be resized like an image, and its content is (initially) an editable text such as any other on the page. Now we'll work on positioning and orientation.

4 With the text box still selected, click Format > Arrange > Align > Use Alignment Guides if it is not already checked.

5   Drag the **rotation handle** clockwise until the text runs straight up and down: a 90 degree rotation (See Figure 3-10.) When you're close to 90 degrees, the box will seem to stick a little bit.

Figure 3-10

Rotating a text box: Word treats 90° as a likely target amount.

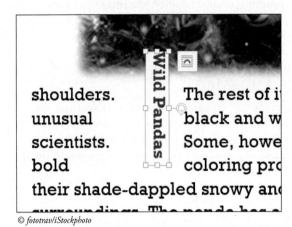

© fototrav/iStockphoto

6   Click the dotted line around the text box to select the box (rather than the text inside it), and drag it over the pandas, positioning it near the image's rightmost edge.

7   Finally, triple-click once more on the *Wild Pandas* text itself. (The text box will rotate temporarily so the text is readable.) The formatting pop-up menu appears; set the text color to white. Then click Drawing Tools > Format > Shape Fill > No Fill.

This series of commands yields a transparent text box with white text running vertically atop the right-hand edge of our panda image. No Fill allows anything that is beneath the text box to show. For more precise control over rotation, we could select the text box and use the Drawing Tools > Arrange > Rotate tool.

8   Without deselecting the text box, Ctrl+click the panda image. Both the panda image and the text box are selected.

9   Click Drawing Tools > Format > Arrange > Align > Align Middle (not Center). The centers of the picture and caption both snap to the same invisible horizontal line, aligning the two objects. Then click Format > Arrange > Group > Group. Only a single selection box remains: the one around the image/caption pair. See Figure 3-11 for a comparison of grouped and individual objects.

Figure 3-11

Grouped (L) and ungrouped (R) objects in Word.

© fototrav/iStockphoto

The caption is nicely placed atop the image, and by **Grouping** them together, we've told Word to move and modify them together, making complex layout tasks somewhat easier. This is just a temporary change; we haven't modified the original image and can use Format > Arrange > Group > Ungroup at a later time if we need to separate image and caption.

Take Note   In Word, Align Middle refers to vertical alignment; Center refers to horizontal alignment. Everyone's familiar with horizontal alignment, which adjusts the position of an element relative to the margins (of the column, page, table cell, or text box). Vertical alignment works the same way, so when you apply the Align Middle command to an object, note carefully what space's middle you're aligning it to. A variety of weird behaviors can be explained by Word performing an action in a different context from what you expect: centering within a column rather than a line, including trailing spaces in a paragraph-select, and so on.

To close, we'll move the image to the right spot on the page. At this point, the Alignment Guides will come into play.

10   Zoom out to around 70% size using the slider on the bottom-right corner of the window, then drag the image to the top of the Habitat section, along the column's right-hand edge. When the image is in position, green lines will appear along its top and right edges, indicating that it's flush against the margin and aligned with the top of the paragraph. Alignment Guides are shown in Figure 3-12.

Figure 3-12

Alignment Guides let you target page and object borders and centers with precision.

© fototrav/iStockphoto

The Alignment Guides feature for Word 2013 appear when you line up two objects in some way: their edges or centers at the same horizontal or vertical position.

Inserting an object directly into a paragraph

Bottom Line   In this lesson, we've worked only with absolute positioning: moving the image and caption freely around the page, forcing the text to flow around them. It's a little tricky, but it gives precise control over the layout of a document. Another way to position objects in a Word document is to insert them directly into the text flow. If you've used previous editions of Word, you've probably used this method of placement. Note the difference in presentation:

STEP BY STEP   **Inserting an object directly into a paragraph**

1   Click the panda image, and then click the Layout Options pop-up menu when it appears.

2   Select the In Line with Text layout method.

3   Drag the image to a different spot in the document.

In a sense, Word treats your image as an unusually large piece of text, and places it on the text baseline just as any other word. There's no Live Preview either: Word just reflows the paragraph around the image. In this case, the output is terrible: the image is too big to sit comfortably on a line with text. In other circumstances, such as placing a sparkline (a word-sized miniature info-graphic), In Line with Text is the right insertion mode.

4   Choose **File > Save** or press **Ctrl+S** to save your work.

5   Close both documents, but only save the changes to **Word03a_work**.

What you learned in this lesson:

• Paragraph and Character Formatting

• Line and Paragraph Spacing

• Styles, Themes, and Live Preview

• Cut, Copy, and Paste

• Using the Format Painter

• Formatting Multi-Column Text

• Adding Text Boxes and Images

Knowledge Assessment

Fill in the Blanks

Complete the following sentences by writing the correct word or words in the blanks provided.

1.   A paragraph in Word is a single _____ of text that's wrapped one or more times.

2.   To start each paragraph 1" to the right of the left margin, drag the _____ to the appropriate spot on the ruler.

3.   To paste text into a document as-is, choose the _____ Paste option.

4.   Select a piece of text, then click the _____ command to grab its formatting info for transfer to another text piece.

5.   In a multi-column layout, Word won't flow text to the next _____ until it's filled all columns in the current one.

6.   Combine several objects to manipulate them all at once for ease of use, using the _____ command.

7.   To place an image on/in a grid alongside text characters, rather than freely position it at a specific spot on the "paper," select the _____ layout option.

8.   The current Style Set is shown at the _____ side of the _____.

9.   The _____ tab of the Paragraph options dialog lets you specify the amount of whitespace before and after each line of text.

10.   To remove text from a document and cache it temporarily for insertion later, use the _____ command.

True/False

Circle T if the statement is true or F it the statement is false.

T F 1. Word has built-in support for "parallel" (independent) multi-column layouts.

T F 2. Align Middle refers to horizontal alignment – the middle of a left-right line through the page.

T F 3. Inserting an object In Line with Text can push it off the printable area of a page.

T F 4. In general, sparklines should be inserted In Line with Text.

T F 5. Word gives no visual indication when the current document theme is modified from its original state.

T F 6. Text emphasis refers to formatting like italics, boldface, and underline.

T F 7. The line count in the Status Bar actually counts paragraphs.

T F 8. The leftmost default tab stop is at the far right of the text block.

T F 9. When pasting text into the middle of a paragraph, it makes sense to use the Merge Formatting paste option.

T F 10. By default, when you place a simple text box in a page full of text, Word will wrap the text around the box.

Competency Assessment

Project 3-1: Paragraph and Character Formatting

In this exercise, edit a document at the character and paragraph levels.

1. Open the project file **glorieta**.
2. Save your document as **project_3-1_formatting**.
3. If you haven't already done so, enable Show Hidden Characters.
4. Click somewhere in the first line of the text and select Bullet formatting.
5. Do the same for the entire document.
6. Italicize the words Glorieta, New Mexico.
7. Add a heading, Capsule History, before the first line, with Style Heading 1. Modify the heading to Right Align.
8. Save and close your work.

Project 3-2: Adding Floats

Here you'll add floating page elements to a Word file.

1. Open the project file **3-2-source**. Save your document as **project_3-2_floats**.
2. Insert a Simple Text Box somewhere in the first paragraph. Type 1862 in the box.
3. Open the text box's Layout Options popup and click See More…
4. Set the text box's characteristics in the dialog box: Right aligned relative to the Margin, Top aligned relative to the Line, size 1" by 1", Square wrapping, Left wrapping only. Click OK. Resize the box vertically so it's just tall enough to fit the text.
5. Select the date in the box and set Format > Align Text to Middle. Select Home > Align Right.
6. Finally, select the box, then select Format > Shape Outline > No Outline.
7. Save your work.

Proficiency Assessment

Project 3-3: More Floats

This exercise makes further use of floats to lay out content on a page.

1. Open project file **3-3-source**. Save your document as **project_3-3_copy_paste**. Copy the text box containing 1862 (not the text itself).

2. Paste copies of it next to all the other timeline entries, using the green guideline to align the right edges of each box. Note that Pasting the text boxes doesn't result in perfectly placed, properly aligned copies.

3. Change the text of each float to reflect the date of the paragraph beside it: Autumn instead of "Late 1862," Christmas instead of "Christmas 1862," the same otherwise.

4. Save and close your work.

Project 3-4: Using Format Painter

In this exercise you'll duplicate text formatting using the Format Painter.

1. Open the project file **3-4-source**. Save your document as **project_3-4_format_painter**.

2. Format the first date entry as follows: Bold, Italic, Red, 10pt Calibri Light.

3. Use the Format Painter to apply the same formatting to all the floats.

   Outside of this exercise context, it would make sense to apply this formatting before copying the floats.

4. Change the bullet points from dots to four-part diamonds.

5. Save and close your work.

Mastery Assessment

Project 3-5: Indentation

This exercise has you tweak the presentation of a text block, including text indentation.

1. Open the project file **3-5-source**. Save your document as **project_3-5_indentation**.

2. Alter the text so it uses a 4" wide text block, with the left margin at the 0.5" mark, fully justified, with no bullets. Delete the boldfaced dates from within the main text block.

3. Insert a rounded rectangle with color Subtle Effect – Green, Accent 6, covering the remaining (red) date entries. Use the Format > Arrange tools to position it behind the dates.

4. Reformat the date floats to have no border and no fill – Shift+clicking will save much time here.

5. Save your work.

Project 3-6: Creating a Custom Style

Here you'll create a custom Text Style for your document.

1. Open the project file **3-6-source**. Save your document as **project_3-6_custom_style**.

2. Create a custom Text Style, Timeline Entry, with the following specs: 11pt Georgia font, left margin 0.75", right margin 5", 12pt spacing before, 8pt after.

3. Apply this custom style to all timeline entries. Save and close your work.

4 Structuring Complex Documents

LESSON SKILL MATRIX

In this lesson, you will learn the following skills:

Folding Text	Adding a Cover Page
Sorting Sections	Viewing Hidden Characters
Building an Outline with Headings	Using Page and Section Breaks
Managing Master Documents and Subdocuments	Adding Cross-References
Adding Captions to Images	Adding and Editing Footnotes and Endnotes
Using Fields	Building a Table of Contents
Hiding and Showing Field Codes	Building a Table of Figures
Editing Document Properties	

KEY TERMS

- Subheading
- Caption
- Table of Figures
- Field code
- Document Properties
- Cover Page
- Date/Time Field
- Page Break
- Section Break
- Hidden Characters
- Cross-Reference
- Footnote
- Endnote
- invisible Field

The Contoso School's annual course catalog is a 200-page collection of tabular data, structured text, hundreds of cross-references, thousands of index items, and a 10-page, three-level table of contents, and the same source files generate the Web and print editions. That kind of complexity is only manageable with the tools discussed in this lesson: Word's wide array of features designed for keeping long, densely interlinked documents under control, from planning to printing.

SOFTWARE ORIENTATION

In this lesson you will discover how to effectively organize table of contents, cross references, fields, captions, and other items to make it easier to work with longer, more complex documents.

Figure 4-1

Commands and controls for creating a table of contents

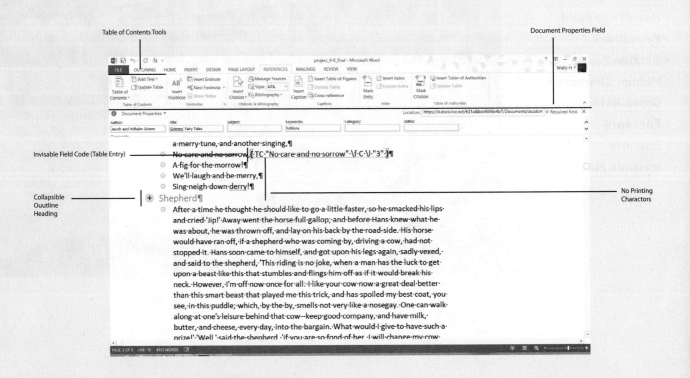

STARTING UP

In this lesson, you'll work with several files from the Word04lessons folder. Make sure that you have loaded the OfficeLessons folder onto your computer.

DOCUMENTS ARE DATA

In this lesson, you'll work on a short but complex document with a variety of endnotes, figures, fields, captions, hyperlinks, and cross-references, a cover page, a table of figures, and a table of contents. While each of these document elements is a useful tool in itself, the goal of the lesson isn't to master any one editing technique or feature. Rather, it's to make a transition from thinking about your .docx file as a block of text on a page with stuff stuck to its edges, to thinking of it as a complex program for generating output that looks like a block of text on a page.

The features discussed in this lesson hook into the structure of your Word document; tools such as headings, styles, and fields blur the line between text and data. The advantage of digital publishing tools over pen-and-paper is the ability to manipulate data programmatically; the closer you get to the software itself, the more power you have over your data. In previous lessons, we've mostly worked with abstractions that resemble physical tools: pages, typefaces, pictures, even backstage. The current lesson is the closest we'll get to thinking about your document data the way Word itself does.

Our task for this lesson is to reformat an informal college class handout as a departmental whitepaper. To that end, you'll add a variety of standard document features: tables of contents and figures, cross-references, document metadata, cover page, and more.

Take a little time before proceeding to preview the lesson file for this exercise.

HEADINGS: LOGICAL DOCUMENT DIVISIONS

As mentioned before, the default behavior in Word 2013 is to treat the built-in Heading styles as special: Word assumes that each heading signifies the beginning of a new section of the document, and uses this assumption to support some best practices for writing and editing. If you use the built-in Heading styles, you can take advantage of a number of tools available in Word to streamline your workflow.

Text folding

Bottom Line

One simple technique for cleanly arranging the content in your workspace is to fold a portion of your document into its heading. In every View mode except Draft, when you mouse over a heading, a triangular handle appears. Clicking the handle temporarily hides all text, images, and other objects between that heading and the next heading of equal level.

STEP BY STEP **Text folding**

1   Open **word04a.docx** found in the Word04lessons folder. Choose File > Save As and navigate to the Word04lessons folder. Name the file **word04a_work** and click Save.

2   Mouse over and click the handle to collapse the first three **subheadings**: Persuasive Strategies, A Note About Cynicism, and The Importance of a Good Title. Figure 4-2 shows the result of this operation.

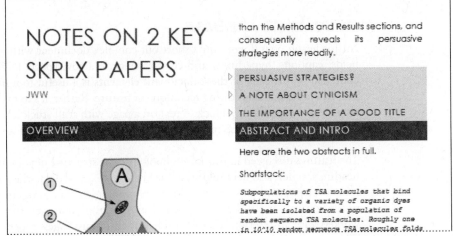

Image used under Creative Commons license, contributor: Dake

3   Mouse over and click to collapse the first top-level heading, Overview.

As you can see, only the Overview heading remains: Word works forward from the heading and stashes everything it finds until it reaches the next Heading 1 text, Abstract and Intro.

4   Mouse over and click the same triangle on the left of the heading to expand the Overview section, and then expand the three collapsed subheadings.

This technique doesn't just clear your workspace: it encourages you to think of your document in terms of high-level organizational units (sections and subsections). In fact, if you triple-click to select a collapsed heading and then Cut it (Ctrl+X), you'll actually cut its entire section, enabling you to move a huge block of laid-out text and images without having to do multiple pages of click-and-drag to select.

Collapsing a section is like grouping multiple objects in a page without changing the data; it just presents it to you in a much more useful way. Because Word is particularly attentive to headings, thinking of a section as a group of objects opens up new possibilities.

Sorting sections

Here's an example of using the programmatic tools available in Word for manipulating document data: you can alphabetize all the sections of your document. For example, if you were working on an encyclopedia, you could give each entry its own heading, and then use the Sort feature in Word to organize the headings from A to Z.

STEP BY STEP   **Sorting sections alphabetically**

1   Open **word04a.docx**. Press Ctrl+A to select the entire contents of your file.

2   Click Home > Paragraph > Sort to bring up a page of options (see Figure 4-3). Select Sort by > Headings from the first drop-down menu, and then click OK.

Figure 4-3

Word's Sort Options screen.

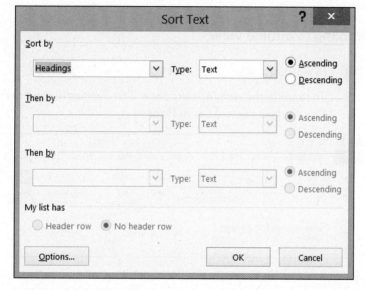

Word automatically rearranges the sections of your document so that it opens with Abstract and Intro instead of Overview. Word won't organize subsections within each section, however; to do so you'll have to switch to Outline View, select the subsections you want to sort, and then click Sort.

3   Press Ctrl+Z, or click Undo in the Quick Access Toolbar, to return to the original section ordering.

4   Choose File > Close to close this document. Do not save your work.

BUILDING AN OUTLINE WITH HEADINGS

In Lesson 2 you saw how the Navigation pane in Word integrates the built-in heading styles; now we'll look quickly at Outline View. Word doesn't provide a full-featured outliner like OmniOutliner or Microsoft OneNote, but the ability to outline and lay out text in the same application makes for a streamlined writing process.

Outline view

Bottom Line

Outline View is something of a legacy option in Word 2013; for most users, collapsible headings and the mini outline in the Navigation pane will provide all the outline-like functionality they need. That said, it's still quite useful for anyone who wants to rapidly build a document skeleton, and then go straight to drafting in the same app. We'll make a quick change to our SKRLX paper in Outline View to get a feel for its usefulness.

STEP BY STEP   **Working in outline view**

1   In **word04a_work.docx**, click View > Views > Outline.

2   To simplify the view, deselect Show Text Formatting and make sure that Show First Line Only is selected , as in Figure 4-4.

Figure 4-4

Make sure Show Text Formatting is deselected and Show First Line Only is selected.

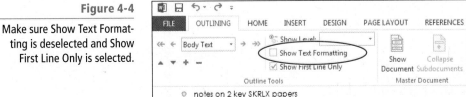

This view is just like any other outline: each level of subheading/subsection is indented slightly from the one above it. For example, and as shown in this exercise file, the Overview section begins with some body text (I'll focus…), which is then followed by three Heading 2 subsections before reaching the next Heading 1 (Abstract and intro). To keep Outline View simple, Word doesn't show our images, but rather a big, potentially confusing bit of whitespace. See Figure 4-5.

Figure 4-5

Outline View is a stripped-down, purely functional angle on your data.

○ I'll focus here on the construction ...
  ⊕ persuasive strategies?
    ○ Journal papers are read by ...
  ⊕ A note about cynicism|
    ○ I do not mean to imply ...
  ⊕ The importance of a good title
    ○ Check it: the Dirk paper1 ...
    ○ Again, this is partly a matter ...

3   Scroll to the top of the document and click the + next to *persuasive strategies?*

Both the subheading and its section text (only a few words of which are visible) are highlighted. The outline is designed to make large-scale changes, like moving this subsection, as easy as possible. Let's switch the order of the selected section and the one following.

4 Drag *persuasive strategies?* to a spot directly above *The importance of a good title.* All three subsections should be vertically aligned as in Figure 4-6, indicating that they have the same heading level.

Figure 4-6

These three subsections have the same outline level.

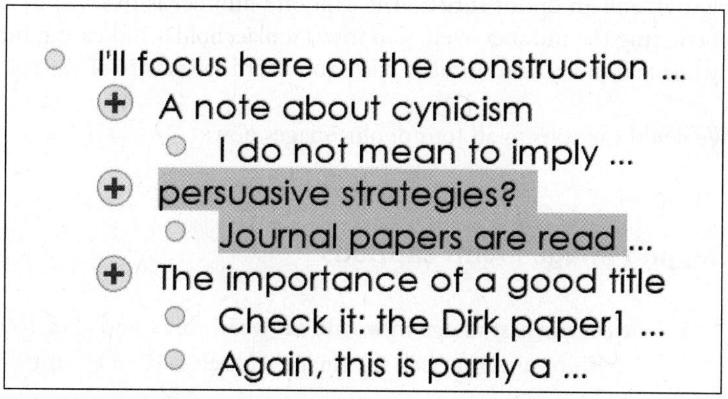

> ○ I'll focus here on the construction ...
>   ⊕ A note about cynicism
>   ○ I do not mean to imply ...
>   ⊕ persuasive strategies?
>   ○ Journal papers are read ...
>   ⊕ The importance of a good title
>   ○ Check it: the Dirk paper1 ...
>   ○ Again, this is partly a ...

5 Finally, select the Overview entry at the top of the document, and then click Outlining > Outline Tools > Collapse (or double-click the + next to Overview).

Just as in Print Layout Mode, you can collapse and expand headings to reduce visual clutter. The Outlining > Show Level command takes this minimalism a step further, for example, by letting you work only with specific text levels: Heading 1 only (level 1), Headings 1-3 (level 3), or all heading and body text (All Levels).

At this point, we've got the basic structure we want.

6 Click Close Outline View to return to Print Layout Mode and press Ctrl+S to save your work.

CAPTIONS

Word 2013 provides special tools to pair **captions** with images; since a caption will never travel alone, it makes sense to treat it as an extension of the image itself. This approach lets you reposition your images and alter your document layout without needing to manually group image and caption every time.

Because Word knows which text pieces are captions, it always has access to an internal listing of paired images and captions, which makes it easy to generate cross-references or a **Table of Figures** (for example, for a scholarly book or technical paper). We'll add captions to our images now and style them; at the end of this lesson we'll add a new subsection to our document with a Table of Figures

Tagging images with captions

You can think of captions as tags for objects (such as images and tables). A caption consists of a unique numerical identifier (automatically generated by Word), an optional label (for example, Figure), and an optional title. The caption's number is inserted as a field; in other words, instead of entering the number itself, you insert a placeholder indicating increase the number of captions by one and insert that number here, and Word takes care of the rest.

We'll add captions to all four of our images now:

STEP BY STEP   **Tagging images with captions**

1   Select the first image in **word04a_work.docx** and click References > Captions > Insert Caption, or right-click the image and select Insert Caption.

2   Set the caption to Figure 1: Neurons and click OK.

3   Click the resulting caption and set its paragraph alignment to Center (Ctrl+E) , as in Figure 4-7.

Figure 4-7

Word formats image captions using the built-in Caption style.

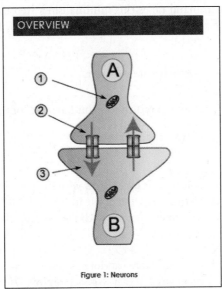

Figure 1: Neurons

Image used under Creative Commons license, contributor: Dake

You can customize Word's handling of captions in the Insert Caption window: the Numbering screen lets you switch from Arabic to Roman numerals, and the Label drop-down menu and New Label button let you switch the word *Field* to another label of your choice. Because there are no other captions in the document, Word assigns this image the number 1.

The Caption style isn't in the Styles gallery by default; it appears when editing a piece of text that uses that style.

Take Note   Captions without numbers- If you don't want figure numbers in your captions, you can add a caption by inserting a text box below your image and formatting the caption text with the Caption style (or any style you want); there's no built-in command to insert a numberless caption.

Let's add captions to our remaining three images, keeping the default label and centering each caption as we go.

Adding captions

1   Insert the caption Figure 2: Macromolecule beneath the second image and center the caption.

2   Insert the caption Figure 3: Knotty Shape beneath the third image and center the caption.

3   Insert the caption Figure 4: No Big Deal beneath the final image and center the caption.

4   Choose File > Save to save your work.

WORKING WITH FIELDS

Bottom Line

Unless you're doing a mail merge (for example, using a database to generate a hundred personalized form letters) you almost certainly won't have to think about how fields (**field codes**) work in Word. But Word uses fields extensively, whether inserting a page number or table of contents, or updating your Document Properties, and the more complex your document, the more useful it is to know what the software is doing behind the scenes.

Viewing field codes

At this point, you've encountered fields in Word several times. A field is just a placeholder for data that can be altered programmatically. The most oft-used field is the page number: the Insert Page Number command tells Word to calculate which page this field appears on, and insert that number in this spot. Word uses field codes to auto-number captions in the current document.

Viewing field codes

1   Click the 1 in *Figure 1: Neurons*. Instead of placing the cursor as usual, Word selects the figure number, indicating that it's a field rather than a regular character.

2   Right-click the 1, and select Toggle Field Codes from the pop-up menu. Figure 4-8 shows the resulting field code display.

Figure 4-8

Field codes are Word's internal representation of your data.

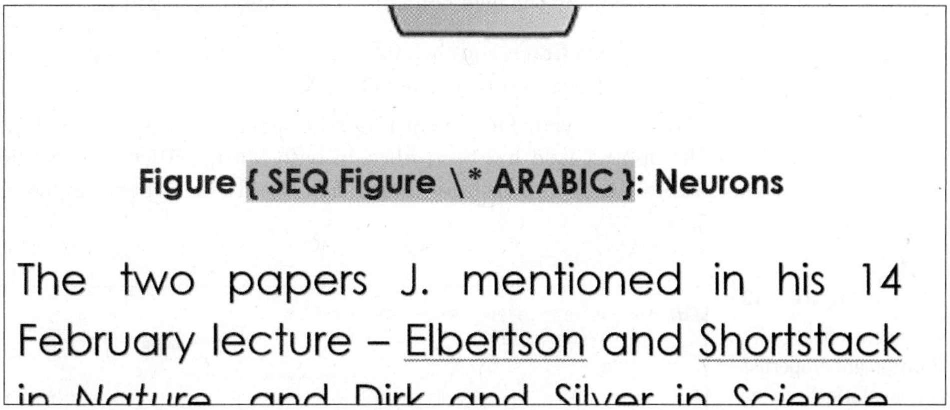

Figure { SEQ Figure * ARABIC }: Neurons

The two papers J. mentioned in his 14 February lecture – Elbertson and Shortstack in Nature and Dirk and Silver in Science

Image used under Creative Commons license, contributor: Dake

The SEQ Figure * ARABIC text is Word's internal code to generate the figure number: it adds an entry to a numerical sequence called *Figure*, and renders the entry as an Arabic numeral. Word uses the same kind of internal counter to number footnotes, pages, and bulleted list entries, but masks its computation with user-friendly abstraction: you look at SEQ Figure * ARABIC and see *1*, a number you can actually use.

3   Right-click the field code and toggle it off to reveal Figure 1.

Setting and accessing document properties

You can also use fields to access your **Document Properties** (or *metadata*), which are viewed through the File > Info command. For instance, if the author's name needs to appear throughout the document, you can insert an Author field anywhere the name should appear; that way the document's writer (or editor) need only type (or change) the document's Author value once, and Word will automatically update every Author field with the corresponding name.

First we'll set the Author and Title properties for the document.

STEP BY STEP   **Setting and accessing documents properties**

1   With **word04a_work.docx** open, click File > Info > Properties, and select Show Document Panel from the drop-down menu.

2   In the Author entry field (see Figure 4-9), type your name. In the title entry field, type **SKRLX notes**.

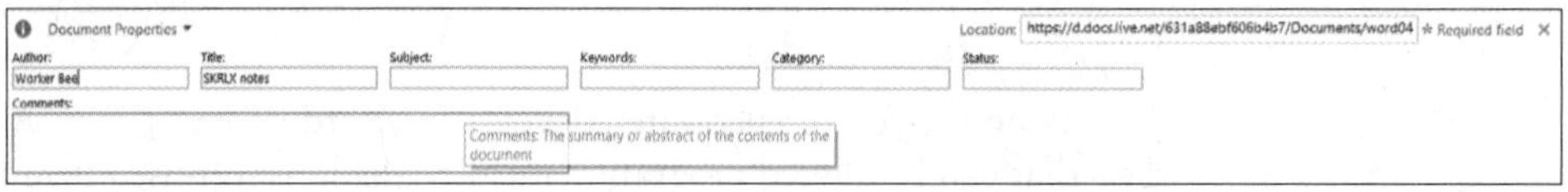

Figure 4-9

Editing Properties (metadata) using the Document Panel.

Now scroll to the top of the document. Currently, we have entered the title manually (Notes on 2 Key SKRLX Papers) and author (JWW) listings; we'll update them to use fields instead. This is a common enough task that Word 2013 provides a tool for it in the Insert tab. We'll also insert a subtitle in between.

3   Triple-click the current manually-entered title. Then click Insert > Text > Quick Parts > Document Property > Title.

4   Triple-click the second line, JWW, and then click Insert > Text > Explore Quick Parts > Document Property > Subject. Word inserts a [Subject] field, not yet filled in.

5   In the [Subject] field, type **Spring 2013**. Then press the right arrow key to switch from editing the field contents to working on the page.

6   Press Enter, and then Click Insert > Text > Quick Parts > Document Property > Author. Apply the Strong style to this line.

Now look at your Document Properties panel still displayed below the Ribbon (see Figure 4-10). The Subject field has been filled in with Spring 2013; you've edited your file's Properties from within the document itself. In general, Word's fields both display data and allow you to edit that data.

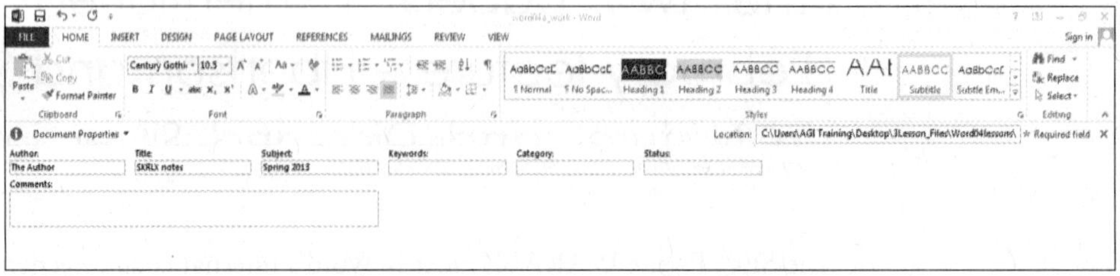

Figure 4-10

The document's field codes and Document Properties panel are two interfaces to the same metadata.

7   Close your Document Panel and then Save your document.

After setting document properties, we can build a cover page and automatically populate it with data.

ADDING A COVER PAGE

In Word 2013, a **cover page** is a bundle of especially-formatted text, fields, and images inserted at the front of your document. When you use the Insert > Cover Page command, Word inserts a page full of text/fields/graphics, assigns it page number zero (to keep the first page of the document proper as page 1), inserts a page break to avoid flowing text between the cover and the document itself, and toggles an option to use a separate header and footer for the cover, which you can see by double-clicking your document's header area.

Ideally, you won't notice this background work; you'll just insert the cover page and continue working on your document, with headers and page numbers and pagination intact. But it's good to know exactly what Word is doing, to avoid surprises and troubleshoot if needed.

STEP BY STEP   **Adding a cover page**

1   With **word04a_work** still open, click Insert > Pages > Cover Page > Whisp.

2   Click the [Date] field on the cover, click the arrow to the right of the text field, and in the drop-down menu select Today.

figure 4-11

When you select a date using the calendar input, it's displayed in the Date field.

Images and templates used with permission of Microsoft

Dates are a different type of field: instead of raw text, Word inserts a **Date/Time field** in MM/DD/YYYY format , as in Figure 4-11. If you prefer a different format, you can easily make a change:

3   Click the label above the field to select the placeholder (the field itself) rather than its contents.

4   Click Insert > Text > Insert Date & Time. In the options screen, choose the style format 22 January 2013 and click OK.

5   At the bottom of the cover page, enter ABC Company in the [Company Name] field.

6   Choose File > Save or press Ctrl+S to save your work.

PAGE AND SECTION BREAKS

In the previous section, we mentioned that Word inserts a **page break** after the cover page to keep the document text from starting before the second page of the file. Page breaks work much like carriage returns, but instead of moving the cursor to the next line, they move it to the next page of the file. A **section break** is a more complicated play on the same basic idea.

Seeing breaks and other hidden characters

To see the page break on your cover page, scroll to the top of the handout document and click Home > Paragraph > Show/Hide ¶ (or press Ctrl+*). As in Figure 4-12, you'll see paragraph marks (meaning new line) and a line marked Page Break.

Figure 4-12

Images and templates used with permission of Microsoft

Viewing **hidden character**s helps with precise layout tasks. The layout of our cover page is interesting: the title, date, and author/company info are laid out as text boxes, which float above the page, separate from the text. The only actual inline text is the dotted burgundy line at the top of the page. After that is a Page Break, meaning any subsequent text fills in starting on the second page; the floating elements on the cover page are treated more like images than text, and can be placed anywhere on the first page.

Section breaks

Bottom Line

We've been using the word section informally in these lessons, but Word 2013 does have a specific feature called the Section Break, which is worth mentioning, though we don't use Sections in our handout. The purpose of Sections in Word 2013 is to allow you to vary formatting within your document: for instance, you could lay out a scholarly paper with a single-column title and abstract, and then switch to two-column layout for the article text (or do a wide newspaper headline the same way).

Alternatively, you could strip out your document's header just for an 8-page section presenting raw data (by deselecting the Link to Previous option in the Header Design tab); place a decorative border around one section, or switch to a new paper size/orientation; or lay out front matter (Intro, Foreword, Preface, and so on) with Roman page numbers and distinct page dressing. You could even instruct your printer to switch to a different paper source, for example, to insert a sales flyer on purple cardstock into your newsletter. In short, Section Breaks are incredibly powerful tools.

They're also very simple: you insert a Section Break with the Page Layout > Page Setup > Breaks tool; any formatting changes you make will apply only to the current section. Taking out the break is simple: click to show hidden characters, and then delete the break as you would any other character.

Take Note

When you delete a section break, the two sections are combined into one, and the formatting of the latter section is used; in other words, if Sections 5 and 6 of a document are separated by a break, and you delete the break, the new section that results will absorb the formatting of Section 6 only.

Try experimenting with inserting Section Breaks in your handout to see the flexibility they can provide; just remember to save the document before you add any sections.

CROSS-REFERENCES

You'll recall that the Insert Caption command is found in the References tab because only specialized documents, such as scholarly papers or technical documentation, tend to make use of image captions. There's a deeper logic at work too: when you add a caption to an image, Word provides hooks to refer to that image or caption using fields; captions are really just labels for referring to images. We'll add a couple of references to see how they work.

STEP BY STEP   **Inserting a cross-reference**

1. Scroll to page 2, to the section *A note about cynicism*. Place the cursor in the middle of the paragraph between the word *decisions* and the comma following it.

2. Insert a space and then the following parenthetical: (consider the outcome in).

3. Now place the cursor before the closing parenthesis, and click References > Captions > Cross-reference.

The Cross-reference dialog box pops up; here you can select the target of your reference and customize its appearance. Unlike most pop-up windows, this one stays open until you close it: clicking Insert really does insert the reference, but it doesn't close the window. (The idea is to make it easy to insert multiple references without reopening the dialog box.)

4. In the Cross-reference window (see Figure 4-13), choose Reference type: Figure, Insert reference to: Only label and number, deselect Insert as hyperlink, and select Figure 4: No Big Deal from the list below.

Figure 4-13

The Cross-reference dialog box.

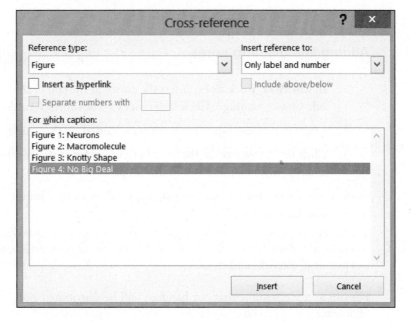

5. Click Insert, and then close the box.

You've now played an in-text reference to a figure located elsewhere in the document. It might seem like a lot of work to insert *See Figure 4*, but consider the case of a document with fifty images and a thousand references, each written by hand; now imagine taking one of those images out, re-numbering the other 49, and then rewriting a thousand references. This method is a lot less work.

FOOTNOTES AND ENDNOTES

Bottom Line

Many technical or scholarly documents include **footnotes** or **endnotes**. Word generates note numbers using fields, but you can customize the appearance and number scheme of your footnotes and endnotes.

Take Note

Sometimes you'll insert a footnote, but it won't appear on the same page; rather, it'll appear several pages later; this tends to happen with very long footnotes, or when a note appears close to the bottom of the text block. Not to worry: you can always travel back and forth between a reference and its associated note by double-clicking their number, and a note will never accidentally appear before its number pops up in the text.

The handout currently contains two footnotes; you should scroll through to see how Word lays them out. Pay special attention to the wrapping and placement: by default, the footnotes are laid out in two-column format, just as the main text, and Word places them beneath the left text column, even if the note number falls in the right-hand column.

In this part of the lesson, we'll make a couple of changes to the notes, but we won't work with Word's bibliography features, which are used by a very small subset of Word users. (If you need a more robust application to manage (shown in Figure 4-14) of scholarly citations, we recommend using an external citations manager such as EndNote; external citations managers are outside the scope of this lesson.)

Adding and deleting notes

We'll begin by adding and deleting notes, and altering their appearance in the text. Footnotes are simple to use, as long as you don't use special formatting.

STEP BY STEP   **Adding and deleting nores**

1   In **word04a_work.docx**, insert the cursor at the end of the handout's first sentence (… side-by-side reading.). Click References > Footnotes > Insert Footnote.

2   In the notes area, type **This work was funded by the Tortle Foundation**.

3   Click the **arrow** icon in the bottom right corner of the Footnotes group to bring up a window with Footnote and Endnote options.

4   Select **Columns: 1 column**, and the symbols in the Number format drop-down. Press **Enter**.

The footnotes revert to a less awkward one-column format, and Word automatically renumbers when we add a new Note 1; finally, the useful note numbers are replaced by visually appealing, but less practical, asterisks and crosses.

For this exercise, assume that our handout will be distributed along with copies of the Dirk and Shortstack papers, so no citations are needed; let's cut the second footnote. To do so, simply delete the note number from the text block.

5   Click and drag to select the second footnote, marked with a cross located in the The Importance of a Good Title section. Delete the note marking; the note text, at the bottom of the page, disappears along with the mark.

Endnotes, briefly

Endnotes work much like footnotes, only Word typesets them at the end of the text rather than the bottom of each page. Word can set your endnotes at the end of each section (as in a textbook or anthology) or in one large listing at the end of your entire document. To work with endnotes rather than footnotes, use the Insert Endnote command in the References tab, and set your layout options by clicking the dialog box icon in the lower right corner of the Footnotes group.

ADDING A TABLE OF CONTENTS

We'll finish this lesson with two consequential mouse clicks: one to generate a Table of Contents (TOC) and one to produce a Table of Figures. The TOC feature in Word makes use of the built-in Heading style hierarchy by default, and mirrors the document structure seen in Outline View, but it offers a high degree of flexibility as well: with a few simple tweaks you could automatically generate a Table of Quotations and Captions, or even a list of First Appearances of Boldfaced Terms.

From headings to table of contents

Bottom Line

The Table of Contents tools are found in the References tab. Each group in the References tab provides tools to generate an analogous table of some resource: the Bibliography, Table of Figures, Index, and Table of Authorities (which lists legal citations): each collect, sort, and nicely lay out every instance of one or more styles in your document. The Table of Figures tool grabs captions; the Index alphabetizes the words you mark as Index Entries, and so on.

By default, the TOC feature in Word builds an outline, with Heading 1 text at the top level, then Heading 2, and so on; just as the Outline View and Navigation pane. Standard-issue TOCs are a single click away.

STEP BY STEP   **Adding and formatting a table of contents**

1 On page 2 of **word04a_work.docx** place the cursor to the right of your name (the Author field). If the field handle (Author) appears, indicating that you're editing the field, press the right arrow to shift focus out of the field.

2 Press Return to move to a new line.

3 Click References > Table of Contents > Table of Contents. From the drop-down gallery, choose Automatic Table 1.

4   Click the new **Contents** heading, and then open **Home > Styles Gallery** (shown in Figure 4-14) to see that a new Style (TOC Heading) has been added.

Figure 4-14

The TOC uses several special-purpose Styles.

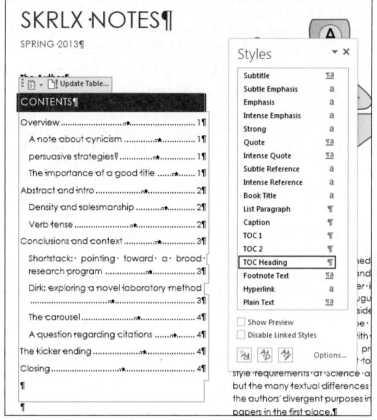

Image used under Creative Commons license, contributor: Dake

A grey handle appears around the entire Table of Contents, indicating that it's a large, complex field. This is how Word visually distinguishes between data you've entered manually, such as text, and data that's programmatically generated, such as the Date field on the cover or the content of the TOC.

Word formats the TOC using a variety of TOC-related Styles, which you can see by opening the Styles pane (Alt+Ctrl+Shift+S). You can change the look of the TOC by modifying those Styles, just as with any other aspect of your document. (See below, "Building a Custom TOC.") As you can see, Word uses your current Theme, Style Set, and page formatting to slot the TOC seamlessly into your document.

A couple of things to note about the Table: First of all, because the text isn't styled in all caps (unlike the article's headings), you can see that many section titles use nonstandard capitalization. You can fix it, but it's irrelevant to this lesson. Second, the field handle includes an Update Table... button: if you click it, you'll bring up a dialog box with options to update the entire TOC (if you've added or deleted headings) or just the page numbers (if you've only changed section length). If you want to keep your TOC up to date, you'll need to periodically refresh it using that button.

If you Ctrl+click one of the TOC entries, you'll jump to that spot in the document; the TOC's entries act as hyperlinks, as in a webpage.

Finally, the TOC field has a drop-down menu icon, which lets you choose from a built-in TOC style or create a Manual Table. The latter is just a skeleton for making and maintaining a TOC by hand; unless you have very specific formatting needs, we do not recommend using this feature.

Building a custom table of contents

Word can restyle an existing TOC, but to set new options, such as how many heading levels to include, you'll need to make a new TOC. We will insert a nonstandard Table of Contents and set its parameters in the Table of Contents dialog.

STEP BY STEP   **Building a custom table of contents**

1   Remove Table of Contents on the TOC field menu, or just select the TOC and insert a new one in its place.

2   Click References > Table of Contents > Custom Table of Contents. A dialog box appears with custom options as shown in Figure 4-15.

Figure 4-15

The Custom Table of Contents dialog box.

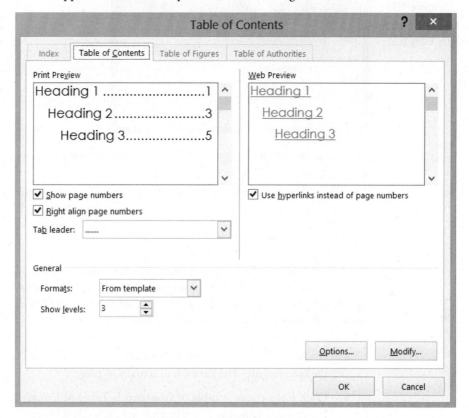

3   Try out as many options as you'd like.

The Web Preview shows how the TOC will be styled if you save your .docx file as an HTML webpage; an HTML Table of Contents without hyperlinks isn't much use, so it's wise to leave the *Use hyperlinks* option checked.

The Modify button lets you modify TOC styles just like paragraph styles.

The Options button enables detailed customization: instead of Word's built-in heading hierarchy, you can build your TOC using any other paragraph styles. Only a small fraction of users will ever need to do so; consult the online help at *office.microsoft.com* for instructions.

Using table fields in your TOC

Finally, the Table Entry fields option lets you add arbitrary text pieces in your TOC by inserting **invisible fields** into your document. We'll add one such field, and then rebuild our TOC.

STEP BY STEP   **Marking text for the TOC**

1   Scroll to the Density and Salesmanship section of the document, and highlight the words *culture does matter*.

2   Press Alt+Shift+O to mark the selected text as a TOC entry. The resulting dialog box is shown in Figure 4-16.

Figure 4-16

Marking text for the TOC with an invisible Table Entry field.

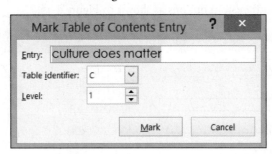

3   In the text field, type handwaving, select 3 from the Level drop-down menu, click Mark, and then click Close.

The Table Identifier option is important only if you use multiple TOCs in a single document, for example, one for chapter headings, another for quotations, a third for dictionary entries, and so on. If so, assign each TOC an identifier and use it to specify which Table your entries will be added to.

Note that Word has turned Show Hidden Characters on; this lets you see the invisible Table Entry code you just entered: {TC "handwaving" \f C \l "3"}. You can edit this text directly, but due to its odd syntax, it's easy to break; to find out what the switches (\f, \l) mean, consult Microsoft's extensive documentation at *office.microsoft.com*.

4   Scroll to the Table of Contents and choose Remove TOC from the drop-down menu on the field handle. The cursor will remain in place.

5   Click References > Table of Contents > Table of Contents > Custom Table of Contents. Make sure Show levels is set to 3. Click Options and make sure Table Entry Fields is selected.

6   Click OK, and then click OK again.

Your new TOC includes an entry marked *handwaving*; this is the only level 3 entry in the whole Table. You can build an entire TOC out of text pieces marked in this labor-intensive fashion, as long as you spend some time up front deciding on a tagging hierarchy; using the built-in heading/outlining tools will save you a lot of work.

ADDING A TABLE OF FIGURES

We've already tagged all our images with captions; now we'll finish our lesson by building a Table of Figures, which lists your document's figures with optional numbers. The process is much the same as adding a TOC:

STEP BY STEP **Adding a table of figures**

1   Place the cursor on the line below the TOC. Select the Heading 1 style and type Table of Figures.

2   Click References > Captions > Insert Table of Figures.

3   Deselect Include label and number. Click OK. The resulting Table of Figures is shown in Figure 4-17.

Figure 4-17

Table of Contents and Table of Figures with hidden characters displayed.

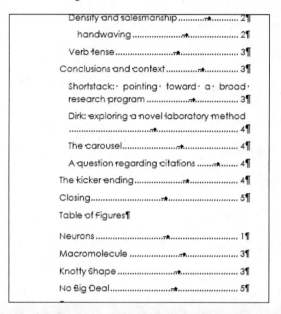

The options for the Table of Figures are almost the same as for the Table of Contents. You can experiment with the Caption label and Include label and number options to vary the appearance of the Table; for example, cutting out the Figure # prefix is important when space and word count are at a premium.

4   Place the cursor directly below the Table of Figures and click Page Layout > Page Setup > Breaks > Column to start the text fresh in the right-hand column.

5   Finally, right-click the Table of Contents, choose Update Field (F9), select Update entire table, and then click OK.

That brings our TOC up-to-date with the latest changes (including a new heading), and brings our lesson to a close.

6   Choose File > Save or press Ctrl+S to save your work. Close this document.

What you learned in this lesson:

- Folding Text

- Sorting Sections

- Building an Outline with Headings

- Managing Master Documents and Subdocuments

- Adding Captions to Images

- Using Fields

- Hiding and Showing Field Codes

- Editing Document Properties

- Adding a Cover Page

- Viewing Hidden Characters

- Using Page and Section Breaks

- Adding Cross-References

- Adding and Editing Footnotes and Endnotes

- Building a Table of Contents

- Building a Table of Figures

Knowledge Assessment

Fill in the Blanks

Complete the following sentences by writing the correct word or words in the blanks provided.

1. The prefix of a caption, like "Figure" or "Equation," is known as its _____.

2. Section 2, with subsections 2.1 and 2.2, is folded in to save space during editing. The next visible section or subsection is _____.

3. To change the order of multiple subsections of a document, switch to _____ view.

4. To quickly insert the title field of a document (using a field code), use the _____ command.

5. Word provides a collection of pre-formatted cover pages, each tied to a specific document _____.

6. By default, page and section breaks are _____ like carriage returns and tabs.

7. Footnotes have _____ numerals by default, but _____ numerals are available from the Footnote and Endnote options dialog.

8. To insert invisible bookmarks into a document and its TOC, use the _____ field tool.

9. Endnotes are automatically inserted at the end of each _____ by default.

10. Master documents and subdocuments are edited in the _____ view.

Matching

Match the document feature to its description.

1. page break
2. section break
3. hidden character
4. footnote
5. endnote
6. caption
7. label
8. field code
9. Table of Figures
10. subdocumenta. collects image captions/labels for quick reference by reader

a. collects image captions or labels for quick reference by the reader
b. portion of a master document, in a separate file
c. identifying or explanatory text attached to an image
d. typeset at bottom of page on which cite appears
e. typesets subsequent content on next page
f. dynamically inserts content into document, doesn't appear in print itself
g. in-text note or cite typeset at bottom of document or section
h. splits document into independently-formatted subparts
i. for instance, a paragraph break or tab, usually invisible to reader
j. optional category prefix for caption (e.g., Figure or Table)

Competency Assessment

Project 4-1: Simple Outlining

1. Open the project file **grimm-source**.
2. Save your document as **project_4-1_outline**.
3. Switch to Outline View. Enable Outline Tools > Show First Line Only.
4. Double click the plus icon next to each section to collapse it into its heading.
5. Expand "Hans in Luck."
6. Before the "After a time he thought" line, insert a new line, Heading 2 (one indent level beyond "Hans in Luck," which has the Heading 1 style), reading Shepherd.
7. Similarly, insert Heading 2 Setting Out right beneath the title "Hans in Luck," Goose before the line "The next man he met was a countryman…," Grinder before the line "As he came to the next village," and Stone after the line "Then who so blythe."

8. Drag the Stone heading down one line, to just above "Hans took the stone."

Feel free to experiment with selecting, reordering, and styling the sections in Outline View.

9. Click Close Outline View.

10. Choose File > Save and then File > Close.

Project 4-2: Document Properties

1. Open the project file 4-2-source. Save your document as project_4-2_document_properties.

2. Open the backstage area and select Info if it's not already selected.

3. In the Properties > Title line, click Add a Title and type Grimms' Fairy Tales.

4. From the Properties dropdown menu, select Show Document Panel.

5. Change the Document Panel's Author: field to Jacob and Wilhelm Grimm.

If prompted to turn AutoComplete on, dismiss the dialog.

6. Set the Keywords: value to folklore.

7. Close the Document Panel.

8. Add a blank line below the document's title line, and select Insert > Quick Parts > Document Property > Author.

9. Choose File > Save and then File > Close.

Proficiency Assessment

Project 4-3: Defining a Custom Field

1. Open the project file 4-3-source. Save your document as project_4-3_custom_field.

2. Click File > Info > Properties > Advanced Properties > Custom tab.

3. In the Name: box, type Edition. In the Value: box, type 1812. Click Add, then OK.

4. Return to the main document editing screen. Add a blank line below the title and place the cursor there.

5. Click Insert > Text > Quick Parts > Field...

6. Select Document Information from the Categories: dropdown, and DocProperty from the Field Names: list.

7. Select the Edition property from the Property: dropdown. Click OK.

8. After the newly-inserted edition date (1812), add a blank space and edition.

If you wish, alter the "edition" line to have no trailing space (Home > Line and Paragraph Spacing).

9. Choose File > Save and then File > Close.

Project 4-4: **Section Breaks and Headers/Footers**

1. Open the project file **4-4-source**. Save your document as **project_4-4_section_breaks**.

2. Insert Odd Page Section Breaks before The Travelling Musicians and Jorinda and Jorindel.

3. Open the document header on the first page and enable both Different First Page and Different Odd & Even Pages in the Header/Footer > Design tab.

   Note that only Section 1's first page will be unique – the other sections of the document will not have unique headers on their first pages.

4. Add the following headers:

   Section 1 Even Page Header: (centered) Hans in Luck

   All Sections, Odd Page Header: (centered) Grimm, {Edition field code} edition

   Section 2 Even Page Header: (centered) Jorinda and Jorindel

   Section 3 Even Page Header: (centered) The Travelling Musicians

   You will have to deselect Header/Footer > Design > Link to Previous for the Section 2 and 3 Even Page headers.

5. Add a centered page number to both the even- and odd-numbered pages (but not page 1), using Insert > Page Number > Bottom of Page > Plain Number 2.

6. Choose File > Save and then File > Close.

Mastery Assessment

Project 4-5: **Adding a Custom Table of Contents**

1. Open the project file **4-5-source**. Save your document as **project_4-5_toc**.

2. Select the first line of each song that appears in the document and tag it as a Table of Contents entry (see the section "Using Table Fields in Your TOC").

3. Below the author line at the top of the document, insert a Custom Table of contents with the Table Entry Fields option selected.

4. Now manually edit the field codes that generate the song entries, to remove the commas from their TOC lines (but not from the printed songs themselves, in the main text), and Update the TOC.

5. Choose File > Save and then File > Close.

Project 4-6: **Bringing It All Together**

1. Open the project file **4-6-source**. Save your document as **project_4-6_final**.

2. Add a cover page including Title, Author, and Edition information.

3. Delete and redo the TOC without the song listings.

4. Add a second table at the end of the document, called Songs, which catalogs only the four song lines you tagged.

5. Select an appropriate document theme to go with your cover page.

6. Save your work and close Word.

5 Working with Tables

LESSON SKILL MATRIX

In this lesson, you will learn the following skills:

Insert and Navigate Tables	Sort Tabular Data
Split and Merge Cells	Use Table Styles
Integrate Tables into Paragraphs	Customize Cell and Table Borders
Position Text Within a Table	Resize Cells and Cell Content
Manipulate Columns and Rows	

KEY TERMS

- Row
- Column
- Heading
- Nested Table
- Table Style
- Select Table Handle
- Merge Cells
- Eraser tool
- Tabular Data
- Database
- Record
- Sort
- Table Style Options
- Tooltip
- Fill
- Border Painter
- AutoFit

Laying out the spring catalog for Northwind Traders's mail-order service means laying out 100 pages full of product descriptions, price lists, images, and other text. To keep this material straight, the designers rely extensively on tables, both for list data and for complex page layout. This lesson covers the somewhat complex behaviors of tables in Word 2013.

SOFTWARE ORIENTATION

Tables provide an easy way to organize and display groups of data. In this lesson you'll gain an understanding of ways you can use Microsoft Word to present, organize, format and style tables in your Microsoft Word documents.

Figure 5-1

Tables and table tools in a Microsoft Word document.

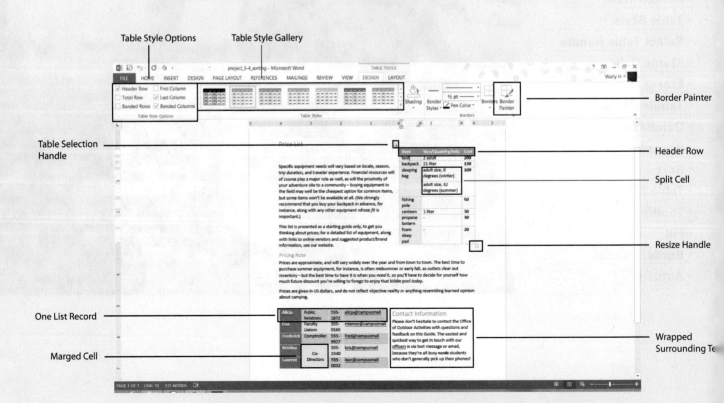

STARTING UP

You will work with files from the Word05lessons folder. Make sure that you have loaded the OfficeLessons folder onto your computer.

THE USES OF TABLES

A table in Word is a matrix of **rows** and **columns** with optional column and row **headings**. There are two kinds of tables you might use: invisible grids used to line up elements of a design (such as the implied grid of a newspaper page), and visible grids meant to highlight a collection of structured data, such as a list of phone numbers appearing in a report. Gridded layout is a popular topic in graphic design, particularly web design, where rendering a page in an ever-changing browser window presents a variety of interesting technical and aesthetic problems; but graphic design is beyond the scope of this book. In this lesson, we'll focus solely on tables that are meant to look like tables.

figure 5-2

Examples of Word's table formatting.

Table 1: Distances between offices, in miles

	Doogle	Frapple	TPC	ACME
Doogle	-	5	3	8
Frapple	5	-	22	7
TPIC	3	22	-	10
ACME	8	7	10	-

December

Sun	Mon	Tue	Wed	Thu	Fri	Sat
						1
2	3	4 concert	5 reception	6 recover	7	8
9	10	11	12	13 India...	14 ...	15 ...
16 ...	17 ...home	18	19	20	21	22
23	24	25	26	27	28	29
30	31					

What?	Where?
Art pencil	Pearl
Codfish	Star
Friendship	Internet
Hip hop	Luna
Keys	Ace
Orangina	Luna
Shirt	Coop
Textbook	Coop

TABLE BASICS

Bottom Line

Table are common elements in technical documents Like spreadsheets, tables consist of rectangular regions call cells, organized in rows and columns; indeed, Excel spreadsheets can be inserted into Word documents as tables. We'll create a few tables from scratch to practice maneuvering through them and making basic edits.

Inserting and navigating tables

A table is an object that can be placed, formatted, and moved just like any other object in Word 2013. But its internal dynamics make it a little more complicated than the average image or text box. We'll start with the commands to insert and navigate tables.

Inserting and navigating tables

1   Open Word 2013 and create a new blank document.

2   Choose File > Save As and navigate to the Word05lessons folder. Name the document **word05_work** and click Save.

3   Click Insert > Table. A drop-down grid appears. Drag your mouse over the grid until a 4 × 4 box is highlighted, and then click.

4   Place the cursor in one of the inner cells of the table and type This is a test of cell spacing. See how the cell stretches to fit?

5   Place the cursor in a different cell of the table. Insert a second 4 × 4 table inside the cell, as in Figure 5-3.

Figure 5-3

Live Preview lets you see the result of the Insert > Table command before you commit to adding the table.

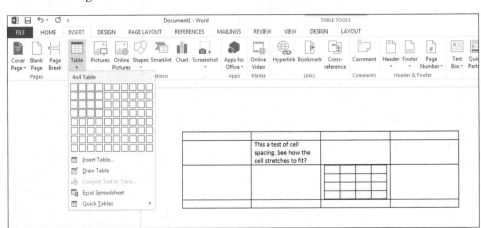

6   Use the arrow keys to move right/left and up/down within the tables; then click in the smaller table and use the Tab key (and Shift+Tab) to navigate instead. Note that pressing Tab in the bottom-right corner of the table adds another row at the bottom.

This is an important but subtle difference: the arrow keys are for traveling around a table, while Tab is assumed to be used for editing the table.

Split cells and table styles

Placing one table inside another is called nesting; if you insert a 3 × 3 table into a particular cell of a table, there will still be space within that cell but outside the nested table. You can create a similar structure by splitting one cell, which doesn't create a new table as such, just a more complex region within the outer table.

One key feature of a split cell, as opposed to a nested table, is that the contents of the split cell still inherit the formatting of the surrounding table. A **nested table** is formatted separately from the table where it's embedded, as the following steps will demonstrate.

STEP BY STEP   **Splitting cells and changing table styles**

1   Click one of the cells of your nested table.

2   Click Table Tools > Layout > Merge > Split Cells. Set both columns and rows to 4, and click OK. The entire split cell, subdivided now into a 4 × 4 matrix, will be selected.

3   Click Table Tools > Design and select Grid Table 5 Dark - Accent 5 from the Table Styles gallery.

As you can see in Figure 5-4, the **Table Style** is applied not just to the selected cells (within the split cell), but to the nested table; yet the outermost table, the one you originally inserted into the blank document, doesn't inherit this formatting.

Figure 5-4

Applying a Table Style to a nested table doesn't affect the outer table.

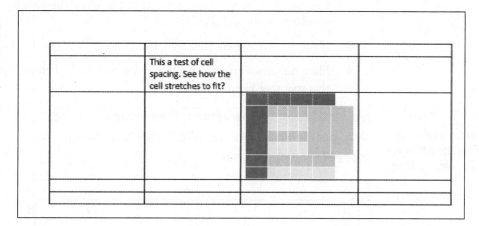

4   Finally, select the cell where you inserted text (This is a test...) and split the cell into a 3 × 3 matrix.

The text is pushed into the upper left cell of the 3 × 3 matrix: our first exposure to the interaction of table and text, which we'll explore in the next section.

5   Choose File > Save and then File > Close.

Working with text in and around tables

You can format text within a table just as you would in the wider space of your document. But the interaction between tables and text can be a little finicky. By default, a table placed with the Insert Table command sits in line with text, but by moving it on the page (or by placing text around it) you turn the table into a floating object, like an absolutely positioned image. The following steps will illustrate this change in behavior.

STEP BY STEP   Inserting a table within text

1   Open **word05a.docx** in your Word05lessons folder.

2   Choose File > Save As and navigate to the Word05lessons folder. Name the file **word05a_work** and click Save.

3   If you haven't already done so, select Home > Paragraph > Show Hidden Characters.

4   Place the cursor after the boldfaced sentence in the first paragraph. Insert a 4 × 4 table at that spot (See Figure 5-5).

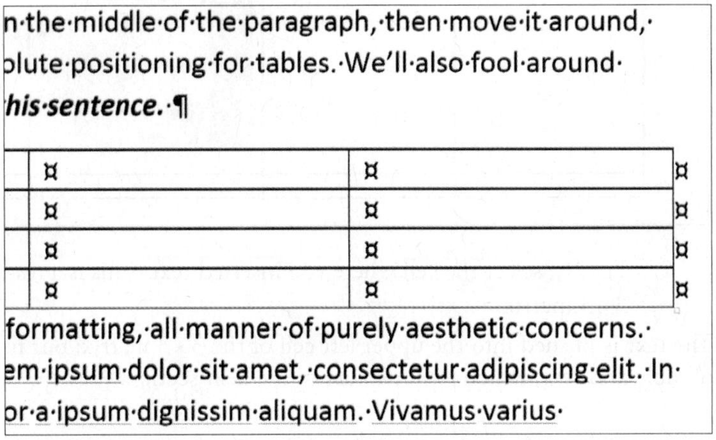

Figure 5-5

Inserting a table into a paragraph also adds a line break.

n·the·middle·of·the·paragraph,·then·move·it·around,· blute·positioning·for·tables.·We'll·also·fool·around· *his·sentence.·¶*

¤	¤	¤
¤	¤	¤
¤	¤	¤
¤	¤	¤

formatting,·all·manner·of·purely·aesthetic·concerns.· em·ipsum·dolor·sit·amet,·consectetur·adipiscing·elit.·In· or·a·ipsum·dignissim·aliquam.·Vivamus·varius·

5   Drag the lower-right handle on the table to resize it; make it as small as possible.

Resizing the table has no effect on word wrapping; it's in line with the text, and Word automatically leaves space below the table. But moving the table turns it into a floating object.

6 Select the table, either by mousing over it to reveal the **Select Table** handle in the upper left, or by clicking in one of the cells and then clicking Table Tools > Layout > Table > Select > Select Table. Drag it down and to the right, placing it in the center of the page, as in Figure 5-6.

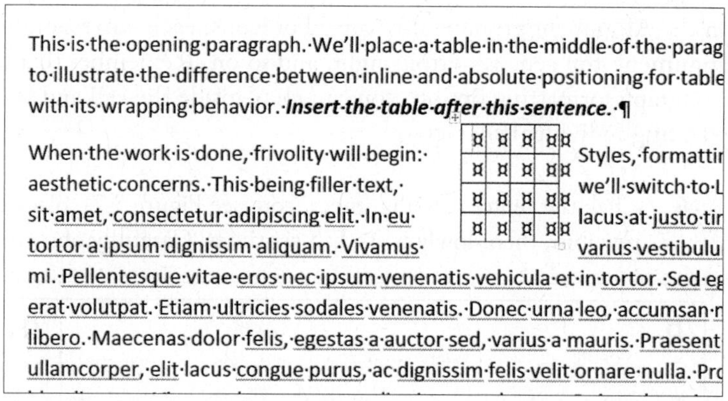

Figure 5-6

Once a table has been moved, Word applies absolute positioning to it, like a floating text box or image.

This·is·the·opening·paragraph.·We'll·place·a·table·in·the·middle·of·the·parag to·illustrate·the·difference·between·inline·and·absolute·positioning·for·table with·its·wrapping·behavior.·***Insert·the·table·after·this·sentence.·***¶

When·the·work·is·done,·frivolity·will·begin:·aesthetic·concerns.·This·being·filler·text,· sit·amet,·consectetur·adipiscing·elit.·In·eu· tortor·a·ipsum·dignissim·aliquam.·Vivamus· mi.·Pellentesque·vitae·eros·nec·ipsum·venenatis·vehicula·et·in·tortor.·Sed·e; erat·volutpat.·Etiam·ultricies·sodales·venenatis.·Donec·urna·leo,·accumsan·r libero.·Maecenas·dolor·felis,·egestas·a·auctor·sed,·varius·a·mauris.·Praesent ullamcorper,·elit·lacus·congue·purus,·ac·dignissim·felis·velit·ornare·nulla.·Pro

Styles,·formattir
we'll·switch·to·L
lacus·at·justo·tir
varius·vestibulu

Now that the table is a float, you can move it around the page much as you would any image or text box. To return it to inline layout, make a change in the Table Properties dialog:

STEP BY STEP   **Using the Table Properties dialog box**

1 Select the table, and then click Table Tools > Layout > Table > Properties.

2 In the dialog box, set Alignment to Left and Text Wrapping to None. Click OK.

Take Note   Why can't I freely move an in-line table ? Why do tables default to inline positioning and seem to resist absolute positioning? Think of it this way: a table squashes and stretches with its contents; it can be used as a container for other page elements; and it is part of the flow of text in the page in a way images and text boxes aren't. It can also add rows and columns, which would screw up line/paragraph spacing. Think of an inline table as part of the page itself, rather than an object on top of it. To freely position the table, open the Table Properties dialog and uncheck "Move with text" on the Positioning page.

Text alignment and merged cells

Bottom Line   After learning how to move a table in the page and move around inside it, we'll look at the tools Word has for altering a table's internal geography. You've seen how to split cells; it's easy to merge them as well, to create complex cell layouts. Merged cells are simply large cells made by joining smaller ones; they occupy multi-cell regions of tables.

STEP BY STEP   **Merging cells and aligning text**

1 Open **word05a_work.docx** if it is not already open and resize the table you inserted so that it's about as wide as the text block using the handles that appear in the corner of the table when selected.

2 Click within the upper left cell, and drag to the right to select the first three cells in the top row.

3 Click Table Tools > Layout > Merge > Merge Cells.

4   Do the same with the four cells in the bottom right corner of the table: click and drag to select, and then Merge Cells.

5   Place the cursor in the new large cell. Type **Centered Text**. Then open the Table Tools > Layout tab.

In the Alignment group is a 3×3 grid of icons, each corresponding to a different text alignment: top center, bottom right, and so on. Remember that text alignment is a paragraph formatting option; you can click inside the cell and set the text alignment without selecting individual characters.

6   Click the center text alignment icon (see Figure 5-7), place the cursor in the first cell in row four, then slowly press **Tab** six times. Carefully observe how the cursor moves.

Figure 5-7

Merged cells occupy a unique position: you can reach the merged cell by tabbing in from the fourth or fifth row.

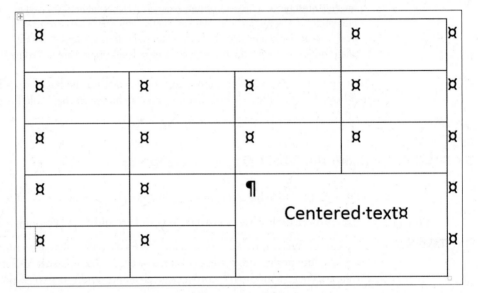

Remember that pressing Tab moves the cursor sequentially through the cells, left to right and top to bottom, until the last cell is reached, at which point Tab inserts a new row. (It doesn't insert a Tab character as it would in a normal paragraph.) Word assigns the newly merged cell the position Row 4, Column 3; as you press Tab repeatedly, the cursor moves along the bottom row, *back* through the merged cell, then on to a brand new row. When you turned the 2×2 region into one cell, Word created an entity that's a single column wide, but resides in two different rows.

Merging cells with the Eraser tool

Bottom Line

There's another way to merge cells: the **Eraser tool**, which eliminates cell borders unless it can't, in which case it simply renders them invisible.

STEP BY STEP	Merging cells with the eraser tool

1   Select the Eraser tool (Table Tools > Layout > Draw > Eraser).

2   Click and drag from the large merged cell upward into the cell directly above it on the left. The top border of the merged cell becomes dotted as in Figure 5-8, meaning it's now a non-printing (invisible) border.

Figure 5-8

The Eraser tool merges cells if possible, but it can't merge cells of different sizes, so it hides their shared border instead.

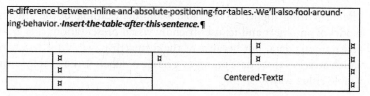

3   Now click and drag the eraser across the vertical line between the two cells above the Centered Text cell. These cells will merge and if they had content, it would be lost.

4   Finally, erase the dotted line between the two merged cells, creating a single empty cell the size of a 3 × 2 region. See Figure 5-9.

Figure 5-9

The Eraser tool knocks down the walls between table cells.

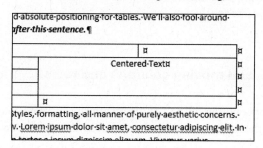

As you can see, you can't merge cells in a table unless their dimensions match; cells must merge horizontally to create a shared two-column southern border before they can merge vertically with the big cell below them.

5   Deselect the Table Eraser and choose File > Save or press Ctrl+S to save your changes.

PRESENTING AND SORTING TABULAR DATA

Bottom Line

The most common use for tables is for presenting **tabular data**. Word treats the contents of a table as a kind of miniature **database**; it will handle each row as a single **record**, for instance with columns corresponding to "fields" (in the database sense, not "field codes"), and can distinguish between records and column/row headings. Our current document contains a small table at the bottom of Page 1 that demonstrates these features: a list of fake chemical elements, along with (fake) Volume/Mass/Energy numbers for each.

The formatting applied to the table is another example of the difference between Word's internal model of an object and its user-friendly visual presentation: this is a 4 × 7 table with a mix of text and numeric data, but because of the formatting, we immediately read it as six records, each of which attaches three data points to a name or label. Word's table formatting tools let you approach a table either way.

Adding, deleting, and moving columns and rows

Bottom Line

Since you can't insert a single cell into the middle of a table without repositioning the columns and rows around it, Word provides hooks to let you manipulate tables by row and by column. We'll alter our chemical data in a handful of ways to see how these tools work: we'll reorder the columns, delete a record, and insert another.

STEP BY STEP   **Adding, deleting and moving columns and rows**

1   Click the upper border of the Volume column; the entire column is selected. (As you mouse over the top border, the pointer should change to a downward-pointing arrow.)

2   Click and drag the column heading to the right and place it in the space between the Mass and Energy columns. The new column order is: Mass, Volume, Energy.

3   Click inside the margin to the left of the Beryllium cell; the entire row is selected. Press Delete; the data in the row will vanish, but the empty cells will remain.

4   Press Ctrl+Z to Undo, restoring the Beryllium data. Then, with the row still highlighted, press Backspace. The row itself will vanish.

Word splits the functions of the Backspace and Delete keys to make a distinction, respectively, between altering the table itself (the size of the database) and altering the contents of a single record. The same behavior occurs when you select a single cell by triple-clicking inside it: you can Delete the data within the cell or Backspace to alter the table grid itself.

Now let's add a replacement record: you can squeeze a record into a table in a couple of ways.

5   Click the word Paramecium. Note that the Table Tools > Layout tab offers a number of icons to Insert Rows and Columns next to the selected cell.

6   Instead, mouse over a space just below and to the left of the Paramecium cell. A small icon with a plus sign appears, as in Figure 5-10.

7   Click the Add Row icon to add an empty row. The entire row is automatically selected; if you begin typing, Word will insert text into the first cell of the row. Type Wampum (press tab), 31 (press tab), 2 (press tab), 9 to populate the row.

Sorting data in a table

Bottom Line

As with a database, you can **sort** the entire contents of a table using one or more columns as keys; for instance, sorting a list of phone numbers by last name, and then first name. We'll sort our table by Energy value (lowest to highest), and then sort Volume from highest to lowest within that ordering.

STEP BY STEP   **Sorting data in a table**

1   Change the Energy value of the Frustrum record to 88.

2   Click anywhere in the table, and then click Table Tools > Layout > Data > Sort.

3   In the dialog box, Sort By: Energy (Ascending), and Then By: Volume (Descending). Click OK The resulting sorted table is shown in 5-11.

Figure 5-11

Sorting our chemical info; the sorted data.

	Mass	Volume	Energy
Wampum	31	2	9
Dilithium	1	9	12
Tristram	86	123	44
Adium	34	23	45
Frustrum	90	87	88
Paramecium	66	44	88

If you wanted to sort a single column of data without altering the entire table (in other words, if the table did not contain records as such, just discrete columns) you could do so by selecting the whole column, clicking the Options button in the Sort dialog box, and then selecting the *Sort column only* check box. Note that after doing so, you could treat the resulting table as a database again; be sure to keep track of the changes you've made to your data!

DESIGNING TABLES

Word 2013 provides a large assortment of Table Styles available from a gallery in the Table Tools > Design tab. Word stocks the gallery with Styles based on the features you select in the Table Style Options group: you decide how your table should be structured, and Word suggests combinations of cell shading, border design, font choices, and so forth. Best of all, once you've chosen a Table Style, Word will modify it if you change the Style Options you want.

Table style options

Bottom Line

The **Table Style Options** group includes six check boxes. You can mouse over each check box to get a **Tooltip** explaining what it does. To see how the various options affect a table's design, start with very basic formatting and iterate through a series of changes.

STEP BY STEP   **Table style options**

1   Click anywhere in the chemical data table and navigate to the Table Tools > Design tab. Open the Table Styles gallery and choose Clear (at the bottom of the gallery).

2   Uncheck all six boxes in the Table Styles Options group. Your table appears without any formatting.

3   From the Styles gallery, select Grid Table 2 (in the Grid Styles section).

4   Click the various Table Styles Options in turn, in various combinations; in particular, try combining Banded Rows and Banded Columns to see how those options conflict.

Our chemical data table suggests a specific set of options: the row and column labels should be set off, and since we're treating the data in terms of records, it makes sense to differentiate table rows rather than columns.

5 Select the **chemical data** table. Check only the **Header Row**, **First Column**, and **Banded Rows** boxes. Open the Table Styles gallery (Figure 5-12) and notice the styles change to reflect the Style options.

Figure 5-12

The Table Styles gallery repopulates to reflect our choice of Style Options.

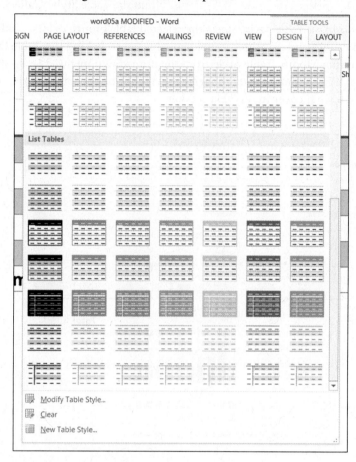

Applying a table style

Bottom Line

After choosing the right Table Styles Options for our data set, we can select a Table Style from the gallery to provide the right visual emphasis. The Grid and List Table Styles vary widely in the intensity of their row/column highlighting and how much emphasis they place on row/column labels. You can experiment with a variety of Table Styles to see how they respond to the constraints you applied in the Table Styles Options group.

1   Select Grid Table 3 – Accent 2 from the Table Styles Gallery.

Choosing a Table Style affects the selected table's fonts, colors, shading, and borders. You can change these features individually by right-clicking the Table Style in the gallery and choosing Modify Table Style from the drop-down menu. The options on this screen (see Figure 5-13) should be familiar by now, with the exception of the border design options, which we'll cover in the next section.

Figure 5-13

The Modify Table Style dialog lets you alter the Table Style using your document's Theme Colors.

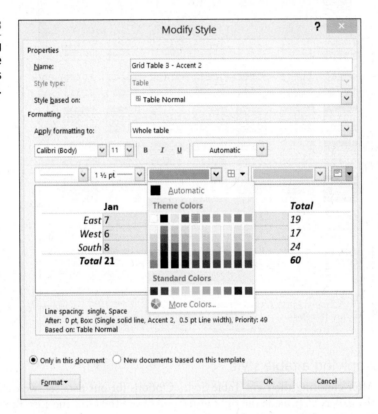

One thing to note on this screen: the border and cell color options are inherited from the document theme; this is another example of how Office 2013 strives for visual consistency across applications and documents. You can now click Cancel to close this dialog box.

Setting cell and table borders

A cell has three parts: its **fill** (background color), content (text/images), and border. A cell border is actually four individual segments; you can specify visibility, style, and color for each segment, or handle them all together, cell by cell. Cell borders are set by column/row according to the Table Style, but you can customize them easily.

STEP BY STEP   Setting cell and table borders

1 Place the cursor in the Volume cell of the Dilithium row.

2 Open the Borders drop-down menu (Table Tools > Design > Borders > Borders) and select No Border.

3 Click and drag to select the Volume cells for Adium and Frustrum; click the Borders icon, which is still set to its last use (No Border).

The borders of the cells you've selected fall away. As you can see in the Borders drop-down menu, you can choose from a variety of border shapes, including diagonal lines.

4 Click and drag to select the data cells (excluding the row/column labels). From the Borders menu, select No Border, and then click to enable Inside Borders. The outer edges of the table will lose their borders, but inter-cell borders remain.

The terms outside and inside refer to your current selection; if you select multiple contiguous cells, Word can differentiate between the outer border of the shape they make together, and the borders between the region's individual cells. If you click within a single cell, there is no inside to speak of, so for that cell alone, the All Borders and Outside Borders options are equivalent.

Resizing a cell (or rather, its entire row or column) is straightforward: just drag the border in question.

Using the Border Painter tool

You can also use the **Border Painter** tool (the opposite of the Eraser tool) to draw in individual borders; the Painter takes its color and line information from the options you select in the Borders group.

STEP BY STEP   Using the Border Painter tool

1 Open the Table Tools > Design tab.

2 From the Line Style drop-down menu, select the double squiggly line style.

3 Select Purple from the Pen Color palette, under Standard Colors.

4 Make sure the Border Painter icon is selected, then click and drag various cell and table borders to paint those borders in the selected style, weight, and color.

5 Change the Line Style to a double line style and apply this border style to various cells. See Figure 5-14 for one possible result.

Unlike the Eraser tool, the Border Painter requires precise placement: you drag along a border to paint, rather than across it, so your initial click has to land right on the border to be recognized. For that reason, it's good to use the Zoom slider, on the Status Bar, when painting cell or table borders.

Figure 5-14

The Border Painter lets you add lines in a variety of styles, colors, and weights.

Mass	Volume	Energy
31	2	9
1	9	12
86	123	44
34	23	45
90	87	88
66	44	88

EDITING CELL CONTENTS

After playing with cell and table borders, we can move on to fills and text. Fills are straightforward: they're just background colors. To change the background color of a cell, select it, and then click Table Tools > Design > Shading. The drop-down palette includes the usual theme colors; clicking the paint icon fills the cell with the selected color.

Cell text and manual cell sizing

Bottom Line

Text formatting within tables is also straightforward; you still use the paragraph/character formatting tools in the Home tab, combined with the cell sizing, alignment, text direction, and margin tools in the Table Tools > Layout tab. We'll add some text to our chemical info table and do some basic formatting.

STEP BY STEP | **Cell text and manual cell sizing**

1 Continue using **word05a_work.docx** and click to drag the border between the Volume and Energy columns to the left, until the Volume cell is just big enough to contain its heading.

2 In the Dilithium Volume cell, type the words 9 cubic liters, measured by ANS. The column will stretch horizontally to fit the word measured, and will stretch vertically to include the full entry.

3 Triple-click the new text and chose Italics from the formatting popup. Then click Bullets in the pop-up menu.

The formatting commands work just as usual, with the added wrinkle of the cell borders shifting slightly around the text. Word started by trying to evenly distribute the four columns, but the column distribution changed when we resized the Volume column.

4   Right-click within the cell you just edited and choose Table Properties. Click Column (see Figure 5-15) and if not already selected, choose Percent in the Measure in drop-down menu. Word is currently trying to apportion 10% of the table's width to Column 3 (Volume). Click OK.

Take Note   If you need a given column or row to have a specific absolute size (for example, 2″ wide), you can set its size in this dialog box.

Figure 5-15

Setting absolute and relative column/row sizes in the Table Properties dialog box.

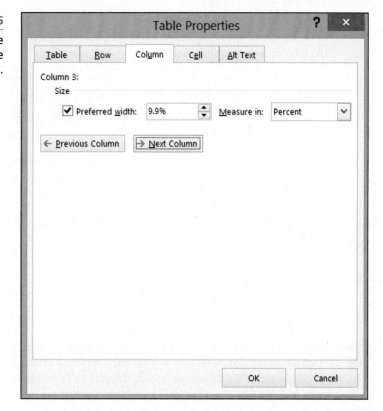

5   With the same cell selected, click Table Tools > Layout > Alignment > Text Direction three times to cycle through the possible orientations for table text.

Note that Word doesn't stretch the column to fit the sideways text entirely into the cell.

6   With the Volume Dilithium cell still selected, type 9. Remove the italics and bullet point.

7   Finally, click Cell Size > Distribute Rows and Distribute Columns to even out the cell spacing.

Distribute Rows and Distribute Columns space the table's rows and columns evenly; if you select multiple rows and Distribute Rows, Word will apportion their current vertical space evenly, but won't even out the whole table.

All these commands involve working within a rigid table shape and size. But how do we adjust size and proportions dynamically to the table's contents? By using the AutoFit feature of Word.

8   Choose File > Save or press Ctrl+S to save your work.

Using AutoFit and Fit Text

Bottom Line

The **AutoFit** tool aims to let you specify general table-sizing behavior without fiddling with absolute sizes or manually tweaking column proportions. By default, a new table will AutoFit Window; it'll stretch between the left and right margins, and stretch and squeeze internally (without changing width) as you change the number of columns. If you manually resize the table, you disable that behavior.

STEP BY STEP   **Using AutoFit and Fit Text**

1   Click anywhere in the table, and select Layout > Cell Size > AutoFit > Autofit Window. The table stretches to full width.

2   Click Autofit Contents. The left-hand column will be widest, then Volume. The Mass column, with its short header, will be narrowest.

3   Click Distribute Columns found in the same Cell Size section of the Layout tab. The left-hand column becomes a jumble, as the labels no longer fit.

4   Click Autofit Contents again to fix the row labels. Select the Mass, Volume, and Energy columns, and click Distribute Columns; now the column headings are too big.

5   Finally, click AutoFit Contents once more.

AutoFit Contents chooses the same optimally efficient spacing every time; because Distribute Columns applies to a subset of the columns, it can produce variable results.

Take Note   It's possible to evenly distribute only the data cells in our table—in which case the headings will be out of sync with the data columns. Reverting to AutoFit Contents will fix this error.

6   Choose File > Save or press Ctrl+S to save your work.

It's worth mentioning one last table text formatting option: Fit Text, which is enabled from the Table Properties dialog box, Cell tab, behind the Options button. Enabling Fit Text will fix the cell's size, and progressively squash or stretch the text to fit inside it. As you can see from Figure 5-16, it tends to adversely affect readability, which is occasionally necessary to fit data to a table's structure.

Figure 5-16

Using Fit Text forces the contents of a cell to squash and stretch.

¤	Mass¤	Volume¤	Energy¤	¤
Wampun¤	3 1¤	2¤	9¤	¤
Dilithium¤	1¤	9¤	1 2¤	¤
Tristram¤	8 6¤	1 2 3¤	4 4¤	¤
A d i u m¤	3 4¤	2 3¤	4 5¤	¤
Frustrum¤	9 0¤	8 7¤	8 8¤	¤
Paromecium¤	6 6¤	4 4¤	8 8¤	¤

This·text·begins·its·fast-moving·life·directly·belo
with·it?·But·life·being·what·it·is·,·we're·left·with·

Images in tables

Images in tables behave exactly like images outside of tables. You can even drag an image in and out of a table as if moving it around the page's object layer. To avoid complications, always choose the In Line with Text layout option (enabled by default when you Insert Image).

What you learned in this lesson:

* Insert and Navigate Tables

* Split and Merge Cells

* Integrate Tables into Paragraphs

* Position Text Within a Table

* Manipulate Columns and Rows

* Sort Tabular Data

* Use Table Styles

* Customize Cell and Table Borders

* Resize Cells and Cell Content

Knowledge Assessment

Matching
Match the function or document element in numbers 1 to 10 to its description in letters a to j.

1. row
2. Eraser tool
3. AutoFit width
4. Border Painter
5. list
6. column
7. fill
8. Tooltip
9. split cells
10. matrix

a 3x3 specimen would start with nine cells
b. in databases this corresponds to one field in a record
c. pattern, color, or image in a cell's background
d. sortable table of one or more columns
e. in-place help and keyboard shortcut information
f. horizontal cell array
g. adds additional rows/columns within a table region
h. stretches cell border rather than cutting off text
i. drag across inner borders to merge cells
j. subdivides cells as lines are drawn in

True/False

Circle T if the statement is true or F is the statement is false.

T F   **1.**   A 4x4 table with a header row and no split cells will contain 12 data cells.

T F   **2.**   Nested tables automatically share Table Styles.

T F   **3.**   The least visually complex Table Style is a Grid style.

T F   **4.**   A descending alphabetical sort will place periwinkle before quiet.

T F   **5.**   To select an entire column, click the top of the header cell.

T F   **6.**   The Split Cells command creates a new nested table within the original, outer table.

T F   **7.**   The Insert > Table command brings up a dialog box to set the size of the new empty table.

T F   **8.**   "Erasing" the border between two cells creates an invisible border in its place.

T F   **9.**   To position text dead center in a cell, select both Center and Align Middle layout options.

T F   **10.**   Like images, tables are floating objects that can be absolutely positioned on the page.

Competency Assessment

Project 5-1: Inserting a Table into a Document

In this exercise you'll add tables to a Word document and work with the text within and around them.

1. Open the project files **table-source** and **table-text-source.**
2. Create a new blank document and save it in the working directory as **project_5-1_inserting_table.**
3. Copy the text from **table-text-source** to your project file.
4. Click the selection handle on the first table in **table-source** and copy the entire table, then paste it directly to the right of the words "Price List" in the project file.
5. Right click the handle on the pasted table and select Table Properties…
6. Select Right alignment and word wrap Around the table, and click OK.
7. Use the lower right resizing handle on the table and make it as small as you can.
8. Use similar techniques to steps 3-6 and paste the second table from table-text-source next to the "Contact Information" section, with Left alignment. You may need to drag the table downward to position it properly.
9. Close the two source files.
10. Save your work and close the file.

Project 5-2: Merging and Splitting Cells

This exercise asks you to alter the structure of a table by merging and splitting cells.

1. Open the project file **5-2-source**. Save your document as **project_5-2_merge_split.**
2. Select the "adult size, 0 degrees" cell in the first table and click Table Tools > Layout > Split Cells.
3. In the dialog box, select 1 row and 2 columns. Click OK.
4. In the newly added cell, type adult size, 32 degrees (summer).
5. Add the word (winter) to the cell you split in step 2.
6. Click and drag to select the Director and Consiglieri cells in the second table. Merge the two cells.

7. Change the merged cell's text to Co-Directors, then click Table Tools > Layout > Alignment > Center.
8. Save your work and close the file.

Proficiency Assessment

Project 5-3: Using Table Styles

In this exercise, customize the presentation of tabular data with Table Styles and Options.

1. Open the project file **5-3-source**. Save your document as **project_5-3_table_styles**.
2. Assign the equipment table a Table Style from the fourth row of the Table Styles gallery's Grid Styles section.
3. Select only the following Table Style Options: Header Row, Banded Columns, Last Column.
4. Select an appropriate Table Style and Options for the second table – remember that it has no header row.
5. Save your work and close the file.

Project 5-4: Sorting List Entries

In this exercise you'll sort data within a table, and alter a table to make sorting easier.

1. Open the project file **5-4-source**. Save your document as **project_5-4_sorting**.
2. Sort the two tables on the page by selecting each in turn and using the Table Tools > Layout > Data > Sort command: sort the equipment list in descending order of price, and alphabetize the names on the contact list.
3. If you are prevented from carrying out step 2, make a small change to each table first in order to facilitate sorting – merging or splitting cells in each table – then correct the data after sorting.
4. Save your work and ("CLOSE") the file.

Mastery Assessment

Project 5-5: Using Draw Table and the Border Painter

In this exercise you'll design a variant tic-tac-toe board in which the center cell is claimed by whichever player wins a mini-game of tic-tac-toe within that cell.

1. Create a new blank document. Save your document as **project_5-5_drawing**.
2. Draw a tic-tac-toe board using the Draw Table, Border Painter, and Eraser tools.
3. Then embed a copy of the complete tic-tac-toe table into the center cell of the original table.
4. Format the cells for visibility of the Xs and Os.
5. Save your work and close the file.

Project 5-6: Laying Out Images in a Table

In this exercise you'll create a "mosaic" using a table to lay out gridded images in a document.

1. Open the project file **5-4-source** (again). Save your document as **project_5-6_images**.

2. Design a background "mosaic" for the document using a table and fill each cell of the table with a camping-themed image. Use the "Washout" Color effect (Picture Tools > Format > Color) to make the different cell images fade into the background as much as possible.

3. Save your work and close Word.

6 Beyond Word: Linking and Collaborating

LESSON SKILL MATRIX

In this lesson, you will learn the following skills:

Tracking Document Edits	Using Document Access Control
Selecting the Right Markup Mode	Combining and Comparing Documents
Incorporating Collaborators' Edits	Embedding and Linking External Data
Using Threaded Comments	

KEY TERMS

- Revert
- Track Changes
- All Markup
- Simple Markup
- No Markup
- Pagination
- Synoptic
- Reviewing Pane
- Accept Changes
- Reject Changes
- Access Control
- Compare Documents
- Combine Documents
- Embedded Object
- Linked Object

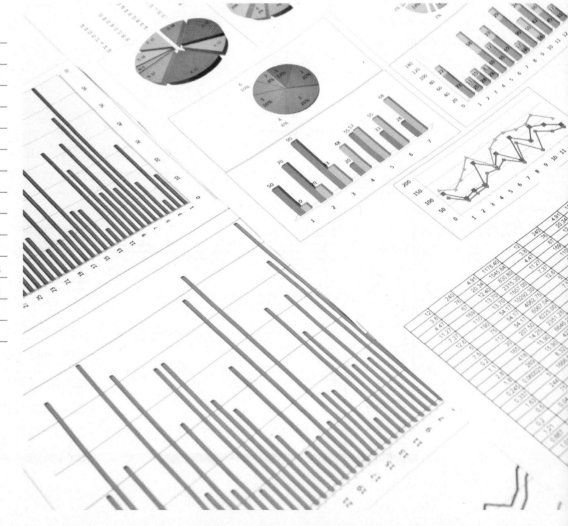

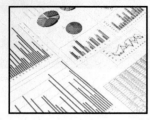

Fabrikam's research whitepapers are group written in-house. Accountability is important – the firm's writers like to keep track of individual contributions and track the evolution of the work across multiple drafts. Because a single draft can cross twelve different desks before the lead author signs off, the ability to smartly merge distributed users' contributions is invaluable. Word's collaboration and versioning tools are built to support precisely this kind of group work.

SOFTWARE ORIENTATION

Documents you create may require feedback and input from multiple people. In this lesson you'll find out how to easily incorporate content from multiple users and organize and use comments and suggestions from reviewers.

Figure 6-1

Tools for collaborating using Microsoft Word.

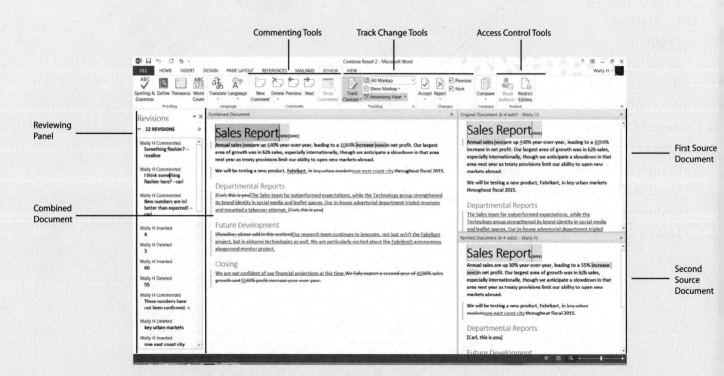

STARTING UP

You will work with files from the Word06lessons folder. Make sure that you computer. If you need further instructions, see "Loading lesson files" in the Starting up section of this book.

GROUP WORK AND GROUPWARE

As part of the Office suite, Word 2013 is built for interoperability: Office works like a single complex app with multiple modules, each suited to a specific kind of work but at its best when connected to the others. A Word file reflects live updates to a linked Excel file; mail merges in Word fill up with records from an Access database, and then get addressed to Outlook contacts; a OneNote notebook turns handwriting into a formatted Word document.

Similarly, Word 2013's collaboration and sharing features keep group-authored projects from getting scattered throughout everyone's hard drives; instead of keeping a mental record of a half-dozen different versions of a file, you can track and combine multiple revisions and even multiple documents from a whole team of authors/editors in a single window.

TRACKING YOUR EDITS

Bottom Line

When you click Review > Track Changes, Word begins to keep a chronological record of your edits (Changes) to the current document, and visually indicates additions, deletions, formatting/style changes, and reviewer comments. Track Changes is doubly useful: as an individual user, it lets you take back edits if you like; in group work, it lets you see each collaborator's changes and choose which to keep and which to throw out.

Take Note

Why can't I **revert** to an earlier version of a document? Previous versions of Microsoft Word let you save multiple versions of a document within the same .docx file. For instance, you could save First Draft, Revision 1, and Revision 2 inside my1stnovel.docx, each with comments explaining the reasoning behind its revisions, and revert to a previous draft if, for example, Revision 2 turned out to be a horrible idea. As of this writing, Word 2013 provides only limited support for document versioning: you can restore an AutoSaved version of a file or revert to its original state (before Track Changes was turned on), but you can't manually create a new version. For proper version control, you'll have to keep multiple copies of the file in Windows Explorer.

As the tooltip for the Track Changes icon notes, you can visually mark every edit made to the document, which can be cumbersome early in the writing process, since your entire document could be marked up as in Figure 6-2. Track Changes really comes into its own when you share a document, or when you finish a draft and want to treat further work as a revision.

A sample workflow

This author uses the following workflow when working in Word:

1 Write first draft front to back without tracking changes, back up first draft.

2 Track changes but hide markup while revising, then display markup to compare first and second drafts.

3 Archive second draft, edit third draft with pen on paper, track changes in new (third) document.

4 Solicit feedback from friends/colleagues (turn on comments, track changes).

5 No need to view markup on final draft (it would only encourage backsliding).

Figure 6-2

An example of a heavily marked-up Word document.

gigantic film/TV tie-in of sorts, opened in 1955. Many people doubted it would last long. However, Disneyland was an immediate success. Instead of ~~having a midway, it~~ featured ~~had~~-themed ~~places~~rides and exhibits. ~~Today~~ Disney's parks ~~are~~still thrive ~~today~~ing.

Six Flags

Many ~~people~~ entrepreneurs tried, unsuccessfully, to copy Disneyland – without Disney's massive financial backing. In 1961, ~~one company finally succeeded:~~ Six Flags[1] over Texas found success with an appeal to regional/cultural identity (plus kitsch). Some traditional amusement parks adopted theme park features to stay alive; some traded on their "old-fashioned" novelty.

Most disappeared.~~As more people grew interested in theme parks, however, traditional amusement parks started to shut down. Some were able to stay open by copying ideas from theme parks.~~

~~Theme parks are still enjoying success. New technology is creating types of rides that were once unattainable. Who knows what the future holds!~~

> **Wally Holland**
> Possibly need more content here

> **Wally Holland**
> Formatted: Heading 2

How Word displays edits

Bottom Line

When you turn on **Track Changes**, you establish the baseline content for the file, which Word treats as the Original document. As long as Track Changes is on, Word will mark any change you've made, and allow you to revert to the original.

You can customize the visual presentation of document edits (markup), but for this lesson we'll assume you're still using the judiciously chosen default markup style.

STEP BY STEP

Viewing edits in Word

1 Open **word0602.docx** in your Word06lessons folder. Click Review > Track Changes to start cataloguing your new edits.

2 Choose File > Save As and navigate to the Word06lessons folder. Enter **word0602_work** in the File name text field and click Save.

3 In the top drop-down menu of the Tracking group, choose All Markup.

4 At the beginning of the title line, add the words A Brief. Save your work.

There are three viewing modes for a document with Track Changes enabled in Word 2013: **All Markup**, which shows a *synoptic* view of the document revisions (i.e., every revision onscreen at once); the new **Simple Markup** mode, which indicates the presence of edits but hides their specific content by default; and **No Markup**, which tracks but doesn't display edits (what you see is the eventual output only). You can toggle between All and Simple Markup modes by clicking the edit bars in the left-hand margin of the page. Figure 6-3 compares the three markup modes, and an unmarked document.

Figure 6-3

Clockwise from upper left: Simple Markup, All Markup, Original, and No Markup.

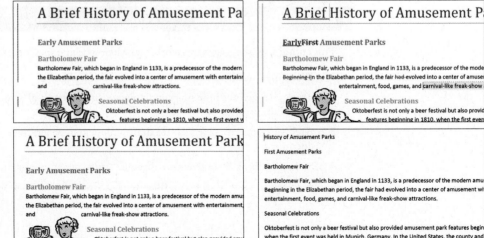

Clip art and template used with permission of Microsoft

5   Toggle between the three markup modes to see the different ways Word can display edits. When you're ready to move on, select Original from the Display for Review drop-down menu.

Selecting the Original view shows you the state of the document immediately prior to the tracked changes; despite appearances, this is *not* the actual content of the document, only a record of its previous appearance.

6   Return to All Markup mode.

There's actually one more viewing mode available: Original: Show Markup, which appears temporarily if you make new changes while in Original document view. This view may be useful if you circulate a copy of your work, solicit feedback/edits from colleagues, and want to see the changes they've made against your baseline document (instead of seeing the live document). In general, though, you'll cycle between the three main viewing modes.

Take Note   Where's the Final display mode? Previous versions of Word used Final to refer to what's now No Markup mode; indeed, Simple Markup is essentially the final document with a little contextual information about which portions have been edited. Arguably, this change in nomenclature reflects contemporary understanding of how digital content is created; after all, Wikipedia pages and live websites don't ever reach final form either.

Tracking new changes

Now you'll make a few more edits to the sample document to see how Word marks them up; in the next section, you'll incorporate these edits permanently into the document, changing Word's definition of the Original content.

STEP BY STEP	**Tracking new changes**

1   Click Home > Paragraph > Show Hidden Characters to reveal invisible characters and breaks.

2   Delete both page breaks, and then switch to Simple Markup mode; the **pagination** *seems* to change.

Figure 6-4

Rendering a page break (L-R): All Markup and Simple Markup. Only the latter accurately reflects the current pagination.

The pagination changes because when you delete a character in All Markup mode, Word renders the character with a strikethrough, and deleting a page break works the same. Word crosses out the break, but the break character (i.e., all the whitespace) is left onscreen, as in Figure 6-4.

The correct pagination (the current state of the document) is reflected in Simple Markup mode.

3   Type the words Toward the Modern World in Heading 1 style below the Pleasure Gardens paragraph; change Pleasure Gaining in Popularity to Heading 2 style. Delete the marked extra space between *heavily* and *influenced* in the Beginning of the Future section.

4   Add the caption **Figure 1: Tilt-a-Whirl** to the photo now on page 2 (select image, then click **References > Insert Caption**). Center the caption text, and then group the image and caption by selecting both using the **Shift** key and clicking **Format > Arrange > Group**.

5   Save your work.

Word doesn't make a note of the image/caption grouping; it's not a change to the document content as such, just a convenience for the author.

Controlling the markup that you see

Bottom Line

As you can see, Word visually distinguishes your edits from other contributors' edits. That's handy, but it can still make for a cluttered document view. Sometimes you'll want to take one reviewer's comments/revisions at a time, or unmark certain reviewers' feedback. (For instance, a colleague might rewrite an entire section of your document; in that case, it's easier to read the new section without markup, as if it were baseline text.)

To toggle certain authors' edits and comments, click Review > Show Markup > Specific People and check only the reviewers whose individual feedback you need right now. To return to a **synoptic** view, click All Reviewers in the same menu. (This tool is also handy when choosing from multiple reviewers' alterations to one portion of a document.)

Similarly, you can use the Show Markup menu to choose to display only specific edits: ignoring insertions/deletions while rectifying section styles, for instance, or hiding comments and formatting changes to concentrate on raw text. How much review/revision/editing information you need depends on what point you've reached in the lifecycle of your document.

The Reviewing pane

Bottom Line

In addition to viewing edits inline (in the context of your document), you can use the Reviewing pane, much like the Navigation pane, to move to specific edit points in your document.

STEP BY STEP   The Reviewing pane

1   Click **Review Tracking > Reviewing Pane > Vertical**. Click several edits in turn to move through the document change by change.

2   In the Reviewing pane, scroll down and click the insertion of *lent their DNA...* to move to that location in the document.

The Reviewing pane isn't just a navigational tool; crucially, it also allows you to Accept and Reject changes without picking them out in the main window:

3 Right-click *Wally H deleted: played a part in...* in the Reviewing pane, and select **Accept Deletion**. Then right-click the *lent their DNA...* insertion and **Accept Insertion** (see Figure 6-5).

Figure 6-5

Incorporating an edit in the
Reviewing pane.

The edits disappear from the Reviewing pane, the struck-through text disappears from the main document window, and the added *lent their DNA* text is now unmarked. Unless you Undo the change, Word will forget that the *played a part...* text was ever there, and accept the new text as part of the Original document state.

EDITING AND COLLABORATING

Word 2013's revision tools are built for collaboration. The Track Changes, Combine, and Compare tools can turn a handful of different document versions, each in a different co-author's hands, into a clean, comprehensive final document. Threaded comments will preserve the details of your collaboration right in the .docx file itself.

Accepting and rejecting changes

Bottom Line

When you use the **Accept Changes** button, you essentially incorporate edits into your document's baseline, folding those changes back into the document's Original state. Accepting and **Rejecting Changes** is usually the job of the document's primary author, though anyone can accept/reject edits unless restricted from doing so.

Accepting and rejecting changes

1   Make sure you have **All Markup** selected and then **close** the Revision pane. Scroll to the top of the document and click the word *Early* in the first heading.

2   Click **Review > Changes > Accept**. The word *Early* loses its underline/coloring, indicating that it's no longer treated as a change, but rather part of the baseline document. The struck word *First* is highlighted: Word has moved on to the next edit.

If you clicked the checkmark Accept icon rather than selecting from the drop-down Accept menu, Word defaults to Accept and Move to Next. In this case, Word treats the insertion of *Early* as having been finalized; it's no longer an edit that needs to be accepted, but a permanent feature of the draft. (If needed, you can press Ctrl+Z to undo Accept Change.)

3   Accept or reject the edits in the first paragraph until you come to the Possible topics comment from Wally H. In the comment bubble located in the right margin, click the **Reply** icon.

4   Type a new comment: **Thanks for suggestion, no time now**. Then right-click the original **Possible** topics comment and select **Mark Comment Done**. See Figure 6-6.

Figure 6-6

Use Mark Comment Done to deemphasize reviewer comments while keeping them around for reference.

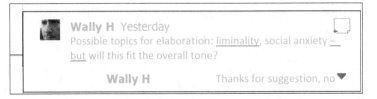

5   Enable Simple Markup view, and if it's still selected, click to deselect **Review > Comments > Show Comments**. A clickable comics-style speech bubble to indicate the conversation.

6   Click **Show Comments** again to display all comment threads (including the one marked Done, still greyed out). Save your work.

COMMENTS AND CONVERSATIONS

Word 2013 treats document review as a kind of augmented conversation (rather than real work and chatter), and a couple of new features have been added to emphasize that view: threaded comments and integrated external communications. You've encountered comments already; we'll quickly review the tools to add, delete, review, and respond to comments here, as well as taking a comment thread to e-mail or instant messenger.

Using Comments and Conversations

1   In the **word0602_work.docx** file, click the word *Oktoberfest* found in the second paragraph and then click **Review > Comments > New Comment**. In the comment box, type **English spelling?** and then press **Escape** to return to the document window.

2   Click the clip art next to it and add a comment with the text **Classier image?** Press **Escape**, and then mouse over the new comment.

3   Click to reply to your own *Classier image?* comment. Enter **Fits document tone** in the box and mark the first comment in the thread **Done**. Save your work.

Taking a comment thread to e-mail or instant messenger

For longer replies, you can respond directly to another author via e-mail, instant messenger, or phone; just mouse over their image in a comment thread to bring up their Person Card, from which you can select a contact method. To update your own contact information, click Sign in (if you are not already signed in) or your account in the upper-right corner of the Office 2013 screen, and then select Account Settings.

ACCESS CONTROL

Sometimes you'll want to place limits on who can edit a document, and how. The Review > Protect group offers two tools to gain **access control.**

Blocking certain edits

Bottom Line

Scroll to the bottom of the document; the final paragraph and its footnote are marked with a little grey Don't Touch! icon and a dotted bracket. This means that one of your colleagues has used the Protect > Block Authors tool to block others from changing that text.

No one else will be able to edit the blocked text until that author takes two steps: unblocking the text by right-clicking the icon and deselecting Block Authors, and uploading the unblocked file to SkyDrive or SharePoint for group review. If the author doesn't have automatic uploading enabled, they have a chance to reconsider before unblocking the paragraph.

The author can also choose Block Authors > Release All of My Blocked Areas to make the entire document unrestricted (once she re-uploads, that is).

Restricting editing

You can also use the Restrict Editing tool to limit others' input on a document. You can access this tool by choosing Review > Protect > Restrict Editing. The Restrict Editing pane, shown in Figure 6-7, offers several levels of access control, largely targeted toward colleagues sharing an intranet.

Figure 6-7

Limiting edit rights to your
document with Restrict
Editing.

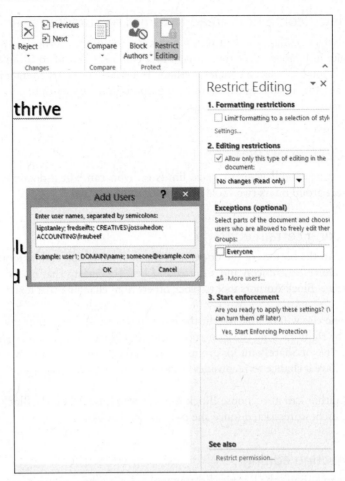

You can place Formatting restrictions, which are useful when using a .docx file as a template (for copying into an advanced layout application such as InDesign, or generating structured XML documents) or adhering strictly to a document theme/template (e.g., when getting feedback on a newsletter). You can also place Editing restrictions: marking a document as Read-only, soliciting comments but no edits, or preventing invisible edits (requiring Track Changes to be on for all reviewers). If your document is a fillable form, you can also prevent other users from changing anything outside of the fillable text boxes.

When you're ready to enforce access limits, you can click Yes, Start Enforcing Protection. When you do so, you're prompted to choose either an unencrypted document password (which you'll distribute manually to reviewers) or user authentication, which requires that you set up Information Rights Management, or IRM.

Take Note   IRM vs passwords - IRM is Microsoft's decade-old system for document access control. If you need IRM, you're almost certainly on a corporate intranet, in which case you should consult your IT department to configure sharing and access. IRM is a good deal more secure (in general) than password protection: anyone with the right password, or able to guess it, can open a password-protected file, but IRM-protected files only open to specific users.

COMPARING AND COMBINING DOCUMENTS

Bottom Line	With the Review > **Compare** tool you can compare two versions of a file to see any points of difference, while flattening out any Tracked Changes in either. **Combine** Documents is a little different: it assumes that each file is a different revision of a common ancestor, and preserves Track Changes info for each.

Comparing documents

Here we'll compare the document you've been working on, **word0602_work.docx**, with **word0604.docx**; both files branched from the same source material, **word0601.docx**. Word doesn't care about the history of either file, only their current states.

STEP BY STEP	**Comparing documents**

1   With the **word0602_work.docx** file open, click Review > Compare > Compare.

2   In the left-hand text box, click Browse and select **word0604.docx**. In the right-hand box, click **word0602_work.docx**.

3   Click More >> and choose to show changes in a New document. Click OK.

4   A dialog box appears, stating that all tracked changes will be treated as accepted, asking whether to proceed. Click Yes.

Word opens a new window called **Compare Result 1** containing a single new document, which essentially treats **word0602_work** as a set of changes to **word0604**.

5   Close the Review pane to make your screen less cluttered. If it's not already selected, click Compare > Show Source Documents > Show Both.

To see how this comparison works, scroll to the Pleasure Gardens paragraph. In the first sentence of the combined document, quotation marks around the phrase *pleasure gardens* have been deleted; but if you look back at your original **word0602_work.docx** file, those quotes were never actually in the source material. They were introduced in **word0604.docx**. Word is treating the former as a modification of the latter, even though they only share a common ancestor.

Figure 6-8

Compare Documents lets you establish any version of a file as the baseline for future edits.

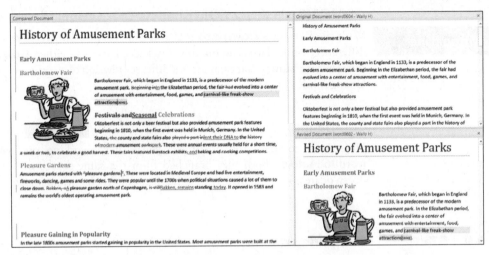

Clip art and template used with permission of Microsoft.

At this point you can go through the edits in the Compared Document window (see Figure 6-8) and accept/reject them as you normally would; this lets you combine two arbitrary files (favoring **word0604** in terms of how the files are presented).

> 6   Leave this file open to use as reference in the next exercise.

Combining documents

Combining documents in Word 2013 is only slightly different from Comparing them: instead of flattening out each source document's internal Track Changes data, it treats both documents as deviations from the same baseline, and throws both documents' Tracked Changes into a new synoptic document. To see the difference, follow the same basic steps as in the previous section.

STEP BY STEP   **Combining documents**

1   Click **Review > Compare > Combine**.

2   In the left source box select **word0604.docx**; on the right, select **word0602_work.docx**.

3   In the dialog box that appears, choose to **Keep** the formatting changes from the original document (**word0604**) and click **Continue with Merge**.

4   Use **Alt+Tab** to toggle back and forth between the Combined and Compared results windows. In each window, scroll to the Festivals and Celebrations/Seasonal Celebrations paragraph.

The Combined document's second paragraph heading is *Festivals and Celebrations*, which it inherits from **word0604**. But the Compared document uses *Seasonal Celebrations*, inherited from **word0602_work**. Why the difference?

Combine Documents sees that both **word0602_work** and **word0604** start with *Seasonal Celebrations*, and **word0604** makes a Tracked Change to get to *Festivals and Celebrations*. Because one file deviates from the shared source document, Word includes that deviation in the Combined file.

But the output of Comparing the files comes from assuming that *Festivals and Celebrations* is the original text, so *Seasonal Celebrations* must be updated. So it preserves that heading instead.

5   Close all the open Word documents and only save the changes to the **word0602_work** file.

Take Note   A Compare or Combine rule of thumb. If you need to see how your first and second drafts differ, use Compare Documents. If two reviewers both send you comments on your second draft and you need to view them side by side, use Combine Documents.

EMBEDDING AND LINKING OBJECTS

For the final piece of this lesson, we'll shift gears to look briefly at how Word connects to external data sources. One such source is an Access database, which you can learn more about in the Mail Merge lesson; here we'll see how live updates to an Excel spreadsheet can be reflected in a Word document without re-embedding the Excel data.

Linking to an Excel spreadsheet

There are two ways to drop an object into a Word file: *embedding* and *linking*. An **embedded object** is added to the .docx file itself, bulking it up; thereafter you'd edit the object through Word itself. A **linked object** is something else: a pointer to an external file, which can be updated to reflect changes to that external file (or broken, if the external file disappears). Each method is useful for different tasks. Embedding is straightforward: drag and drop or cut and paste. Linking is only slightly more complicated.

STEP BY STEP	Linking to an Excel spreadsheet

1   Navigate to the Word06lessons folder and double-click **word0603.xlsx** which will open in Excel 2013.

2   Click in the upper-left corner cell (**A1**) and either shift-click or drag down and to the right to H8 so the entire table is selected. Press **Ctrl+C** to copy the data. A moving dotted outline will surround the copied cells.

3   Open a blank new Word document and save it as **word0603_work**. Right-click in the document area and under Paste Options choose **Link & Keep Source Formatting**.

The Excel data appears in the new Word doc in an organized way. To view a read-only copy of the source data, right-click the table and choose Linked Worksheet Object > Open Link.

4   Back in the Word document, right-click the table and select **Linked Worksheet Object > Edit Link** to open the spreadsheet for editing in Excel.

5   In **word0603.xlsx**, change the January Employees count to **350** and save the document.

6   Switch back to your Word document. Right-click the inserted Excel data and select **Update Link**. The cell values change to reflect alterations to the original.

7   Finally, in the Word document, click the table and select a new Table Style from the Table Tools > Design tab.

The spreadsheet object formats its cell data just like the source file (or Excel file), but its table formatting and style from Word's own table tools.

Unlinking a linked object

If you want to stop dynamically updating the data in your spreadsheet, right-click the spreadsheet object, click Linked Worksheet Object > Links, and select Break Link. There's not much more to it; naturally, if you move or rename the source file you'll break the link, which is the main hazard when you choose to link (vs. embed) external data. But for many work situations, with a little care and feeding of your files and folders, live data will be preferable.

What you learned in this lesson:

- Tracking Document Edits

- Selecting the Right Markup Mode

- Incorporating Collaborators' Edits

- Using Threaded Comments

- Using Document Access Control

- Combining and Comparing Documents

- Embedding and Linking External Data

Knowledge Assessment

True/False

Circle T if the statement is true or F it the statement is false.

T F   1. A .docx file grows over time to hold every version of the document since its creation.

T F   2. No Markup is another name for the Original version of a document.

T F   3. A linked spreadsheet automatically updates the moment its source data changes.

T F   4. User access restrictions go into effect when you click the Start Enforcing Protection button.

T F   5. When you have acted on a comment, the next step is to delete the comment.

T F   6. Track Changes treats each individual character changed as a separate edit.

T F   7. To see whether a file has been changed in Simple Markup, hover over its text.

T F   8. In No Markup mode, Word continues to track changes.

T F   9. Jaime edits section of a chapter and Margeret edits section to form the complete final version of the chapter, use the Compare Documents function.

T F 10. The Compare Documents tool preserves Track Changes data for all versions in the comparison.

Fill in the Blanks

Complete the following sentences by writing the correct word or words in the blanks provided.

1. Red bars in the margin indicate the presence of edits in a document in _____ mode.

2. Turning on Track Changes establishes the current state of the document as its "_____," and any subsequent edits as tracked changes.

3. To undo a colleague's tracked change in the Reviewing Pane without incorporating it, click the _____ command.

4. "Final" Markup mode is now called _____ mode.

5. A comment and its replies, displayed together in a single pane, are called a _____.

6. Comment and edit-tracking tools reside in the _____ tab.

7. Page breaks, both present and edited out, are visible when _____ is enabled.

8. When multiple collaborators work on the same document, each user's edits has a different _____.

9. The _____ command fades, but doesn't delete, a comment thread.

10. To stop reflecting edits to a spreadsheet's source file, select its representation in the Word file and select the _____ command.

Competency Assessment

Project 6-1: Using Track Changes

In this exercise you'll enable Track Changes on a document and add comments and edits.

1. Launch Word and open the project file **markup-source**.

2. Save your document in your working directory as **project_6-1_markup.**

3. With Track Changes enabled in All Markup mode, select the table of contents and click Review > New Comment.

4. In the comment box, type Move to separate page?

5. Delete the table of contents. Note that the TOC remains visible but struck through.

6. Switch to Review > Tracking > Simple Markup.

   The TOC vanishes, reflecting its current deleted status.

7. Save your work and close the file.

Project 6-2: Comment Threads

This exercise explores Word's threaded reviewer comments.

1. Open the project file **6-2-source**. Save your document as **project_6-2_comments**.

2. Switch to All Markup mode.

3. Mouse over the "Capitalized" comment and click the Reply button. Type I prefer original format.

4. Click the Reply button again and add the comment Will revert unless boss objects.

5. Highlight what in the first paragraph and click Review > Changes > Reject > Reject Change. Note that the comment thread disappears as well.

6. Save and close your document.

Project 6-3: Accepting/Rejecting Changes

In this exercise you'll accept and reject reviewer modifications to a document using Track Changes.

1. Open the project file **6-3-source.** Save your document as **project_6-3_review_pane.**
2. Right click the "Move to separate page?" comment and choose Mark Comment Done.
3. Open the Reviewing Pane.
4. Select the first edit in the Pane, the TOC deletion, and click Review > Changes > Accept.
5. Similarly accept the next two edits, the Americanization of "neighbour" to "neighbor."
6. Reject the next change. Note that no record is kept of accepted/rejected changes – they are implemented and "forgotten."
7. Scroll down to reject both edits in the blythe/blithe change, and reject any travelling/ traveling or traveller/traveler edits as well.
8. Accept the rest of the changes and mark all comments done.
9. Save and close the document.

Project 6-4: Combining Documents

In this exercise you'll use the Combine Documents tool and choose which edits you want to keep.

1. If it's not open already, launch Word 2013.
2. Click Review > Compare > Combine.
3. Select **6-4-source1** and **6-4-source2** as the documents for combination and click OK.

   You can consult the exercise file **6-4-original** to see the source material for these two exercise files.
4. Turn off Show Comments to save space.
5. Place the cursor at the beginning of the Combined Document. Click Next Change to cycle through the comments and edits made by the two reviewers.
6. In paragraph 1, accept the more optimistic numbers from edit1, and dismiss Rosaline's comment about confirmation. Accept all changes until the last paragraph – reject edit1's revised projections and instead accept edit2's "We are not confident…"
7. Give the document a flashier title in keep with both reviewers' suggestions.
8. Save the document to your working directory as **project_6-4_combined.** Close the file.

Project 6-5: Linking and Embedding Excel Data

This exercise explores linked and embedded Excel data in Word documents.

1. Create a new blank Word document. Save your document as **project_6-5_link_embed**.
2. Embed the **ratings_source** project file in the document. Then insert a link to **sales_source** below it.
3. Use the Edit Link command to edit the **sales_source** file itself, listing every representative as having 8 January and 8 June sales calls.
4. Use the Save As command in Excel to save the edited source file in your working directory as **project_6-5_sales**.

    The Word file should automatically update and change the link target as you edit and Save As in Excel.
5. Save and close your Word document.

Project 6-6: Access Control

This exercise challenges you to protect a Word document from prying eyes.

1. Open the project file **6-4-original**. Save your document as **project_6-6_access**.
2. Use the Block Authors command to prevent Carl and Rosaline from editing the headings, and use Restrict Editing to allow only tracked changes in the document.
3. Begin enforcing protection on the file, with password sesame.
4. Save your work and close Excel.

LESSON SKILL MATRIX

In this lesson, you will learn the following skills:

Linking to a Merge Data Source

Inserting Merge Fields into a Word Document

Using If-Then Conditional Field Codes

Previewing Merge Documents

Conditionally Inserting Images into a Merge Document

Finalizing and Saving a Merge Document

KEY TERMS

- **Mail Merge**
- **Form Letter**
- **Wizard**
- **Data Source**
- **SQL**
- **Address Block**
- **Conditional Field**
- **Syntax**

Contoso's community outreach program forges links between dozens of area businesses and thousands of local students. To raise funds and seek community involvement, Contoso puts out upward of 5,000 targeted form letters a year, using a database listing every business in the greater metro area. To assemble these letters is the work of just two data files: the database itself, and a single carefully constructed Word file, whose text and design vary from letter to letter depending on the recipient.

SOFTWARE ORIENTATION

Personalizing documents for a group of people can be an easy task, as you'll discover in this lesson. You will discover how to work with a list and combine it with a document to create personalized documents.

Figure 7-1

The tools for creating a mail merge.

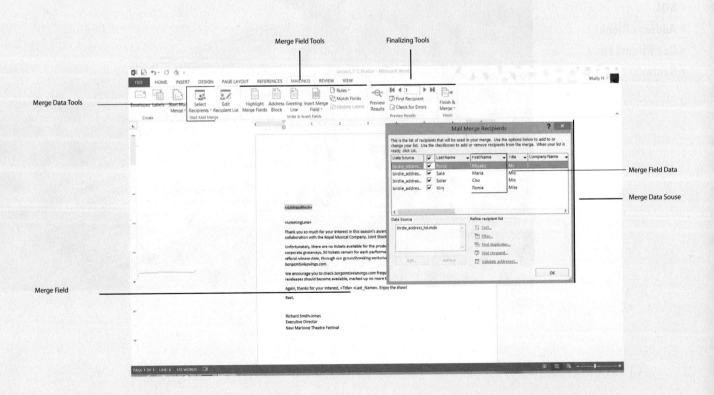

STARTING UP

You will work with files from the Word07lessons folder. Make sure that you have loaded the OfficeLessons folder onto your

MAIL MERGES

Bottom Line

You've already seen how fields can be used to insert content into a Word 2013 document, but until now, you've worked with fields that contain just a single piece of data: the current date and time, a document's author and title, or the page/section numbers of a given location in the document. Moreover, in previous lessons you worked only with field codes and document properties specific to a given document, you haven't had to make Word look outside your .docx to fill any field with data.

But Word is designed to work hand-in-hand with other applications in the Office suite. In particular, an action called a **mail merge** lets you fill a Word document with fields, map each field to a column in an Access database, and then create multiple versions of the Word doc, one for each database record. In this way you can make a hundred personalized **form letters** (for example), one for each entry in an address book in Access, using a single document skeleton in Word.

Word provides a Mail Merge **Wizard** to take you step-by-step through the mail merge process; we'll follow the same steps without using the Wizard.

Take Note

By far, the most common use for Office's merge tools is mass mailings: form letters and bulk envelopes. But you could just as easily use a merge to generate flash cards, invoices, course listings, board game counters, or print labels. This lesson isn't just about form letters; it's about applying a consistent visual format to every record in a database

Linking to a data source

Bottom Line

The first step when building a mail merge is to link your Word document to a **data source**, such as an address book, though any database will do. We'll use an Access database, which mixes text fields (title, name, address, and so on) and a single currency field (donation amount). In this exercise, we won't edit the database itself, but you can look over its contents.

STEP BY STEP   **Linking to a data source**

1   Open the **word07a.docx** file and read it over, noting the pieces of text that will need to be converted to fields for the form letter.

2   Choose File > Save As and navigate to the Word07lessons folder. Name your file **word07a_work** and click Save.

3   Click Mailings > Select Recipients > Use an Existing List (Note that most of the icons in the Mailings tab are greyed out.)

A dialog box appears, in which you'll select a file to use as your data source. From this box, you can alternatively choose to connect to an existing SQL database or create a new file; both processes follow the same general contour as the following.

4   Navigate to your Word07lessons folder and select **word07b.mdb**. Click Open.

5   If the Confirm Data Source dialog box appears, select the first option (OLE DB Database Files) and click OK. Save your work.

Choosing a data source and connection method returns you to your document screen, but with the icons in the Mailings tab active. Your Word file is now linked to the data source, and you can use its fields and records to build your form letter (shown in Figure 7-2).

Figure 7-2

Our form letter: highlights indicate text to be converted into fields.

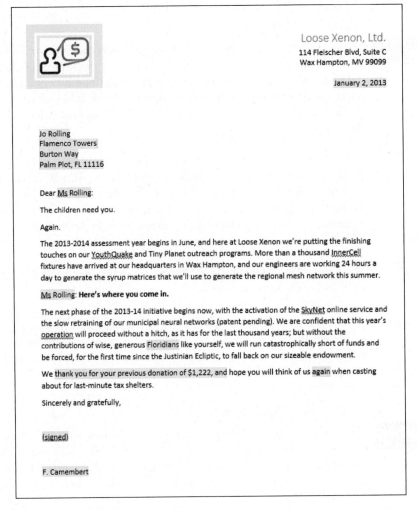

Loose Xenon, Ltd.
114 Fleischer Blvd, Suite C
Wax Hampton, MV 99099

January 2, 2013

Jo Rolling
Flamenco Towers
Burton Way
Palm Plot, FL 11116

Dear Ms Rolling:

The children need you.

Again.

The 2013-2014 assessment year begins in June, and here at Loose Xenon we're putting the finishing touches on our YouthQuake and Tiny Planet outreach programs. More than a thousand InnerCell fixtures have arrived at our headquarters in Wax Hampton, and our engineers are working 24 hours a day to generate the syrup matrices that we'll use to generate the regional mesh network this summer.

Ms Rolling: **Here's where you come in.**

The next phase of the 2013-14 initiative begins now, with the activation of the SkyNet online service and the slow retraining of our municipal neural networks (patent pending). We are confident that this year's operation will proceed without a hitch, as it has for the last thousand years; but without the contributions of wise, generous Floridians like yourself, we will run catastrophically short of funds and be forced, for the first time since the Justinian Ecliptic, to fall back on our sizeable endowment.

We thank you for your previous donation of $1,222, and hope you will think of us again when casting about for last-minute tax shelters.

Sincerely and gratefully,

(signed)

F. Camembert

Clip art and template used with permission of Microsoft

Data sources for mail merges

When performing a merge, you can draw on a wide variety of tabular data sources; indeed, you can even pull data from a table within another Word document. Your options include:

- An HTML or Word document containing a single table

- An online **SQL** database

- An Outlook contacts list or other electronic address book

- A short Office Address list you create directly in Word

- An Excel worksheet (many people, use Excel as an ultra-lite database program)

- A tab-delimited or comma-delimited text file, such as a .csv file

Sometimes, when you select a source file for your recipients list, the Confirm Data Source dialog asks you for a connection method; the default choice for Access databases requires no further input from you, whereas connecting to an Oracle database over a corporate intranet would require additional configuration steps. (For more details on connecting to a database or other data source, consult Office online help.)

Take Note   Creating an address/data list is no more complicated than creating a database; indeed, it's just like filling out a table. The Mail Merge toolkit enables you to build such a list right inside Word 2013

INSERTING MERGE FIELDS INTO A DOCUMENT

Looking over the highlighted regions of the fundraising letter, you can assemble a list of the dynamically-generated text pieces we'll need:

• Title, first name, and last name for each recipient

• Mailing address: the word *Floridians* will need replacing

• Date: we want Word to insert the data on which the document is printed

• Closing: original author *F. Camembert* should be switched out for an Author field

• Iconic image: only Boston-area recipients should see the clip art

• Finally, the *previous donation* line (and the word *again*) are only appropriate for previous donors

• Inserting simple merge fields

Inserting simple merge fields

Bottom Line   **Merge fields** work just like other fields in Word, except that they're designed to refer to a specific external data source. You'll start by fitting in standard date/author fields and those that link to columns in the database without conditionals.

STEP BY STEP   **Inserting simple merge fields**

1   Select the entire date line at the top right of the document. Click Insert > Text > Date & Time. Select the 5 February 2013 format (see Figure 7-3), and make sure Update automatically is checked. Click OK.

Figure 7-3

Inserting a date/time field into our document.

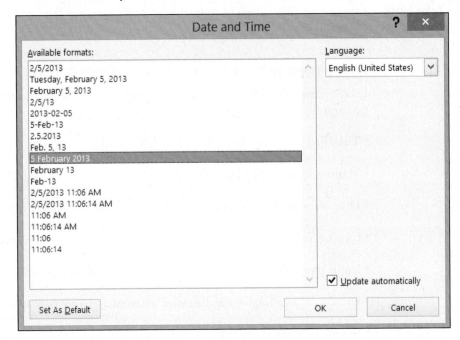

2   Select the *F. Camembert* text and replace with an Author Document Property (Insert > Text > Quick Parts > Document Properties).

3   Now delete the four-line address block below the image, and without moving the cursor, click Mailings > Write & Insert Fields > Address Block.

Figure 7-4

Formatting an address block for a mail merge.

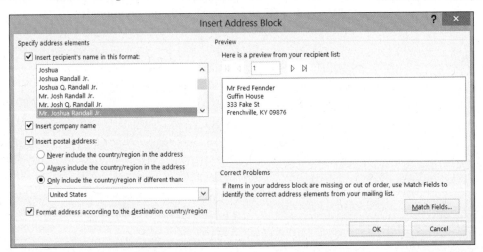

The Insert Address Block dialog box (see Figure 7-4) lets you tailor your **address block** to the data; the controls above the preview pane can cycle through each record in the data source to confirm that, for instance, our solitary UK address displays properly despite having a slightly different format from our US records. In particular, note that checking Format address according to the destination country/region, moves the UK postal code to its own line, but pairs US zip codes with city and state.

4   Select the Mr. Joshua Randall Jr. name format, and make sure all four check boxes are marked. Cycle through the preview to see how the different records are formatted. When you're ready to proceed, click **OK**.

Because you haven't yet merged the data into the form letter, your document displays a field code as a placeholder: <<AddressBlock>>. When you create the final merged document, you'll see each address block in its proper place.

Take Note   If we were sticklers about our document layout, we could use conditional fields to vary the amount of space between our recipient address block and our greeting, to compensate for the US/UK address formatting difference. Alternatively, we could just lay out the address block in a text box big enough for a UK address. That kind of precise layout is left as an exercise for you.

5   Select the words *Ms Rolling* in the middle of the page. Use the Insert Merge Field tool to insert a <<Title>> field, then a <<Last_Name>> field, making sure to leave a blank space between, and to preserve the trailing colon.

6   Finally, delete the greeting line. In its place, click Mailings > Greeting Line to insert a flexible greeting field. Select the colon from the third drop-down menu. Click OK. Make sure the text *The children need you.* is on its own line. You may need to press Enter.

7   Choose File > Save to save your work.

Using if-then conditional fields

Bottom Line   The final paragraph of our fundraising appeal mentions a previous donation, but we don't have donation amounts for all our recipients. Instead of adjusting merged letters by hand, we can use **conditional** (if-then) **field** programming in that paragraph to mention an earlier donation only if the database contains such information. Conditional fields choose from two values to output -- IF a condition is met, THEN return value A, ELSE return value B.

STEP BY STEP   **Using if-then conditional fields**

1   Select the highlighted passage in the final paragraph (*thank you for…*) and press Ctrl+X to cut it. Then click Mailings > Write & Insert Fields > Rules > If...Then...Else.

2   Set the Field name to Donation and Comparison field to is not blank. In the Insert this text box, press Ctrl+V to paste the *thank you for…* sentence. Make sure there's a blank space after the word *and*.

This logic should be easy to follow. The next step is a bit more complex: if we have a previous donation on file, the personalized text should include the amount. To get this effect, we'll insert a field (nested inside our conditional) that pulls the Donation amount from the database if necessary.

3   Delete the 1,222 amount (not the dollar sign) in the Insert this text box. In its place, press Ctrl+F9 to manually insert a field code. Type Mergefield Donation in the brackets. Then click OK.

The **syntax** here is the same as for all fields: Mergefield tells Word what kind of field we're inserting; Donation is the column name we want. Now we'll finish the sentence by making the word *again* similarly contingent upon a previous donation.

4   Use the Mailings > Write & Insert Fields > Rules > If...Then...Else tool (shown in Figure 7-5) to replace the word *again* in the letter's final sentence with a conditional, using the same If criteria as in step 2, but inserting the word **again** with a trailing space if a previous donation exists. Click **OK**.

Figure 7-5

Figure Customizing the text of each form letter with if-then-else rules

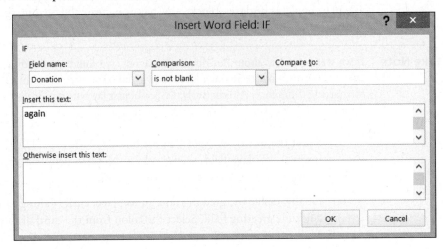

5   Press **Alt+F9** to reveal field codes.

Figure 7-6

Alt+F9 reveals the internal code to generate an address block.

```
{ ADDRESSBLOCK \f "<<_TITLE0_ >><<_FIRST0_ >><< _LAST0_ >><< _SUFFIX0_ >>
<<_COMPANY_
>><<_STREET1_
>><<_STREET2_
>><<_CITY_>><<, _STATE_ >><< _POSTAL_>><<
_COUNTRY_>>" \l 1033 \c 2 \e "United States" \d }
```

Pressing Alt+F9 toggles field codes, showing the internal code that Word uses to programmatically generate output such as page numbers, address blocks (see Figure 7-6), today's date, or, as shown in the sentence you just edited, a text string with an additional field embedded in it, all wrapped up in a conditional.

Take Note   This is the only time we'll directly edit field codes in the Word 2013 portion of this book, but expert Office users will need to learn more. The syntax for fields allows a lot of customization; the If/then/else tool is just a front end to a special-purpose programming language of sorts. If you want to go deeper with fields, you'll find tutorials and reference material at *office.microsoft.com*

We'll close out this part of the lesson by making one more change: adding a bit of personalization in place of the word *Floridian*, to distinguish between corporate and individual contributors.

STEP BY STEP   **Adding personalization**

1   Delete the word *Floridian* and in its place insert an If/then/else rule.

2   Use the following conditions: If the Company_Name field is blank then insert the word **citizen**, otherwise insert the word **professional**.

USING FILL-IN PROMPTS

Word's merge field Rules go beyond if/then conditionals. You can also use a field to solicit input from the document creator – a useful technique if, for instance, you want to add a short personalized message to each merged document but don't want to hardcode those messages in the document skeleton itself.

To display a prompt to get text to replace a field, insert a Fill-In field using the Mailings > Rules command.

PREVIEWING A MERGE

Bottom Line

Now we can begin to get a sense for how our document will look when we perform the final merge operation. In the Mailings > Preview Results group you'll find a button to Preview Results; this will perform a kind of provisional merge to let you know whether you've provided the proper spacing in and around text fields (for example). By cycling through your data records using the record counter tool, you can see whether your form design is robust. (In other words, whether your document skeleton is flexible enough to accommodate the different data values you're going to insert during the merge.) But the Preview Results tool doesn't actually create a merged file; you're still in editing mode, so to speak.

STEP BY STEP   **Previewing a merge**

1   Press Alt+F9 to hide field codes.

2   Click Preview Results and cycle through the six records to see how the field values change. Take special note of the conditional fields in the final paragraph.

As you can see, Word treats standard fields and merge fields a bit differently: if you turn off Preview Results, the Date/Author fields still update as normal, and more importantly, the conditional fields do too, even if they contain nested Mergefields. But standalone Mergefields (such as <<Title>> and <<Last_Name>> in the *Here's where you come in* line) don't populate with table data until you turn Preview Results on.

3   Click to disable Preview Results before moving on, and save your work.

CONDITIONALLY INSERTING AN IMAGE

Bottom Line

Our last step in turning our static letter into a flexible document template of sorts is to wrap the image in a conditional, which is no more complex than inserting text, though it must be done manually as Word provides no simple tool for conditional image insertion. Our plan is to include the image only if a recipient lives in Massachusetts (in other words, if the State mergefield value is *MA*).

To make the exercise easier to complete in regards to formatting, we'll insert the image into the header rather than the main body of the document.

STEP BY STEP   **Conditionally inserting an image**

1   Click to select the icon in the top-left corner and delete it. Press Ctrl+Home to place the cursor at the beginning of the document (to the left of *Loose Xenon*).

2   Double-click in the header to open it for editing, and place the cursor on the far left of the header text area.

3   Type Ctrl+F9 to insert a field. Type IF followed by a space, and then insert a second field inside it by pressing Ctrl+F9 again. Type Mergefield State within the nested field. Place the cursor just to the right of the nested field and type = "MA".

4   Press the spacebar, then click Insert > Pictures. Navigate to the Word07lessons folder and select the image **word07icon.png**, and click Insert. Resize the image to make it just a line or two high. The result is shown in Figure 7-7.

Figure 7-7

Conditionally inserting an image.

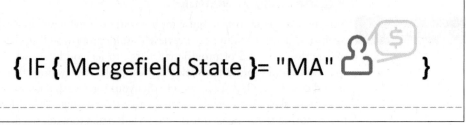

Clip art used with permission of Microsoft

Now using the Preview Results, you can cycle through the six database records to see that only the two Massachusetts residents get an icon. Two cleanup steps remain, and then we can merge the Word skeleton and Access database.

5   Triple-click to select the word (signed) at the bottom of the document. In the Home > Font group, click the small popup icon to open the Font formatting dialog. Check the Hidden effect and click OK.

6   Press Ctrl+A to select all, and choose Home > Font > Highlight > No Color to remove the remaining yellow highlighting.

FINALIZING THE MERGE

Now we're ready to perform the merge. We have three options under the Finish & Merge tool for merging our data into our Word document. All three options preserve the original Word document (the skeleton) and the Access database:

• **Edit Individual Documents** produces a single Word file with every individual form letter included on its own page. You can then continue to edit the merged letters individually without worrying about field codes and conditionals, but you can't easily make global changes to formatting in this mode.

• **Print Documents** skips that step and carries out a single big print job.

• **Send E-mail Messages** does the same, but instead of print copies it creates a large batch of e-mail messages in Outlook. You just fill in the subject line and name a database field to pull addresses from. (This option won't work for our current project: our database doesn't have e-mail information.)

We'll take the first option, just to have a chance to look at the final output.

1   Click Mailing > Finish > Finish & Merge > Edit Individual Documents. In the Merge to New Document dialog box, make sure All is selected, and click OK.

2   Save the resulting merge output file in the Word07lessons folder and call it **word07completedmerge.docx**.

One thing to note about the resulting single large file: the date field beneath the sender address is still a field, though all the other fields have been converted to pure text. Since it is a date/time field, you can bring its contents up to date periodically by clicking the Update button/icon on its field handle.

What you learned in this lesson:

* Linking to a Merge Data Source

* Inserting Merge Fields into a Word Document

* Using If-Then Conditional Field Codes

* Previewing Merge Documents

* Conditionally Inserting Images into a Merge Document

* Finalizing and Saving a Merge Document

Knowledge Assessment

Fill in the Blanks

Complete the following sentences by writing the correct word or words in the blanks provided.

1. Snippets of code that insert data from a merge's data source are called _____.
2. Mail merge tools reside within the _____ tag in Word 2013.
3. A .csv file separates cells with _____.
4. The name, street address, city/state, and optional title/phone number of a form letter's recipient will all be folded under a complex field called an _____.
5. The basic structure of a conditional field is IF, THEN, _____.
6. To use a personalized greeting line for each of 100 recipients, you can insert a _____ prompt and type in a different text string for each recipient when you finalize your merge.
7. The field code {IF {MergeField FirstName}= "Bill" "Hi Bill" "Hello stranger"} inserts different text depending on the value of the current data record's _____ field.
8. When finalizing a merge, choose the _____ option to make changes to specific merged letters after the merge is complete.
9. If you don't have an external data source file, you can create an _____ directly in Word at the outset of the mail merge process.
10. To insert the document author's name in place of a closing in a mail merge document, use the _____ command.

Matching

Match each term numbered 1 to 10 to its description or definition in letters a to j.

1. conditional field
2. Mailings > Rules
3. Ctrl+F9
4. Mail Merge Wizard
5. Preview Results
6. Insert Merge Field…
7. Alt+F9
8. Mailings > Greeting Line
9. Finish & Merge > Print Documents…
10. Edit Individual Documents

a. used when skipping merge preview, or after individual documents are edited

b. inserts a field code

c. inserts equivalent of the To: line in an email

d. toggle field codes

e. shows merge output without finalizing

f. e.g., tweak wording in a handful of merged docs before printing

g. step-by-step merge creator

h. commands to output variable merge data

i. uses IF/THEN/ELSE structure

j. selects from fields relevant to merged docs only

Competency Assessment

Project 7-1: Creating a Data Source

In this exercise you'll create an address list within Word to act as a merge data source.

1. Launch Word and open the project file **merge-text-source.**
2. Save your document in your working directory as **project_7-1_data_source**.
3. Click **Mailings > Select Recipients > Type a New List…**
4. Add the following four records to the address list:

    Ms Miyako Porra, 33 Fake St, Springfield IL, 00293

    Mrs Maria Sala, 99 Hinman Hollow, Rampling MI, 12340

    Mrs Cho Soler, 1 Great White Way, Merryway TX, 74747

    Miss Ronia Kim, Alcor Village, Apartment 2D, Anchorage, AK, 39962

5. Save the address list as **birdie_address_list**.
6. Click **Mailings > Select Recipients > Use an Existing List…** and select the address list you just created.
7. Save your document.

Project 7-2: Editing the Merge Document

In this exercise you'll replace pieces of a letter (a .docx file) with merge fields.

1. With **project_7-1_data_source** still open, save it as **project_7-2_edit**.
2. Delete the three generic address block lines. In their place, click **Mailings > Write & Insert Fields > Address Block**.
3. Use the default recipient name format, exclude the company name and country/region, and click **OK**.
4. Click **Mailings > Preview Results > Preview Results**.
5. Select the newly-inserted address block and **Remove Space After Paragraphs** (in Home > Paragraph). Then insert a blank line before the greeting line.
6. Similarly replace the current greeting line with **Mailings > Write & Insert Fields > Greeting Line** in the default format.
7. Change the final line "thanks for your interest" to "**thanks for your interest, <<title>> <<Last Name>>**" (inserting the appropriate merge fields before the period).
8. Save the document.

Proficiency Assessment

Project 7-3: **Finalizing the Merge**

In this exercise you'll complete a mail merge and create an output .docx file with all your merged form letters.

1. Continue using **project_7-2_edit**. Save your document as **project_7-3_finalize**.

2. Add a return address block (Richard Smith-Jones, etc.) in the upper right of the document, and insert a Current Date field below it, set to update automatically. Save your document.

3. Select Finish & Merge > Edit Individual Documents… to merge all records to a new .docx file.

4. Add a short personalized message before "Enjoy the show" in each of the four documents.

5. Maria Sala inquired about Camelot, not Bye Bye Birdie; edit the appropriate merged page to reflect this change.

6. Save the merged document as **project_7-3_merged_printable**.

7. Save and close all open documents.

Project 7-4: **Creating Other Documents with Mail Merge**

In this exercise you'll create math flash cards using Word's Mail Merge tools.

1. Create a new blank Word document. Save your document as **project_7-4_flashcards**.

2. Use the Mail Merge feature to create a set of 10 simple multiplication flashcards, each 3" square, with a simple multiplication problem on each, in the following format:

   7

   x 5

   35

   Generate the numbers for the flashcards in a 3-column Excel sheet, with columns labeled Mult1, Mult2, and Product; merge them into a Word document whose page dimensions are 3"x3".

3. Save the merged printable output as **project_7-4_printable**, and the Excel document as **project_7-4_numbers**.

Mastery Assessment

Project 7-5: Using Excel Data for a Merge

In this exercise you'll create a mail merge using an Excel worksheet as your data source.

1. Open the project file **merge-text-source** in Word, and then launch Excel 2013.
2. Save your Excel document as **project_7-5_source**, and your Word document as **project_7-5_text**.
3. Create an Excel worksheet with columns labeled Title, First, Last, Street, Street2, City, State, and Zip Code.
4. Populate the Excel spreadsheet with the following data:

   Ms Miyako Porra, 33 Fake St, Springfield IL, 00293

   Mrs Maria Sala, 99 Hinman Hollow, Rampling MI, 12340

   Mrs Cho Soler, 1 Great White Way, Merryway TX, 74747

   Miss Ronia Kim, Alcor Village, Apartment 2D, Anchorage, AK, 39962
5. Save and close the Excel document.
6. Set up a mail merge in Word using the Excel document as your data source, and use the Mailings > Match Fields command to map Excel columns to merge fields. Insert an address block and finalize the merge.
7. Save and close your Word document.

Project 7-6: Conditional Image Formatting

In this exercise you'll wrap an image in a conditional field code, so it only appears in certain merge documents.

1. Open the project file **7-6-source** and save it as **project_7-6_conditional**.
2. Use the instructions in the lesson to insert an image at the top of the document, which will only appear if the recipient's last name is Porra.
3. Preview the merge to make sure the conditional has been entered properly.
4. Save and close your document.

Blogging in Word

LESSON SKILL MATRIX

In this lesson, you will learn the following skills:

Setting up a Blog Account

Editing a Blog Post

Setting a Post's Categories

Uploading Posts and Drafts

KEY TERMS

- blog
- blog post
- category
- hyperlink

The staff at Northwind Traders is encouraged to blog about their work projects – new products, new designs, new ways of using Northwind gear. Because they're already used to using Office for document creation, it makes sense that Northwind's staff would use Word 2013 for blogging. Word supports popular blog platforms, and posting rich blog content from Word is no different from creating a .docx file.

SOFTWARE ORIENTATION

You can use Microsoft Word to manage and format online blogs as you'll discover in this lesson.

Figure 8-1

Microsot Word blog tools.

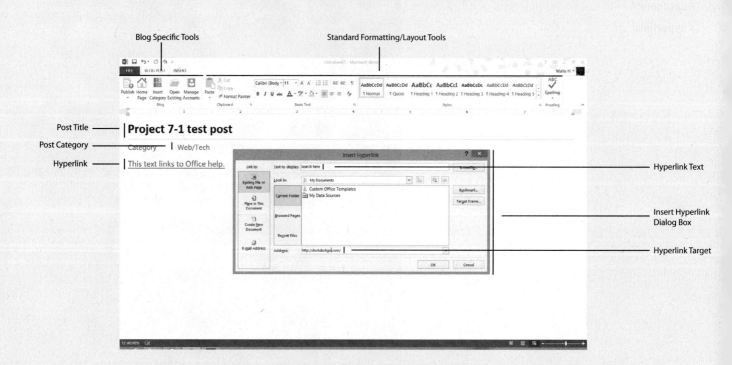

STARTING UP

You will not need to work with any files for this lesson.

How blogs work

The difference between **blogs** and the rest of the Web has disappeared since the first blogs appeared more than a decade ago; almost every website you visit is now a front-end for one or more databases of continually refreshed information, from weather reports to news articles to Wikipedia entries. That's all Web 2.0 really means: tools for dynamically generating web content. (The social web is just content generated by users, for free.)

A blog is just a database of **posts** (articles, essays, journal entries, quotations, or links to pictures) turned into HTML and laid out in reverse chronological order by a web server. Blog posts are tagged with a title, one or more **categories** (Yoga, Toddlers, Recipes), a time/date stamp, and author information (many of the most popular blogs have multiple authors).

If you think of a blog post as a .docx file, the text is just that, text, the post's other features are just document properties, which can be edited through fields. This is exactly how Word 2013 edits blog posts.

Setting up a blog account

Bottom Line

Blogging in Word is similar to editing any other kind of file: you create a document using the Blog Post template, edit a couple of fields, write your text, and save your document. The only unique aspect of blogging (compared to editing any other .docx file) is setting up an account with a blog provider. We'll do that first.

Take Note

If you have your own blog, just use your own account information while working through the lesson; if your blogging service isn't supported by Word 2013 out-of-the-box, check online for the information you need to set up the app. If you don't have a blog, set up a free account at *wordpress.com* or *blogger.com*. (You will not be able to do the exercises in this lesson without an active blog account.)

STEP BY STEP   Setting up a blog account

1   Launch Word 2013. From the Backstage View, click New, and then select the Blog template from the gallery.

2   Click Blog Post > Manage Accounts. At the Register a Blog Account dialog box, click Register Now. In the New Blog Account dialog box, click New. In the Blog Accounts dialog box, click New.

Figure 8-2

A variety of popular blog services are supported by Word out of the box.

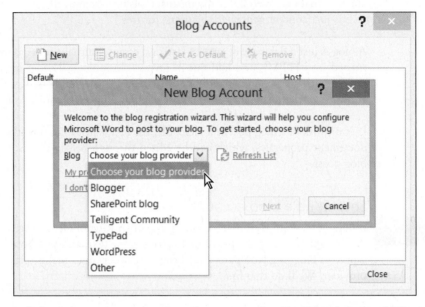

A dialog box appears with a drop-down menu (see Figure 8-2) from which you can select a blog provider. Blogger and WordPress are popular free services; Typepad is a venerable pay service; Telligent and Microsoft SharePoint are corporate intranet/groupware services. Regardless of which provider you set up your account with, posting works the same way.

3   Select your blogging service, and then provide a username and password. If you don't have a blog account and want to set one up, select *I don't have a blog yet*.

If you store your images at a separate site (for example, a gallery on your own website), enter that information by clicking Picture Options.

4   Click OK to close the dialog box(es).

CREATING A BLOG POST

Bottom Line

Word's blog post editing interface looks much like any other .docx file. The obvious differences are the altered Ribbon (only Blog Post and Insert tabs are present) and the [Enter Post Title Here] field, shown in Figure 8-3. We'll set the categories and title for our post, add some text and an image, and upload the post to our blog.

Figure 8-3

Word 2013's blog editing interface.

STEP BY STEP

Creating a blog post

1 Click the **title** field and type **Flop Flip**.

2 Click within the main text area and type **From space, flip and flop look the same.** Press **Return**.

3 Click **Insert > Online Pictures**. At the royalty-free clip art prompt, search for **flip flop**, then select an image from the gallery and click **Insert**.

4 Select the word *space* and click **Insert > Hyperlink**. Type **http://nasa.gov** in the Address text field. Click **ScreenTip...**, enter **...is the place** and click **OK**. In the Insert Hyperlink dialog (see Figure 8-4), click **OK** again.

Figure 8-4

Inserting a hyperlink.

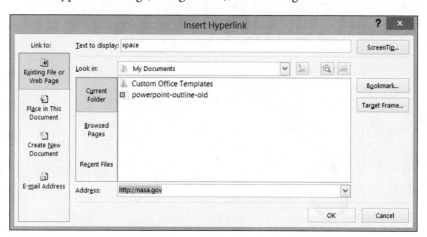

The **hyperlink** dialog box offers several options to link to files and locations within our document (which will be a webpage in a few moments).

Formatting text

    1   Click to insert your cursor below the image of flip flops and then press Enter.

    2   Type Further Information and hit Enter. On the next line type The title says it all. In the Blog Post tab, apply the Heading 2 style to the *Further Information* line.

    3   Select the words *The title* and choose Insert > Hyperlink.

    4   In the Link to: pane, choose Place in This Document. Select Top of the Document from the outline that appears. Click OK.

You can format your text just as you normally would with any .docx file; Word provides a stripped-down set of character and paragraph formatting tools in Blog Post mode.

Setting your blog post's categories

Bottom Line

The last step before posting is to set the categories of your blog post; these are a form of metadata that your blogging service will use to organize your posts (for example, to display all your blog posts marked with the Alien Visitation category). In Word, categories are set by entering data into one or more fields.

Setting categories

    1   Click Blog Post > Blog > Insert Category. When prompted, enter the login and password for your blog.

You can only insert categories if you have set up a blog account. If so, Word will retrieve the categories from your blog.

    2   Select an appropriate category from the Category drop-down menu (which is just a special field). See Figure 8-5.

Figure 8-5

Word downloads the category listing from your blog.

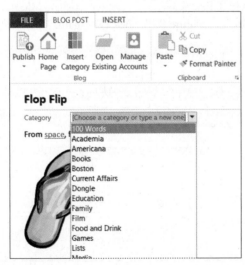

Clip art and template used with permission of Microsoft.

You can add multiple categories if you want; indeed, that's smart practice in general. Your post will still appear just once on the front page of your blog, but will be included in multiple category archive listings.

UPLOADING POSTS AND DRAFTS

Bottom Line

When you're ready to upload your test post, click Publish, and then give your username and password when prompted. To view your post, click Home Page to launch your default web browser and load the front page of your blog.

The Publish button also has a drop-down menu from which you can choose to Publish as Draft. If you do so, your post won't appear on your blog site, but will be stored on the server for later editing. Your blogging service should offer a web interface for browsing, editing, and publishing drafts.

Editing posts stored on the server

You can also use Word to edit posts that reside on the web server after uploading: click Blog Post > Open Existing, provide login/password information, and select a post from the dialog box. Beyond that, all the commands are the same; when you publish your edited post, you'll overwrite the one on the server.

What you learned in this lesson:

• Setting up a Blog Account

• Editing a Blog Post

• Setting a Post's Categories

• Uploading Posts and Drafts

Knowledge Assessment

Fill in the Blanks

Complete the following sentences by writing the correct word or words in the blanks provided.

1. Clickable text that opens a browser on a specific page is called a _____.
2. Blog posts might begin as Word documents, but they render in web browsers as _____ data.
3. Blogs are hosted on remote computers called _____.
4. Display the main screen of your blog, as a reader would see it, by clicking the _____ button in Word.
5. A post that's been uploaded but not yet published to the blog is called a _____.
6. To indicate the topic(s) of a post, set one or more _____ with the dropdown menu in Word.
7. Editing a blog post in Word involves only the File, Blog Post, and _____ tabs.
8. To make a hyperlink to a webpage, choose the _____ option in the Insert Hyperlink box's Link to: pane.

Competency Assessment

Project 8-1: Creating a Blog Post

In this exercise you will create a new blog post, assign it to a category, insert a hyperlink, and publish it.

1. Launch Word and create a new Blog Post from the launch screen.
2. Add the title Project 8-1 test post.
3. Click Insert Category and select an appropriate category from the drop-down menu.
4. Click Insert > Hyperlink.
5. In the Insert Hyperlink dialog box, create a link to the webpage http://office.microsoft.com with link text This text links to Office help.
6. Click Blog Post > Publish to upload the file, and view it by clicking the Home Page button.

Project 8-2: Hyperlinks

In this exercise you'll practice creating hyperlinks in Word.

1. Create a blank Word document and save it as **project_8-2_hyperlinks**.
2. Type the sentence This file contains a link to Microsoft, and one to online Office support.
3. Select the word Microsoft and click Insert > Links > Hyperlink. Create a link to http://google.com.
4. Select the words online Office support and create a hyperlink to http://office.microsoft.com.
5. Insert ten blank lines, then type This links back to the first sentence.
6. Select the words This file and click Insert > Links > Bookmark. Name the bookmark opening.
7. Select the final sentence and add a hyperlink with the target Place in this document. Select the bookmark from the list and click OK.
8. Save and close your document.

Proficiency Assessment

Project 8-3: Formatting Blog Posts

In this exercise you'll use Word's formatting features to style a blog post.
If you haven't set up a blog account yet, feel free to skip this exercise.

1. Open Word and create a blank blog post with the title Style Test.
2. Add a Heading 1 line and several Heading 2 lines, each with some Normal text below it. (The text can be about anything you like.)
3. Next to the first Heading 1 line, insert an online image appropriate to the text, with Tight Wrapping turned on.
4. Add a <blockquote> (Quote style) paragraph somewhere in the document. If you're able, add appropriate Category listings to the document.
5. Upload your post to your blog, or save it as regular Word document **project_8-3_formatting**.

Project 8-4: Drafts

In this exercise you'll upload a blog post as a draft. If you haven't set up a blog account yet, skip this exercise.

1. Create a blank blog post in Word, complete with title, categories, and some body text.
2. Use the Blog Post > Publish > Publish as Draft command to upload the post to your blog provider without publishing.
3. Take a screenshot of the post listing interface of your blog provider and save it to your working directory as **project_8-4_draft**.
4. Close your document (there is no need to save it locally).

Mastery Assessment

Project 8-5: HTML Tables

In this exercise you'll insert a table into a blog post and upload it to your blog. If you haven't set up a blog account, skip this exercise.

1. Create a new blank blog post in Word. Give it a title and add one or more categories.
2. Add a 4x5 table, filled however you like, with style Grid Table 5 Dark – Accent 4.
3. Upload your post and close your document (no need to save).

Project 8-6: Linking Between Blog Posts

In this exercise you'll create two blog posts, each with a link to the other. If you haven't set up a blog account, skip this exercise.

1. Create two blank blog posts in Word, with whatever content you like.
2. Upload the first post and view it in your browser.
3. Open the second post in Word and add a hyperlink to the first (get its post URL from your browser). Upload the second post.
4. Now edit the first post in Word to include a link to the second, so that each post links to the other. Re-upload the post.
5. Close Word without saving the files.

Microsoft Excel 2013

LESSON SKILL MATRIX

In this lesson, you will learn the following skills:

Getting to Know the Workspace	Using the Quick Access Toolbar
Getting to Know the Cell Pointer	Using the Formula Bar
Using the Ribbon	Moving Around the Worksheet
Exploring the Status Bar	Exploring What's New in Excel 2013

KEY TERMS

- **Workbooks**
- **Worksheet**
- **Columns**
- **Rows**
- **Ribbon**
- **Status bar**
- **Quick access toolbar**
- **Quick analysis**
- **Sparklines**
- **Flash fill**
- **Slicers**

The accounting department of Fabrikam, Inc. needs to track revenue and expenses for the entire firm and maintain a large volume of employee data. It's also responsible for creating revenue projections and visualizations for the other departments within the firm. Microsoft Excel is an ideal tool for organizing and analyzing such data. In this lesson, you will learn how to enter text and numbers into an Excel worksheet to keep up-to-date employee records.

SOFTWARE ORIENTATION

This lesson provides you with an introduction to many of the essential tools and capabilities you'll need to use when working in Microsoft Excel.

Figure 1-1

The Microsoft Excel interface.

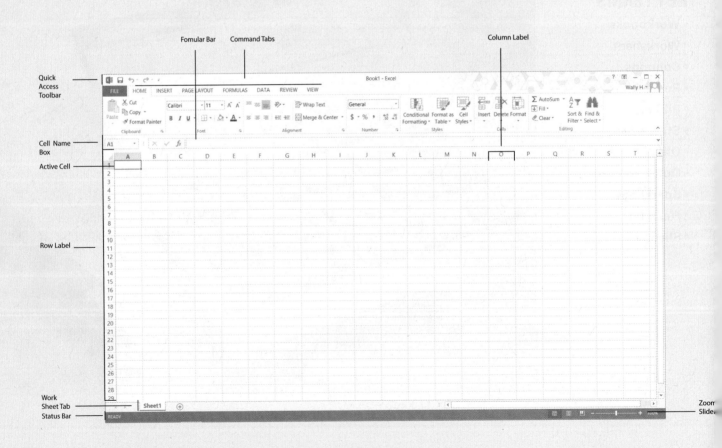

STARTING UP

In this lesson, you'll work with several files from the Excel01lessons folder. Make sure that you have loaded the OfficeLessons folder onto your computer.

GETTING TO KNOW THE WORKSPACE

In Microsoft Excel, files are called **workbooks**. In Excel 2013, you can create a new, blank workbook or select from a set of predesigned workbook templates that enable you to quickly get to work. Templates exist for budgets, invoices, lists, reports, and much more. Templates are discussed in greater detail In Lesson 7, "Working with Excel 2013 Templates."

When you create a new file, a blank workbook containing a single **worksheet** is displayed (Figure 1-2). A workbook consists of individual worksheets, each capable of containing its own set of data. By default, each workbook you create contains a single worksheet although a workbook can contain as many as 256 separate worksheets. At the bottom of each worksheet is a tab initially named Sheet1. You can easily rename worksheets by double-clicking the tab and typing the name you wish to use.

Figure 1-2

A. Status Bar. B. Row. C. Cell. D. Ribbon Bar. E. Name Box. F. Column. G. Formula Bar.

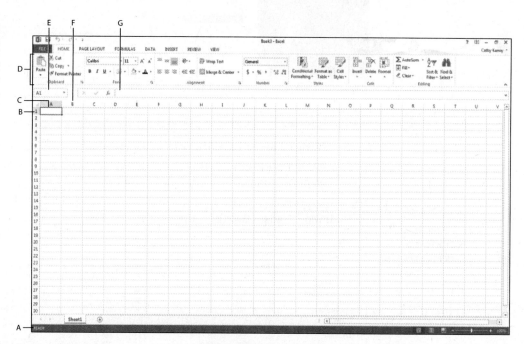

An Excel worksheet is constructed of **columns** and **rows** and is similar in appearance to a grid or bookkeeping ledger. Column headings are arranged along the top of the worksheet window and are labeled alphabetically. Row headings are displayed down the left edge of the worksheet window and are listed numerically.

The basic unit of a worksheet is the **cell**, formed by the intersection of a row and column. Every cell has a cell address named for that intersection, such as A4 or G11. When you click a wcell, the column and row headings appear highlighted, indicating the cell's address. The cell address also appears in the Name box, located just above column A.

Bottom Line

To work efficiently in Excel, you need to become familiar with its primary user interface. Knowing your toolkit will let you work more efficiently, and get to work more quickly.

STEP BY STEP   **Opening an Excel document**

1   Launch Microsoft Excel and see the Backstage view (Figure 1-3).

Figure 1-3

The Backstage displays the files you have recently opened.

Templates used with permission of Microsoft

2   Choose Open Other Workbooks from the Backstage.

3   Navigate to the Excel01lessons folder and double-click **excel01**. An Excel document opens to display a worksheet containing three different venue quotes for a fictitious event planning company as shown in Figure 1-4.

Figure 1-4

The file named excel01 contains three different pricing quotes for a fictitious events planner.

	A	B	C	D	E	F	G	H	I	J	K	L	M
1	Northwind Traders Events												
2	Event	McGrath-Jameson Wedding											
3	Date	6/12/2013											
4													
5													
6		Sapphire Ballroom				Plaza Hotel				Henderson's on the Bay			
7		Unit Price	Person	Total		Unit Price	Person	Total		Unit Price	Person	Total	
8	Cocktail Hour												
9	Cheese/Crackers	3.95	100	395.00		4.50	100	450.00		4.00	100	400.00	
10	Crudites	3.95	100	395.00		4.50	100	450.00		4.00	100	400.00	
11	Fruit Platter	2.95	100	295.00		3.95	100	395.00		3.25	100	325.00	
12	Dinner												
13	Ceasar Salad	2.50	200	500.00		4.00	200	800.00		3.25	200	650.00	
14	Antipasto	5.95	100	595.00		7.95	100	795.00		6.00	100	600.00	
15	Pasta	5.75	200	1150.00		7.25	200	1450.00		6.50	200	1300.00	
16	Beef	550	2	1100.00		750	2	1500.00		625	2	1250.00	
17	Turkey	200	3	600.00		550	3	1650.00		425	3	1275.00	
18	Ham	195	3	585.00		425	3	1275.00		375	3	1125.00	
19	Potatoes/Veg	2.00	200	400.00		4.00	200	800.00		3.50	200	700.00	
20	Coffee	32.00	6	192.00		50.00	6	300.00		40.00	6	240.00	
21	Subtotal			$ 6,207.00				$ 9,865.00				$ 8,265.00	
22	18% Admin			1117.26				1775.70				1487.70	
23	Subtotal			$ 7,324.26				$ 11,640.70				$ 9,752.70	
24	6.25% Meal Tax			457.77				727.54				609.54	
25	Grand Total			$ 7,782.03				$ 12,368.24				$ 10,362.24	
26													
27													

4   Choose File > Save As and navigate to the Excel01lessons folder. Name the file **excel01_work** and click Save.

GETTING TO KNOW THE CELL POINTER

Before we begin exploring the Excel workspace, it helps to get to know the mouse pointer as it takes many different forms in Excel. The pointer appears as the familiar arrow when you are choosing commands. When you move the mouse pointer within the worksheet area the mouse pointer changes its shape to that of a plus sign. As you enter data in a cell, the mouse pointer takes the shape of a cursor.

Since the mouse pointer takes so many different forms depending on the task you are performing it helps to take a moment to review the most basic shapes. The table below describes the mouse pointer shapes in more detail.

Mouse pointer shapes

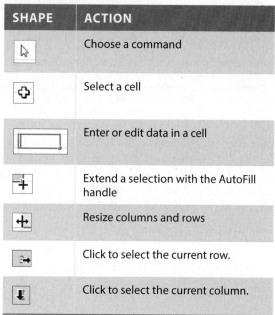

SHAPE	ACTION
	Choose a command
	Select a cell
	Enter or edit data in a cell
	Extend a selection with the AutoFill handle
	Resize columns and rows
	Click to select the current row.
	Click to select the current column.

USING THE RIBBON

Bottom Line

The **Ribbon**, which runs along the top of the worksheet window, contains context-sensitive tools and commands to help you organize, calculate, and format your data. It is made up of a series of named tabs, each of which contains a set of related commands. For instance, the Home tab contains a set of frequently-used commands such as Copy and Paste. The names of the tabs are Home, Insert, Page Layout, Formulas, Data, Review, and View. Additional tabs are also displayed when working Charts, Images, and PivotTables.

Figure 1-5

Use the Ribbon to choose commands.

The table below describes the options on the Ribbon in more detail.

TAB	DESCRIPTION
Home	Contains commonly used commands such as format cells, copy and paste, text alignment, and number formats.
Insert	Commands that enable you to insert items into your worksheet including charts, images, text boxes, and SmartArt.
Page Layout	Contains commands that enable you to change the appearance of your printed page. You can set margins, apply themes, change the page orientation, and insert page breaks
Formulas	Contains function library and other commands related to performing calculations.
Data	Contains commands for managing lists of data.
Review	Contains commands such as Spell Checker, Grammar Checker, etc.
View	Commands that enable you to change the display of the worksheet window.

Customizing the Ribbon display

You can collapse the Ribbon, by clicking the Ribbon Display Options button located in the far right corner of the title bar, so that only the named tabs appear across the top of the worksheet window. When you need to choose a command, just click the tab to redisplay the Ribbon and its options. You can also choose to Auto-Hide the Ribbon when you need additional viewing space. When you click the top of the worksheet window the Ribbon is redisplayed.

Figure 1-6

Collapse the Ribbon to display the named tabs only.

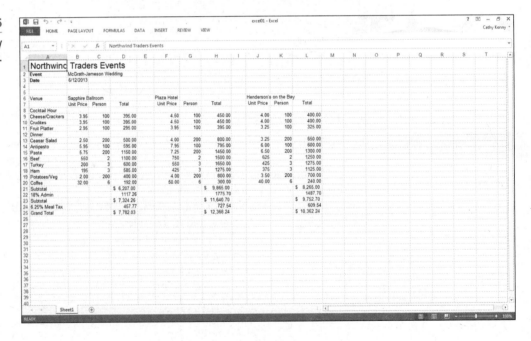

The table below describes the Ribbon Display Options found in the top-right corner of Excel.

OPTION	ICON	WHAT IT DOES
Auto-Hide Ribbon		Hides the Ribbon. Click at the top of the Excel window to redisplay it.
Show Tabs		Display tabs only. Click a tab to redisplay the Ribbon.
Show Tabs and Commands		Displays both the Tabs and Commands at all times.

STEP BY STEP   **Collapsing the Ribbon**

1 Click the Ribbon Display Options button.

Figure 1-7

The Ribbon Display Options button allows you to alter the Ribbon's appearance.

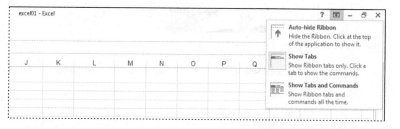

2 Choose Show Tabs and then select cell A1.

3 Click the Home tab to redisplay the Ribbon and choose Bold in the Font group.

The Show Tabs command shows the tabs but doesn't display the Ribbon unless a specific tab is selected. Once a command is selected on the Ribbon or you click elsewhere on the worksheet, the Ribbon disappears.

STEP BY STEP   **Hiding the Ribbon**

1 Click the Ribbon Display Options button.

2 Choose Auto-Hide Ribbon.

3 Click the top of the Excel window to redisplay the Ribbon.

The Auto-Hide Ribbon command hides the Ribbon from view. When you click the top of the worksheet window, the Ribbon is redisplayed.

Once you choose a command or click elsewhere on the worksheet, the Ribbon disappears.

Take Note To quickly collapse the Ribbon, right-click anywhere within the Ribbon and choose Collapse the Ribbon.

EXPLORING THE STATUS BAR

Bottom Line

The **Status bar** appears at the bottom of the worksheet window and provides updates on the current worksheet. Messages appear in the lower left corner to tell you what a command does, or what you should do next, to execute a command. For instance, when entering data in a cell the

Status bar displays ENTER in the lower left corner.

Figure 1-8

The Status bar displays the word ENTER when entering data in a cell.

	A	B	C	D	E	F	G	H	I	J	K	L
1	Northwind Traders Events											
2	Event	McGrath-Jameson Wedding										
3	Date	6/12/2013										
4												
5												
6	Venue	Sapphire Ballroom				Plaza Hotel				Henderson's on the Bay		
7		Unit Price	Person	Total		Unit Price	Person	Total		Unit Price	Person	Total
8	Cocktail Hour											
9	Cheese/Crackers	3.95	100	395.00		4.50	100	450.00		4.00	100	400.00
10	Crudites	3.95	100	395.00		4.50	100	450.00		4.00	100	400.00
11	Fruit Platter	2.95	100	295.00		3.95	100	395.00		3.25	100	325.00
12	Dinner											
13	Caesar Salad	2.50	200	500.00		4.00	200	800.00		3.25	200	650.00
14	Antipasto	6.95	100	695.00		7.95	100	795.00		6.00	100	600.00
15	Pasta	5.75	200	1150.00		7.25	200	1450.00		6.50	200	1300.00
16	Beef	550	2	1100.00		750	2	1500.00		625	2	1250.00
17	Turkey	200	3	600.00		550	3	1650.00		425	3	1275.00
18	Ham	195	3	585.00		425	3	1275.00		375	3	1125.00
19	Potatoes/Veg	2.00	200	400.00		4.00	200	800.00		3.50	200	700.00
20	Coffee	32.00	6	192.00		50.00	6	300.00		40.00	6	240.00
21	Subtotal			$ 6,207.00				$ 9,865.00				$ 8,265.00
22	18% Admin			1117.26				1775.70				1487.70
23	Subtotal			$ 7,324.26				$ 11,640.70				$ 9,752.70
24	6.25% Meal Tax			457.77				727.54				609.54
25	Grand Total			$ 7,782.03				$ 12,368.24				$ 10,362.24

The Status bar also contains a set of buttons that enable you to change the view of your worksheet. You can switch between Normal, Page Layout, and Page Break Preview modes. Using the Zoom slider, you can enlarge or reduce the size of the worksheet display.

Switching display modes

The default viewing mode in Excel is the Normal mode, and it is primarily used when you are working with your data. There are times when you want to switch the display to see what your worksheet will look like when printed, or you may just want to view where the page breaks will occur, and you can use various display modes to see these things. You can quickly change the viewing mode of your worksheet by using the buttons in the Status bar. You'll learn more about printing in Lesson 2, "Creating a Worksheet in Excel 2013."

STEP BY STEP   **Switching display modes**

1   Switch to Page Layout mode by clicking the Page Layout button.

Figure 1-9

Choose the Page Layout mode.

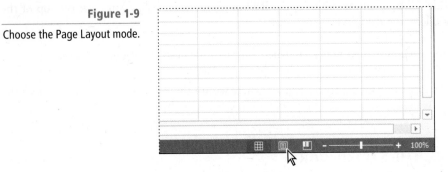

   2   Switch to Page Break Preview mode by clicking the Page Break Preview button.

   3   Click Normal to return the regular viewing mode.

Change the size of the worksheet display

You may need to change the size of your worksheet display, especially if you are working with data that extends beyond the visible area. Using the Zoom tool in the Status bar, you can quickly reduce or enlarge the worksheet display.

Figure 1-10

Change the size of your worksheet display by dragging the Zoom slider.

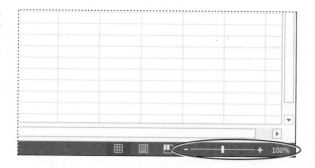

STEP BY STEP   **Changing the size of the worksheet display**

   1   Click and drag the Zoom slider to enlarge the display area to 125%.

   2   Drag the slider to 100% to return the view to its original size.

USING THE QUICK ACCESS TOOLBAR

Bottom Line

The **Quick Access Toolbar** is displayed at the top left of the Excel window and provides single-click access to frequently-used commands such as Save and Undo. You can customize the toolbar to add additional commands that you use frequently.

STEP BY STEP   **Customizing the Quick Access Toolbar**

   1   Click the Customize Quick Access Toolbar button.

Figure 1-11

Add your favorite commands to the Quick Access Toolbar to gain single-click access.

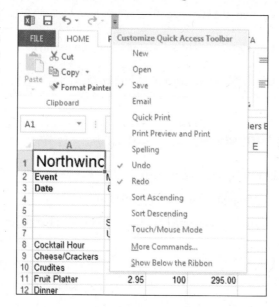

2 Click New to add the New command to the toolbar.

3 Click the Customize Quick Access Toolbar again and click Open to add the Open command to the toolbar.

USING THE FORMULA BAR

Bottom Line

The Formula bar appears just below the Ribbon and displays the contents of the active cell. When you type data in a cell, the Formula bar activates and displays the data as you type.

STEP BY STEP   Using the Formula bar

1 Click in cell A6 and type Venue.

Figure 1-12

As you type, the data appears in the Formula bar.

Notice also the appearance of three buttons to the left of the Formula bar. These buttons enable you to confirm or cancel what you are entering or a Function within the cell. Formulas will be discussed in greater detail In Lesson 4, "Using Formulas in Excel 2013."

The buttons in the Formula bar

BUTTON	ACTION
✓	Confirms the current entry. Equivalent to pressing Enter.
✗	Cancels the current entry. Equivalent to pressing Esc.
fx	Opens the Insert Function dialog box.

STEP BY STEP   Activating the Formula bar

1 Activate the cell by clicking it.

2 Move the mouse pointer to the Formula bar area.

3 When the cursor appears, click within the Formula bar to set the insertion point.

MOVING AROUND THE WORKSHEET

The active cell in a worksheet always appears with a dark outlined border. To activate another cell using the mouse, move the mouse pointer to the cell you wish to use and click it. For example, you can click cell F13 to make it active.

If you wish, you can navigate through an Excel worksheet using only its wide variety of keyboard commands, but the mouse remains an option for selecting cells and regions.

Figure 1-13

The active cell in a worksheet appears with an outlined border.

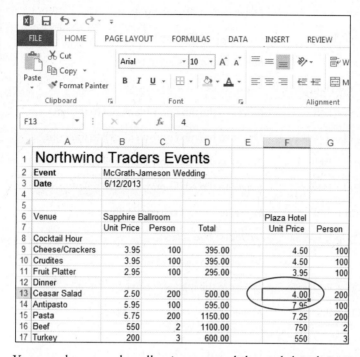

You can also move the cell pointer around the worksheet by using the keyboard. The table below discusses the keys for navigating the worksheet with the keyboard.

Navigating the worksheet with the keyboard

KEY	MOVEMENT
Up, Down, Left, Right	Moves one cell to the left, right, up or down
Ctrl Up, Down, Left, Right	Moves to the next cell of data separated by a blank cell
Tab	Moves one cell to the right
Shift Tab	Moves one cell to the left
Home	Moves to the first cell in the row
Ctrl + Home	Moves to cell A1
End + Left	Moves to the next non-blank cell to the left
End + Right	Moves to the next non-blank cell to the right
End + Up	Moves to the next non-blank cell above.
End + Down	Moves to the next non-blank cell below.
Ctrl + End	Moves to the last cell containing data
PgUp	Moves up one screen
PgDn	Moves down one screen
Ctrl + PgUp	Moves to the next worksheet
Ctrl + PgDn	Moves to the previous worksheet

Moving to a specific cell

You can quickly move to a specific cell within a worksheet by typing the cell address in the Name box that appears to the left of the Formula bar.

STEP BY STEP   **Moving to a specific cell**

1   Click the **Name** box.

Figure 1-14

To quickly move to a specific cell, type the cell address in the Name box.

2   Type **D11** and press **Enter** or **Return** on your keyboard to move to cell D11.

Using the scroll bars

The scroll bars, located along the right edge and bottom of your worksheet window, offer the quickest way to navigate a worksheet with the mouse or touch screen. Each scroll bar consists of a scroll box, scroll arrows, and the scroll bar. The scroll box, located within the scroll bar, changes size depending on where you are in the worksheet. When you are at cell A1, the scroll box fills the entire scroll bar. As you drag the bar further away from A1, the scroll box decreases in size.

Figure 1-15

A. Scroll Arrow. B. Scroll Box. C. Scroll Bar.

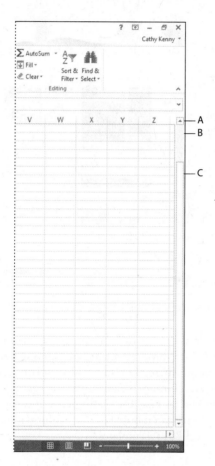

EXPLORING WHAT'S NEW IN EXCEL 2013

Microsoft has been busy adding new features designed to help you display your data visually, and has provided you with a new streamlined interface. Let's take a quick look at some of the new features Excel 2013 has to offer.

Templates help you get started right away

Excel's Backstage view, which appears whenever you launch Excel or choose File > New, displays a set of professionally designed worksheet templates. When you create a worksheet from a template, you need only plug in your data and the worksheet will update automatically.

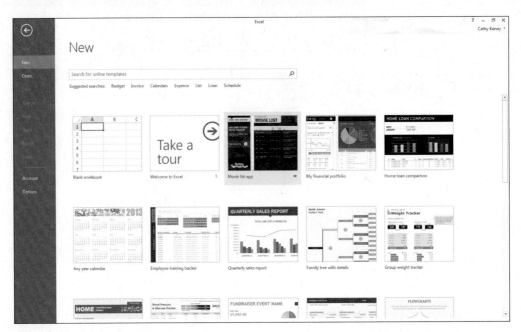

Figure 1-16

Excel's Templates take the design-work out of your hands and let you get started immediately.

Templates used with permission of Microsoft

Excel offers thousands of template choices to help you get up and running. From Invoices and Budgets, to Sales Reports and Cash Flow Statements, Excel has templates for virtually every type of business or organizational need. There are also a wide assortment of personal templates, such as a Home Construction Budget, a Group Weight Loss Tracker, and the ability to keep track of your movie collection with the Movies List. Excel also makes it easy to search through thousands of online templates with its built in Search box. For more information on using Excel's templates, see Lesson 7, "Working with Excel 2013 Templates."

Quick analysis gets down to business

With the new **Quick Analysis** button, you can instantly produce visual snapshots of your data. After selecting a range of data, click the Quick Analysis Button and choose from the selected options. Add special Formatting, create a quick Chart, add a line of Totals, produce a PivotTable, or add **Sparklines**. For more information on the Quick Analysis Tools, see Lesson 8, "Advanced Data Analysis in Excel 2013."

Figure 1-17

Get a quick visual of your data with the new Quick Analysis tools.

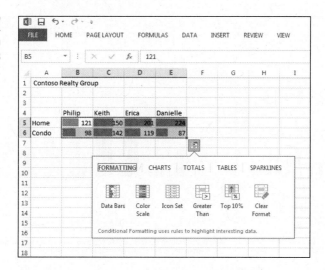

Flash Fill reduces data entry drudgery

One of the more tedious aspects of working with a program like Excel is that before you can analyze your data, you first have to enter it into your worksheet. Excel 2013 introduces **Flash Fill**, which aims to reduce the drudgery that is data entry. As you enter data, Excel analyzes the data for any patterns that may exist and if it detects any, fills the rest of the Information for you. For more information on using Flash Fill, see Lesson 6, "Working with Data."

Figure 1-18

Excel aims to reduce data entry time by anticipating patterns and filling the remainder in for you.

	A	B	C	D	E	F
1	**Contoso Realty Group**					
2	Customer Contact List					
3						
4						
5		First Name	Last Name	City	State	Zip
6	Stephen Tran	Stephen	Tran	Boston	MA	02124
7	Eric Donaldson	Eric	Donaldson	Arlingto	MA	02474
8	Dante West	Dante	West	Brighto	MA	02135
9	Linda McMann	Linda	McMann	Boston	MA	02124
10	Jennifer Ponson	Jennifer	Ponson	Woonsc	RI	02895

Chart recommendations remove the guesswork

Not sure which chart type is the best fit for your data and the message you want to convey? With Excel's new Chart recommendations, you needn't ever second guess yourself again. Just select the data you want to chart and choose Recommended Chart's, from the Insert tab. Excel will recommend a set of charts based on your data. For more Information on charts, see Lesson 5, "Working with Charts."

Figure 1-19

Use Chart Recommendations when you are not sure which chart type best suits your data.

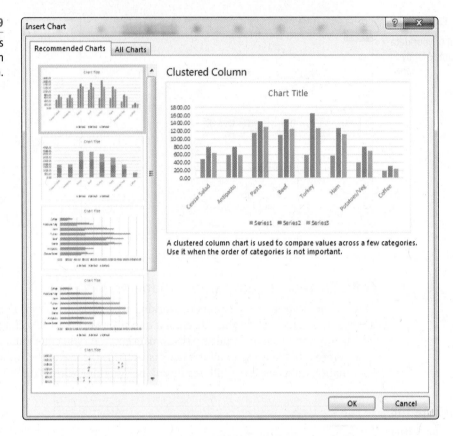

Filter your data with slicers

You can use **slicers** to filter your data using more than one value. The slicer is built-in to the Table feature and an icon is displayed to let you know when your data has been filtered. To learn more about Data Slicers, see Lesson 8, "Advanced Data Analysis in Excel 2013." While the slicer functionality first appeared in Office 2010, it has been streamlined significantly for Office 2013.

Figure 1-20

Filter your data on multiple values using the new Data Slicers.

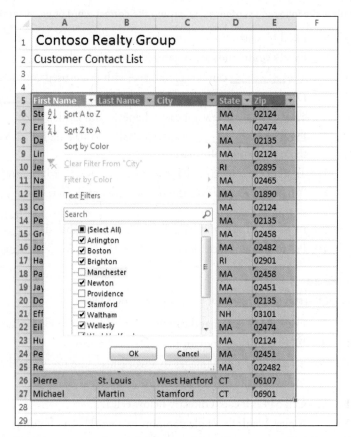

You've now completed this lesson. Now that you are familiar with the workspace in Excel, you are ready to begin creating new worksheets and working with your data.

What you learned in this lesson:

- Getting to Know the Workspace
- Getting to Know the Cell Pointer
- Using the Ribbon
- Exploring the Status Bar
- Using the Quick Access Toolbar
- Using the Formula Bar
- Moving Around the Worksheet
- Exploring What's New in Excel 2013

Lesson 1 Knowledge Assessment

Fill in the Blank

Complete the following sentences by writing the correct word or words in the blanks provided.

1. Excel files are also known as _____.
2. Excel's commands are organized by topic in the _____.
3. The _____ can be customized with often-used commands like Quick Print.
4. Data can be entered directly into a cell, or into the _____.
5. The _____ view appears whenever you launch Excel.
6. Excel's new _____ tool will analyze your data for patterns and attempt to fill in the rest of your information.
7. To jump to a specific cell in the worksheet, enter its address in the _____.
8. When you mouse over the row number at the left of the screen, the pointer changes to a _____.
9. Rows are labeled numerically; columns are labeled _____.
10. Pre-formatted Excel documents can be downloaded through the _____ Gallery.

True/False

Circle T if the statement is true or F it the statement is false.

T F 1. Every Excel command can be accessed from the Home tab.

T F 2. Workbooks can contain multiple worksheets.

T F 3. To add charts and images to a worksheet, use the View tab.

T F 4. The zoom slider is located within the Status Bar.

T F 5. Cell M4 is located directly below cell L4.

T F 6. A new, blank Excel file contains two workbooks holding two worksheets each.

T F 7. When you input data in a cell, the Status Bar displays the word ENTER.

T F 8. A command like "add cells F5 and F6 and display the result here" is called a function.

T F 9. Pressing the Home button moves the cursor to the top left cell.

T F 10. As you type data into a cell, it also appears in the Address bar.

Competency Assessment

Project 1-1: Creating and Saving a Workbook

Use this exercise to familiarize yourself with the Save function and Backstage view.

1. Launch Excel if it is not already open and create a new document by selecting **Blank workbook** from the launch screen, or pressing **Ctrl+N**.
2. Add two worksheets (Sheets 2 and 3) by clicking the ⊕ symbol at the bottom of the Excel window.
3. Click in cell A1 and drag to C3 to select nine cells.
4. In the Font group of the Home tab, click the **paint bucket** icon to change the color of the selected cells.

5. Click the File tab to open the Backstage view, then select Save. Note that "Save As" remains highlighted.

6. In the left column, select Computer. Then click Browse.

7. Browse to the Excel01lessons folder on your computer.

8. In the File name: text area, type **1_1**. Click the Save as type: drop-down to view the many save formats available in Excel 2013.

9. Select Excel Workbook from the Save as type: drop-down and click Save.

10. Close the workbook.

Project 1-2: Utilizing the Ribbon

In this exercise you'll work with the Ribbon tabs.

1. Open Excel and create a new blank document. (No need to save.)

2. Click the File tab (Backstage) and survey the file-management options available.

3. Press Escape to return to the main editing screen. Add a title to Slide 1, then select the new title text.

4. In the Home tab, expand the font gallery. Press T to jump down the font list. Choose Times New Roman and note the font change in the title box.

5. Select Undo from the Quick Access Toolbar (or press Ctrl+Z).

6. Experiment with commands in the Insert, Design, and other tabs.

7. Click File > Exit. When prompted, elect not to save the document.

Proficiency Assessment

Project 1-3: Entering Data

You will create an Excel worksheet containing a list of items sold at a recent garage sale. Excel's tools for quick data entry speed up the process.

1. Create a new workbook. Click the File tab, choose Save, navigate to Excel01lessons folder, and name the workbook **Sale_Items_1**.

2. In cell A1, type Item. Press Tab.

3. In cell B1, type Cost. Press Tab.

4. In cell C1, type Quantity. Press Tab.

5. In cell D1, type Total Cost. Press Return to move the cursor to A2.

6. Type each of the following item names and press Return after each: sneakers, shirt (L), shirt (S), books. The last entry will appear in A5.

7. Click in B2, type $5, and press Return.

8. Type $2, then click on the small handle at the lower right of the selected cell, called the AutoFill handle, and drag it down to B5. All three cells will display $2.

9. Click in cell C2, then click in the Formula bar and type 2.

10. Hit Return. Type the following values, hitting Return after each one: 1, 3, 10.

11. Save the file and close the workbook.

Project 1-4: Editing and Extending a Workbook

In this exercise, you will add formulas to the previously created workbook.

1. Click the File tab. A list of recent locations and documents will appear. Under Recent Workbooks, select **Sale_Items_1**.
2. Select cell **D2**. In the Formula bar, type **=product(** but do not press Return.
3. Click and drag from B2 to C2 to select those cells. The Formula bar now reads =product(B2:C2.
4. Press Return. Cell D3 is selected, and D2 displays the number 10.
5. Click cell D2 and drag its AutoFill handle down to D5. The column fills with numbers representing total sales cost: 2, 6, and 20.
6. Click cell **B4** and type **5**, then press Return. The values in B4 and D4 will update.
7. Choose Save As and name the file **Sales_Items_2**. Close the file.
8. Leave Excel open for the next exercise.

Mastery Assessment

Project 1-5: Using Display Modes

1. Hit **Ctrl+N** to create a new file.
2. In cell A1, type **Sample entry 1**.
3. Drag its AutoFill handle down to populate the first 60 cells of column A.
4. Open the View tab and click Page Layout. Note that Excel fills up the entire first page with dozens of rows before breaking for page 2.
5. Select Page Break Preview. Drag the blue dotted line, which indicates a page break, up to roughly row 10.
6. Reselect Page Layout. Excel has moved the page break to its new location.
7. Press **Ctrl+W** to close the document. When prompted to save, select Don't Save. Leave Excel open for the next exercise.

Project 1-6: Customizing the Quick Access Toolbar

1. Click the arrow on the Quick Access Toolbar to open the Customize Quick Access Toolbar drop-down menu.
2. Select Sort Ascending from the menu.
3. Reopen the dropdown menu and select More Commands...
4. From the left-hand list, select Create Chart and click Add>>.
5. Click Customizations: Reset and select Reset only Quick Access Toolbar. Click Yes at the prompt, then click OK.
6. Close Excel.

LESSON SKILL MATRIX

In this lesson, you will learn the following skills:

Creating a Worksheet	Using Undo/Redo
Entering Data in a Cell	Working with Rows and Columns
Working with Cell Ranges	Creating Additional Worksheets
Saving Workbooks	Printing Worksheets and Workbooks
Opening Workbooks	
Editing Data	

KEY TERMS

- **AutoFill**
- **AutoSum**
- **Cell Address**
- **Copy**
- **Cut**
- **Footer**
- **Formula**
- **Freeze (row or column)**
- **Handle**
- **Header**
- **Operator**
- **Page Layout Mode**
- **Page Orientation (portrait, landscape)**
- **Paste**
- **Print Area**
- **Range**

The staff at Contoso Partners are preparing a report on campaign contributions, broken down geographically and by age group. They lay out Excel documents that combine scratch data-entry spaces, complex calculations, and carefully sorted final numbers. Excel's data-entry and analysis tools, screen/print layout tools, and features like AutoSum and AutoFill let the staff build these complex documents quickly and efficiently.

SOFTWARE ORIENTATION

Understanding how Microsoft Excel helps you organize and compute data saves you time while helping you to be more accurate in the work you perform.

Figure 2-1

New document workspace.

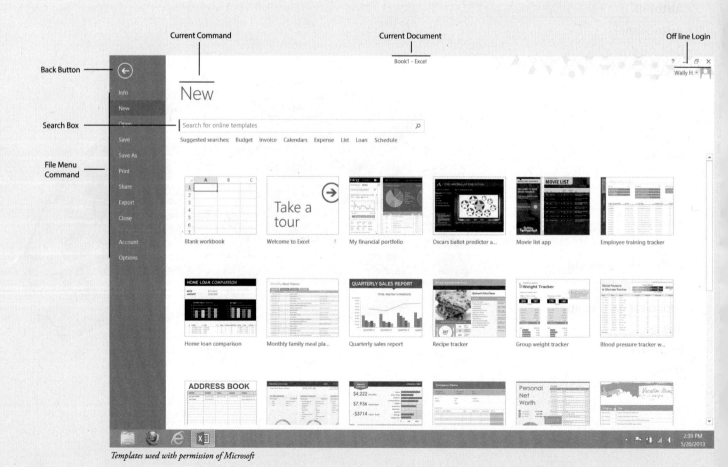

Templates used with permission of Microsoft

STARTING UP

In this lesson, you'll work with several files from the Excel02lessons folder. Make sure that you have loaded the OfficeLessons folder onto your computer.

Bottom Line

CREATING A WORKSHEET

In this first lesson, we will create a new blank workbook to practice some basic data entry skills.

STEP BY STEP | **Creating a new workbook**

1   Launch Microsoft Excel.

2   Choose Blank workbook from the New Backstage (See Figure 2-2.).

Figure 2-2

Excel 2013 offers thousands of predesigned templates to choose from. Choose Blank Workbook to start from scratch.

Templates used with permission of Microsoft

3   Excel opens a new window and displays a blank workbook containing a single worksheet.

ENTERING DATA IN A CELL

Bottom Line

Entering data in Excel is fairly straightforward, once you understand a few simple concepts. Before you can enter data, you must first select the cell in which you want the data to appear. As discussed in Lesson 1, "Getting Started with Excel 2013," the active cell appears outlined and the cell pointer changes its shape to that of a plus sign when it is within the worksheet window. To select a cell, click it or use the arrow keys on your keyboard to move the cell pointer to that cell.

When you start typing, the data appears in both the active cell and in the Formula bar. You can enter text, numbers, dates, times, or formulas in a cell.

Entering text

As you enter text within a cell, the text continues to be displayed in adjacent columns until it meets a non-blank cell. Although the text appears to be in more than one cell, it is contained within the active cell only. Note also that Excel aligns the text to the left edge of the cell border.

Entering text in cells

1   Click cell **A1**.

2   Type **Contoso Realty Group** and press **Enter**.

3   In your Excel spreadsheet, enter the words shown in the right column (Type) into the cells indicated by the left column (Cell), as in Figure 2-3.

Cell	Type
B4	Philip
C4	Keith
D4	Erica
E4	Danielle
A5	House
A6	Condo
A7	Total
F4	Total

Figure 2-3

Use text to label the data in your worksheets.

	A	B	C	D	E	F	G
1	Contoso Realty Group						
2							
3							
4		Philip	Keith	Erica	Danielle	Total	
5	House						
6	Condo						
7	Total						
8							

Entering numbers

When you type numbers or values in a cell, you can type them with or without accompanying symbols, such as commas, decimals, or dollar signs. You can format the cell after the fact to display the symbols that we discuss in Lesson 3, "Formatting Excel Worksheets." If you do enter the value with accompanying symbols, Excel automatically assigns the appropriate numeric format. In addition, Excel automatically aligns the values to the right side of the cell.

Entering numbers in cells

1   Click cell **B5**.

2   Type **121** and press **Enter**.

3 In your Excel spreadsheet, enter the values shown in the right column (Type) into the cells indicated by the left column (Cell). The resulting table is shown in Figure 2-4.

Cell	Type
B6	98
C5	150
C6	142
D5	201
D6	119
E5	224
E6	87

Take Note If you enter a large value, Excel displays the symbols ##### in the cell, indicating that the value is wider than the current column width

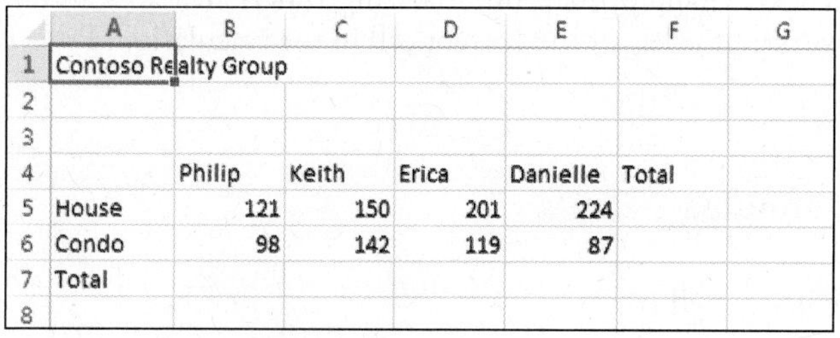

Figure 2-4

Values appear right-aligned within a cell.

	A	B	C	D	E	F	G
1	Contoso Realty Group						
2							
3							
4		Philip	Keith	Erica	Danielle	Total	
5	House	121	150	201	224		
6	Condo	98	142	119	87		
7	Total						
8							

Entering dates and times

Excel accepts a number of different formats for entering date and time values. You can enter dates and times with accompanying symbols, such as dashes (-), slashes (/), or colons (:) or type the entry as text, for example, March 30, 2013 or 12:15 PM. Excel recognizes any of these entries as a date or time and applies the appropriate date format.

STEP BY STEP **Entering numbers in cells**

1 Type 3/20/13 in cell A2.

2 Press Enter to enter the date.

Take Note To quickly enter Today's date, select a cell and press Ctrl+;.

Entering formulas

The final type of data you can enter into Excel is a **formula**, which is a calculation using a combination of values and mathematical **operators**. Formulas must follow a particular syntax to be recognized by Excel, and they begin with the equal sign (=) followed by the values and operators. For example, the formula =750*34 multiplies the value 750 by 34. When you press Enter, Excel displays the result, or in this case, the product of the two values. Formulas will be discussed in greater detail in Lesson 4, "Using Formulas in Excel 2013."

If you don't want to enter fixed, specific values into your formula, you can enter the cell address of applicable values. When you use **cell addresses** in a formula, Excel refers to them as cell references, and uses whatever value is in the cell. If the value contained in the cell changes, Excel automatically updates the formula.

To perform quick calculations in Excel, you can use the **AutoSum** command. To use it, click in a cell directly adjacent to the values you want to summarize. Choose AutoSum from the Home tab and click the appropriate summarizing function. Excel automatically includes the range of cells above or to the left of the current cell in the calculation. Press Enter to complete the formula.

STEP BY STEP   **Using formulas**

1   Click in cell B7.

2   Choose AutoSum from the Editing group in the Home tab, and click Sum from the resulting menu.

AutoSum options

BUTTON	WHAT IT DOES
Sum	Sums the value of a range.
Average	Finds the average value in a range.
Count Numbers	Counts up the numbers in a range.
Max	Finds the maximum value.
Min	Finds the minimum value.

Excel automatically selects cells B5 and B6, the values directly above the current cell.

3   Press Enter to calculate the sum.

4   Click in F5, choose AutoSum again, and click Sum from the resulting menu.

5   Excel automatically selects cells B5 through E5, the cells directly to the left of the current cell (see Figure 2-5).

Figure 2-5

The AutoSum command selects the values in adjacent cells.

	A	B	C	D	E	F	G	H	I
1	Contoso Realty Group								
2	20-Mar-13								
3									
4		Philip	Keith	Erica	Danielle	Total			
5	House	121	150	201	224	=SUM(B5:E5)			
6	Condo	98	142	119	87	SUM(number1, [number2], ...)			
7	Total	219							
8									

6   Press Enter to calculate the Total amount.

Rather than enter the same formula for columns C, D, and E, you can copy the formula instead.

When you do, Excel automatically updates the cell addresses in the formula to refer to the proper range of cells.

7   Click cell **B7** and choose *Copy* from the Home tab.

8   Click and drag from cell C7 to cell E7 and choose *Paste*. Excel calculates the total amounts for columns C, D, and E.

9   Click in cell F5, choose *Copy* from the Home tab, click and drag from cell F6 to F7 and choose *Paste*.

WORKING WITH CELL RANGES

Bottom Line

Before you can use many of the features in Excel, you must first select the cells with which you want to work. Excel refers to a collection of selected cells as a range. Cell **ranges** are designated by first and last cell in the range, separated by a colon. For instance, a selection of cells spanning from A1 through cell G8 would be referred to as A1:G8.

When you select a range of cells, the selection appears highlighted and a dark border surrounds the entire range. Once you select a cell or range of cells, any command or action you perform affects the entire selection.

Selecting a range of cells

The easiest way to select a range of cells is to click the first cell in the range and drag to the last cell in the range. You can also use the keyboard to select a range of cells. To do so, move to the first cell in the range, press and hold the Shift key, and move to the last cell in the range.

STEP BY STEP   **Selecting a range of cells**

1   Click in cell A4, drag to cell F7 and release. The range is now selected.

2   Select cell **B5**, press and hold the **Shift** key, use the right arrow key to extend the selection to cell F5, and release the Shift key. This is another method of selecting a range of cells.

When you need to select more than one range of cells at a time that are not contiguous, you can use the Ctrl key.

STEP BY STEP   **Selecting multiple ranges**

1   Click in cell B4 and drag to cell F4 to select the first range of data.

2   Press and hold the **Ctrl** key, click in cell B7 and drag to cell F7. Both ranges appear selected, as in Figure 2-6.

Figure 2-6

Press and hold the Ctrl key to select multiple ranges of cells that are not contiguous

⊿	A	B	C	D	E	F	G
1	Contoso Realty Group						
2	20-Mar-13						
3							
4		Philip	Keith	Erica	Danielle	Total	
5	House	121	150	201	224	696	
6	Condo	98	142	119	87	446	
7	Total	219	292	320	311	1142	
8							

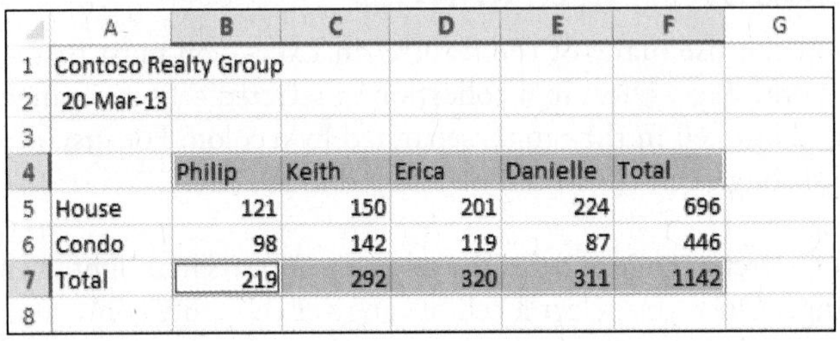

STEP BY STEP   **Select an entire row**

1   Point at the row heading such as row 4.

2   Click to select the row when the pointer turns into a forward-facing arrow (⇥).

Excels selects the entire row.

STEP BY STEP   **Select a column**

1   Point at the column heading such as column E.

2   Click to select the column when the pointer turns into a downward-facing arrow (⬇).

Excel selects the entire column.

STEP BY STEP   **Select the entire worksheet**

1   Click the area just below the Name box (see Figure 2-7) to select the entire worksheet.

Figure 2-7

Select the entire worksheet
with one click

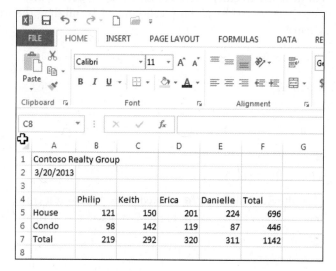

Take Note   Use caution after selecting the entire worksheet, since any action you perform affects the entire selection.

Selecting Cells using the Keyboard

KEY	ACTION
Shift+left arrow	Selects the cell to the left
Shift+right arrow	Selects the cell to the right
Shift+up arrow	Selects the cell above
Shift+down arrow	Selects the cell below
Shift+Spacebar	Selects the current row
Ctrl+Spacebar	Selects the current column
Ctrl+Shift+Spacebar	Selects the entire sheet

Using AutoFill to fill a range with data

One of the quicker ways to enter data in a worksheet is to use the **AutoFill** feature. With AutoFill, Excel looks for patterns in your data and quickly fills in the remainder of the data based on that pattern. For instance, to enter a series of dates each a week apart, enter the first date followed by the next date 7 days later. Select both cells and click and drag the AutoFill handle to fill in the remaining dates.

STEP BY STEP	Using AutoFill

1   Enter the value 1 in cell J1.

2   Enter the value 2 in cell J2.

3   Select cells J1 and J2.

4   Click the AutoFill **handle**, located at the lower-right corner of the selected range, and drag down to cell A20 as in Figure 2-8. Excel fills in the values 1 through 20 in the range of cells.

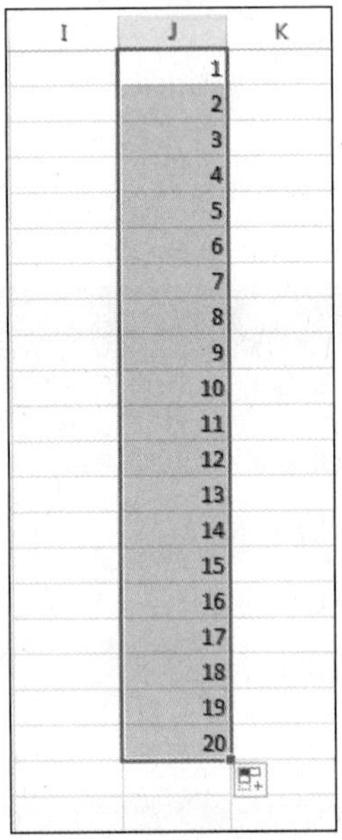

Figure 2-8

AutoFill quickly fills in a range of data when it senses a pattern.

SAVING WORKBOOKS

Bottom Line

When you save a workbook for the first time, Excels prompts you to assign a name to the file and indicate where you want the file stored. Once you assign a name to the file, it appears in the title bar of your workbook. You don't need to assign a name each time you save a file. After a file has been named, the next time you save the file Excel will not prompt you for a name and will simply save it using the assigned name.

STEP BY STEP   **Saving Workbooks**

1   Choose Save from the File tab.

2   Click Computer in the Office Backstage, and then click the Browse button.

3   In the Save As dialog box, navigate to the Excel02lessons folder.

4   Type **excel_practice** in the File name text box (See Figure 2-9.).

Figure 2-9

In the Save As dialog box, enter a name for the file and indicate where it should be saved.

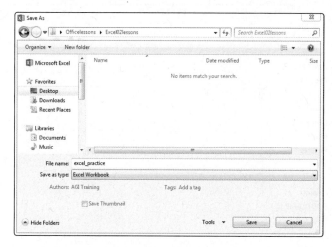

5   Click Save to save the file and choose File > Close to close this file.

A word about Save vs. Save As

The Save As command and the Save command can be confusing because the first time you use the Save command to save your file, Excel displays the Save As dialog box instead of a Save dialog box. Excel doesn't really have a Save dialog box; when you choose the Save command for the first time, Excel displays the Save As dialog box because you have not yet specified a name or location.

If you use the Save As command when you want to save a file, Excel will again ask you to supply the name and location and this is where you may run into some trouble. The Save As command should really only be used if you want to make a copy of the file with a new name, leaving the original file intact.

OPENING WORKBOOKS

There are two ways to open an Excel workbook. You can navigate to the file in your Documents folder and double-click the icon to both launch Excel and open the file. Alternatively, you could launch Excel and then use the Open command to open a file within the Excel window.

STEP BY STEP   **Opening an existing worksheet**

1   Launch Microsoft Excel if it is not already opened.

2   From the Backstage, choose **Open** (see Figure 2-10) and navigate to the Excel02lessons folder on the desktop.

Figure 2-10

The Open dialog box appears to allow you to find an Excel file.

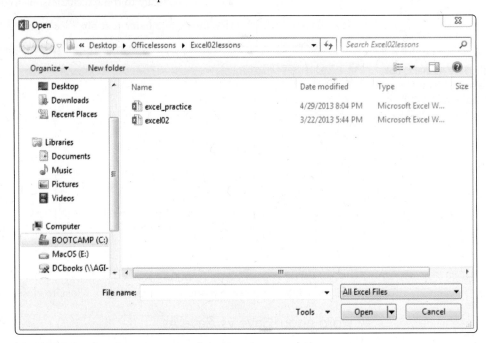

3   Double-click the file named **excel02**, shown in Figure 2-11. An Excel document opens to display a worksheet containing the customer list for a fictitious real estate company.

Figure 2-11

Open an existing file in Excel using the Open command in the File tab.

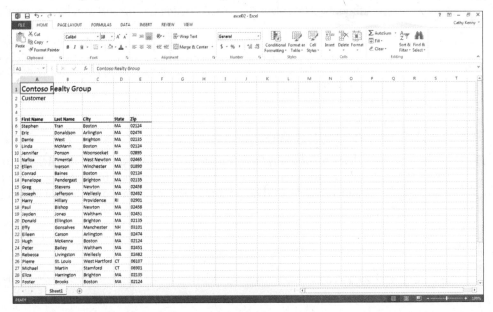

Since we will be altering the file in this lesson, we will use the Save As command to save the file with a new name. By doing so, the original file will remain intact and the changes that we will make throughout the course of the lesson will only be saved in the new version.

STEP BY STEP	**Using Save As**

1   Choose **Save As** from the File tab.

2   From the Office Backstage, choose **Computer** and then click **Browse** and locate the Excel02lessons folder.

3   In the File Name text box, add **_customers** to the end of the file name.

4   Click the **Save** button.

EDITING DATA

Bottom Line

A common occurrence when constructing worksheets is the need to edit, rearrange, or work with data that has already been entered. For instance, you might need to move a range of cells from one location to another, copy a collection of cells so they can be reused in another section, or even clear a selection of cells altogether.

Editing data in a cell

To edit existing data in a cell, you have two options. You can edit the data directly in the cell, or you can use the Formula bar. Before you can edit data, though, you must first select the cell containing the data.

To edit data directly in the cell, double-click the cell you want to edit. When the cursor appears in the cell, make your changes.

STEP BY STEP	**Editing data in a cell**

1   In the file **excel02_customers**, double-click cell **A2**.

2   Type **List** after Customer and press **Enter**.

To edit data in the Formula bar, click the cell you want to edit and move the pointer up to the Formula bar. When it changes into the cursor shape, click to set the insertion point and make your changes.

STEP BY STEP	**Editing data in the Formula bar**

1   Click cell **A2**.

2   Click in the Formula bar to set the insertion point between Customer and List.

3   Type **Contact**, add a space and press **Enter**.

Using cut, copy, and paste

The Cut, Copy, and Paste commands allow you to rearrange existing worksheet data. With **Cut**, you can move data from one location to another; **Copy** allows you to make multiple copies of a range of data. When you use Cut and Copy, Excel uses the Clipboard to temporarily store the data until the next time you use the Cut or Copy command. Data you have selected to be cut or copied appears highlighted by a dashed line border instead of the usual solid border.

To move a range of data from one location to another, use the Cut and **Paste** commands. Excel removes the selected data from its original location and inserts it into the new one. Note that you can only paste a range of data that has been cut once.

STEP BY STEP | **Using Cut**

    1   Select range A5:E37 (see Figure 2-12).

    2   Choose Cut from the Clipboard group on the Home tab.

Figure 2-12

When you select a range of cells to Cut or Copy, Excel uses a dashed border to indicate the selected range.

	A	B	C	D	E	F
1	Contoso Realty Group					
2	Customer Contact List					
3						
4						
5	First Name	Last Name	City	State	Zip	
6	Stephen	Tran	Boston	MA	02124	
7	Eric	Donaldson	Arlington	MA	02474	
8	Dante	West	Brighton	MA	02135	
9	Linda	McMann	Boston	MA	02124	
10	Jennifer	Ponson	Woonsocket	RI	02895	
11	Nafisa	Pimental	West Newton	MA	02465	
12	Ellen	Iverson	Winchester	MA	01890	
13	Conrad	Baines	Boston	MA	02124	
14	Penelope	Pendergast	Brighton	MA	02135	
15	Greg	Stevens	Newton	MA	02458	
16	Joseph	Jefferson	Wellesly	MA	02482	
17	Harry	Hillary	Providence	RI	02901	
18	Paul	Bishop	Newton	MA	02458	
19	Jayden	Jones	Waltham	MA	02451	
20	Donald	Ellington	Brighton	MA	02135	
21	Effy	Gonsalves	Manchester	NH	03101	
22	Eileen	Carson	Arlington	MA	02474	
23	Hugh	McKenna	Boston	MA	02124	
24	Peter	Bailey	Waltham	MA	02451	
25	Rebecca	Livingston	Wellesly	MA	02482	
26	Pierre	St. Louis	West Hartford	CT	06107	
27	Michael	Martin	Stamford	CT	06901	
28	Eliza	Harrington	Brighton	MA	02135	
29	Foster	Brooks	Boston	MA	02124	

    3   Click in cell B5 and choose Paste.

To reuse a range of cells in another area of your worksheet, use Copy and Paste. Excel keeps the original selection intact and inserts a copy in the new location. You can paste as many copies of the selected data as you need.

STEP BY STEP | **Using Copy and Paste**

    1   Select range B37:F37.

    2   Choose Copy from the Home tab.

    3   Click in cell B38 and choose Paste.

    4   Enter Kelvin in cell B38 and Davis in cell C38.

Take Note Notice that the contents of column D have been truncated. This occurs because the contents are longer than the current column width can accommodate. To resize the column width, double-click the border separating column D and E. Excel automatically adjusts the width to the widest entry. (For more information on changing column widths, see Lesson 3, "Formatting Excel Worksheets.")

Inserting cells

Another way to reorganize a worksheet is to insert cells within an existing range of data when you need to add new information. You can insert a new cell one at a time or insert a range of cells all at once. When you do, you can shift existing cells to the right or down to accommodate the new cells.

STEP BY STEP   **inserting cells**

---

    1   Select range **B8:F8**.

    2   Click the arrow just below the Insert command in the Cells group on the Home tab.

    3   Choose **Insert Cells** from the resulting menu.

    4   From the Insert dialog box (see Figure 2-13), click **Shift cells down**.

Figure 2-13

Insert a range of cells to add data to an existing worksheet.

    5   Click **OK** and then choose **File > Save** to save your work.

Deleting cells

When you need to remove a range of cells from a worksheet altogether, you can delete them. Excel then automatically adjusts the existing data.

STEP BY STEP   **Deleting cells**

---

    1   Select range **B8:F8**.

    2   Click the arrow just below the Delete command in the Cells group of the Home tab.

    3   Choose **Delete Cells** from the resulting menu.

    4   From the Delete dialog box, click **Shift cells up** and then click **OK**. Excel shifts the existing cells automatically.

Clearing cells

If you need to remove data from a range of cells without deleting them from the worksheet range, you can choose to clear them.

STEP BY STEP	Clearing cells

1   Select range **B8:F8**.

2   Click the arrow just below the Clear command in the Editing group on the Home tab.

3   Select **Clear Contents** from the resulting menu.

USING UNDO AND REDO

Bottom Line

The Undo command is an extremely important tool when working in Excel. As its name implies, Undo allows you to reverse the last action you have performed. For example, if you mistakenly delete a range of cells, you can immediately click Undo to have them reinserted.

Excel records the last 100 actions performed, allowing you to cycle through the commands until you restore the worksheet to its intended order. You can click the arrow to the right of the Undo button to see the list of actions performed. Click the action you want to Undo; Excel reverses all actions up to that point. If you realize that you really did mean to do what you did, Redo will redo the action that you undid.

Perform the following set of steps to see how the Undo and Redo commands work.

STEP BY STEP	Using undo and redo

1   Select range **B8:F8**.

2   Choose **Insert** from the Cells group on the Home tab and select **Insert Sheet Rows**.

3   Click the **Undo** button (⬏) found on the Quick Access Toolbar to reverse the action.

4   Click the **Redo** button (⬐) to re-insert the range of cells.

5   Click **OK** and then choose **File > Save** to save your work.

WORKING WITH ROWS AND COLUMNS

Bottom Line

As discussed in Lesson 1, a worksheet is constructed of a series of rows and columns, the intersection of which forms a cell. When constructing worksheets, you might need to rearrange your existing data to accommodate new information.

While you could use the Cut and Paste commands to move your data, many times the simplest way to add new information is to insert a new row or column into the existing data structure. When you do, Excel automatically moves existing data and updates formulas as necessary. (For more details on formulas, see Lesson 4, "Using Formulas in Excel 2013.")

Inserting rows and columns

Before inserting a new row or column, you must first indicate where you want the new row or column to appear. To do so, select a cell in the row *below* where you want the new row to appear. For example, to insert a new row between rows 1 and 2, click any cell in row 2. Prior to inserting a new column, select a cell in the column *to the right* of where you want the new column to appear. For example, if you want to insert a column between columns B and C, click any cell in column C to select it.

STEP BY STEP	Inserting rows and columns

1 Click in cell B8.

2 On the Home tab, in the Cells group, choose **Insert** and select **Insert Sheet Rows** from the resulting menu.

3 In cell B8, type **Stephanie**; in cell C8 type **Walker**; in cell D8 type **Boston**; in cell E8 type **MA**; and in cell F8 type **02124**.

4 Move the cell pointer to cell D6, choose **Insert** from the Home tab, and select **Insert Sheet Columns** from the resulting menu. Excel inserts a column between columns C and E.

Take Note To quickly insert a row or column, right-click the row or column heading and choose Insert from the resulting menu. To insert more than one row or column at a time, select the number of rows or columns you want to insert before you choose the Insert command. For example, if you want to insert two rows, select two existing rows, and then choose Insert.

Deleting rows and columns

Before you can delete a row or column, you must select a cell within the row or column to be deleted.

STEP BY STEP	Deleting rows and columns

1 Click cell **B3**.

2 From the Home tab, choose **Delete**, and then select **Delete Sheet Rows** from the resulting menu.

Excel removes the row and shifts existing data up one row.

3 Click cell **D2**.

4 From the Home tab, choose **Delete**, and select **Delete Sheet Columns** from the resulting menu.

Excel removes the column and shifts existing data one column to the left.

5 Delete any blank rows that may appear in the middle of your chart.

Hiding and unhiding rows and columns

Another option available when constructing worksheets is to hide certain rows or columns from view. By hiding rows and columns rather than deleting them, the data remains within the worksheet, but no one will see it.

The following set of steps illustrate how hiding a row or column works.

STEP BY STEP   **Hiding rows and columns**

1   Select column **D**.

2   Choose **Format** from the Home tab, choose **Hide & Unhide** from the resulting menu as in Figure 2-14, and click **Hide Columns**.

Figure 2-14

Hide a column or row when you want to prevent the data from being displayed.

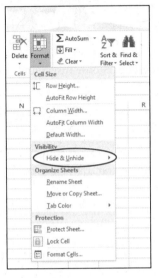

3   Select row **6**, choose **Format** from the Home tab, choose **Hide & Unhide**, and click **Hide Rows**.

Redisplaying columns is a little trickier. You must first select cells on either side of the hidden row or column before you can unhide them.

Figure 2-15

When columns and rows are hidden in the worksheet, you must select a range of cells on either side before you can redisplay them.

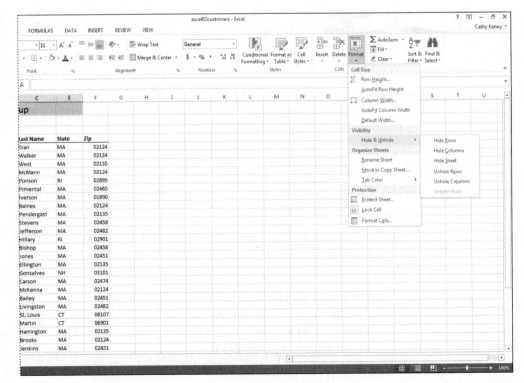

STEP BY STEP	**Redisplaying rows or columns**

1   Select range C1:E1 as shown in Figure 2-15.

2   From the Home tab, choose Format, choose Hide & Unhide, and click Unhide Columns.

3   Select range A5:A7.

4   Again from the Home tab, choose Format, choose Hide & Unhide, and click Unhide rows.

Freezing and unfreezing rows and columns

If your worksheet data spans beyond a single screen display, you can **freeze** the column and row headings so they continue to be displayed when you scroll to other areas of the worksheet. You can specify that the top row or first column of the worksheet be frozen or select a specific range of cells to remain displayed.

STEP BY STEP	**Freezing and unfreezing rows and columns**

1   Select range B5:F5.

2   Choose Freeze Panes from the View tab.

3   From the resulting menu choose Freeze Panes.

4   Excel freezes everything above row 5.

5   Scroll down to row 25 and notice that the titles at the top of the worksheet remain displayed.

6   Choose Freeze Panes from the View tab and choose Unfreeze Panes.

Freeze options

OPTION	ACTION
Freeze Panes	Keeps rows and columns visible above the current selection
Freeze Top Row	Keeps the first row in the worksheet visible.
Freeze First Column	Keeps the first column in the worksheet visible.

CREATING ADDITIONAL WORKSHEETS

Bottom Line

Each new workbook file you create consists of a single worksheet. You can insert additional worksheets into a workbook file when you need to manage a new set of related data.

Inserting worksheets

STEP BY STEP	**Inserting worksheets**

1   Choose Insert from the Home tab and select Insert Sheet.

2   A new blank worksheet is displayed to the left of the current worksheet named Sheet2.

You can also click the plus sign located at the bottom of the worksheet window, adjacent to the worksheet tab. Excel inserts a new worksheet to the right of the current worksheet tab (see Figure 2-16).

Figure 2-16

A. Worksheet tab.

B. New Sheet button.

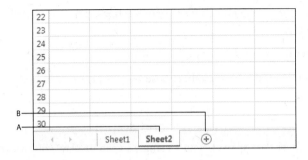

Renaming worksheets

Each worksheet you create is assigned a consecutively numbered name, such as Sheet1, Sheet2, and Sheet3. You can assign more meaningful names to your worksheets.

STEP BY STEP   Renaming worksheets

1   Click the tab labeled Sheet1.

2   Choose Format from the Home tab and select Rename Sheet.

3   Excel highlights the current worksheet tab. Type Customers and press Enter.

4   Double-click the tab labeled Sheet2.

5   Type Listings and press Enter.

Moving and copying worksheets

When you are working with multiple worksheets in a workbook, you might need to rearrange the order of their appearance. Moving a worksheet requires you to click and drag the tab to the new location in the workbook. You can also make a copy of a worksheet in your workbook.

STEP BY STEP   Moving and copying worksheets

1   Click and drag worksheet Customers and drop it right before tab Listings. Notice that as you drag the tab, a small black triangle appears as a guide. When the triangle is at the point where you want it, let go of the tab to drop the worksheet into place. The result is shown in Figure 2-17.

Figure 2-17

Move the Customers tab in front of the Listings tab.

21	Effy	Gonsalves	Manchester	NH	03101
22	Eileen	Carson	Arlington	MA	02474
23	Hugh	McKenna	Boston	MA	02124
24	Peter	Bailey	Waltham	MA	02451
25	Rebecca	Livingston	Wellesly	MA	02482
26	Pierre	St. Louis	West Hartford	CT	06107
27	Michael	Martin	Stamford	CT	06901
28	Eliza	Harrington	Brighton	MA	02135
29	Foster	Brooks	Boston	MA	02124

Customers   Listings   ⊕

READY

2   Choose File > Save to save your work.

Changing the color of worksheet tabs

You can color code your Excel worksheet tabs for organization purposes just as you would paper-based filing systems. When managing data in a workbook containing multiple tabs, you can rely on color coding to help you find your information quickly and easily. For instance, in a Budget worksheet, you could change the color of a tab containing Income to Blue and the tab containing expenses to Red.

STEP BY STEP **Changing the color of worksheets tabs**

1 Click the Customers worksheet.

2 From the Home tab, choose Format.

3 Choose Tab Color and select Blue from the resulting color menu, as in Figure 2-18.

4 Change the color of the Listings worksheet to Orange.

Figure 2-18

Assign color-coding to worksheet tabs to help keep data organized.

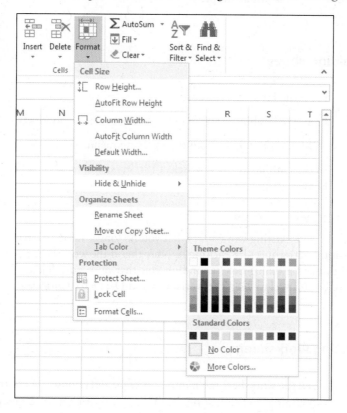

Hiding sheets

You can hide worksheets from view just as you do with rows and columns.

STEP BY STEP   Hiding sheets

1   Click the Listings tab.

2   From the Home tab, choose Format.

3   From the Visibility section of the Format menu, choose Hide & Unhide.

4   Select Hide Sheet from the resulting menu. Excel removes the worksheet and its tab from view.

Unhiding sheets

Unhiding sheets is just as simple as hiding them.

STEP BY STEP   Unhiding sheets

1   From the Home tab, choose Format.

2   From the Visibility section of the Format menu, choose Hide & Unhide.

3   Select Unhide Sheet from the resulting menu.

4   In the Unhide dialog box, select Listings, and then click OK. Excel redisplays the hidden worksheet.

Deleting worksheets

You can delete existing worksheets that you no longer need. To delete a worksheet, you must first make it the active sheet by clicking it. Note that if the worksheet you want to delete contains data, Excel displays a dialog box reminding you that once you delete a worksheet, you cannot get it back. Click Cancel to keep the worksheet and Delete to continue deleting the worksheet.

STEP BY STEP   Deleting worksheets

1   Click the worksheet tab named Listings and choose Delete from the Home tab. You can also right-click Listings to display a context-sensitive menu. Select Delete.

2   Choose Delete Sheet from the resulting menu.

PRINTING WORKSHEETS AND WORKBOOKS

If you want to print your worksheet, you might find that you have more data than easily fits onto a standard piece of paper. When your worksheets contain a great deal of information, you'll need to specify details about the data you want to print and how you want it to fit on the page. This makes the printing process a bit more detailed than many other applications.

Printing a range of data

By default, Excel prints the entire worksheet. If you want to print a specific range of data, you need to select it.

STEP BY STEP   **Printing a range of data**

1   Select range A1:F38.

2   Click the File tab and choose Print.

Figure 2-19

Excel shows you a static preview of what your worksheet will look like when printed.

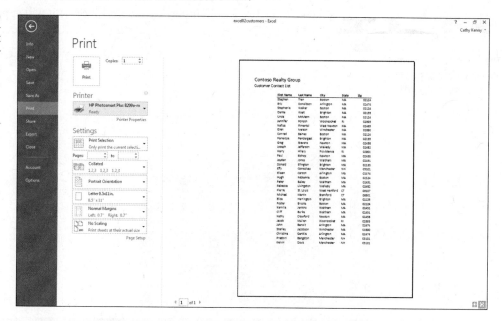

3   In the Settings section of the Print Backstage view (see Figure 2-19), click the drop-down arrow and choose Print Selection.

4   In the Printer section, specify your printer.

5   Click Print to print your worksheet.

Defining the print area

If you frequently need to print the same range of data, define it as the **Print Area** so you don't have to select the same range every time you're ready to print.

STEP BY STEP   **Defining the print area**

1   Select range A1:F38.

2   From the Page Layout tab, choose Print Area.

3   Select Set Print Area from the resulting menu. Each time you elect to print, Excel automatically selects the range you defined as the Print Area.

4   To clear the print area, choose Print Area from the Page Layout tab and select Clear Print Area from the resulting menu.

Viewing the page layout

As stated above, the Print menu option now incorporates a preview of the worksheet as it will appear when printed. If you need to make changes to the worksheet based on your preview, you'll need to exit Preview mode.

The **Page Layout** mode in Excel displays a fully-editable preview of your printed page. When you switch to Page Layout, guides indicate the current margins and page breaks, and you can continue working on your worksheet as well.

Viewing the page layout

1   Select range A1:F38.

2   In the Status bar, click the Page Layout button. Excel switches to Page Layout mode (shown in Figure 2-20), displaying the worksheet as it will appear when printed.

Figure 2-20

The dynamic Page Layout Mode allows you to preview and work on your data.

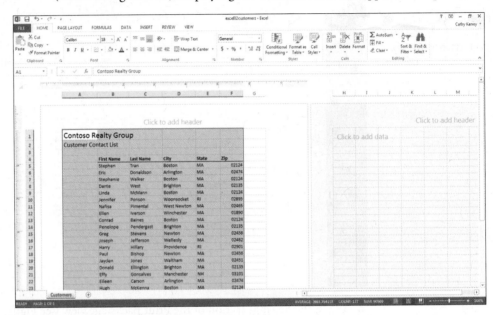

3   Click Normal on the Status bar to return to the default worksheet display mode.

Adding headers and footers

Headers and **footers** are text that appear in the top and bottom margins of your worksheets. You can add the current date and time, page numbers, and other specific text to this area. The easiest way to add headers and footers to your worksheet is to switch to Page Layout mode.

Adding headers and footers

1   In the Status Bar, click the Page Layout button.

2   On your preview page, click the area labeled Click to add header to display the Header & Footer Tools tab.

3   From the Design tab, choose Header to display a list of sample headers (See Figure 2-21.).

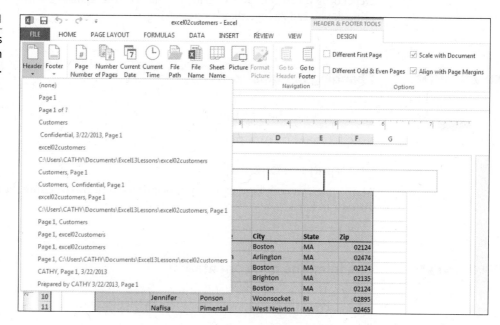

4   Choose excel02_customers from the displayed list to add the file name to the header.

Header and footer tools

TOOL	ACTION	EXAMPLE
Page Number	Inserts the current page number	Page 1
Number of Pages	Inserts the current page out of the total number of pages	Page 1 of 3
Current Date	Inserts the current date	3/20/2013
Current Time	Inserts the current time	2:30 pm
File Path	Inserts the file name, including the entire path	C:\users\username\document\budget2013
File Name	Inserts the file name only	Budget2013
Sheet Name	Inserts the name of the current sheet	Expenses
Picture	Inserts an image	

5   Scroll to the bottom of the Page Layout view and click the area labeled Click to add footer to display the Header & Footer Tools tab.

6   From the Design tab, choose Footer to display a list of sample footers.

7   Choose Page 1 from the displayed list.

8   Click the Normal view button from the Status bar.

Changing margins

Depending on the amount of data you have or the manner in which you want your worksheet printed, you can change the margin settings.

STEP BY STEP   **Changing margins**

1   Choose Margins from the Page Layout tab.

2   Choose Narrow from the resulting menu.

Changing the orientation

Many times, you can fit more data on the printed page by switching the **Page Orientation** from Portrait to Landscape.

STEP BY STEP   **Changing the page orientation**

1   From the Page Layout tab, choose Orientation.

2   Choose Landscape.

Printing titles

If the data in your worksheet spans multiple pages, you can add print titles to your print job so the column or row headings appear on each page of the printout. To indicate Print Titles, select the row or column that contains the headings.

STEP BY STEP   **Printing titles**

1   From the Page Layout tab, choose Print Titles.

2   Click Rows to repeat at top to set the insertion point inside the text box.

3   Click the row heading for row 4. You will see the range $4:$4 indicated, as in Figure 2-22.

4   Click **OK**.

5   From the File tab, choose **Print** and then click the **Print** button to print the worksheet.

6   To turn off Print Titles, choose **Print Titles** again and remove the row reference from the Rows to repeat at top box.

Turning gridlines off and on

Excel automatically turns off the worksheet gridlines when you print. You can, however, elect to include the gridlines in your printout.

STEP BY STEP   **Turning gridlines off and on**

1   Click the Page Layout tab.

2   Select **Print** in the Gridlines section to have Excel print the gridlines on your paper.

3   Select **Print** again to turn them off in the printouts.

4   Choose **File > Save** to save your work.

You've now completed this lesson. Now that you are familiar with entering and editing data and selecting worksheet ranges, you are ready to begin learning how to format your worksheets to give them a professional appearance.

What you learned in this lesson:

* Creating a Worksheet

* Entering Data in a Cell

* Working with Cell Ranges

* Saving Workbooks

* Opening Workbooks

* Editing Data

* Using Undo/Redo

* Working with Rows and Columns

* Creating Additional Worksheets

* Printing Worksheets and Workbooks

Knowledge Assessment

Matching

Match the Excel function in numbers 1 to 10 to its keyboard or mouse command in letters a to j.

1. Turn gridlines on/off in printed output
2. Unhide a worksheet
3. Print only specific cell range
4. Insert a worksheet into a workbook
5. Print short, wide pages
6. Select a range of cells
7. Reduce printed whitespace
8. Enter formula into a cell
9. Delete a row
10. Freeze a range of cells

a. Print > Settings > Print Selection
b. Page Layout > Margins > Narrow
c. Home > Delete > Delete Sheet Rows
d. Type =, function name, then parameters
e. Page Layout > Orientation > Landscape
f. Page Layout > Gridlines > Print
g. Shift+click opposite corners
h. Home > Insert > Insert Sheet
i. Select cells, then View > Freeze Panes
j. Home > Cells > Format > Visibility > Unhide Sheet...

Fill in the Blanks

Complete the following sentences by writing the correct word or words in the blanks provided.

1. To create a new workbook at any time, press _____.

2. When you type $15 into a cell, Excel automatically applies the _____ data format.

3. The range A6:D6 includes _____ cells.

4. Hold the _____ key while click/dragging to select multiple cell ranges.

5. The _____ command adds data to the clipboard while removing the original content.

6. To add a row or column to a worksheet, use the _____ command.

7. The _____ command, found in the Quick Access Toolbar, returns the document to a previous state.

8. A _____ column heading stays visible even when you scroll several pages down the worksheet.

9. When you create a workbook and add two additional worksheets, the worksheets' default names are _____ and _____.

10. The _____ command to recolor worksheet tabs is found in the _____ group of the _____ tab.

Competency Assessment

Project 2-1: Rapidly Populating a Worksheet

In this exercise you will use AutoFill to fill two columns of a worksheet.

1. Create a new document by selecting Blank workbook from the launch screen, or pressing Ctrl+N if Excel is running.

2. Select cell A1. Type Date and press Tab.

3. Type Amount and press Return or Enter.

4. Type mar 11 <Tab> 3 <Enter>.

5. Type mar 12 <Tab> 6 <Enter>.

6. Select cell A3 and drag the AutoFill handle straight down until the date 4-Apr appears.

7. Click and drag to select both B2 and B3.

8. Drag the AutoFill handle straight down until the number 75 appears next to the date 4-Apr.

9. Save your file as **project_2-1_autofill** and close it.

Project 2-2: Using Undo and Redo

In this exercise you will modify a document and experiment with the Undo/Redo tools.

1. Open the project file **2-2-source** and save it as **project_2-2_undo**.

2. Select cell C27 and type April total. Press Tab.

3. Click Formulas > AutoSum > Sum.

4. Click and drag to select the range B2:B26. Press Enter or Return.

5. Click on the row number 27 to select the entire row, and press Ctrl+B. Now we will use the Undo function to "take back" steps 4-5.

6. Click the drop-down arrow beside the Undo command in the Quick Access Toolbar.

7. Select Typing '=SUM(B2:B26)' in D27 from the Undo dropdown menu.

8. Select cell D27.

9. Click Formulas > AutoSum > Sum, then select the range B23:B26. Press Return.
10. Save and close your document.

Proficiency Assessment

Project 2-3: Working with Rows

In this exercise you will work with several rows of data at once.

1. Open the project file **2-3-source** and save it as **project_2-3_rows**.
2. Select row 1 by clicking on the row label "1." Apply boldface formatting to the row (Ctrl+B).
3. Freeze row 1 (View > Freeze Panes > Freeze Top Row).
4. Select row 23. Right click the label and select Insert Row.
5. Insert three more empty rows in the same spot.
6. Select row 31 and Copy its contents.
7. Select row 23 and Paste the clipboard contents.
8. Change the contents of cell C23 to March total.
9. Select cell D23. Click in the Formula bar. Drag the handles of the blue bounding box to change the selected cell range to B2:B22. Press Return.
10. Select the column C heading and click Home > Cells > Format > AutoFit Column Width to resize the column.
11. Select rows 2 through 22. Right click in the selected range and choose Hide.
12. Repeat step 11 for rows 27 through 30 (the April data).
13. Save and close your document.

Project 2-4: Rows and Columns

In this exercise you will reformat rows and columns in a worksheet.

1. Open the project file **2-4-source** and save it as **project_2-4_columns**.
2. Click and drag to select the labels for rows 26 and 31 (and the hidden rows between). Right click one of the labels and select Unhide.
3. Click and drag to select the headings for columns C and D.
4. Press Ctrl+X to cut.
5. Click the heading for column E and press Ctrl+V to paste.
6. Select cells A27:A30. From the Home > Number group, select Short Date from the drop-down menu. Note that applying the Date data format to the whole column would mislabel the header cell as a Date.
7. Save and close your document.

Project 2-5: **Worksheet Layout**

In this exercise you will experiment with Excel's formatting tools: AutoFit, page breaks, gridlines, and so forth.

1. Open the project file **2-5-source** and save it as **project_2-5_layout**.
2. Copy all the data from Sheet1 to a new sheet in the same workbook, Sheet2. You will work with Sheet2 for the rest of this exercise.
3. Rename Sheet2 Printable.
4. Change the fill color of row 1 to Grey 25% - Background 2.
5. Fix column E's width with AutoFit.
6. Insert a page break between rows 26 and 27 (above the April monthly data).
7. Turn off gridlines.
8. Save and close your document.

Project 2-6: **Print Layout**

In this exercise you'll prep a document for print.

1. Open the project file **2-6-source** and save it as **project_2-6_layout2**.
2. Hide Sheet1.
3. Add a centered Header: Daily Totals.
4. Add a footer to the lower right of every page: <page number> of <total pages>.
5. Resize column A so all its data appears in Page Layout view (rather than ####).
6. Select Narrow margins and Landscape orientation.
7. Use the Print Titles tool to repeat row 1 at the top of every page.
8. AutoFit column E's width.
9. Click File > Export and create a PDF, using all default options, also entitled **project_2-6_layout2**.
10. Save and close your Excel document.

3

Formatting a Worksheet

LESSON SKILL MATRIX

In this lesson, you will learn the following skills:

Understanding Cell Formats	Copying Cell Formats
Changing Number Formats	Working with Cell Styles
Changing the Font and Font Size	Using Conditional Formatting
Modifying Row Heights and Column Widths	Using Page Themes
Cell Alignment	
Borders & Shading	

KEY TERMS

- Accounting Format
- Alignment
- AutoFit
- Color Scheme
- Conditional Formatting
- Effects
- Fill Color
- Font Set
- Format
- Format Painter
- Merge (cells)
- Separator
- Cell Style
- Text Attributes
- Theme
- Values
- Wrap

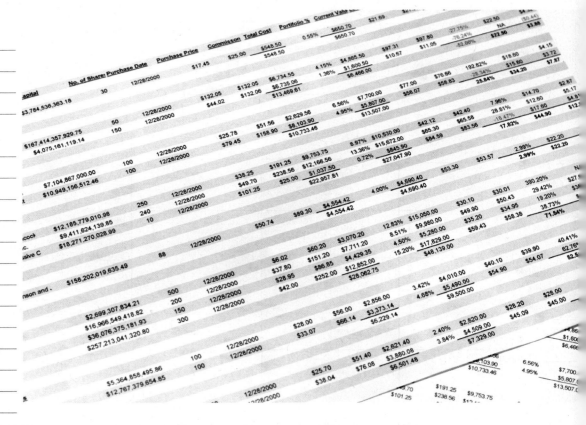

A large crew of contractors submit complex data sheets several times a day to the central desk at Northwind Traders, which a small team then cleans up and consolidates into a daily master spreadsheet for the analysts downstairs. Smart, robust, consistent data formatting is essential to this process. Excel 2013's cell and document formatting tools help the Northwind team produce readable, flexible documents as quickly as possible.

SOFTWARE ORIENTATION

Data needs to be clear and easily understood. Formatting your spreadsheets helps readers understand and work with the data you organize in Microsoft Excel.

Figure 3-1

Formatting controls

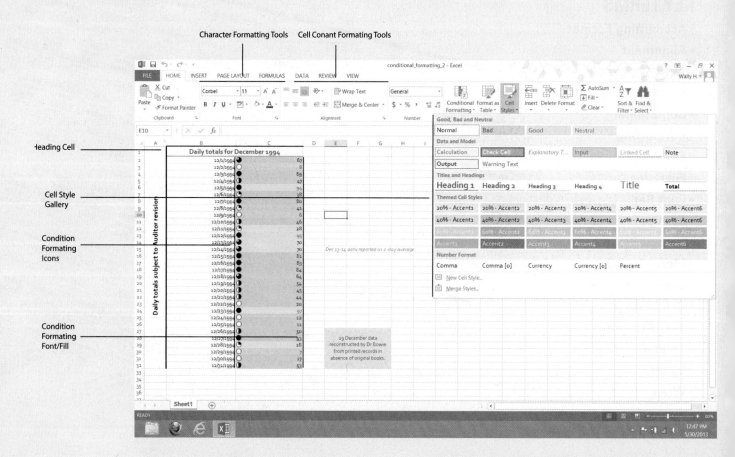

STARTING UP

In this lesson, you'll work with several files from the Excel03lessons folder. Make sure that you have loaded the OfficeLessons folder onto your computer.

UNDERSTANDING CELL FORMATS

Bottom Line

Before we talk about cell formatting, you must understand how Excel treats data. Excel categorizes data into three different types: numbers, text, and dates or times. Numbers, or **values**, consist of numeric data that will be used in calculations or formulas. There are also numbers on which you would never perform calculations, such as zip codes, social security numbers, product codes, or phone numbers.

Text also appears to be a straightforward concept. Text includes alphanumeric data that can be used in headings and other descriptive labels, for example, Sales 2001 or Northwest Region. When you enter a date, you might also think of it as a text-based entry, for example, March 27, 2013 or even 3/27/2013. Dates, in all actuality, are converted to a date value when entered, since you can perform calculations with dates.

When numbers are entered in a worksheet cell, Excel automatically applies a General format, unless it recognizes the value in some other way. For instance, if you enter a dollar ($) sign with the value, Excel assigns the Currency format. If you enter a percent (%) sign, it applies a percentage format. If you enter a value with a decimal point, Excel assigns the Number format.

When you enter numbers such as zip codes and social security numbers in a cell, Excel thinks they are values and treats them as such. In the case of zip codes, Excel automatically removes any leading zeroes from the number, (for example, 02124 becomes 2124), and converts it to a number. In these cases, you must intervene and let Excel know that the data you are entering is actually a text entry.

The following table explains the different types of cell formats that Excel uses.

Cell formats

FORMAT	DESCRIPTION
General	Applies no specific format. Will display decimal point if initially entered.
Number	Displays decimal point and two decimal places.
Currency	Displays the currency symbol to the immediate left of the value and a minus sign in front of negative numbers.
Accounting	Displays the currency symbol to the left edge of the cell, lines up decimal points, and encloses negative values in parentheses.
Short Date	Displays the date in mm/dd/yyyy format: 3/24/2013
Long Date	Displays date in expanded format: Monday, March 25, 2013
Time	Displays time in hh:mm:ss format: 12:19:20 PM
Percentage	Displays the percent symbol and rounds up
Fraction	Displays the value as a fraction
Scientific	Displays the value using scientific notation
Text	Data entered will be treated as text and will not be used in calculations.

CHANGING NUMBER FORMATS

Bottom Line

You can format your numeric entries using a variety of predefined formats. You can also create and apply custom numeric formats for values such as phone numbers and zip codes.

In this first lesson, we will format a range of values using a variety of number formats.

Applying a numeric format

The next steps show an example of how to use this feature.

STEP BY STEP   **Applying a numeric format**

1   Launch Excel and open the file named **excel03** from the Excel03lessons folder.

2   Select range **B9:B20**.

3   In the Number section of the Home tab, click the arrow to display the Format drop-down menu (See Figure 3-2.).

Figure 3-2

First select the range of cells and then assign a format to your values.

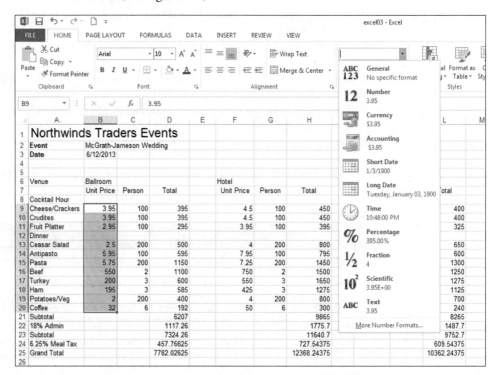

4   Choose **Number**.

Excel adds a decimal point and two digits (two decimal places) after each value in the range.

Commonly-used numeric formats

ICON	NAME	ACTION
$	Accounting (Currency)	Adds the currency symbol and two decimal places
%	Percent	Adds the percent sign and zero decimal places
,	Comma	Adds the thousands separator and two decimal places
⬅.0 .00	Increase Decimal	Increases the decimal place setting by 1
.00 ➡.0	Decrease Decimal	Decreases the decimal place setting by 1

Changing the number of decimal places

By default, Excel rounds values with the Number format to two decimal places. You can increase or decrease the decimal place value accordingly. The following steps show an example of how to use this feature.

STEP BY STEP   **Changing the number of decimal places**

1   Select range **D24:D25**. Notice that all numbers in this range have four decimal places.

2   In the Number section of the Home tab, click the **Decrease Decimal** button (.00 ➡.0) three times.

3   Excel rounds down the value and displays the result with two decimal places instead of the original four. The value in cell D25 now reads 7782.03.

4   Perform steps 1–3 for ranges H24:H25 and range L24:L25.

Adding the thousands separator

Excel automatically adds the thousands **separator** when the Currency or Accounting format is applied. The Comma Style format can be used when you want the thousands separator but not a currency symbol. Follow the next steps for an example of how to use this feature.

STEP BY STEP   **Adding the thousands separator**

1   Select range **D9:D20**.

2   Press and hold the **Ctrl** key and select ranges **H9:H20** and **L9:L20**.

3   In the Number section of the Home tab, click the **Comma Style** button. Excel adds the thousands separator to the values and adds two decimal places.

4   Click the Decrease Decimal button on the Home tab twice to remove the decimal place setting. The result is shown in Figure 3-3.

Figure 3-3

Click the Decrease Decimal button to remove the two decimal spaces.

Ballroom Unit Price	Person	Total
3.95	100	395
3.95	100	395
2.95	100	295
2.50	200	500
5.95	100	595
5.75	200	1,150
550.00	2	1,100
200.00	3	600
195.00	3	585
2.00	200	400
32.00	6	192
		6207
		1117.26
		7324.26
		457.77
		7782.03

Assigning the currency format

The next steps show an example of how to assign the currency format.

STEP BY STEP   Assigning the currency format

1   Select range D21:D25.

2   Press and hold the Ctrl key and select ranges H21:H25 and L21:L25.

3   From the Home tab, choose Number Format.

4   From the Number Format list, choose **Currency** to apply this style to the selected cells, as in Figure 3-4.

Figure 3-4

Assign the Currency format to a range of cells.

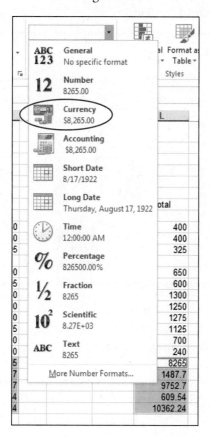

Assigning the accounting format

The next steps show an example of how to assign the **accounting format**.

STEP BY STEP	Assigning the accounting format

1   Select range **D21:D25**.

2   Press and hold the **Ctrl** key and select ranges **H21:H25** and **L21:L25**.

3   From the Home tab, choose **Number Format**.

4   From the Number Format list, choose **Accounting**. See Figure 3-5. Notice how the Accounting format looks slightly different than the Currency format but the dollar signs, commas and decimals remain.

Figure 3-5

Values assigned the Accounting format look slightly different than the Currency format.

	A	B	C	D	E	F	G	H	I	J	K	L	M
1	Northwinds Traders Events												
2	Event	McGrath-Jameson Wedding											
3	Date	6/12/2013											
4													
5													
6	Venue	Ballroom				Hotel				Restaurant			
7		Unit Price	Person	Total		Unit Price	Person	Total		Unit Price	Person	Total	
8	Cocktail Hour												
9	Cheese/Crackers	3.95	100	395		4.5	100	450		4	100	400	
10	Crudites	3.95	100	395		4.5	100	450		4	100	400	
11	Fruit Platter	2.95	100	295		3.95	100	395		3.25	100	325	
12	Dinner												
13	Ceasar Salad	2.50	200	500		4	200	800		3.25	200	650	
14	Antipasto	5.95	100	595		7.95	100	795		6	100	600	
15	Pasta	5.75	200	1,150		7.25	200	1450		6.5	200	1300	
16	Beef	550.00	2	1,100		750	2	1500		625	2	1250	
17	Turkey	200.00	3	600		550	3	1650		425	3	1275	
18	Ham	195.00	3	585		425	3	1275		375	3	1125	
19	Potatoes/Veg	2.00	200	400		4	200	800		3.5	200	700	
20	Coffee	32.00	6	192		50	6	300		40	6	240	
21	Subtotal			$ 6,207.00				$ 9,865.00				$ 8,265.00	
22	18% Admin			$ 1,117.26				$ 1,775.70				$ 1,487.70	
23	Subtotal			$ 7,324.26				$ 11,640.70				$ 9,752.70	
24	6.25% Meal Tax			$ 457.77				$ 727.54				$ 609.54	
25	Grand Total			$ 7,782.03				$ 12,368.24				$ 10,362.24	
26													
27	The above bids are based on a head count of 200 guests. Should the guest list head count change the administration fee will also change based on the new nu												
28													

Assigning the text format

The next steps show an example of how to format the text.

STEP BY STEP **Assigning the text format**

1   Type the label **Contact Number** in cell A4.

2   Click in cell **B4**.

3   From the Home tab, choose **Number Format**.

4   From the Number Format list, choose **Text**.

5   Type **(800) 555-1212** in cell B4 and press **Enter**.

Creating custom formats

When formatting data, you can choose from among the built-in formats or you can assign a custom format for specialized data. Follow the next set of steps for an example of how to create custom formats.

STEP BY STEP **Creating custom formats**

1   Click in cell B4.

2   From the Editing group on the Home tab, choose **Clear**.

3   From the Clear list, choose **Clear All**.

4   Type **8005551212** in cell B4 and press the **Enter** key.

5   Click back on cell B4 and from the Home tab, choose **Number Format**.

6 In the drop-down menu choose More Number Formats.

Figure 3-6

Use Special Formats for items such as zip codes and phone numbers.

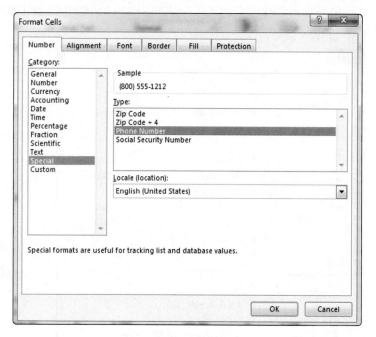

7 In the Format Cells dialog box (shown in Figure 3-6), select Special as the Category.

8 From the Type section, select Phone Number.

9 Click OK to apply the format.

CHANGING THE FONT AND FONT SIZE

Bottom Line

In addition to changing the display of numeric data, you can add visual interest to your worksheets. Some of the changes you can make include font and font size, the color of the text, the background color of the cell, and text attributes such as bold, italic, and underline.

Changing the font

The following set of steps show an example of how to change the font.

STEP BY STEP | **Changing the font**

1 Select range A1:L27.

2 From the Home tab, choose Font from the Font group.

3 Select Calibri from the list (shown in Figure 3-7). Notice that your selected worksheet cells display a preview of the font as you move over a font name in the list.

Figure 3-7

Change the manner in which your data is displayed with the Font option.

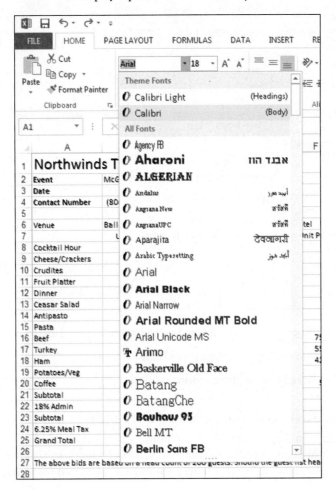

Changing the font size

The following set of steps show an example of how to change the size of the font.

STEP BY STEP	Changing the font size

1 Select range A2:L27.

2 From the Home tab, choose Font Size to display the drop-down list of font sizes.

3 Select 12.

Take Note Click the Increase Font Size or Decrease Font Size buttons to quickly adjust the size accordingly.

Changing the color of your text

The following set of steps show an example of how to change the color of text.

STEP BY STEP   **Changing the color of your text**

1 Select range A1:B4.

2 From the Home tab, click the arrow to the right of the Font Color button to display the color palette, as in Figure 3-8.

3 Select Blue. Notice that the Font Color icon now reflects the change in color. You can apply the same color to another range of cells by clicking the icon because Excel saves the color that was last used.

Figure 3-8

For on-screen displays, make use of color.

Changing the background color of cells

The following set of steps show an example of how to change the background color of cells.

STEP BY STEP   **Changing the background color of cells**

1 Click cell D25.

2 From the Home tab, click the arrow to the right of the Fill Color button to display the color palette See Figure 3-9.

3 From Standard Colors, select *Orange*. Notice that the Fill Color icon now displays the paint color you selected.

Figure 3-9

Change the background color of cells to draw attention to important data.

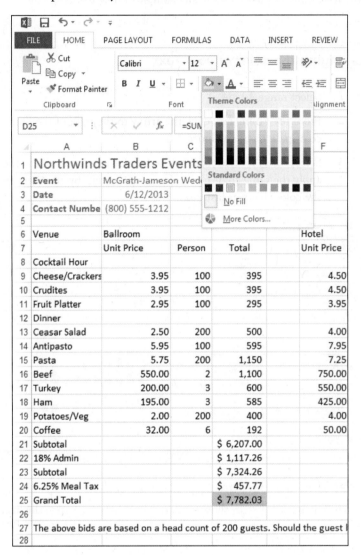

Changing text attributes

Another way to add visual interest to your worksheets is to use **text attributes**, which works regardless of the font you have chosen. Your choices are bold, italics, underline, and double-underline (See Figure 3-10 for an example of formatting a heading.). The next set of steps show an example of how this feature works.

STEP BY STEP   **Changing text attributes**

1 Select range B7:D7.

2 Press and hold the Ctrl key and select ranges F7:H7 and J7:L7.

3 From the Home tab, choose Bold.

4   Select ranges **A9:A11** and **A13:A20**.

5   From the Home tab, choose **Italic**.

Figure 3-10

Text attributes can help set headings apart from the rest of the worksheet data.

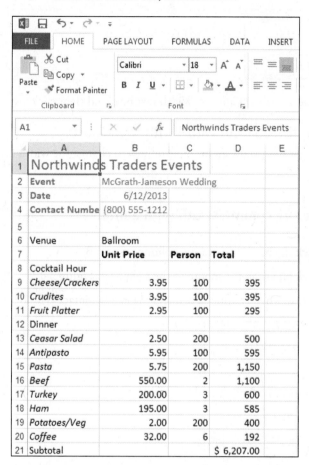

MODIFYING ROW HEIGHTS AND COLUMN WIDTHS

Bottom Line

By default, column widths and row heights are set to predefined measurements. If the data in a worksheet is larger than the column width or row height allows, Excel will alert you depending on the data type. If text is longer than the column width, Excel truncates the text if the cell to the immediate right contains data. Otherwise, the text continues to be displayed. If a numeric entry is longer than the current column width, Excel displays a series of number signs (########) in the cell. Row heights are set to adjust automatically when you change the size of your data.

Change the column width

The next set of steps show an example of how to change the width of columns.

STEP BY STEP   **Change the column width**

1   Click in cell L25.

2   From the Cells group on the Home tab, choose **Format**.

3   Select **Column Width** from the resulting menu to display the Column Width dialog box, shown in Figure 3-11.

Figure 3-11

Change the width of a column by typing an amount in the Column Width dialog box.

4   Type **12** In the Column Width text box, and then click **OK**.

Changing the column width with the mouse

The next set of steps show an example of how to change the width of columns with the mouse.

STEP BY STEP   **Changing the column width with a mouse**

1   Click the border separating columns A and B.

2   Click and drag the mouse to the right as in Figure 3-12.

3   Release when column A displays the label Contact Number in its entirety.

Figure 3-12

Change the width of a column by clicking and dragging the column border.

Changing the column width automatically

You can quickly adjust the column width to accommodate the longest entry.

STEP BY STEP   **Changing the column width automatically**

1   Select any column from the worksheet.

2   From the Cells group on the Home tab, choose **Format**.

3   Select **AutoFit Column Width** to set that column to auto-fit the width depending on the contents.

Take Note You can also double-click the border between the column headings to adjust the column width to the widest entry

Changing the row height

The next set of steps show an example of how to adjust the height of a row.

STEP BY STEP **Changing the row height**

1 Click the border separating rows 5 and 6.
2 Click and drag the mouse down.
3 Release when the row is the height you desire.

Take Note Excel automatically adjusts the height of a row when you change the size of the data within the row.

Changing the row height automatically

You can quickly adjust the row height to accommodate the tallest entry.

STEP BY STEP **Changing the row height automatically**

1 Select row 5 from the worksheet.
2 Choose Format from the Cells group of the Home tab.
3 Select AutoFit Row Height.

Take Note Double-click the border between the row headings to automatically adjust the height of a row.

CELL ALIGNMENT

Bottom Line

By default, Excel automatically **aligns** numeric data to the right edge of a cell and text entries to the left. For the most part, numeric entries generally stay aligned to the right for consistency's sake (See Figure 3-13.). There are many different options for aligning text within a worksheet. Text can be aligned within a cell or across a range of cells. You can change the horizontal and vertical placement of text within a cell and you can also wrap extra-long text entries within a single cell.

Figure 3-13

Excel automatically aligns text to the left edge of the cell and numbers to the right.

	A	B	C	D	E	F
1	Northwinds Traders Events					
2	Event	McGrath-Jameson Wedding				
3	Date	6/12/2013				
4	Contact Number	(800) 555-1212				
5						
6	Venue	Ballroom			Hotel	
7		**Unit Price**	**Person**	**Total**		**Unit Price**
8	Cocktail Hour					
9	Cheese/Crackers	3.95	100	395		4.50
10	Crudites	3.95	100	395		4.50
11	Fruit Platter	2.95	100	295		3.95
12	Dinner					
13	Ceasar Salad	2.50	200	500		4.00
14	Antipasto	5.95	100	595		7.95
15	Pasta	5.75	200	1,150		7.25

Aligning text within cells

You can change the alignment of text both within the columns and rows. That is, between the column widths and the row heights. When you increase the **width** of a row, data can be aligned between the top and bottom edges of the cell.

STEP BY STEP   **Aligning text within cells**

1   Select range **B7:D7**.

2   Press and hold the **Ctrl** key and select ranges **F7:H7** and **J7:L7**.

3   On the Home tab in the Alignment group, click the **Center** button. Excel centers the headings within the selected cells.

Merging and centering columns

You can center a heading over multiple columns with the Merge and Center command. When you **merge** a range of cells, all the cells are converted to a larger single cell. For instance, in our example we want the heading for the venue type to be centered over the column headings Unit Price, Person, and Total.

STEP BY STEP   **Merging and centering columns**

1   Select range **B6:D6**, which contains both the heading we want to center and the columns to center it over.

2   From the Home tab, choose the **Merge & Center** command from the Alignment group.

3   Excel merges cells B6, C6, and D6 and centers the heading Ballroom over all three columns.

4   Merge and Center range F6:H6 and J6:L6. The result is shown in Figure 3-14.

Figure 3-14

When a heading spans multiple columns, use the Merge & Center command to center the heading over all the columns.

5										
6	Venue		Ballroom			Hotel			Restaurant	
7		Unit Price	Person	Total	Unit Price	Person	Total	Unit Price	Person	Total
8	Cocktail Hour									
9	Cheese/Crackers	3.95	100	395	4.50	100	450	4.00	100	400
10	Crudites	3.95	100	395	4.50	100	450	4.00	100	400
11	Fruit Platter	2.95	100	295	3.95	100	395	3.25	100	325

Wrapping text

Excel has a number of sophisticated text handling tools that you would normally only find in a word processing program such as Microsoft Word. As Excel has grown more powerful and easier to use, it has added the ability to manipulate text within worksheet cells. For example, the Wrap Text command allows you to wrap extra-long text within a single cell.

The following set of steps shows an example of how to wrap text.

STEP BY STEP   **Wrapping text**

1   Click cell **A27**.

2   Choose **Wrap Text** from the Alignment group on the Home tab.

Excel enlarges the height of row 27 and wraps the extra-long notation within cell A27.

Rotating text

Another advanced text editing tool is the ability to rotate text within a cell. This can be useful when a heading is much longer than the data it is describing, or when you'd like to fit more data on a single page.

Follow the next set of steps for an example of how to rotate text.

STEP BY STEP	**Rotating text**

1   Select range **B7:D7**.

2   Choose **Orientation** from the Alignment group on the Home tab.

3   Select **Angle Counterclockwise**. The result is shown in Figure 3-15.

Figure 3-15

Text alignment helps when you need to make more room on a page.

Take Note   When you apply formatting to a cell, the format is either On or Off. A format that is applied to the current cell will appear highlighted to indicate that it is on.

4   Click the **Orientation** button again and choose **Angle Counterclockwise** again to turn off the format from range B7:D7.

BORDERS AND SHADING

Bottom Line   Just as text and number formats can help guide the eye in a worksheet, so too can the use of borders. A border can be applied to all four sides of a cell in a variety of line styles.

There are two ways to add a Border: you can add a predesigned border to a selected range of cells or you can draw your own, changing the line style and color yourself.

Applying a border

The following steps show an example of how to add a border.

STEP BY STEP	**Applying a border**

1   Select range **B6:D7**.

2   Choose **Borders** from the Font group on the Home tab.

3   Select **Outside Borders**, as in Figure 3-16.

Figure 3-16

Add borders to your worksheet
to help draw the eye.

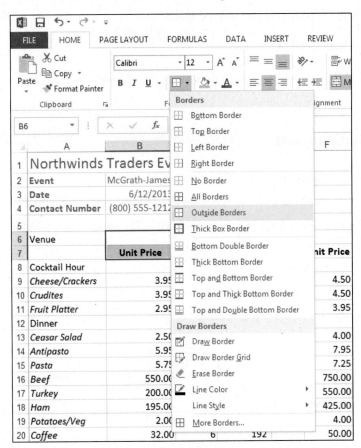

4   Click another cell so you can view the thin border.

Take Note   Once you select a Border style, the Border icon maintains that style until you pick a new one. Select each range of cells and click the Border icon to apply the style.

Drawing a border

Excel automatically uses a single black line style when you draw a border. You can change both the line style and color of a border you drawn, as illustrated by the next set of steps.

STEP BY STEP   **Drawing a border**

1   From the Font group choose **Borders**.

2   Choose Line Style and select the **Thick-Dashed** line style. The cell pointer changes its shape into that of a pencil.

3   Choose **Borders** again, click **Line Color** and select **Green**.

4 Click and drag the pencil around range F6:H7 to add the border See Figure 3-17.

5 Press the Esc key on the keyboard when you have finished to remove the pencil cell pointer.

Figure 3-17

Draw a custom border around a range of cells.

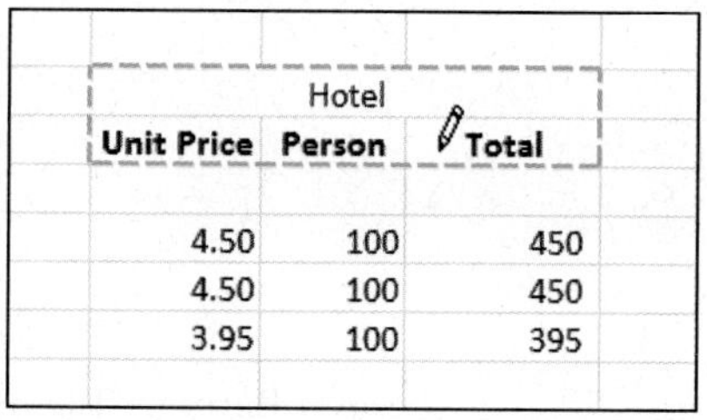

	Hotel	
Unit Price	Person	Total
4.50	100	450
4.50	100	450
3.95	100	395

Erasing a border

Just as there are two ways to add a border, there are two ways to remove a border. When you apply a border, you select the range of cells and then pick the border you want to use. To remove a border, select the range of cells and choose No Border from the Border command. You can also use the Erase Border command to erase the border by clicking each cell that has a border.

Here is an example of erasing a border using the No Border option:

STEP BY STEP   **Removing a border**

1 Select range B6:D7.

2 From the Home tab, choose Border.

3 Choose No Border from the displayed list.

STEP BY STEP   **Erasing a border**

1 From the Home tab, choose Border.

2 Choose Erase Border. The mouse pointer is displayed as an eraser , as in Figure 3-18.

3 Click the eraser on the edge of each cell in range F6:H7 to remove the border.

Figure 3-18

Remove a border from a range of cells with the Eraser.

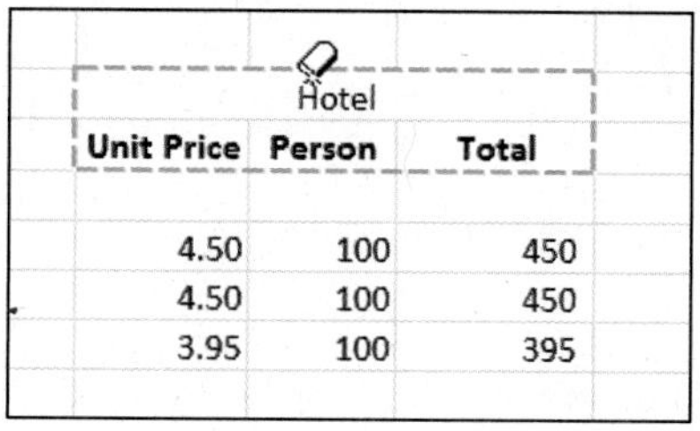

	Hotel	
Unit Price	Person	Total
4.50	100	450
4.50	100	450
3.95	100	395

4 Press the Esc key when finished to return the pointer back to normal.

COPYING CELL FORMATS

Bottom Line

Excel's **Format Painter** tool is essential when formatting a worksheet. With this tool, you can quickly and easily copy a format from one cell to another with a single click. Follow the next set of steps for an example.

STEP BY STEP   **Copying cell formats**

1   Select cell D25.

2   In the Clipboard group, choose the Format Painter. The mouse pointer now includes a paint brush, shown in Figure 3-19.

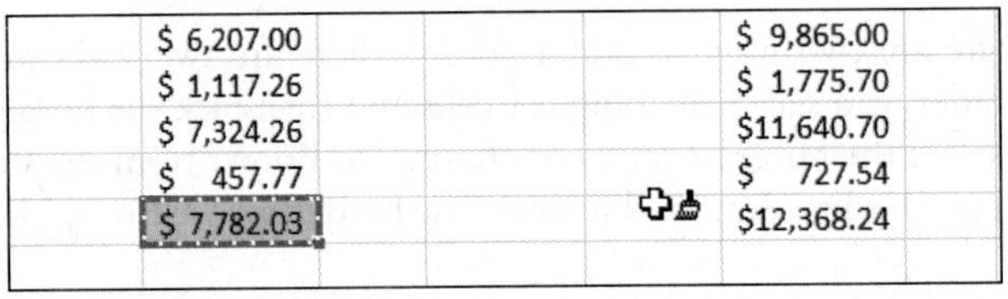

Figure 3-19

Copy formats from one cell to another with the Format Painter command.

$ 6,207.00			$ 9,865.00	
$ 1,117.26			$ 1,775.70	
$ 7,324.26			$11,640.70	
$ 457.77			$ 727.54	
$ 7,782.03			$12,368.24	

3   Click cell H25 to apply the formatting.

4   Repeat step 2 and 3 to copy the format to cell L25.

Take Note   To apply formatting to multiple cells, double-click the Format Painter and click each cell to apply. Press Esc when you are done.

WORKING WITH CELL STYLES

Bottom Line

A **style** is a collection of formatting stored under a single name. A style can consist of alignment, numeric formats, borders, fonts, shading, and a host of other attributes. To apply that collection of attributes, you need to assign the style rather than each attribute individually.

Excel comes with a number of predefined styles from which to choose; you can also create your own.

Applying cell styles

Follow the next set of steps for an example of how to apply styles to cells.

STEP BY STEP	**Applying a style to a range of cells**

1 Select range A8:A11.

2 From the Styles group choose **Cell Styles**. The drop-down gallery is shown in Figure 3-20.

Figure 3-20

Assign cell styles to maximize visibility.

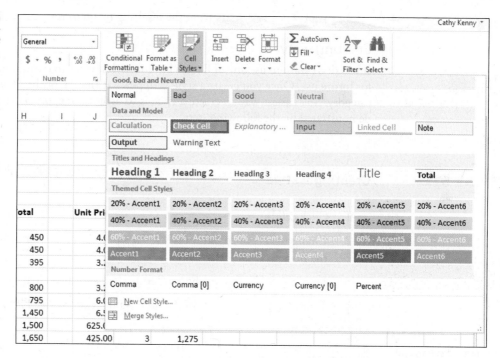

3 Select **40% - Accent 2**.

4 Select range A12:A20.

5 From the Home tab, choose **Cell Styles**.

6 Select **40% - Accent 1**.

7 Click cell **A8**, press and hold the **Ctrl** key, and click cell **A12**.

8 From the Home tab, choose **Cell Styles**.

9 Select **Heading 3**.

10 Click on cell **A21**. Hold the **Ctrl** key and click cells **A21** and **A25**.

11 From the Home tab, choose **Cell Styles**.

12 Select **Total**.

Clearing a style

You can easily remove the formatting from a cell without removing its contents with the Clear command, as the following set of steps illustrates.

STEP BY STEP   **Clearing a style**

1   Select range A9:A11.

2   From the Editing group, choose Clear.

3   Select Clear Formats from the resulting menu to remove the themed cell style.

Creating a style

If you don't want to use any of Excel's built-in styles, you can create your own styles and save them for future use. Once you create a style, it appears at the top of the Styles menu under the Custom category. The easiest way to create a style is to assign the appropriate formats to the cell first, as demonstrated by the following steps.

STEP BY STEP   **Creating a style**

1   Click cell B6.

2   Change the Font to Bauhaus 93, the size to 14, the color to Blue, and add a Border to the Bottom of the cell.

3   From the Styles group, choose Cell Styles, and then click New Cell Style.

4   Type Heading Column in the Style name text box (see Figure 3-21) and click OK.

Figure 3-21

You can create your own custom styles and save them for future use.

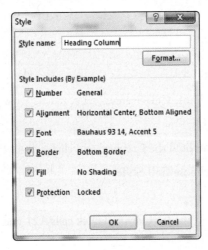

Modifying a style

Another way to create a custom style is to take an existing style, change an attribute or two, and save it as a new style.

Modifying a style

1 From the Styles group, choose **Cell Styles** to display the Style Gallery.

2 Right-click the new **Heading Column** style at the top of the Style Gallery and choose **Modify** (See Figure 3-22.).

Figure 3-22

Rather than start from scratch, modify an existing style to suit your needs.

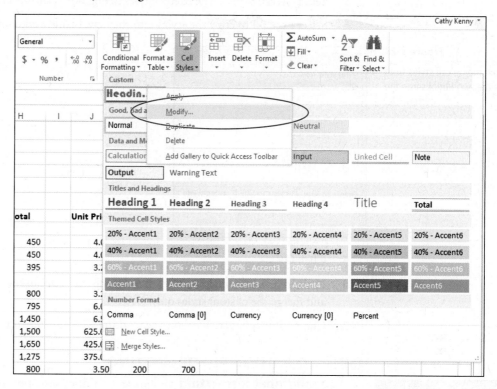

3 Click **Format** in the resulting dialog box, and then click the **Font** tab.

4 Change the size to **12**.

5 Click **OK** twice to save the modifications.

Merging styles from other worksheets

When you create a style, Excel stores the style in the worksheet in which it was created. You can use custom styles with other worksheets, but you must first merge them in to the current worksheet.

STEP BY STEP   **Merging styles from other worksheets**

1   Open a new worksheet using the **File > New** command. Choose **Blank workbook**.

2   Choose **Cell Styles** from the Styles group.

3   Select **Merge Styles**. The Merge Styles dialog box is shown in figure 3-23.

4   Select **excel03** to copy the styles into the new, blank workbook.

Figure 3-23

You can merge cell styles from other workbooks into the current file.

5   Click **OK**.

6   In the resulting dialog box, click **No** to keep the styles in the current workbook intact and merge the custom styles only.

7   Choose **File > Close**. We won't be working with this file so you don't need to save it.

USING CONDITIONAL FORMATTING

Bottom Line

Excel's **conditional formatting** options let you draw attention to important points in your data set based on a certain set of criteria. You could, for instance, highlight values that are greater than a certain value; highlight sales data that falls within the top 10%; or highlight testing values that are above average. By using color, symbols, and other special attributes, you can show data at a glance that might be on the rise or falling below expectations.

Conditional formatting is based on a set of predefined rules. For instance, the rule that states Format All Cells Based on Their Values formats cells using a graduated color scale based on a set of defined values. There are five different categories of rules and a number of options within each category that you can use.

Conditional formatting rules

ICON	HIGHLIGHT CELL RULES	DESCRIPTION
	Highlight Cells Rules	Highlights cells based on a defined value.
	Top/Bottom Rules	Highlights values based on a defined ranking.
	Data Bars	Adds a data bar to the cell to represent the value; the longer the bar, the larger the value.
	Color Scales	Applies a gradient color scale to a value and the color indicates where the value falls within a range.
	Icon Sets	Adds a set of icons to represent the values in a range of cells.

To demonstrate conditional formatting, we will open a new worksheet from the Excel03lessons folder. But first, save and close the current event planning worksheet we have been using.

STEP BY STEP   **Saving a worksheet**

1   Go back to the **excel03** worksheet and choose File > Save As.

2   In the Office Background, click Computer and navigate to the Excel03lessons folder.

3   In the file name text box, type _formats at the end of the current file name.

4   Click Save, and then choose File > Close.

Using conditional formatting

Follow the next set of steps for an example of how to use this feature.

STEP BY STEP   **Using conditional formatting**

1   Choose File > Open.

2   Navigate to the Excel03lessons folder and double-click the file named **excel03_grades**.

3   Select range A4:E37.

4   From the Style group, choose Conditional Formatting.

5   Select Top/Bottom Rules (see Figure 3-24) and select Top 10%.

Figure 3-24

Instantly highlight important data with Conditional Formatting.

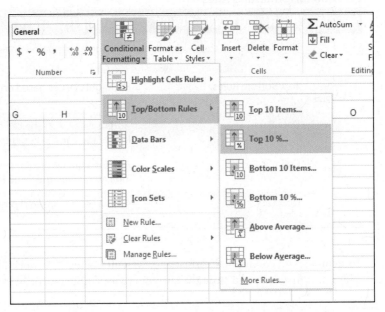

6   Click OK. Excel highlights the grades that fall within the Top 10%.

Removing conditional formatting

You can remove conditional formatting from an entire worksheet or a specified range, as the follow example indicates.

STEP BY STEP   **Removing conditional formatting**

1   Select range A4:E37.

2   Choose Conditional Formatting again.

3   Choose Clear Rules.

4   Select Clear Rules from Selected Cells.

Creating a new rule

If the predefined rules are not what you are looking for, you can create your own, including specifying the formatting you want to apply should the conditions be met. The next set of step shows you an example of how to use this feature.

STEP BY STEP   **Creating a new rule**

1   Select range E4:E37.

2   From the Style group choose Conditional Formatting again.

3   Choose New Rule.

4   From the Rule list, select Format only cells that contain.

5   In the **Format only cells with:** section, select Greater Than from the drop-down menu adjacent to the Cell Value field (See Figure 3-25.).

Figure 3-25

Create a New Rule to make your data standout when it meets specific criteria.

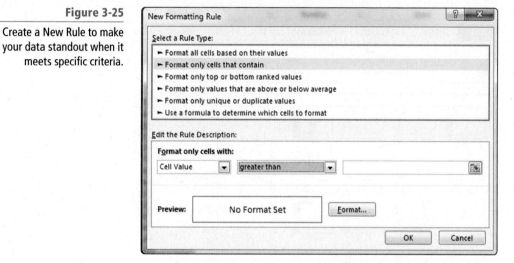

6   Type 2000 in the box adjacent to Greater Than.

7   Click Format and choose the Fill tab.

8   Select the color Blue.

9   Click OK twice. Excel highlights all scores that are higher than 2000.

USING PAGE THEMES

Page **themes** are a collection of color-coordinated color schemes and font families for use in a single worksheet. Each theme contains a set of predefined colors, fonts, and attributes that have been professionally designed and coordinated. You can also swap out different parts of each theme to suit your individual needs. You can, for instance, pick a new font set to use or select a different color scheme. You can also adjust the settings for objects added to your worksheets with the Drawing tools.

Applying a theme

Follow the next set of steps for an example of how to apply a theme.

STEP BY STEP	Applying a theme

1   From the Page Layout tab, choose Themes from the Themes group.

Figure 3-26

Use Page Themes to design color-coordinated worksheets.

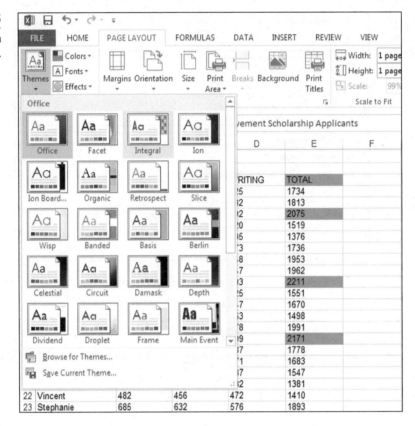

2   Select Integral from the gallery, shown in Figure 3-26

Excel changes the appearance of your worksheet, including any cells that make existing use of Cell Styles or colors.

Changing the color scheme

Follow the next set of steps for an example of how to change the **color scheme** of your worksheet.

Changing the color scheme

1   From the Page Layout tab in the Themes group, choose Colors.

2   Select Blue Green (See Figure 3-27.).

Figure 3-27

Swap out one color set for another in the Page Theme.

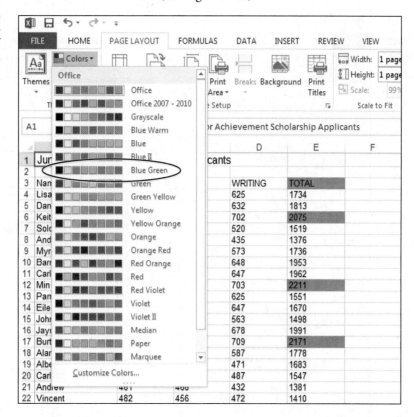

Changing the font set

Follow the next set of steps for an example of how to change the **font set** used by your worksheet.

STEP BY STEP   **Changing the font set**

> 1   From the Page Layout tab, choose Fonts.
>
> 2   Select Corbel from the Fonts gallery, shown in Figure 3-28.

Figure 2-28

Pick a new Font family to use in the Page Theme.

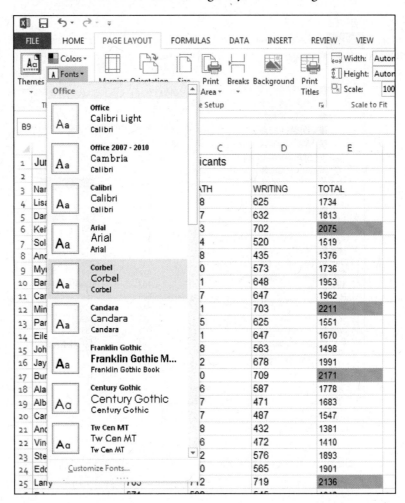

Changing the effects

Follow the next set of steps for an example of how to change the **effects** used in your worksheet.

Changing the effects

1   From the Page Layout tab in the Themes group, choose Effects.

Figure 3-29

Select the effects to add to drawn objects in a worksheet.

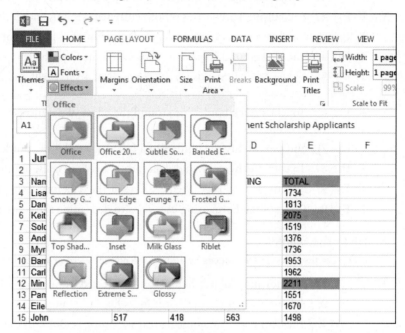

2   Select Glow Edge from the gallery. See Figure 3-29.

3   Choose File > Save As, and navigate to the Excel03lessons folder. Type **excel03_grades_format** as the file name, and click Save.

What you learned in this lesson:

- Understanding Cell Formats

- Changing Number Formats

- Changing the Font and Font Size

- Modifying Row Heights and Column Widths

- Cell Alignment

- Borders & Shading

- Copying Cell Formats

- Working with Cell Styles

- Using Conditional Formatting

- Using Page Themes

Knowledge Assessment

True/False

Circle T if the statement is true or F it the statement is false

T F 1. A number with a thousands separator but no currency symbol has the Comma Style.

T F 2. Accounting Format aligns both currency symbols and decimal points.

T F 3. Excel offers Social Security and Phone Number format support.

T F 4. The background color of a cell is called the Cell Shade.

T F 5. Merge & Center adds up the contents of several cells and displays the sum in a single large cell.

T F 6. To add a thick borderline around the edges of a multi-cell selection, use the All Borders option.

T F 7. You can modify the borders of a cell range using the Border Eraser tool.

T F 8. To copy the fill color and data format between cells, use the Format Painter.

T F 9. Selecting a new Page Theme will clear the data formatting in a document.

T F 10. Conditional Formatting uses rules to determine the content or style of a cell.

Fill in the Blanks

Complete the following sentences by writing the correct word or words in the blanks provided.

1. Themes and Color Schemes can be selected from galleries in the _____ tab.

2. A Font Set consists of default fonts for _____ and _____ cells.

3. The command for adjusting text wrapping is found in the _____ group of the _____ tab.

4. To automatically expand a column to display its entire contents, use the _____ tool.

5. In addition to changing font, size, and color, you can alter your data's text attributes. Options include _____, _____, _____, and _____.

6. Data formatted with the Text format will not be used in _____.

7. To display $5 as $5.00, apply the _____ command twice.

8. Calendar entries can be formatted as _____ (e.g., 2/13/1979) or _____ (e.g., Tuesday, February 13, 1979).

9. In Excel, numbers are also known as _____.

10. To format a calendar date like 21 /:/ December /:/ 2005, use a _____ number format.

Competency Assessment

Project 3-1: Formatting Numeric Data

In this exercise you will apply a variety of number formats to the same data.

1. Create a new blank workbook.

2. Fill the range A1:A7 with the following text labels, one per cell: **General**, **Date**, **Currency**, **Percentage**, **Scientific**, **Accounting**, **Time**.

3. Type the number 4509.334 in cell B1.

4. Drag the AutoFill handle down to fill cells B2:B7 with the same number.

5. Select cell B2.

6. From the drop-down menu in the Home > Number group, select **Short Date**.

7. Repeat steps 6-7 to format cell B3 with the Currency format, B4 as a Percentage, B5 with Scientific notation, B6 with Accounting, and B7 with the Time format.

8. AutoFit column A's width to its contents.

9. Press Ctrl+W. Save your file as **project_3-1_numberformats**.

Project 3-2: **Simple Conditional Formatting**

In this project you'll use conditional formatting to highlight top and bottom 10% values.

1. Open the exercise file **cond_formatting_1** and save it as **project_3-2_conditional**.

2. Select cells B2:B32.

3. Click Home > Styles > Conditional Formatting. From the Top/Bottom Rules list, select Top 10%.

4. Format the top 10% of cells with Green Fill with Dark Green Text. Click OK.

5. Repeat steps 3-4 to format the bottom 10% of cells with Light Red Fill with Dark Red Text.

6. Finally, from the Conditional Formatting dropdown, select the 5 Quarters icon set.

7. Save and close your document.

Proficiency Assessment

Project 3-3: **Applying Themes and Styles**

In this exercise you'll apply themes and styles to your worksheet data.

1. Open the project file **3-3-source** and save it as **project_3-3_themes**.

2. Apply the Heading 1 style to cell A1.

3. Select cells B2:B32.

4. Apply the "40% - Accent 4" themed cell style.

5. In cell D15, type Dec 13-14 data reported as 2-day average.

6. Apply the Explanatory Text style to cell D15.

7. Select the Basis theme from the Page Layout tab.

8. Save and close your document.

Project 3-4: **More Cell Formatting**

In this exercise you'll format cell contents.

1. Open the project file **3-4-source** and save it as **project_3-4_cellformatting**.

2. Insert a column to the left of column A.

3. In any cell in the range A1:A32, type the text Daily totals subject to Auditor revision.

4. Select the cell you edited in step 3 and rotate the text 90 degrees counterclockwise, so it reads bottom to top.

5. Apply the Merge and Center tool to A1:A32.

6. Middle Align the newly merged cell.

7. Select the thickest Line Style from the Cell Borders tool, then draw a border along the right hand edge of the merged cell.

8. Click on the merged cell B1 and determine its font size and text characteristics from the Home > Font group.

9. Format merged cell A1 with the same font size and boldface type.

10. Save and close your document.

Mastery Assessment

Project 3-5: Custom Cell Styles

In this exercise you will create custom cell styles.

1. Open the project file **3-5-source** and save it as **project_3-5_customcellstyles**.
2. Merge cells E27:G32.
3. Open the exercise file bowie_data.
4. Copy the cell text ("29 December data...") from bowie_data into the newly merged cell in themes_styles_3.
5. Format the new merged cell as follows: Text data format; Word Wrap on; 9pt Corbel; "Red, Accent 2, Lighter 80%" fill; red text; Center text; Middle Align text.
6. Select the new merged cell and save its formatting as a custom Cell Style called data_notice.
7. Save and close your document.

Project 3-6: Advanced Conditional Formatting

In this exercise, create more complex conditional formatting rules.

1. Open the project file **3-6-source** and save it as **project_3-6_conditional2**.
2. Select the data in column C.
3. Create a new Conditional Formatting rule to add a bright yellow fill to any cells with duplicate daily values.

   (Four cells should be emphasized with this rule, in rows 12, 14, 15, and 29.)
4. Open the Manage Cells... dialog and change the order in which conditional formatting rules are applied, so the duplicate cells rule is applied last. (This will not affect the spreadsheet's formatting.)
5. Save and close your document.

LESSON SKILL MATRIX

In this lesson, you will learn the following skills:

Understanding Formulas	Using Common Functions
Entering Simple Formulas	Working with Ranges
Referencing Cells from Other Worksheets/Workbooks	Copying Formulas
Using Functions	Formula Auditing
Using the Function library	Using the AutoSum Tool

KEY TERMS

- **Absolute Cell Reference**
- **Arguments**
- **Auditing (tools)**
- **Average**
- **Cell Reference**
- **Comparison Formula**
- **COUNTIF**
- **Formula**
- **Function Library**
- **If**
- **Max**
- **Median**
- **Min**
- **Name Manager**
- **NOW**
- **PMT**
- **Range Name**
- **Relative Cell Reference**
- **Sum**

ResearchersField researchers at Fabrikam receive enormous amounts of raw sensor data each day. To turn it into something meaningful for humans, they must transform the data in a variety of ways, ranging from simple sums and averages to advanced statistical analysis. Excel's Function Library offers the combination of Excel's robust Function Library contains the tools they need for their mathematical work – and back at HQ, the financial and HR teams will use the same Library for their own ends.

SOFTWARE ORIENTATION

You can use formulas to perform basic or complex calculations within Microsoft Excel.

Figure 4-1

Formula controls in Microsoft Excel 2013.

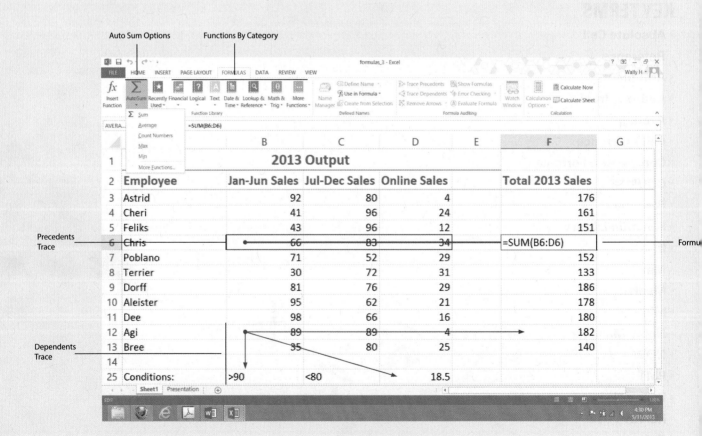

STARTING UP

In this lesson, you'll work with several files from the Excel04lessons folder. Make sure that you have loaded the OfficeLessons folder onto your computer.

The most useful feature of Excel is its ability to perform calculations. Through formulas, you can use Excel to calculate any range of values. Excel's extensive Function library, which is a set of predefined formulas, enables you to perform sophisticated data analysis with little or no experience.

FORMULAS

Bottom Line

A **formula** is a mathematical equation used to calculate a value. In Excel, a formula must always begin with the equal sign (=), which indicates to Excel that it must interpret the data in the cell as a formula.

When you enter a formula, Excel displays the result of the formula in the cell rather than the formula itself. For example, if you type =2+6 in a cell, Excel displays the result of that calculation (8). The Formula bar, located at the top of the worksheet window, is the area in which you can view, enter, and edit formulas.

Excel also provides hundreds of predefined functions that allow you to perform calculations, from easy to complex, without having to build the formulas from scratch. For instance, the SUM function quickly adds together a range of cells, so you don't have to add each cell individually.

Before we begin creating formulas, you should become familiar with some key terms.

Operator

An operator is a sign or symbol that specifies the type of calculation that should be performed, such as an addition (a plus sign +) or a multiplication (*). For example, in the formula =150+25, the operator is the plus sign, and it adds together the values 150 and 25.

Operand

Every Excel formula includes at least one operand, which is the data that Excel uses in the calculation. The simplest type of operand is a number; however, you can also include a reference to worksheet data, such as a cell address (B1), as an operand.

Arithmetic formula

An arithmetic formula combines a numeric operand (a number or a function that returns a numerical value as a result) with an operator to perform a calculation. As you can see in the following table, there are six arithmetic operators you can use to construct arithmetic formulas.

Mathematical operators in formulas

OPERATOR	PURPOSE
+	Addition
-	Subtraction
*	Multiplication
/	Division
%	Percentage
^	Exponentiation

Order of operations

Many errors occur in formulas when mathematical operators are not entered in the proper order. When creating formulas, you must keep in mind the *order of operations*: exponentiation occurs before multiplication or division, and multiplication occurs before addition and subtraction. You can alter the order of operations by enclosing segments of the formula in parentheses. For example, the formula =(4+10)*2 forces Excel to first add 4 and 10 and then multiply the result by 2.

Comparison formula

A **comparison formula** combines a numeric operand, such as a number, with special operators to compare one operand to another. The most common comparison operators are greater than (>), less than (<), and equal to (=) or some combination thereof. A comparison formula returns a logical result of 1 or 0. If the comparison is true, the formula returns a value of 1. If the comparison is false, the formula returns a value of 0.

Comparison formulas often consist of *If...Then* statements. For example, the formula =IF(C2>D2,"Yes","No") returns the label Yes if the value in cell C2 is greater than the value in cell D2; otherwise, it returns the label "No."

ENTERING SIMPLE FORMULAS

You can create formulas by using the mouse or the keyboard.

Building a formula by typing

The following example shows how to build a formula by typing.

STEP BY STEP	Entering a formula

1   Launch Microsoft Excel and open a Blank workbook.

2   Type 24 in cell A2 and 12 in cell A3.

3   Type =24*12 in cell A4, as in Figure 4-2.

Figure 4-2

When you enter a formula, Excel displays the result of the formula in the cell and the formula in the Formula bar.

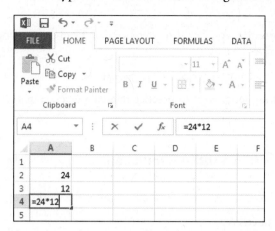

4   Press Enter. Excel displays the result of the formula, 288, in cell A4.

Another way to create a formula is to refer to the cell that contains the value, rather than enter the value itself. When you do, Excel updates the formula automatically when the original value changes. For instance, the values used for the formula in cell A4 actually reside in cells A2 and A3. Note that Excel also color-codes each cell reference in the formula to help you keep track of the data in your worksheet.

Follow the next set of steps to see how this feature works.

STEP BY STEP   **Using a formula**

1   Type = in cell A5.

2   Continue typing A2*A3 in cell A5 and press Enter. Excel displays the result of 288.

3   Type 57 in cell A2 and press Enter. Excel updates the result in cell A5 to 684.

Building a formula by pointing

In addition to typing the **cell reference**, you can also build a formula by pointing to the cell that contains the data you want to use, as shown by the following set of steps.

STEP BY STEP   **Building a formula by pointing**

1   Type = in cell A6.

2   Using the arrow keys or the mouse, move the cell pointer to cell A2.

3   Type the multiplication operator, (*) and move the cell pointer to cell A3.

4   Press Enter on your keyboard. Excel displays the result 684.

REFERENCING CELLS FROM OTHER WORKSHEETS OR WORKBOOKS

Bottom Line

When building formulas, you can also reference data from other worksheets or workbooks.

Referencing a cell in another worksheet

Perform the following set of steps to practice referencing a cell in another worksheet.

STEP BY STEP   Referencing a cell in another worksheet

1   Click the New Sheet button at the bottom of the worksheet window.

2   Type 823 in cell A2.

3   Type = in cell B2.

4   Click cell A2 and type *.

5   Click the tab labeled Sheet1.

6   Click cell A2. Excel appends the sheet name to the cell address in the formula bar. Your formula should now read: =A2*Sheet1!A2.

7   Press Enter on your keyboard. Excel switches back to Sheet2 and multiplies the value in cell A2 of Sheet1 by the value in cell A2 of Sheet2.

Referencing a cell in another workbook

Perform the following set of steps to practice referencing a cell in another workbook.

STEP BY STEP   Referencing a cell in another workbook

1   Choose File > Open, click Computer in the Backstage view, and click Browse.

2   Navigate to the Excel04lessons folder and open the file named **excel04_formulas**.

3   Point to the Excel icon in the Windows Taskbar at the bottom of your screen (see Figure 4-3) and click the file named Book1 to maximize the workbook.

Figure 4-3

Switch between open workbooks in the Windows Taskbar.

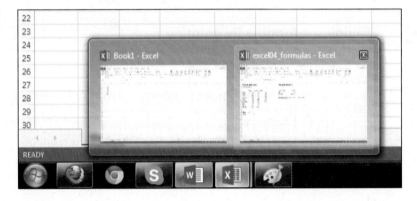

4   On Sheet1 of **Book1**, click in cell A7 and type =.

5   Point to the Excel icon in the Windows Taskbar, and click the file named **excel04_formulas** to maximize the workbook.

6   Click in cell B5. Excel appends the file name, sheet name, and cell address to the formula. Your formula should now read: =[Excel04_formulas.xlsx]Sheet1!$B$5.

7   Type *.

8   Switch back to Sheet1 in the workbook named **Book1** and click in cell A6.

9   Press Enter on your keyboard. Excel multiplies the value in cell B5 of the workbook named **excel04_formulas** by the amount in cell A6.

USING FUNCTIONS

Bottom Line

Functions are predefined formulas that perform a specific calculation, such as determining the average value in a range or calculating a mortgage payment. Excel includes over 200 functions in categories such as financial, statistical, scientific, and engineering. The table below details some of the most commonly-used functions.

Common Excel functions

FUNCTION	DESCRIPTION	SYNTAX AND EXAMPLE OF SYNTAX
SUM	Adds together values within a range	=SUM(*range*) =SUM(A1:A50)
IF	Tests whether a condition is met and returns the first result if the value is true and the second result if the value is false	=IF(*test,true,false*) =IF(A1>B1,500,5000)
AVERAGE	Returns the average of a range	=AVERAGE(*range*) =AVERAGE(A1:A10)
MAX	Returns the largest value in a range	=MAX(*range*) =MAX(A1:A30)
MIN	Returns the smallest value in a range	=MIN(*range*) =MIN(A1:A10)
MEDIAN	Returns the median value in a range	=MEDIAN(*range*) =MEDIAN(A1:A10)
DATE	Returns the value that represents the date	=DATE(*year,month,day*) =DATE(2013,4,23)
NOW	Returns the current date and time	=NOW()
COUNTIF	Counts the number of cells within a range that meet a given condition	=COUNTIF(*range,criteria*) =COUNTIF(A1:A45,">20")
PMT	Calculates the payment for a loan	=PMT(*rate,nper,fv*) =PMT(.08/12,12,100000)

USING THE FUNCTION LIBRARY

Bottom Line

The **Function Library** in the Formulas tab, shown in Figure 4-4, organizes functions by type. To use the Function Library, select the category containing the function you want to use, and click it. When you do, Excel displays the list of functions assigned to that category. Select the function you want to use by clicking it. Excel displays a Function Arguments dialog box, where you can indicate the ranges containing the arguments.

Figure 4-4

The Function Library group on the Formulas tab.

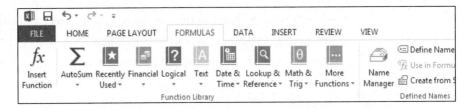

Take Note

If you know the Function you want to use and its syntax, you can type the function and its required arguments directly in the cell, without using the Function Library at all.

The Function Library

TYPE	DESCRIPTION
AutoSum	Commonly-used functions such as SUM, AVERAGE, COUNT, MAX, and MIN.
Recently-Used	The most recently-used functions.
Financial	Financial calculations such as loan payments (PMT) and net present value (NPV).
Logical	Formulas that perform logical tests including IF, TRUE, and NOT.
Text	Formulas that manipulate text strings including FIND, EXACT, and SEARCH.
Date & Time	Date and time calculations including NOW, MONTH, and DAYS.
Lookup & Reference	Formulas that help find matching values, including VLOOKUP, MATCH, and CHOOSE.
Math & Trig	Mathematical calculations, including SUM, PRODUCT, and COS.

Creating a formula with a function

Creating formulas with functions is very similar to creating regular formulas, with the exception that each function follows a specific syntax. All functions consist of the equal sign followed by the function name and the **arguments** within a set of parentheses. For instance, the formula to calculate the average in a range of data would be similar to: =AVERAGE(A1:A50).

You can create a formula using a function by typing the function name and arguments yourself, or you can use the Function Library to build the function step by step. In the following example, we will use the NPER function to determine how long it will take to pay back a loan of $15,000 if monthly payments of $100 are made and the interest rate is 2.5% per year.

STEP BY STEP   **Creating a formula with function**

1 In **Book1**, click in cell A8.

2 Choose Financial from the Formulas tab.

3 Select NPER from the Function list. In the formula bar Excel displays a description and the syntax for the NPER function, which calculates the number of payment periods to pay off a loan.

The Function Arguments dialog box for the selected function NPER is displayed. See Figure 4-5.

4 Enter .025/12 in the Rate box; enter 100 in the Pmt box; and 15000 in the Pv box.

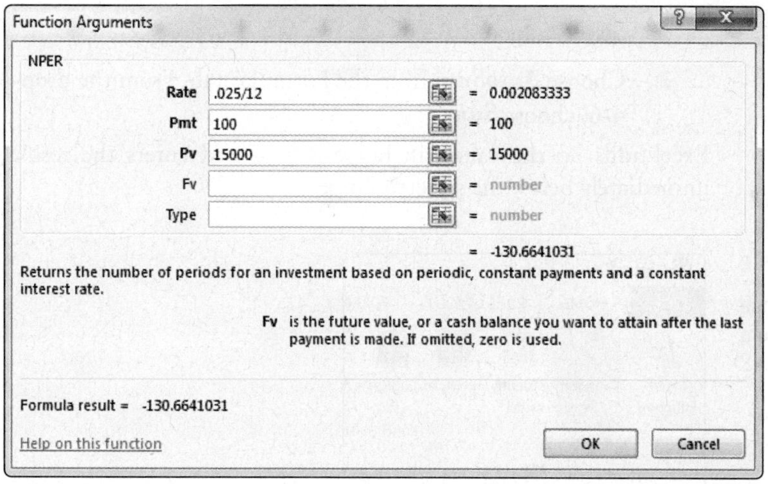

Figure 4-5

The Function Arguments dialog box helps you build a formula step by step.

5 Click OK. Excel enters the formula in cell A8 and calculates the result of 130 pay periods.

USING THE AUTOSUM TOOL

Bottom Line

The AutoSum tool, which you'll find on both the Home tab and Formulas tab of the Ribbon, contains a set of quick single-click functions. To use these commands, select the range of data and then choose the appropriate function. The following table describes what each function does.

The AutoSum functions

COMMAND	DESCRIPTION
AutoSum	Adds up the values in a range.
Average	Finds the average value in a range.
Count Numbers	Counts the number of values in a range.
Max	Returns the maximum value in a range.
Min	Returns the minimum value in a range.

Quickly adding up a range of values

Perform the next set of steps to understand how you can quickly add up a range of values in Excel using the AutoSum function.

STEP BY STEP   ## Using the AutoSum Tool

1   Select range **A2:A8**.

2   Choose **AutoSum** from the Formulas tab. From the drop-down menu shown in Figure 4-6, choose **Sum**.

Excel adds up the values in range A2:A8 and enters the result in cell A9, which is the cell immediately below the selected range.

Figure 4-6

Quickly calculate a range of values with the AutoSum command.

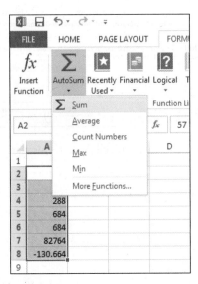

USING COMMON FUNCTIONS

Before we review some of the more commonly-used functions and how to use them, we need to save the worksheet we have been using to experiment with creating formulas.

Saving your work

1   Choose File > Save, and choose Computer.

2   Click the Browse button, navigate to the Excel04lessons folder, name the file
    excel04_sample, and click Save.

3   Choose File > Close to close the worksheet. We will continue working with the file
    named **excel04_formulas**.

SUM

The **Sum** function adds together the values in a range of cells, as the following steps show.

Using the SUM function

1   Click in cell B9.

2   Click the arrow next to the AutoSum button in the Editing group of the Home tab, and
    select Sum from the drop-down menu, shown in Figure 4-7.

Figure 4-7

AutoSum button found in the
Editing group of the Home tab.

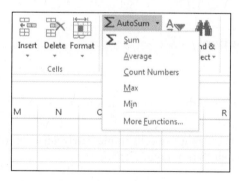

3   Excel automatically selects the range of cells immediately adjacent to the current cell, in
    this case the values directly above cell B9, or range B5:B8 (See Figure 4-8.).

Figure 4-8

Excel automatically selects the
range of cells adjacent to the
current cell.

	A	B	C	D	E
1	**Monthly Sales Figure**				
2	*Northwest Region*				
3					
4		**House**	**Condo**	**Total**	
5	*Philip*	121	98		
6	*Keith*	150	142		
7	*Erica*	201	119		
8	*Danielle*	224	87		
9	**Total**	=SUM(B5:B8)			
10	**Average**	SUM(number1, [number2], ...)			
11	**Max**				
12	**Min**				
13	**Median**				
14					
15					
16	**Bonus**				
17	**Quota**				
18					

NPER   fx   =SUM(B5:B8)

4   Press Enter on your keyboard to sum the range.

AVERAGE

The **Average** function finds the average value in a range of cells, as the following example shows.

STEP BY STEP   **Using the AVERAGE function**

    1   Click in cell B10.

    2   Click the arrow next to the AutoSum button in the Editing group, and select Average from the drop-down menu.

Excel automatically selects the range of cells immediately adjacent to the current cell, in this case the values directly above cell B10, or range B5:B9.

    3   Change the range to B5:B8.

    4   Press **Enter** on your keyboard. Excel displays the average amount in cell B10.

MAX

The **Max** function finds the maximum value in a range of cells, as the following example shows.

STEP BY STEP   **Using the MAX function**

    1   Click in cell B11.

    2   Click the arrow next to the AutoSum button, and select Max from the drop-down menu.

Excel automatically selects the range of cells immediately adjacent to the current cell, in this case the values directly above cell B11, or range B5:B10.

    3   Change the range to B5:B8.

    4   Press **Enter** on your keyboard. Excel displays the Maximum value in cell B11.

MIN

The **Min** function finds the minimum value in a range of cells, as the following example shows.

STEP BY STEP   **Using the MIN function**

    1   Click in cell B12.

    2   Click the arrow next to the AutoSum button and select Min from the drop-down menu.

Excel automatically selects the range of cells immediately adjacent to the current cell, in this case the values directly above cell B12, or range B5:B11.

    3   Change the range to B5:B8.

    4   Press **Enter** on your keyboard. Excel displays the minimum value in cell B12.

MEDIAN

The **Median** function finds the middle value in a range of cells, as shown by the next set of steps.

STEP BY STEP   **Using the MEDIAN function**

1   Click in cell B13.

2   Type =MEDIAN(.

3   Select range B5:B8.

4   Type) and press Enter on your keyboard.

5   Excel displays the median value in cell B13.

IF

The **If** function performs a logical test on a cell or range of cells to determine whether a specified condition has been met. For example, suppose you have decided that a Bonus will be granted to the individual who sells more than 700 units of certain product. The example below shows how you can use the If function to calculate whether the value in cell B9 meets this criteria.

STEP BY STEP   **Using the IF function**

1   Click in cell B16.

2   Type =IF(B9>700,"Yes","No") and press Enter on the keyboard.

Figure 4-9

Perform logical tests on data using IF and COUNTIF functions. Here, data is analyzed to see if sales quotas have been met.

	B16	▼	:	× ✓	fx	=IF(B9>700,"Yes","No")	
	A	B	C	D	E	F	
1	**Monthly Sales Figure**						
2	*Northwest Region*						
3							
4		House	Condo	Total			
5	*Philip*	121	98				
6	*Keith*	150	142				
7	*Erica*	201	119				
8	*Danielle*	224	87				
9	**Total**	696					
10	**Average**	174					
11	**Max**	224					
12	**Min**	121					
13	**Median**	175.5					
14							
15							
16	**Bonus**	No					
17	**Quota**						
18							

Excel evaluates the Total amount in cell B9 to determine whether more than 700 units have been sold (in other words, whether the value in B9 is greater than 700). If the value in B9 is greater than 700, (meaning that more than 700 units have been sold), the formula returns the label Yes, and you can give the individual his or her bonus. However, if the value in B9 is 700 or less as in Figure 4-9,, the function returns the label No, and you can decide not to grant the individual his or her bonus.

COUNTIF

COUNTIF is similar to IF in that the function evaluates a cell or range of cells to test for a specific condition. However, the COUNTIF function returns the number of times the condition has been meet in the range, not whether the condition has been met at all. For example, suppose you want to figure out how many brokers have met a sales quota of 200 units. The following set of steps illustrates how to apply the COUNTIF formula to make this determination.

STEP BY STEP   **Using the COUNTIF function**

1   Click in cell B17.

2   Type **=COUNTIF(B5:B8,">200")** and press **Enter** on the keyboard.

Excel evaluates the values in range B5:B8 to determine how many of the cells within this range have values that are greater than 200 (in other words, how many brokers met the sales quota of 200 units.)

NOW

The **NOW** function enters the current date and time in a worksheet cell and it's updated whenever the workbook is opened. An example is shown below.

STEP BY STEP   **Using the NOW function**

1   Click in cell G2.

2   From the Formulas tab, choose **Date & Time**.

3   From the drop-down list that appears, select **NOW**. Note that the function does not take any arguments.

4   Click **OK** in the resulting dialog box.

Excel enters the current date and time in cell G2.

PMT

The **PMT** function calculates the monthly payment amount on a loan. The arguments it uses are the Interest Rate (*rate*), Term (*nper*), and Principal (*pv*) amount. You must adjust the interest rate period and payments to use the same number units. For example, if you make monthly payments on the loan, the interest rate needs to be adjusted to *rate*/12 and the term or Nper adjusted to *nper**12. In the following example, you will calculate the monthly payment for a 30-year loan of $425,000 at a 4.25% interest rate.

STEP BY STEP   **Using the PMT function**

1   Click in cell H8.

2   From the Formulas tab, choose **Financial**.

3   From the list of functions that appears, select **PMT**.

4   In the Functions Argument dialog box (see Figure 4-10), enter the following: **H4/12** in Rate; **H5*12** in Nper; and **H6** in Pv.

5   Click OK. Excel calculates the monthly payment of -$2,090.74. (The amount is displayed as a negative number to indicate that it is a payment.)

Figure 4-10

Calculate the monthly payment on a loan using the PMT function.

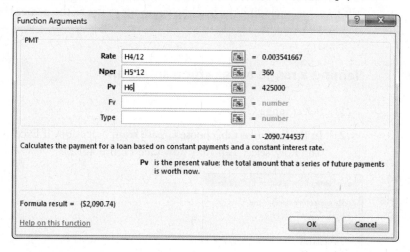

WORKING WITH RANGES

Bottom Line

You can assign names to particular ranges within a worksheet. By assigning a name to a range, you can more easily describe data. In particular, you can use **range names** in formulas rather than cell references to describe the data being used in the formula.

For instance, in the worksheet shown in the figure below, range B5:B8 contains data for the number of individual houses sold. If you assign the name House to that range, we can easily construct the formula =SUM(House) to calculates the total number of houses sold.

Naming a range of cells

The following set of steps shows an example of how to name a range of cells.

STEP BY STEP   **Naming a range of cells**

1   Select range **B5:B8**.

2   From the Formulas tab, choose **Define Name**.

3   In the Name box (see Figure 4-11), type **House**.

Figure 4-11

Name a range of cells to describe the data in your worksheet.

4   Click OK.

Naming a range of cells from a selection

You can quickly convert row or column headings to range names. To do so, first select the range of cells to name, including the heading you want to use as the name. Here's an example.

STEP BY STEP	Naming a range of cells for a selection

1   Select range C4:C8.

2   In the Formulas tab, choose Create from Selection. If Excel doesn't automatically select Top Row, select Top Row now (See Figure 4-12.).

Figure 4-12

Quickly name a range of cells using existing headings.

3   Click OK. Excel creates the range name *Condo* for range C5:C8.

4   Select range A5:C8.

5   In the Formulas tab, choose Create from Selection. Excel automatically selects Left column.

6   Click OK. Excel creates range names for each row of broker's sales.

Using a range name in a formula

When using a name in a formula, you can type the range name or select the name from a list, as the next set of steps illustrates.

STEP BY STEP	Using a range name in a formula

1   Click in cell C9.

2   Type =SUM(to begin the formula.

3   From the Formulas tab, choose Use in Formula.

4   From the list that appears (see Figure 4-13), select Condo, and then type).

Figure 4-13

Select the Range Name to use in the formula instead of typing the cell addresses.

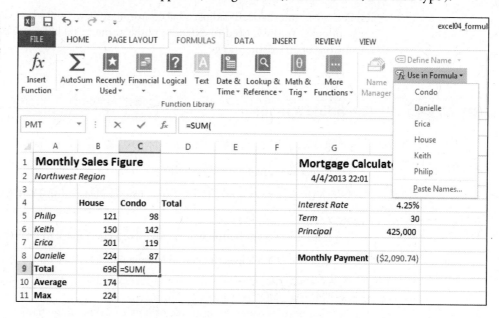

5   Press Enter. Excel calculates the Total number of Condo units sold.

Editing a range name

You can use the **Name Manager** in the Formulas tab to adjust the range addresses or to rename your range names. Note that when you rename a range, you must update any formulas that use the range names.

STEP BY STEP   **Editing a range name**

1   From the Formulas tab, choose Name Manager. The resulting dialog box is shown in Figure 4-14.

Figure 4-14

The Name Manager is used to modify existing range names.

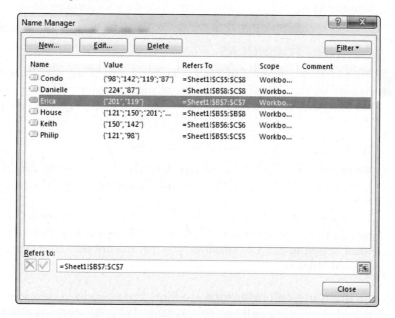

2   Select the range name Erica and click Edit.

3   Type EricaM in the Name box and click OK.

4   Click Close to close the Name Manager.

Extending a range

Range names automatically adjust to accommodate new cells when you add a cell to an existing range of cells. You will need to extend a range name to include new data if you add that data to the bottom of an existing range.

STEP BY STEP   **Extending a range**

1   From the Formulas tab, choose Name Manager.

2   Select the range name Danielle.

3   In the Refers to box, edit the range to include column D. (Change the C in the range to a D.)

4   Click the Accept button which looks like a checkmark to the left of the Refers to text box.

5   Click Close to close the Name Manager.

Deleting a range name

The next set of steps shows an example of how to delete range names.

STEP BY STEP   **Deleting a range name**

1   From the Formulas tab, choose Name Manager.

2   Select Philip and click Delete.

3   Click OK in the resulting dialog box to confirm the deletion.

4   Click Close to close the Name Manager.

Take Note   When you delete a range name, any formula that refers to that range name will result in an Error. (The error message #NAME? is returned in the cell.) To correct the error, you must redefine the name or replace the range name in the formula with the appropriate range address.

COPYING FORMULAS

Bottom Line   After creating a formula in Excel, you can use the Copy and Paste commands to duplicate or transfer the formula in/to other areas of your worksheet. When you copy formulas that contain cell references, the references adjust to their new location, unless you specify otherwise.

Using absolute and relative cell references

When you use cell references in your formulas, Excel uses the data stored in that location in its calculations. The benefit is that when you change the original data, the formula is updated as well.

If you copy a formula from one location to another, Excel adjusts the cell reference based on its new location. For instance, the formula =B2*B3 entered in cell B5 would be adjusted to =C2*C3 when copied to cell C5. However, you can modify the cell reference so it remains fixed to its original location.

An **absolute cell reference** in a formula remains fixed even when the formulas are copied or moved. A **relative cell reference adjusts to its new location.**

The dollar sign ($) is used to indicate that the cell reference should remain absolute. Use the dollar sign to indicate the portion of the address (the row reference, the column reference, or both) that should remain fixed. The following table shows some examples.

Absolute and relative cell references

REFERENCE	WHAT IT MEANS
$A6	Column A remains fixed, row 6 adjusts
A$6	Row 6 remains fixed, column A adjusts
$A$6	Cell A6 remains fixed
A6	The reference to column A and row 6 adjusts to its new location

Making a cell reference absolute

The following example shows how to make a cell reference absolute.

STEP BY STEP   **Making a cell reference absolute**

1. Type = in cell D5.

2. Point to cell B5 and then press the F4 function key on your keyboard. Excel inserts a dollar sign ($) between the row and column reference.

3. Type + and point to cell C5.

4. Press Enter on the keyboard. The formula in cell D5 now reads =$B$5+C5.

Take Note   When you use a range name in a formula, Excel automatically makes the range absolute. In other words, when you copy a formula that makes use of a range name, the range reference will not adjust to its new location

Copying formulas with AutoFill

The AutoFill command lets you quickly copy a formula to a range of adjacent cells. Perform the following set of steps to practice using the AutoFill command.

STEP BY STEP   **Copying formulas with AutoFill**

1. Click in cell D5.

2. From the Formulas tab, choose AutoSum. Excel adds up the cells immediately adjacent to the current cell, which in this case is range B5:C5. Press Enter.

3   Click in cell D5 and drag the AutoFill handle (see Figure 4-15) down to cell D9 and release. Excel copies the formula from cell D5 and adjusts the cell references accordingly.

Figure 4-15

The AutoFill feature lets you quickly copy a formula to adjacent cells.

	A	B	C	D	E
	Monthly Sales Figure				
1					
2	Northwest Region				
3					
4		House	Condo	Total	
5	Philip	121	98	219	
6	Keith	150	142		
7	Erica	201	119		
8	Danielle	224	87		
9	Total	696	446		
10	Average	174			
11	Max	224			
12	Min	121			
13	Median	175.5			
14					
15					
16	Bonus	No			
17	Quota	2			
18					

Cell D5 formula: =SUM(Philip)

Copying formulas with Copy and Paste

When you use the Copy command, Excel stores a copy of the selection on the clipboard, allowing you to paste the data multiple times. Perform the following set of steps to practice copying and pasting data.

STEP BY STEP   **Duplicating data with Copy and Paste**

1   Click in cell B10.

2   From the Home tab, choose **Copy** from the Clipboard group.

3   Select range **C10:D10**.

4   Choose **Paste** from the Clipboard group. Excel pastes the formula from cell B10 and adjusts the cell references accordingly.

Take Note   You can also press the Enter key on your keyboard to paste the data in a worksheet cell. However, Excel will remove the stored item from the clipboard.

Pasting formula results

With the Paste Values command, you can copy a formula and then paste the results of the formula in another cell. Perform the following set of steps to practice copying and pasting formula results.

STEP BY STEP   **Pasting formula results**

1   Select cell **H8** and choose **Copy** from the Home tab.

2   Click in cell I8, choose **Paste** from the Clipboard group, and then select **Paste Special**. The Paste Special dialog box appears. See Figure 4-16.

Figure 4-16

Paste the results of formulas in a separate cell.

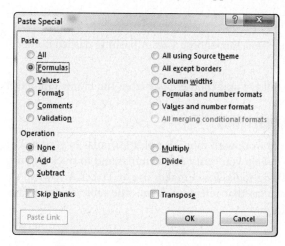

3   Select **Values** from the Paste Special dialog box and click **OK**. Excel pastes the result of the PMT formula, (2,090.74) in cell I8.

Moving worksheet formulas

Unlike copying a formula, Excel does not adjust cell references when a formula is moved. There are two ways to move a formula in Excel: with the Cut and Paste command, or by dragging and dropping the formula to its new location.

To drag and drop a formula:

STEP BY STEP   **Moving worksheet formulas**

1   Select range **D4:D10**.

2   Position the mouse pointer on the edge of the selected range; when the mouse pointer changes to a four-headed arrow, click and drag the selection to cell E4, as in Figure 4-17.

Figure 4-17

Quickly move a range of cells to a new location with click, drag and drop.

D4		▼	:	×	✓	fx	Total	
	A	B	C	D	E			
1	**Monthly Sales Figure**							
2	*Northwest Region*							
3								
4		House	Condo	Total				
5	*Philip*	121	98	219				
6	*Keith*	150	142	292				
7	*Erica*	201	119	320				
8	*Danielle*	224	87	311				
9	**Total**	696	446	1142				
10	**Average**	174	111.5	285.5				
11	**Max**	224						
12	**Min**	121						
13	**Median**	175.5						
14								
15								
16	**Bonus**	no						
17	**Quota**	2						
18								

3   Release to drop the range in its new location.

To move a formula with Cut and Paste:

Moving a formula with Cut and Paste

1   Select range E4:E10.

2   From the Home tab, choose Cut. A flashing dashed border appears around the selected range.

3   Click in cell D4 and choose Paste from the Home tab. Excel pastes the selected range.

FORMULA AUDITING

Bottom Line

When you begin to work with more complex formulas in your worksheets, Excel provides a set of **Auditing** tools to help you verify cell formulas and to track down errors in syntax or use. When you use the Auditing tools, Excel makes use of Tracer Arrows to show the relationship between cells and the formulas that reference them. The table below details the Auditing tools and the actions they perform.

Excel formula auditing tools

COMMAND	TOOL	ACTION
Trace Precedents		Indicates cells that are referred to in the formula.
Trace Dependents		Indicates cells that are dependent on the formula.
Remove Arrows		Removes the auditing arrows from the worksheet.
Show Formulas		Displays the formulas in the worksheet instead of the results.
Error Checking		Runs through the worksheets looking for errors.
Evaluate Formula		Runs through a formula argument by argument to ensure its accuracy.

Tracing formula precedents

The following is an example of how to trace formula precedents.

Tracing formula precedents

1   Click in cell B9 and choose Trace Precedents from the Formula Audition group on the Formulas tab See Figure 4-18.

Figure 4-18

Choose Trace Precedents.

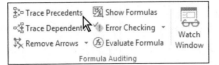

Excel overlays a tracer arrow on range B5:B8, showing the cells that are used in the SUM function in cell B9.

Tracing formula dependents

The following is an example of how to trace formula dependents.

STEP BY STEP **Tracing formula dependents**

1 Click in cell B9 and choose **Trace Dependents** from the Formulas tab.

Excel overlays a tracer arrow from cell B9 pointing to cell B16; the IF function that relies on data in cell B9 for its conditional formula; and cell D9, which calculates the total amount. See Figure 4-19.

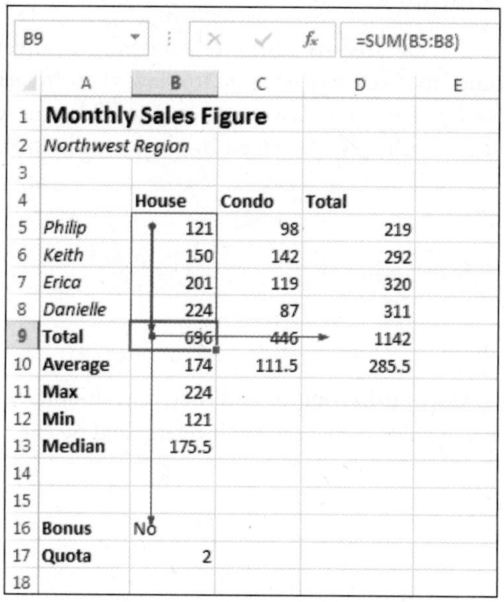

Figure 4-19

The Trace Precedents and Trace Dependents tools display the relationships between formulas and the cells that the formulas reference.

Removing tracer arrows

Tracer arrows can be removed from the entire worksheet or one at a time from specific cells.

STEP BY STEP **Removing tracer arrows**

1 Click in cell B9 and then click the arrow to the right of the Remove Arrows command on the Formulas tab.

2 Choose **Remove Precedent Arrows**.

STEP BY STEP   **Removing dependent arrows**

1   Click in cell B9 and then click the arrow to the right of the Remove Arrows command on the Formulas tab.

2   Choose **Remove Dependent Arrows**.

STEP BY STEP   **Removing all tracer arrows**

1   From the Formulas tab, choose **Remove Arrows**.

Viewing formula references

The Tracer Arrows offer a visual display of the relationships between formulas and the cells that reference them, but sometimes the easiest way to view these relationships is to switch to Edit mode. To do so, double-click the cell you want, press the F2 key on your keyboard, or click in the formula bar. When you do, each cell referenced by the formula is displayed.

STEP BY STEP   **Viewing formula references**

1   Click in cell H8.

2   Press the **F2** key on your keyboard. Alternatively, double-click in the Formula bar or on the cell itself. Excel color-codes each cell referenced by the formula, as in Figure 4-20.

Figure 4-20

When you enter Edit mode, Excel color-codes each cell referenced by the formula.

F	G	H	I
	Mortgage Calculator		
	4/4/2013 22:33		
	Interest Rate	4.25%	
	Term	30	
	Principal	425,000	
	Monthly Payment	=PMT(H4/12,H5*12,H6)	

3   Press **Esc** on your keyboard to exit Edit mode.

Displaying worksheet formulas

As mentioned previously, Excel displays the result of the formula in a cell rather than the formula itself. With the Show Formulas auditing tool, you can switch the worksheet display so that it displays the formulas as entered.

STEP BY STEP   **Displaying worksheet formulas**

1   From the Formulas tab, choose Show Formulas. Excel displays all formulas in the cells as entered. See Figure 4-21.

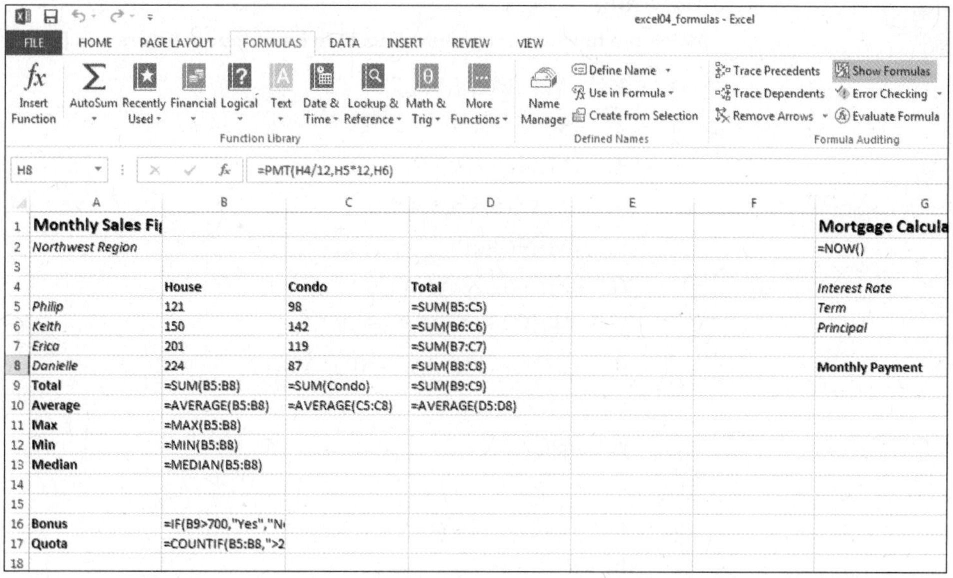

Figure 4-21

Switch the worksheet view to Show Formulas when you want to view the formulas and not the results.

2   Choose Show Formulas again display the formula results.

3   Choose File > Save As, navigate to the Excel04lessons folder.

4   Type **excel04_formulas_final** as the file name, and click Save.

You've now completed this lesson. Now that you have learned how to work with formulas to perform calculations, you are ready to learn how to produce charts and graphs with your worksheet data, which you will learn in Lesson 5, "Working with Charts."

What you learned in this lesson:

- Understanding Formulas

- Entering Simple Formulas

- Referencing Cells from Other Worksheets/Workbooks

- Using Functions

- Using the Function library

- Using the AutoSum Tool

- Using Common Functions

- Working with Ranges

- Copying Formulas

- Formula Auditing

Knowledge Assessment

Matching

Match the function in numbers 1 to 10 to its output in letters a to j.

1. =AVERAGE(5,6,7)
2. =SUM(2,4,9)
3. =MIN(4,2,8,3,0)
4. =MAX(5,5,5,3,4,9,6)
5. =MIN(B4:B9)
6. =MEDIAN(A1:A10)
7. =IF(B1=5, "yes", "no") ; B1=7
8. =COUNTIF(A5,">10"); A5=12
9. =NOW()
10. =NOW

a. no
b. 15
c. 6
d. returns an error
e. shows current date/time
f. 0
g. displays lowest value in range
h. 1
i. displays middle value in range
j. 9

Fill in the Blanks

1. The AutoSum tool offers quick access to sum, count, _____, _____, and _____ functions.
2. Indicate a range of cells by listing the first and last cells separated by a _____.
3. Cell A4 of Sheet3 in the file data.xlsx is indicated by the cell reference _____.
4. Calculations like loan payments, interest rates, and security yields are performed using functions from the _____ category of the Function Library.
5. Excel recognizes the contents of a cell as a formula if it begins with the _____ character.
6. The RAND() function generates a random number. To paste the number's value rather than the formula, use the _____ command.
7. To see the cells that a formula refers to, use Excel's Auditing command to trace its _____.
8. Cell C3 contains a formula, but displays its output value. To edit the formula itself, highlight cell C3 and press _____.
9. The _____ function traverses a cell range and returns a count of how many values in that range meet an IF/THEN condition.
10. A formula's _____ is the symbol of the operation it performs (e.g., multiplication); its _____ are the numbers, cells, or ranges it acts upon.

Competency Assessment

Project 4-1: Basic Formulas

In this exercise you will build formulas using text, numeric data, and cell references.

1. Open the practice file **2013_output** and save your document as **project_4-1_formulas.**
2. In cell F3, type =SUM(.
3. Select cells B3:D3 and type).
4. Drag F3's AutoFill handle down to reuse its formula in F4:F13.
5. Select B15 and use the AutoSum > Sum command over the range B3:B13.
6. Drag B15's AutoFill handle to C15.
7. Select cell C15 and press Ctrl+C to copy.
8. Select D17 and press Ctrl+V, then edit D17's formula to =SUM(D3:D13).
9. Select F19 and click AutoSum.
10. Select B23 and add the formula =COUNTA(A3:A13).
11. Click B24.
12. Type =. Click cell F19. Type /. Click cell B23. Press Return.
13. Save and close your document.

Project 4-2: Range Names

In this exercise you'll create named ranges for ease of use.

1. Open the project file **4-2-source** and save it as **project_4-2_range_names.**
2. Press Ctrl+A and change the fill color to No Fill.
3. Select B3:D3.
4. Click Formulas > Define Name and name the range AstridSales. Note that Astrid-Sales appears in the Name Box.
5. Select B3:B13 and name the range JanJunSales.
6. Do the same for C3:C13 (JulDecSales) and D3:D13 (OnlineSales).
7. Open the Name Manager. Double click the Astrid entry and add a comment ("label not included").
8. Close the Name Manager.
9. Save and close your document.

Project 4-3: Cell References

In this exercise you'll use cell references to simplify formula building.

1. Open the project file **4-3-source** and save it as **project_4-3_references**.
2. Create a new worksheet within the file and name it Presentation.
3. Select the Presentation worksheet. In cell A1, type Astrid total sales:.
4. In cell C1, type =AstridSales. The error message indicates that Excel expects a single value; you've inserted a reference to a range of cells.
5. Change C1's content to =SUM(AstridSales). You can insert the range name with the Formulas > Use in Formula command.
6. Type Bree total sales: in A2.
7. In C2, add a Sum formula, and select Sheet1!B13:D13 as the range.
8. Save and close your document.

Project 4-4: Formula Auditing

In this exercise you'll perform Formula Audits on a worksheet.

1. Open the project file **4-4-source** and save it as **project_4-4_trace**.
2. Switch to Sheet1. Select Formulas > Formula Auditing > Show Formulas.
3. Select cell F19, then select Trace Precedents.
4. Do the same for F3:F13 to generate a complete map of the 2013 Sales Total's formula precedents.
5. Run Trace Precedents for Presentation!C1 and Presentation!C2.
6. Clear Arrows, deselect Formulas, then Trace Precedents for Sheet1!B24.
7. Save and close your document.

Project 4-5: Advanced Formulas

In this exercise you'll construct a complex formula using the Function Library.

1. Open the project file **4-5-source** and save it as **project_4-5_formulas2**.
2. Hide rows 15-24 in Sheet1.
3. Type Conditions: in A25.
4. Type >90 in B25 and <80 in C25.
5. Click D25 and use Insert Function to call the AVERAGEIFS function.
6. Build the function using the Online Sales data (OnlineSales) as the Average_range, JanJunSales as Criteria_range1, B25 as Criteria1, JulDecSales as Criteria_range2, and C25 as Criteria2.

   The output of this function is the average online sales of those employees who sold >90 units Jan-Jun but <80 units Jul-Dec – the average of D10 and D11.
7. Save and close your document.

Project 4-6: **Operations with Text**

In this exercise you'll perform some complex operations on text data.

1. Open the project file **4-6-source** and save it as **project_4-6_text**.

2. In I3, use the REPLACE(…) function to replace the first letter in Astrid's name with X, then use AutoFill to extend that operation down column I to all 12 employee names.

   Hint: the first letter in Astrid is character 1, and the replacement string must be in quotes: "X."

3. Add a single cell that displays the average length of the employee names.

   Hint: the LEN() command will prove useful here, as will the "Search for a function" feature of the Insert Function command.

4. Choose File > Save and then File > Close.

5 Working with Charts

LESSON SKILL MATRIX

In this lesson, you will learn the following skills:

Understanding Chart Types	Editing a Chart
Creating a Chart	Customizing the Chart
Understanding Chart Elements	Printing a Chart
Using Chart Recommendations	Enhancing a Chart
Moving and Resizing Charts	

KEY TERMS

- Linked data
- Chart area
- Chart title
- Data series
- Vertical axis
- Gridlines
- Horizontal axis
- Legend
- Plot area
- Data marker
- Plot
- Data source
- Scale (i.e. chart scale – along axis)
- Sparkline

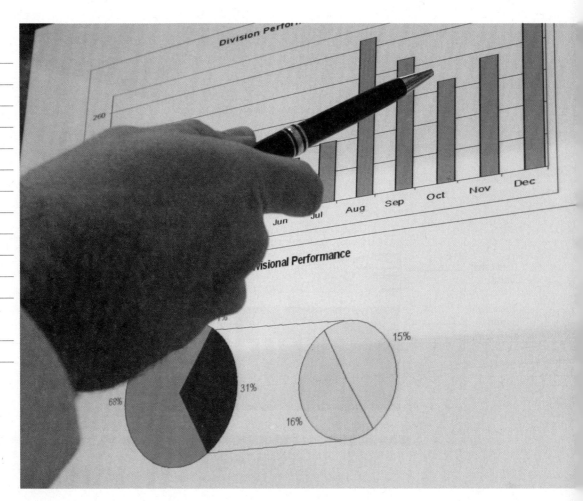

The new management team at Northwind Traders needs to quickly get a handle on the yearly financial data – but they're in Springville and Northwind's accountants are in Ellicottville, so meeting time is in short supply. Turning the raw data into memorable visuals is the solution.

Luckily, Excel has an extensive suite of tools to do just that – and an even wider variety of tools to nudge, tweak, style, and emphasize infographic elements in order to make sure the managers know exactly what the data means, and why it matters.

SOFTWARE ORIENTATION

Charts and graphs help you to express numbers and data visually.

Figure 5-1

Working with charts in Excel.

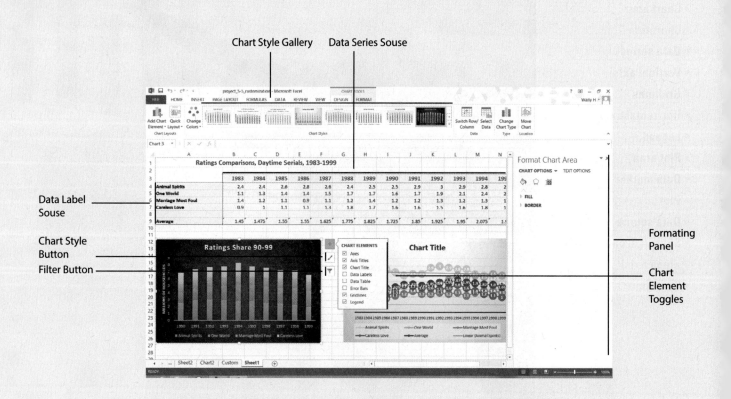

STARTING UP

In this lesson, you'll work with several files from the Excel05lessons folder. Make sure that you have loaded the OfficeLessons folder onto your computer.

UNDERSTANDING CHART TYPES

Bottom Line

Excel offers a number of different chart types. From bar graphs and pie charts to scatter plots and area charts, Excel provides a chart type for the data you want to present. The new Recommended Charts feature helps to remove some of the guesswork by offering a number of chart types based on your selected data. You can also change the chart from one type to another once it is complete. The following table lists the 12 chart types that Excel offers.

Chart types

TYPE	ICON	DESCRIPTION
Area		Shows the relative importance of values over time. An area chart emphasizes the magnitude of change over time more than a line chart does.
Bar		Illustrates individual values at a specific point in time.
Bubble		A type of XY chart that uses three values instead of two. In the third data series, Excel displays the plot points as bubbles; the larger the bubble, the larger the value.
Column		Shows variations in data over time or compares individual items.
Combo		Highlights different types of information in a single chart.
Doughnut		Shows how individual parts relate to a whole. A doughnut chart can display multiple data series, with each ring representing a different series.
Line		Illustrates changes in a large number of values over time.
Pie		Shows the relationship of each part to the whole.
Radar		Shows changes in multiple data series relative to a center point as well as to each other.
Stock		Shows the fluctuation of values over a certain time period, such as stock prices or temperature fluctuations.
Surface		Plots trends in values across two dimensions in a continuous curve, and applies color to indicate where data series are in the same range. This is useful for comparing two data series to find the best combinations between them.
XY Scatter		Shows the relationship between numeric values in multiple data series that may not be apparent from looking at the data.

CREATING A CHART

Bottom Line

Charts enable you to present worksheet data in graphical form. They also allow you to highlight trends, see the parts that make up a whole, or show comparisons. When you create a chart, the source worksheet data is **linked** to the chart. So when you update the data in your worksheet, the chart gets updated, too. In Excel, you can add a chart directly to the worksheet as an object or you can create a separate chart worksheet.

STEP BY STEP   **Creating a chart**

You will now create a Clustered Column type of chart from a range of data contained within the exercise file.

1   Choose File > Open, click Computer in the Backstage view, and click Browse.

2   Navigate to the Excel05lessons folder and open the file named **excel05_charts**.

3   Choose File > Save As, and choose Computer.

4   Click the Browse button, navigate to the Excel05lessons folder, name the file **excel05_charts_final**, and click Save.

5   Select range A4:C8.

6   From the Insert tab, choose Insert Column Chart as shown in Figure 5-2

Figure 5-2

Convert your worksheet data into easy-to-read charts.

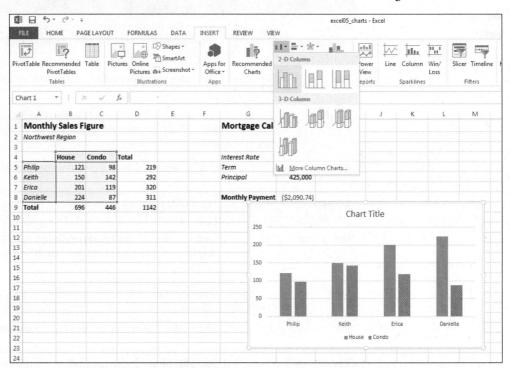

7   From the 2-D Column section of the drop-down menu, select Clustered Column.

Excel adds the chart to the worksheet and highlights the source data used by the chart.

Take Note   When you select the data for a chart, include headings and labels but do not include totals and subtotals.

UNDERSTANDING CHART ELEMENTS

Bottom Line

When you create a chart, Excel adds it to the worksheet as an object, which then sits on top of the worksheet and can be manipulated separately from the worksheet data. The Key Charting Terms table details key terms related to working with charts and are also displayed in Figure 5-3.

Figure 5-3

A. Legend. B. Chart Area. C. Horizontal Axis. D. Vertical Axis. E. Gridline. F. Chart Title. G. Data Marker. H. Plot Area.

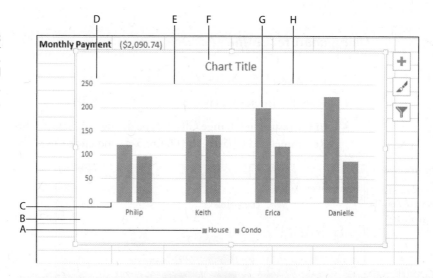

TERM	DEFINITION
Chart area	Everything inside the chart window.
Chart title	Identifies the subject of the chart.
Data Series	A set of values used to plot the chart.
Vertical (value) axis	Also known as the value or y-axis, shows the data values in the chart, such as hours worked or units sold.
Gridlines	Horizontal and vertical extensions of the tick marks on each axis; they make the chart easier to read.
Horizontal (category) axis	Also known as the category or x-axis, shows the categories in the chart, such as months of the year or branch offices.
Legend	A key that identifies patterns, colors, or symbols associated with a data series.
Plot area	The area in the chart where the data is plotted; includes the axes and data markers.
Data marker	A symbol on the chart that represents a single value in the worksheet, such as a bar in a bar chart or a wedge in a pie chart. A group of related data markers (such as all the green columns in the example on the previous page) constitute a single data series.

USING CHART RECOMMENDATIONS

Bottom Line

The most difficult part in creating charts is deciding the type that best suits your data and the message you want to convey. When you use Recommended Charts, Excel suggests a set of chart types based on your selected data. Follow the steps below for an example of how this works.

STEP BY STEP   **Using chart recommendations**

1   Using **excel05_charts_final**, select range A4:C8.

2   From the Insert tab, choose Recommend Charts.

3   In the resulting Change Chart Type dialog box, select Clustered Bar from the Recommended Charts tab (Figure 5-4) and click OK.

Figure 5-4

Chart recommendations suggest chart types based on your data.

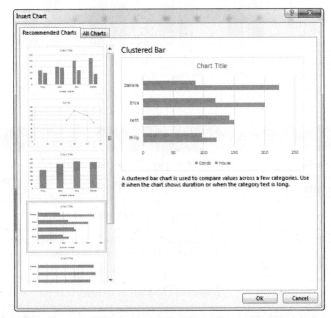

Excel inserts a clustered bar graph in your worksheet. Note that the bar graph is now sitting directly on top of the column chart you created in the previous exercise.

MOVING AND RESIZING CHARTS

Bottom Line

When you add a chart to a worksheet, Excel adds it to the middle of the workspace area. To move the chart to another location, click and drag the chart object. Alternatively, you can manually move the chart to a new worksheet.

When you click a chart, Excel displays a set of selection handles around the chart area and a set of Chart Tools appear in the Ribbon bar (Figure 5-5). The Design and Format tabs contain context-sensitive tools for editing and formatting charts.

Figure 5-5

When you click a chart to select it, two new tabs appear in the Ribbon bar.

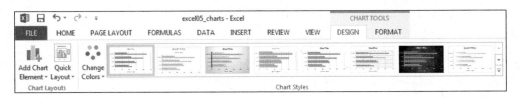

For the next four exercises (Moving a Chart, Resizing a Chart, Creating a Chart Sheet, and Deleting a Chart), use the same Excel exercise file that you used for the previous exercises, so don't close the file at the end of each set of steps.

Moving a chart

STEP BY STEP	Moving a chart

1 Click near the outside edge of the Clustered Bar chart to select it.

2 Position the pointer within the chart area. When the pointer changes into a four-headed arrow, click and drag the chart to the vicinity of B13.

Figure 5-6

Click and drag the chart object to move it to a new position.

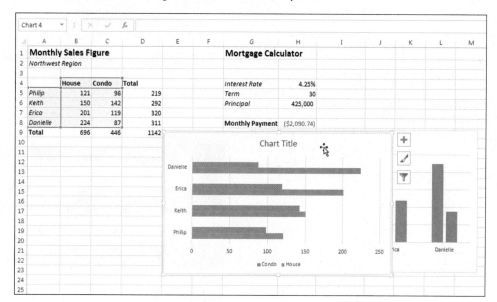

3 Click and drag the Clustered Column graph to the vicinity of I13.

Resizing a chart

STEP BY STEP	Resizing a chart

1 Click the Clustered Bar chart to select it.

2 Point at the corner of the chart area. When the pointer changes into a double-headed arrow, click and drag to resize the chart. Release when the chart is the desired size.

Creating a chart sheet

STEP BY STEP	Creating a chart sheet

1 Make sure the Clustered Bar chart is still selected.

2 From the Design tab, choose Move Chart in the Location group.

3   In the Move Chart dialog box, select New Sheet and type Total Sales in the name box as shown in Figure 5-7.

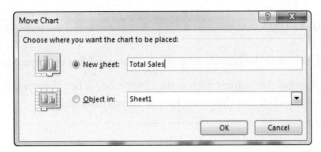

4   Click OK. The Clustered Bar chart appears on a Chart Sheet (Figure 5-8).

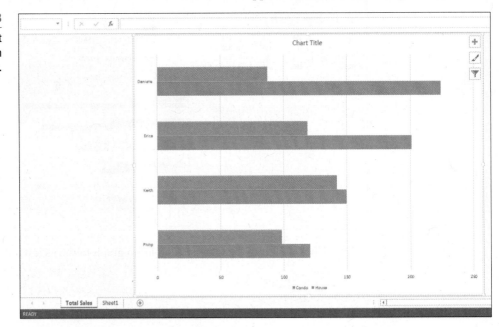

5   From the Design tab, choose Move Chart.

6   From the Move Chart dialog box, select Object in and click OK. The Clustered Bar is moved back to the worksheet.

Take Note   When you move a chart from a chart sheet to a worksheet, Excel deletes the chart sheet from the workbook.

Deleting a chart

STEP BY STEP   **Deleting a chart**

1   Click the Clustered Bar chart to select it.

2   Press the Delete key. Excel removes the chart object from the worksheet.

3   Save your exercise file, but don't close it. You will continue using it in the next section.

ENHANCING A CHART

An important step when creating charts is to provide adequate explanations of the data represented in the chart. Excel enables you to add descriptive titles and legends, adjust the scale and orientation, and add data labels and gridlines. These chart elements are in either an on or off state. That is, to add an element, click the check box to mark it; to remove an element, click the check box to clear it.

For all seven exercises in this section, use the same exercise file you have been using till now. Don't close the file at the end of each exercise.

Using Quick Layouts

The Quick Layouts feature contains a set of predefined layout options that you can assign to a chart with a single click.

STEP BY STEP   **Using Quick Layouts**

1   Click the Clustered Column chart to select it.

2   From the Chart Layouts group on the Design tab, choose Quick Layout.

3   As you hover over each option, your chart is updated to reflect the layout as displayed in Figure 5-9.

Figure 5-9

Quick Layouts allow you to quickly change the layout of the chart.

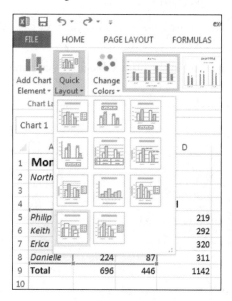

4   Click Layout 10 to select it.

Adding a chart title

STEP BY STEP   **Adding a chart title**

1   In the Clustered Column chart, click the text box labeled Chart Title.

2   Click inside the box to set the insertion point.

3   Type Monthly Sales (Figure 5-10).

Figure 5-10

Click to set the Chart Title.

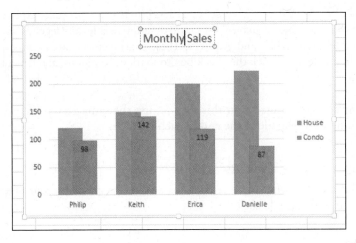

Displaying a data table

When you add a data table to your chart, Excel adds the source data to the chart area in table form.

| STEP BY STEP | Displaying a data table |

1   Click the Monthly Sales chart to select it.

2   From the Design tab, choose Add Chart Element; or click the Chart Elements button that appears to the right of the chart.

3   Select Data Table and and in the Data Table drop-down menu, choose No Legend Keys (Figure 5-11).

Figure 5-11

Data tables display the source data used to generate the chart.

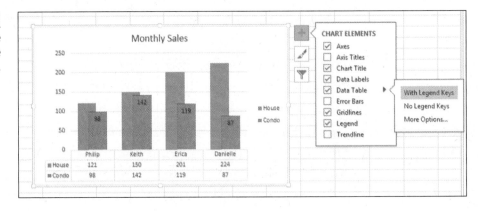

Adding data labels

With Data Labels, Excel labels each data marker in the chart with the source value. The Quick Layout we selected before added Data Labels to the Condo Data Series. Here, we will add Data Labels to the House Data Series.

| STEP BY STEP | Adding data labels |

1   Click the Monthly Sales chart to select it.

2   From the Design tab, choose Add Chart Element; or click the Chart Elements button.

3 Click the drop-down arrow next to Data Labels and choose Inside End as shown in Figure 5-12.

Figure 5-12

Data Labels include the data values behind the chart.

STEP BY STEP   Adding gridlines

1 Click the Monthly Sales chart to select it.

2 From the Design tab, choose Add Chart Element; or click the Chart Elements button.

3 Click the drop-down arrow next to Gridlines and choose Primary Minor Horizontal as shown in Figure 5-13.

Figure 5-13

Gridlines help to guide the eye along the data points.

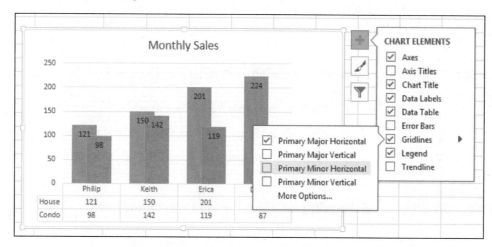

Adding or moving legends

Legends describe the color-coded data series in each chart.

STEP BY STEP   Adding and moving legends

1 Click the Monthly Sales chart to select it.

2 From the Design tab, choose Add Chart Element; or click the Chart Elements button.

3   Click the drop-down arrow next to Legend and choose Left to place the Legend box to the left of the chart area (Figure 5-14).

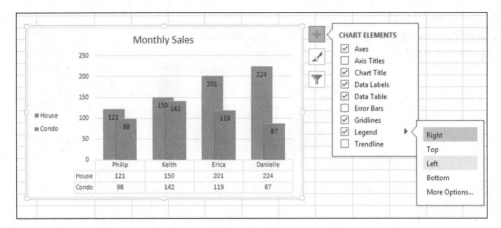

Removing chart elements

You can remove chart elements from the chart display by deselecting the item. For instance, when you click the Chart Elements button, any element that is currently employed has a check mark indicating it is selected. To remove the element, deselect it.

You can also remove a chart element by selecting the element you want to remove and pressing the Delete key. When you select an element, selection handles are displayed around the selected object.

STEP BY STEP — **Removing an element with the Delete key**

1   Click the Monthly Sales chart to select it.

2   Click the gridlines and press Delete. Excel removes the gridlines from the chart object.

3   Click Undo to revert the action and place the gridelines back into the chart.

STEP BY STEP — **Removing an element via Chart Elements**

1   Click the Monthly Sales chart to select it.

2   Click the Chart Elements button.

3 Deselect **Data Labels** and **Data Table** as shown in Figure 5-15.

Figure 5-15

To remove an element from the chart, deselect the option.

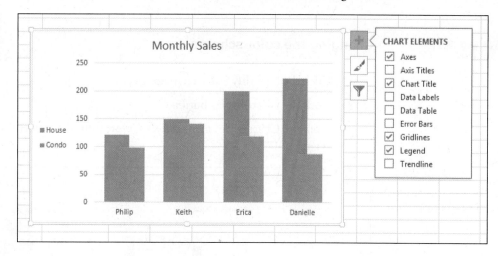

4 Save the exercise file, but don't close it.

FORMATTING A CHART

Bottom Line

Excel provides many formatting options and commands that allow you to make charts visually appealing. You can change the colors used by the data series, change text attributes, and adjust alignment, among other options. You can also apply a chart style, which is a set of predefined formatting options that help to maintain uniformity of design.

Take Note

For all four exercises in this section, use the same exercise file you have been using till now. Don't close the file at the end of each exercise.

Applying chart styles

STEP BY STEP **Applying chart styles**

1 Click the **Monthly Sales** chart to select it.

2 Click the **Chart Styles** button (Figure 5-16) and select the second style option displayed.

Figure 5-16

Chart styles consist of a collection of related formatting options.

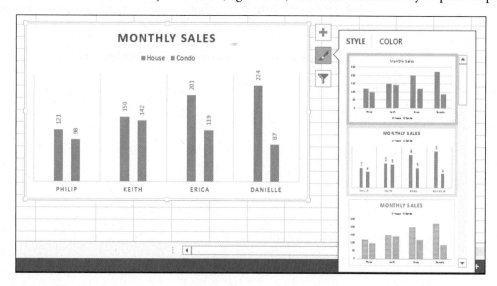

3 Click the **Chart Styles** button again to close the menu.

Changing the color scheme

STEP BY STEP **Changing the color scheme**

1 Click the Monthly Sales chart to select it.

2 Click the Chart Styles button.

3 From the Chart Styles menu, select Color; from the Colorful section, choose Color 4 (Figure 5-17).

Figure 5-17

Change the color scheme used by your chart style.

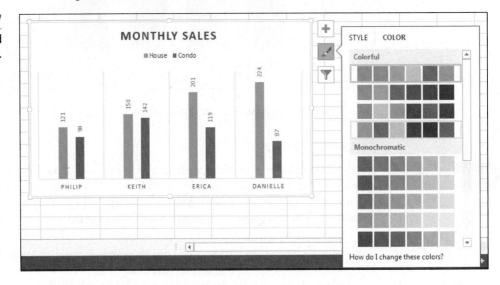

4 Click the Chart Styles button again to close the menu.

Adding borders

STEP BY STEP   **Adding borders**

1 Click the Monthly Sales chart to select it.

2 From the Format tab, choose Format Selection in the Current Selection group.

3 In the Format Chart Area window, select Chart Options.

4 Click Border, select Solid Line, and change the width to 4 pt.

5   Click the Outline Color button and select Black as shown in Figure 5-18.

Figure 5-18

Add borders to the chart area to set it apart from the rest of the worksheet.

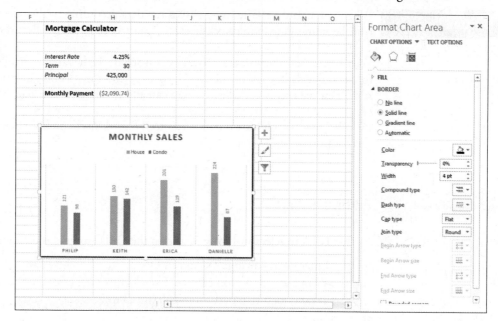

6   Close the Format Chart Area window by clicking the X in the upper-right corner.

Formatting text

STEP BY STEP   **Formatting text**

1   Click the Monthly Sales title box.

2   On the Home tab, click the Font button.

3   Select the Candara font and Blue for the text color as displayed in Figure 5-19.

Figure 5-19

Change the text in your chart using the Font menu.

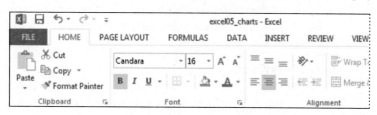

EDITING A CHART

Bottom Line

When you create a chart, Excel **plots** the data according to the selected data range. When you edit the source data in the worksheet, the chart is updated to reflect those changes.

You can also add a new data set to an existing chart. If the range of data you want to add is adjacent to the source data, you can click and drag to extend the selection so it includes the additional data. If the new data set is not adjacent, you can add the data via the Data Source dialog box.

First, let's add an additional data series to the worksheet you have been using for all the previous exercises.

STEP BY STEP   **Editing a chart**

1   Click to select Column D, and in the Cells group of the Home tab, choose Insert.

2   Enter the following: Apt in cell D4, 75 in cell D5, 112 in cell D6, 98 in cell D7, and 42 in cell D8. As you can see, Excel's automatic error checker detects problems with the Total values we moved from column D to E.

3   Click in cell E5 and choose Update Formulas to Include Cells from the Error Check menu.

4   Do the same for cells E6:E8.

5   Finally, copy the formula in cell C9 to range D9:E9.

STEP BY STEP   **Adding a data series by selecting the adjacent data**

1   Click the Monthly Sales chart to select it. Excel highlights the source data, range A4:C8, in the worksheet.

2   Click and drag the sizing handle to include the new data in range D4:D8 as displayed in Figure 5-20. The chart is automatically updated.

Figure 5-20

Click and drag to extend the data range to add a new data series to the chart.

	A	B	C	D	E	F
1	Monthly Sales Figure					
2	Northwest Region					
3						
4		House	Condo	Apt	Total	
5	Philip	121	98	75	294	
6	Keith	150	142	112	404	
7	Erica	201	119	98	418	
8	Danielle	224	87	42	353	
9	Total	696	446	327	1469	
10						

3   Click Undo to revert the action so the Monthly Sales chart only shows the data in range A4:C8. (You need the Monthly Sales chart to only show this data for the next exercise.)

STEP BY STEP   **Adding a data series manually**

1 Click the **Monthly Sales** chart to select it. Excel highlights the source data, range A4:C8, in the worksheet.

2 From the Design tab, choose **Select Data** in the Data group.

3 In the Select Data dialog box that appears (Figure 5-21), choose **Add**.

Figure 5-21

Use the Data Source dialog box when the data you want to add to the chart is not nearby.

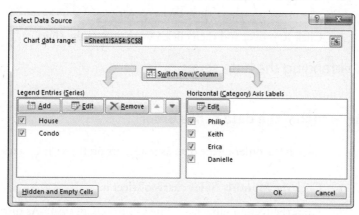

4 Click in the **Series Name** box and select cell D4.

5 Click in the Series Values box removing any text that was prepopulated and select range D5:D8. Then click **OK**.

6 Click **OK** to close the dialog box. The Monthly Sales chart now includes the new data series.

STEP BY STEP   **Changing the order of a data series**

You can rearrange the order of the data series in your chart.

1 Click the **Monthly Sales** chart to select it.

2 From the Design tab, choose **Select Data**.

3 From the Legend Entries box, select **Condo** as done in Figure 5-22.

Figure 5-22

Rearrange the order of the series by clicking the Move Up and Move Down buttons.

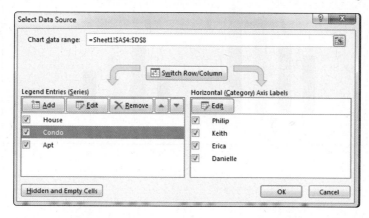

4 Click the **Move Up** button to move the Condo series to the first position, and then click **OK**.

Removing a data series

The easiest way to remove a data series from a chart is to click the data series in the chart window and then press Delete; Excel adjusts the chart accordingly. You can also remove a data series via the Data Source dialog box.

STEP BY STEP   **Removing a data series**

1   Click the Monthly Sales chart to select it.

2   From the Design tab, choose Select Data, click in the Chart data range text box and select range A4:D8. Then click Apt series.

3   Click Remove, and then click OK to update the chart.

Rearranging the data series order

STEP BY STEP   **Rearranging the data series order**

You can switch the order of the data as it appears on the x and y axes.

1   Click the Monthly Sales chart to select it.

2   From the Design tab, choose Switch Row/Column. As displayed in Figure 5-23, Excel swaps the order of the data.

Figure 5-23

Swap out the series on the axis to get another look at your data.

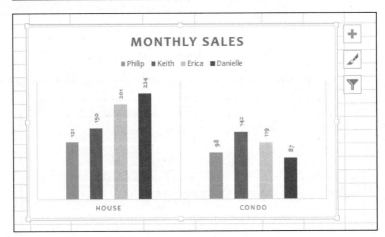

	A	B	C	D	E
1	**Monthly Sales Figure**				
2	Northwest Region				
3					
4		House	Condo	Apt	Total
5	Philip	121	98	75	294
6	Keith	150	142	112	404
7	Erica	201	119	98	418
8	Danielle	224	87	42	353
9	Total	696	446	327	1469
10					

Filtering data in a chart

When you filter data in a chart, you can hide the display of the data series rather than remove it outright.

STEP BY STEP   **Filtering data in a chart**

1   Click the Monthly Sales chart to select it.

2   Click the Chart Filters button as shown in Figure 5-24.

Figure 5-24

Filter your charts to only display the series or categories you want.

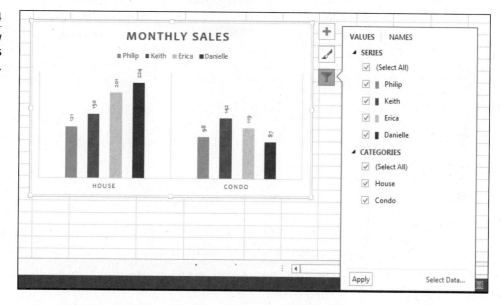

3   Click the check box adjacent to Erica to remove her data from the chart, and then click Apply. Erica's data no longer appears in the chart.

4   Click the Chart Filters button again to close the tab.

Changing the chart type

STEP BY STEP   **Changing the chart type**

1   Click the Monthly Sales chart to select it.

2   From the Design tab, choose Change Chart Type.

3   Select **Bar**, choose **Clustered Bar** (Figure 5-25), and then click **OK**.

Figure 5-25

Switch the Chart Type via the
Change Chart dialog box.

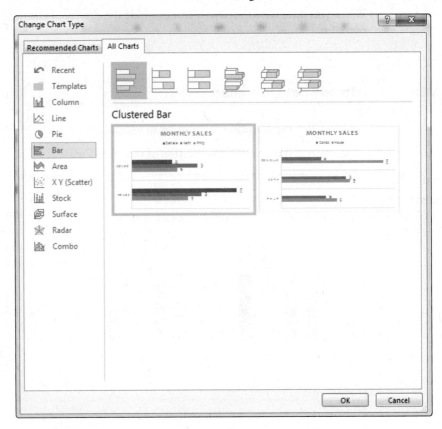

4   You can choose to save the exercise file, but don't close it, since you will need it for the
next section.

CUSTOMIZING THE CHART

Bottom Line

Excel automatically plots the data along the axes according to the data used to create the chart.
You can adjust the values used in the chart **scale** and change the numeric format of those values.
Before we customize the chart, we will revert some earlier changes.

Take Note   For this section, use the same exercise file you have been using till now. Don't close the file at the
end of each exercise.

STEP BY STEP   **Reverting earlier changes**

1   Click the **Monthly Sales** chart to select it and choose **Switch/Row Column** from the
Design tab.

2   Choose **Change Chart Type** and select **Column > Clustered Column** and click **OK**.

3   Click the **Chart Elements** button and deselect the **Data Labels** option.

4   Click the **Chart Filters** button, select **Erica** and click **Apply** to add her data back to the
chart.

Changing the chart scale

1 Click the **Monthly Sales** chart to select it.

2 Click the **Chart Elements** button, select **Axes**, and choose **Primary Vertical**.

3 Choose **Gridlines**, select **Primary Major Horizontal**, and deselect **Primary Major Vertical**. Click the **Chart Elements** button again to close the menu.

4 Double-click the vertical axis scale.

5 Select the **Axis Options** tab and under Bounds enter **300** as the Maximum value.

6 Change the Major value to **25** in the Units section as shown in Figure 5-26.

Figure 5-26

Adjust the values in the chart scale to highlight your data.

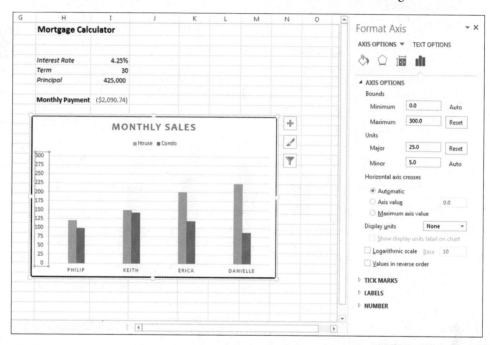

7 Click the **X** to close the Format Axis pane.

Formatting the scale

1   Click the Monthly Sales chart to select it.

2   Double-click the Vertical Axis scale.

3   From the Axis Options tab and at the very bottom of the tab, select Number.

4   From the Category box, choose Number and change the number of decimal places to 0 as displayed in Figure 5-27.

Figure 5-27

Change the numeric format of your axis scales.

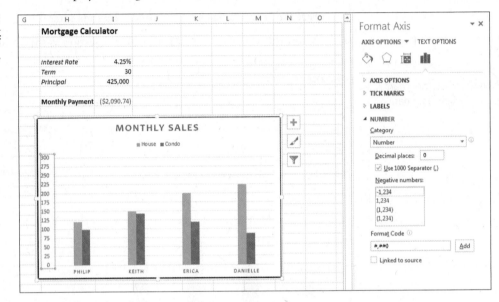

5   Click the X to close the Format Axis pane.

6   You can choose to save the exercise file, but don't close it, since you will need it for the next section.

PRINTING A CHART

Bottom Line

You have two options for printing charts. You can print the chart alongside the worksheet data, or you can print the chart itself. When you choose the latter, the chart is printed in full page version.

Printing with worksheet data

1   Select range A1:M29.

2   Choose File > Print.

3   From the Printer Properties menu, select the printer you want to use.

4   In the Scaling box, choose Fit Sheet On One Page; then click Print.

STEP BY STEP | **Printing the chart**

1   Click the Monthly Sales chart to select it.

2   Choose File > Print.

3   From the Printer Properties menu, select the printer you want to use, and then click Print.

4   Choose File > Save to save your work.

5   Choose File > Close to close the worksheet.

USING SPARKLINES

Bottom Line

Sparklines are mini charts placed in a single cell, each representing a row of data in your worksheet. They are useful when you want to show trends in your data without having to create a full-blown chart. You can add markers, such as high points and low points, and adjust the color to draw attention to important details.

Sparkline chart types

TYPE	ICON	DESCRIPTION
Line	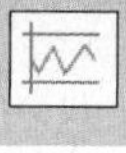	Illustrates change.
Column	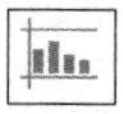	Compares items.
Win/Loss	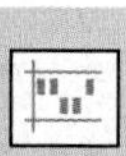	Compares items, with all of the positive values displayed above the line and negative values below.

STEP BY STEP | **Creating a Sparkline**

In this exercise, you will create a Sparkline.

1   Choose File > Open, click Computer, and click Browse.

2   Navigate to the Excel05lessons folder and open the file named **excel05_MonthlySalesCharts**.

3   Choose File > Save As, and choose Computer.

4   Click the Browse button, navigate to the Excel05lessons folder, name the file **excel05_MonthlySalesCharts_final**, and click Save.

5   Select range B6:M9.

6   Click the Quick Analysis button that appears in the bottom right corner of the chart.

7 Choose **Sparklines** and select **Line** as shown in Figure 5-28.

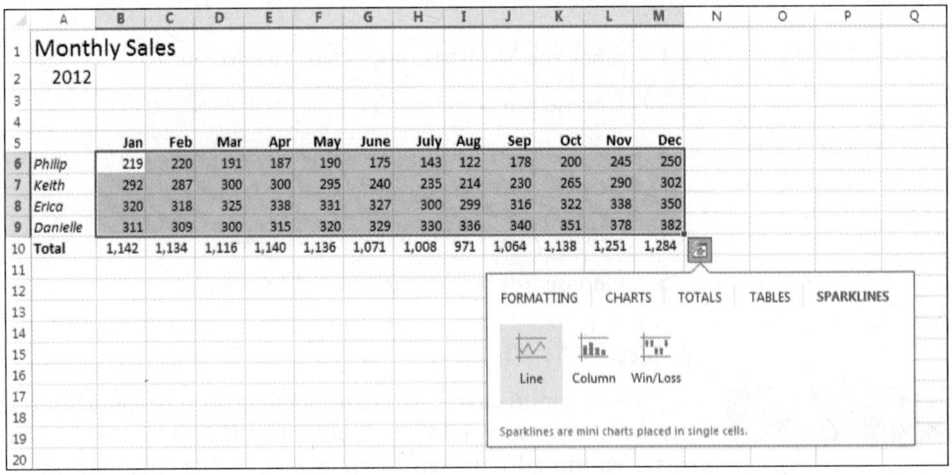

Figure 5-28

Choose Sparkline from the Quick Analysis button to add a Sparkline to the worksheet.

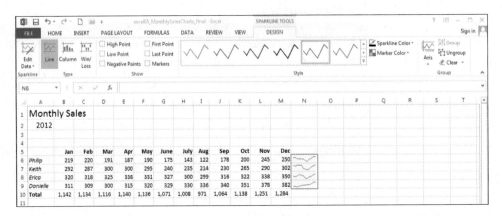

As shown in Figure 5-29, Excel adds the Sparkline to the cells immediately adjacent to the selected range, beginning in cell N6 and a Sparkline Tools tab is added to the Ribbon.

Figure 5-29

The Sparkline Tools tab is added to the Ribbon bar when you add a Sparkline to the worksheet.

Take Note Excel treats Sparklines applied to a multi-row range as a single group, so any changes you make affects the entire group. To treat the charts individually, you must first ungroup them by choosing Ungroup from the Sparkline Tools tab.

STEP BY STEP | **Adding data markers**

1 Using **excel05_MonthlySalesCharts_final**, select cell **N6**. Notice that N6 through N9 are selected.

2   From the Show group of the Sparkline Tools tab, select **High Point**, **Low Point**, and **First Point**. As displayed in Figure 5-30, Excel adds these details to your Sparkline.

Figure 5-30

Add details such as High Point and Low Point values to make your Sparkline pop.

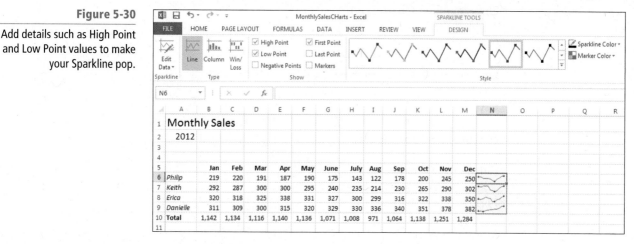

STEP BY STEP   **Changing the Sparkline type**

1   Make sure N6:N9 is still selected.

2   From the Sparkline Tools tab, choose **Column** from the Type group. As shown in Figure 5-31, Excel switches to a columnar display and retains the Marker options.

Figure 5-31

When you switch the Sparkline type, Excel retains the Marker settings.

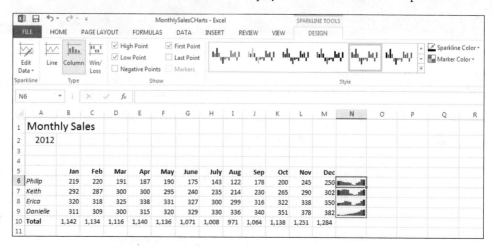

STEP BY STEP   **Removing the Sparklines**

1   Make sure N6:N9 is selected.

2   Choose **Clear** from the Sparkline Tools tab and choose **Clear All** from the drop-down menu. Excel removes the Sparklines from the worksheet.

3   Choose **Undo** to place the Sparklines back into the spreadsheet.

4   Choose **File > Save** to save the current worksheet.

What you learned in this lesson:

- Understanding Chart Types

- Creating a Chart

- Understanding Chart Elements

- Using Chart Recommendations

- Moving and Resizing Charts

- Enhancing a Chart

- Formatting a Chart

- Editing a Chart

- Customizing the Chart

- Printing a Chart

Knowledge Assessment

True/False

Circle T if the statement is true or F it the statement is false.

T F 1. The collection of values used to plot a chart is called the data series.

T F 2. A chart must remain on the worksheet that contains its source data.

T F 3. Quick Layouts for charts are found in the Page Layout tab.

T F 4. Chart Style and Chart Color can be selected independently.

T F 5. A chart's vertical axis is marked in increments called Labels.

T F 6. You can customize a sparkline with titles and labels.

T F 7. Bar graphs are also known as area charts.

T F 8. The vertical axis of a graph generally tracks magnitudes or values.

T F 9. By default, Excel creates a new workbook for each new chart.

T F 10. You can enhance a chart with a display of its numeric source data, called a Chart Sheet.

Fill in the Blanks

Complete the following sentences by writing the correct word or words in the blanks provided.

1. A _____ chart plots points with three values, using X and Y coordinates and points of different sizes.

2. The _____ includes the entire contents of the chart window.

3. Select a chart, then click on its _____ button to toggle the title, gridlines, and data labels.

4. Text formatting commands for charts are found in the _____ tab.

5. Commands for styling an entire chart are found in the _____ contextual tab; commands to style individual chart elements reside in the _____ contextual tab.

6. Temporarily remove individual elements from a chart's data series with the _____ tool.

7. The command to switch a chart from Bubble Chart to Clustered Bar is _____.

8. A _____ sparkline displays positive values above a dividing line and negative values below it.

9. Create a sparkline without opening the Ribbon by selecting a data range and clicking the _____ button.

10. A single graph with both line and column plots is called a _____ Chart.

Competency Assessment

Project 5-1: Creating a Simple Chart

In this exercise you will create a simple chart in a new worksheet.

1. Open Excel and create a new blank worksheet.

2. Save your document as **project_5-1_simple_chart.**

3. In A1, type Date. In B1, type Calls.

4. Populate A2:A9 with the dates December 1-8.

5. Populate B2:B9 with the data series 6, 4, 4, 9, 6, 2, 6, 9.

6. Apply the Heading 2 cell style to A1:B1.

7. Select A1:B9. Click the Quick Analysis button, then select Charts > Line.

8. Save and close your document.

Project 5-2: Chart Elements

In this exercise you'll begin to customize the content and presentation of your chart.

1. Open the document 5-2-source and save it as **project_5-2_elements.**

2. Click on the chart's Chart Elements button.

3. Deselect Gridlines. Select Axis Titles > Primary Vertical (not Horizontal).

4. Select the chart's title (Calls), the double click it to edit the text. Type Daily Sales Calls.

5. Similarly edit the vertical axis title to Only completed calls are counted.

6. Click the Chart Styles button and select Style 2.

7. Under Chart Styles > Color, select Color 3 (orange).

8. Press Ctrl+W to close the document. When prompted, save your work.

Proficiency Assessment

Project 5-3: Recommended Charts

In this exercise you'll take advantage of Excel's ability to recommend chart types.

1. Open the practice file **ratings_comparison**.
2. Save the file as **project_5-3_recommended_charts**.
3. Use AutoFill to extend the =AVERAGE() function to the other cells in row 9.
4. Select A3:R7 and preview Recommended Charts. Add a **Line Chart** to the worksheet.
5. Select A3:R9 and preview Recommended Charts. Add a **Clustered Column Chart** for the new range.

   Note the difference in Excel's handling of the raw yearly data and the AVERAGE() output.

6. Experiment with selecting different ranges (e.g., R4:R7, P3:R7) to see which chart styles Excel recommends.
7. Save and close your document.

Project 5-4: Altering Meaning with Chart Elements

This exercise will demonstrate how the meaning of a chart can be altered by a subtle change to its construction.

1. Open the project file **5-4-source** and save it as **project_5-4_chart_elements_2**.
2. Move the chart with no AVERAGE() data to worksheet Chart1, and the other chart to Chart2.
3. Change Chart1's Chart Type to **100% Stacked Area**.
4. Hide the data series for Animal Spirits with the **Select Data** command.

   The graph now depicts the other three shows' share of the "leftover" viewers not watching the top-rated series.

5. Copy Chart1 to a new worksheet (Sheet2). In the new version of the graph, restore the fourth data series and switch rows/columns. What kind of relationships does the new chart in Sheet2 depict?
6. Save and close your document.

Mastery Assessment

Project 5-5: Further Chart Customization

In this exercise you'll carefully tailor a pair of charts to project specifications.

1. Open the project file **5-5-source** and save it as **project_5-5_customization**.
2. Add a sheet to your document and name it **Custom**.
3. Create two new charts in the Custom sheet, each from the full data set, according to the following specifications:
   * Stacked Column, Layout 10, Style 8, Title **Ratings Share 90-99**, Vertical axis **Millions of households**, exclude Average data series and dates 1983-1989
   * Line, Layout 1, Style 2, Color 16, no gridlines, no title, add bright orange trend-line for Animal Spirits
4. Save and close your document.

Project 5-6: Choosing the Right Chart

This exercise challenges you to build a chart to achieve a specific informational effect.

1. Open the project file **5-6-source** and save it as **project_5-6_design**.
2. Experiment with different types of charts available and use different chart and text options to creatively style your charts.
3. Save and close your document.

LESSON SKILL MATRIX

In this lesson, you will learn the following skills:

Working with Lists	Sorting Records
Filtering Records	Searching Records
Deleting Records	Removing Duplicates
Extracting Records	Subtotaling Data
Grouping Records	Using Data Validation
Converting Text to Columns	Using Flash Fill

KEY TERMS

- List
- Database
- Field
- Record
- Custom sort
- Filter
- Criteria range
- Subtotal
- Grand total
- Data validation
- Input message
- Error alert
- Columnar form
- Delimiter
- Flash fill

CUSTOMER SATISFACTION SURVEY

n a scale of 1 to 5 where 1 represents "Extremel

ow would you rate your level of overall satisfac

1 ☐   2 ☐   3 ☐   4 ☑   5 ☐   na ☐

How likely are you to recommend our Com

☐ Excellent
☑ Very Good
☐ Good

Contoso's customer database has grown unwieldy – ten thousand records, each with thirty fields, some updated weekly. Their data handlers can only work with a subset of the data at once, and need to reorder and cut down the data for quick reading. Excel's sorting, filtering, and data validation tools keep the database under control, and prevent errors from sneaking in where they'll be impossible to fix.

SOFTWARE ORIENTATION

You can use powerful tools to sort, organize, and manage data within Microsoft Excel.

Figure 6-1

Filtered data

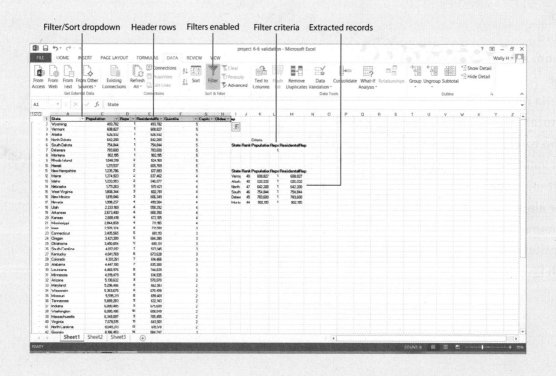

STARTING UP

In this lesson, you'll work with several files from the Excel06lessons folder. Make sure that you have loaded the OfficeLessons folder onto your computer.

WORKING WITH LISTS

Bottom Line

With Excel, you can easily manage data in a **list**. After information is organized into a list format, you can find and extract data that meets certain criteria. You can also sort information in a list to put into a specific order, and you can extract, summarize, and compare data.

Database terms

A list, also known as a **database**, is information that contains similar sets of data, such as a phone directory. Information in a list is organized by categories or **fields**. Each column in a list contains a heading or field name that determines the type of information entered in that column. You enter data in a row to form a record. Once information is organized in a list, you can filter, sort, extract, and summarize the data. Figure 6-2 shows 24 records of a database containing four fields.

Figure 6-2

A list contains similar sets of data.

	A	B	C	D	E
1	**Northwind Traders**				
2	*Employee Expense Reports*				
3					
4					
5	**First Name**	**Last Name**	**Department**	**Amount**	
6	Stephen	Tran	Sales	$245	
7	Eric	Donaldson	Accounting	$300	
8	Dante	West	Marketing	$260	
9	Linda	McMann	Editorial	$320	
10	Jennifer	Ponson	Marketing	$140	
11	Nafisa	Pimental	Marketing	$340	
12	Ellen	Iverson	Sales	$180	
13	Conrad	Baines	Editorial	$280	
14	Penelope	Pendergast	Editorial	$254	
15	Greg	Stevens	Sales	$167	
16	Joseph	Jefferson	Accounting	$100	
17	Harry	Hillary	Sales	$189	
18	Paul	Bishop	Marketing	$349	
19	Jayden	Jones	Marketing	$415	
20	Donald	Ellington	Editorial	$620	
21	Effy	Gonsalves	Editorial	$430	
22	Eileen	Carson	Editorial	$300	
23	Hugh	McKenna	Sales	$150	
24	Peter	Bailey	Accounting	$780	
25	Rebecca	Livingston	Marketing	$450	
26	Pierre	Louis	Sales	$309	
27	Michael	Martin	Accounting	$500	
28	Eliza	Harrington	Editorial	$550	
29	Foster	Brooks	Sales	$425	

CREATING A LIST

Bottom Line

Creating a list is very simple. The first step is to determine the categories of information that you want to capture, and then enter a label in each column of the list. For instance, you could have a file with information about your sales force, where the columns are labeled First Name, Last Name, Department, and Amount.

The row that contains the column headings or field names is referred to as the Header Row. The header row is important when you begin to work with your data, since it is used to specify fields to sort by or records to filter.

STEP BY STEP   **Adding records to a list**

When creating a list, the first step is to create the header row; you can then enter **records** in the rows directly beneath.

To move to the next field in the list, press the Tab key on your keyboard. To move down the list, you can press the Enter key: Excel recognizes the data entry pattern as a list and automatically moves the cell pointer to the first field in the next row.

Here's an exercise for you to practice creating lists in Excel.

1   Open Excel, choose File > Open and navigate to the Excel06lessons folder. Open the file named **excel06_list.**

2   Choose File > Save As and navigate to the Excel06lessons folder again. Name the file **excel06_list_work.**

3   Click in cell A38 and type James.

4   Press Tab and type Gilford in cell B38.

5   Press Tab and type Sales in cell C38. Notice that when you begin typing Sales, Excel automatically fills in the remainder for you with its AutoComplete feature.

6   Press Tab and type 345 in cell D38.

7   Press Enter to move to cell A39. See Figure 6-3.

8   Save the file, but don't close it; you'll use it in the next section.

Figure 6-3

When you press the Enter key, Excel moves the cell pointer to the next record.

	A	B	C	D	E
1	**Northwinds Traders**				
2	Employee Expense Reports				
3					
4					
5	**First Name**	**Last Name**	**Department**	**Amount**	
30	Kamilla	Jenkins	Accounting	$375	
31	Cliff	Burke	Accounting	$345	
32	Kathy	Crawford	Sales	$125	
33	Jacob	Mullen	Marketing	$600	
34	John	Benoit	Marketing	$450	
35	Stanley	Jacobson	Marketing	$235	
36	Christine	Gentile	Marketing	$350	
37	Preston	Bangston	Editorial	$230	
38	James	Gilford	Sales	$345	
39					
40					

SORTING RECORDS

Bottom Line

Excel enables you to organize the data in a list to suit your needs. You can sort the data so it appears in a certain order, either alphabetically or numerically, and in ascending or descending order. You can also create a custom sort to arrange records on multiple fields.

Take Note   For all four exercises in this section, use the same exercise file you used in the previous section. Don't close the file at the end of each exercise.

STEP BY STEP ## Sorting records in ascending order

1. Position the cell pointer in cell B6 to sort the records by Last Name.

2. From the Data tab, choose Sort A to Z. Excel sorts the list alphabetically by last name, as in Figure 6-4.

Figure 6-4

Sort records in a list to rearrange the order alphabetically.

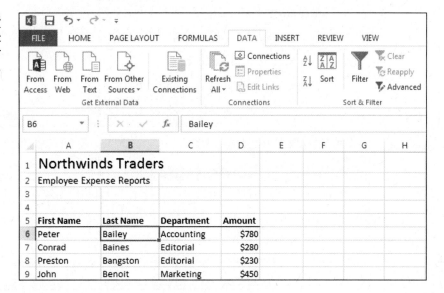

STEP BY STEP ## Sorting records in descending order

1. Position the cell pointer in cell D6 to sort by the Amount field.

2. From the Data tab, choose Sort Z to A. Excel sorts the list from highest to lowest by the Amount field. (See Figure 6-5.)

Figure 6-5

Sort numeric values in a list in descending order to rearrange the order from highest to lowest.

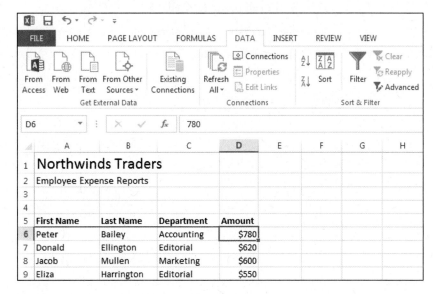

STEP BY STEP   Sorting selected records

You can also sort a subset of records rather than the entire list. When you sort a select group and choose the Sort A to Z or Sort Z to A commands, Excel automatically sorts by the first field in the list. To sort by a different field you must use the Sort command.

1   Select range A6:E16.

2   From the Data tab, choose Sort. (See Figure 6-6.)

3   In the Sort By field, select Last Name.

4   Change the Order to A to Z and click OK.

Figure 6-6

Sort a subset of records with the Sort command.

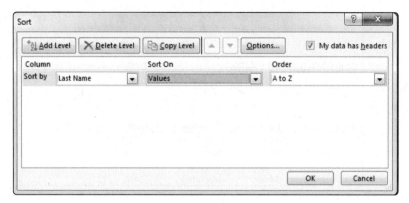

STEP BY STEP   Creating a custom sort

When you want to sort records by more than one field, (for instance, by Department and then Last Name), you can create a **custom sort**.

1   Position the cell pointer in cell A6.

2   From the Data tab, choose Sort; then, select Department in the Sort by field.

3   Click the Add Level button.

4   In the Then By field, select **Last Name**, and then click **OK**. The data is now sorted alphabetically by the department and then alphabetically by the last name.

Figure 6-7

With the Sort command, you can sort records by more than one field.

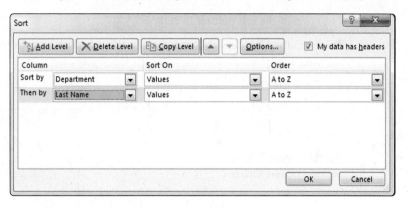

Figure 6-8

Sort records by more than one field when you want view records by multiple order.

	A	B	C	D	E
1	**Northwinds Traders**				
2	Employee Expense Reports				
3					
4					
5	**First Name**	**Last Name**	**Department**	**Amount**	
6	Peter	Bailey	Accounting	$780	
7	Cliff	Burke	Accounting	$345	
8	Eric	Donaldson	Accounting	$300	
9	Joseph	Jefferson	Accounting	$100	
10	Kamilla	Jenkins	Accounting	$375	
11	Michael	Martin	Accounting	$500	
12	Conrad	Baines	Editorial	$280	
13	Preston	Bangston	Editorial	$230	
14	Eileen	Carson	Editorial	$300	
15	Donald	Ellington	Editorial	$620	
16	Effy	Gonsalves	Editorial	$430	
17	Eliza	Harrington	Editorial	$550	
18	Linda	McMann	Editorial	$320	
19	Penelope	Pendergast	Editorial	$254	
20	John	Benoit	Marketing	$450	
21	Paul	Bishop	Marketing	$349	
22	Christine	Gentile	Marketing	$350	
23	Stanley	Jacobson	Marketing	$235	
24	Jayden	Jones	Marketing	$415	
25	Rebecca	Livingston	Marketing	$450	
26	Jacob	Mullen	Marketing	$600	
27	Nafisa	Pimental	Marketing	$340	
28	Jennifer	Ponson	Marketing	$140	
29	Dante	West	Marketing	$260	

Bottom Line

5   Save the file, but don't close it; you'll use it in the next section.

FILTERING RECORDS

By **filtering** records, you can select the records to view in your list. Filtering records is similar to sorting in that you indicate the field by which you want to filter. You can also create multiple levels of filtering so you can view records by more than one criterion. For example, you can view records by specific departments or by a certain amount. When you apply a filter, Excel hides the records that do not meet the filter.

Take Note   For all exercises in this section, use the same exercise file you have been using till now. Don't close the file at the end of each exercise.

STEP BY STEP   Creating a filter

1   Position the cell pointer in cell A6.

2   From the Data tab, choose **Filter**. Excel adds filter buttons to the field names in row 5 in your list.

3   Click the **Department** filter button.

4   Click **Select All** to deselect it; select **Marketing**, as in Figure 6-9.

Figure 6-9

Filtering allows you to designate the records you want to view.

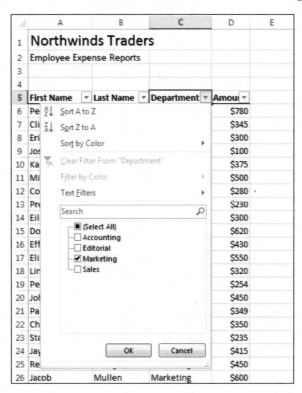

5   Click **OK**. As in Figure 6-10, Excel displays only the records from the Marketing department.

Figure 6-10

Filtered records only display the records containing the filter you specified.

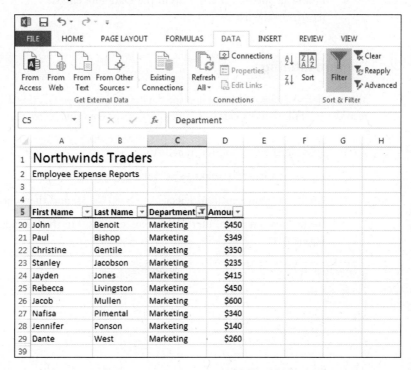

Clearing a filter

Excel indicates when a filter is in place by adding the filter symbol to the field heading you are filtering by. When you hover the pointer over the field heading, a box pops up telling you the current filter that is in place.

1   Click in cell A20.

2   From the Sort & Filter group in the Data tab, choose Clear. Excel redisplays all the records in the list.

STEP BY STEP   **Custom filtering**

You can define a custom filter when the data must meet specific criteria. For instance, you can locate records that fall within a certain range of values or contain a certain string of text.

1   Position the cell pointer in cell A6.

2   From the Data tab, make sure Filter is selected.

3   Click the Amount filter, select Number Filters, and then choose Greater Than.

4   In the Custom AutoFilter dialog box, type 400 in the box adjacent to is greater than. See Figure 6-11.

Figure 6-11

AutoFilters let you search for specific records.

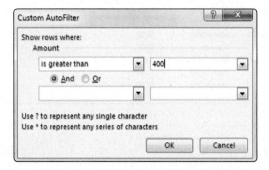

5   Click OK to only show records that have amounts over $400, as in Figure 6-12.

Figure 6-12

Filtered records display only those where the amount is greater than $400.

	A	B	C	D	E
1	**Northwinds Traders**				
2	Employee Expense Reports				
3					
4					
5	First Name	Last Name	Department	Amou	
6	Peter	Bailey	Accounting	$780	
11	Michael	Martin	Accounting	$500	
15	Donald	Ellington	Editorial	$620	
16	Effy	Gonsalves	Editorial	$430	
17	Eliza	Harrington	Editorial	$550	
20	John	Benoit	Marketing	$450	
24	Jayden	Jones	Marketing	$415	
25	Rebecca	Livingston	Marketing	$450	
26	Jacob	Mullen	Marketing	$600	
30	Foster	Brooks	Sales	$425	
39					

6   Save the file, but don't close it; you'll use it in the next section.

SEARCHING RECORDS

Bottom Line

To quickly find records in your list, use the Search feature.

STEP BY STEP | **Using the Search filter**

1   Click in cell A6.

2   From the Data tab, click **Filter** twice. Excel removes the last filter setting and then adds filter buttons to the field names in your list again and removes the current filter.

3   Click the **Last Name** filter.

4   In the Search box, type **Gonsalves** and click **OK**. (See Figure 6-13.) Excel displays only those records that meet the specified search criteria.

Figure 6-13

Find specific records with the Search filter.

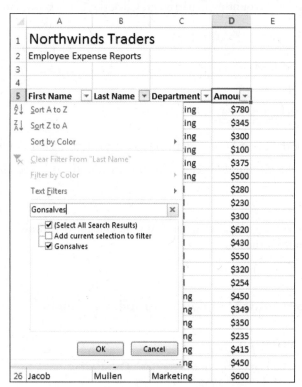

5   Save the file, but don't close it; you'll use it in the next section.

DELETING RECORDS

Bottom Line

When you need to delete records from a list, you can delete them directly from the worksheet, just as you would any data you no longer need. If you're working with a large list, you should first filter the list to display only those records you want to delete. Use the Delete command to remove the filtered records from the list.

STEP BY STEP **Deleting Records**

1 Click in cell A16.

2 From the Data tab, click Filter twice to clear the previous filter settings and begin a new filter.

3 Click the Department filter.

4 Click Select All to deselect it and choose Accounting.

5 Click OK. Excel filters the list to display only those records from the Accounting department.

6 Highlight range A6:E11 and in the Cells group on the Home tab, choose Delete.

7 Click OK when prompted to delete the rows (see Figure 6-14). Excel removes the records from the Accounting department. Click the Undo button to restore the deleted records.

Figure 6-14

Delete filtered records from a list with the Delete command.

8 Click the Filter button on the Data tab to clear the current filter.

9 Save the file, but don't close it; you'll use it in the next section.

REMOVING DUPLICATES

Bottom Line

Excel can scan a list and search for duplicate entries. If it finds any, you can instruct Excel to remove them from the list.

STEP BY STEP **Removing records that contain duplicate values**

1 Click in cell A6.

2 From the Data tab, choose Remove Duplicates.

3 Click the Unselect All button.

4 From the Columns section of Remove Duplicates dialog box, shown in Figure 6-15, select First Name and Last Name.

Figure 6-15

Remove records that contain duplicate values.

5   Click **OK**. If there were records with duplicate first name and last name entries, they would be removed.

6   In the resulting dialog box, click **OK** to acknowledge that no duplicate values were found.

EXTRACTING RECORDS

Bottom Line

Organizing data in a list is very important, and so is pulling data out when needed. With Advanced sort, you can pull data from a list and store it in another area of the worksheet. By extracting specific records, we can analyze a subset of the data.

Before you can use the Advanced Sort feature, you must define a **criteria range** in the worksheet. The criteria range is identical to the header row in the list in that it contains a copy of the field names used in the list. To define the criteria, enter the data or criteria you want to find immediately below each column heading. You can indicate that the records be copied to another location for further analysis.

STEP BY STEP   **Defining the criteria range**

1   Select range A5:D5 and choose **Copy** from the Home tab.

2   Click in cell G5 and press **Enter** to paste the copied headings.

3   In cell J6, enter >400.

STEP BY STEP   **Extracting records defined in the criteria range**

1   Click in cell L5.

2   From the Sort & Filter group of the Data tab, choose **Advanced**. Excel automatically selects range A5:D38 as the List range.

3   Change Excel's automatic selection to indicate range G5:J6 as the Criteria range.

4   Select **Copy to Another Location**.

5   Indicate cell L5 as the Copy to range. (See Figure 6-16.)

Figure 6-16

Use Advanced Filter to extract a range of records from a list.

6   Click OK. Excel pulls the records that match the criteria and copies them over under cell L5, as in Figure 6-17.

Figure 6-17

Extract a range of records for further analysis.

First Name	Last Name	Departme	Amount
Peter	Bailey	Accountin	$780
Michael	Martin	Accountin	$500
Donald	Ellington	Editorial	$620
Effy	Gonsalves	Editorial	$430
Eliza	Harrington	Editorial	$550
John	Benoit	Marketing	$450
Jayden	Jones	Marketing	$415
Rebecca	Livingston	Marketing	$450
Jacob	Mullen	Marketing	$600
Foster	Brooks	Sales	$425

7   Save the file, but don't close it; you'll use it in the next section.

SUBTOTALING DATA

Bottom Line

Excel's Subtotal command allows you to summarize data in your lists by calculating **subtotal** and **grand total** amounts for numeric fields. When you summarize a list in such a manner, Excel calculates subtotals on subsets of data. For example, you can quickly determine sales revenue by department or determine the average number of units sold by branch.

STEP BY STEP   **Alphabetically sort the list**

Prior to adding subtotals, you must sort the list by the appropriate field.

1   Click in cell C6.

2   From the Home tab, choose Sort A to Z. Excel sorts the list by department if this was not already done.

STEP BY STEP   **Adding subtotals**

1   Click in cell A6.

2   From the Outline group on the Data tab, choose Subtotal.

3   From the "At each change in" drop-down menu, select Department.

4 In the Add subtotal to box, select **Amount**. See Figure 6-18.

Figure 6-18

You can add subtotal amounts at each change in Department.

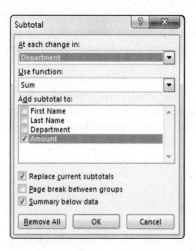

5 Click **OK**. As Figure 6-19 shows, subtotals are now added to the list below each department.

Figure 6-19

Subtotal amounts are added to the list.

GROUPING RECORDS

Bottom Line

When Subtotals are added to an Excel list, each set of records is automatically grouped on the field by which they are subtotaled. When records are grouped in such a way, you can collapse the details of the group to display the subtotals only, and you can expand each group to display the detailed data.

Excel automatically applies an outline view to the worksheet list after subtotals are added. This view offers you single-click access to hiding and expanding details. You can collapse and expand outline levels with the Outline symbols or with the Show Detail and Hide Detail commands from the Data tab.

STEP BY STEP   **Hiding and showing details**

1   Click in cell C7 and choose Hide Detail (⊟) from the Data tab. Excels hides rows 6 through 11 and displays the Subtotal amount for the Accounting department in row 12. (See Figure 6-20.)

Figure 6-20

Hiding the rows will adjust the total of your spreadsheet.

2   Choose Show Detail (⊞) to expand the detail items for the Accounting group; in this case, rows 6 through 11.

Take Note   Click the Level 1 symbol to hide all details and display the Grand Total amount only. Click the Level 2 symbol to show subtotal amounts for each group. Click the Level 3 symbol to display all detail data.

STEP BY STEP   **Removing an outline**

You can remove the outline from your worksheet list without removing the subtotal and grand total calculations. However, prior to removing the outline, make sure you expand the outline to include all your worksheet data. The quickest way to do this is to click the lowest level number displayed in your outline. For the exercise file you've been using throughout this lesson, this would be Level 3.

1   Click the drop-down arrow under the Ungroup button from the Data tab.

2   Select Clear Outline. Excel clears the outline from the display and retains the subtotal rows and data.

3 Choose Subtotal from the Data tab and click OK to add the Outline back to the list. Choose Subtotal and click Remove All from the resulting Subtotal dialog box. Excel removes both the outline and subtotals from the list.

4 Save the file, but don't close it; you'll use it in the next section.

USING DATA VALIDATION

Bottom Line

Excel's **Data Validation** tools enable you to restrict the type of data that users enter into the field of a list. By doing so, you can streamline data entry and ensure that the data meets a certain level of authentication. Data Validation can also help cut down on data entry errors. For instance, you can create a list of choices from which users can make a selection for a field such as Department. Or impose a restriction on the highest amount that can be entered into a field that captures expense-related items.

STEP BY STEP | **Creating data validation rules**

1 In cell E5, type Date Submitted and press Enter.

2 Select range E6:E38 and click Data Validation in the Data tab.

3 Select Date in the Allow field; select between in the Data field.

4 Type 1/1/13 in the Start Date field; type 1/31/13 in the End Date field. Click OK. (See Figure 6-21.)

Figure 6-21

Restrict data entry to specific dates with Data Validation.

STEP BY STEP | **Entering data using data validation**

1 Click in cell E6.

2 Type 1/2/13 and press Enter.

3 Type 1/4/13 in cell E7 and press Enter.

4   Type 2/2/13 in cell E8 and press Enter. Excel displays an error message (Figure 6-22) alerting you that the value you entered is not valid.

Figure 6-22

Error messages are displayed when a user breaks a Data Validation rule.

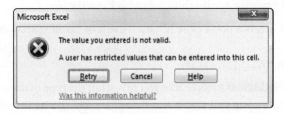

5   Click Cancel and enter 1/2/13 in cell E8 and press Enter.

STEP BY STEP   **Creating an input message**

You can define the message that a user sees when the cell pointer moves to a range that has data validation enabled.

1   Select range E6:E38.

2   In the Data tab, choose Data Validation, and then click the Input Message tab.

3   Type Date Submitted in the Title field; type Enter dates for the current month only. in the Input message field, as in Figure 6-23.

Figure 6-23

Define the message that users will see when they point to a cell with data validation rules.

4   Click OK. The custom message you created is displayed explaining the data validation rules as in Figure 6-24.

Figure 6-24

Define the message that users will see when they point to a cell with data validation rules.

	A	B	C	D	E	F	G
1	**Northwinds Traders**						
2	Employee Expense Reports						
3							
4							
5	**First Name**	**Last Name**	**Department**	**Amount**	**Date Submitted**		
6	Peter	Bailey	Accounting	$780	1/2/2013		
7	Cliff	Burke	Accounting	$345	1/4/		
8	Eric	Donaldson	Accounting	$300	1/2/		
9	Joseph	Jefferson	Accounting	$100			
10	Kamilla	Jenkins	Accounting	$375			
11	Michael	Martin	Accounting	$500			
12	Conrad	Baines	Editorial	$280			

STEP BY STEP   **Creating the error alert**

In addition to creating a specialized message when users enter a cell using Data Validation, you can create a custom error message when users break the data entry rule.

1   Make sure range E6:E38 is selected.

2   In the Data tab, choose Data Validation.

3   Click the Error Alert tab and select Stop from the Style drop-down menu.

4   Type Invalid Date in the Title field; type Enter a date from the current month only. in the Error Message field. See Figure 6-25.

Figure 6-25

Create a custom error message for when users type the incorrect data.

5   Click OK. Test by typing 2/5/13 in cell E9 and press Enter. The resulting dialog box is shown in Figure 6-26.

Figure 6-26

A custom error message alerts the user to invalid entries.

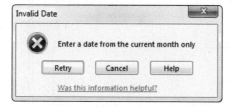

6   Click Retry and type 1/5/13 and press Enter.

7   Choose File > Save and then File > Close.

CONVERTING TEXT TO COLUMNS

Bottom Line

Many times, the data we want to work with in an Excel list comes from other sources. To manipulate the information in the column and row worksheet structure of Excel, we need to clean up the data and convert it so that it can be more readily used.

For example, suppose that you import a mailing list that contains both the first and last name of the customer in the same field. In a list such as this, you can't sort the records by last name. The best option is to split the complete name into two separate fields: First Name and Last Name.

STEP BY STEP   **To convert text into columnar form**

Before you convert text into multiple columns, you must make sure that there are enough blank columns to hold the split data; otherwise, existing information will be overwritten.

In this exercise, you will begin by opening the practice file, save it, and rename it so you have your own working copy. Then you will add a blank column to your working copy so you have enough columns to hold the split data; and finally, you will split the data.

1   Choose File > Open and navigate to the Excel06lessons folder on your Computer. Open the file named **excel06_customers**.

2   Choose File > Save As and navigate back to the Excel06lessons folder. Name the file **excel06_customers_work**.

3   Click in column B and click the down arrow below Insert from the Home tab. Select **Insert Sheet Columns**.

4   Select range A4:A32 and choose Text to Columns from the Data tab.

5   In the Covert Text to Columns wizard, choose Delimited. (See Figure 6-27.) Then, click Next.

Figure 6-27

Convert text entries into multiple columns.

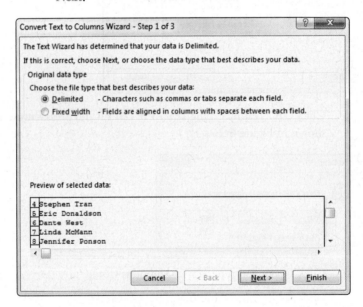

6   Select Space as the only **Delimiter** and click Next. Click Finish. As in Figure 6-28, Excel splits the names from column A into first and last name entries in columns A and B.

Figure 6-28

Convert multi-word text entries into separate columns for easy manipulation.

	A	B	C	D	E	F
1	Contoso Realty Group					
2	Customer Contact List					
3						
4	Stephen	Tran	Boston	MA	02124	
5	Eric	Donaldson	Arlington	MA	02474	
6	Dante	West	Brighton	MA	02135	
7	Linda	McMann	Boston	MA	02124	
8	Jennifer	Ponson	Woonsocket	RI	02895	
9	Nafisa	Pimental	West Newton	MA	02465	
10	Ellen	Iverson	Winchester	MA	01890	
11	Conrad	Baines	Boston	MA	02124	
12	Penelope	Pendergast	Brighton	MA	02135	
13	Greg	Stevens	Newton	MA	02458	
14	Joseph	Jefferson	Wellesly	MA	02482	
15	Harry	Hillary	Providence	RI	02901	
16	Paul	Bishop	Newton	MA	02458	
17	Jayden	Jones	Waltham	MA	02451	
18	Donald	Ellington	Brighton	MA	02135	
19	Effy	Gonsalves	Manchester	NH	03101	
20	Eileen	Carson	Arlington	MA	02474	

7   Save the file, but don't close it; you'll use it in the next section.

USING FLASH FILL

Bottom Line

The **Flash Fill** command is another time-saving technique for working with data imported from other programs. Flash Fill evaluates a range of cells for any patterns or consistencies that it might find. When it senses a pattern, it automatically fills in the remainder of the data for you.

For example, in the following exercise, column A will contain the first and last name in the same field. We will use Flash Fill to fill column B with the first name and column C with the last name.

1   Click the Undo button two times to revert the worksheet you used in the previous exercise back to its original state.

2   Click in cell B4 and choose Insert > Insert Sheet Columns twice from the Home tab.

3   Click in cell B4 and type Stephen.

4   Click in cell B5 and type **Eri**. Excel senses the pattern and fills in the remainder of first names in column B, as in Figure 6-29. To accept the fill, press **Enter**.

Figure 6-29

Flash Fill cuts down on data entry by sensing patterns in your data.

	A	B	C	D	E	F	G
1	Contoso Realty Group						
2	Customer Contact List						
3							
4	Stephen Tran	Stephen		Boston	MA	02124	
5	Eric Donaldson	Eric		Arlington	MA	02474	
6	Dante West	Dante		Brighton	MA	02135	
7	Linda McMann	Linda		Boston	MA	02124	
8	Jennifer Ponson	Jennifer		Woonsocket	RI	02895	
9	Nafisa Pimental	Nafisa		West Newton	MA	02465	
10	Ellen Iverson	Ellen		Winchester	MA	01890	
11	Conrad Baines	Conrad		Boston	MA	02124	
12	Penelope Pende	Penelope		Brighton	MA	02135	
13	Greg Stevens	Greg		Newton	MA	02458	
14	Joseph Jefferso	Joseph		Wellesly	MA	02482	
15	Harry Hillary	Harry		Providence	RI	02901	
16	Paul Bishop	Paul		Newton	MA	02458	
17	Jayden Jones	Jayden		Waltham	MA	02451	
18	Donald Ellington	Donald		Brighton	MA	02135	
19	Effy Gonsalves	Effy		Manchester	NH	03101	
20	Eileen Carson	Eileen		Arlington	MA	02474	
21	Hugh McKenna	Hugh		Boston	MA	02124	
22	Peter Bailey	Peter		Waltham	MA	02451	
23	Rebecca Livings	Rebecca		Wellesly	MA	02482	
24	Michael Martin	Michael		Stamford	CT	06901	
25	Eliza Harrington	Eliza		Brighton	MA	02135	
26	Foster Brooks	Foster		Boston	MA	02124	
27	Kamilla Jenkins	Kamilla		Waltham	MA	02451	
28	Cliff Burke	Cliff		Waltham	MA	02451	
29	Kathy Crawford	Kathy		Newton	MA	02458	

5   Click in cell C4 and type **Tran**.

6   Click in cell C5 and type **Dona**. Again, Excel senses the pattern and fills in the remainder of last names in column C. Press **Enter** to accept the pattern.

7   Select range **A4:A32** and choose **Delete > Delete Cells** from the Home tab.

8   Select **Shift cells left** and click **OK**. This removes the data in column A, which had become obsolete.

You've now completed Lesson 6. In our next lesson, "Using Templates," you will learn how to use and customize the templates included in Excel 2013.

What you learned in this lesson:

- Working with Lists

- Sorting Records

- Filtering Records

- Searching Records

- Deleting Records

- Removing Duplicates

- Extracting Records

- Subtotaling Data

- Grouping Records

- Using Data Validation

- Converting Text to Columns

- Using Flash Fill

Knowledge Assessment

Matching

Match the function in numbers 1 to 10 to its output in letters a to j.

1. database
2. input message
3. delimiter
4. record
5. filter
6. field
7. columnar form
8. custom sort
9. descending order
10. subtotal

a. single line in a database
b. character that separates entries in a series
c. orders data based on multiple criteria
d. list of entries, each w/several fields
e. splitting data into multiple fields per line
f. sorting from Z to A, or greater to lesser numbers
g. prompt for data entry
h. one column/category in a database
i. criteria for viewing records
j. summary of part of a dataset

Fill in the Blanks

Complete the following sentences by writing the correct word or words in the blanks provided.

1. An Ascending Sort of the series (3, 5, 1, 8, 2, 2, 0, 4) produces the series _____.

2. To enable the Hide/Show Detail commands, you must _____ data in your spreadsheet, or calculate _____ for some subset of the data.

3. The _____ tool can, for instance, force the user to enter dates in a certain range into a cell.

4. The most flexible way to include mailing addresses in an Excel list is to first break them into _____ form.

5. Using the / (forward slash) character as a delimiter when breaking up the string "3:00pm on 5/30/99" yields the following entry: _____.

6. The Data Validation will throw up an _____ when data outside its acceptable range is entered.

7. After subtotals are applied to a list, Excel converts it automatically to _____ view.

8. To create an Advanced sort, first preselect or _____ part of the data.

9. The _____ command lets you clear redundant/repeated data within a column.

10. Clicking the dropdown arrow in a column's header cell displays a set of commands to _____ the entries in the column.

Competency Assessment

Project 6-1: Filtering Lists

In this exercise you'll filter and sort data in a list.

1. Open the practice file **state_rankings** and save a copy called **project_6-1_filters**.

2. Select cell **A1** and click **Data > Filter**.

3. Hide column B.

4. Select the **filter** dropdown arrow for column C, and choose **Number Filters > Top 10**. In the Top 10 Autofilter dialog box, click **OK**.

5. Click the column **A** filter dropdown and select **Sort Z to A**.

6. Save and close your document.

Project 6-2: More Sorts

In this exercise you'll create a custom sort for your database.

1. Open the exercise file **6-2-source** and save your document as **project_6-2_sorting**.

2. Click **Data > Sort & Filter > Clear**, then Unhide column B.

3. Open the project file **state_reps** and copy column A.

4. Paste the copied column into your working document.

5. Select cell **D1**, select **Data > Filter**, then reselect it.

6. Click **Data > Sort**.

7. On the first sort line, sort by Reps, from largest to smallest.

8. Add a Level. Sort by Population, smallest to largest. Click OK.

This sort uses state population as a "tiebreaker" when two states have the same number of representatives.

9. Save your work and close all open files.

Project 6-3: Extracting Records

In this exercise you'll extract a handful of records meeting specific numeric criteria.

1. Open the exercise file **6-3-source** and save your document as **project_6-3_extracting**.
2. Clear the filter/sort settings for the worksheet.
3. Add the heading Residents/Rep to column E and AutoFit the column's width.
4. In E2, add a formula that divides the state's population by its representative count.
5. Format E2 as a Number, comma style, with no decimal spaces. Use AutoFill to apply the E2 formula/formatting to the whole column.

    Note that District of Columbia shows a "divide by zero" error in this field.
6. Copy A5:D5 to I7:M7.
7. Type >5000000 in K8 and <600000 in M8.
8. Click anywhere in the main dataset and select Data > Sort & Filter > Advanced.
9. Select Copy to Another Location, use I7:N8 for the Criteria range, and Copy to: I12. Click OK.

    Excel automatically uses the main dataset, A1:E52, as the List Range.
10. Save and close your document.

Project 6-4: Subtotals and Groups

In this exercise you will sort, filter, and add subtotals to a database.

1. Open the exercise file **6-4-source** and save your document as **project_6-4_subtotals**.
2. Sort the dataset by Population, smallest to largest.
3. Click the State dropdown, and filter the list so only District of Columbia is displayed. Delete its row.
4. Clear the filter/sort info, then sort the dataset by Rank.
5. Add column F, heading Quintile.

    "Quintile" simply means "fifth": the bottom or 5th quintile is the 1/5 of the dataset with the lowest population.
6. Fill F2:F11 with the number 5, F12:F21 with 4, F22:F31 with 3, and so forth.
7. Click in the main dataset, and select Data > Subtotal.
8. At each change in Quintile, use function Average, add subtotal to Residents/Rep.
9. AutoFit column F's width.
10. Save and close your document.

Project 6-5: **Advanced Filtering**

In this exercise you'll extract records from a list according to a complex set of criteria.

1. Open the exercise file **6-5-source** and save your document as **project_6-5_filters_2**.
2. Delete the subtotal and grand average rows and hide the Rank column.
3. Use a combination of filter dropdowns and new filter criteria to extract all records of states with a single representative and an above average residents/reps ratio. Copy the results to I11.
4. Save and close your document.

Project 6-6: **Data Validation**

This exercise challenges you to add data validation to a column in a database.

1. Open the exercise file **6-6-source** and save your document as **project_6-6_validation**.
2. Add two new columns to your worksheet, header cells Capital and Oldest Rep.
3. Set up Data Validation for the Oldest Rep column, allowing only Date entries in the 20th century, with Input title oldest rep's birthdate, message Please enter a valid 20th century date, and Stop-style error alert (title invalid date, message Please try again!).
4. Save and close your document.

7

Working with Excel 2013 Templates

LESSON SKILL MATRIX

In this lesson, you will learn the following skills:

Working with Templates	Saving a Workbook as a Template
Opening a Custom Template	Protecting Workbooks
Protecting Worksheets	Unlocking Cells in a Protected Worksheet
Hiding and Protecting Formulas	Searching for Templates

KEY TERMS

- Custom template
- Protected mode
- Workbook protection
- Password protection
- Locked cell
- Template library

Fabrikam's internal financial data adheres to strict content and style guidelines to maintain consistency and security throughout the firm. User rights management, data protection, and carefully controlled custom templates make for efficient, reliable data entry and help safeguard the data no matter whose desk it crosses. Excel provides fine-grained control over who edits which data, and how.

SOFTWARE ORIENTATION

Templates make it easy to re-use formatting and formulas.

Figure 7-1

Template workspace.

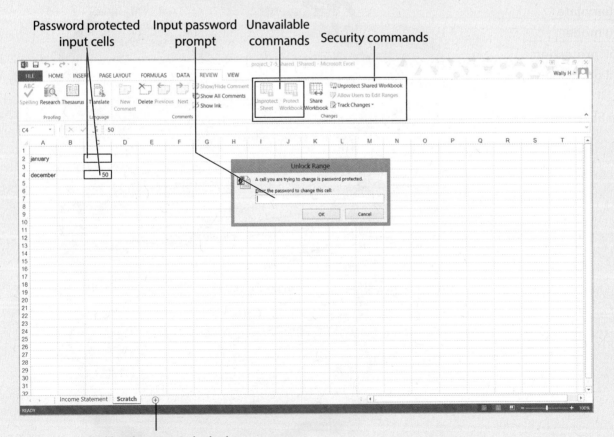

STARTING UP

In this lesson, you'll work with several files from the Excel07lessons folder. Make sure that you have loaded the OfficeLessons folder onto your computer..

EXCEL TEMPLATES

Bottom Line

A template is a worksheet that contains formatting, data, and other standard worksheet elements saved as a boilerplate. Excel offers a set of professionally-designed worksheet templates that you can use over and over again. Among the default templates offered by Excel are calendars, budgets, sales reports, and financial statements.

You can also search through the thousands of templates available from *Office.com*. When you use the Search tool, Excel displays a long list of categories from which to choose.

The Backstage view (Figure 7-2) displays a number of predesigned templates when you choose the File > New command. When you click a template, Excel displays a preview of the template. To choose it, click Create. Excel then opens a copy of the template file.

Figure 7-2

Worksheet templates offer fill-in-the-blank functionality.

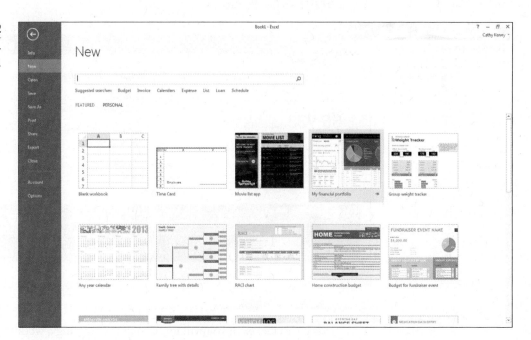

STEP BY STEP   **Opening a template**

1   Open Excel or choose File > New if you already have Excel open. Excel displays a number of templates from which you can choose.

2   In the Search for online templates text box, type **generic family budget** and select the only result, shown in Figure 7-3.

Figure 7-3

Preview a template file before you open it.

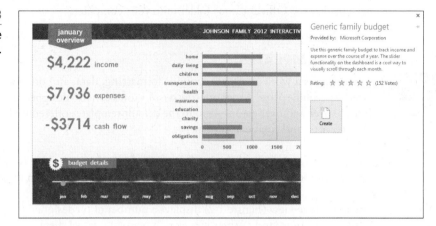

3   In the resulting window, click **Create**. Excel opens a new workbook file with the selected template. See Figure 7-4.

Figure 7-4

The Generic Family Budget template collects data for a family budget.

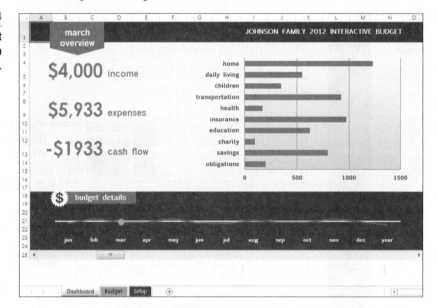

4   Keep this file open; you will use it to practice saving a workbook as a template.

When you create a new workbook based on a template, Excel does not open the original template file, but a copy of it. Sample data, explanatory text, and setup worksheets can also be contained within the file to offer guidelines on how to work with the template.

Take Note   Caution: When working with template files, use care when you encounter formulas. Do not delete or otherwise disrupt formulas, since the data in your worksheet could become unreliable.

The Generic Family Budget template contains three separate worksheets: Dashboard, Budget, and Setup. Within each sheet are a series of text boxes and explanatory text detailing how to work with the various elements in the file, shown in Figure 7-5.

Figure 7-5

The Generic Family Budget template contains three separate sheets that explain how to work with the file.

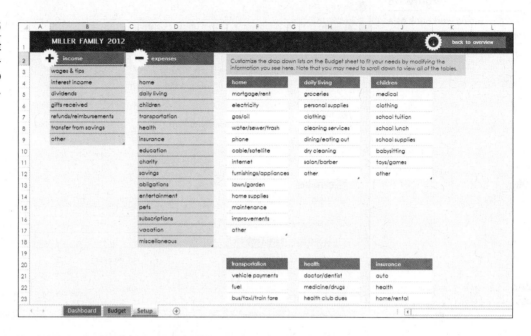

SAVING A WORKBOOK AS A TEMPLATE

Bottom Line

If you have an existing workbook that you use on a frequent basis, you can save the file as a template. When you do, the template appears under the Personal templates page of the Office Backstage.

Workbooks saved as template files are stored in the default personal templates directory (C:\users\<*user name*>\Documents\Custom Office Templates.)

STEP BY STEP **Saving a workbook as a template**

1   Using the budget file you created in a previous exercise, choose File > Save As.

2 Select **Computer** under the Save As section and click **Browse**. Navigate to the Custom Office Templates folder, seen in Figure 7-6.

Figure 7-6

Save a workbook as a template so that you can use it over and over again.

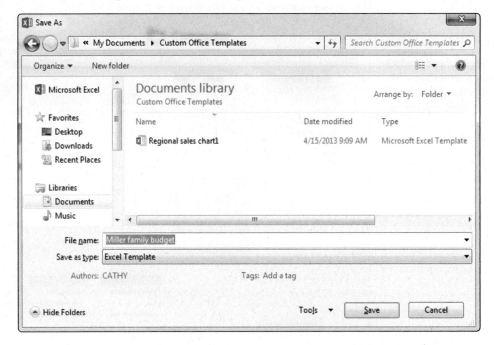

3 Select **Excel Template** from the Save as type drop-down menu.

4 Type **Miller Family Budget** in the file name box and click **Save**.

5 Choose **File > Close** to close this file.

OPENING A CUSTOM TEMPLATE

Bottom Line

After saving a worksheet as a template, you can select your custom template from the Personal tab of the New Office Backstage.

STEP BY STEP **Opening a custom template**

1 Choose **File > New**.

2   Click the Personal tab and then click the **Miller Family Budget** template. (See Figure 7-7.)

Figure 7-7

Saved templates appear under the Personal tab of the New Backstage.

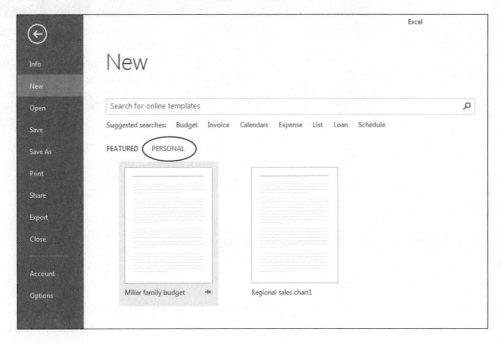

3   Choose File > Save As and select Computer.

4   Click Browse and navigate to the Excel07lessons folder.

5   In the Save As Type box, select Excel Workbook; name the file **Miller_Budget_work**.

6   Click Save and then choose File > Close.

Take Note   Once you've opened a template from the Personal page, Excel displays it with the rest of the templates on the File New page. You do not need to switch to the Personal page every time you want to use it.

PROTECTING WORKBOOKS

Bottom Line

When you create a new workbook based on a template, Excel allows you to freely edit the file. You can customize the template to suit your personal needs by changing formats, adjusting categories, and entering your own data. When you create templates to be shared with other users, you can use a variety of protection methods to prevent the template from experiencing unintentional damage.

By protecting workbooks, you can prevent other users from accidentally deleting important formulas or worksheets. Protecting a workbook is especially useful when working with templates, because this can help prevent accidental deletions or misuse.

You can protect workbooks at the file level or at the worksheet level. There are three levels of password protection in Excel: password protection to open a file, password protection to change data, or password protection for changing the file's structure, such as adding, deleting, or hiding worksheets.

There are three other levels of protection in Excel: workbook, worksheet, and specific cells. When you enable workbook protection, Excel greys out the menu items that are not available in **protected mode**. You can also assign a password that users would be required to enter in order to disable worksheet protection.

Workbook protection levels

Protection	Description
Workbook	Prevents users from altering the structure of the workbook, including adding or deleting sheets and displaying hidden worksheets. You can also prevent users from changing the size or position of worksheet windows.
Sheet	Prevents users from making changes to a worksheet. You can specify the elements that users are allowed to change.
Cells	Cells are locked by default in a protected worksheet. Users cannot edit, insert, delete or formats cells. You can unlock cells that users are able to edit.

STEP BY STEP   **Enabling workbook protection**

1 Open any Excel file.
2 Choose Protect Workbook from the Review tab.
3 Select Structure in the Protect Structure and Windows dialog box, as in Figure 7-8.

Figure 7-8

Prevent users from making changes to the structure of a workbook by turning on workbook protection.

4 Click OK. When a workbook is protected, the Protect Workbook tool in the Ribbon remains selected.
5 Close the file. You can choose not to save it.

STEP BY STEP   **Adding password protection**

When you protect a workbook at the Workbook level so that the workbook's structure can't be modified, you can add an additional layer of protection by assigning a password. When you do, users are unable to turn off workbook protection unless they have the password.

Take Note Make sure you write down the password, since you will be unable to retrieve a forgotten password by means other than the slip of paper you wrote it on.

1 Open any Excel file.
2 From the Review tab, choose Protect Workbook.
3 Select Structure in the Protect Structure and Windows dialog box.

4   In the Password text box, type sesame, and then click OK. See Figure 7-9.

Figure 7-9

Add a password to your workbooks to prevent users from turning off workbook protection.

5   In the Confirm Password dialog box, retype sesame, and then click OK to assign the password.

STEP BY STEP   Disabling workbook protection

1   Using the file from the previous exercise, choose Protect Workbook from the Review tab.

2   In the Password text field of the Unprotect Workbook dialog box, type sesame (see Figure 7-10), and then click OK.

Figure 7-10

Enter the password to disable workbook protection.

STEP BY STEP   Protecting a file

1   Using the file from the previous exercise, click File > Save As.

2   From the Save As section, choose Computer, and click Browse.

3   In the Save As dialog box, click the Tools drop-down list, and click General Options. (See Figure 7-11.)

Figure 7-11

Prevent users from opening or modifying a workbook by assigning a password to the file.

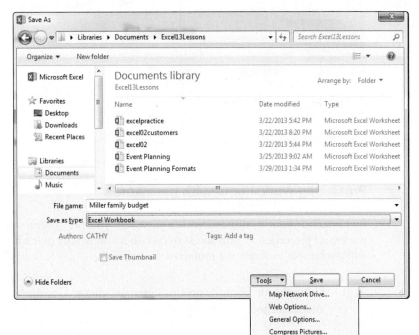

4   Type *sesame* in the Password to open box.

5   Type *sesame1234* in the Password to modify box, shown in Figure 7-12.

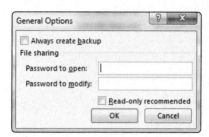

6   Click **OK** and click Save to the save the workbook with a password.

PROTECTING WORKSHEETS

Bottom Line

Within a workbook, you can protect a worksheet so that users cannot make any changes to the sheet. When you assign sheet protection, every cell in the sheet is locked unless you unlock specific cells. You can also provide users with a certain level of rights so they can work with data in the sheet. For instance, you can specify that users can insert columns, but are not allowed to delete them.

STEP BY STEP   **Protecting worksheets**

1   Using the file from the previous exercise, choose **Protect Sheet** from the Review tab.

2   Make sure that Protect worksheet and contents of locked cells is selected.

3   In the Allow all users of this worksheet to area, select **Format Cells** and **Sort**, as in Figure 7-13, and then click **OK**.

Figure 7-13

Indicate the specific tasks that
users are allowed to and are
not allowed to perform with
worksheet protection.

STEP BY STEP   **Protecting worksheets with passwords**

By protecting your worksheets with a password, you can control who can be allowed to turn off worksheet protection to gain access to certain sections. Any user who does not know the password will not be able to access the protected worksheets.

1   Using the file from the previous exercise, choose **Unprotect Sheet** from the Review tab and then choose **Protect Sheet**.

2 In the Password to unprotect sheet box, type sesame, and then click OK. Re-enter sesame in the Confirm Password dialog box, shown in Figure 7-14.

Figure 7-14

Use passwords to prevent users from disabling worksheet protection.

UNLOCKING CELLS IN A PROTECTED WORKSHEET

Bottom Line

When you protect a sheet, every cell in the sheet is **locked** unless you specify otherwise. By unlocking a specific range of cells, the worksheet remains protected, but users are allowed to enter data. You can add an additional layer of preventative measures by assigning a password to the range of cells. That way, only those with the password can enter data in the unlocked cells.

STEP BY STEP   **Unlocking cells**

Cells must be unlocked prior to enabling worksheet protection.

1 Using the file from the previous exercise, choose **Unprotect Sheet** from the Review tab. Then type sesame when prompted for the password.

2 On the Budget worksheet, click in cell C5 to select the Starting Balance amount. Press and hold the **Ctrl** key, and then select range **C13:N17**.

3 From the Review tab, choose **Allow Users to Edit Ranges**.

4 In the resulting dialog box, shown in Figure 7-15, click **New**.

Figure 7-15

Select a range of cells that users are allowed to edit in a protected sheet.

5   In the Title, type Income (see Figure 7-16), and then click OK.

Figure 7-16

Assign a range name to the range of unprotected cells.

6   Click OK in the Allow Users to Edit Ranges dialog box.

STEP BY STEP   **Protecting ranges with passwords**

1   Using the file from the previous exercise, choose Allow Users to Edit Ranges from the Review tab.

2   From the list of named ranges, choose Income, and then click Modify.

3   In the Range Password box, shown in Figure 7-17, type sesame, and then click OK.

Figure 7-17

Add a password to a specific range of unprotected cells in your workbooks to prevent unauthorized users from entering data.

4   In the Confirm Password dialog box, retype sesame, and then click OK and OK again to assign the password.

5   Choose Protect Sheet from the Review tab. Type sesame in the Password to Unprotect Sheet text box and click OK.

STEP BY STEP   **Entering data in a locked cell**

To enter data in a locked cell:

1   Using the file from the previous exercise, click in cell C13.

2   Type 3; Excel displays the Unlock Range dialog box.

3   In the text box, type sesame, and then click OK.

4   Type 3000 in cell C13. The resulting dialog is shown in Figure 7-18.

Figure 7-18

Before you can enter data in a locked cell, you must enter the password.

HIDING AND PROTECTING FORMULAS

Bottom Line

Another method of protecting data in worksheet templates is to hide important formulas from view in the cell or formula bar. When you hide formulas, the result of the formula appears in the cell, and the formula gets updated as the data changes, but users are prevented from viewing or editing the contents of the formula. When you hide a formula, you can also choose to lock the cell so it cannot be edited.

STEP BY STEP　**Hiding and Protecting formulas**

1　Using the file from the previous exercise, choose Unprotect Sheet from the Review tab and type sesame when prompted for the password.

2　Select range C6:N9; from the Home tab, choose Format, and then select Format Cells.

3　Click the Protection tab (Figure 7-19) and select Locked and Hidden.

Figure 7-19

Hide worksheet formulas from view in a protected worksheet so the formula itself is not displayed, just the result.

4　Click OK. From the Review tab, choose Protect Sheet, and click OK to turn on worksheet protection.

5　Choose File > Save and File > Close to save and close the file.

SEARCHING FOR TEMPLATES

Bottom Line

In addition to the templates that ship with Excel 2013, you can search through the hundreds of templates available at Office.com. The **template library**, accessible via the File > New command, displays a number of categories from which you can choose.

STEP BY STEP　**Searching for a template**

1　Choose File > New.

2   In the Search box, type **Budget**, and then press **Enter**. The results are shown in Figure 7-20.

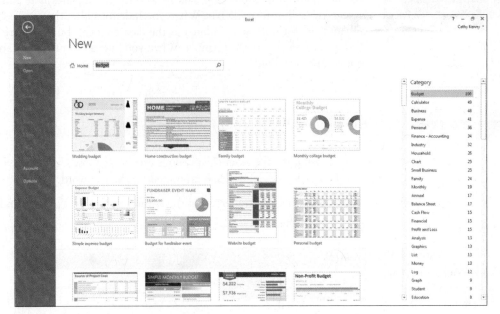

3   Click **Simple Budget**, and then click **Create**.

4   Choose **File > Save**, select **Computer**, and click **Browse**.

5   Point to the Excel07lessons folder, type **excel07_budget** and click **Save**.

6   Choose **File > Close** to close the worksheet.

You've now completed this lesson. In the next lesson, "Advanced Data Analysis," you will learn how to work with data tables and pivot tables.

What you learned in this lesson:

• Working with Templates

• Saving a Workbook as a Template

• Opening a Custom Template

• Protecting Workbooks

• Protecting Worksheets

• Unlocking Cells in a Protected Worksheet

• Hiding and Protecting Formulas

• Searching for Templates

Knowledge Assessment

Matching

Match the term or concept in numbers 1 to 10 with a definition in letter a to j.

1. Range Password
2. opening template
3. custom template
4. New > Personal
5. Hide Formulas
6. Review tab
7. Sheet Protection
8. Save as type
9. unlocked cell
10. protected file

a. houses permission/protection tools
b. can be edited even if sheet is protected
c. creates copy of file rather than modifying original
d. keeps users from viewing functions, allowing only output
e. must be entered to edit any cells in protected range
f. where to specify storing of workbook as template
g. only specified changes to worksheet allowed
h. prebuilt file made by the user
i. requires passwords to open and/or modify
j. template gallery tab housing custom templates

True/False

Circle T if the statement is true or F it the statement is false.

T F 1. A template contains a single pre-filled worksheet.
T F 2. Saving a commonly-used document as a template creates a custom template.
T F 3. In a protected worksheet, cells are unlocked by default.
T F 4. You can password-protect a workbook's structure (adding/deleting sheets, etc.).
T F 5. You can separately set which data is protected and what kinds of changes are permitted.
T F 6. To protect a file when saving, open Tools > General Options in the Save As dialog box.
T F 7. The Review > Protect Sheet command allows you to specify which editing commands remain available to users of the worksheet.
T F 8. The Office template library is a list of templates housed on your hard drive.
T F 9. Custom templates are saved by default to the user's Documents library.
T F 10. In a protected worksheet, all cells must be locked or unlocked at once.

Competency Assessment

Project 7-1: Selecting and Opening a Template

In this exercise you'll create a custom template based on an existing template.

1. Open Excel. Type income statement in the gallery search box and press Enter.
2. Select the first result (template name: income statement) and click Create.
3. Replace [Name] with your name and [Time Period] with 2013. Apply the General number format to B3.
4. Delete rows 24-47.
5. Press Ctrl+S to bring up the Save As dialog.
6. Choose Excel Template from the Save as type list and name the file project_7-1_select. Note that the template will save by default to your Documents > Custom Office Templates folder.
7. Close the document.

Project 7-2: Using Custom Templates

In this exercise you'll work with a custom template to create a new template document.

Note: If you haven't completed Project 7-1, complete steps 1-4 of Project 7-1 now, then skip to step 3 of this exercise.

1. Select File > New and open the Personal tab.
2. Select the project_7-1_select template.

   Unlike built-in templates, this personal template generates no preview pane.
3. Type 1000000 in G6 and 50000 in G7.
4. Press Ctrl+S and save the file (as a standard Excel workbook) to your working directory. Name the document project_7-2_save.
5. Close your document.

Proficiency Assessment

Project 7-3: Protecting Workbooks and Worksheets

In this exercise you'll add workbook- and sheet-level protection to a file.

1. Open the project file 7-3-source and save your document as project_7-3_protect.
2. Click Review > Protect Workbook. Make sure Structure is checked, and type safe into the Password box. Reenter safe when prompted.
3. Click Review > Protect Sheet and add the password safe sheet.
4. Confirm sheet protection by attempting to delete row 8, and providing Protect Sheet password.
5. Confirm workbook protection by attempting to add a worksheet to the workbook and providing Protect Workbook password.
6. Save and close your document.

Project 7-4: **Locking and Unlocking Cells**

In this exercise you'll take advantage of Excel's ability to lock and unlock specific cell ranges.

1. Open the project file 7-4-source and save your document as **project_7-4_range**.
2. Unprotect the workbook and worksheet.
3. Select Review > Allow Users to Edit Ranges.
4. Create a New range called revenue referring to G6:G7 with password safe range. Click **Protect Sheet...**
5. Add the password safe sheet to the worksheet.
6. Confirm the protection and save and close the document.

Mastery Assessment

Project 7-5: **Protecting and Sharing Files**

In this exercise you'll add password protection to prevent unauthorized users from opening a file at all.

1. Open the project file 7-5-source and save your document as **project_7-5_shared**.
2. Clear all protections on the file.
3. Add a new worksheet, Scratch, with labeled cells for December and January revenues.
4. Lock and password protect both worksheets, permitting editing only in the labeled input cells you created in step 3 (range password=input).
5. Lock and password protect the workbook's structure.
6. Optionally edit the Sheet1 Revenues cell to reflect the sum of the input cells on the Scratch sheet.
7. Use the Protect and Share Workbook command and password protect(password=safe share) the Track Changes data.
8. Exchange your work with a colleague, if possible, to confirm the level of security on your documents.
9. Save and close the document.

Project 7-6: **Putting It All Together**

This exercise challenges you to design a security scheme for a file to be shared with several departments at a company, each with different levels of access and editing rights.

1. Design a security configuration for a multi-sheet workbook with the following conditions:
   - IT department can edit one column (they have dept-specific password)
   - PR dept can edit one column (same)
2. Save this workbook as **project_7-6_security**.
3. Share your work with a colleague, along with any passwords you use, to compare your approaches.

8 Advanced Data Analysis

LESSON SKILL

In this lesson, you will learn the following skills:

Introduction to PivotTables	Creating, Rearranging, and Formatting PivotTables
Editing and Updating a PivotTable	Changing PivotTable Calculations
Hiding and Showing Data in a PivotTable	Adding Subtotals to a PivotTable
Using Recommended PivotTables	Working with PivotCharts
Working with Tables	Using Data Validation
Converting Text to Columns	What-If Analysis

KEY TERMS

- PivotTable
- PivotTable field
- Slicer
- What-If Analysis
- Goal Seek
- Scenario
- Data table

A mayoral candidate's enormous registered-voter spreadsheet is a useful resource, but drawing inferences from that mass of data is difficult. It's hard to get a visual sense of the raw data. PivotTables help the candidate's team simplify, filter, and visualize relationships between data entries, helping the team draw lessons from the mass of names and numbers.

SOFTWARE ORIENTATION

You can work with more complex data sets to produce reports, summarize and filter data.

Figure 8-1

PivotTable workspace.

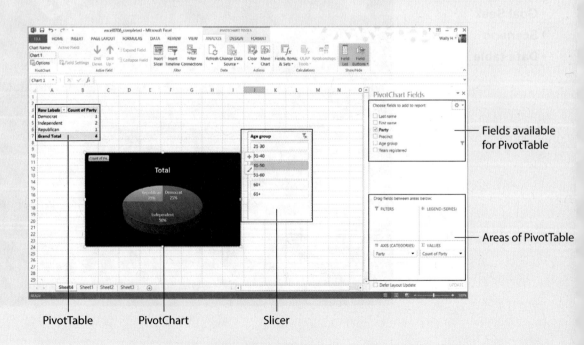

Fields available for PivotTable

Areas of PivotTable

PivotTable   PivotChart   Slicer

STARTING UP

In this lesson, you'll work with several files from the Excel08lessons folder. Make sure that you have loaded the OfficeLessons folder onto your computer.

INTRODUCTION TO PIVOTTABLES

Bottom Line

As discussed in Lesson 6, "Working with Data," Excel offers an excellent set of tools to track and manage lists of information. The real dilemma occurs when you need to quickly summarize the data or produce informative reports. A PivotTable allows you to do just that.

A **PivotTable** is an interactive table that summarizes data in an existing worksheet list or table. You can quickly rearrange the table by dragging and dropping fields to create a new report without changing the structure of your worksheet.

When you create a PivotTable from a list, column labels are used as row, column, and **filter fields**, and the data in the list become items in the PivotTable. When the data in the list contains numeric items, Excel automatically uses the SUM function to calculate the values in the PivotTable.

PivotTable fields

Area	Description
Columns	Items arranged in a columnar orientation. Items in this field appear as column labels.
Rows	Items arranged in a linear orientation. Items in this field appear as row labels.
Filters	Field is used to filter the data displayed. Items in this field appear as labels.
Values	Summarized numeric data.

STEP BY STEP   **Creating a PivotTable**

A PivotTable is made up from data entered in a list format. (See Figure 8-2.) The column labels contained in the header row of the list are used to construct the table. Once you have indicated the range of data to include, you can select how to organize the data in the PivotTable. When you click within any cell of a list, Excel automatically detects the table.

1. Choose File > Open, click Computer, and click Browse. Navigate to the Excel08lessons folder and open the file named **Sales_Report**.

2. Choose File > Save As, navigate to the Excel08lessons folder, and name the file **Sales_ Report_work**.

3 Click in cell A6 and choose PivotTable from the Insert tab.

Figure 8-2

Quickly summarize large data sets with the PivotTable.

	A	B	C	D	E	F
1	**Contoso Realty Group**					
2						
3						
4						
5	**Rep**	**Type**	**Town**	**Price**	**Month**	
6	McGrath	House	Boston	$325,000	Apr	
7	Reynolds	House	Boston	$375,000	Apr	
8	Ryan	Condo	Brighton	$229,000	Jan	
9	Ryan	House	Brighton	$320,000	Jan	
10	Sloane	House	Brighton	$340,000	Jan	
11	McGrath	Condo	Brighton	$235,000	Feb	
12	Reynolds	Condo	Brighton	$242,000	Feb	
13	Sloane	Condo	Brookline	$430,000	Apr	
14	McGrath	Condo	Boston	$419,000	Apr	
15	Reynolds	Condo	Boston	$360,000	Mar	
16	Sloane	Condo	Brighton	$245,000	Mar	
17	McGrath	Condo	Brookline	$550,000	Jan	
18	McGrath	Condo	Brookline	$490,000	Feb	
19	Reynolds	House	Brighton	$402,000	Mar	
20	Ryan	House	Boston	$550,000	Feb	
21	Reynolds	Condo	Cambridge	$559,000	Feb	
22	Reynolds	House	Brighton	$315,000	Jan	
23	McGrath	House	Cambridge	$575,000	Jan	
24	McGrath	House	Cambridge	$602,000	Feb	
25	Sloane	Condo	Brookline	$435,000	Mar	
26	Ryan	Condo	Brookline	$418,000	Feb	
27						

4 Select Existing Worksheet and click in cell H6 (see Figure 8-3).

Figure 8-3

PivotTables can be added directly to the worksheet.

5   Click **OK** to open the PivotTable Fields pane, shown in Figure 8-4.

Figure 8-4

Select the fields you want to summarize in the PivotTable.

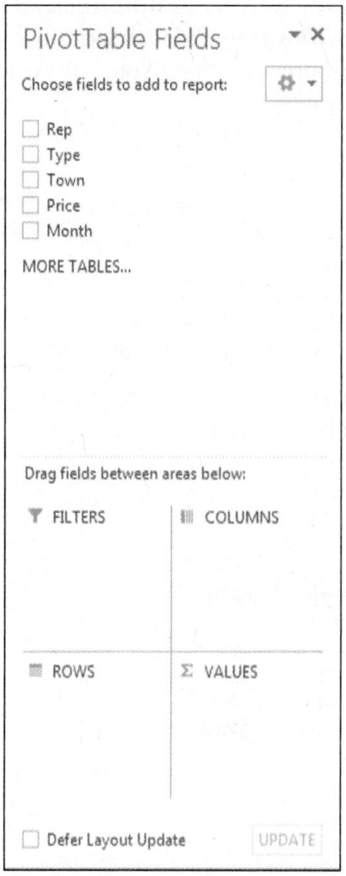

6   Select **Rep**, **Type**, **Town**, and **Price** in the Choose fields to add to report. As you select the fields, Excel automatically places them into the report layout in a single column layout.

7   To arrange the PivotTable in a more readable layout, click and drag **Town** to the Filters box, **Rep** to the Columns box, and leave Type in the Rows box and Price in the Values box. Excel redraws the PivotTable to display data organized by Type, as in Figure 8-5.

Figure 8-5

Arrange the layout of a PivotTable by dragging the fields to the appropriate location.

Town	(All)				
Sum of Price	Column Labels				
Row Labels	McGrath	Reynolds	Ryan	Sloane	Grand Total
Condo	1694000	1161000	647000	1110000	4612000
House	1502000	1092000	870000	340000	3804000
Grand Total	3196000	2253000	1517000	1450000	8416000

8   Choose **Field List** from the Show group on the Analyze tab to close the PivotTable Fields pane.

9   Save the file, but don't close it; you will use it the next section.

REARRANGING A PIVOTTABLE

Bottom Line

Once you have constructed a PivotTable, you can easily rearrange it through click and drag. When you drag fields to new locations, the PivotTable is automatically redrawn. To nest levels of data, add more than one field to the appropriate section. Note that removing fields from a PivotTable does not remove the data from the worksheet.

STEP BY STEP   **Rearranging fields**

1   Click in the **PivotTable**.

2   Choose **Field List** from the Analyze tab to redisplay the PivotTable Fields pane.

3   Drag **Type** to the Columns area and **Rep** to the Rows area. Excel redraws the PivotTable so that the data is arranged by Rep as in Figure 8-6.

Figure 8-6

Rearrange the layout of a PivotTable by dragging the fields to different locations.

Town	(All)		
Sum of Price	**Column Labels**		
Row Labels	**Condo**	**House**	**Grand Total**
McGrath	1694000	1502000	3196000
Reynolds	1161000	1092000	2253000
Ryan	647000	870000	1517000
Sloane	1110000	340000	1450000
Grand Total	**4612000**	**3804000**	**8416000**

STEP BY STEP   **Adding fields to a PivotTable**

1   Click in the PivotTable.

2   Select **Month** in the PivotTable Fields pane. Excel automatically adds it to the Rows area of the PivotTable. See Figure 8-7.

Figure 8-7

Nest data in a PivotTable by adding a new field to the column or row area.

Town	(All)		
Sum of Price	**Column Labels**		
Row Labels	**Condo**	**House**	**Grand Total**
⊟McGrath	1694000	1502000	3196000
Jan	550000	575000	1125000
Feb	725000	602000	1327000
Apr	419000	325000	744000
⊟Reynolds	1161000	1092000	2253000
Jan		315000	315000
Feb	801000		801000
Mar	360000	402000	762000
Apr		375000	375000
⊟Ryan	647000	870000	1517000
Jan	229000	320000	549000
Feb	418000	550000	968000
⊟Sloane	1110000	340000	1450000
Jan		340000	340000
Mar	680000		680000
Apr	430000		430000
Grand Total	**4612000**	**3804000**	**8416000**

3   Drag **Rep** to the Columns area and **Type** to the Rows area, below the Month field. Excel rearranges the PivotTable to display the data from the Rep field in each column and the data from the Type field in each row.

Removing fields from a PivotTable

1   Click in the PivotTable.

2   In the Rows area, click the arrow next to Type to display the drop-down menu, and then choose **Remove Field**. See Figure 8-8.

Figure 8-8

Remove a field from the PivotTable by deselecting its name from the Fields List.

3   From the fields list, select **Type** to add it back to the Rows area to add the Type data back to the PivotTable.

4   Save the file, but don't close it; you'll use it in the next section.

Take Note   A quicker way to remove a field from a PivotTable is to deselect it from the Fields list in the Pivot-Table Fields pane.

FORMATTING A PIVOTTABLE

You can format a PivotTable through any of the customization options available in Excel, which include changing the style of the table, adjusting number formats, and altering font and font sizes. The Design tab, a context-sensitive menu, appears in the Ribbon bar whenever the cell pointer is within a PivotTable.

Figure 8-9

PivotTables automatically nest multiple layers of data.

Town	(All)				
Sum of Price	**Column Labels**				
Row Labels	**McGrath**	**Reynolds**	**Ryan**	**Sloane**	**Grand Total**
⊟ Jan	1125000	315000	549000	340000	2329000
Condo	550000		229000		779000
House	575000	315000	320000	340000	1550000
⊟ Feb	1327000	801000	968000		3096000
Condo	725000	801000	418000		1944000
House	602000		550000		1152000
⊟ Mar		762000		680000	1442000
Condo		360000		680000	1040000
House		402000			402000
⊟ Apr	744000	375000		430000	1549000
Condo	419000			430000	849000
House	325000	375000			700000
Grand Total	3196000	2253000	1517000	1450000	8416000

Changing the layout

When you change the layout of the PivotTable, you can elect to display as little or as much information as you need to. (See Figure 8-9.) By default, Excel automatically applies the Compact layout to any new PivotTable you create.

Layout	Description
Compact	Keeps related data together in a nested format rather than spread out horizontally.
Outline	Data is displayed in a hierarchy across columns.
Tabular	Shows all data in table form, including subtotal and grand total amounts.

STEP BY STEP   **PivotTable layouts**

1   Using the file you used in the previous exercises, click in the PivotTable.

2   From the Design tab, choose Report Layout and select Show in Outline Form (Figure 8-10).

Figure 8-10

Change the Report Layout of your PivotTable to display more or less detail.

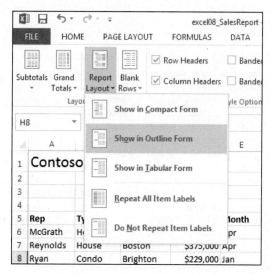

The data in the PivotTable appears with a column for each field, as in Figure 8-11.

Figure 8-11

Data in Outline form is displayed with a column for each field.

Town	(All)				
Sum of Price		Rep			
Month	**Type**	**McGrath**	**Reynolds**	**Ryan**	**Sloane**	**Grand Total**
Jan		1125000	315000	549000	340000	2329000
	Condo	550000		229000		779000
	House	575000	315000	320000	340000	1550000
Feb		1327000	801000	968000		3096000
	Condo	725000	801000	418000		1944000
	House	602000		550000		1152000
Mar			762000		680000	1442000
	Condo		360000		680000	1040000
	House		402000			402000
Apr		744000	375000		430000	1549000
	Condo	419000			430000	849000
	House	325000	375000			700000
Grand Total		3196000	2253000	1517000	1450000	8416000

3   From the Design tab, choose Report Layout once again.

4　Select **Show in Tabular Form**. All the data in the PivotTable appears, including subtotals and grand totals. See Figure 8-12.

Figure 8-12

The Tabular Layout displays all of the data in the PivotTable, including sub and grand totals.

Town	(All)					
Sum of Price		**Rep**				
Month	**Type**	**McGrath**	**Reynolds**	**Ryan**	**Sloane**	**Grand Total**
⊟Jan	Condo	550000		229000		779000
	House	575000	315000	320000	340000	1550000
Jan Total		**1125000**	**315000**	**549000**	**340000**	**2329000**
⊟Feb	Condo	725000	801000	418000		1944000
	House	602000		550000		1152000
Feb Total		**1327000**	**801000**	**968000**		**3096000**
⊟Mar	Condo		360000		680000	1040000
	House		402000			402000
Mar Total			**762000**		**680000**	**1442000**
⊟Apr	Condo	419000			430000	849000
	House	325000	375000			700000
Apr Total		**744000**	**375000**		**430000**	**1549000**
Grand Total		**3196000**	**2253000**	**1517000**	**1450000**	**8416000**

5　From the Design tab, choose **Report Layout** for the third time.

6　Select **Show in Compact Form**. The PivotTable appears in the default layout that Excel uses when you create a new PivotTable.

STEP BY STEP　　**Applying a style**

The PivotTable Styles are predefined formatting options that you can apply to the PivotTable for clarity. For example, adding banded columns or banded rows make large tables easier to read with shading.

1　Make sure your cell pointer is still in the PivotTable.

2　From the PivotTable Style Options group of the Design tab, choose **Banded Rows**.

3   From the PivotTable Styles group (Figure 8-13), select Pivot Style Light 16 if its not already selected.

Figure 8-13

Add banding and shading to a PivotTable to make large tables easier to read.

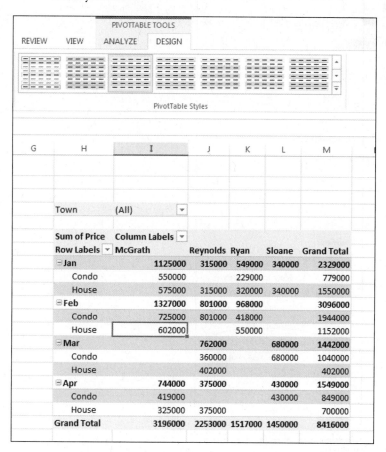

Town	(All)				
Sum of Price	**Column Labels**				
Row Labels	**McGrath**	**Reynolds**	**Ryan**	**Sloane**	**Grand Total**
⊟ Jan	1125000	315000	549000	340000	2329000
Condo	550000		229000		779000
House	575000	315000	320000	340000	1550000
⊟ Feb	1327000	801000	968000		3096000
Condo	725000	801000	418000		1944000
House	602000		550000		1152000
⊟ Mar		762000		680000	1442000
Condo		360000		680000	1040000
House		402000			402000
⊟ Apr	744000	375000		430000	1549000
Condo	419000			430000	849000
House	325000	375000			700000
Grand Total	3196000	2253000	1517000	1450000	8416000

STEP BY STEP   **Changing number formats in a PivotTable**

The values area of a PivotTable displays the numeric data from a worksheet list. The data displayed here is assigned the General numeric format by default.

1   Click in the PivotTable.

2   From the PivotTable Fields pane, click the Sum of Price button in the Values area.

3   Choose **Value Field Settings** from the resulting menu (see Figure 8-14).

Figure 8-14

Change the numeric format of the Values data.

4   In the Value Field Settings dialog box, click **Number Format**.

5   Choose **Currency** and decrease the Decimal Place setting to **0**.

6   Click **OK** in the Format Cells dialog box and click **OK** in the Value Field Settings dialog box. The Price values are now displayed in the Currency format, as in Figure 8-15.

Figure 8-15

Change the numeric format of the Values data in a PivotTable.

Town	(All)				
Sum of Price	**Column Labels**				
Row Labels	**McGrath**	**Reynolds**	**Ryan**	**Sloane**	**Grand Total**
⊟**Jan**	$1,125,000	$315,000	$549,000	$340,000	$2,329,000
Condo	$550,000		$229,000		$779,000
House	$575,000	$315,000	$320,000	$340,000	$1,550,000
⊟**Feb**	$1,327,000	$801,000	$968,000		$3,096,000
Condo	$725,000	$801,000	$418,000		$1,944,000
House	$602,000		$550,000		$1,152,000
⊟**Mar**		$762,000		$680,000	$1,442,000
Condo		$360,000		$680,000	$1,040,000
House		$402,000			$402,000
⊟**Apr**	$744,000	$375,000		$430,000	$1,549,000
Condo	$419,000			$430,000	$849,000
House	$325,000	$375,000			$700,000
Grand Total	$3,196,000	$2,253,000	$1,517,000	$1,450,000	$8,416,000

EDITING AND UPDATING A PIVOTTABLE

Bottom Line

When you create a PivotTable, a link is established between the source data in the worksheet and the PivotTable. If you make changes to the source data by adding new records or editing existing records, you need to update the PivotTable to reflect the changes.

STEP BY STEP | ### Updating data in a PivotTable

When you make changes to the source data in the worksheet, you must update the data in the PivotTable to reflect those changes.

1 Click in cell D23.

2 Type 975000 and press Enter.

3 Click any cell in the PivotTable.

4 From the Analyze tab, click the arrow below Refresh.

5 Select Refresh All to update the PivotTable with the latest data. See Figure 8-16.

Figure 8-16

Use the Refresh All command to update data in a PivotTable.

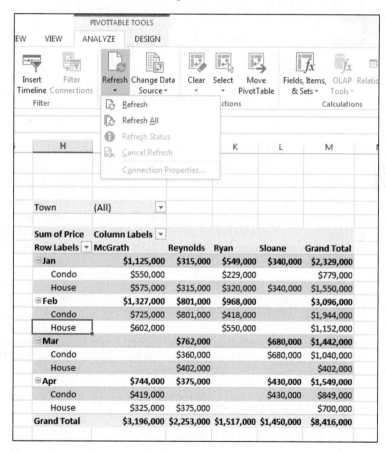

STEP BY STEP   **Expanding the source data range**

Whenever you add more records to the source range in the worksheet, you must update the data in the PivotTable.

1   Click in cell A27 and type **Sloane**; in cell B27 type **House**; in cell C27 type **Cambridge**; in cell D27 type **778000**; and in cell E27 type **Mar**.

2   Click any cell in the PivotTable.

3   From the Analyze tab, choose **Change Data Source**. Excel automatically highlights the source data range.

4   Press and hold **Shift** and press the **Down Arrow** key on your keyboard to extend the selection by one row. See Figure 8-17.

Figure 8-17

You must change the source range after adding new records in the source list.

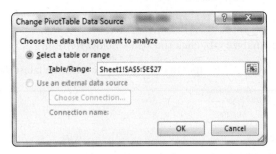

5   Click **OK** to change the data source. You can see that Sloane's house sale in Mar is updated in cell L16.

CHANGING THE CALCULATION

Bottom Line

After generating a PivotTable, you can change the way you choose to summarize the values and the way you choose to display them. When the items displayed in the Values area of the PivotTable are numeric, Excel automatically uses the SUM function to summarize the data. However, there are several other functions that you can use in the values area. The most commonly used function is SUM, but you can also use COUNT to display the number of items in the table; AVERAGE to find the Average amount; or MAX and MIN to find the maximum or minimum amounts.

STEP BY STEP   **Changing the summary function**

In the sample sales worksheet that you've been using for all the previous exercises, you will switch the summary function from SUM to COUNT so you can see how many total units were sold by each sales rep.

1   Click in cell I8.

2   From the Active Field group of the Analyze tab, choose **Field Settings**.

3   From the Summarize Value Field by list, choose Count and then click OK.

Figure 8-18

Change the Summary Function to calculate different values.

Town	(All)				
Count of Price	Column Labels				
Row Labels	McGrath	Reynolds	Ryan	Sloane	Grand Total
Jan	$2	$1	$2	$1	$6
Condo	$1		$1		$2
House	$1	$1	$1	$1	$4
Feb	$3	$2	$2		$7
Condo	$2	$2	$1		$5
House	$1		$1		$2
Mar		$2		$3	$5
Condo		$1		$2	$3
House		$1		$1	$2
Apr	$2	$1		$1	$4
Condo	$1			$1	$2
House	$1	$1			$2
Grand Total	$7	$6	$4	$5	$22

Excel changes the summary function to calculate the total items sold by each sales rep. Note in Figure 8-18 that the currency format is still in effect.

4   Choose Field Settings, click Number format, and select General.

5   Click OK twice to return to the worksheet. See Figure 8-19.

Figure 8-19

Count the number of items sold.

Town	(All)				
Count of Price	Column Labels				
Row Labels	McGrath	Reynolds	Ryan	Sloane	Grand Total
Jan	2	1	2	1	6
Condo	1		1		2
House	1	1	1	1	4
Feb	3	2	2		7
Condo	2	2	1		5
House	1		1		2
Mar		2		3	5
Condo		1		2	3
House		1		1	2
Apr	2	1		1	4
Condo	1			1	2
House	1	1			2
Grand Total	7	6	4	5	22

STEP BY STEP   Changing the summary type

By changing the summary type, you can choose the manner in which the values in the PivotTable are displayed. For example, you could calculate values based on the values of other cells; you could calculate the difference between items; or calculate the items as a percentage of a total. In our example, we will calculate the values as a percentage of total sales.

1   Click in cell I8.

2   From the Active Field group of the Analyze tab, choose Field Settings.

3   In the Summarize value field by, select Sum.

4   Click the Show Values As tab.

5   In the Show Values As box, select **% of Grand Total**, and then click **OK**. Sales are calculated as a percentage of Total. (See Figure 8-20.)

Figure 8-20

Calculate sales as a percentage of Total.

Town	(All)				
Sum of Price	**Column Labels**				
Row Labels	**McGrath**	**Reynolds**	**Ryan**	**Sloane**	**Grand Total**
⊟Jan	15.90%	3.28%	5.72%	3.54%	28.44%
Condo	5.73%	0.00%	2.39%	0.00%	8.12%
House	10.16%	3.28%	3.34%	3.54%	20.33%
⊟Feb	13.83%	8.35%	10.09%	0.00%	32.27%
Condo	7.56%	8.35%	4.36%	0.00%	20.26%
House	6.27%	0.00%	5.73%	0.00%	12.01%
⊟Mar	0.00%	7.94%	0.00%	15.20%	23.14%
Condo	0.00%	3.75%	0.00%	7.09%	10.84%
House	0.00%	4.19%	0.00%	8.11%	12.30%
⊟Apr	7.75%	3.91%	0.00%	4.48%	16.15%
Condo	4.37%	0.00%	0.00%	4.48%	8.85%
House	3.39%	3.91%	0.00%	0.00%	7.30%
Grand Total	37.48%	23.48%	15.81%	23.22%	100.00%

HIDING AND SHOWING DATA IN A PIVOTTABLE

Bottom Line

Working with data in a PivotTable is similar to working in outline mode. If your PivotTable is large, you can collapse some areas and expand others, or you can build additional structure into the table by grouping related items together. For instance, if you would like to summarize data at a level that is not present in the source data, you can group the data together in the PivotTable. In our sample worksheet, we can group the months into fiscal quarters and view the data that way.

STEP BY STEP   **Grouping items**

1   Click in cell H8, press and hold the **Ctrl** key, and then click **H11** and **H14**.

2   From the Analyze tab, choose **Group Selection**. Excel adds a new layer, Group1 to the PivotTable. (See Figure 8-21.)

Figure 8-21

Group similar items into a new category with the Group Selection command.

Town	(All)				
Sum of Price	**Column Labels**				
Row Labels	**McGrath**	**Reynolds**	**Ryan**	**Sloane**	**Grand Total**
⊟Group1					
⊟Jan	15.90%	3.28%	5.72%	3.54%	28.44%
Condo	5.73%	0.00%	2.39%	0.00%	8.12%
House	10.16%	3.28%	3.34%	3.54%	20.33%
⊟Feb	13.83%	8.35%	10.09%	0.00%	32.27%
Condo	7.56%	8.35%	4.36%	0.00%	20.26%
House	6.27%	0.00%	5.73%	0.00%	12.01%
⊟Mar	0.00%	7.94%	0.00%	15.20%	23.14%
Condo	0.00%	3.75%	0.00%	7.09%	10.84%
House	0.00%	4.19%	0.00%	8.11%	12.30%
⊟Apr					
⊟Apr	7.75%	3.91%	0.00%	4.48%	16.15%
Condo	4.37%	0.00%	0.00%	4.48%	8.85%
House	3.39%	3.91%	0.00%	0.00%	7.30%
Grand Total	37.48%	23.48%	15.81%	23.22%	100.00%

3   Click in the Active Field box in the Active Field group of the Analyze tab, type **Quarter**, and press **Enter**. The cells you selected are grouped together into a new category.

STEP BY STEP   **Ungrouping items**

1   Click in cell H8.

2   Choose Ungroup from the Analyze tab. Excel removes the group heading from the PivotTable and the Quarter field.

STEP BY STEP   **Collapsing and expanding PivotTable data**

The expand and collapse buttons, similar to those displayed in Outline mode, are added to a Pivot-Table when multiple levels of data are displayed. For instance, in the sales report, data is organized by month and then by type. You can collapse the level of detail when you want to see the big picture and expand it again to view the details.

1   Click the Collapse button, located to the left of the Jan field label, to collapse data for January.

2   Do the same for Feb, Mar, and Apr fields. See Figure 8-22.

Figure 8-22

Collapse detailed levels when you only want to view the big picture.

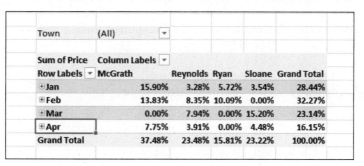

3   Click the Expand button for each month to display detail levels of data.

STEP BY STEP   **Filtering PivotTable data**

When you add a field to the Filter area of a PivotTable, data is automatically filtered by that field. Initially, all data is displayed in the PivotTable. To switch to the filter, click the Filter button and select the label by which you want to filter data.

1   Click the Filter button adjacent to the Town field in cell I4 (Figure 8-23).

2   Select **Boston** and click **OK**. Excel displays sales data for the Boston area only.

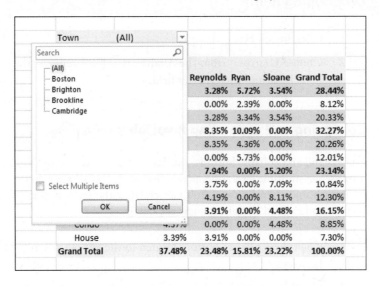

		Reynolds	Ryan	Sloane	Grand Total
		3.28%	5.72%	3.54%	28.44%
		0.00%	2.39%	0.00%	8.12%
		3.28%	3.34%	3.54%	20.33%
		8.35%	10.09%	0.00%	32.27%
		8.35%	4.36%	0.00%	20.26%
		0.00%	5.73%	0.00%	12.01%
		7.94%	0.00%	15.20%	23.14%
		3.75%	0.00%	7.09%	10.84%
		4.19%	0.00%	8.11%	12.30%
		3.91%	0.00%	4.48%	16.15%
Condo	4.37%	0.00%	0.00%	4.48%	8.85%
House	3.39%	3.91%	0.00%	0.00%	7.30%
Grand Total	37.48%	23.48%	15.81%	23.22%	100.00%

3   Click the filter next to Boston and choose **(All)** and click **OK**.

You can also filter records using the filter buttons for the row and column fields.

STEP BY STEP   **Filtering records at the column level**

1   Click the **Filter** button adjacent to the Column Labels field.

2   Click **Select All** to deselect the option.

3   Select **McGrath** and click **OK**. Excel filters the PivotTable to display data for sales rep McGrath only. See Figure 8-24.

Town	(All)	
Sum of Price	Column Labels	
Row Labels	McGrath	Grand Total
Jan	42.41%	42.41%
Condo	15.29%	15.29%
House	27.11%	27.11%
Feb	36.90%	36.90%
Condo	20.16%	20.16%
House	16.74%	16.74%
Apr	20.69%	20.69%
Condo	11.65%	11.65%
House	9.04%	9.04%
Grand Total	100.00%	100.00%

4   Click the **Filter** button next to Column Labels, choose **(Select All)** so all check boxes are filled, and click **OK**.

ADDING SUBTOTALS TO A PIVOTTABLE

Bottom Line

When you create a PivotTable, subtotal and grand total amounts are automatically generated for each level of data. You can decide where and when these amounts should be displayed.

Before adding subtotals to the Sales Report PivotTable, perform the following steps to redisplay the data as sales values instead of percentages.

STEP BY STEP | **Adding subtotals to a PivotTable**

1 Click cell I9 and choose Field Settings from the Analyze tab.

2 Click the Show Values As tab and select No Calculation from the drop-down menu.

3 Click Number Format and select Currency with 0 decimal places and click OK. Click OK again.

4 Click in cell I14 and choose Options from the PivotTable group on the Analyze tab.

5 In the Format section of the PivotTable Options dialog box, type 0 in the For empty cells show box. Click OK. (See Figure 8-25.)

Figure 8-25

Here the PivotTable displays a zero rather than a blank cell.

Town	(All)				
Sum of Price	Column Labels				
Row Labels	McGrath	Reynolds	Ryan	Sloane	Grand Total
Jan	$1,525,000	$315,000	$549,000	$340,000	$2,729,000
Condo	$550,000	$0	$229,000	$0	$779,000
House	$975,000	$315,000	$320,000	$340,000	$1,950,000
Feb	$1,327,000	$801,000	$968,000	$0	$3,096,000
Condo	$725,000	$801,000	$418,000	$0	$1,944,000
House	$602,000	$0	$550,000	$0	$1,152,000
Mar	$0	$762,000	$0	$1,458,000	$2,220,000
Condo	$0	$360,000	$0	$680,000	$1,040,000
House	$0	$402,000	$0	$778,000	$1,180,000
Apr	$744,000	$375,000	$0	$430,000	$1,549,000
Condo	$419,000	$0	$0	$430,000	$849,000
House	$325,000	$375,000	$0	$0	$700,000
Grand Total	$3,596,000	$2,253,000	$1,517,000	$2,228,000	$9,594,000

STEP BY STEP　　　**Formatting subtotal amounts**

1　Click in cell H9.

2　From the Design tab, choose Subtotals.

3　Choose Show all Subtotals at Bottom of Group. See Figure 8-26.

Figure 8-26

Subtotal amounts are displayed at the bottom of each group.

Town	(All)				
Sum of Price	**Column Labels**				
Row Labels	**McGrath**	**Reynolds**	**Ryan**	**Sloane**	**Grand Total**
Jan					
Condo	$550,000	$0	$229,000	$0	$779,000
House	$975,000	$315,000	$320,000	$340,000	$1,950,000
Jan Total	**$1,525,000**	**$315,000**	**$549,000**	**$340,000**	**$2,729,000**
Feb					
Condo	$725,000	$801,000	$418,000	$0	$1,944,000
House	$602,000	$0	$550,000	$0	$1,152,000
Feb Total	**$1,327,000**	**$801,000**	**$968,000**	**$0**	**$3,096,000**
Mar					
Condo	$0	$360,000	$0	$680,000	$1,040,000
House	$0	$402,000	$0	$778,000	$1,180,000
Mar Total	**$0**	**$762,000**	**$0**	**$1,458,000**	**$2,220,000**
Apr					
Condo	$419,000	$0	$0	$430,000	$849,000
House	$325,000	$375,000	$0	$0	$700,000
Apr Total	**$744,000**	**$375,000**	**$0**	**$430,000**	**$1,549,000**
Grand Total	**$3,596,000**	**$2,253,000**	**$1,517,000**	**$2,228,000**	**$9,594,000**

STEP BY STEP　　　**Formatting grand total amounts**

When you add grand total amounts to a PivotTable, they are calculated at the row and column level. Excel allows you to dictate where these amounts are added.

1　Click in cell H9.

2　From the Design tab, choose Grand Totals. See Figure 8-27.

Figure 8-27

Grand Totals are added at the row and column level.

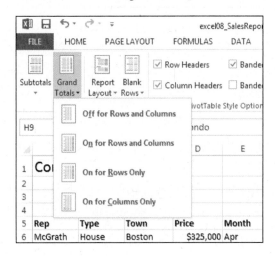

3 To display grand total amounts for rows only, choose **On for Rows Only**. See Figure 8-28.

Figure 8-28

Display Grand Total amounts for rows only in the PivotTable.

Town	(All)				
Sum of Price	**Column Labels**				
Row Labels	**McGrath**	**Reynolds**	**Ryan**	**Sloane**	**Grand Total**
Jan					
Condo	$550,000	$0	$229,000	$0	$779,000
House	$975,000	$315,000	$320,000	$340,000	$1,950,000
Jan Total	**$1,525,000**	**$315,000**	**$549,000**	**$340,000**	**$2,729,000**
Feb					
Condo	$725,000	$801,000	$418,000	$0	$1,944,000
House	$602,000	$0	$550,000	$0	$1,152,000
Feb Total	**$1,327,000**	**$801,000**	**$968,000**	**$0**	**$3,096,000**
Mar					
Condo	$0	$360,000	$0	$680,000	$1,040,000
House	$0	$402,000	$0	$778,000	$1,180,000
Mar Total	**$0**	**$762,000**	**$0**	**$1,458,000**	**$2,220,000**
Apr					
Condo	$419,000	$0	$0	$430,000	$849,000
House	$325,000	$375,000	$0	$0	$700,000
Apr Total	**$744,000**	**$375,000**	**$0**	**$430,000**	**$1,549,000**

4 From the Design tab, choose **Grand Totals** again.

5 To display grand total amounts for columns only, choose **On for Columns Only**. See Figure 8-29.

Figure 8-29

Display Grand Total amounts for columns in the PivotTable.

Town	(All)			
Sum of Price	**Column Labels**			
Row Labels	**McGrath**	**Reynolds**	**Ryan**	**Sloane**
Jan				
Condo	$550,000	$0	$229,000	$0
House	$975,000	$315,000	$320,000	$340,000
Jan Total	**$1,525,000**	**$315,000**	**$549,000**	**$340,000**
Feb				
Condo	$725,000	$801,000	$418,000	$0
House	$602,000	$0	$550,000	$0
Feb Total	**$1,327,000**	**$801,000**	**$968,000**	**$0**
Mar				
Condo	$0	$360,000	$0	$680,000
House	$0	$402,000	$0	$778,000
Mar Total	**$0**	**$762,000**	**$0**	**$1,458,000**
Apr				
Condo	$419,000	$0	$0	$430,000
House	$325,000	$375,000	$0	$0
Apr Total	**$744,000**	**$375,000**	**$0**	**$430,000**
Grand Total	**$3,596,000**	**$2,253,000**	**$1,517,000**	**$2,228,000**

6 To display grand total amounts for rows and columns again, choose **On for Rows and Columns from the Grand Totals** command.

7 Choose **File** > **Save** and then **File** > **Close**.

USING RECOMMENDED PIVOTTABLES

The Recommended PivotTables command, similar to the Recommended Charts command, assists in creating PivotTables by selecting an appropriate layout based on the data in the list. When you use this command, Excel automatically creates the PivotTable on a new worksheet.

STEP BY STEP | **Using recommended PivotTables**

1   Choose File > Open, navigate to the Excel08lessons folder and double-click **Sales_Report_B**.

2   Choose File > Save As, navigate to the Excel08lessons folder, name the file **Sales_Report_B_work**, and click Save.

3   Click in cell A6 and choose Recommended PivotTables from the Insert tab. See Figure 8-30.

Figure 8-30

Recommended PivotTables creates a layout based on the data in the list.

4   Select Sum of Price by Month and Type and click OK. The result is shown in Figure 8-31.

Figure 8-31

Excel inserts the PivotTable on a new worksheet.

	A	B	C	D	E
1					
2					
3	Sum of Price	Column Labels			
4	Row Labels	Condo	House	Grand Total	
5	Jan		779000	1950000	2729000
6	Feb		1944000	1152000	3096000
7	Mar		1040000	1180000	2220000
8	Apr		849000	700000	1549000
9	Grand Total		4612000	4982000	9594000
10					
29					
30					

Sheet2 | Sheet1

STEP BY STEP   Moving a PivotTable

Once you've created a PivotTable, you can move it to a new location in the current worksheet or to a new, blank worksheet. You can also move a PivotTable to an existing worksheet.

1   Click in cell B5 of the newly constructed worksheet.

2   From the Analyze tab, choose Move PivotTable.

3   In the resulting Move PivotTable dialog box, click the Sheet1tab, and click in cell N6. See Figure 8-32.

Figure 8-32

Excel inserts the PivotTable on a new worksheet.

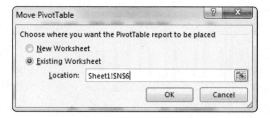

4   Click OK. Excel moves the PivotTable to cell N6 of Sheet1.

5   Click Undo to move the PivotTable back to Sheet2.

WORKING WITH PIVOTCHARTS

Bottom Line

A PivotChart is an interactive chart based on data in a PivotTable. Unlike a regular chart, which displays static data, a PivotChart is dynamic. Simply click the field buttons within the chart window and redisplay the data accordingly. You can filter data and change the summary function of the data values. You can also add and remove data fields and watch the chart update automatically. Note that any changes you make in the PivotChart, such as removing fields or filtering data, is also reflected in the PivotTable.

STEP BY STEP   Creating a PivotChart

1   Click in cell H9 on Sheet1 and choose PivotChart from the Analyze tab.

2   Click **OK** to accept the Clustered Column chart type. Excel adds the PivotChart to your worksheet, shown in Figure 8-33.

Figure 8-33

A PivotChart is a dynamic representation of a PivotTable.

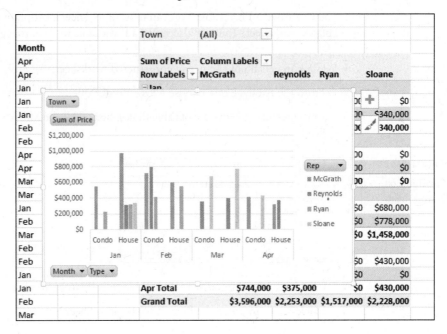

STEP BY STEP   Updating a PivotChart

1   Click and drag the **PivotChart** down to cell F26.

2   Use the scroll bars to scroll down so that the entire chart is displayed.

3   Resize the chart so that it is a little bigger by clicking and dragging a corner of the chart window. Release when the chart spans the range F26:M46.

4   Select **Month** in the PivotTable Fields pane to remove the field from the chart. Excel redraws the charts without the data for Month.

Note in Figure 8-34 that the data displayed in the chart reflects the data in the PivotTable so that when you remove the Month field from the chart the Month field is also removed from the Pivot-Table.

Figure 8-34

Remove data from the chart by deselecting the field name in the PivotTable Fields pane.

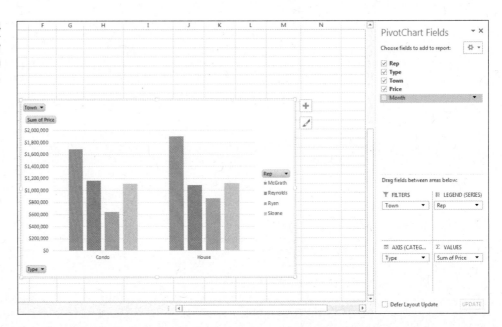

STEP BY STEP   **Filtering a PivotChart**

1   Click the Rep field button found directly above the legend on the right side of the chart. (Figure 8-35)

Figure 8-35

Filter data in the chart by selecting the items you want to see.

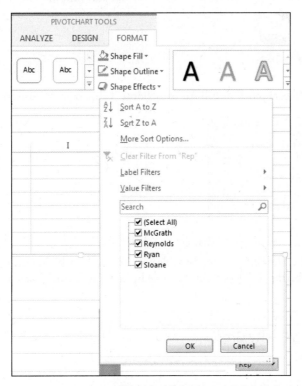

2   Deselect the Select All option.

3   Click McGrath and Sloane and click OK. As shown in Figure 8-36, Excel redraws the chart and displays data for Reps McGrath and Sloane only.

Figure 8-36

The PivotChart is redrawn to display filtered data.

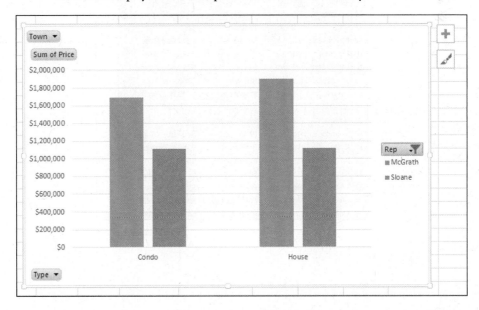

4   From the Analyze tab, choose Clear, and then choose Clear Filters. All the data is redisplayed.

WORKING WITH TABLES

Bottom Line

Data arranged in a list format, which we discussed in Lesson 6, can also be converted to an interactive table. When you convert a list to a table, Excel adds the filter buttons to the header row, and the data in the table is automatically selected. Once a list has been converted to a table, you can filter records, apply special table formatting, and add subtotal amounts to the data.

STEP BY STEP   **Creating a table**

1   On Sheet1, click in cell A6 and choose Table from the Insert tab. See Figure 8-37.

Figure 8-37

Indicate the range containing the table in the Create Table dialog box.

2   In the Create Table dialog box, click OK.

Excel adds the filter buttons to the table and selects the table range. (See figure 8-38.) These filters are used to rearrange the data in the table by clicking the appropriate filter button.

Figure 8-38

Filter buttons are automatically added to the header row in the table.

Rep	Type	Town	Price	Month
McGrath	House	Boston	$325,000	Apr
Reynolds	House	Boston	$375,000	Apr
Ryan	Condo	Brighton	$229,000	Jan
Ryan	House	Brighton	$320,000	Jan
Sloane	House	Brighton	$340,000	Jan
McGrath	Condo	Brighton	$235,000	Feb
Reynolds	Condo	Brighton	$242,000	Feb
Sloane	Condo	Brookline	$430,000	Apr
McGrath	Condo	Boston	$419,000	Apr
Reynolds	Condo	Boston	$360,000	Mar
Sloane	Condo	Brighton	$245,000	Mar
McGrath	Condo	Brookline	$550,000	Jan
McGrath	Condo	Brookline	$490,000	Feb
Reynolds	House	Brighton	$402,000	Mar
Ryan	House	Boston	$550,000	Feb
Reynolds	Condo	Cambridge	$559,000	Feb
Reynolds	House	Brighton	$315,000	Jan
McGrath	House	Cambridge	$975,000	Jan
McGrath	House	Cambridge	$602,000	Feb
Sloane	Condo	Brookline	$435,000	Mar

STEP BY STEP **Inserting slicers**

Slicers are similar to the filter buttons in that they allow you to dictate how you want to view the data in the table. Slicers are added to the worksheet in the form of an interactive button that makes it easy to change the views.

1   With the table still selected, choose Insert Slicer from the Design tab.

2   From the Insert Slicers dialog box, select Rep and Town. Then click OK. Excel adds two slicer objects to the worksheet: one for Rep and another for Town. See Figure 8-39.

Figure 8-39

Slicers offer a more visual way to filter worksheet data.

3   Click and drag the Rep slicer to cell F5 so that it is adjacent to the table. Click and drag the Town slicer so that it sits directly below the Rep slicer. (see Figure 8-40)

Figure 8-40

Since the buttons sit on top of your worksheet, you can clearly see which item is filtering the data.

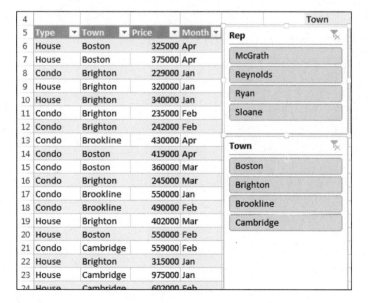

4   Click the McGrath button in the Rep slicer. Only those records containing McGrath as the rep are displayed in the table.

5   Press and hold the Ctrl key, and then click the Reynolds button. Only those records containing sales for McGrath and Reynolds are displayed, as in Figure 8-41.

Figure 8-41

Slicers appear highlighted when they are in use.

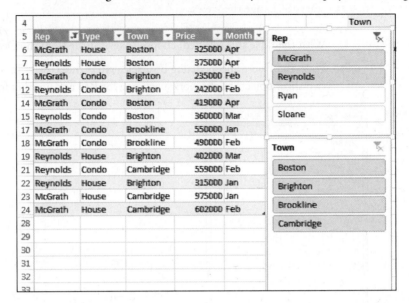

6   To clear the filters in use, click the Clear Filter button in the upper right area of the Slicer object.

STEP BY STEP   **Formatting a table**

With Table Styles, you can apply styles to the range of data in the table. You can also change the color of the slicer objects.

1   Select **A5:E27** the Design tab, choose **Table Styles**. Notice in Figure 8-42 that styles are categorized by Light, Medium, and Dark color.

Figure 8-42

Table Styles are categorized according to color.

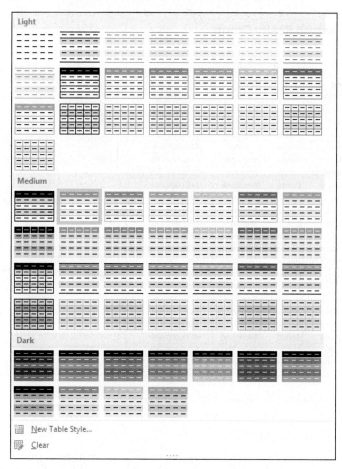

2   Choose **Table Style Light 21**.

3   Click the **Rep** slicer and click the Options tab.

4   Choose **Slicer Style Light 6**.

5   Click the Town slicer and choose Slicer Style Light 6 from the Options tab. (See Figure 8-43.)

Figure 8-43

Slicers and Tables can use the same style for consistency.

6   Choose File > Save and File > Close.

WHAT-IF ANALYSIS

Bottom Line

As discussed in Lesson 4, "Using Formulas," you can use formulas to calculate values based on data stored in worksheet cells. Whenever you change the values in the referenced cells, Excel re-calculates the formula to reflect that change. **What-if analysis** enables you to test possible end results by entering a series of different values in those referenced cells.

Excel offers three tools for performing What-If analysis: Goal Seek, Scenarios, and Data Tables. With **Goal Seek**, you can achieve a desired result by changing values used within the formula. Scenarios allow you to store the result of each what-if analysis for comparison. A Data Table allows you to create a range of results by substituting multiple variables in the formula.

STEP BY STEP   **Using Goal Seek**

With the Goal Seek command, you can test out a specific result by changing a variable in a formula. For example, you can find out how much of a mortgage you could afford based on a budgeted monthly payment by adjusting the mortgage amount variable.

1   With Excel open, choose File > Open and click Computer in the Backstage view. Navigate to the Excel08lessons folder and open the file named **What_If**.

2 Choose **File > Save As**, navigate back to the Excel08lessons folder, name the file **What_If_work**, and click **Save**.

3 Click in cell B11 and choose **What-If Analysis** from the Data tab.

4 Choose **Goal Seek** from the resulting drop-down menu. (Figure 8-44)

Figure 8-44

Alter data in formulas to achieve specific results with Goal Seek.

5 In the To value field, type **1800**.

6 In the By changing cell field, type **B9**. See Figure 8-45.

Figure 8-45

Adjust the principal amount so the monthly payment can be met.

7 Click **OK**. Excel recalculates the formula until a result is found that meets the monthly payment variable. See Figure 8-46.

Figure 8-46

Goal Seek adjusts the amount of the principal to meet the monthly payment requirement.

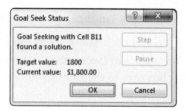

8 Click **OK** to close the Goal Seek Status dialog box.

STEP BY STEP **Managing scenarios**

Scenarios allow you to save a set of variables and the resulting formulas. You can then compare results by flipping through each saved scenario. For example, you could find out how much a monthly mortgage payment would be based on a 30 or 15-year fixed interest rate.

1 Select range **B7:B8** and choose **What-If Analysis** from the Data tab.

2 From the resulting drop-down menu, choose **Scenario Manager**.

3 In the Scenario Manager dialog box, click the **Add** button.

4   In the Scenario Name box, type **30 YR Fixed** and click **OK**. See Figure 8-47.

Figure 8-47

Save a set of variables as a
scenario.

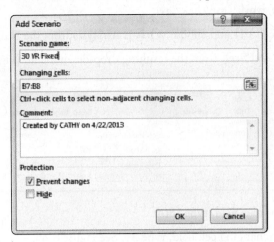

5   In the first variable box, Type **.0345** and click **Add**. See Figure 8-48.

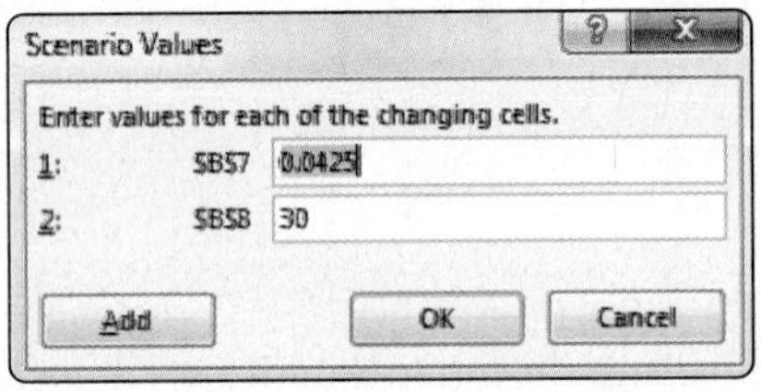

Figure 8-48

Enter the variables in the
Scenario Values dialog box.

6   In the Scenario Name box, type **15 YR Fixed** and click **OK**.

7   Type **.02625** in the first variable box, **15** in the second variable box, and then click **OK**.

8   Click the **15 YR Fixed** scenario and click **Show**. Excel switches the data in the worksheet to reflect the data variables in the scenario. You may need to click and drag the Scenario Manager dialog box over to the right so you can see the data changes.

9 Click the 30 YR Fixed Scenario and click Show (see Figure 8-49) to switch back to the 30 YR Fixed amount.

Figure 8-49

Show the results of a scenario in the worksheet.

10 Click Close to close the Scenario Manager.

Create a data table

Bottom Line

A **data table** is made up of a single formula and a range of input values that are substituted for a specific variable in the formula. A two-variable data table allows you to substitute two separate variables in the formula. For example, in a one-variable table, you could enter a series of interest rates and Excel would calculate the monthly payment based on the interest rate amount. In a two-variable table, you could enter a series of interest rates and principal amounts to return a table of monthly loan payments.

STEP BY STEP   **Creating a one-input variable table**

1 Click in cell F8, type .020, and press the Tab key.

2 In cell G8, type .025 and press Enter.

3 Select range F8:G8 and click and drag the Fill handle to the left to cell M8.

4 Type =PMT(B7/12,B8*12,B9) in cell E9 and press Enter. Note that Excel automatically applies the Currency format to the cell.

5   Select range **F8:M8** and choose **Percentage** from the Number Format drop-down menu on the Home tab. Then, click the **Decrease Decimal** button to remove one decimal space.

6   Select range **E8:M9** and choose **What-If Analysis** from the Data tab.

7   Choose **Data Table** from the resulting drop-down menu, shown in Figure 8-50.

Figure 8-50

Enter a range of Input variables.

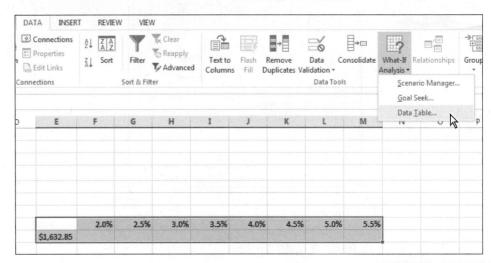

8   In the Row input cell box, type **B7** and click **OK**. Excel generates a table of monthly payments based on the Interest rate amounts, shown in Figure 8-51.

Figure 8-51

A Data Table generates a table of values based on the input variables.

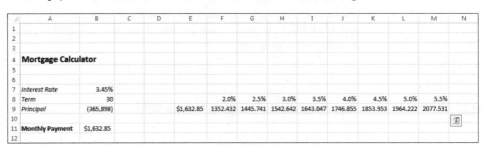

STEP BY STEP   Create a two-Input Variable Table

1   Select range **F8:M8**, choose **Copy** from the Home tab, click in cell F12, and press **Enter**.

2   In cell E12, type **=PMT(B7/12,B8*12,B9)** and press **Enter**.

3   In cell E13, type **300000**; in cell E14, type **325000**.

4   Select range **E13:E14** and click and drag the **Fill** handle downwards to cell E25.

5   Select range **E12:M25** and choose **What-If Analysis** from the Data tab.

6   Choose **Data Table** from the resulting menu.

7   In the Row Input box, type **B7**; in the Column Input box, type **B9**. Click **OK** to generate the results. See Figure 8-52.

Figure 8-52

The data table generates monthly payments based on the interest rate and principal amount.

$1,632.85	2.0%	2.5%	3.0%	3.5%	4.0%	4.5%	5.0%	5.5%
300000	-$1,108.86	-$1,185.36	-$1,264.81	-$1,347.13	-$1,432.25	-$1,520.06	-$1,610.46	-$1,703.37
325000	-$1,201.26	-$1,284.14	-$1,370.21	-$1,459.40	-$1,551.60	-$1,646.73	-$1,744.67	-$1,845.31
350000	-$1,293.67	-$1,382.92	-$1,475.61	-$1,571.66	-$1,670.95	-$1,773.40	-$1,878.88	-$1,987.26
375000	-$1,386.07	-$1,481.70	-$1,581.02	-$1,683.92	-$1,790.31	-$1,900.07	-$2,013.08	-$2,129.21
400000	-$1,478.48	-$1,580.48	-$1,686.42	-$1,796.18	-$1,909.66	-$2,026.74	-$2,147.29	-$2,271.16
425000	-$1,570.88	-$1,679.26	-$1,791.82	-$1,908.44	-$2,029.02	-$2,153.41	-$2,281.49	-$2,413.10
450000	-$1,663.29	-$1,778.04	-$1,897.22	-$2,020.70	-$2,148.37	-$2,280.08	-$2,415.70	-$2,555.05
475000	-$1,755.69	-$1,876.82	-$2,002.62	-$2,132.96	-$2,267.72	-$2,406.76	-$2,549.90	-$2,697.00
500000	-$1,848.10	-$1,975.60	-$2,108.02	-$2,245.22	-$2,387.08	-$2,533.43	-$2,684.11	-$2,838.95
525000	-$1,940.50	-$2,074.38	-$2,213.42	-$2,357.48	-$2,506.43	-$2,660.10	-$2,818.31	-$2,980.89
550000	-$2,032.91	-$2,173.16	-$2,318.82	-$2,469.75	-$2,625.78	-$2,786.77	-$2,952.52	-$3,122.84
575000	-$2,125.31	-$2,271.95	-$2,424.22	-$2,582.01	-$2,745.14	-$2,913.44	-$3,086.72	-$3,264.79
600000	-$2,217.72	-$2,370.73	-$2,529.62	-$2,694.27	-$2,864.49	-$3,040.11	-$3,220.93	-$3,406.73

8   Choose **File > Save** and then **File > Close**.

What you learned in this lesson:

- Introduction to PivotTables

- Creating, Rearranging, and Formatting PivotTables

- Editing and Updating a PivotTable

- Changing PivotTable Calculations

- Hiding and Showing Data in a PivotTable

- Adding Subtotals to a PivotTable

- Using Recommended PivotTables

- Working with PivotCharts

- Working with Tables

- What-If Analysis

Knowledge Assessment

True/False

Circle T if the statement is true or F it the statement is false.

T   F   1. A PivotTable updates automatically when its source data changes.

T   F   2. Once a dataset has received table formatting, it can't be converted back to a regular list.

T   F   3. Multiple slicers can be enabled for a single table.

T   F   4. To remove data series from a PivotChart, deselect their labels in the PivotChart Fields pane.

T   F   5. The entire data range must be selected before you can invoke the Insert > PivotTable command.

T   F   6. Removing a PivotChart from a worksheet is as simple as selecting it and pressing Delete.

T   F   7. Data tables can be created with up to two variable inputs.

T   F   8. Excel's default summary function for numeric data is the AVERAGE function.

T   F   9. Excel will automatically extend a PivotTable's source data range when new records are added.

T   F   10. The Scenario Manager tool lets you save sets of variable values and formula outputs with an identifying scenario name.

Fill in the blanks

Complete the following sentences by writing the correct word or words in the blanks provided.

1. PivotTables contain _____ different kinds of fields.

2. Creating a PivotTable establishes a _____ between the source data and the PivotTable itself.

3. A PivotTable full of numeric data will automatically use the _____ function to summarize that data.

4. You can choose which PivotTable rows to display with the expand and _____ buttons.

5. To apply a slicer to a dataset, first convert the data to a _____.

6. Slicer settings are adjusted from the _____ ribbon tab.

7. The _____ tool iterates the value of a formula variable until the function generates a desired outcome.

8. Excel displays a range of variable values and their associated function outputs in a _____ table.

9. To add a field to a PivotTable, drag its name from the _____ section of the PivotTable pane to the _____ section.

10. A _____ is a dynamically-generated interactive graph or chart.

Competency Assessment

Project 8-1: Creating a PivotTable

In this exercise you'll create and manipulate a PivotTable.

1. Open the project file **pivot_source**. Save your document as **project_8-1_pivot**.
2. Click somewhere in the data region of Sheet1.
3. Select Insert > PivotTable. Target it to an Existing Worksheet, in cell H3. Click OK.
4. In the PivotChart Fields pane, drag Party to Filters, Precinct to Rows, and Years Registered and Last name to Values.
5. In the Values box in the lower right of the pane, click the Sum of Years registered drop-down. Select Values Field Settings...
6. Change Sum to Average in the dropdown list. Click OK.
7. Change Row Labels to Precinct in cell H3. Set J3's text to # of Voters.
8. Experiment with the Party filter dropdown in cell H1.
9. Save and close your document.

Project 8-2: Creating a PivotChart

In this exercise you'll create a PivotChart from a dataset and experiment with different arrangements of the data.

1. Open the project file **8-2-source**. Save your document as **project_8-2_chart**.
2. Click somewhere in the data region of Sheet1.
3. Select Insert > PivotChart > PivotChart, and place the chart on a new worksheet.
4. Add the following fields: Legend=Precinct, Axis=Party, Values=Party.

   This graph highlights strong precincts for each party affiliation – the taller the bar, the more voters have that affiliation in that precinct.
5. Select Design > Change Chart Type, and choose the Pie chart type.
6. Rearrange fields: Axis=Party, Values=Party, Filters=Precinct.
7. Click the Count of Party dropdown arrow. Choose Values Field Settings, and from the Show Values As tab and dropdown, select % of Grand Total.
8. Select the chart itself, and in the Chart Elements pane, select Data Labels.
9. Experiment with filtering the PivotChart to see percentage breakdowns for each precinct.
10. Save and close your document.

Proficiency Assessment

Project 8-3: Using Goal Seek

In this exercise you'll use Goal Seek to determine the appropriate yearly interest rate, compounded monthly, to double your savings in five years.

1. Open project file **goal_seek** and save your work as **project_8-3_goal_seek**.
2. Select Data > Data Tools > What-If Analysis > Goal Seek...
3. In the dialog box, set cell C11 to **6000** by changing cell C9. Click OK.
4. Copy the column C data to column F.
5. In column F, use Goal Seek to find the appropriate annual interest rate to turn $10,000 into $100,000 in five years. Display the answer in F9.
6. Save and close your document.

Project 8-4: Using Data Tables

In this exercise you'll create a data table to compare payouts for an interest-bearing security, for varying interest rates and lengths of time.

1. Open the project file **8-4-source**. Save your document as **project_8-4_data_table**.
2. Double click cell **F7** and copy its formula (not the cell itself) to F15.
3. In F15, replace ^60 with ^(J8*12), and type **5** in cell J8.
   This allows you to vary the length of the investment.
4. Fill G15:K15 with the values **1**, **2**, **3**, **10**, and **20**.
5. Fill F16:F19 with the values **5%**, **10%**, **15%**, and **20%**.
   Now create the data table in the space outlined by the values you just input.
6. Select **F15:K19**. Then select Data > What-If Analysis > Data Table...
7. For the row input cell, select J8; for column input, F3. Click OK.
8. Confirm that cell I17, which duplicates the original interest rate and length of time from F15 (10%, 5 years), generates the same value as F15.
9. Save and close your document.

Mastery Assessment

Project 8-5: The Scenario Manager

In this exercise you'll carry out What-If Analysis using the Scenario Manager.

1. Open the project file **monthly_costs**. Save it as **project_8-5_scenario**.
2. Use the Scenario Manager (under Data > What-If Analysis) to create two scenarios, called City Center and Suburb. Use the following values:

Line item	City Center	Suburb
Rent	1200	950
Food	650	450
Charity	50	50
Transport	80	150
Internet	50	50
TV	0	50

3. Display the total annual cost for each below the data region on Sheet1.
4. Save and close your document.

Project 8-6: PivotTables and PivotCharts Part 2

This exercise challenges you to duplicate a PivotChart given a dataset.

1. Open the project file **pivot_source_3**. Save it as **project_8-6_pivot2**.
2. Use the data on Sheet1 to duplicate the following PivotChart:

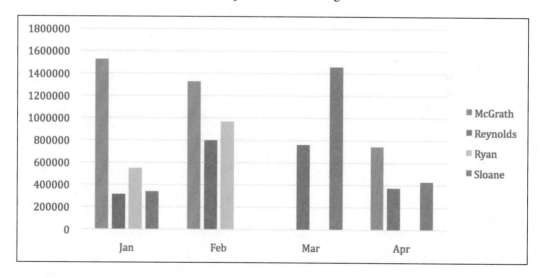

Note which categories have been used for Legend, Axis, and Value in the PivotChart – for instance, the Legend lists the four representatives' names.

3. Save your work and close Excel.

Microsoft PowerPoint 2013

1 Microsoft PowerPoint 2013 Jumpstart

LESSON SKILL MATRIX

In this lesson, you will learn the following skills:

Selecting and Opening a Template	Adding Animations and Transitions
Adding Slides	Switching presentation Themes
Editing Slide Text	Presenting a Slide Show
Placing Images into Slides	Adding Speaker Notes

KEY TERMS

- Variant
- Widescreen
- Change Case
- WYSIWYG
- Speaker Notes
- Exit Animation
- Transition
- Slide Sorter

Contoso's one thousand employees are spread over four buildings and a dozen departments. Staying on top of other groups' progress, even within a single project, can be daunting, especially when two groups have wildly different areas of expertise. Workplace presentations – from slide shows online to point-by-point in-person talks – are vital to Contoso's operations. PowerPoint helps engineers, marketers, researchers, admins, accountants, and managers make their ideas "stick." It's a tool for that most memorable workplace activity: show-and-tell.

SOFTWARE ORIENTATION

You'll quickly create your first presentation using PowerPoint in this lesson where you'll discover the process for adding slides, editing text, importing images, and using presentation themes.

Figure 1-1

Microsoft PowerPoint 2013 Workspace.

STARTING UP

In this lesson, you'll work with several files from the PPT01lessons folder. Make sure that you have loaded the lesson files onto your computer.

This Jumpstart lesson contains minimal explanation of the basic functions you'll use in every PowerPoint 2013 presentation: selecting a theme, adding slides, editing text, inserting images, applying basic animations, and starting a slide show. Most PowerPoint presentations are no more complicated than the sample file in this lesson. The remaining lessons explore these functions in greater detail, introduce some of PowerPoint's more advanced features, and introduce you to topics such as presentation style and visual design.

After completing the work in this lesson, you'll have a file that looks like **pp01c-finished.pptx**; feel free to consult that file at any point. Now launch PowerPoint 2013. The launch screen is shown in Figure 1-2.

Figure 1-2

Rather than a blank document, PPT 2013's launch screen offers templates and recent files.

Choosing a template

Bottom Line

We'll use one of PowerPoint's ready-made templates to structure and style our slides. Templates are premade documents, ready to be filled in with your content. Office 2013 offers templates with multiple color schemes (**Variants**), providing some flexibility within each design.

Choosing a template

1   From the Template Gallery, select the Ion template.

2   A window pops up with four color choices. Select the purple variant (see Figure 1-3) and click Create.

Figure 1-3

Select the purple variant of the Ion template.

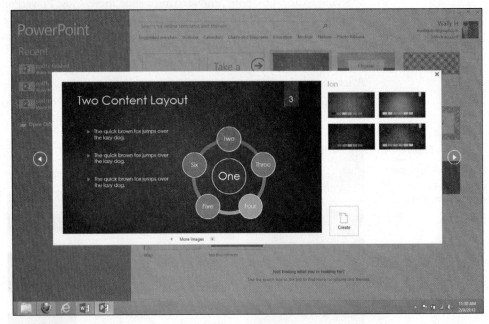

The main document screen appears, initially split into three parts: Ribbon and toolbar at the top, a pane containing all the presentation's slides at left, and the document editing area taking up most of the screen.

Take Note   Previous editions of PowerPoint supported **widescreen** presentations as a supplementary option: you had to tweak aspect ratios manually to get to a widescreen format. As you can see, we're starting the lesson with a widescreen template, and you can move fluidly between widescreen (16:9) and old-fashioned TV (4:3) formats with the Design > Slide Size button.

Editing the title slide

By default, templates open with a Title Slide. The title slide skeleton contains two text boxes (title and subtitle) with minimal empty space for visual decoration. The Slides pane displays a preview of the slide with all elements in place: the placeholder text (Click to add title) appears only in the editing area.

Editing the title slide

1   Click in the Title text box and type Digital Publishing.

2   Click in the Subtitle text box and type From raw text to printed output.

Note that the subtitle is formatted in all caps. You can change the look of the subtitle with the Home > Font > Change Case command.

3   Choose File > Save As and navigate to the PPT01lesson folder. Name the document **Publishing-Markup** and press Enter.

Adding slides

Bottom Line

To add a slide, you can select a slide type from the New Slide drop-down menu or press Ctrl+M to insert a new slide with the current slide's layout, then change its layout afterward.

STEP BY STEP   **Adding slides**

1   Press Ctrl+M three times to insert three slides after the current slide. Leave slide 2 as is.

Pressing Ctrl+M with the title slide selected inserts a blank heading/content block slide. PowerPoint is smart enough to know you don't want two title slides.

2   Select slide 3 in the Slides pane and change its layout by clicking Home > Slides > Layout > Comparison. (You can also right-click the slide preview and choose Layout from the context menu.)

3   Use the same command to change slide 4 to the Panoramic Picture with Caption layout.

Adding text to your presentation

Bottom Line

Now we can add content to our slides. As you've already seen from adding slides after the title slide, PowerPoint makes some simplifying assumptions about your document; these will streamline the process of building your presentation.

STEP BY STEP   **Adding text to your presentation**

1   Select slide 2. Click in the slide title box and type why work with plain text?

2   Select the text you just entered and select Home > Font > Change Case > Capitalize Each Word, and then correct the resulting capitalization by changing With to with.

PowerPoint can also automatically capitalize certain paragraph styles (for instance, the title slide's subtitle) but the **Change Case** command is for quick changes.

3   Click in the main text area of slide 2, which is formatted to produce bulleted text by default. Enter the following text (remember that Tab increases indent level, Shift+Tab decreases it):

- Portable

- Easy to Edit

- Modern markup

  - Single source

  - Human readable

Take Note   Picking a font size for a PowerPoint presentation is slightly more complex than sizing for the printed page; 12 point text should be the same size on notebook paper and in a 6×9 trade paperback, but the readability (indeed, the size) of slide text is highly dependent on the size and quality of the projection screen. We strongly suggest following this general principle: go big for those in the back row of the auditorium.

4   Select all the text in the bulleted list and click **Home > Font > Increase Font Size** (**Ctrl+Shift+>**) five times; the list should nearly fill the text area, as in Figure 1-4.

Figure 1-4

Increase the font size five times.

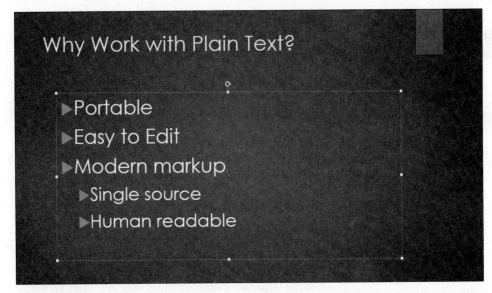

Now we'll add the slide number to all but the first slide; since we're using a built-in template, there's already a spot set aside for it on every slide.

5   Click **Insert > Text > Header & Footer**. Make sure the Slide number and Don't show on title slide check boxes are marked as in Figure 1-5. Click **Apply to All**.

Figure 1-5

Adding slide numbers to our presentation.

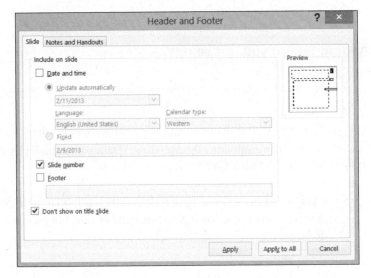

6   Choose **File > Save** or press **Ctrl+S** to save your work.

Adding visuals to a slide

Most built-in PowerPoint 2013 slide layouts include content areas with buttons to add standard visual elements: images, video, Excel data, charts, etc. (Title slides, on the other hand, are laid out with the assumption that they'll include only text.) Just as in the other Office 2013 applications, you can use the Insert tools to add objects to a slide, but if you don't want to bother with formatting, the content area controls (shown in Figure 1-6) will let you add visuals easily.

Figure 1-6

Use the content controls to insert charts, graphs, images, spreadsheets, and video in a slide content area.

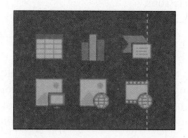

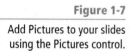

STEP BY STEP   **Adding visuals to a slide**

1   Switch to slide 3. In the title box, type Visual Editing vs Markup.

2   Type WYSIWYG (short for What You See Is What You Get) in the heading area to the left, and Markup in the right.

3   In the content area to the left, click the Pictures control. Navigate to your PPT01lessons folder and select **pp01a.png**. Click Insert.

4   Do the same in the box to the right, but insert the image **pp01b.png**.

Figure 1-7

Add Pictures to your slides using the Pictures control.

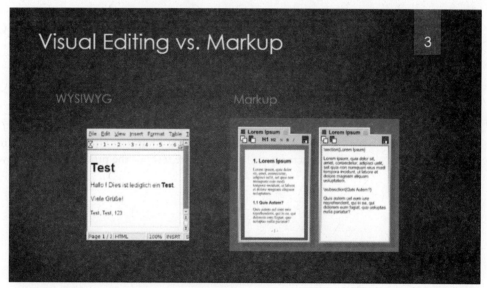

The two images aren't the same size or proportion (see Figure 1-7), so the slide is currently unsightly. With help from PowerPoint's layout guides and basic image editing tools, you can quickly and easily make rudimentary layout corrections.

5   Click View > Show > Guides to turn on responsive guidelines. Drag the left hand image up and to the left until its top edge is flush with the other image's and its left edge is flush with the word **WYSIWYG**. Orange dotted guidelines will appear when you get close. (You can Use the zoom slider on the Status Bar to zoom in on the slide for fine control over positioning.)

6   Use the image handles to make the right image (Markup) the same height as the WYSIWYG image; again, an orange guideline will appear along the bottom edge of the two images to indicate when you've matched the size.

7   Choose File > Save to save your work.

The Show Guides feature works the same in PowerPoint and Word; it's most obviously useful when laying out complex pages, but PowerPoint slides are rarely as complex as, say, a newsletter. We'll see its full usefulness in later lessons.

FROM SLIDE DECK TO PRESENTATION

As you build your slide deck, we recommend stopping periodically and clicking through the presentation as if you were presenting to an audience; even without your commentary, this practice will give you a sense for the flow of the slides. Viewing the presentation without busy user interface elements like the Ribbon and Status Bar will also let you see and think about the look and feel of the slides themselves.

Including speaker notes

Bottom Line

Speaker notes are additional text pieces attached to your slides. You can use them as prompts or scripts while you give your talk. They're for your eyes only; the audience won't see them. We'll add an image and caption to slide 4, and then start to annotate our presentation with speaker notes. When we've finished designing the slides and making notes, we'll run through the rough draft of the presentation.

STEP BY STEP   **Adding speaker notes**

1   Turn off guidelines by deselecting View > Show > Guides. Click to select slide 4. In the large content area, click the icon to add a picture. Navigate to the PPT01lessons folder and select **pp01d.png**. Click Insert or press Enter to add the image.

2   In the title box, type **Live Preview: best of both worlds**. In the bottom content area, type **Modern apps let you see multiple (beautiful) outputs from a single readable text source**.

As you can see from Figure 1-8, this is a fairly lengthy piece of text, and probably too small for easy reading onscreen; we'll see when we test out the presentation. Next we'll add notes to each slide.

3 Click View > Show > Notes to display a pane with speaker notes. Add the following note to slide 4: **Stress cross-platform for corporate audience.**

Figure 1-8

Add speaker notes to each slide.

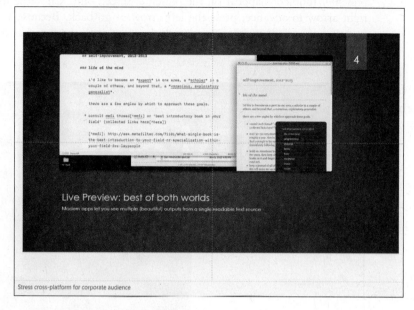

4 Add the note **Final bullet: analogy to HTML** to slide 2, and **Dynamic numbering makes outlining less stressful** to slide 3.

5 Finally, add the following note to the title slide: **MAKE SURE TO THANK THE MONEY GUYS** (don't forget all caps). Save your work.

Practicing the slide show

Bottom Line

The Slide Show tab is full of tools to configure and run the presentation (Slide Show) itself. The Set Up Slide Show command lets you configure the presentation for different viewing modes: projecting onscreen at a talk, running repeatedly at a kiosk, or simply viewed on a single user's screen. We'll use the default options for now, and view the slide show in Presenter Mode to see what the tool offers.

STEP BY STEP   **Playing the slide show**

1 Using the **Publishing-Markup** file, open the Slide Show tab and select Start Slide Show > From Beginning to start the presentation. The slide show runs in full screen mode; to return to the editing screen, press Escape.

What you see in the basic Slide Show view is essentially the same as what an audience would see on a mirrored display device; but when you mouse over the lower-left part of the screen, a set of presenter tool icons appear on the presenter screen only. Click the mouse or press space/return/ right arrow to advance; press the left arrow to go back. Because your presentation doesn't yet contain animations or transitions, each time you press the spacebar or right arrow you'll advance one slide.

Figure 1-9

Presenter tools in the basic Slide Show view.

When you move the mouse in the Slide Show, a set of controls is revealed in the lower left of your (presenter) screen, but hidden from the audience. These controls, shown in Figure 1-9, provide access to the Pen Tools (laser pointer, highlighter, pen), zoom mode (zoom in on part of the screen), slide selector, and an options screen that includes Presenter View, shown in Figure 1-10.

STEP BY STEP   **Using the Presenter View**

1   Click the (...) button and select Show Presenter View.

Figure 1-10

The revamped Presenter View emphasizes presentation flow along with the current slide content.

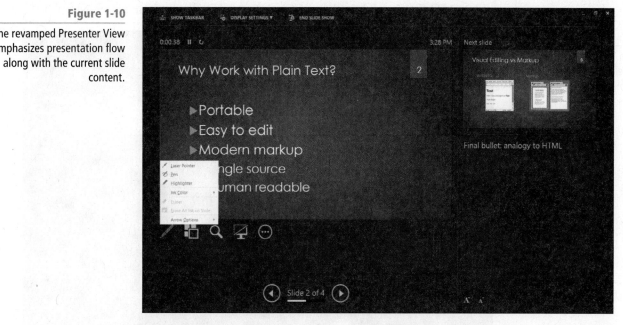

Presenter View is a private view of your presentation: a control center for the presenter. It provides ready access to speaker notes, a view of the next slide, a timer and clock, an overall status bar, and access to pen tools, zoom, and slide sorter. It's meant to keep you abreast of your presentation as an audience (theatrical) event rather than a series of static images.

Take special note of the timer; it can be paused and reset, letting you time individual slides while you practice your talk, or pause while you clean up some infelicity of text or speech.

Take Note   Of all the Office 2013 applications, PowerPoint is the obvious candidate for deep touchscreen integration: slides can naturally be manipulated directly by fingertips or pen. If you're working on a Surface or other Windows tablet, Presenter View provides a nice showcase for Office 2013's new touch-based UI.

2 Advance to slide 2. From the Pen Tool menu, select the Highlighter and highlight a couple of bulleted lines. Then select the pen tool and circle the words *Modern markup*. This is the point where, according to your speaker notes, you'd emphasize the ease of translating between markup languages for humans and those for machines (like HTML). The slide with handwritten annotations is shown in Figure 1-11.

Figure 1-11

Pen Tools let you emphasize slide elements during your live presentation.

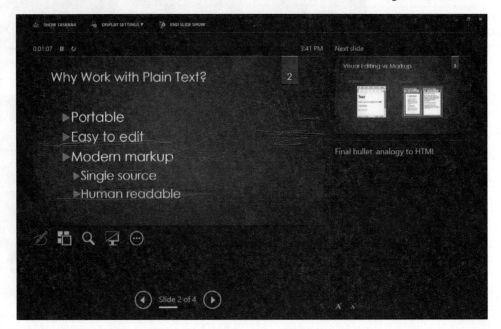

3 Click the Zoom tool and zoom in on one part of the slide, then move around the screen. The audience would see only the zoomed portion of the screen.

4 Finally, press Escape to leave Zoom mode, and then press Escape again to leave Presenter View. Click Discard to throw out your pen annotations.

ANIMATING YOUR PRESENTATION

PowerPoint (PowerPoint's default behavior is to start new animations on mouse click; time-delayed animations require a little configuration.) slides don't need to be static cards; you can add visual emphasis by judiciously applying animations and transitions to slides and individual image/text objects. Remember: a little visual flair goes a long way. In this lesson, we'll emphasize bullet points and include flashy transitions, but we recommend using fewer visual effects when creating professional PowerPoint presentations.

STEP BY STEP	Animating your presentation

1 Switch to slide 1 and open the Animations tab. Click in the subtitle, then in the Animation group, select the Float In animation from the Animation Styles gallery. As soon as this is selected, the slide will preview the animation assigned to the subtitle.

2 Press F5 to start the Slide Show from the beginning. When you click to advance, the subtitle will drift onscreen. Your second click will move to slide 2.

3 Press Escape to return to editing slides and select slide 1. A box containing the numeral 1 appears next to the subtitle, indicating that it will animate on your first click to this slide.

4   Add the Shape animation to the subtitle (this is animation #2) using the Add Animation drop-down menu in the Advanced Animation group. Then click **Advanced Animation > Animation Pane**. In the Animation pane, switch the order of the two animations using the up or down arrow. You can press F5 to run the beginning of the slide show again, to see how the animations add up. Remember to save your work afterward.

Making the most of animations

The idea of animating every square inch of a slide is appealing. But some animations have more impact than others: revealing bullet points one by one, for instance, to focus attention on the current line, or fading in images. A couple of points in our miniature slide deck could profit from that kind of treatment.

STEP BY STEP   **Adding animations**

1   Select slide 2. Click in the main text area, the bulleted list, and add the Fade animation. Note that the last three lines appear together as animation #3.

2   In the Animation pane, expand the list of events. Select the last entry in the list, and from the drop-down menu choose **Start on Click**. See Figure 1-12.

Figure 1-12

Configure the last entry in the Animation pane to Start on Click.

3   Repeat step 2 for the animation for Single source. All five lines now have separate click-triggered animations.

4   Press Shift+F5 to start the slide show from slide 2, and click to advance through the bullets one by one. When you're finished, press Escape to return to editing mode.

5   Select slide 3. Shift+click the two headings (WYSIWYG and Markup) to select them both. Give them the Bounce entrance animation.

6   Shift+click to select the two images, and give them the Fade animation. Press **Shift+F5** to run the slide show from slide 3, clicking through the animations.

Revealing the images together (but separate from the headings) gives the slide a little drama, and the relative subtlety of the Fade animation is a nice contrast with the sillier Bounce animation. To close this part of the lesson, we'll add exit animations to take away the slide's visual elements before transitioning to the closing slide.

7   Select the two headings and two images, and give them the Fly Out **exit animation**. Preview the animations by running the slide show.

8   Choose File > Save or Ctrl+S to save your work.

Take Note   You can tell Slide A to transition to Slide B automatically after displaying for a certain number of seconds (you could make a whole PowerPoint movie that way) but what if Slide A also includes animations? Happily, PowerPoint won't advance the slide to Slide B until Slide A's animations have played.

Linking slides with transitions

Transitions work much like animations, but it's the entire slide that transforms. When you apply a transition to Slide B, Slides A and B are linked by a visual effect more complicated than the usual cut-on-click. Like animations, transitions can easily be abused; but a well-chosen transition can powerfully emphasize the relationship between the contents of two slides, or signal a shift in focus within the presentation.

We'll close the lesson by adding a couple of transitions, including sound effects. Then we will reorder the slides to alter the narrative flow of the presentation. In this task we'll make use of the Slide Sorter view, which offers a wide-angle look at the entire presentation, like a visual outline.

STEP BY STEP   **Linking slides with transitions**

1   Using the **Publishing-Markup** file, click the View tab and select Slide Sorter view. Beneath the slides that contain animations, a start icon is present; click each star to preview the animations.

2   Select slide 2. Open the Transitions tab and select the Fly Through transition. In the Timing group, check the After: check box, and set the After: value to 00:05.00.

3   Add the Shape transition to slide 3 and the Ferris Wheel to slide 4. Adjust the look of the Ferris Wheel animation by clicking Transitions > Effect Options and choosing From Left.

4   Add sound to the slide 4 transition by selecting Voltage from the Transitions > Timing > Sound drop-down menu.

Grouping and ordering slides in Slide Sorter

Bottom Line

Slide Sorter is useful after you've finished your individual slides and need to work on the overall architecture of your presentation. With the Home > Slides > Section tool, you can group slides logically into sections, which can help you think about the structure and pace of the slide show. (Sections are handy when you collaborate on a presentation too: Bob and Tim, clean up the 'Accounts' section, is clearer and less likely to suddenly make no sense during editing, than Bob and Tim, work on slides 53–70.

STEP BY STEP   **Grouping and ordering slides in Slide Sorter**

1. Click slide 1 in the Slide Sorter, then click Home > Slides > Section > Add Section. Press F2 or right-click Untitled Section to rename the section and type Intro and click Rename to commit the change and close the dialog box.

2. Select slides 2 and 3 by Shift+clicking, and add them to a new section called Setup.

3. Finally, make a section called Synthesis that includes only slide 4.

Right now we go straight to a bulleted list from our title slide. To add a bit of visual variety, we can move slide 3 to slide 2's spot.

4. Click and drag slide 3 to the left to switch the slide order within the Setup section. Finally, save your work. (See Figure 1-13.)

Figure 1-13

Shuffling the Slide Deck in the Sorter view.

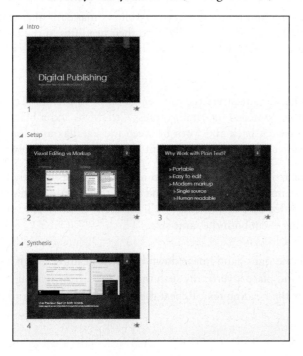

5. Choose File > Save or press Ctrl+S to save your work.

SETTING YOUR OVERALL LOOK WITH DOCUMENT THEMES

Bottom Line

The overall look and feel of a presentation is set with a Document Theme. Themes provide a matched set of fonts, colors, backgrounds, and visual effects, which can apply to any layout in a PowerPoint template. Indeed, themes can be used across Office 2013 applications to give a consistent visual identity to your work. In theory, a single click should switch your slide deck's theme with no additional work needed on your part; but if you've tweaked any document elements (such as an embedded image's layout) you may need to make further tweaks once you've applied the new theme.

We'll switch our presentation's theme to see what changes, and what needs changing afterward.

STEP BY STEP   **Setting your overall theme**

1   While in Slide Sorter view, open the Design tab. Select a handful of themes from the Themes gallery, one by one, to see what changes they make to your slide deck. (You may need to zoom out using the zoom slider on the taskbar to see the entire presentation at once.)

2   Select the Parallax theme found near the bottom of the Themes gallery. Then click each of the Variants, in the second gallery, to sample color choices. (Variants change only the theme's color scheme.) Choose the second variant, with the orange and grey stripes. Double-click slide 2 to switch to slide editing mode, then save your work.

What happened to our headings? As you recall, we manually altered the layout of this slide to line up the two images a little better relative to their headings in the Ion template. But headings and content have moved relative to each other in the switch to Parallax theme: now the images overlap the headings.

Take Note   Blank slides handily illustrate the differences between themes. To see exactly what happened to slide 2 when we switched to Parallax, press Ctrl+M to add a blank slide (it will inherit slide 2's layout), then switch back and forth between the Parallax and Ion themes. The different aspect ratios and relative locations of the content areas account for the obscured headings

The easiest fix for the slide 2 layout is to move the images directly below the headers. You could also delete the images from the slide and place them again without tweaking their layout until after you've settled on a final theme. We'll manually position the images, and further balance the slide by making them both the same size.

3   Drag the right-hand image down below its heading. Align its left edge with the heading text, and place it vertically such that double-arrow spacing guides appear above and below the heading text. Repeat the process for the left-hand image.

4 Right click the left-hand image and select Size and Position. In the Format Picture pane, deselect Lock Aspect Ratio and set the width to 4.81". The result is shown in Figure 1-14.

Figure 1-14

Balanced image sizes make for more forgiving layouts.

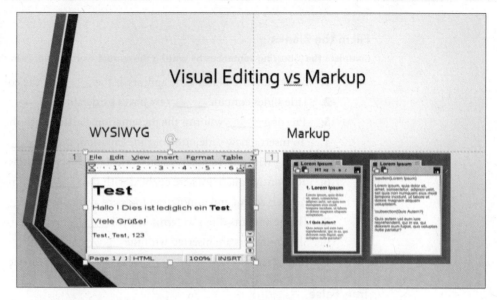

5 Choose File > Save and then File > Close to close the file.

What you learned in this lesson:

- Selecting and Opening a Template

- Adding Slides

- Editing Slide Text

- Placing Images into Slides

- Adding Speaker Notes

- Adding Animations and Transitions

- Switching presentation Themes

- Presenting a Slide Show

Knowledge Assessment

Fill in the Blanks

Complete the following sentences by writing the correct word or words in the blanks provided.

1. By default, the Notes Pane appears at the _____ of the editing screen.
2. Title slides contain _____ text boxes by default.
3. Pressing _____ will run the presentation starting with the current slide.
4. To insert a new slide into your presentation, press _____.
5. Along with the Template Gallery, the launch screen shows a list of _____ documents.
6. Responsive guidelines are enabled with the _____ command.
7. Pointer, zoom, and annotation tools are available in the _____ View.
8. Theme variants differ in terms of their _____.
9. Slide numbers are inserted with the _____ command.
10. Empty text boxes display _____ which won't print on the final document output.

True/False

Circle T if the statement is true or F it the statement is false.

T F 1. Widescreen slides are no longer supported in PowerPoint 2013.

T F 2. Selecting two images at once and applying an animation will animate first one, then the other.

T F 3. PowerPoint is a WYSIWYG document editor.

T F 4. The Change Case command increases or decreases the indent level of bulleted text.

T F 5. The Pictures content control brings up a text box for Bing image search.

T F 6. Most built-in PowerPoint templates open with a title slide.

T F 7. Presenter View is another name for Slide Show View.

T F 8. By default, animations begin five seconds after their slide displays.

T F 9. Transitions are actually specialized full-slide animations listed in the Animations Gallery.

T F 10. Grouped slides can be named for ease of editing and search, or assignment to collaborators.

Competency Assessment

Project 1-1: Using PowerPoint Templates

Here you'll practice picking templates and switching themes.

1. Launch Powerpoint. At the launch screen, click the search box and search for business wireframe building.
2. Select the template that appears in the gallery and create a new document with the template. The presentation template will download.
3. When the document opens, select slide 1. Change the words Title Layout to First Presentation Project.

   Note that the text is laid out in all caps no matter what capitalization you apply.

4. Change the subtitle to Building Wireframe Template.

5. Open the Themes gallery in the Design tab and mouse over several themes. Select one you like.

   Note that the wireframe template's theme is not available from the Themes gallery.

6. Click the Undo button or press Ctrl+Z until the building wireframe template is restored.

7. Press Ctrl+W to close the document. When prompted, save your file as **project_1-1_wireframe**.

Project 1-2: Editing Slide Text

In this exercise you'll add and edit some slide text.

1. Open the project file **1-2-source**. Save your document as **project_1-2_text_edit**.

2. Select slide 2. Click each text item in turn and change the slide's text to:

   SAMPLE BULLETED LIST

   First claim

   Supporting evidence

   Second claim

3. Click the second bullet point, then click Home > Paragraph > Increase List Level to indent it one level.

   The text of the "supporting evidence" line will resize to reflect its new list level.

4. Change slide 3's title to Infographic.

5. Reselect slide 2. Click Insert > Text Box and click to place a text box in the lower right quadrant of the slide.

6. Type Quotation or anecdote in the text box and italicize the new text.

7. Save and close your document.

Proficiency Assessment

Project 1-3: Sorting and Presenting Slides

Here you'll work on grouping slides in the Slide Sorter.

1. Open the project file **1-3-source**. Save your document as **project_1-3_sorting**.

2. Open the Slide Sorter.

3. Select slides 7-11, right click, and choose Hide Slide.

4. Select slides 1-3 and right click to create a new section. Then right click its section name and rename it Main Content.

5. Create two more sections: 4-6 (Supporting) and 7-11 (Other).

6. Collapse the section Other.

7. Press F5 to run the presentation; click each slide to move through to the next. Note which slides are excluded.

8. Select the Supporting section and give it the Ion Boardroom theme, orange variant.

9. Save and close your document.

Project 1-4: Adding and Styling Images

This exercise focuses on image styles and visual effects.

1. Open the project file **1-4-source**. Save your document as **project_1-4_images**.
2. Change slide 2's layout to Two Content.
3. Insert an online picture in the new content area: search for action item clip art (not Bing) and insert the resulting image.
4. Shift+drag the image straight upward until its top edge aligns with the top edge of the bulleted list content area – an alignment guide will appear.
5. Add the Drop Shadow Rectangle Picture Style to the image, and the Watercolor Sponge Artistic Effect.
6. Save and close your document.

Mastery Assessment

Project 1-5: Animations and Transitions

Here you'll add animations and transitions to a presentation.

1. Open the project file **1-5-source**. Save your document as **project_1-5_animations**.
2. Hide slides 4-6.
3. Add the Shape animation to the "Things to Do" image, and the Fly Out exit animation to the bulleted list.
4. Change the slide 2➔3 transition to Random Bars with a 5-second duration, and remove the slide 1➔2 transition entirely.
5. Run your presentation. Save and close your document and quit PowerPoint.

Project 1-6: Creating an Animation...with Transitions

In this final exercise you'll force PowerPoint to do something it wasn't designed for: create a short animation using slide transitions.

1. Create a new blank file and save it as **project_1-6_animation**.
2. Find or create a series of photographs you'd like to "animate."
3. Add each image to a different slide in your deck and use slide transitions to quickly cycle through them without needing to click.
4. Search for a command to loop the presentation indefinitely, then run it full-screen to see your short animation.
5. Save and close your document.

LESSON SKILL MATRIX

In this lesson, you will learn the following skills:

Navigating the PowerPoint UI	Inserting and Formatting Text and Images
Quickly Finding Design, Layout, Content, and Presentation Tools	Reordering Slides and Add Transitions
Choosing the Right Document View for a Task	Choosing and Customizing Themes
Building an Outline	

KEY TERMS

- **Tab Bar**
- **Notes Page**
- **Animation**

Fabrikam's sales presentations are carefully targeted to individual investors and clients. Though much of their content is fixed, the presentations are edited up to the last minute to respond to new information. Knowing PowerPoint's interface and workflow are essential to this process of shaping and reshaping – when the basic material is nailed down, the sales folks are free to experiment, edit, and see how new or revised content affects the pitch.

SOFTWARE ORIENTATION

This lesson helps you gain an understanding of outlining, along with the design, layout, and presentation tools. You'll reorder slides and customize themes.

Figure 2-1

Outline view and the Themes Gallery

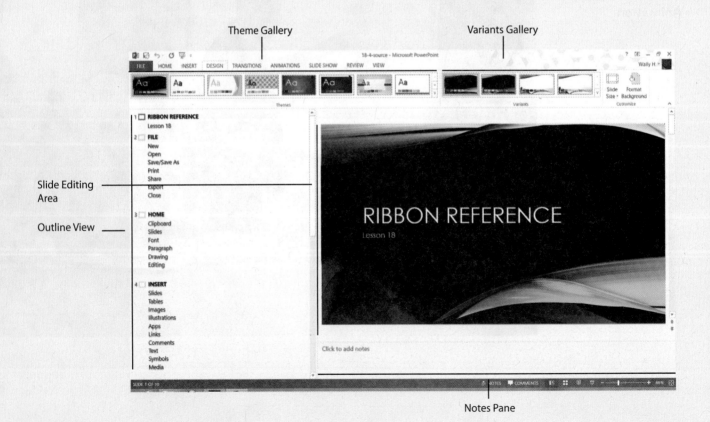

STARTING UP

In this lesson, you'll work with several files from the PPT02lessons folder. Make sure that you have loaded the OfficeLessons folder onto your computer.

YOUR WORKSPACE AND YOUR TOOLBOX

PowerPoint shares several features with the other Office 2013 apps, but it's purpose-built for a variety of specific tasks: writing, designing, and laying out slides; developing a presentation flow; generating handouts and presenter cues; refining and rehearsing the presentation; and sharing the presentation, whether live on stage or privately in a kiosk. Each task has an associated editing/viewing mode. Once you have a feel for your work environment and the tools it offers, you can focus all your attention on making useful content.

This lesson walks through the creation of a short presentation, focusing on the way the different features of PowerPoint work together. You won't present the slide show itself just yet; you will create it now and present the live act in a later lesson.

Take Note   This lesson looks at PowerPoint's content creation and editing workflow; as such, it's divided into common tasks: outlining, writing, structuring, animating, and styling a presentation. Even leaving out custom slide layouts, presenter tools, and document sharing, this lesson contains a lot of information; it'll take several lessons to cover in depth all the material introduced here. We strongly suggest you take your time and stop as needed to explore the tools the lesson introduces.

To begin, launch PowerPoint and open the sample document for this lesson.

STEP BY STEP   **Opening a PowerPoint document**

1   Launch PowerPoint 2013. From the Launch Screen, click Open Other Presentations, navigate to your PPT02lessons folder, and then select **pp02a.pptx**.

POWERPOINT AND THE OFFICE 2013 USER INTERFACE

PowerPoint 2013 presents the basic Office 2013 user interface (UI) optimized for creating presentations of slide decks. In this section, we'll map out the various tools in the UI, and see how PowerPoint's tailored interface helps support a smooth workflow.

The Ribbon and Backstage view

Bottom Line   The Ribbon, which appears by default atop the application screen, contains PowerPoint's many editing, viewing, and presenter tools. The Home tab, which is the default toolset, is where you can find the usual font/paragraph formatting tools (but no paragraph Styles; see below). In the Home tab, you can also find commands to add and edit slides, and quick shape-drawing tools. The Insert and Review tabs will be familiar to Office users, though PowerPoint is missing Word's Styles and Track Changes features. Several Ribbon tabs are shown in Figures 2-2, 2-3, and 2-4.

PowerPoint's file-management tools are found in the Backstage View (the File tab). The key PowerPoint-specific features are the theme variants for new documents, which let you preview different visual schemes for a given theme right in the New Document gallery, and the options for exporting your presentation as a video or web document (complete with animations, transitions, and audio).

Figure 2-2

The Design tab houses the Themes gallery and slide design tools.

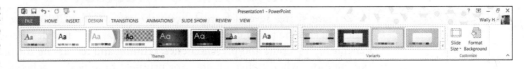

Figure 2-3

Configure and run your presentation from the Slide Show tab.

Figure 2-4

The View tab houses tools to customize your PowerPoint workspace.

Take Note   PowerPoint's review/collaboration tools are minimal: you can't Track Changes within a document, though you can generate a set of changes by comparing two different versions of a slide show. Collaboration takes place in Comments, which are now threaded, just as in Word 2013

Choosing a look with the Design tab

The Design tab illustrates a major conceptual difference between Word and PowerPoint. Word's Design tab lets you choose a theme, but hides the Themes gallery: you're expected to settle on one theme, then pick from its Style Sets to suit your taste. PowerPoint doesn't use Word's Styles; it has a simplified text style collection, which you edit with the Slide Master tools. The Design tab offers a Theme gallery and a second Variants gallery, which offers several color/background choices for each Theme.

Take Note   A template includes a selection of slide designs and placeholders, along with default visuals: for instance, a calendar template might include Monthly Calendar and Weekly Appointment Book slides with dummy images where your preferred pictures would go. Themes set default text, image, background, and color options for the slide deck. You can choose from a variety of different themes for a given template. PowerPoint's built-in Themes generally include several Variants, providing several options for the same basic aesthetic.

Moving from content to performance

Moving from left to right across PowerPoint's **tab bar**, you get a sense for the application workflow. First you generate your basic slide show content: the Home and Insert tabs support you in adding text, images, and data to your individual slides. Then comes aesthetics: you select a look and feel with the Design tools, link the slides into a series using the Transitions tools, and give individual slides some movement with Animations.

Transitions and Animations also help you think about your individual slides as tools for performance: as content is finalized, the workflow shifts from your slide deck to the slide show. In the Slide Show tab, you'll find controls for your presentation; crucially, this includes rehearsal and timing tools. The Review tools let colleagues respond to your work.

Finally, the View tab is a kind of master switch for shifting between different editing or viewing modes. The Master views let you set up document-wide formatting. The Slide Master sets default paragraph formatting values (font, color, emphasis), which propagate to all slide layouts; you can then customize each layout in turn. (The Slide Master is PowerPoint's rough equivalent to Word's Style Set.) Handout and Notes Masters determine the look for audience and speaker printouts, respectively.

Each of PowerPoint's Presentation Views is best suited to a specific part of the workflow:

- **Outline View:** quickly build a presentation skeleton

- **Normal View:** fill in individual slide content

- **Slide Sorter:** pull back to focus on overall flow

- **Notes Page:** turn slide deck into speaker script

- **Reading View:** review the slides as the audience would see it outside PowerPoint's interface

To see how the different parts of the PowerPoint workflow interact, we'll now quickly fill in our sample document, one viewing mode at a time.

BUILDING YOUR PRESENTATION CONTENT

Just as is the case with Word, the fastest way to get started with PowerPoint presentations is to begin with an outline, flesh out each section, and only then work on style and visual presentation. We'll follow this pattern to turn our sample document skeleton into an internal marketing pitch.

Building an outline

Bottom Line

Outline View shows the text content of your slides and nothing more: no images, no careful layout, and no design. PowerPoint presentation outlines work the same, in principle, as Word document outlines: top-level headings correspond to individual slides (rather than Word headings/sections), and each successive outline level maps to bulleted slide content. Since bulleted lists are the most common form of PowerPoint text content, drafting your presentation in Outline View is the fastest way to generate a lot of rough-and-ready slides.

We'll use Outline View to change our slide order and add a couple of new slides.

STEP BY STEP   **Building an outline**

1   In the file **pp02a.pptx**, choose View > Presentation Views > Outline View.

2   Select slide 5 by clicking the white box next to its slide number, and drag it to its new position right after the title slide so it becomes slide 2, as in Figure 2-5.

Figure 2-5

Use the Outline View to move slide 5 under the title slide.

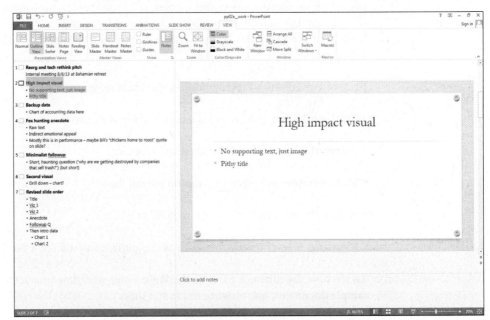

3   Select slide 6, Second visual, and press Ctrl+X to cut the entire slide. Place the cursor at the end of slide 2 in the outline and press Ctrl+V to insert the cut slide in its new position.

4   Resize the outline pane until it's about half the width of the screen to fit more slides onscreen at once by clicking and dragging the separating line to the right. Select View > Normal to flip back to slide editing mode, and then return to Outline View.

In Outline View, it makes sense to place the text content in the foreground by downsizing the slide visuals; after all, we haven't thought about layout and design, yet.

5   Finish reordering the existing slides according to the new order in slide 7 and then switch to Normal editing view.

6   Choose File > Save As. Navigate to the PPT02lessons folder and name this file pp02a_work.

Editing slide content

Bottom Line

In Normal View, the content of individual slides is front and center. However, when editing slide content, you can temporarily shift from thinking of your presentation as a continuous narrative, and make each slide impactful in itself.

STEP BY STEP   Editing slide content

1   Select slide 1 and change the title and subtitle to Reorienting Our IT Approach and A Modest Proposal, respectively.

2   Delete the text content and title from slide 2. The controls to insert visuals appear. Right-click slide 2 in the slides pane, and choose Layout > Blank.

If you're switching to a blank slide layout, it's good to clear out all its text content first; otherwise it will carry over to the new layout, with text boxes appearing in odd places (and you'll have to delete the boxes themselves).

3   Still working on the now-blank slide 2, click Insert > Online Pictures. In the royalty-free clip art search box, search for bad news. From the gallery of results, choose the image of the woman frowning on the phone and click Insert.

4   Clear the title and content from slide 3 and change the layout to Blank. Click Insert > Online Pictures again, and in the clip art search box (not Bing), search for charts and graphs. Shift+click any two images and insert them both.

5   Finally, Insert > Online Pictures again and search office.com clip art for graphs and charts. Insert one more resulting image.

SLIDES BACKGROUNDS AREN'T TEXT AREAS

PowerPoint differs from Word in several respects -- among them its assumption that slide content is always either background or <italic>floating elements</italic>. PowerPoint text always resides in a text box; there's no "text block" to act as a default location for text, as in Word.

Formatting inserted images

Bottom Line

After inserting dramatic visuals in a blank slide, you can change their appearance and layout using the Format Picture pane.

STEP BY STEP   **Formatting inserted images**

1   Right-click one of the inserted images and select Format Picture. Switch to its Size and Properties tab.

2   Under Size, make sure that Lock aspect ratio is checked (so images will keep the same proportions), then type 1.5 in the Height box and press Return. PowerPoint reads the unlabeled numeral as 1.5".

3   Do the same for the other two images. Then enable View > Show > Guides.

4   Drag one of the resized images to the very center of the slide. (With Guides turned on, it will stick when it's near the center.) Drag a second image to a spot directly to the right of the center image so that an orange span arrow appears between them. Drag the third image to the spot opposite the second, on the left side of the slide, as in Figure 2-6.

Figure 2-6

PowerPoint's drawing guides help you visually line up objects in the slide.

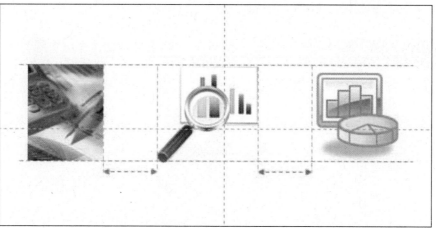

Clip art used with permission of Microsoft

5   If Notes are not already displayed, select View > Show > Notes.

The other commands in the Format Picture pane are reasonably self-explanatory; we'll return to them in a later lesson.

6   Edit the remaining slides as per these specifications:

* **Slide 2**: Add speaker note Average IT response time: 4 years

* **Slide 3**: Add speaker note Move slowly through images – drama!

* **Slide 4**: Set layout to Section Header, delete all text, change title to "The chickens come home to roost...in the lion's den...among the eagles" (including quotation marks)

* **Slide 5**: Set layout to Two content; change title to Key Question, and change slide content areas: We trail ACME sales by 400% (left) and Why? (right). No bullets in content area to the right (Home > Paragraph > Bullets)

* **Slide 6**: Set to Picture with caption layout, make title Year-over-year numbers. Text content: $2B short of projections!

We'll add a chart to slide 6 in a later section and make the visuals more interesting with animations and transitions.

7   Choose File > Save to save your work.

Creating notes pages

If you don't want to look at your screen while you deliver your presentation, you can print out **Notes Pages**, which let you control the layout of your speaker notes on a per-slide basis. This is handy if you want to alternate between improvisatory phrases or suggestions, and word-for-word reading of a complete slide script. We'll edit a single slide's notes to see how it works.

STEP BY STEP   Creating notes pages

1   Switch to View > Presentation Views > Notes Page. Scroll through the presentation and select slide 6.

2   Navigate to your PPT02lessons folder and open **pp02b.docx**. Copy the text of the document, and then Paste it into the notes area of slide 6.

3 Resize the image of the slide on the notes page, making it much shorter, and then resize the text box to fill the remaining page space. Select all the text and set it to 16pt type in Home > Font > **Font Size**, as in Figure 2-7.

Figure 2-7

Notes Pages help place your written presentation in its performance context.

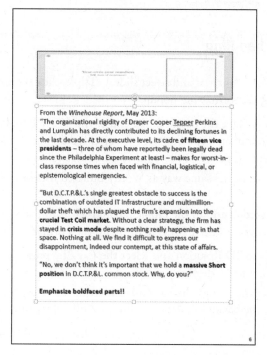

You can tailor the Notes Page for each slide in the same way: sometimes the most helpful visual aid is the slide itself; sometimes more textual detail is important.

Reading view

Reading View, new in Office 2013, lets you view your presentation as a series of flat slides with no visual chrome (no animations or transitions, just single screens). Crucially, Reading View also hides the entire PowerPoint interface: there is nothing around the slides to distract you, not even presenter tools.

For a clean look at your presentation, click View > Reading View. Use the usual navigation controls: Space/Return/Right arrow to advance, left arrow to move back. When you've got a feel for the way the draft slides present visually, press Escape or navigate past the last slide to return to editing mode, then click Normal View.

WORKING WITH TEXT, IMAGES, AND VISUAL EFFECTS

PowerPoint's text editing tools are more like Excel's than like Word's: simple, not meant to handle large-scale text pieces. (The general rule for slide text is: *Less Is More*.) Its image formatting tools are also streamlined. In this section, we'll briefly describe the different panes and toolbars.

Simplified text handling

Bottom Line

PowerPoint uses a simplified Style model: you define a style by formatting the text on the Slide Master (for instance, declaring that all title boxes should default to boldface italic text); make changes to layouts using the Slide Layout (for example, no boldface title on a specific slide layout only); and then inherit that formatting when you fill in the slide itself. In complexity and flexibility, PowerPoint's editing tools are more similar to Excel's than to Word's.

Applying character and paragraph formatting works the same way in PowerPoint as it does anywhere else in Office. In this section, we'll make changes to the Slide Master and to individual slides using a variety of formatting tools.

STEP BY STEP   **Simplified text handling**

1   Choose View > Normal and select slide 1. Triple-click the subtitle and set the text color to red using the formatting popup.

2   Select slide 5. Place the cursor at the end of the 400% line. Press Return to add a line. Press Tab to indent. Type 600% in fiscal Q4. Add another line; press Shift+Tab to reduce indent. Type ...while winning customer satisfaction war.

Tab and Shift+Tab work the same way as Word's bulleted lists or PowerPoint's outline mode.

3   Select the word *Why?* In the Home tab and set its font size to 96pt. Right-click *Why?* and select Format Text Effects to bring up the Format Shape pane.

4   Scroll down to 3D Rotation and select the Parallel preset, Isometric Left Down. Set the Z rotation to 15 degrees.

The Format Shape pane brings the various formatting tools together in a single toolbox; from there, you can alter the background, shape, line and fill colors, and texture of the text box, along with its contents.

5   Choose File > Save or press Ctrl+S to save your work.

Inserting images

Bottom Line

Inserting images works consistently across Office apps. You can either click one of the controls in a content area, or use the tools in the Insert tab. We'll illustrate the principle by inserting a single piece of clip art from online.

1   Select slide 6. Click in the image area, not on the Insert Image control, and then select Insert > Online Pictures.

2   Search the Office.com Clip Art collection for magnifying glass bar graph. Select the image that appears in the gallery, and click Insert.

Take Note

You can reformat an image (apply visual effects, add or edit a border, change its size/location properties, and more) using the Picture Tools > Format menu, or the Format Picture command in the image's context menu. The picture formatting tools are self-explanatory and work the same way in PowerPoint as they do in Word; we encourage you to experiment with them. We'll provide more detailed treatment in a later lesson

Adding and editing animations

Bottom Line

Animations apply to individual elements within a slide: images, boxes, even individual lines of text. The Animations tab contains the basic animation tools, whereas the Animation pane lets you organize the animations within a slide.

Take Note

This lesson uses the Fade entry/exit animations exclusively: they're the most elegant of all, and altering the length of a fade won't make it look inane compared to a sped-up Fly In animation (for example). For sheer flexibility, the best option is the Custom Path animation, which lets you really animate an object by moving it around like a cartoon character.

STEP BY STEP   **Adding Animation**

1   In slide 5, click the word ACME. (Don't select the text, just place the cursor.) Open the Animations tab and apply the Fade animation. Then open the Animation pane. In that pane, click the double caret (⌄) to expand the animation list.

PowerPoint automatically animates the entire bulleted list: the first two lines appear on your first click, then the third line when you click again. We'll uncouple the first two lines, add a dramatic pause before the second, and draw out the animation on the third.

Figure 2-8

Animation order is indicated by numbered labels in the slide.

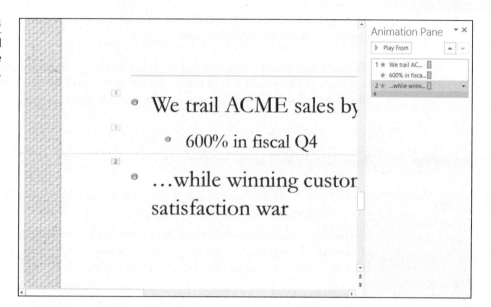

STEP BY STEP   **Editing Animation**

1   Select animation #2 in the Animation pane (the ...*while winning* bullet, marked in Figure 2-8). From its drop-down menu, make sure Start After Previous is selected. In the Timing group, set Delay to three seconds (type 3 in the entry box). Set the Duration to one second. What was animation #2 is now folded in to animation #1.

2   By Shift+clicking select both the title and the text box on the left. Click Add Animation, scroll down to the Exit Animations and choose Fade.

3   In the Animations pane, make sure animation #3 (the ...*while winning* exit animation) is set to Start with Previous. The slide now contains three animation events on the slide, in two groups: (1) add top two bullets on click, then add third bullet three seconds later, (2) dismiss all text except *Why?* on click.

4   Click *Why?* and add the Fade (entry) animation. Make sure it is set it to Start After Previous, with a 4-second duration and 1-second delay.

5   Choose File > Save or press Ctrl+S to save your work.

Now preview your work by pressing Shift+F5 to start the slide show from the current slide. The slide starts out displaying just the title, awaiting your input. Click through the various animations (remember to wait for the two delayed entrances) to see how a bit of customization can give a sequence of animations a slightly cinematic quality.

Take Note   The hardest part of using time-delayed animations is setting the actual delay. Four seconds can feel like an eternity during a presentation. By cycling through edits and test runs, you can develop a flow for each slide that makes sense for your presentation style.

6   To close out this section, animate slide 3: fade in the image on the left 0.5 seconds after loading the slide, then load the other two images one by one.

The easiest way to apply the same animation to multiple objects is with the Animation Painter: after animating the first image, select the image, press Alt+Shift+C to copy its animation, and then click the next image to paint the animation onto it. Repeat this process for image #3.

Transitions and slide sorter

Bottom Line

Adding a transition is like animating an entire slide. Think of it as a scene change in a movie: a transition tells the audience to prepare for a new context. The bigger the transition, the bigger the expected context change. This is why we don't recommend using splashy transitions for every single slide: they tire the audience out.

We'll add a couple of simple transitions to key points in the presentation and group slides to give us a sense of the presentation's proportions. For this task we want the Slide Sorter view, which affords a bird's eye view of the presentation. (In fact, you can't edit slide content in the Sorter.)

STEP BY STEP   **Transitions and slide sorter**

1   Switch to Slide Sorter view. Right-click slide 4 and select Add Section. Do the same with slide 6 to make three sections in total.

Sections don't materially affect the presentation: unlike Word 2013, you can't reformat individual sections of a PowerPoint presentation. The purpose of sections is to aid with slide organization, for instance, when distributing the presentation to authors.

2   Click the Default Section heading and press F2 to bring up the Rename Section dialog. Rename the first section The Trailer.

3   Rename the first Untitled Section Make it personal, and call the third Hard data.

The section divisions can be used to lay out the slides for printing later. Now let's focus on the movement of the presentation by adding a couple of slide transitions. The presentation starts jaunty and turns to finger-pointing later, so we'll start with some quick transition moves and give the last slide some melodrama with a long fade.

4   Select slide 2 and apply the Push transition (from the Transitions to This Slide gallery). Then apply the Airplane transition to slide 4, modifying it slightly by choosing Left from the Effect Options drop-down menu.

5   Select slide 6 and apply the Fade transition. Add the Through Black effect with the Effect Options tool, then set the transition duration to six seconds (type 6 in the Timing > Duration text box and press Enter).

6   Save your work, then press F5 and walk through the presentation to see how the transitions and animations appear. Note that you can click to skip to the end of a lengthy transition.

The sprightly transitions in the early slides keep the tone light before slowing down on slide 5. Then the slow, dramatic crossfade divides the first section of the presentation, which builds to the question Why are we trailing ACME, from the data-driven second section.

The same basic steps apply to any transition: add the animation, tweak any effect settings, and alter timing if necessary.

DESIGN TOOLS

You can find PowerPoint's design tools in the Design tab. To establish the look of a slide show, begin by choosing (or editing) a template, then apply a theme, and finally, make fine-grained edits to formatting.

What's in a template?

Bottom Line

The easiest way to see how templates work is to open one up. The idea is the same as in any other Office 2013 app: a template is a skeleton that you fill in with your content. We'll peek inside a built-in template to see how much work a well-chosen template can save you.

Take Note   Microsoft can always replace the template in this section with another, differently-named template; in such a case, follow along in this section using another calendar template from the Office template gallery.

STEP BY STEP   **Customizing slide layouts**

    1   Click **File > New**, and select **Suggested Searches: Calendars**.

    2   From the template gallery, select **2013 Photo calendar (Sun-Sat)**. Click **Create**.

Looking at slide 1 (of 12) of the calendar template, you can see how this slide layout works: each calendar day is a content box waiting for text. The *Click to edit master styles* text is a dummy placeholder: when you click a day it disappears to make way for your own text.

A template can include custom slide layouts to avoid repeatedly and heavily editing the standard layouts; in a later lesson we'll create a custom Employee Bio layout to illustrate how this works.

    3   In the Design tab's Themes Gallery, select **Ion**. Note that the slide layout doesn't change.

    4   Switch to Slide Master view. Mouse over the current slide to see which layout is in use.

If you completed Lesson 1, you'll remember that switching themes altered the content layout, obscuring some heading text. The calendar's slide layout doesn't change when you change themes, though, because slide 1 uses a slide layout (see Figure 2-9) that's not overwritten by the Ion theme. We'll work more with the Slide Master view later.

Figure 2-9

Custom slide layouts in a monthly calendar template.

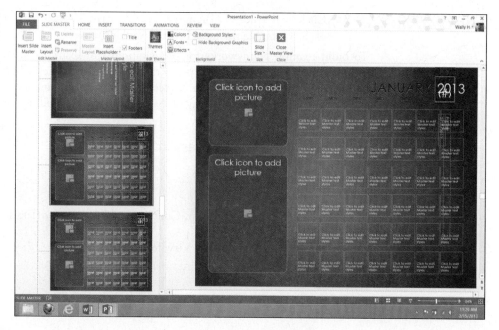

5 Close the calendar document without saving.

Applying themes to a slide show

Bottom Line

The Design tab's main features are two galleries: Themes and Variants. A Theme is a slide deck's look, combining fonts, slide layouts, and theme colors into an aesthetically-pleasing overall design. Variants offer alternative color schemes for a given theme. Using standard slide layouts (as we are in this exercise) allows you to switch between themes without damaging your document layout.

We'll apply a theme to our slide show, tweak fonts and colors a bit, and then save our customizations.

STEP BY STEP | **Applying a theme to a slide show**

1 Return to your **pp02a_work.pptx** document.

2 In the Design tab's Themes Gallery, select the Quotable theme (they are listed alphabetically). Then choose the red color Variant.

Take Note We're trying to minimize our labor, so we're avoiding themes that format slide Titles in all caps. Why? Select slide 1 and preview the striking Integral theme: our presentation title includes the acronym IT, which reads as "it" when the whole title's in all caps. If you still prefer the Integral theme, try switching IT to red characters to set it off from the rest of the line.

Customizing a theme in the Slide Master view

Bottom Line

Slide Master View is built for editing custom slide layouts, but it's also where you customize PowerPoint's themes. At a basic level, customizing a theme is as easy as selecting a new font, color scheme, and visual effect.

STEP BY STEP | **Customizing a theme in the Slide Master view**

1 Switch to Slide Master view.

2 In the Background group, change the color scheme to Red Violet; select Garamond-TrebuchetMS from the Fonts menu; and choose Frosted Glass from the Effects menu.

3 Click Edit Theme > Themes > Save Current Theme. Save your now-modified version of the Quotable theme as **Frosted Violet Quote**.

To build reusable frameworks for presentations (for example, a corporate visual identity and standard slide layout for in-house presentations) you would use these tools to create custom themes and slide layouts. We'll do so in a later lesson; for the moment, save your work and take this opportunity to further explore any of the editing tools covered in this lesson.

What you learned in this lesson:

• Navigating the PowerPoint UI

• Quickly Finding Design, Layout, Content, and Presentation Tools

• Choosing the Right Document View for a Task

• Building an Outline

• Inserting and Formatting Text and Images

- Reordering Slides and Add Transitions

- Choosing and Customizing Themes

Knowledge Assessment

True/False

Circle T if the statement is true or F it the statement is false.

T F   1. The background of each PowerPoint slide is a text area, as on a Word 2013 page.

T F   2. PowerPoint themes are selected from the Layout tab.

T F   3. Normal View focuses attention on the content of an individual slide.

T F   4. The Format Picture pane is the central location for tools to fine-tune an inserted image's appearance.

T F   5. A Notes Page is a printed sheet that helps the audience follow along with a presentation on paper.

T F   6. PowerPoint uses the same Style Sets as Word.

T F   7. Animations can be triggered by mouse click, or activate after a specified period of time.

T F   8. Switching a presentation's Theme will erase any custom slide layouts you've created.

T F   9. Reading View provides quick access to all PowerPoint's document editing tools.

T F 10. In Outline View, each top-level heading corresponds to a new slide.

Matching

Match each term to its description or definition.

1. Outline View

2. Slide Sorter

3. transition

4. title slide

5. Insert > Online Pictures

6. Notes Page

7. exit animation

8. Template Gallery

9. empty slide

10. Themes Gallery

a. presents collection of prebuilt document skeletons

b. despite open space, contains no text area as such

c. high-level view of presentation, for reordering and grouping slides

d. prompts, quotes, and directions for speaker, not audience

e. maps top-level headings onto slides

f. collects overall presentation aesthetics in Design tab

g. has boxes for title and subtitle only

h. "fly out" and other effects remove elements from slide

i. like an animation that turns one slide into another

j. takes search string, returns clip art/Bing image results

Competency Assessment

Project 2-1: Outlining

In this exercise you'll create a reference of the various command groups in the Ribbon.

1. Launch PowerPoint and create a new blank presentation.
2. Save your document as **project_2-1_outline.**
3. Open the outliner (View > Outline View) and click in the outline pane next to the orange box indicating slide 1.
4. Create an outline with each slide's title corresponding to a Ribbon tab.
5. For each slide, add bullets (one level down) for that tab's Ribbon command groups.
6. Insert a new title slide, and change the "File" slide's layout to Title and Content.
6. View the presentation in Normal and Slide Show views.
7. Save and close your document.

Project 2-2: Visual Elements

Here you'll alter several slide elements and add appropriate images.

1. Open the project file **2-2-source**. Save your document as **project_2-2_visuals.**
2. Set the title of the presentation to Ribbon Reference, and its subtitle to Lesson 2.
3. Assign a document theme from the Themes gallery.
4. Change all non-title slides' layouts to Content with Caption.
5. Move each slide's caption text to the caption box beneath its title, rather than the main content box where it presently resides.
6. In each slide's content box, insert an image related to its Ribbon tab (e.g., a file cabinet for the File tab).
7. Save and close your document.

Proficiency Assessment

Project 2-3: Notes Pages

In this exercise you'll create and format Notes Pages for a slide deck.

1. Open the project file **2-3-source**. Save your document as **project_2-3_notes.**
2. Expand the Notes Pane at the bottom of the editing area, to make room for a few lines of typed notes.
3. On each slide, type a brief description of what the tools on that Ribbon tab do (in general; no need to go command-by-command).
4. Select View > Notes Master. Click Check Out.
5. Select the top-level notes text ("Click to edit master text styles") and change it to 20pt text in any font you like.
6. Click Notes Master > Close Master View, then select Notes Page view to see the new large notes page text.
7. Close and save your document.

Project 2-4: The Presentation

Here you'll run a slide show and experiment with the Presenter View interface.

1. Open the project file **2-4-source**. Save your document as **project_2-4_presentation**.
2. Add optional transitions between slides; use the delay/duration controls to alter the dynamics of the transitions.
3. Run the presentation in Presenter View (Alt+F5). Experiment with resizing panes and toggling screen elements like the Windows taskbar. Experiment too with ink annotations (the Pen tool); if you make pen marks on the slides, elect to keep them when you close your presentation.
4. Save and close your document, and quit PowerPoint.

Mastery Assessment

Project 2-5: Matching Interface to Workflow

Here you'll use custom Ribbon tabs to streamline your PowerPoint workflow.

1. Create a new blank document (no need to save).
2. Create a single custom Ribbon tab called Tweaks.
3. Add commands to the new tab to quickly do the following repetitive tasks:
    *   Create a new file
    *   Select a Theme
    *   Modify the header
    *   Add a new slide
    *   Insert an online image
    *   Run the slide show in Presenter View
    *   Save the document
4. Close your document.

Project 2-6: Putting It All Together

The final exercise asks you to quickly assemble a presentation to order.

1. Create a new blank presentation called **project_2-6_final**.
2. Craft a "marketing presentation" with four slides:
    *   Title/creator/date, snazzy image
    *   Good news re: recent sales
        *   o   add sales figure chart from online image search
        *   o   Fade transition to...
    *   Future challenges
        *   o   animated bulleted list of new markets
        *   o   image that suggests "look out for challenges!"
    *   Request for audience questions; speaker contact information
3. Run through the presentation in Presenter View and save your document.

3

Designing a Presentation

KEY TERMS

- Placeholder Text
- Title Slide
- Shape Style
- Format Pane
- Gradient
- WordArt
- Slide Master
- Slide Layout

The PR team at Northwind Traders handed a hefty assignment to an intern: quickly make 25 poster designs for an upcoming in-store event series, each using a variant of the same basic design, with modified text and images on every poster. The intern hit on a clever response: build each poster as a PowerPoint slide, using the Slide Master and flexible, ready-to-fill custom layouts to generate the basic look and varying colors/effects from slide to slide. The work was done in no time flat.

SOFTWARE ORIENTATION

This lesson helps you understand effective ways to create presentations using PowerPoint.

Figure 3-1

Parts of a PowerPoint presentation

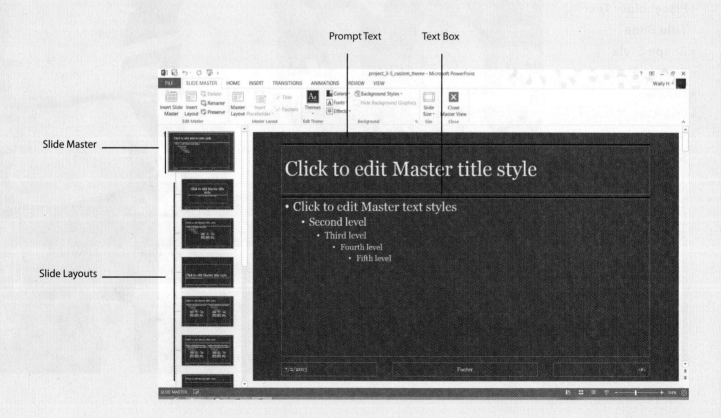

STARTING UP

In this lesson, you'll work with several files from the PPT03lessons folder. Make sure that you have loaded the OfficeLessons folder onto your computer.

BUILDING BETTER SLIDES

A good PowerPoint presentation isn't really about the slides; it's about a person communicating with an audience. A well-designed slide deck can illustrate a point that might be difficult to express in words, or subtly reinforce the speaker's message; it can flash hard data behind an impressionistic speech, or put mood lighting on a technical talk. It can even tell a story all by itself, not needing a speaker at all. Lots of presentations are boring; but they can also be beautiful.

The previous lesson explored PowerPoint's slide show creation workflow, from initial outline to final style touches. The next three lessons walk through specific aspects of slide building: text and layout, tabular data and SmartArt, and audiovisual elements. In this lesson, we'll discuss working with text, style and layout tools, and translating a presentation to print (as notes pages and audience handouts).

The finished project for this lesson, a short presented slide show, is saved as **pp03a-finished.pptx** in your PPT03lessons folder if you would like to take a look before getting started.

WORKING WITH TEXT

The text handling tools available in PowerPoint are fairly simple. Whereas a middleweight layout program such as Word 2013 needs flexible paragraph- and character-level formatting tools, slide text is more constrained. The most common use for PowerPoint is to accompany a talk.

In the first part of the lesson, you'll build individual text-heavy slides, and then you will establish default formatting for your slides using the Slide Master tool. Our text-heavy sample document for this lesson is a rules and regulations talk for new interns.

Filling in an existing text area

Bottom Line

Nearly every blank PowerPoint presentation starts with the same content: a blank Title Slide with two text areas for a title and subtitle, each with **placeholder text** (such as *Click to add title*). Within these text boxes, you can format your text much as you would in a Word 2013 text box (for example), applying character and paragraph formatting, but no Styles. You can also insert special dynamic text, such as the slide number or current date and time.

STEP BY STEP | **Filling in an existing text area**

1   Launch PowerPoint 2013 and create a new Blank Presentation.

2   In the title box of slide 1, type LSC Intern Orientation. Right-click the new title text and choose Font. In Figure 3-2, note that instead of a font name, the Latin text font value is actually +Heading, which is inherited from the Theme. Click Cancel.

Figure 3-2

The Title Slide layout inherits the Theme's default Heading font.

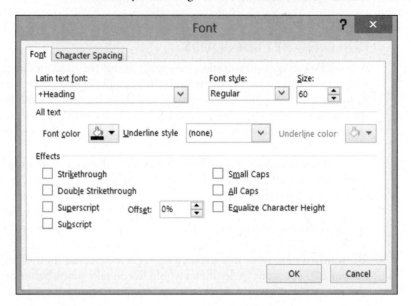

3   Place the cursor in the subtitle text area. Type your name (for example, John Q. Superuser), press Enter, and then click Insert > Text > Date & Time. Make sure Update Automatically is selected and click OK.

4   Press Ctrl+M to add the next slide. Set slide 2's title to Agenda and add four bullet points: Logistics, Housing, Lab practices, and Project schedule.

5   Finally, click Home > New Slide > Title Only to add slide 3.

6   Choose File > Save As and navigate to the PPT03lesson folder. Name the new file pp03a_work and click Save.

The style and formatting for these slides came from the Document Theme, which bundles color scheme, default fonts, backgrounds, and slide layouts. **Title Slide** is a standard layout in Microsoft's built-in themes (see Figure 3-3), so by changing a theme, you'll automatically alter the slides' layouts (though the built-in themes make bigger changes to style than to layout).

Figure 3-3

The layout and style of the title slide depend on the Theme you choose.

Adding and styling text boxes

The default Office theme, which the Blank Presentation template uses, includes the nine slide layouts found in the Home > Slides > Layout gallery (or the Slide Master view). In contrast, the Organic theme has 15 built-in layouts. On rare occasions, none of the included layouts will do, and you'll need to customize your own slide layout, with text boxes, images, and other content areas. For this, it's back to the Insert tab.

STEP BY STEP   **Adding and styling text boxes**

1   Set slide 3's title to Carpool Assignments.

2   Click Insert > Text > Text Box to active the Text Box tool, then click somewhere just below the title. Enter four names, each on its own line: Andy, Beth, Carlos, Dave.

3   Insert two more text boxes in the slide, each with four names on four lines: Ezra, Feliks, Gaffer, Hedges and Ibsen, Jake, Klaatu, Lopes.

4   Click in the first box, and then open the Format tab. From the Shape Styles gallery, select Colored Fill – Black, Dark 1.

Note that when you mouse over an icon in the gallery, Office's Live Preview feature lets you see how your text box will look in that style. Applying a **Shape Style** to an object sets its line, fill, gradient, effects, and text formatting properties all at once. You can also set those properties one at a time. We'll change the look of one of our text boxes to show some favoritism:

5   Apply the Shape Styles Blue, Accent 1 and Orange, Accent 2 to the second and third text boxes respectively.

6   With the orange box selected, click the small icon in the bottom right corner of the Shape Styles group to open the Format Shape pane. Select its Shape Options > Effects tab and apply the following Shadow effect: Offset Diagonal Top Right preset, 120% size, 20 pt. blur, 18 pt. distance. See Figure 3-4. Then close the Format Shape pane.

Figure 3-4

The Format Shape pane is your primary tool for styling individual objects.

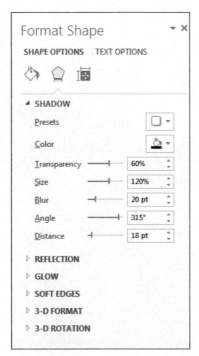

Take Note If you make changes to the placeholders on a slide, for example, move the title box, restyle an image placeholder, or delete a content area, you can revert to the default layout for that slide by clicking Home > Slides > Reset. Doing so won't affect the slide background or the elements you've added to the layout.

The Format pane

Bottom Line

The **Format pane** is where you fine tune the appearance of slide elements such as text boxes, images, or the slide background. When you use it to style a text box, the Format Pane's tabs are grouped under two headings: Shape Options and Text Options, each with three tabs (fill and line, visual effects, and size/shape/margins/alignment). If you select nothing at all while the Format pane is open (for example, by clicking outside the slide or in an empty region of the slide), the Format pane will display formatting options for the background: solid color, a color **gradient**, an image (or texture made of tiled images), or a pattern.

STEP BY STEP **Formatting with the Format pane**

1 Right-click in an empty region of slide 3 or right-click the margin. Select Format Background from the context menu.

2 Select Gradient fill from the menu, and then choose the Preset gradient Top Spotlight – Accent 6.

3 In the Gradient Stops slider, click to add a fourth gradient stop halfway between the second and third; set its color to White. This will give the slide a blown-out appearance as in Figure 3-5.

Figure 3-5

Add a green gradient fill background to slide 3.

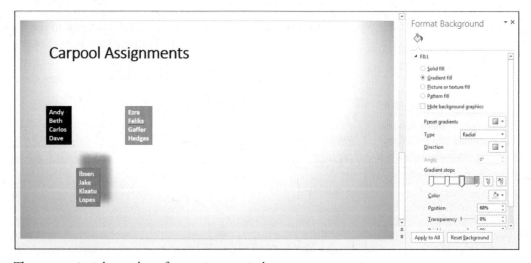

The same principles apply to formatting text in boxes.

4   Select the entire heading. In the Format Shape pane, click **Text Options > Text Effects** in the Format pane. Apply the **Reflection Variation Half Reflection**, **4 pt.** offset, and the **Glow Preset Blue**, **8 pt. Glow**, **Accent color 5**.

5   Finally, Shift+click to select all three shaded text boxes (not the slide title, which is actually a text box, too). Turn on alignment guides (**View > Show > Guides**) and drag the text boxes to the center of the slide to give the vertically-extended heading text more room.

Take Note   If you're in the habit of deselecting text after modifying it to get a clean look at the results, make sure you reselect the text before applying your next formatting change, or you may end up styling your slide background by mistake.

Autofit and text boxes

You may have noticed, as you entered the carpool information, that the text boxes expand to fit the text inside them. Indeed, even if you draw a text box at the size you want, PowerPoint's default behavior is to collapse the text box around the text you're typing. This is Office's Autofit feature at work. The Format pane offers three options for Autofitting text in a text box: squeeze the text, stretch the box, or do nothing (spill over). Figure 3-6 compares the three.

Figure 3-6

Autofit options: Shrink Text (L), Resize Shape (C), Do Not Autofit (R).

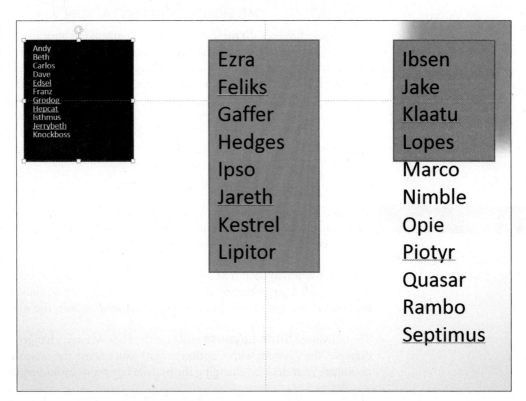

STYLING TEXT WITH WORDART

Bottom Line   Adding complicated visual effects to a piece of text can be time consuming; PowerPoint speeds up the process with its **WordArt** feature, which bundles font, line, fill, shadow, and other effects into WordArt Styles that can be applied to text just as Paragraph Styles can be applied in Word.

You can use the WordArt tool in three ways: by selecting a piece of text and layering effects with the Format > WordArt Styles > Fill/Outline/Effects tools; selecting a ready made WordArt Style from the gallery; or choosing Insert > WordArt to add pre-styled dummy text to your slide. (By choosing the latter option with a piece of text selected, you will create a new text box that contains a copy of that text, but in the appropriate style.) The WordArt Styles group is an alternate front-end to the Format pane.

1   Add a new slide (slide 4) with layout Content with Caption. In the content area to the right, click the Pictures icon. Navigate to the PPT03lessons folder and select **pp03c.png** and click Insert.

2   Type Dormitories for the title. Navigate to the PPT03lessons folder and open **pp03b.docx**. Select the first paragraph and press Ctrl+C to copy the text. Switch back to **pp03a_work** and place the cursor in the text area below the title. Press Ctrl+V to paste.

3   Select the words, *Aim for the oddly-shaped reflective tower*, in the text area. Use Live Preview to see how the various WordArt styles will look with this content. Choose the Gradient Fill – Gray WordArt Style from the Format > WordArt Styles gallery to apply it to the selected text.

Note the following about WordArt Styles: some apply their bundled formatting options to the entire paragraph, some only to the selected characters. Live Preview will help you see how your selected style will be applied.

FORMATTING THE WHOLE PRESENTATION

Sometimes a project calls for slides that don't fit any of the built-in layouts. In that case, you'll have to design your own layout. If you need a single custom slide, start with a blank slide, or one that's close to what you want, and build from there: assemble your text and images, tables, charts, audio, or video. If you later need to reuse that layout, you can duplicate the slide and change the content.

If you know you will need multiple custom slides with the same design, you can save yourself time and effort by building a reusable layout in the Slide Master view. In this part of the lesson, we'll do just that.

The Slide Master view

The Slide Master View is where you set the visual standards for your entire presentation: the slide elements and formatting options that will be included on every slide. In the Slide Master View, you can edit two elements of your presentation:

The **Slide Master** itself is a template for every other layout in the deck; if you insert a background image or visual ornament, or alter the body or heading fonts, those changes will propagate to all the slides that inherit from the Slide Master (in other words, the whole deck).

The individual **Slide Layouts** build on the Slide Master; changes to one of a deck's layouts (for example, the Content with Caption layout) won't affect the others in the deck. You can further customize your deck by changing the built-in layouts or by adding one or more custom layouts.

If your presentation calls for multiple visual feels, you can insert multiple slide masters and assign each slide layout to a slide master depending on what visual feel it calls for.

Editing the slide master

To quickly make the same visual edit to every slide, make changes directly on the slide master.

Bottom Line

Slide Master View

1   Open Slide Master View by selecting View > Master Views > Slide Master. In the left pane, scroll to the very top and select the Office Theme Slide Master.

2   Select the title text *Click to edit Master title style*. Using the formatting pop-up menu or the Home > Font > Color tool, set its color to Blue, Accent 1.

As you can see from the tree diagram in the left pane (Figure 3-7), all the other layouts inherit formatting from the Slide Master; the change you've made to the Title style in the Slide Master affects all text formatted with that style in the whole deck. You can click the different layouts to see that all of them now include blue title text. This is the equivalent of editing the Title or Heading Style in Word 2013.

Figure 3-7

Formatting changes to the Slide Master are immediately reflected in all layouts.

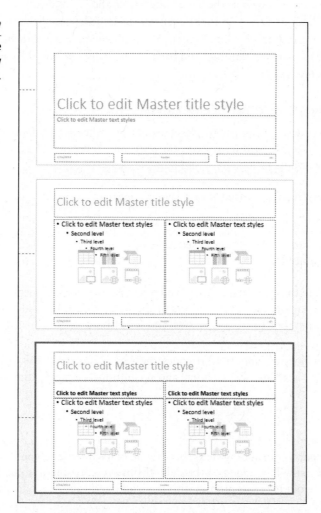

If you scroll down to the Comparison layout in the left pane, you'll see that its subheadings haven't turned blue; you can right-click those subheadings and choose Font from the context menu to see that they're formatted with the +Body font, rather than +Heading.

Now let's add a small logo to the Slide Master at the bottom of the slide, but not strictly in the Footer text area.

STEP BY STEP   **Editing the Slide Master**

1.   Return to the Slide Master at the top of the left pane. Click Insert > Illustrations > Shapes > Basic Shapes > Lightning Bolt.

2.   Shift+click+drag anywhere in the slide to place the image without modifying its proportions. (Note that it appears on every slide in the left pane.)

3.   Drag the image to the bottom of the slide, over the footer area. Shift+drag one of its handles to resize the image to roughly the height of the footer. Place it at the bottom center of the slide; alignment guides will appear to help you place the image precisely. Save your work.

4.   Now scroll down to the Title Slide layout and try to delete its lightning bolt logo; you will notice that you can't. It's part of the basic layout of the entire deck. Images and text placed in the Slide Master can't be edited on a per-slide basis; the Slide Master is for formatting, framing, and background; content should be edited in the slide layouts themselves.

CREATING CUSTOM SLIDE LAYOUTS

Custom slide design helps your deck stand out from other nearly identical PowerPoint presentations that your colleagues will have seen prior to yours. You can add new layouts in the Slide Master View. Slide layouts include fixed and mutable elements:

- **Text** and **visuals** inserted into a layout appear in every slide using that layout and can't be edited.

- **Placeholders** are blank spaces set aside for content, and can be removed from any slide where they're not needed.

If you click in the Slide Master itself, you'll see that the Insert Placeholder command is greyed out. Adding and laying out content occurs in the slide layouts; the slide master is for formatting and ornamentation (borders, backgrounds, and so forth).

Take Note   PowerPoint doesn't support field codes the way Word does; the only fields available are slide number and date/time. Expert users and programmers can get around this limitation with VBA code.

Bottom Line

Adding a custom slide layout

Adding layouts is like adding slides, but instead of fixed content, you'll generally insert placeholders (where content will be added on the slides themselves). To demonstrate how they work, we'll make a reusable layout for tutor profiles with headshots and capsule biographies.

STEP BY STEP   **Adding a custom slide layout**

1.   Use the Slide Master > Edit Master > Insert Layout command to add a custom layout to your deck, and then use Slide Master > Rename to change its name to Profile.

2.   Drag one of the handles on the right side of the Title box such that you resize the box to about half the width of the slide. Then change the title placeholder text to Add tutor name here.

Custom placeholder text is only visible while editing slides: the words, *Add tutor name here*, will prompt you for text, but won't appear on the final slides. Now add an image placeholder:

3   Click **Master Layout > Insert Placeholder > Picture** and Shift+click+drag to place a square image, roughly 2" high, in the upper-right corner of the slide. Click **Format > Insert Shapes > Edit Shape > Change Shape** to make the image placeholder an oval, then give it the **Colored Outline – Blue, Accent 1** Shape Style from the gallery. Use the **Shape Outline > Weight** command to make the new circular border 4.5 pt. wide.

4   Make sure that **View > Show > Guides** is checked, and place the image so that its top edge aligns with the top of the Title box, and its right side with the right side of the right most footer. Then replace its prompt text with **Tutor pic here** as in Figure 3-8. Save your work.

Figure 3-8

Adding an image placeholder to a custom slide layout.

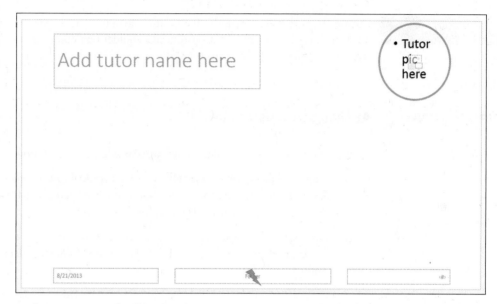

At this point, you should take a look at your slide layout in progress.

5   Choose **Slide Master > Close > Close Master View** to close this view.

6   Insert a new slide and give it the new Profile layout. The main editing window shows your custom prompts, but only the image border appears on the final slide. Don't delete the new slide.

7   Choose **File > Save** to save your work.

Completing the custom layout

You now have all the tools you need to finish the new Profile layout.

STEP BY STEP	**Completing the custom layout**

1   Go back to the Slide Master view by choosing **View > Master Views > Slide Master**. Select the **Profile** layout.

2   Add a tall thin text placeholder below the image to hold a quote from each tutor. Format its top-level Master text style in **18 pt. italic blue-gray non-bulleted text**. Change the top-level prompt text to **Pithy quote here** and delete the remaining placeholder text.

3   Fill the remaining slide space with a large text area, leaving the fonts unmodified. Set its top-level dummy text to **Bulleted bio here**. Align both new text boxes with the already-existing slide elements.

4   Right-click in an empty slide region, add a **Pattern** fill to the slide background, and select the **5%** (dotted) pattern.

5   When you're finished adding slide elements, click Slide Master > Close Master View and return to editing your presentation.

6   Note that slide 5, the blank Profile slide, still uses the old layout: dummy text and background update, but new placeholders don't appear.

7   To refresh slide 5's layout layout, reapply the Profile layout (Home > Slides > Layout > Profile).

8   Add two slides to the end (slides 6 and 7), also with the new Profile layout

Applying the custom layout

Bottom Line

Custom layouts behave exactly like built-in layouts. You're set to fill in three slides, each with a different tutor Profile. Now the custom placeholder text comes in handy: it'll help prevent clerical error when importing data into the slides.

STEP BY STEP   Applying the custom layout

1   If it is not already open, reopen **pp03b.docx** and scroll down to the Tutor Profile Text.

2   Copy and paste the tutor profile text from **pp03b.docx** into the appropriate content areas on slides 5 to 7. Make sure not to insert a blank line at the end of the tutor name, or it'll alter the vertical alignment of the text.

3   For each profile's image, click the Insert Picture control in the profile slide's blue circular border, and then navigate to the PPT03lessons folder to select the image listed in the Tutor Profile Text.

Figure 3-9

Slide 7 after inserting information into a Profile layout.

Mark Fathersbaugh

- Hobbyist crudité experimenter
- Clerical work
- Wrote the theme to a popular cartoon show
- IT support engineer, diagnostic team
- Lead on Raleigh-Durham Retrofit

Q: Are we not interns? A: We are interns.

© Fuse/Getty Images

4   Save your work.

The picture placeholder seamlessly crops and styles the profile images as in Figure 3-9; no change is needed. You could generate this series of slides without using the Slide Master or creating custom layouts, but that's a poor long-term solution; next time you need something like this Profile layout, you'd be starting from scratch again. The power of custom layouts is their ability to scaffold your next several presentations.

CUSTOMIZING A PRESENTATION THEME

If you want to edit the color scheme, font selection, background style, or visual effects for your whole presentation, you'll do so in the Slide Master View. The Slide Master > Background group contains tools to customize the various parts of your document's Theme. Once you've chosen a Theme, you have a collection of slide layouts and visual elements designed to work together, but small changes to color scheme or font pairing can personalize your presentation's look without compromising the structure of its slides.

Best of all, once you've worked out an overall visual scheme for your presentation, you can save it or share it, for instance, as a corporate visual identity. In this last part of the lesson, we'll apply a theme to the slide deck, make a couple of unobtrusive changes to its visual scheme, and export the theme for later use.

CHANGING A THEME'S VISUAL SCHEME

Bottom Line

The difficulty with applying a theme to our document at this point in our slide deck design is that we've already styled several slides to taste; switching themes will change the way the slide elements work together, so it's good to watch out for oddities resulting from reskinning the presentation. You can preview the effects of a theme change by flipping to different slides in the deck and using Live Preview to see how the new background, layout, fonts, and color scheme affect the slides' look. The best slides for this purpose are custom slides, especially those dense with visual elements.

STEP BY STEP | **Changing a theme**

1   Open the Design tab. Select slide 4, and then mouse over several themes in the gallery. Do the same with slides 3 and 5, which are already heavily visually customized.

As you change the theme, Take special note of the way the various elements in slide 5, which uses a custom layout, change appearance while holding position, and compare to what occurs in slide 4: the elements change size and switch places with the text column.

2   Select the Wood Type theme.

Several changes take effect: the logo disappears from the title slide; a circular red seal (meant to contain the slide number) appears in the lower right of each slide; the layout of slide 4 mirrors with the map moving left; the background on slide 3 takes on the Wood Type colors and a different gradient; and every slide's color/font settings are switched to the Wood Type settings. See Figure 3-10.

Figure 3-10

Wood theme applied to a Profile template slide.

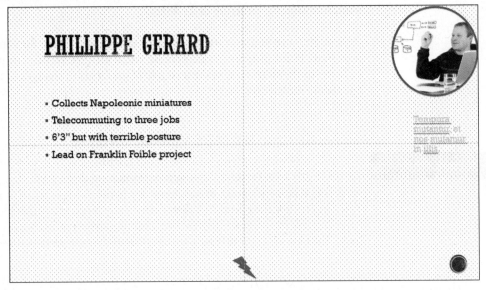

Image used with permission of Microsoft.

Experimenting with alternate color and font schemes is straightforward:

3   Open Slide Master View. Set Slide Master > Background > Colors to Green Yellow, and set Background > Fonts to Tw Cen MT-Rockwell.

4   Still in the Slide Master tab, select Themes > Save Current Theme. Assign to the modified theme the name Intern Green Yellow.

Your new Intern Green Yellow file includes not only the new color/font settings, but your new Profile slide layout, meaning you can send the exported theme to a colleague who might want to work with your overall aesthetic and your custom content.

5   Choose File > Save and then File > Close.

What you learned in this lesson:

• Adding, Styling, and Filling Text Boxes

• Using the Format Pane

• Adding Styled Text with WordArt

• Creating Custom Layouts in the Slide Master

• Customizing Document Themes

Knowledge Assessment

Matching

Match each term to its description or definition.

1. WordArt
2. Format Pane
3. placeholder text
4. Slide Master
5. gradient
6. slide layout
7. text box
8. title slide
9. AutoFit
10. slide background

a. Floating slide element lacking image controls
b. Not a "page" in the Word 2013 sense; can't directly add text here
c. e.g., black fades to white from left to right in slide background
d. Default starting slide for most templates
e. Each template contains several of these; user can also custom design
f. Consolidates fine-grained formatting tools for slide elements
g. Sets visual basis for deck; slide layouts further specify
h. Squashes or stretches text boxes to fit contents
i. Appears in unfilled text box, e.g., as prompt or instructions
j. Complex text styles available regardless of theme

Fill in the Blanks

Complete the following sentences by writing the correct word or words in the blanks provided.

1. To add a current Date field to a slide, use the _____ > Text > Date & Time command.
2. Adjust text/text box proportions automatically as you type with the _____ function.
3. PowerPoint lets the user set default +Heading and _____ fonts.
4. Slide _____ inherit background and placeholder information from the Slide _____.
5. To create a square (not just rectangular) content placeholder, hold down _____ while you drag to insert its border.
6. Complex fill/outline/effects combinations are achieved with one click in the _____ Styles menu.
7. To add the current date to a title slide along with the title itself, add it to the _____ text box.
8. Slide title boxes in the Slide Master contain the boilerplate text "Click to edit _____."
9. To leave a fillable box for an image in a slide layout, click Master Layout > _____ > Picture.
10. The Format > Insert Shapes > _____ > _____ command can be used to alter the shape of a slid element placeholder.

Competency Assessment

Project 3-1: Text Boxes

This exercise involves creating a new document from a template and adding/editing several text boxes.

1. Launch PowerPoint and create a new presentation using the Berlin template. Save your document as **project_3-1_textbox**.
2. Fill in Text Box Test (title) and Lesson 3 (subtitle) on the title slide.
3. Add a blank slide, and add a text box to it. Add two paragraphs of text to the text box.
4. Experiment with resizing the text box to change the word wrapping. Open the Format Pane (right click text box) and adjust the AutoFit options in its Text Options > Text Box tab.
5. Experiment with multi-column text and turning off text wrap entirely (Text Options > Text Box > Wrap text in shape).

    Note the efficient use of space in a two-column format.
6. Experiment with adding text boxes in other shapes and proportions to the slide deck. Alter the backgrounds of your text boxes with Format Shape > Shape Options > Fill commands.
7. When you're comfortable with the text box editing controls, save and close your document.

Project 3-2: WordArt and Text Style

Here you'll try out several Style Options for newly-created WordArt.

1. Open the project file **3-2-source**. Save your document as **project_3-2_wordart**.
2. Add a new slide with layout Title and Content, entitled WordArt Samples.
3. Add five lines of bulleted text (varying bullet levels) to slide 4's text area.
4. Select the final bulleted line and apply a WordArt Style (Drawing Tools > Format > WordArt Styles gallery) to the text. Try out several different WordArt Styles for the five lines of text.

    Note that WordArt Styles are character-level formatting – several styles can be applied to a single line of text.
5. Select the slide title and manually choose Text Fill, Text Outline, and Text Effects options (Drawing Tools > Format), along with a Shape Style for the slide title's text box.
6. Feel free to experiment further with these tools. When you're finished, save and close your document.

Proficiency Assessment

Project 3-3: The Format Pane

In this exercise you'll tweak the formatting options in PowerPoint's Format Pane.

1. Open the project file **3-3-source**. Save your document as **project_3-3_format_pane**.
2. Add a new slide. Open the Format Background Pane.
3. Switch to a Picture/Texture fill. Open the Picture Corrections tab of the Format Pane and choose the Brightness -40%/Contrast +40% preset.

4. Select the main content box on the slide and apply a Top Spotlight – Accent 5 preset gradient fill.

5. In the main content box, do an Online Picture clip art search for office stapler, and insert one of the returned images.

6. Save and close the document.

Project 3-4: Custom Slide Layouts

This exercise challenges you to create a custom slide layout to spec.

1. Create a new blank document. Save your document as **project_3-4_custom_layout**.

2. Follow the general outline of the instructions in this lesson to create a custom slide layout in the Slide Master. It should meet the following specifications: radial gradient background fill, one text box (besides title area), one circular image placeholder, two styled geometric shapes (not placeholders), one piece of WordArt (not a placeholder).

3. Add a slide using your custom slide layout and fill in the various content areas. (Pressing Ctrl+A while editing the new slide will highlight only editable content areas, leaving fixed (background) elements unselected.)

4. Save and close your document.

Mastery Assessment

Project 3-5: Customizing a Theme

Here you'll customize a document theme to taste, and save it to your hard drive.

1. Create a new blank document. Save your document as **project_3-5_custom_theme**.

2. Create a custom theme with the following features: subtle black/purple pattern in background, serif font, Milk Glass visual effects scheme.

3. Save your custom theme (Slide Master > Edit Theme > Save Current Theme) with the filename **project_3-5_blackpurple**.

4. Save your document and quit PowerPoint.

Project 3-6: Custom Calendar Layout

This exercise challenges you to create a complex custom slide layout.

1. Create a new blank document and save it as **project_3-6_calendar**.

2. In the Slide Master, create a generic monthly calendar layout. It should contain five rows (for five weeks), a large space at the top for the name of the month, and placeholders for two images, one in a circular frame.

3. Use your new generic layout to create a 9- or 12-month calendar, with seasonally-appropriate images.

4. Save and close your document.

LESSON SKILL MATRIX

In this lesson, you will learn the following skills:

Transforming Bulleted Lists into SmartArt	Linking and Embedding Excel Worksheets
Visually Editing and Tweaking SmartArt	Creating Charts from Tabular Data
Styling SmartArt	Editing and Styling Charts

KEY TERMS

- SmartArt
- Infographic
- Text Pane (SmartArt)
- Bitmap
- Major Gridline

At Northwind Traders, organizational information, sales data, process outlines, and marketing plans are shared between all the company's departments. Status updates need to be quick, plans need to be unambiguous, and org charts need to be crystal clear. To efficiently share all this information, Northwind's employees turn to infographics and other visuals, recasting complex data as memorable images. PowerPoint helps them turn out custom infographics quickly and easily.

SOFTWARE ORIENTATION

In this lesson you will discover how to incorporate images, tables, and Smart Art in your PowerPoint presentations.

Figure 4-1

Smart Art tools and
formatting functions

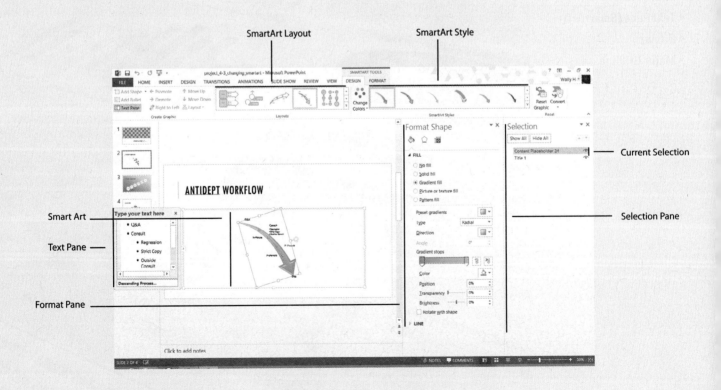

STARTING UP

In this lesson, you'll work with several files from the PPT04lessons folder. Make sure that you have loaded the OfficeLessons folder onto your computer.

GIVING STRUCTURE TO YOUR CONTENT

Tables, charts, and SmartArt occupy a middle ground between straight text and graphics: tables and SmartArt turn structured text content into styled visuals, while charts represent relationships between data points with shapes and colors. Tables can also be used to fit an entire slide's layout to a grid, turning cell text into a visual element.

In this lesson, you'll build slides around tabular data, format structured text as editable **SmartArt**, and transform spreadsheet data into graphs and charts. You'll also link a chart to an Excel document to include live external data in your slide.

TRANSFORMING TEXT INTO SMARTART

The SmartArt feature available in Office lets you format lists as flowcharts, Venn diagrams, cycle diagrams, family trees, and other **infographics**. Moreover, if you build an organization chart from a bulleted list (for example), any later edits you make to the list will be reflected automatically in the diagram. And like other visual slide elements, SmartArt is easily styled using document themes.

1 Begin the lesson by launching PowerPoint 2013.

2 Open the document for this lesson, **pp04a.pptx**, located in the PPT04lessons folder. (For a look at its finished form, open **pp04a-finished.pptm**.)

Take Note For a Microsoft article that lists of all the SmartArt types, see the Descriptions of SmartArt graphics article in Microsoft's Support page at the following URL:

http://office.microsoft.com/en-us/powerpoint-help/descriptions-of-smartart-graphics-HA010057065.aspx

Formatting lists as SmartArt

Bottom Line Unsurprisingly, the most common text format in PowerPoint slides is used as the building block of PowerPoint SmartArt: the bulleted list. In this part of the lesson, we'll take a handful of lists and transform each into a different kind of diagram. (Note that lists needn't actually be bulleted to generate SmartArt, but bullets make a nice clear distinction between text levels 1 and 2.)

STEP BY STEP **Formatting lists as SmartArt**

1 In **pp04a.pptx**, select slide 2, *Mamet Code Process Outline*.

2 Right-click the text of the bulleted list and select Convert to SmartArt > More SmartArt Graphics.

3 From the Cycle group, select the Cycle Matrix type near the bottom and click OK.

PowerPoint automatically styles top-level bullets as cycle elements and treats level 2 as text. The original list is preserved in the SmartArt's Text pane if it did not open automatically, from which you can directly edit the SmartArt's contents as well.

4   If the **Text pane** isn't already open, do so now: Click the cycle diagram, and then click the small arrow handle on the left edge of the selection box.

5   In the Text pane, change the Free heading to Reset.

Because the diagram and its source list remain linked (see Figure 4-2), editing either the Text pane or the image text will automatically update the other.

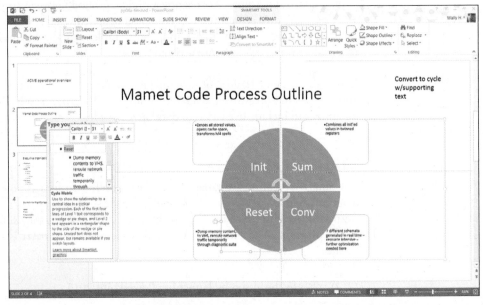

Note that the two lower level 2 text pieces are set too close to the cycle diagram. You can easily fix this, since the various components of a SmartArt diagram can be formatted just as any other floating slide element with the Format pane.

6   Right-click the SmartArt's lower-right label and choose Size and Position to open the Format Shape pane. In the Text Box section, set Vertical alignment (of the text) to Bottom; then click in the lower-left label and do the same to it.

7   Choose File > Save As and navigate to the PPT04lessons folder. Type **pp04a_work** in the File name text field and click Save.

Visually editing a flowchart

Bottom Line

Slide 3 in the sample deck can be turned into a flowchart without making changes to it, but you can customize its content and visual style with the SmartArt Design and Format tabs.

STEP BY STEP   **Visually editing a flowchart**

1   Advance to slide 3. Transform the list of names into an organization chart (Home > Paragraph > Convert to SmartArt Graphic > Organization Chart).

2   Click the Robeson box in the chart, and then click SmartArt Tools > Design > Add Shape > Add Assistant to insert an assistant box beneath it. Enter the name Paul in the new text box.

3   Right-click Pilfer and choose Add Shape > Add Assistant from the context menu. Enter Drudge in the text box.

4   Open the org chart's Text pane if it is not already opened. In the text pane, select Atchison and the lines below and press Ctrl+X to move them to the clipboard. Then Paste them between Paul and Pilfer in the Text pane by moving your cursor before Pilfer and pressing Ctrl+V. The entire Atchison branch of the chart moves to the center of the graphic.

5   Click Atchison in the SmartArt itself, and select SmartArt > Design > Create Graphic > Layout > Right Hanging to switch that branch to a narrower layout, as in Figure 4-3.

Figure 4-3

SmartArt layouts affect not just the look, but the meaning of your diagram.

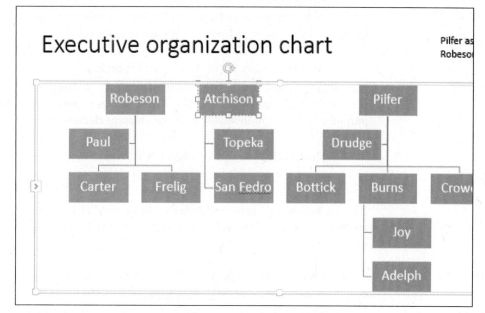

The other two branches in this SmartArt can't switch to the compact Right or Left Hanging layouts without confusing assistants with lower branches; not all layouts are created equal in terms of the information they format. That said, this new layout might not be the best choice: at present, it's reasonable to (incorrectly) read Topeka as Atchison's assistant. We may need a different visual scheme.

6   Click Undo in the Quick Access Toolbar to change the layout back.

Styling a piece of SmartArt

Bottom Line

PowerPoint provides three sets of tools for altering the appearance of a piece of SmartArt. As usual, the document theme establishes the baseline appearance of your diagrams. The SmartArt Design tab lets you add structural elements (for example, additional nodes in an org chart), try out diagram variants, switch between sets of Theme Colors, and apply visual effects to the whole diagram with a SmartArt Style. Finally, the SmartArt Format tab provides access to the usual formatting tools for slide elements: lines, fills, colors, and so on.

We'll use each of these tools to give our org chart a coherent visual scheme; then we will discard the standard Org Chart format to make our organizational hierarchy clearer.

1   Deselect the SmartArt and delete the small text box in the upper right of the slide. In the Design tab, apply the Banded theme (it has a white stripe through the middle) and select the third (charcoal/white) variant. All four slides take on the new look.

2   Reselect the SmartArt. In the SmartArt Design tab, change to the Hierarchy List layout found near the bottom. Then click Change Colors > Colorful – Accent Colors.

The available color schemes draw from the Theme Colors; you can further customize the SmartArt's coloration by going block by block through the chart, but that's not really a sustainable method.

3   Apply the Brick Scene 3-D SmartArt Style.

Note that Paul and Drudge, the assistants, have been dropped to the bottom of their respective branches; the Hierarchy List and Org Chart treat assistants differently. This works for our present purposes: we'll just individually style the assistant elements to show their special status.

4   Shift+click Paul and Drudge. Click SmartArt > Format > Shapes > Smaller five times. Then click Shape Styles > Subtle Effect – Brown, Accent 6 to give the assistant nodes an appropriately modest look.

You can individually move and style the components of a piece of SmartArt, but the entire graphic appears as a single entry in the Selection pane. We'll use the pane to grab the whole SmartArt object at once.

5   Open the Selection pane (Home > Editing > Select > Selection Pane) and select the Content Placeholder entry, which refers to the SmartArt. Close the Selection pane and Format Shape pane to clear screen real estate, then drag the diagram to center it in the charcoal region of the slide. Figure 4-4 shows the result.

Figure 4-4

A more readable, less ambiguous org chart built from the same data.

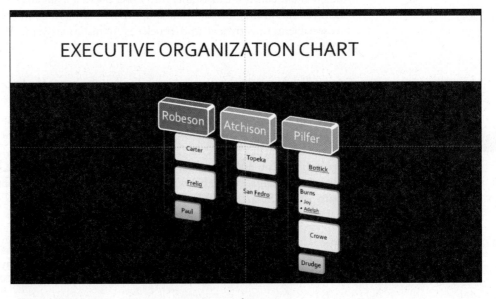

6   Choose File > Save to save your work.

Piecing together SmartArt

Bottom Line

Slide 4 of our test presentation requires some adjustments, mostly Cut and Paste, before you can transform it from text to SmartArt. To see what the slide will look like when you're done, see slide 4 of **pp04a-finished.pptm** in the PPT04lessons folder.

STEP BY STEP   **Piecing together SmartArt**

1   To start with, select the left bulleted list and convert it to the Balance SmartArt graphic (Home > Paragraph > Convert to SmartArt Graphic > More SmartArt Graphics > Relationship > Balance). With its Text pane open (see Figure 4-5), you can see what's happening: the Balance graphic takes two level 1 paragraphs (Fast and Dependable) to compare them and leaves out any other level 1 text.

Figure 4-5

Studying the text pane provides insight into how to structure text for future SmartArt conversion.

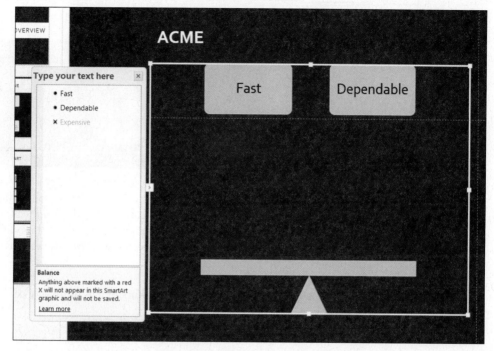

To make this SmartArt graphic work, we'll need a bulleted list with two level 1 entries (ACME and FredCo), each with several pros/cons at level 2.

2   Right-click the bounding box of the SmartArt and choose Convert to Text to turn the SmartArt back into a bulleted list, then make the necessary changes to the list.

3   Cut and Paste the list to the right (FredCo) to the bottom of the ACME list. When you have a single list of seven lines, select all the text in the list and click Home > Paragraph > Increase List Level.

4   Insert the word ACME as a level 1 line at the top of the list, and insert FredCo at level 1 between Expensive and Sluggish.

5   Delete the ACME and FredCo headings above the two content areas, and then change the layout of slide 4 to Title and Content (Home > Slides > Layout > Title and Content).

6   Now place your cursor in the list and reapply the Balance SmartArt graphic (in the Relationships collection).

The balance tilts to the right, but the balance is dynamically set to tilt toward the side that has more level 2 text. Now let's make a frivolous change to the image and have *Future-proof* tip over and fall off the scale altogether.

7   Drag the Future-proof box a bit to the right, and use its rotate handle to tip it roughly 45 degrees clockwise, as in Figure 4-6. Then open the Text pane and change *Future-proof* to Open format.

8   To close, give the SmartArt a bit of panache by applying the Intense Effect SmartArt Style from the SmartArt Styles in the Design tab.

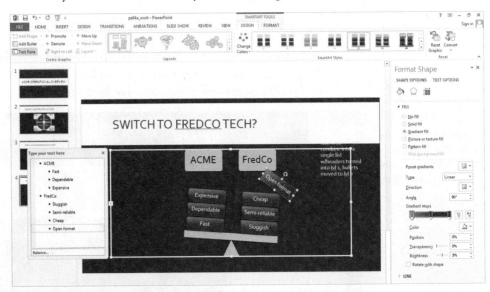

As you can see, the *Open format* text box is still linked to its source list line despite having moved around; bullet order is unrelated to, and unaffected by, any graphical manipulations you might do. But deleting text (or a text box) from the graphic itself will still modify the bulleted list. In fact, if you delete the *Cheap* box from our teeter totter, the *Open format* box will snap into its place, and the balance will tilt back to the center.

To help you understand SmartArt better, think of it as unusually complicated text formatting, not as graphics with text labels.

LINKING AND EMBEDDING EXTERNAL DATA

Because PowerPoint presentations are often used to show off other work, PowerPoint 2013 lets you link and embed external data in a presentation. A table in a slide can pull its contents from an Excel file, for instance, and automatically update when changes are made in Excel. You can even insert an entire Word 2013 document into a slide, which opens a copy of Word within PowerPoint, to bring the full power of Word's formatting and layout abilities to that slide.

Take Note   For step-by-step details of linking to external data, see the section on Embedding and Linking Objects in Word Lesson 6, "Beyond Word: Linking and Collaborating" in the first part of this book. This section will cover the Insert Object command, which lets you edit a slide element using applications such as Photoshop or MS Paint, while providing an alternate method to link to external data

In this part of the lesson, you'll use Excel, Word, and MS Paint to edit directly the contents of your presentation.

Embedding an Excel worksheet as an object

Bottom Line   The Insert > Object command lets you create objects representing external data and add them to your presentation. An embedded object becomes part of the .pptx file itself (significantly increasing file size); double-clicking the object within the presentation launches the appropriate editing application. For instance, double-clicking an Excel worksheet embedded in a slide opens an instance of Excel 2013 right inside PowerPoint. If you embed an object created from an external file, changes to the original file won't affect the copy inside the presentation because the embedded version is a copy of the original.

A linked object, on the other hand, stays connected to its source data. If you create a link to an Excel spreadsheet in your slide deck, editing the object opens the original file (if it can still be found).

Embedding data as a slide object is as simple as inserting an image.

STEP BY STEP   **Embedding an Excel worksheet as an object**

1   Add a new slide, slide 5, to **pp04a_work.pptx**, with layout Title Only and title it Stock Holdings.

2   Select Insert > Text > Object. Select Create from file, and Browse to your PPT04lessons folder. Select **pp04b.xlsx** and click OK. Click OK again to insert the object.

3   Resize the object to fit in the content area and place it at the center of the slide.

Excel objects can be minimally formatted; if you click the embedded worksheet, the Drawing Tools > Format tab is mostly greyed out. However, the Shape Fill is still available.

4   Click Format > Shape Styles > Shape Fill and select White.

Notice in Figure 4-7 that the cells that fill in with white are the ones that haven't otherwise been colored in the original Excel document; this occurs because the unformatted cell are effectively transparent from PowerPoint's perspective.

Figure 4-7

Unformatted cells in the original Excel file match the charcoal presentation background; white fill affects only those cells.

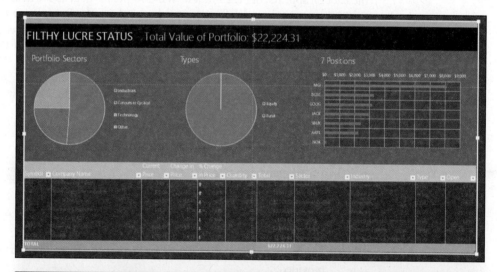

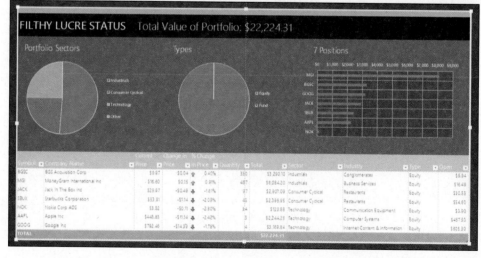

Editing embedded objects

To edit an embedded object, double-click it. If it's an Office document (in this case, an Excel worksheet), Windows launches an embedded version of the appropriate app within PowerPoint, as in Figure 4-8.

STEP BY STEP   **Editing embedded objects**

1   Double-click the portfolio spreadsheet object.

Figure 4-8

The File menu returns, along with a full Excel Ribbon, when you edit an Excel object within PowerPoint.

2   Click the word FILTHY (cell B2). Change the words FILTHY LUCRE STATUS to CURRENT HOLDINGS.

3   Press Escape to return to PowerPoint. The Excel object updates to reflect the new heading.

The editing interface for an embedded Excel worksheet can be a bit confusing: Excel's version of the Ribbon appears, but the File and Window menus float above it, and the PowerPoint application menu appears in the top left corner of the window. The PowerPoint Ribbon vanishes utterly; you can't change the enclosing presentation while you edit the embedded object. Remember that the Escape key functions literally here: pressing Escape pops you out of the embedded editor back to PowerPoint proper.

The same principles apply when you insert a Paint object, but to edit a **bitmap** image, Windows launches a full version of MS Paint.

STEP BY STEP   **Editing a bitmap image**

1   Select Insert > Text > Object > Create new > Bitmap Image and click OK. MS Paint launches.

2   Switch to a dark green color. Draw a picture of a dollar sign ($) in the white space provided.

3   Press Alt+F4 to close Paint and return to PowerPoint. Place the new image, resized to fit in the white band, in the upper-right corner.

You don't need to save your Paint document; you're not working on a separate Paint file as such, you're editing an object within your PowerPoint (.pptx) file using Paint as its borrowed editing interface (See Figure 4-9.) In fact, if you keep both PowerPoint and Paint visible at once while editing the bitmap, you'll see any changes you make in Paint reflected instantly in the slide.

Figure 4-9

An embedded object differs from a linked file in that its data exists only within the .pptx file

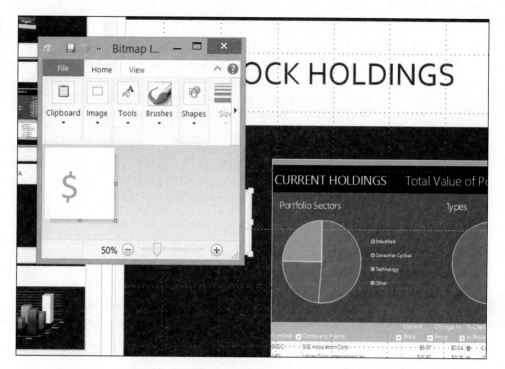

4   Choose File > Save to save your work.

Creating a linked object

Bottom Line

Linked objects can be created using the Paste Special command to link to data on the clipboard, or with the Insert Object command. We'll use Insert Object in this section, building on the exercises you've just completed.

1   Add a new slide to your presentation with the title Expectations Management Plan.

2   Click Insert > Object. Select Create from file, and click Browse. Select **pp04c.docx** in your PPT04lessons folder, and click OK and click OK again.

PowerPoint takes a snapshot of the contents of the Word document and inserts it into the current slide, but leaves the data in the source file (keeping the presentation document itself slim). To edit, just double-click as usual; the original file opens in Word.

You can also choose to create a linked file, rather than an embedded one, when using the Insert Picture control in a slide: instead of clicking Insert after selecting your image, select Insert and Link, or Create a Link, from the Insert drop-down menu.

CREATING A CHART FROM TABULAR DATA

Sometimes an audience wants to see raw data, but more often it wants a visual that highlights relationships between data: a graph or chart instead of a table (however cleverly designed). Excel offers a suite of powerful tools for representing data visually; PowerPoint borrows some of these tools to let you include charts and graphs in your slides.

Take Note   Additional details on tables are found in Word Lesson 5, "Working with Tables," in the first part of this book. The commands for adding, navigating, styling, and editing tables are the same between Word and PowerPoint 2013; given the similarities between the two interfaces, you're encouraged to practice linking/embedding/drawing tables in both apps.

We'll add charts to our presentation in two ways: directly in PowerPoint (in an embedded Excel editing window), and by pasting in an Excel chart linked to its source data.

Generating charts in PowerPoint

Bottom Line   If you create a chart from scratch in PowerPoint, a mini Excel worksheet opens to let you enter data. This is a great way to quickly add simple info graphics to your slide show.

STEP BY STEP   **Generating a chart in PowerPoint**

1   Add a new Title and Content slide (slide 7) to your open presentation, with layout Title and Content. Title it **Fall Semester Sales**.

2   Click **Insert Chart** in the content area. Select the **3-D Column** layout and click **OK**.

3   Insert the following data into the Excel sheet that appears:

	CPU	Monitor	RAM
Wilson	4.3	2.4	2
Johnson	2.5	4.4	2
Clarkson	3.5	1.8	3
Wolfson	4.5	2.8	5

4   Close the embedded Chart in the Microsoft PowerPoint window. Click the chart area, open the Chart Elements handle (+), and uncheck **Legend**.

5   Apply **Chart > Design > Quick Layout > Layout 7** and **Chart Style 11** to the chart.

6   Finally, right-click anywhere on the chart and select **Edit Data > Edit Data** to reopen the worksheet.

If you need the full features of Excel to edit your data, you can open Excel 2013 through the Edit Data mini-sheet or the Edit Data context command.

Editing individual chart elements

Just as SmartArt pieces stay connected to elements in an underlying bulleted list, the individual pieces of PowerPoint charts (such as the red and orange bars in our sample chart) are linked to cell data in the associated table; you can tailor a chart's appearance and content by editing individual chart elements. To see how this works, let's give Wolfson and Johnson's RAM sales some extra emphasis:

STEP BY STEP   Editing chart elements

1   If **pp04a_work.ppt** isn't open, open the file now. In the chart, click Johnson's yellow RAM sales bar in the back row; the entire RAM row is selected. (Hovering your mouse over the bar will bring up a tooltip identifying the bar and showing its source data.) Click the bar again to select the individual bar.

2   Click Chart > Format > Shape Styles > Colored Outline – Orange, Accent 2 to format that individual bar.

3   Do the same with Wolfson's much larger RAM sales bar (Figure 4-10).

Figure 4-10

PowerPoint's chart tools offer fine-grained control over both aesthetics and content.

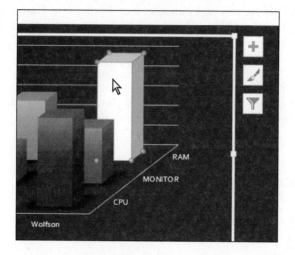

4   Close the worksheet.

Every element of the chart is equally customizable. Indeed, you can even right-click the tiny gridlines that run along the edges of the graph, and then open the Format pane (Format Gridlines) to change any of their visual parameters. Clicking through the various components of the graph with the Format pane open will show you how customizable your graph's visuals are. The Chart Design and Format tabs remain available, as they would for any floating slide element.

Linking a chart to external Excel data

Bottom Line

Naturally, you can paste a chart directly from an existing Excel document, just as any other image. Since Excel charts are linked to the sheets that generate them, you can choose to maintain that link when you copy the chart into PowerPoint. Your presentation can then update to reflect changes to the underlying chart data.

STEP BY STEP   **Linking a chart to external Excel data**

1   Add another slide (slide 8) to your presentation, entitled Sales Comparison.

2   Navigate to your PPT04lessons folder and open **pp04e.xlsx** in Excel 2013. Select the Seasonal Beverage Sales graph and press Ctrl+C to copy it. Make sure you're selecting the entire chart and not just one element; click in an empty region of the image to be sure.

3   In PowerPoint, click Home > Paste > Use Destination Theme & Link Data.

4   Place the chart near the lower left corner of the slide, then drag the upper right handle further up and to the right to fill the slide's content area.

5   Navigate back to **pp04e.xlsx** and change the PepDrink Spring sales value to 20. Save the file as **pp04e_work** in the PPT04lessons folder and close Excel.

The data should automatically refresh, but in case it has failed to do so, we'll manually refresh the data in PowerPoint.

6   In PowerPoint, click the chart and choose Chart Tools > Design > Data > Refresh Data.

Take Note   If you click Refresh Data with the Excel source file open, you may get an error message to indicate that the file is locked for editing by another user. In that case, Cancel the refresh and close the file in Excel. Note that a linked local file mirrored to SkyDrive may need to upload to the cloud before a data refresh will work.

Styling charts and graphs

Bottom Line   As with a chart created directly in PowerPoint, double-clicking a chart linked to Excel opens the Format pane. From there you can make subtle or dramatic changes to your graphics' look.

STEP BY STEP   **Styling charts and graphs**

1   Double-click the graph to open the Format pane. Select one of the gridlines; the Pane's heading changes to Format Major Gridlines.

2   In the Fill & Line subpane, click the Gradient line option button; PowerPoint recolors the gridlines along a gradient, using an accent color from the current theme.

3   With the gridlines still selected, click the drop-down menu beside the **Major Gridline** Options heading in the pane (see Figure 4-11). Select Chart Area from the drop-down menu.

Figure 4-11

From the Format pane, you can select any chart element for styling.

The Chart Options drop-down menu displays a list of every editable chart element so you don't have to search for half-hidden objects in the chart's back row. There's also space to translate your content for visually impaired audiences:

4   In the Chart Options > Size & Properties tab, edit the Alt Text: set the Title to Seasonal Beverage Product Sales by Product and the Description to Breakdown of 5 soda product sales by season.

As is the case with text and SmartArt, when you need to do fine-grained editing of floating slide elements such as charts and graphics (which you'll do in the next lesson), you'll spend a lot of time inside the Format pane. If you have the screen real estate, you could leave several editing/formatting panes open all the time, and switch back and forth between Normal Mode and Reading Mode to get a wide-angle look at your slides. As always, your location in PowerPoint's natural workflow will shape how you use the application's interface.

5   Choose File > Save to save your work.

What you learned in this lesson:

- Transforming Bulleted Lists into SmartArt

- Visually Editing and Tweaking SmartArt

- Styling SmartArt

- Linking and Embedding Excel Worksheets

- Creating Charts from Tabular Data

- Editing and Styling Charts

Knowledge Assessment

Fill in the Blanks

Complete the following sentences by writing the correct word or words in the blanks provided.

1. To create a piece of SmartArt, begin with text in _____ form.
2. Double clicking a linked object in a slide allows the user to _____ the object.
3. The _____ popup lets you customize which components (gridlines, axis labels, etc.) are included in an infographic.
4. Chart elements like gridlines are styled in the _____ Pane.
5. Information in row/column form, such as a spreadsheet, is called _____ data.
6. The data behind a SmartArt infographic is accessible from the SmartArt's _____ Pane.
7. Inserting "live" data from an external file into a PowerPoint document is called _____ the data.
8. SmartArt Styles take their color choices first from the current document _____.
9. To show who works for whom within a corporation, use an infographic called an _____.
10. Clicking a piece of SmartArt adds the _____ and _____ tabs to the Ribbon.

True/False

Circle T if the statement is true or F it the statement is false.

T F 1. Double clicking a piece of text in a SmartArt object brings up the Text Pane.
T F 2. The Paste Special command can be used to create a linked Excel spreadsheet within a presentation.
T F 3. Double clicking an embedded Excel file opens an Excel interface "inside" PowerPoint.
T F 4. Navigating PowerPoint tables works just the same as navigating Word tables.
T F 5. Photoshop files and MS Paint images can be embedded in PowerPoint slides.
T F 6. Editing embedded Office data in a PowerPoint document adds old-fashioned File and Window menus atop the PowerPoint window.
T F 7. Moving one shape within a piece of SmartArt "unlinks" the SmartArt from its source data.
T F 8. Linked data exists in a separate file, independent of the PowerPoint data itself.
T F 9. All SmartArt types can be made from bulleted lists of any length and depth.
T F 10. In an Office org chart, "child" means the same thing as "assistant."

Competency Assessment

Project 4-1: Adding SmartArt to a Slide

In this exercise you'll insert SmartArt graphics into several presentation slides.

1. Open the exercise file **4-1-source**. Save your document as **project_4-1_smartart**.

2. Select slide 3 of the Northwind "Interoffice Mtg" presentation. Click somewhere in the bulleted list and choose Format > Paragraph > Convert to SmartArt. Select the org chart.

3. In the text pane, indent all the lines below "Cameo."
   The SmartArt automatically updates to reflect the new bulleted list structure.

4. Right click the flowchart on slide 2 and select Convert to Text.

5. Indent lines 3-5, then convert the list to Basic Timeline SmartArt.

6. Select several pieces of the SmartArt in turn – the blue dots, arrow, and text pieces – and move them around the screen.

7. Click SmartArt Tools > Design > Reset Graphic.

8. Save and close your document.

Project 4-2: Changing SmartArt Layouts

In this exercise you'll modify pieces of SmartArt in a presentation.

1. Open the project file **4-2-source.** Save your document as **project_4-2_changing_smartart.**

2. Select the SmartArt on slide 2. In the SmartArt Tools > Design tab, mouse over several entries in the Layouts gallery to see the changes the different layouts make to the chart's information.

3. Select the Circle Process layout.

4. Right click slide 2 in the slide selection pane and click Duplicate Slide. (The duplicate is now slide 3.)

5. On slide 3, select the SmartArt and in the SmartArt Design tools tab, click Reset > Convert > Convert to Shapes.

6. Rotate the new image 45 degrees counterclockwise.

7. Add a gradient fill to slide 3's background, Linear gradient, from bottom left to top right (like the image), color Orange – Accent 2.

8. Save and close the document.

Project 4-3: Styling SmartArt

This exercise focuses on using SmartArt Styles and layouts.

1. Open the project file **4-3-source.** Save your document as **project_4-3_styling_smartart.**
2. Switch to the Integral document theme.
3. Click the SmartArt graphics on slides 2 and 4 and experiment with different SmartArt Styles, Layouts, and color schemes in the Design tab.

    Note that the converted graphic on slide 3 can no longer be styled like SmartArt, though its fonts still update with any theme/font changes to the file.

4. Open the Format Pane and experiment with tweaking the appearance of individual pieces of the SmartArt graphics – the lines in the org chart, for instance. You can click Reset Graphic to return the SmartArt to its original appearance.
5. When you're finished experimenting, save and close your document.

Project 4-4: Embedding Excel Data

In this exercise you'll embed an Excel worksheet in a slide show.

1. Create a new blank document. Save your document as **project_4-4_embedding.**
2. Look over project file **4-4-source.xlsx.**
3. Add a blank slide to the project file and use the Insert Object command with the Create from File option to embed the 4-4-source.xlsx worksheet into your presentation.
4. Double click the embedded data to edit; choose Home > Styles > Format as Table, pick a table formatting style, and give the range A3:C9 to change the appearance of the embedded data.
5. Update the "Books" data to 60 units for 200 total income, and format the column C data using the Currency number format.
6. Save and close your document.

Mastery Assessment

Project 4-5: Charts from Tabular Data

In this exercise you'll generate a chart from new tabular data, right in PowerPoint.

1. Create a new blank document. Save your document as **project_4-5_tabular**.
2. Add a pie chart to slide 2 entitled Percentage of Sector Profits, 2013, with the following data behind it:

Company	Profit
Northwind	3.3
ProductCo	4.1
ObjectCo	2.5
FasterCo	4.2
FastestCo	4.8

3. Delete the title placeholder from slide 2.
4. Save and close your document.

Project 4-6: PowerPoint Genealogy

In this exercise you'll build a family tree within PowerPoint.

1. Create a new slide show and save it as **project_4-6_genealogy**.
2. Create a family tree on paper going back to your grandparents, then use SmartArt to turn that drawing into an infographic in PowerPoint.
3. Save and close your document and PowerPoint.

LESSON SKILL MATRIX

In this lesson, you will learn the following skills:

Recolor, Adjust, Crop, and Stack Images	Add Media Triggers to Slide Objects
Heighten Visual Impact with Animations	Embed Online and Local Video
Enrich Slides with Sound Effects and Background Sound	Use Grids and Guides to Lay Out Slides

KEY TERMS

- Crop
- Selection Pane
- Motion Path
- Codec
- Compress
- Alignment Guides

The sales and marketing team at Northwind Traders often needs to show their upcoming commercials and video presentations to stores that sell their products and other marketing partners. To easily share upcoming sales and marketing efforts, Northwind's communications and design teams integrate their multimedia content into dynamic and rich PowerPoint presentations. They can include sales data, planning information, and video all into a single PowerPoint file that is easy to share with their sales and marketing team.

SOFTWARE ORIENTATION

This lesson helps you effectively incorporate graphics and multimedia into your PowerPoint presentations.

Figure 5-1

Animation and
timing controls

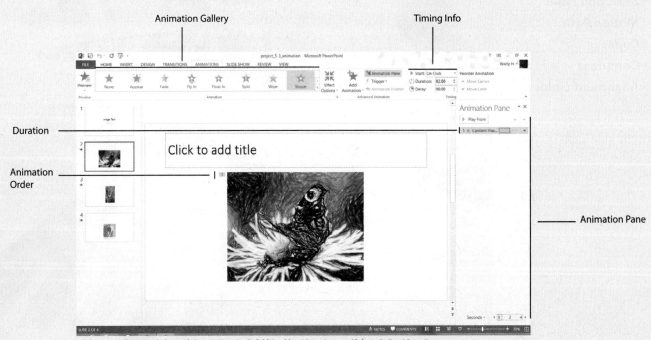

Slide 1: © enduro/iStockphoto; Slide 2: © Tom Brakefield/Stockbyte/Getty Images; Slide 3: © Fuse/Getty Images

STARTING UP

In this lesson, you'll work with several files from the PPT05lessons folder. Make sure that you have loaded the OfficeLessons folder onto your computer.

BEYOND BULLETED LISTS AND BAR GRAPHS

Now we come to the final elements of a slide builder's toolkit: graphics, sound, and video. PowerPoint handles images and video objects just as any other floating visual elements, with the standard Design and Format tools. Sound effects and music, much less common in presentations for a variety of reasons, work a little like animations or transitions: you can cue a sound up with a fixed time delay or start it with a mouse click.

In this lesson, you'll also explore PowerPoint's image-editing toolkit, which lets you make simple adjustments to images embedded in your slides. Finally, you'll add some custom animations to your slide elements, turning a single text block into a swirl of motion.

Your final product will look something like **pp05a-finished.pptx**; feel free to use it as a visual guide while you work through the exercises in this lesson. Read the comments in the sample file, which walk through the design choices behind the presentation.

Recoloring and adjusting images

Bottom Line

The Picture Tools > Format tab in PowerPoint contains a collection of tools to set the layout, framing, size, and shape of an image; the same tools can be applied to clip art, SmartArt, and text boxes. But Word provides a set of tools to alter the content of an image (the Format tab's Adjust group), which you can use to obtain fine-grained control over the look of an image when attention to detail could have a huge impact on a slide's effectiveness.

Crucially, these are nondestructive editing tools: no matter how many edits you make to an embedded image, you can return to the original with a single click.

We'll use the image formatting tools available in Word to blend the image in slide 2 into the muted palette of the presentation.

STEP BY STEP | **Recoloring and adjusting images**

1   Open the file called **pp05a.pptx** found in the PPT05lessons folder.

2   Choose File > Save As and navigate to the PPT05lessons folder. Name the file **pp05a_work** and click Save.

3   Select slide 2 in your presentation and click the blue image.

4   Click **Picture Tools** > **Format**. Recast the image in black and white by clicking **Adjust** > **Color** > **Grayscale** (Figure 5-2 shows the gallery of Color options.).

Figure 5-2

Choose Grayscale from the Color options.

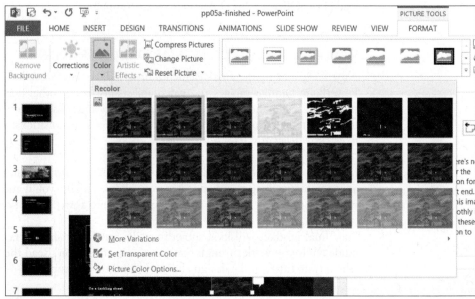

Slides 2, 3, and 5: Photos used with permission of Microsoft

5   Click **Adjust** > **Corrections** > **Brightness –20% Contrast –20%** to further mute the image.

6   Finally, click **Picture Styles** > **Picture Effects** > **Soft Edges** > **Soft Edges Options** to bring up the Format pane. Set the Soft Edges value to **17pt**.

The Format pane is your main tool for tweaking individual slide and floating element parameters.

7   Save your work, and then preview this slide only by pressing **Shift+F5** (then **Escape** when you're done).

Take Note   At this level of blend, brightness, and contrast, the image is hard to make out, but in a dark room it will demand attention without stealing from the recurring blue text. Indeed, that's our main purpose in pulling the color out of the image in slide 2: it pulls focus into the slide while leaving the word *house* prominent.

Cropping an image

Bottom Line

The Format tab includes a **Crop** tool for paring away unwanted parts of an image to keep viewer emphasis on the most important visual content. The image on slide 5 image stands out too much from its background; instead of blending it, we'll crop away the bright background.

STEP BY STEP   **Cropping an image**

1   Select slide **5** and click the image of the keys.

2   Click **Format** > **Size** > **Crop** > **Crop to Shape** > **Oval** (in the Basic Shapes section).

3   Right-click the cropped image and choose **Format Picture**.

4   In the Size & Properties tab, deselect Lock aspect ratio and enter 1.25 for both width and height. Then go to the Effects tab and apply the Paint Strokes effect (shown in Figure 5-3) from the Artistic Effects gallery .

The Paint Strokes effect makes the image a little difficult to parse at first; this is not ideal for a conventional presentation, but it fits the visual tone of our narrative slide deck.

Figure 5-3

The image of the keys with cropping and effects applied.

Photo used with permission of Microsoft

5   Drag the resized image to center right, a little closer to the right edge of the slide. Save your work.

Reordering images in the object stack

Bottom Line

At times, images and text will overlap, either because a slide is crowded or because you're using one element as background for another. You can alter the order of objects in the stack with the Format > Arrange tools, and use the **Selection pane** to grab an object hidden behind other slide elements.

STEP BY STEP   **Reordering images in the object stack**

1   Select slide 3. Click Insert > Text > Text Box and then click an empty region of the slide.

2   In the text box, type It willed as it was.

3   Click Format > Arrange > Selection pane. Click the eye icon next to Picture Placeholder 7 (to hide the image), then click to select the TextBox 1 entry (Figure 5-4), and click again to edit its name. Rename TextBox 1 to will-text.

Figure 5-4

Toggling the visibility of slide elements in the Selection pane.

4   Rename Picture Placeholder 7 to house-img. Keep it invisible for the moment.

5   Position the new text box an inch below the midline of the slide, above *It breathes where it will.*

6   In the Selection pane, drag will-text to the bottom of the stack, then click to make house-img visible, obscuring the text box. Close the Selection pane, and then save your work.

The Selection pane works a little like a visual outline of the slide; just as is the case with outlines and text, the Selection pane lets you change the relative positions of objects without using the object's handles or selecting objects in the slide area itself. In this case, we're hiding the new text behind the image in order to reveal it later by fading the image out. We'll add that effect next.

HEIGHTENING VISUAL IMPACT WITH ANIMATIONS

The basic commands for adding animations and transitions to a slide show were covered in Lesson 2, "Getting Started with PowerPoint 2013"; in this section, we'll add a single exit animation to generate a novel visual effect (revealing hidden text), then fill a slide with a complex jumble of animations using custom movement paths.

Creating a crossfade effect with stacked slide elements

Bottom Line

First we'll finish slide 3 with a subtle animation effect. A "crossfade" is just a combination of two animations: one object fades out, another fades in, in its place.

STEP BY STEP | **Creating a crossfade effect**

1   Click to select the house image in slide 3.

2   Open the Animations tab and scroll down the Animation gallery to apply the Fade exit animation.

3   In the Timing group, set the animation's duration to 3 (seconds). Save your work.

Preview the slide with Shift+F5. PowerPoint doesn't offer a crossfade animation equivalent to the Fade transition (which fades out one slide and fades in another), but this stack/fadeout combination accomplishes the same thing.

Take Note   It's easy to add a sound to play along with an animation: just select Effect Options in the Animation pane and select the sound file. You can also play audio over a slide transition by selecting Transitions > Timing > Sound. Feel free to experiment with these commands on your own; you'll work with PowerPoint's audio tools in a later section of this lesson.

Creating complex scenes by clustering animations

Motion Paths let you control the movement of an object around the space of the slide. Moving a single object draws attention to it; moving several objects simultaneously draws attention to the quality of the movement rather than any one moving part. The fifth slide of our storybook slide show offers an interesting opportunity to use a cluster of animations for dramatic purposes. (Important: This is a lengthy process; save your file often as you work through this section.)

STEP BY STEP | **Creating complex scenes by clustering animations**

1   Select slide 5. Click the title, *Still it stands*. Apply the Custom Path animation (under Motion Paths in the gallery) in the Animations tab.

The mouse pointer now switches to a reticle. (On a touch device there's no pointer and the next step will be quite natural; this is another example of how touchscreens work great with PowerPoint 2013.)

2   Click and drag to draw a smooth arch shape from the current title's location to the lower-right corner of the slide. Press Enter when the line is drawn. Preview the new animation by pressing Shift+F5.

3   Now click the main text area located underneath the title, and then click Advanced Animation > Add Animation > Custom Path. Draw a wide flat loop that circles to the right, down a bit, then back to a spot just below its start. Press Enter when the arc is drawn, and then open the Animation pane in the Advanced Animation group.

Figure 5-5

PowerPoint animates a text block line by line.

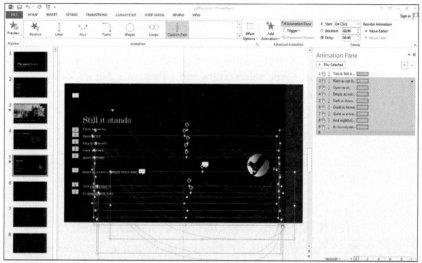

Slides 2, 3, and 5: Photos used with permission of Microsoft

As you can see in Figure 5-5, PowerPoint applies the animation to the entire contents of the text box, but by default, it splits the animation up by line. (You can customize this behavior under Effect Options > Sequence.) Our eight-line text box is now animated in eight separate steps, one line at a time. We're going for a different effect.

4   Click the double caret in the Animation pane to expand the animation list. The eight grouped animations are selected by default. Ctrl+click *Plain as can be* in the pane to deselect it, and then right-click and choose Remove to remove the remaining animations. Only two remain: the title and *Plain as can be*.

The rest of the work for this slide follows the same principle: animate the text block, then delete every new entry from the Animation pane except the line you want to apply the new animation to. Notice that these animations are pulling the short poem apart: for the purposes in this lesson, we'll sacrifice readability for the sake of visual drama.

Take Note   PowerPoint can't animate a single word from a line of text; its chosen level of abstraction is the paragraph. If you need to animate one word from a text string, you'll have to do extra work: for instance, you might just animate a second text box with only that word in it, or with all the other text in the background color instead of the text color. Alternatively, you could download scripts online to split up a line of text into individual text boxes. As always, deciding in advance the kind of visual effect you want to generate can save you a lot of work when you start the actual animating.

5   Repeat steps 3 and 4 for four or five more lines of the main text block, drawing a motion path for the block and then deleting all the newly-added Animation pane entries except the one you want to keep.

Take Note   Make sure to use Add Animation rather than the gallery when applying additional motion paths; otherwise, you'll replace the existing text animation instead of adding a second animation.

6 Select every animation in the Animation pane except the first two (title and first text line), right-click the selection, and choose Start With Previous. Save your work, then press Shift+F5 to preview.

The slide animates in two parts: the title curves to bottom-right corner on your first click, and then the lines of text fly apart all at once on second click. Now we'll change the slide further, for drama's sake: we'll have these two effects occur without a click, as if the text were moving on its own.

Take Note   To add more drama to our animation design, we might have moved each line of the text box just a handful of pixels very slowly, perhaps an inch over ten seconds. However, for the purposes of this exercise, it's more useful to see quick dramatic movement.

7 Click in the Animation pane to clear your selection. Then right-click entry 1 in the pane, and select Start After Previous. Set its Delay in the Timing group of the Animations tab to 2 seconds. Preview the slide with Shift+F5, and then save your work.

It takes a lot of work to generate this effect, but remember that PowerPoint isn't really an animation program. That said, it's a pleasantly odd visual effect that seems right for this particular slide deck.

After working on an appropriate set of visuals, we'll work on another of our audience's senses: hearing.

ENRICHING SLIDES WITH SOUND EFFECTS

Most PowerPoint presentations support and accompany talks in front of audiences, and sound effects and music are generally a secondary concern at talks, if they're present at all. But a well-chosen musical transition or subtle background sound can have a big effect on an attentive crowd, or grab hold of an inattentive one.

PowerPoint 2013 offers basic support for including audio files in slide shows as both clickable objects and background sounds, and some basic editing commands (though nothing on the level of its image-editing commands). You can trim, fade, and trigger your sounds, but actual audio content editing has to be done in an external app; as a result, smart sound selection and pre-editing make a big difference to the effectiveness of your presentation audio.

In this section, you'll add both background and triggered sounds to your slide deck.

Adding background sounds to a presentation

Bottom Line   Adding background music or sound effects to an entire presentation is as simple as embedding an audio object in slide 1 (see Figure 5-6) and ordering it to play automatically on a loop.

STEP BY STEP   **Adding background sounds to a presentation**

1 Select slide 1. Click Insert > Media > Audio > Audio on My PC. Navigate to your PPT05lessons folder and select **pp05c.mp3**. Click Insert.

2 Drag the inserted speaker icon to the lower-right corner of the slide (just for convenience while editing). In the Audio Tools > Playback tab, select Play in Background and Volume > Low.

3 Set both the Fade In and Fade Out values to 2 seconds.

Now preview the presentation from the beginning by pressing F5. As you can see, selecting an Audio Style toggles several audio settings at once: the Play Across Slides and Loop until Stopped options are now selected, for instance, to keep the sound rolling through the entire presentation.

Figure 5-6

Editing playback parameters for embedded audio.

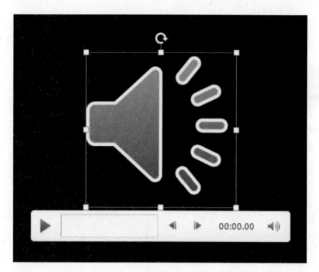

Take Note When choosing ambient background sounds, look for consistent volume levels; an unexpected, unwanted spike in volume can interrupt the momentum of a presentation.

Trimming and triggering sound effects

Bottom Line Sound effects in PowerPoint are triggered just as animations are: either cued up to begin after a delay, or set to play on a click. They can also be set to play along with animations or over slide transitions. We'll add an eerie heartbeat sound to one of our later slides, with a long fadeout. (Remember that the background sound will be playing quietly the whole time.)

The animation on slide 5 takes six or seven seconds from slide transition to final state; we'll trim our sound file to last just a bit longer than that, but instead of playing the sound automatically, we'll leave it to trigger when the user clicks the key image.

Take Note We've approached this slide show as a kind of storybook, for viewing on a computer or at a kiosk, but it could also work as an oddball public presentation. By triggering the sound on slide 5 to occur on a click rather than playing it automatically, we generate an interesting effect: a presenter can use the eerie sound to accentuate the animation or underscore additional narration; an onscreen reader exploring the slide would see the pointer change as it passed over the image, and get a strange surprised when she clicked.

STEP BY STEP **Trimming and triggering sound effects**

1 Select slide 5 and click Insert > Media > Audio > Audio on My PC. Select **pp05d.mp3**.

2 Move the audio icon to the corner of the slide as before. Select Playback > Audio Options > Hide During Show to make the icon invisible during the presentation.

3 Click Editing > Trim Audio. Set the clip's End Time to 10 (seconds) and click OK or press Enter. Then set the Fade Out value (in Playback > Editing) to 10.

Neither of the edits in step 3 affects the original file; as with nondestructive image adjustments, you can always return to the unaltered original file. Now we'll customize the trigger, linking the sound to a click on the key image.

4   Open the Animation pane. Right-click the sound **pp05d** and select **Timing** (See Figure 5-7.).

5   In the Timing dialog, select **Start effect on click of Content Placeholder 9**. Click **OK** or press **Enter**. Save your work, and then preview the slide with **Shift+F5**.

Figure 5-7

Linking audio playback to a trigger object in the Animation pane.

One nice side effect of linking the sound effect to a specific trigger object, rather than a click anywhere in the slide, is that the sound can play even while the text block animation is playing. This fits the off-kilter quality of the slide deck as a whole.

Adding custom actions to slide objects

Bottom Line

In the previous section you linked audio playback to a click event. The process can also work in reverse: you can add an Action to a slide element, which triggers anything from a simple hyperlink to launching an external application. In this section, you'll add hyperlinks to the first and last slides by adding two invisible Shape objects and attaching a Hyperlink Action to each.

Take Note

PowerPoint does allow you to style your hyperlink text to an extent (by customizing font and color by modifying the Theme), but there's no option to turn off hyperlink underlines for text objects. This section shows you how to perform two effects: illustrate triggered actions, and generate non-underlined hyperlinks through a workaround.

STEP BY STEP   Adding custom actions to slide objects

1   Select slide 1 and click **Insert > Illustrations > Shapes > Rectangle**. Draw a tight rectangle over the word *house*.

2   Click the rectangle and select Insert > Links > Action. Select Hyperlink to: Last slide as in Figure 5-8.

Figure 5-8

Associating a hyperlink action with a slide element.

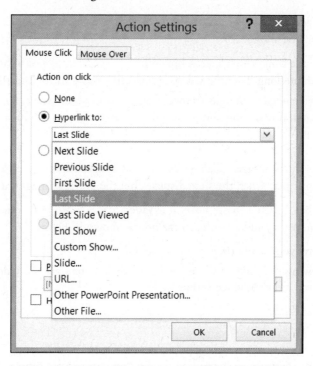

3   Click OK. Select the new rectangle shape. In the Format tab, select Shape Fill > No Fill and Shape Outline > No Outline.

4   Repeat steps 1–3 to add a similar hyperlinked rectangle over the question mark in slide 8. Point the hyperlink toward the First Slide.

5   Save your work and test the links by previewing the slide show.

The Action Settings dialog box can also run macros (chains of actions), load external apps, or edit OLE objects (such as a linked Excel spreadsheet), either on mouse click or on mouse over. This lesson only scratches the surface of what a dedicated presentation designer could do in terms of interactivity, but the tools themselves don't get any more complex than what you've already seen.

INTEGRATING VIDEO INTO A PRESENTATION

Fast processors, cheap bandwidth, big hard drives, and high-quality screens mean using video in a presentation is now neither a gimmick nor a hassle. Online media files (video, audio, images, templates) are easily incorporated into Office 2013 files, and adding a YouTube video into your presentation is no more complicated than embedding a local file.

In this final section, you'll embed, style, and trigger videos in your slide show.

Embedding and formatting videos

Bottom Line

Microsoft's Bing video search is built into PowerPoint 2013, and YouTube can be added as an online video source. We'll use a video from Bing and another from a local file.

Take Note

YouTube videos appear in Bing search (you'll find a YouTube video with Bing in this section), but you can also link your Live login to your YouTube account, if you have one, for access to account-specific information. Regardless, to add YouTube search to the Online Video screen in Office, click the Also Insert From YouTube icon in the Insert Video screen.

STEP BY STEP   **Embedding and formatting a video**

1   Add an empty slide to the end of the presentation. Click Insert > Media > Video > Online Video.

2   In the Bing Video Search box, type house of leaves intro. Select the first result (the minute-long YouTube video, House of Leaves – Intro) and click Insert.

PowerPoint embeds a single frame of the video, which serves as a preview image. Clicking the preview frame during the presentation brings up the YouTube player, which streams from *youtube.com*. We can skip the preview frame, however:

3   Select the image. Click Video Tools > Playback > Start > Automatically. The video won't play when the slide displays, but the preview image won't appear.

4   Click Video Tools > Format > Video Styles > Slope Beveled Rectangle in the Subtle categoryto add a border to the image, shown in Figure 5-9.

5   Save your work, then preview the slide.

When viewing the slide, click the embedded player to start the video, and press Escape to stop playback and clear the video frame.

Figure 5-9

PowerPoint treats video display and playback as animation events.

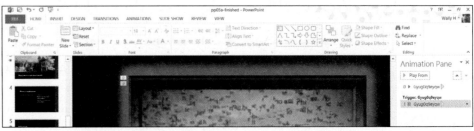

Slides 2, 3, and 5: Photos used with permission of Microsoft

PowerPoint has no control over the content of videos; you can alter the preview image with the standard image-adjustment tools (Video Tools > Format), but during playback, PowerPoint only draws the border and effects such as glow, shadow, and 3-D rotation. Note that the Trim Video command is greyed out.

Considerations for embedding local video

Trimming and formatting local video works the same as for audio: select an embedded video clip, set playback options in Video Tools > Playback, adjust the frame and preview image in Video Tools > Format, and go. Unlike YouTube and other online videos, local video files can be altered to fit the needs of the presentation: Playback > Trim Video and the Fade tools become available, along with Bookmarks (which let you jump to specific spots in the Trim window) and Volume controls.

One extra consideration arises with local video: media format compatibility. PowerPoint 2013 works best with .mp4 video (H.264 **codec**) and .m4a (AAC) audio, but also supports the following video formats:

• **.avi, .wmv, and MPEG (.mpg/.mpeg):** common local video formats

• **.swf:** Flash video, intended for online streaming

• **.asf:** a multimedia streaming format for Windows

PowerPoint RT, on the Microsoft Surface, is less robust; Microsoft encourages Windows RT users to use .mp4 and .m4a media. PowerPoint 2013 can also play Apple's QuickTime video formats (.mov, .mp4, .qt) through the external QuickTime Player app.

As you can see, keeping up with video formats takes a bit of work; your best bet is to get your video file into exactly the shape you want using an external editor such as Premiere or Final Cut, then export to PowerPoint's preferred format.

Media compression and compatibility

 # Workplace **Ready**

<table>
<tr><td>**Bottom Line**</td><td>If disk space is at a premium (on a tablet or USB key, for instance), you could **compress** the audio and video in your slide show; doing so also makes for smoother playback on older machines. Since workplace ready embedded media are stored within the .pptx file itself, compressing your media will directly reduce the size of your presentation.</td></tr>
<tr><td>**Take Note**</td><td>Comparing **pp05a.pptx** and **pp05a-finished.pptx** gives a sense of the relative size of embedded media files: the presentation with three small embedded images comes to less than 200KB the uncompressed final presentation adds another megabyte or so. Nearly the entire difference in size comes from a single audio file. Optimizing embedded media compatibility nearly doubles the file size, and compressing doesn't make any difference, since the media files are already in low-bitrate mp3 format. With larger, higher-quality media files, compression will be more useful.</td></tr>
</table>

Moreover, if you end up presenting your slide show using someone else's computer, media compatibility may become an issue. Fortunately, PowerPoint's File > Info tab includes tools to improve portability and performance. To see them in action, just open up the File tab:

STEP BY STEP   **Media compression and compatibility**

1   If you haven't already done so, open your presentation and click the File tab to reach the Backstage View.

2   Click **Optimize Compatibility**. In the Media Size and Performance text below, note that embedded media files now measures 3MB.

3   Click **Compress Media** > **Presentation Quality** to eliminate wasted space in the file without obviously affecting playback quality. This saves 0.1MB. Save your work.

The more you compress the presentation, the more image and audio quality can degrade. Because you can undo a compression step, it's easy to e-mail a minimum-size presentation to a colleague for review, and burn the uncompressed file to disc (or upload it to the cloud) for actual presentation.

The other tools in the Info tab will come in handy in the next lesson, when you learn how to deliver your presentation.

LAYING OUT SLIDE ELEMENTS

In earlier lessons, you learned about PowerPoint's alignment guides and layout tools. In this final section, you'll get a closer look at a crucial slide layout tool: PowerPoint's hidden grid, which guides object placement as gently or forcefully as you need. The grid and guides are shown in Figure 5-10.

Figure 5-10

Alignment guides and the slide grid are invaluable aids for relative positioning of slide elements

Photos used with permission of Microsoft

Taking advantage of the grid

Bottom Line

Slide elements occupy space in a ¹⁄₁₂″ grid, which can be made magnetic with the Snap to Grid setting. When Snap to Grid is enabled, objects in a slide will automatically stick to the nearest gridline rather than sliding pixel by pixel, making alignment and layout much less fiddly and a little less flexible. In this section, you'll vary PowerPoint's grid settings to see the kind of flexibility that they permit.

STEP BY STEP   **Aligning items to the grid**

1   Add a new empty slide, slide 10. Use **Insert > Images > Pictures** to add three images to the new slide from your PPT05lessons folder: **pp05f.jpg**, **pp05g.jpg**, and **pp05h.jpg**.

2   Right-click an empty part of the slide and select **Grid and Guides**.

3   Select all the check boxes in the dialog box, and set the Spacing to 1/2". Click **OK**.

Open the View tab and notice that Show > Gridlines and Show > Guides are now enabled; they're equivalent to the Display grid and Display drawing guides toggles in the dialog box.

Now try dragging the images around the slide. There are two features to note here. The images stick instead of moving smoothly across the slide, naturally falling into grooves that are ½″ apart from each other; when the centers or edges of the images are aligned, red **alignment guides** appear.

4   Set the grid back to ¹⁄₁₂″. Place the smaller image near the center of the slide, and place one of the ghost images directly below it.

5 Shift+click to select both images, then click Picture Tools > Format > Arrange > Align > Align Center to align their centers vertically. Then drag to align the centers of the two images with the dotted vertical line down the middle of the slide, and place the small image dead center in the slide. (It will snap into place.)

6 Deselect the images and click only the lower large image. Shift+drag it vertically until its top edge is aligned with the bottom grid line on the slide as in Figure 5-11.

Figure 5-11

When two images' centers are horizontally aligned, they can move freely straight up and down without breaking the alignment.

Photos used with permission of Microsoft

When you press and hold Shift while moving a slide element, it sticks to one cardinal direction of movement: either straight up and down or right and left. This is handy when you've already lined up image centers or edges, and need to vary just one positional axis.

Working with alignment guides

Bottom Line

PowerPoint's layout guides appear when the centers or edges of two objects are in alignment. They're sticky meaning objects will gravitate toward them,, though their effect is much less dramatic than a coarse grid. To see them at work, drag one image slowly past another:

Using alignment guides

1   Place the three images in a rough L-shape with roughly an inch between them and the small image at the joint of the L, as in Figure 5-12

Figure 5-12

For fine-grained object placement, make frequent use of the Zoom slider.

Photos used with permission of Microsoft

2   Align the left edges of the small image and the one below it. Then align the top edges of the small image and the one beside it, and place the side image roughly an inch away from the small image.

3   Shift+drag the lower image vertically until it's aligned with both of the other images.

With the image edges aligned, an off-kilter grid layout emerges. Image guides are more helpful when you place the three images in a line:

4   Zoom out. Drag the bottom image to the left side of the slide, positioned so all three top edges are aligned.

5   Shift+drag the smaller image to the right; when the three images are horizontally balanced, two equidistant markers will appear in the gaps between them.

6   Finally, select the current slide in the left pane of the screen and delete it from the presentation. (It doesn't quite fit the lonely house storybook theme.)

What you learned in this lesson:

- Recolor, Adjust, Crop, and Stack Images

- Heighten Visual Impact with Animations

- Enrich Slides with Sound Effects and Background Sound

- Add Media Triggers to Slide Objects

- Embed Online and Local Video

- Use Grids and Guides to Lay Out Slides

Knowledge Assessment

Matching

Match each term to its description or definition.

1. Picture Tools > Format
2. crop
3. Artistic Effects
4. alignment guides
5. Custom Action
6. compression
7. View > Show
8. Animation Pane
9. trigger
10. Selection Pane

a. downsizing embedded media to keep .pptx file manageable
b. indicate even spacing/distribution of slide elements
c. toggles for positioning guides like ruler, gridlines
d. extract just one region of an image
e. lists animations in order w/sparklines indicating duration
f. lists objects in slide, front to back
g. Image adjustment, style, stacking tools
h. interaction (e.g., click) to set off effect (e.g., play audio)
i. run program, open hyperlink, play sound (etc.) on click
j. blur, glowing edges, pen strokes, etc.

Fill in the Blanks

Complete the following sentences by writing the correct word or words in the blanks provided.

1. Shortening an audio file is called _____ the file.
2. An animated object's trajectory is called its _____.
3. To include only part of an embedded image, _____ the image to the desired dimensions.
4. The _____ Pane lets users move objects forward and backward in the object "stack."
5. The frame, color, and shape of an image are edited in the Picture Tools > _____ tab.
6. The _____ > _____ > _____ > Grayscale command converts a color image to black, white, and grey.
7. PowerPoint's favored video format is _____ files.
8. When images are evenly spaced across the slide while dragging, _____ will appear between them.
9. Toggle alignment guides and the grid in the _____ > _____ group.
10. Office's Online Video search command uses the _____ service by default, rather than searching (e.g.) YouTube directly.

Competency Assessment

Project 5-1: Adding Images to a Presentation

In this exercise you will search for images online and insert them into a new slide show.

1. Create a new blank presentation and save it as **project_5-1_images**.
2. Add the text Image Test (title) and PPT Lesson 5 (subtitle) to slide 1.
3. Add a new slide (Ctrl+M) and in its content area click the Online Pictures control.
4. Do a clip art (not Bing image) search for butterfly on flower. Insert one of the resulting images.
5. Add a third slide with the same layout; insert online clip art using the search string orangutan hanging.
6. Add a new slide, slide 4, with the Blank layout. Click Insert > Online Pictures to add a piece of clip art using the search string safari lion.

   Note the way PowerPoint lays out the image on blank vs structured slides.
7. Save and close your document.

Project 5-2: Styling and Cropping Images

This exercise utilizes PowerPoint's image formatting and style tools.

1. Open the exercise file **5-2-source** and save it as **project_5-2_crop**.
2. Select the image on slide 2.
3. Click Picture Tools > Format > Artistic Effects > Pencil Grayscale.
4. Select the image on slide 3.
5. Click Format > Crop.
6. Drag the sides and top of the cropping frame toward the orangutan in the image, to make a "tightly cropped," tall, thin frame.
7. When you have the crop you want, press Escape.
8. Crop the lion image on slide 4 to a tight 3.5"x3.5" square. Apply the Orange, Accent color 2 Light color correction and Reflected Rounded Rectangle Picture Style.
9. Save and close your document.

Proficiency Assessment

Project 5-3: Animating Slide Elements

In this exercise you'll add a couple of animations to slide elements.

1. Open the exercise file **5-3-source** and save it as **project_5-3_animation**.
2. Select the modified butterfly image on slide 2. Apply the Shape animation with the Diamond Effect Option.
3. Add a Fade transition from slide 2 to slide 3 with duration 3 seconds.
4. Select the slide 4 image and click the Lines motion path animation.
5. After the preview plays, drag the red destination dot to the upper right of the slide. Then press Enter.
6. Preview the slide 4 animation by clicking the Play Animations icon next to slide 4 in the slide selector pane.
7. Save and close your document.

Project 5-4: Setting Transition Timing and Duration

This exercise involves PowerPoint's slide transitions, including duration and delay parameters.

1. Create a new blank presentation and save it as **project_5-4_pictureshow**.
2. Delete the title slide and add four (4) slides with Blank layouts. In the Design menu, change the slide size to 5"x5".
3. Insert an image into each slide.
4. Create a "photo montage" effect by applying Fade transitions into each slide, with 2 second duration, and Advance each Slide after 2 seconds.
5. Set up the slide show to loop continuously (Slide Show > Set Up Slide Show).
6. Save and close your document.

Mastery Assessment

Project 5-5: Triggering Media

In this exercise you'll add custom actions to a button image in a slide.

1. Create a new blank document and save it as **project_5-5_trigger**.
2. Insert a forward arrow icon on slide 1, and some image on slide 2.
3. Use the Insert > Action command to give the button special properties:

   On click, advance to slide 2

   Highlight on mouse over
4. Save and close your document.

(Note what happens if you add a transition into slide 2 – it will play whether you advance from 1 to 2 regularly or by clicking the button.)

Project 5-6: Using Alignment Guides

This exercise challenges you to use alignment guides and the Format Pane to precisely lay out a slide full of images.

1. Open the project file **5-6-source** and save it as **project_5-6_alignment**.
2. Resize each image in your document to be 1"x1" square.
3. Turn on alignment guides and arrange the slide so each image is the corner of a square, with 1" separating each pair of images along the square's edge.

   You will need to use the Format Picture > Size & Position tools for this task along with the alignment guides.
4. Save and close your document.

6

Delivering Your Presentation

LESSON SKILL MATRIX

In this lesson, you will learn the following skills:

Customizing Your Presentation Setup	Using the Laser Pointer, Highlighter, and Ink Annotations
Precisely Controlling Your Presentation	Rehearsing Timings and Recording Narration
Using Slide Show and Presenter Views	Delivering a Presentation Online
Creating Speaker Notes and Handouts	

KEY TERMS

- **Kiosk**
- **Set Up Show**
- **Custom Slide Show**
- **Presenter View**
- **Slide Show view**
- **Notes Page**
- **Notes Master**
- **Handout Master**
- **Laser Pointer**
- **Ink Annotations**
- **Narration**

Contoso internships end with a presentation to the project heads: "What I Accomplished This Summer." Impressing the heads isn't easy...especially when each talk is just 10 minutes long. There's no room for stumbling, being surprised by which slide is next, not being able to find a laser pointer, or not having printed notes to hand when a strong presentation might mean future employment. Fortunately, PowerPoint gives presenters control over even the finest details of their talks. "Are there any questions?"

SOFTWARE ORIENTATION

This lesson helps you understand how to deliver effective presentations using PowerPoint.

Figure 6-1

The Presenter View collects PowerPoint's full suite of presenter tools in a clean multi-pane interface.

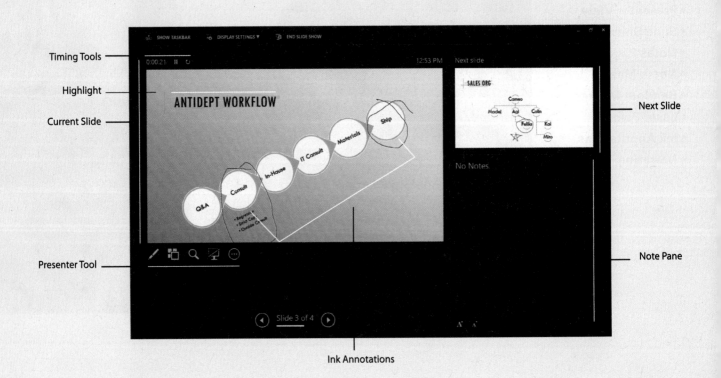

STARTING UP

In this lesson, you'll work with several files from the PPT06lessons folder. Make sure that you have loaded the OfficeLessons folder onto your computer.

PRESENTATIONS ARE PERFORMANCES

Presentations are meant to be *presented* your slides don't work unless they work for an audience. Regularly previewing and practicing your presentation while building your slide deck will give you a clear sense of whether the slides form an effective whole, and rehearsing will make for a much smoother and more confident presentation, too.

Your workflow should build toward an outstanding talk, not just perfect slides. Fortunately, PowerPoint 2013 offers a full suite of presentation tools to structure and improve the performance side of your slide show, including a totally redesigned Presenter View. In this lesson, you'll start from a finished slide deck, rehearse your presentation (and put your slide notes to use), pin down the timing of your talk, and use PowerPoint's pen tools and hand-drawn annotations to put audience focus right where it belongs. Then you'll learn to assemble multiple custom presentations from a single slide deck and shape your printed notes and audience handouts to your needs.

Take Note   Most PowerPoint slide shows are used to accompany talks. Designing for a public kiosk is a separate but related concern, and this lesson gives an overview of kiosk aesthetics and usability. If you don't have access to a second screen or projector, you can go ahead and skip the material. Finally, the art of giving a strong presentation is rich enough to fill several books on its own; we will only cover the essentials in this one.

PREPARING FOR YOUR PRESENTATION

Before you begin your talk, you need to configure your hardware (presenter console and display screen) and PowerPoint (the presentation app). As far as your hardware is concerned, the best advice we can give is to get to the room early and test out your projector because it rarely just works. Configuring the presentation itself is much more under your control.

Setting up the slide show

Bottom Line   The Set Up Slide Show command (see Figure 6-2) offers several options to customize your slide deck and the dynamics of your presentation: looping, graphics settings, pen/pointer settings, slide controls, and monitor configuration will vary based on the type of slide show you're preparing:

- **Presented by a speaker (full screen)**: the standard big-slides-behind-the-speaker view, to accompany a talk.

- **Browsed by an individual (window)**: the full presentation running in a window with limited interactivity (for example, click to advance doesn't work); ideal for integrating presentations with work in other apps.

- **Browsed at a kiosk (full screen)**: an unattended presentation, minimally interactive, meant to transition automatically between slides and loop endlessly (for example, on a trade show floor or as advertising).

A **kiosk** presentation, for instance, always loops automatically, while a windowed screen slide show loops by default, but isn't required to; windowed presentations automatically display on your primary monitor; Presenter View is (naturally) disabled for kiosk and windowed slide shows; the laser pointer is available for kiosk/windowed shows, but the pen is disabled.

Figure 6-2

Configuring your slide deck for different presentation types.

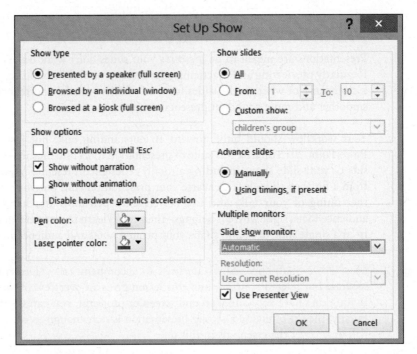

The **Set Up Show** dialog box offers a few additional options to customize your presentation. If you've recorded practice narration, or designed your slide deck for both unattended and live presentations, you can turn off the narration in the dialog box. You can also specify a subset of the deck to use in your presentation and disable automatic timings.

If you have multiple monitors connected (for instance, a laptop screen or tablet for the presenter and a projector facing the audience), you can also specify in this dialog box which screen will display which information.

Controlling your presentation from the keyboard

Bottom Line

If you're using a Surface or other Windows tablet while presenting, touch commands will likely be the most convenient way to interact with your slide show; on a PC, however, the keyboard is probably your fastest input method. Rather than printing a complete list here, we'll mention the most common presentation commands, and refer you to the support pages at *office.microsoft.com* (from which this information is taken) for a full accounting:

Common presentation commands

COMMAND	KEYBOARD SHORTCUT
Next Trigger or Slide	N, Enter, PgDown, Right Arrow, Down Arrow, Space
Previous Trigger or Slide	P, PgUp, Left Arrow, Up Arrow, Backspace
Go to slide #	Type #, press Enter
Black screen	B, period
White screen	W, comma
Stop/restart	S
End	Escape
Pen	Ctrl+P
Arrow	Ctrl+A
Slide Sorter	G
Erase annotations	E

You can also get in and out of your slide show using only the keyboard: F5 starts your slide show from the beginning; Shift+F5 starts from the current slide; and Alt+F5 jumps right into Presenter View from the beginning.

Note that the only way to navigate directly between slides, skipping over triggered animations and effects, is by selecting a slide directly, either by typing its number or using the Slide Sorter.

Creating custom slide shows

Bottom Line

Sometimes you'll want to give several different presentations using only parts of a single slide deck; for instance, you might give roughly the same talk to both a team of engineers and the middle managers who supervise them, and want to leave out your raw data in the nontechnical talk. PowerPoint offers the **Custom Slide Show** tool for just such situation.

STEP BY STEP | **Creating a custom slide show**

1 Open **pp06a.pptx** located in the PPT06lessons folder. Click Enable Content to enable embedded media.

Take Note Slide shows that contain links to external media, such as YouTube videos, open in Protected mode by default. To automatically enable embedded media, make your file a Trusted Document.

2 Choose File > Save As and navigate to the PPT06lessons folder. Name the file **pp06a_work** and click Save.

3 Click Slide Show > Custom Slide Show > Custom Shows.

4 Click New. Enter children's group in the Slide show name text area (see Figure 6-3).

5   Select slides 1 through 3 and click Add.

Figure 6-3

Custom Slide Shows include a subset of the full slide deck.

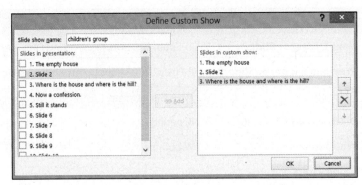

Now a children's group show appears in the list under Custom Slide Show, which cuts out the last three slides. You can create as many custom slide shows as you need; the slide list is simply saved in the .pptx file.

6   Click OK and then Close the Custom Shows dialog box.

Take Note   If your slide deck contains a transition from slide 2 to slide 3, the transition will be included in any custom show that contains slide 3; transitions move into slides rather than out of them. A custom slide show that skips from slide 2 to slide 4 would include a transition only if slide 4 has a transition in. (Exit animations are contained within slides and aren't affected.)

Take careful note: custom slide shows renumber the individual slides. A custom show that skips slide 3 will renumber slide 4 as 3. If you've memorized specific slide numbers from your full deck, you may have to remember a whole new set of numbers for each custom show. When navigating a custom show, the Slide Sorter, with its slide thumbnails and section headings, becomes extremely helpful.

PRESENTING IN SLIDE SHOW VIEW

Bottom Line   You've used the basic **Slide Show** command throughout this book's PowerPoint lessons. As you've seen, Slide Show gives you the audience's view of your presentation; it's especially well-suited to showing the slides in action during editing. If you give the same talk multiple times, you could find it easier to present straight from Slide Show mode; the stripped-down interface will minimize distraction.

The keyboard command and onscreen tools in the Slide Show are the same as for Presenter View; the difference is the amount of information on the screen. Crucially, Slide Show mode offers neither speaker notes nor a preview of the upcoming slide.

STEP BY STEP   **Presenting in Slide Show view**

1   Begin the Slide Show by pressing F5. Use any of the shortcut keys to advance to slide 3.

2   Press Ctrl+H to hide the pointer.

Oddly enough, Ctrl+H does not act as a toggle: pressing it twice won't make the pointer visible again. To do so, you have two options: switch to Pen mode and then back to arrow mode (press Ctrl+P twice), or right-click and select Pointer Options > Arrow Options > Visible from the context menu.

3   Press Ctrl+P to enter pen mode, circle the word *house*, and then press Escape to switch
    the pointer to an arrow.

4   Press Escape again to end the Slide Show; Discard your ink annotations.

MISSION CONTROL: POWERPOINT'S PRESENTER VIEW

Bottom Line

PowerPoint's standard Slide Show mode (invoked by pressing F5) shows you the presentation as
the audience would see it: the current slide is displayed with no notes or additional information.
Your Pen Tools are available in Slide Show mode, along with the Slide Sorter and Zoom tool, but
the focus is on the slide and the audience experience.

In contrast, **Presenter View** is like Mission Control for presentations. It splits the screen to
display slide notes, a preview of the next slide, and a handful of display options for your second
(audience) screen. Your presenter tools are hidden from the audience unless you deliberately switch
the Presenter and Audience screens. If you're giving the same presentation over and over (or prefer
printed Notes pages) you may not need the full Presenter View, but for your early efforts at giving
a talk, it's an essential tool.

Take Note

PowerPoint 2013 launches Presenter View in a separate window from the Slide Show view, so you
can press Alt+Tab to switch between the two views.

Figure 6-4

Presenter View gives you
a big picture view of your
presentation.

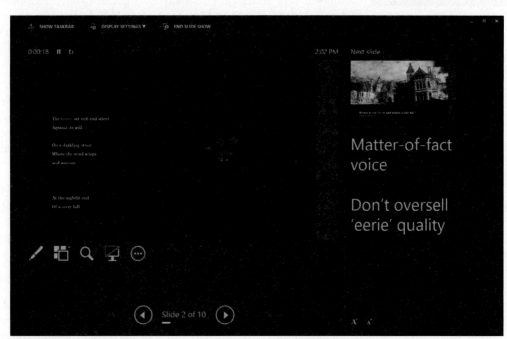

Photos used with permission of Microsoft

In this section, you'll quickly tour the Presenter View Interface , shown in Figure 6-4.

STEP BY STEP   **Using PowerPoint's presenter view**

1   Activate Presenter View by pressing Alt+F5.

Note the large right and left arrows at the bottom of the screen. They do **not** let you skip from
slide to slide without triggering animations. To move by the slide rather than interact with it by
clicking, use the Slide Sorter. By default, Presenter View is split into three panes:

• a large display of the current slide with timing, annotation, and zoom tools nearby;

• a small preview of the next slide; and

• resizable speaker notes.

2   Drag the borders between the three panes to resize the current and next slides and the slide notes.

Figure 6-5

Resizing the Presenter View panes lets you focus on different aspects of your performance.

Moving the speaker notes and slide preview to the side (see Figure 6-5) can help you focus on tabular data or images; downsizing both slide images brings you speaker notes to the fore, which is important when you're reading lengthy or precisely worded text pieces.

USING SPEAKER NOTES

Bottom Line

Speaker notes are easily overlooked during slide show construction. Even with animations and transitions, your slides are essentially static; slide-to-slide movement will come from you, the presenter, as you link presentation across slides and draw connections between ideas. The glue that holds your slide deck together (in other words, the logic that gets you from Slide A to Slide B) goes into your Speaker Notes.

Take Note

One useful technique for building a presentation (or a piece of writing) is to outline its dynamic elements along with static content. Filling in a slide is often easier than figuring out how it transforms into the slide that follows: its implications, its relationship to the wider presentation. Including a single transition sentence between outline entries is extremely helpful when you need to flesh out your presentation. If you don't have time to rehearse, aiming for the transition sentence will make your improvisation a lot smoother.

In Presenter View, you can resize the text of your slide notes by clicking the two icons at the bottom of the Notes pane. If you don't want to be bound to a screen during your presentation, you can print out Notes Pages instead, which present a slide thumbnail with a large formatted notes pane. You can customize the look and layout of your notes pages with the Notes Master.

How detailed should speaker notes be?

You can think of presentations as a form of theatrical performance: if you rely too heavily on your script, you could end up with a stiff performance. Obviously, you should tailor your notes to your personal taste and level of preparation, but ideally, by the time you reach the podium, your notes will be nothing more than prompts or reminders to help you move smoothly through natural, conversational spoken delivery.

For that reason, you should revise your speaker notes as you rehearse your presentation, refining scattered notes down to a telling word or phrase. If you're comfortable improvising or even memorizing, a written-out presentation can work too; but remember, you're writing a one-person stage performance, not a book report.

Incorporating direct quotes is another consideration. In general, long text passages fit awkwardly on slides. If you need to read verbatim text aloud, it's often best to leave a telling excerpt on the slide and leave the full text off to your speaker notes.

The most important guideline for speaker notes is this: *Focus on the talk, not the text.* Write only and exactly the notes that let you give the most fluid, memorable talk you can.

FORMATTING AND PRINTING NOTES PAGES

Bottom Line

The notes pane in Presenter View can't be formatted like slide text; indeed, slide notes can only be formatted for the **Notes Page** view, and then only minimally (at the paragraph level). Such a limitation fits the approach suggested in this lesson: your speaker notes are notes, not a script, and great talks don't rely on notes for their impact; if you can wean yourself off speaker notes entirely, all the better.

That said, printed speaker notes can be of great benefit during a talk, freeing you from staring at your laptop or tablet screen. You can format your speaker notes (both the text itself and the layout of the printed notes page, including header and footer areas) in the **Notes Master** view.

STEP BY STEP **Formatting and printing notes pages**

1   Select **View > Notes Master**.

2   Click in the Footer box at the bottom of the notes page and type **Not for distribution**.

3   Triple-click to select the entire first line in the notes pane (Click to edit...styles). Use the mini formatting pop-up menu (or the Home > Font group in the Ribbon) to format the line as 20pt boldfaced blue text.

4   Use the resizing handles to make the top content area (the slide image) about 2″ square, and drag the top of the notes text box upwards to fill the added space and give the text more breathing room. Click to select the notes content area itself and apply the **Colored Outline – Blue, Accent 1** style from the Drawing Tools > Format > Shape Styles gallery.

5   Click outside of the notes content area to deselect it. Finally, select **Notes Master > Close Master View** and save your work.

If you've worked through Lesson 3, "Designing a Presentation," this process will seem familiar; designing a notes page is exactly like making changes to a slide layout in the Slide Master. You can print your formatted notes page by selecting File > Print and selecting Notes Pages under Print > Settings; use the controls at the bottom of the screen (Figure 6-6) to flip through the slides in your deck. Note that Print Comments and Ink Markup is selected by default; this will insert separate pages containing only comments on each slide.

Take Note   With the style options in the Notes Master > Background group, you can quickly change the overall look and feel of your notes page. Feel free to experiment with adjusting the look of your notes page using these commands, though you're more likely to need custom page formatting for printed handouts, instead.

Figure 6-6

Printing speaker with
additional background
formatting added to the
Notes Master.

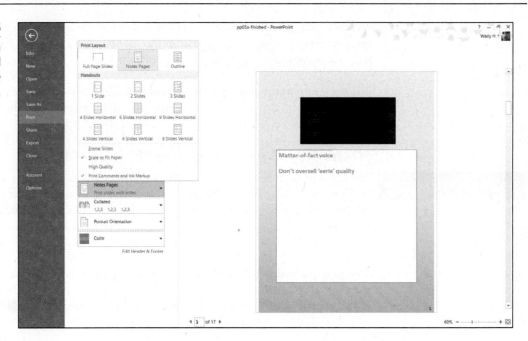

DESIGNING A PRINTED HANDOUT

Bottom Line

Printed handouts are useful tools for presentation audiences as material for connecting their handwritten notes to slide content. But poorly formatted handouts (for example, many slides per page on an intrusively busy background), are worse than none at all. You can use the **Handout Master** to design a printout of your presentation for the audience to take away. The process is largely the same as for the Notes Master and printed notes page, except that the Handout Master > Page Setup group has a Slides Per Page button to set that crucial parameter. The layout for each Slides Per Page option is fixed, so handouts are less customizable than notes pages in that sense, but a subtle background or distinctive color scheme can make a printed handout more sticky in terms of audience retention.

STEP BY STEP | **Designing a printed handout**

1   Select **View > Handout Master** to edit the handout's layout.

2   Establish the layout by choosing **Handout Orientation > Landscape** and **Slides Per Page > 4 Slides**.

3   Click **Background Styles > Style 4**, then close the **Handout Master**. Save your work.

4   Click **File > Print**. Select **4 Slides Horizontal** from the third drop-down menu, and deselect **Print Comment Slides and Ink Markup** from the same menu.

5   Now preview the printed handout using the controls at the bottom of the screen. When you've done so, press **Escape** to cancel the print. (The black background uses a lot of ink.)

Take Note   You can quickly generate a handout layout from the Print options screen.

Navigating with the slide sorter

The Slide Sorter works the same in Presenter View as in editing mode: it shows thumbnails of your entire slide deck organized by section and navigable with the arrow keys. To invoke the Slide Sorter from Slide Show or Presenter modes, press G or click the See all slides icon. When the right slide is highlighted, press Enter to drop back into presenting.

Note that, as is the case with Presenter View, the Slide Sorter won't appear on the audience screen, just the presenter's.

Take Note When you compose and edit your slide show, sections are a handy organizational tool; especially if you're collaborating and wish to assign tasks to colleagues by section. During your presentation, sections are only relevant in the Slide Sorter.

Going to a black or white screen

At times during a presentation, you'll want to clear the audience screen of content. PowerPoint provides commands to black out or white out the screen, rather than quitting the presentation entirely (popping back out to the edit window). This is extremely useful for the very end of your talk as a way of signaling to the audience that you're finished, without the awkward anticlimax of accidentally showing off your Windows desktop.

To black out the screen during a presentation, press B (or the period key); to white it out, press W or the comma. Press the same key to restore the slide content. The onscreen buttons to accomplish the same effects are shown in Figure 6-7

Figure 6-7

Black out your screen by clicking the highlighted icon beneath the slide; whiteout is only accessible from the keyboard.

FOCUSING AUDIENCE ATTENTION WITH PEN TOOLS

No matter how much time you spend on slide design, there are plenty of uses for PowerPoint's pen tools during a presentation. A moving laser pointer can draw the audience's eyes to a specific region in a chart or a graph, or make the contour of a scatter plot clear. Ink circles can help listeners to later recall a specific fact. Subtle yellow highlights can make crucial words or phrases pop out of a paragraph or bulleted list. And you can save or print your pen annotations, making the live performance part of the written record of your talk.

Crucially, interacting with a slide can be an effective tool for you as the presenter; among other things, it lets you focus on specific physical action rather than staring over the heads of the crowd or fidgeting with papers at the podium. In this section, you'll mark up your presentation and save your pen annotations for later.

Using the laser pointer and highlighter

Bottom Line The **laser pointer** tool is available in both Slide Show and Presenter Views. It doesn't leave marks on the slide, just draws attention to a given slide element.

STEP BY STEP   **Using the laser pointer and highlighter**

1 Press F5 to enter the Slide Show.

2 Click the pen icon in the lower left of the screen, and then click Laser Pointer. Move the glowing red ring around on the screen to draw attention to features of the slide.

3 Press the right-arrow key to advance to the next slide. The laser pointer remains up.

4 Now press Ctrl+P to switch to Pen mode. Click and drag to circle the word *house*. Then click the pen icon and select Erase All Ink on Slide. Press Ctrl+P to return to pointer mode. Advance to the next slide.

Keeping ink annotations

Bottom Line

If you want to distribute a version of your slide show with live penstrokes included, choose to Keep **ink annotations** (and then save the file) when you finish marking up your slides.

1 Click the pen icon and select Highlighter. Highlight several words on the slide. Then switch to the pen tool (Ctrl+P) and handwrite hotel over the image.

2 Press Escape to return to pointer mode, then Escape again to exit your presentation. When asked to save your annotations, click Keep. Save your work.

The ink remains on the slide. This is an image object; indeed, when you select the lines you just drew in the editing window, an Ink Tools > Pens tab appears along with Drawing Tools > Format. Note that all the strokes you make on a single slide during a given presentation are combined into a single graphic object (See Figure 6-8.).

The easiest way to change the color of a pen stroke after the fact is with Drawing Tools > Format > Shape Outline; you can change the stroke weight with Ink Tools > Pens > Thickness.

Once you choose to keep your ink annotations from a given talk, the only way to remove them is in the editing window; the next time you run through the presentation, PowerPoint will treat them as part of the slide (in other words, the eraser tool won't alter pen strokes from previous run-throughs).

Figure 6-8

Saved ink annotations transform into graphic objects when you exit the Slide Show.

Photo used with permission of Microsoft

REHEARSING YOUR PRESENTATION

Rehearsals are essential to the process of creating and shaping your talk and the slide deck itself. (After all, how can you know your slide show is working if you don't experience it in its proper context?) PowerPoint provides a suite of rehearsal tools to help you iron out the timing of your presentation and pre-record narration and pointer movements.

Bottom Line

Recording slide and presentation timings

With the tools in the Slide Show > Set Up group, you can record your timings and spoken narrations, and play back the entire presentation with prerecorded narration, or just display slide timings while you run through the deck again. In this section, you'll start by recording timings; use the timings to run a hands-free slide show; and then record narration and laser pointer movements.

STEP BY STEP **Recording slide and presentation timings**

1   Click **Slide Show > Set Up > Rehearse Timings** to begin the slide show in practice mode. A small timer appears in the upper-left corner of the screen. Presenter View is unavailable in this mode.

2   Click through the presentation, taking five or so seconds per slide.

3   When the dialog box appears at the end of the slide show (Figure 6-9), click **Yes** to save your timings. Save your work.

Figure 6-9

You can save one set of slide timings at a time.

Photos used with permission of Microsoft

After saving your timings, you can run through your presentation with the transitions playing automatically behind you. This is useful for rehearsing, but if you can give a smooth presentation without relying too much on the slides, you can also run the slide show at a fixed rate during the talk itself.

4   Now press **F5** to run your slide show again. Animations and transitions will run automatically at the previously recorded tempo. Press **Escape** when you're ready to move on.

Recording narration and pointer movements

Bottom Line

Once you've fixed your slide timings to your satisfaction, you can record voice-over **narration** and pointer movements. This is an especially useful feature for kiosk slide shows, which can play like mini movies. But you can also use it to make recorded presentations for online distribution, or record a live presentation (for instance a team meeting) with listener feedback as a kind of audiovisual archive.

Take Note   PowerPoint 2013 RT doesn't allow you to record narration. If you're working through this lesson on a Windows RT device such as a Surface, skip any steps that don't apply to your version of Office 2013. Surface Pro users have a full version of Office 2013 and should be able to follow the steps in this section.

STEP BY STEP   **Recording narration and pointer movements**

1   Click Slide Show > Record Slide Show. In the dialog box, make sure only Narrations and laser pointer is checked. Click Start Recording. Speak some of the slide text aloud as you click through the presentation.

PowerPoint is now recording audio (from your system's default audio input; usually a built-in microphone), and will record any laser pointer movements you make.

2   Enable the laser pointer (using the button at the lower left of the screen) and move the pointer over some of the slides, holding still during others.

Take Note   If you don't move the laser pointer at all during a slide, it won't be visible on playback, since only movements are recorded. Don't use the point if you don't need it.

3   When the slide show is finished, press Escape to quit.

4   Make sure Play Narrations and Use Timings are selected in Slide Show > Set Up. Then adjust your computer's volume to a comfortable level and press F5 to play back the presentation.

The slide show plays back using your rehearsal timings (recorded earlier) and the narration and laser pointer moves you just recorded.

5   Choose File > Save or press Ctrl+S to save your work.

Tweaking and removing timings, narration, and laser pointer movements

Bottom Line   Your rehearsal timings are saved as automatic transitions: look under Transitions > Timing and you'll see that each slide now has an Advance Slide After value. You can tweak these timings as you would any other transition. (If you only want to use recorded timings and don't want to be able to break them by skipping quickly through slides, deselect the On Mouse Click timing option.)

Recording rehearsal timings overwrites any Advance Slide After timings you might have already set. The only way to remove rehearsal timings is to delete them from the slides themselves. We'll do that now, to make the presentation timing more flexible.

STEP BY STEP   **Tweaking and removing timings, narration, and laser pointer movements**

1   In the Normal edit view, select all the slides by clicking in the slide pane on the left and pressing Ctrl+A.

2   In the Transitions tab, deselect Timing > Advance Slide After. Save your work.

PowerPoint saves your narrations as audio objects, one per slide. If you don't need narration during a given presentation, you can always disable the narration in the Set Up Show dialog box; to reduce file size and speed up PowerPoint's performance, we'll remove the narration we've just recorded.

3   Click Slide Show > Record Slide Show > Clear > Clear Narrations on All Slides. Save your work.

PRESENTING ONLINE

At times, you might need to present to someone across town or in a different time zone. Microsoft offers a couple of channels for online presentations:

- **Lync,** a paid groupware service offering integrated audio/video conferencing, instant messaging scheduling, and media sharing.

- **Office Presentation Service (OPS),** a free public service for making slide shows viewable in the PowerPoint Web.

From the speaker's standpoint, presenting online is similar to presenting in person. One key difference is that online viewers can flip back through the slide deck during the presentation without interrupting the presenter or anyone else in the audience. The potential downside to using OPS for presentations is that there's no speech integration: the audience gets the slide deck and embedded media, but your actual talk can only go out over an external service such as Skype and there's no built-in video presence. The Lync service provides these additional features.

You can also embed your slide show in a webpage using SkyDrive. This option gives you the least control over access or the viewer experience, but it's the easiest way to share your slide deck; you could use it to post a multimedia photo album to a blog, for example. An OPS presentation is only viewable as long as you're actually presenting (see Figure 6-10), and though it's theoretically open to the public, only invited viewers will be able to find it. Lync offers the most control over who can see your presentation and how.

Delivering a presentation using Office Presentation service
You can present a slide show using OPS directly from the Slide Show tab.

STEP BY STEP	**Delivering a presentation using Office Presentation service**

1 Click Slide Show > Start Slide Show > Present Online > Office Presentation Service.

2 Uncheck the option to make the slide deck downloadable (Enable remote viewers). Then click Connect.

The Enable remote viewers option does just what it says: if you leave it checked, your audience will be able to download the source file for your presentation.

The Optimize Media option appears because **pp06a_work.pptx** contains a link to a YouTube video, which might not display properly on older Flash-disabled computers. For our purposes, we needn't worry about it. PowerPoint now generates the online presentation. When it's finished, a Present Online pane appears.

3 Click Copy Link, then click Start Presentation.

4 Open a web browser, but don't stop the presentation by pressing Escape. Paste the URL into the location bar of the browser to view your presentation.

5 Return to your slide show in PowerPoint and advance to the next slide, and then switch back to your web browser; the presentation will have advanced there as well.

6   Return to PowerPoint and stop the presentation by pressing Escape. Select Present Online > End Online Presentation, then confirm your choice in the pop-up dialog box.

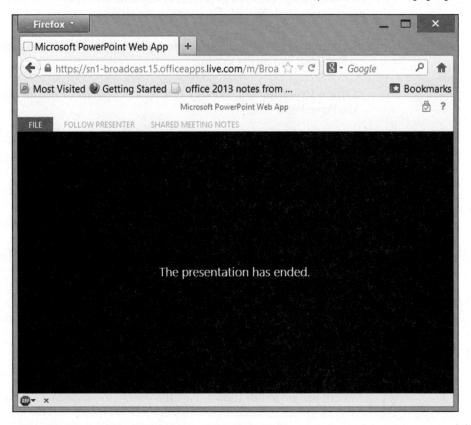

Take Note   Your online audience might need to install or upgrade Silverlight or Flash in order to view a multimedia presentation. To ensure compatibility, follow the suggestions in Lesson 5, "Adding Graphics and Multimedia to Your Presentation."

Bottom Line

Presenting in Lync

If you have a Lync account set up, the steps to present via Lync are much the same as the previous. Note that Lync sharing is not available on Windows RT devices, such as Microsoft Surface.

STEP BY STEP   **Presenting in Lync**

1   Select Slide Show > Present Online > Microsoft Lync.

2   If you have a Lync meeting set up, select it from the list of scheduled meetings; otherwise, click Start a new Lync meeting and add invitees.

3   When the meeting is underway, begin the presentation as you normally would.

Take Note   For more details on using Lync for online presentations, see the Lync documentation at onlinehelp.microsoft.com.

The important takeaway in this section is that the mechanics of presenting your slides are the same regardless of the physical or online venue.

Embedding your slide show in a webpage

If you want to publish a standalone slide deck online, or let colleagues peruse your deck as a work in progress, you can embed your slide show in a webpage by sharing it directly from SkyDrive. (If you don't have a place to host your slideshow online, just read along, or skip to the next section.)

STEP BY STEP	Embedding your slide show in a webpage

1   If you haven't already done so, save the practice presentation to your SkyDrive folder by doing one of the following:

Log in to *skydrive.com* in your web browser, click the Upload button in the SkyDrive screen, and navigate to the file; or

Use the desktop SkyDrive or SkyDrive Pro app to upload the file to your SkyDrive.

2   Open *skydrive.com* in your web browser and navigate to where your presentation is stored.

3   Right-click the presentation's icon in the browser, and select Embed.

4   SkyDrive will generate HTML to embed the presentation in a web page, along with a preview of the embedded slide show. Press Ctrl+C to copy the embed code.

5   Paste the HTML code into the blog editor of your choice; for instance, into a new Blog Post document in Word 2013. Then upload the file to your blog, and view the post in a web browser to see the embedded presentation.

If you want to share the original file via e-mail instead of embedding it on a webpage, follow steps 1 and 2 above, then choose Sharing in step 3 and e-mail a link to the original file instead. You can also open the file from your SkyDrive directory using the PowerPoint Web App, and selecting File > Sharing > Embed from the Web App to generate HTML embed code.

6   Choose File > Save and File > Close.

GIVING EXCELLENT PRESENTATIONS

There's no single recipe for a great PowerPoint presentation except to practice, practice, practice. Of course you need to master the basics first. Speak to the audience, not the slide. Practice stringing multiple sentences together to avoid *um* and *uhh*. Spread text out over several sparse slides, rather than one crowded one. Pick a simple font/visual scheme and stick to it.

Once you have the basics down you start getting into style, where your presentations (ideally) begin to look less like everyone else's, because you're finding personal solutions to technical problems.

Great talks are always unique and personal. Some speakers put a single word on a slide; some do original art for every talk; and some rely entirely on infographics and speech. Great presenters never stick to the trusty title + bullet points + clip art scheme; there's always some twist, and the twist is what lets the talk hook into the audience's minds in the first place, and keeps it there long after you get to the end of your presentation.

That said, here are a few principles to keep in mind as you develop your first few presentations. Our hope is that this advice will scale up to stay relevant as your skill increases.

- **Slides aren't novels—they're paintings.** A slide crammed full of complete sentences is one of the classic PowerPoint blunders. If you're giving a talk, think of your slides as visuals competing with your speech for audience attention; if everyone's reading a well-crafted prose paragraph off the screen, they're not listening to your talk.

- **It's a visual medium—make sure the visuals are visible.** Use high-contrast colors, legible fonts (and not too many at once), and uncluttered layouts. The audience shouldn't have to figure out what you're saying.

- **Themes help you and your audience.** Every time you switch look and feel in the middle of a slide show, you impose a kind of cognitive tax on your audience as they adapt to change. Settling on a visual theme early lets you build text and images around the theme's layout library; designing your own theme gives you even more control, matching aesthetics and informational content. A theme isn't just a paint job; it's a tool for information design.

- **In general, use more images and less text per slide.** As text piles up, it loses immediate visual impact and gets harder to remember, but images can gain power in combination. Try splitting a slide into four quarters and filling each quarter, one by one, with images: you're building a collage, and the images talk to one another. Do the same with blocks of text, and you're just making a mess. If you need four blocks of text, use four slides.

- **Don't just read slides aloud.** Unless you must share a verbatim text passage, you should design your slides for visual impact and stickiness in memory and design your spoken lines for ease and fluency of speaking. Just talk to your audience; this generally involves looking at them.

- **A little flash goes a long way.** Every blinking doodad or complex animation draws attention from the content of the talk to the visual flash itself. Sometimes a slide needs an animated object or two; truly rare is the slide that needs any more than that.

- **Leave time for revision.** Your first idea is only special because it comes first, and you won't see the problems with your first draft until you get into your second. You'll often have an easier time revising a broken talk than starting from none at all, and revision takes time.

- **Leave time for rehearsal.** The first time you read through your slides, you'll notice weird juxtapositions, odd grammar, and plain old factual errors. You can do this in front of your audience if you insist, but the other way is better. Rehearsing out loud is part of the design process. The same goes for designing a kiosk presentation: if you haven't tested the talk at an actual kiosk, you won't know whether it'll work.

What you learned in this lesson:

- Customizing Your Presentation Setup

- Precisely Controlling Your Presentation

- Using Slide Show and Presenter Views

- Creating Speaker Notes and Handouts

- Using the Laser Pointer, Highlighter, and Ink Annotations

- Rehearsing Timings and Recording Narration

- Delivering a Presentation Online

True/False

Circle T if the statement is true or F it the statement is false.

T F 1. Slide Show View provides a complex presenter-facing tools display.

T F 2. PowerPoint provides a single command to clear all rehearsal timings.

T F 3. Kiosk-mode presentations are designed to run automatically, without a human attendant.

T F 4. To move to the next slide, hit Enter, Space, right arrow, or down arrow (among others).

T F 5. To run the presentation, press F1 plus any desired modifier keys.

T F 6. The notes page's orientation can be set directly in the Notes Master tab.

T F 7. Notes pages can be styled all at once with document themes.

T F 8. Pressing G during a presentation brings up the Slide Sorter.

T F 9. Ink annotations are saved in a separate file, which can be layered on top of any presentation.

T F 10. Saved rehearsal timings are stored as Advance Slide After: data.

Matching

Match each term to its description or definition.

1. ink annotation
2. narration
3. Notes Page
4. Notes Master
5. kiosk mode
6. laser pointer
7. Office Presentation Service
8. windowed presentation
9. Custom Slide Show
10. Slide Sorter

a. can add (e.g.) headers/footers to notes page

b. press G during show to display; allows quick selection of slides from any group

c. stored as audio files, one file per slide; can optionally play during presentation

d. hosts online slide shows; viewer join in from their browsers

e. includes a subset of slides from a deck; list resides in Slide Show tab

f. presentation loops automatically, keyboard/mouse not used except for hyperlinks

g. stored as graphic object in .pptx file, embedded in its slide

h. not intended for distribution; text styling/layout available from master

i. full presentation w/limited interactivity, keeping other apps available

j. this pen tool doesn't affect file, only draws attention during presentation

Competency Assessment

Project 6-1: Setting Up a Presentation

In this exercise you will tailor slide show options for a specific venue using the Set Up Show dialog.

1. Open the project file **6-x-source.**
2. Click Slide Show > Set Up Slide Show to open the Set Up Show dialog box.
3. Run the presentation first in regular full-screen mode, then windowed, and finally in kiosk mode.
4. Edit each slide to advance after two seconds, then run the presentation in kiosk mode again.

   Note that you can't interact with the presentation in kiosk mode at all.
5. Experiment, in the Set Up Show dialog, with using a subset of the slides, looping in speaker/individual modes, and altering pen/pointer colors.
6. When you're finished experimenting, close the file.

Project 6-2: Custom Slide Shows

This exercise reviews the Custom Slide Show command.

1. Open the project file **6-x-source.** Save it to your project directory as **project_6-2_custom.**
2. Open the Slide Show tab and click Slide Show > Custom Slide Show > Custom Shows...
3. Create a new custom show called Title/Org containing slides 1 and 4 only. Click OK.
4. Select Title/Org from the Custom Slide Show dropdown menu in the Slide Show tab.
5. Create a second custom show called Processes Only including slides 2 and 3.
6. Save and close your document.

Proficiency Assessment

Project 6-3: Presentation Views

In this exercise you'll explore the different presentation viewing modes in PowerPoint 2013.

1. Open the project file **6-x-source.**
2. Run the slide show from the beginning (F5).
3. Select slide 3. Run the presentation from there, stopping it on slide 4 (Escape). Enable looping in the Set Up Show dialog and loop through the presentation a few times.
4. Press Alt+F5 to run the slide show in Presenter View. Experiment with resizing the notes pane and current/next slides in Presenter View.
5. While in Presenter View, press Alt+Tab to switch between all three PowerPoint windows – Presenter View, Slide Show View, and the main editing window.
6. While in Presenter View, click the ... button to invoke a custom slide show.
7. When you're finished experimenting, close the file.

Project 6-4: **Adding Ink Annotations to a Presentation**

In this exercise you'll add ink annotations to a presentation and save them to the .pptx file.

1. Open the project file **6-x-source** and save it to your working directory as **project_6-4_ink.**

2. Run the presentation in Slide Show or Presenter View.

3. In slides 2 and 3, circle the Consult and Ship steps using the pen tool.

4. On the final slide, circle Feliks and place a star next to his name. Keep the annotations when prompted.

5. Rerun the presentation and highlight the title of each slide except the first. Again, keep the annotations when prompted.

   Note that slide annotations are additive – the second round won't replace the first.

6. Close and save your document.

Mastery Assessment

Project 6-5: **Rehearsal Timings**

In this exercise you'll use saved rehearsal timings to nail down your presentation delivery.

1. Open the project file **6-x-source** and save it to your working directory as **project_6-5_timings**.

2. Use the Slide Show > Rehearse Timings command to add slide timings (a few seconds per slide) to the file.

3. When prompted, keep the timings.

4. Run the presentation, making sure Slide Show > Use Timings is selected.

5. If you have a microphone, rerun the slide show, recording both narration and ink/ laser pen marks. Keep your narration and markup.

6. Save and close your document.

Project 6-6: **Presenting Online**

In this exercise you'll deliver a brief presentation using the Office Presentation Service.

1. Open the project file **6-x-source**. Save it as **project_6-6_online.**

2. Add a slide with your name and image, and save the document.

3. Set up an online presentation using the Office Presentation Service. Set it up so that remote viewers can download the presentation.

4. Deliver the presentation to your instructor online. When you're finished, close the file.

Microsoft Outlook 2013

LESSON SKILL MATRIX

In this lesson, you will learn the following skills:

What is Microsoft Outlook?	Sending messages
Setting up Outlook	Archiving old messages
Outlook 2013 interface	Contacts and the Address Book
Composing e-mail	Calendar
Inserting attachments	Using tasks
Adding recipients	

KEY TERMS

- Configuration process
- Recipient
- Attachment
- Contacts
- Appointment
- Meeting
- Tasks

Craig has just started working for a company that uses Microsoft Outlook 2013 as their e-mail and scheduling management program. Craig has used other e-mail programs but is new to Outlook. He needs to quickly become familiar with the e-mail, calendaring, and people management tools of Outlook 2013.

SOFTWARE ORIENTATION

This lesson helps you to start working with Microsoft Outlook to manage your email and schedule.

Figure 1-1

Configuring Microsoft Outlook
for your user.

Signature and Stationaries- Used to add personal signatures lines to email messages and personalized stationary background to email messages.

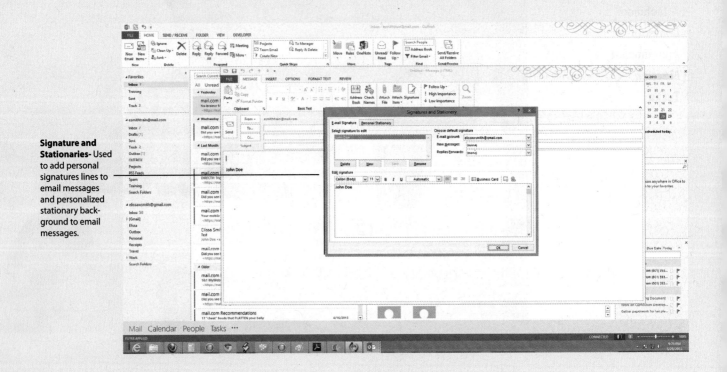

STARTING UP

In this lesson, you'll work with several files from the Outlook01lessons folder. Make sure that you have loaded the OfficeLessons folder onto your computer.

WHAT IS MICROSOFT OUTLOOK?

In today's modern world, sending and receiving e-mail is an integral part of almost every business and personal life. Programs such as Outlook help you send and receive e-mail, but they also keep track of contacts, including office numbers, mobile numbers, and e-mail addresses. Outlook can also help schedule meetings and appointments. It can also create tasks for you and others, and then allow you to use e-mail to check on the status of those tasks. Many Outlook users would consider themselves lost without it, because it does a great job of keeping people organized in today's fast-paced work environment.

SETTING UP OUTLOOK

Before you start using Outlook, you need to ensure that it's set up to receive and send e-mail. Outlook needs to know your e-mail address and e-mail password so it can retrieve and display your e-mail. If you have an IT department that has already set up Outlook for you, you can skip this section and move on to Composing E-mail. But if you are starting Outlook for the first time, you'll need to tell the program where your e-mail is stored and how it is sent. If you use a Microsoft Exchange server, this can be as simple as entering your e-mail address and password, but other e-mail servers may require a bit more work on your part. You'll start the **configuration process** of setting up a new e-mail account in the Control Panels of your computer. You can do this directly within Outlook, but there are some e-mail server configuration steps that are more efficient when you access them through the Control Panel. For this exercise, you will configure Outlook via the Mail Control Panel, which is part of the Windows operating system.

Take Note   You need to ensure that Outlook is installed on your computer and that you have opened your Outlook software, at least once, before performing these steps

STEP BY STEP	**Setting up Outlook**

1   Make sure Outlook is closed.

2   Within the Windows operating system, click the Start menu, then choose Control Panel. Double-click to open the Mail control panel.

Figure 1-2

The Mail Setup control panel.

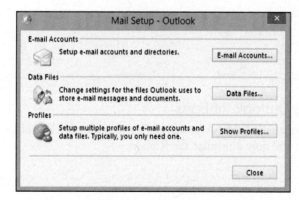

3   In the Mail Setup control panel, click the E-mail Accounts button. The Account Settings Window opens.

4   In the Account Settings window, using the E-mail tab, click the New button. Then click the E-mail account option button, and click Next to open the Add New Account window.

5   In the Add New Account window, enter your full name as you would like it to appear when sending messages. Also enter your e-mail address, such as *me@mydomain.com*, and enter the password provided by your IT department or Internet service provider.

Outlook will attempt to locate your e-mail server and configure your e-mail for you. If it cannot locate your e-mail server, it will ask you additional questions about the type of e-mail account you are using. If necessary, obtain the additional information from the Internet service provider that hosts your e-mail account, your IT department, or click the Help button (**?**) in the main Outlook window.

Using more than one e-mail account

If you have multiple e-mail accounts, you can configure Microsoft Outlook to receive mail from all your accounts. To do this, repeat the steps described above to configure Outlook to communicate with each additional e-mail server. Each e-mail account functions the same way for sending, receiving, and managing messages.

OUTLOOK 2013 INTERFACE

Microsoft Outlook 2013 has a user interface that is very similar to the other programs in Microsoft Office 2013. The following sub-sections describe important aspects and features of the Outlook interface that are found in other office programs.

The Ribbon tabs

• **File:** takes you into the Backstage view and main functions, including opening and printing items from Outlook.

• **Home:** contains the most common functions for the portion of Outlook you are in, such as E-mail, Calendar, People (Contacts), or Tasks.

• **Send/Receive:** for controlling how e-mail and other information is received into Outlook.

• **Folder:** controls the creation of new folders.

• **View:** customizes the Outlook window and the panes and tools that are visible.

Figure 1-3

Outlook 2013 Ribbons.

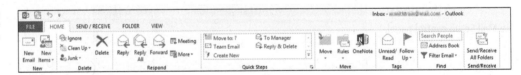

Minimizing Outlook Ribbons

You can minimize the Ribbons so that the buttons are not viewable and all you see are the tabbed headings. You will now minimize the Ribbon.

STEP BY STEP	**To minimize the Ribbon**

    1   Click any Ribbon tab to make it active, and then double-click the same tab to minimize the Ribbon. You will only see the tabbed headings.

    2   To peak at the Ribbon without entirely opening it, click any of the Ribbon tabs. The Ribbon appears; however, it covers up the top part of the Outlook window. To open the Ribbon tabs completely, double-click the Ribbon tab.

You can turn on and off the individual tabs in the Outlook Ribbon. You can also create your own Ribbon tabs that contain the Outlook buttons you use the most. You will do this in Lesson 2, "Getting Started with Microsoft Outlook 2013."

The Quick Access Toolbar

Outlook has a Quick Access Toolbar, just as other Microsoft Office 2013 applications do. You can add your favorite Outlook shortcuts to the Quick Access Toolbar so you can have quick and easy access to them from the main Outlook screen. The Quick Access Toolbar is located in the top-left corner of the Outlook screen, and by default, it contains four buttons: Send/Receive All Folders, Undo, Redo, and Customize Quick Access Toolbar. (The Redo button only becomes available after the Undo button has been used.)

Moving the Quick Access Toolbar

You can't move the Quick Access Toolbar in the same way that you could move other toolbars in previous versions of Microsoft Office. However, you can change the location of the Quick Access Toolbar to sit below the Ribbon, and then you can move it back to its default position in the top-left corner of the Outlook window. To move the Quick Access Toolbar to appear below the ribbon, right-click anywhere on the Quick Access Toolbar, and from the shortcut menu that appears, choose Show Quick Access Toolbar Below the Ribbon. To move it back to its default location, right-click anywhere on the toolbar, and from the shortcut menu that appears, choose Show Quick Access Toolbar Above the Ribbon.

Customizing the Quick Access Toolbar

The fastest way to add your own shortcuts to the Quick Access Toolbar is to click the Customize Quick Access Toolbar button (⩒) to expose a list of popular shortcuts that you can add to the toolbar. From this list, you can choose the options you want to add, and they will be automatically added to the toolbar.

You will now use the Customize Quick Access Toolbar button to add buttons to the toolbar.

STEP BY STEP	**Customizing the Quick Access Toolbar**

    1   Click the **Customize Quick Access Toolbar** button (⩒).

    2   From the list that appears, choose the Delete option. A black X is added to the toolbar as the Delete shortcut. Repeat the process to add another shortcut.

If you want to add shortcuts to the Quick Access Toolbar that aren't available when you click the Customize Quick Access Toolbar button, you can use the More Commands option to find those shortcuts.

3   Click the Customize Quick Access Toolbar button. From the list that appears, choose More Commands (it's the option second from the bottom of the list). The Outlook Options—Customize the Quick Access Toolbar dialog box appears.

Figure 1-4

Outlook Options—Customize the Quick Access Toolbar

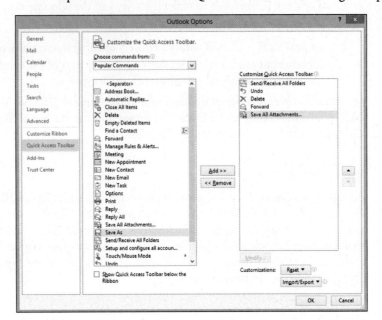

4   On the left side of the Customize the Quick Access Toolbar pane, you will see a drop-down list with the entry Popular Commands. Immediately below it, you will see a column with a list of Popular Commands. On the right side of the Customize the Quick Access Toolbar pane, you will see a column with a list of the buttons currently available in your Quick Access Toolbar. To add one of the Popular Commands to your Quick Access Toolbar, select one of the Popular Commands from the list on the left, and then click the Add button located between the two columns. The Popular Command you choose is added to the list of buttons currently available in your Quick Access Toolbar.

5   Repeat the process to add more buttons. When you are done, click OK to close the Outlook Options box. The buttons you selected now appear on the Quick Access Toolbar.

Creating a new e-mail message

1   From the New group located at the far left side of the Home Ribbon tab, click the New E-mail button. A new, untitled message box appears.

Figure 1-5

New Untitled Message Box Opens.

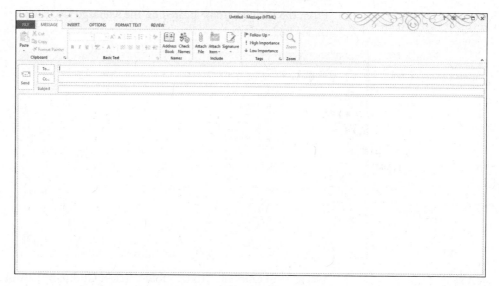

2   In the field to the right of the To button, enter the e-mail address of the **recipient** of the message. You can separate additional recipients with a semicolon (;).

Take Note   If the recipient of the message works at a different company or has a different domain (the part of the e-mail address after the @ symbol), you will need to enter the complete address. For example, to send an e-mail address to Jennifer Smith at work, you might enter **jsmith@company.com**. If you work at the same company, you might only need to enter the first part of her e-mail address, not the entire domain address, since Outlook would try to complete it for you.

3   In the field to the right of the Subject Heading, enter a Subject for the message. We recommend entering a short, descriptive subject that summarizes the content of the message.

4   In the large white area below the Subject field, enter the Body of the e-mail message, and then click the Send button, located on the top-right portion of the message box, beneath the Ribbon.

Adding attachments to e-mail messages

Another important function of e-mail is sending **attachments**. Attachments are files such as a Word document, Excel spreadsheet, or even a photograph that are sent along with your e-mail message. Attachments can be opened and used as needed by the recipients of your e-mail message.

STEP BY STEP   **Adding attachments to e-mail messages**

1   From the Home tab, click New E-mail to create a new e-mail. Click the text box next to To and type in an e-mail address.

2   From the Include group located on the Message tab, click Attach File. The Insert File dialog box appears.

Figure 1-6

Insert File dialog box.

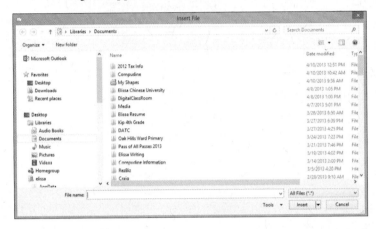

3   Navigate to Outlook01lessons folder, select **CompanyVolunteerSign-Up.docx**, and choose Insert.

Take Note   You can also click and drag a document into the body portion of the e-mail message you are composing to attach it to the message. If you attach multiple files to your e-mail message, each file appears on the attached line separated by a semicolon (;).

4   The Insert File window closes and you are back to your e-mail message. A new line called Attached appears under the Subject line, and displays the file you have selected.

5   Click the Send button; your e-mail message is sent with the attached file included.

Take Note   When sending files as attachments, be careful not to send anything too large. Some e-mail systems are not able to accommodate e-mail messages more than a certain size. The upper limit tends to be 25 MB, although this varies by the policies set by the recipient's e-mail administrator.

Adding signatures

Besides adding signatures, the second tab of the Signature and Stationeries dialog box(Personalized Stationary) has a themes button that allows users to add customized background colors and fonts to the body of their e-mail messages.

Workplace Ready

You might want to add your contact information and company name to the bottom of the e-mail messages you send. You can avoid typing this information each and every time you send a message if you create an e-mail signature. When you create an e-mail signature, you can save it, and then apply it as needed at the bottom of your e-mail messages.

STEP BY STEP   **Creating a new e-mail signature**

1   Open a new e-mail and click the Signature button in the Include group of the Message tab. A menu appears.

2   In the menu that appears, click Signatures. The Signatures and Stationery window appears.

3   In the Signatures and Stationery window, click New. Enter a name for the signature. For example, if you want to have a work e-mail signature and a personal signature, you would name your work signature work. The name is for your use only and is not visible to the people you e-mail.

4   Enter the information you want to appear at the end of your messages. For example, if your name is John Doe, you might enter

John Doe
jdoe@trainingrus.com
1-800-222-1234

Figure 1-7

Adding a new e-mail signature to the Signatures and Stationery window.

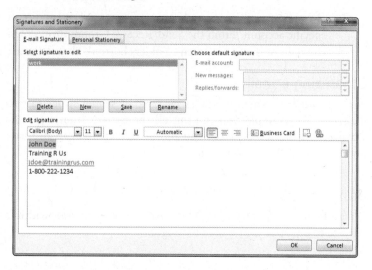

Take Note   Go to *http://office.microsoft.com* for different e-mail templates that you can download and use. When you access the site, type Outlook E-mail Signature Templates in the Search field. A group of different e-mail templates appears.

5   After entering the e-mail signature information, you can indicate the type of messages that should use the e-mail signature. For example, to apply the signature to new messages, select the signature name from the New messages drop-down menu. To apply the signature to your e-mail replies and to messages you forward, select the signature name from the Replies/forwards drop-down menu. If you want to apply the signature manually and not have it appear automatically when you create a new message, reply to a message, or forward a message, choose (none) from the New messages and Replies/ forwards drop-down menus.

6   Click OK. In the e-mail message window, and from the Signature drop-down menu at the top of the message window, choose the signature you just created. If necessary, choose Signatures from this menu again to edit or modify the signature.

If you set your signature to apply automatically to your messages, the next time you create a new message, you will see that the signature is added automatically to the body section of your new e-mail message.

Receiving e-mail

Once you configure Outlook, it will automatically attempt to receive e-mail messages from your account at a specified interval. You can disable this option, and manually check for e-mail more regularly. If you are connected to a Microsoft Exchange e-mail server, your account will automatically update immediately upon receipt of a message.

STEP BY STEP	Receiving e-mails

1   To send and receive all e-mail messages outside the regular schedule, click the **Send/Receive** Ribbon tab, then click the **Send/Receive All Folders** button (⬚), which is the very first button on the far left side of the Ribbon tab.

2   If you have multiple e-mail accounts, you can send and receive messages only for one specific account. From the Send/Receive Groups drop-down menu (located directly to the right of the Send/Receive Folders button), choose the account you want to use.

Organizing e-mail

You can organize e-mail messages by topic or sender so it's easier to locate and work with the messages. For example, you can put all the e-mails from a specific sender in one folder, or all e-mails regarding a certain topic in another folder. You can also have Outlook detect and remove junk e-mail (spam) for you.

Using folders

E-mail folders act just as other folders on your computer or within a filing cabinet, and it's what you use to organize your e-mail messages.

STEP BY STEP   **Creating a new folder**

1   Along the left side of your Outlook in the Folder pane, right-click the name of your e-mail account. From the context menu that appears, choose *New Folder.*

2   Your new empty folder appears as a white box in the Folder pane with a blinking cursor. Type *Training* and then press *Enter.* By default, the new folder appears listed in alphabetical order with the other items in the Folder pane. Drag it up or down to relocate it to a more convenient position.

3   Click and drag an e-mail message into the new folder. Click the folder to view its contents in the middle area of your screen. Click the Inbox to view your e-mail again.

4   Repeat this process to create as many folders as you need to effectively organize your e-mail.

Take Note   You can automatically route e-mail messages to specific folders using Rules. From the File Ribbon tab, select **Manage Rules and Alerts**, then create a new rule. For example, you can route all the e-mail messages you receive from the professional association to which you belong to a folder that's just for correspondence from that association. You will learn more about rules in the next lesson.

ARCHIVING OLD MESSAGES

You can archive any or all your old messages if you want to save them for future reference. The contents of folders are archived at different intervals. Some folders are archived after two months, while others are archived after six months. You can change the time Outlook waits before archiving a folder, or specify that a folder is not to be archived at all. You can also have outlook delete old messages.

If you work in a company, you should check to see whether the company has a records' retention policy before deleting messages. Some organizations require employees to retain messages for legal or compliance reasons. Note that an IT administrator can disable these settings if you are using an Exchange e-mail server. If you do not see the settings below and work in a corporate environment, the settings might have been disabled because they have already been applied for you.

STEP BY STEP   **Specifying how often Outlook should archive your e-mail messages**

1   Choose the File Ribbon tab to go into the Backstage view of Outlook. Then click **Options**. The Outlook Options box appears.

2   Click the **Advanced** tab on the left side of the box. In the Advanced tab, click the **AutoArchive Settings** button. The AutoArchive Settings dialog box appears.

3   In the AutoArchive Settings dialog box, specify the frequency with which the folder should be archived, the age of items before they are archived, and whether the items should be moved or deleted. When you're done, click **OK** to close the AutoArchive settings dialog box.

Figure 1-9

AutoArchive Setting dialog box is open.

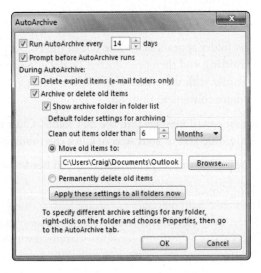

4   You can also specify different Auto Archive settings for an individual folder: from the Folder pane, right-click a folder, and then choose **Properties**. The Properties dialog box appears.

5   From the Properties dialog box, click the third tab over, **AutoArchive**. The AutoArchive tab contains the following options:

• **Do not archive items in this folder**: this is the default option for every new folder; when this option is selected, none of the items in the folder will be archived at all.

• **Archive items in this folder using the default setting**: this option lets you archive the items in the folder using standard settings.

• **Archive this folder using these settings**: this option allows you to select your options for archiving this specific folder. You can select how old items are before they're archived, where to move items to when archiving, or have items be permanently deleted when archived.

6 Click the second button, Archive items in this folder using default settings. Click **OK** to close the folder properties dialog box.

Figure 1-10

Setting Auto Archive settings for a specific folder.

Bottom Line

Bottom Line Summary:The first half of this lesson discusses the e-mail portion of Outlook 2013. The Outlook 2013 interface is introduced including the Ribbon tabs and Quick Access Toolbar. Next, creating, sending, and responding to e-mail messages is covered. Attaching files to e-mail messages, archiving e-mail, and also file management within Outlook is also discussed.

CONTACTS AND THE ADDRESS BOOK

Microsoft Outlook contains a contact management tool called People. In older versions of Outlook, this part of the program was called **Contacts**. People is similar to an electronic address book in that it allows you to save information about the individuals with whom you communicate. The information you can track in the Contacts area includes names, e-mail addresses, phone numbers, addresses, and other basic contact information. If you use a Microsoft Exchange Server or work in a company that uses Outlook for e-mail and contacts management, Outlook will already contain contact information for employees of the organization. This information is usually maintained by the organization's IT department.

You can also attach files to contacts and add notes regarding them in a Contact box. You can manually add contacts for individuals that Outlook has not automatically placed in your Contacts list.

Adding contacts

> 1   Click the **People** button at the bottom-left corner of the Outlook window.
>
> 2   In the upper-left corner of the Home tab, click **New Contact**. Enter the contact information you want to save, including e-mail address and phone information.

Figure 1-11

New Contact Box is open.

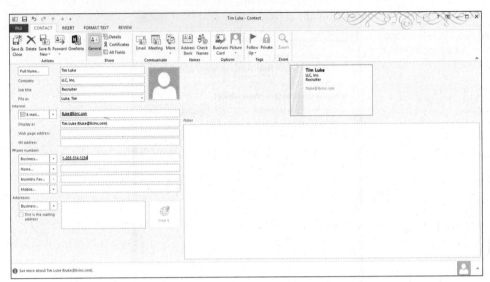

> 3   Click **Save** and **Close**, located on the far left side of the Contacts tab. The new contact appears in the middle pane of your Outlook window.

Finding contacts

You can use the Search bar whenever you need to quickly find a specific person from your list of contacts. You can also use the Search bar to look for e-mails, tasks, and appointments in other areas of the program.

STEP BY STEP | **Finding contacts**

1   If you aren't already in the People area of Outlook, click the **People** button in the lower-left corner of the Outlook window to see your contacts.

2   At the top of the Outlook window, enter **part or the entire name of the person you want to locate.**

3   When the correct contact's name is displayed in the list under the search box, the right side of the Outlook screen displays the corresponding details in the Contact Information box, as well as options to Schedule a meeting or Send E-mail.

4   Under the Send E-mail heading, click the contact's e-mail address; an untitled message box appears already addressed to the correct contact. Click the **X** in the top-right corner of the untitled message box to close it.

Figure 1-12

Using Search box to find a contact.

Creating groups

If you frequently send messages to the same group of people, you can create a group to simplify the process. For example, if you frequently send e-mails to five colleagues in the sales department, you can create a single group that includes all five colleagues, and then just enter the group name to e-mail all five people.

STEP BY STEP | **Creating a group**

1   If you aren't already in the People part of Outlook, click the **People** button in the lower-left corner of the window.

2   In the Home tab, click **New Contact Group**. An untitled contact group appears.

3   Enter **Sales Department**.

4 From the Member group in the Contact Group tab, click **Add Members**. Click **From Outlook Contacts**; the Select Members dialog box appears. Double-click the contacts you need to add to your new group; they will appear at the bottom of the box in the Members area, separated by semi-colons.

Figure 1-13

Select members to add to the new group.

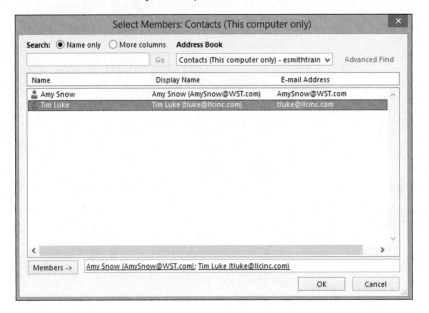

5 Click **OK** to close the Select Members box and return to the New Group box.

6 From the Contacts Group tab, click **Save & Close** to save the new contact group.

CALENDAR

You can use Outlook to organize your schedule, set-up meetings, and keep track of anything that needs to be done by a specific date or time.

Appointments and meetings

If you need to schedule time for your own activities, Outlook considers it an **Appointment**. If you want others to participate, it becomes a **Meeting**.

Creating appointments and setting up reminders

Follow these steps to create a new appointment from the Calendar portion of Outlook. Many companies create preset locations for meetings to be held in like company conference or meeting rooms. These locations are permanently saved in the Outlook Calendar and meetings can be assigned to a company location when a meeting is scheduled.

STEP BY STEP   **Creating appointments and setting up reminders**

1 Click the **Calendar** button in the bottom-left corner of the Outlook window. In the Home tab, click **New Appointment**. If you are in the Mail portion of Outlook, click the **New Items** button, located on the Home Ribbon tab, and then click **Appointment**.

2 In the Subject field, enter **Dentist Appointment**. This title is added to the calendar.

3 In the Location field, enter **123 Main Street, Anytown, NY**.

4 Enter a **start and end time** for the appointment.

5   On the Appointments tab, set a Reminder. The default is 15 minutes before the appointment is due to begin. Turn the reminder off by clicking the arrow next to the 15 minutes and setting it to 0.

Figure 1-14

Setting a reminder in a new Appointment box.

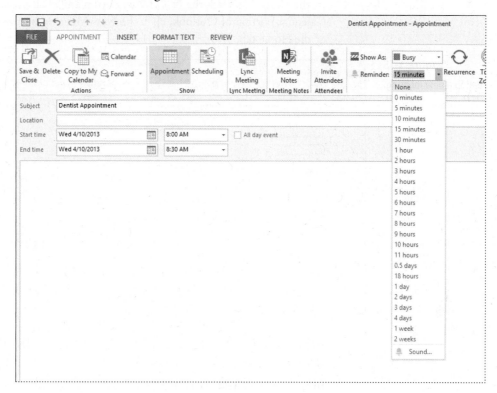

6   Click the Save & Close button, located on the far left side of the Appointment tab.

Setting up meetings and inviting attendees

Follow these steps to create a new meeting and invite other participants to attend. The process is almost identical to creating an appointment, except you invite other participants to the meeting. The meeting invitations are then sent to the participants as an e-mail message.

STEP BY STEP   Setting up meetings and inviting attendees

1   In the Home tab, click the New Items button and click Meeting. If you are in the Calendar portion of Outlook, click the New Meeting button located on the far left side of the Home tab.

Figure 1-15

Creating a new meeting.

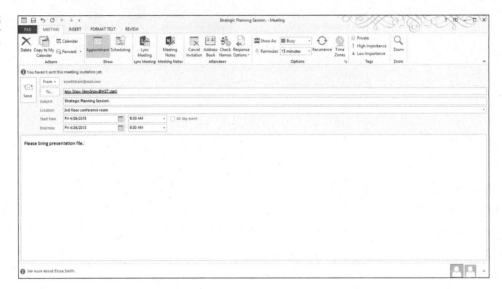

2   In the Subject field, enter Strategic Planning Session. This title is also added to the calendar.

3   In the Location field, enter 3rd floor conference room.

4   In the To field, enter the e-mail addresses or contact names of all participants. If your colleagues share a group calendar such as Microsoft Exchange, click the Scheduling button in the Show group of the Home Ribbon tab to see the times when the attendees are available for a meeting.

5   Enter a start and end time for the appointment.

6   In the large white area at the bottom of the message, type a note that describes the purpose of the meeting. You can also attach files, just as you would attach files to an e-mail message.

7   Click Send to e-mail the meeting invitation to your recipients.

Those you send the meeting invitation to will receive the invite in their Inbox. As those that you've invited respond to the meeting invitation, Outlook keeps track of who has accepted and declined the meeting request. You will see individual e-mails back in your own Inbox indicating who has accepted or declined the meeting invitation.

Using tasks

With **Tasks**, you can keep track of activities in much the same way you would a to-do list. (The difference between tasks and appointments is that appointments occur at a specific time and location; tasks have a start date and an due date, but no real location.) You can create tasks for yourself, and you can e-mail task assignments to others.

If you e-mail a task assignment to another individual, you can receive a message back if the assignee accepts or rejects the assignment. You can also receive a message back when the task assignment is completed.

STEP BY STEP   **Creating a task**

1   From the Home tab, click the New Items button and click Task. An Untitled Task dialog box appears. If you are in the Task portion of Outlook, click the New Task button on the far left side of the Home tab.

2   In the Subject field, enter Gather paperwork for tax planning.

3   Choose a priority of normal, high, or low for the task.

4   Enter the start date for the task and the due date.

Figure 1-16

Creating a new task.

5   Click the Save & Close button. The task is displayed in the task list, along the left side of the Outlook Window, if you are in the Tasks portion of the program. If you are in the Mail portion, the tasks can appear on the To Do pane, which you can open on the right side of the View Ribbon tab.

Bottom Line

The Outlook Address book, now called People, is introduced and how to create contacts and groups. Next, the Outlook Calendar and how to create appointments and meetings is covered. Finally, Outlook tasks are discussed.

What you learned in this lesson:

• What is Microsoft Outlook?

• Setting up Outlook

• Outlook 2013 interface

• Composing e-mail, inserting attachments, adding recipients

• And sending messages

• Archiving old messages

• Contacts and the Address Book

• Calendar

• Using tasks

Knowledge Assessment

True/False

Circle T if the statement is true or F it the statement is false.

T F 1. Microsoft Outlook 2013 is a full business management and communication tool with e-mail, contact, scheduling, and task management tools.

T F 2. Before you can send and receive e-mail items in Outlook, you may need to complete some configuration steps that are easier to complete from your computer's Control Panel.

T F 3. You can only configure Outlook to receive e-mail from one account at a time.

T F 4. It doesn't matter how large your e-mail attachments are, they will still be sent.

T F 5. Archiving allows old e-mail items to be moved to a different folder, so the Inbox area doesn't become so cluttered.

T F 6. In older versions of Outlook, the People portion of Outlook was referred to as, the Address Book.

T F 7. When you frequently need to e-mail groups of different people/contacts, you can create Group to simplify this process.

T F 8. A meeting is a calendar event scheduled for one person.

T F 9. On the Appointment Ribbon tab of a new Appointment, you can set a Reminder to trigger for a set amount of time before an appointment or meeting is scheduled to begin.

T F 10. There are no differences between Appointments and Tasks.

Multiple Choice

Select the best response for the following statements.

1. Which Outlook Ribbon tab controls how e-mail items and sent and received into Outlook?
   a. Folder Ribbon tab
   b. View Ribbon tab
   c. Send/Receive Ribbon tab
   d. Home Ribbon tab

2. When entering multiple e-mail addresses into the To field of an e-mail message, they need to be separated with:
   a. A common
   b. A semicolon
   c. A period
   d. An apostrophe

3. If you want e-mail messages to automatically be routed to a specific folder, you can create a:
   a. text box to put them in
   b. folder named Routing to put them in
   c. a task to remind you to create a folder for them
   d. Rule from the File Ribbon tab, Rules and Alerts

4. How do you access the People portion of Outlook 2013?
   a. Click People in the bottom left hand corner of the Outlook window
   b. Click People on the Home Ribbon tab
   c. Click the People short cut button in the bottom right hand corner of the Outlook window
   d. None of the above

5. To use the Search box to find contacts in the People portion of Outlook, you need to:
   a. copy and paste the information from Word into Outlook
   b. type the search term into the search box and hit enter on your keyboard
   c. hit F1 on your keyboard to open the search box
   d. find Search on your Home Ribbon tab

6. When creating a new contact Group, what button do you use to pick the members of your group?
   a. Add Tasks
   b. Create New E-mail
   c. Insert File
   d. Add Members

7. When you send a Meeting Invitations to someone, how do you know if they can attend or not?
   a. They call you.
   b. They schedule the meeting in a global calendar for you.
   c. Outlook sends a meeting response back to your e-mail showing whether the meeting invitee either accepts or declines the meeting invitation.
   d. They text you.

8. In the default Task view, when a task is Marked Complete, it is:
   a. Moved to the Task Complete folder
   b. Moved to the Inbox
   c. E-Mailed to the IT Department
   d. Removed from the Task list

9. The default time for a meeting reminder is:

    a. 30 minutes

    b. 15 minutes

    c. 20 minutes

    d. 5 minutes

10. What information should be entered in the Body section of an e-mail message:

    a. The text and information of the e-mail message

    b. E-mail addresses

    c. Contacts

    d. Meeting location

Competency Assessment

Project 1-1: Creating an e-mail message and signature

You will create an e-mail message and an e-mail signature to go in your Outlook e-mail messages.

1. If you aren't in the Mail portion of Outlook, click Mail in the bottom left hand corner of the Window.

2. From the Inbox, on the Home Ribbon tab, click New Email in the New group.

3. In the Untitled Message box, type an e-mail address of your choice in the To field.

4. In the Subject section, type a subject of your choice.

5. In the Body section, type a message of your choice.

6. On the Message Ribbon tab, in the Include group, click Signature and Signatures….

7. In the Signatures and Stationary box, in the Email Signature tab, click New.

8. In the New Signature box, type a name of the new Signature, and click OK.

9. Back in the Email Signature area, at the bottom of the box under Edit Signature, Type your Signature and use the toolbar under Edit Signature to edit your signature. See the example below:

    Suzie Stuff

    Trading Manager

    Northwind Traders, Inc.

    suzie@northtraders.com

    1-888-22-TRADE

10. Click OK to close the Signatures and Stationary box.

11. To enter the new signature into your e-mail message, click the Signatures button, and select the name for your new signature. It will be entered in the body of your e-mail message wherever your cursor is blinking.

12. Click Send to send the e-mail message.

Project 1-2: Creating and saving a new contact

In the People portion of Outlook, you will create and save a new contact, and also view it in different ways in the People window.

1. From the Home Ribbon tab, in the New group, click New Contact.
2. In the Untitled Contact box, type a Full Name for the contact.
3. In the Email field, type an e-mail address for the contact.
4. Under the Phone numbers: section, type a Business Phone number.
5. On the right hand side of the contact in the Notes field, type some notes about the contact.
6. Under Addresses and next to Businesses, type a business address for the contact.
7. On the Contact Ribbon tab, click Save & Close button.
8. View your new contact in the People window. On the Contact Ribbon tab, in the Current View group, click Business Card. Your view will change, so the contacts resemble digital business cards.
9. In the Current View group, click Phone.
10. Double-click the contact, you just create, and add a Home phone number to the contact.
11. Click Save & Close to close the contact.

Proficiency Assessment

Project 1-3: Creating a new appointment

You will create a new appointment for yourself and a meeting request for at least two other people.

1. Click Calendar. On the Home Ribbon tab, open an Untitled Appointment.
2. Type a Subject and Location for the new appointment.
3. In the Options group of the Appointment Ribbon tab, set a Reminder for 30 minutes before the appointment begins.
4. Set an appropriate Start and End Time for the Appointment.
5. Click the Save & Close button.
6. On the Home Ribbon tab, click New Meeting to open an Untitled Meeting.
7. In the To field, enter two or three e-mail addresses to send the Meeting to.
8. Complete filling out the Meeting.
9. Click the Send button to send the Meeting to meeting invitees.

Project 1-4: Creating and managing a task list

You will create a task list, mark some tasks as complete, and customize your task view.

1. Click Tasks. On the left hand side, where it says, Type a new task.
2. Type 5 new tasks (hit enter between tasks).
3. Double-click one of the tasks to open the individual Task Information box.
4. On the Task Ribbon tab, in the Manage Tasks group, click Mark Complete.
5. The Task dialog box will close.
6. To customize the view of tasks, on the Home Ribbon tab, in the Current View group, click Detailed. Notice, the completed task has a line through it, indicating its completion.
7. Click on another task, on the Home Ribbon, click Mark Complete.
8. Mark another task complete.

Mastery Assessment

Project 1-5: Adding contacts and creating a contact group

You need to add some new business contacts into your People location of Outlook and create a Contact Group to manage them.

1. From the People area of Outlook, create three new business contacts of your choice and be sure to enter the following fields for each: Full Name, Business Phone, Business Address, Home Address, Business Email, and notes.
2. From the People area, create a new Contact Group. Be sure to add your three new contacts to the new group.
3. Create a new meeting and mail it to your new contact group.

Project 1-6: Managing files in your Inbox

You will manage the file properties of your Inbox in Outlook.

1. From your Outlook Inbox, create two new folders for your choice. Add at least two Outlook items to your new folders. Drag some un-needed items to the deleted items folder.
2. Go into your Outlook Autoarchive Settings and set the default archive settings to your personal preferences.
3. Add three buttons of your choice to the Outlook Quick Access Toolbar.

LESSON SKILL MATRIX

In this lesson, you will learn the following skills:

Outlook Views	Using Rules to manage incoming items
Printing in Outlook Views	Recurring appointments and meetings
Customizing the Mail View	Junk e-mail options
Forwarding and replying to e-mail	

KEY TERMS

- **Folder Pane**
- **Junk E-mail or Spam**
- **Recurring appointment or meeting**
- **To Do bar**
- **Replying**
- **Forwarding**

Jerome has been using Outlook for a few months. He wants to be able customize Outlook's views, especially in the Calendar and People areas, to fit his own needs. He also needs to be able to Print different Outlook items like Calendar events and specific e-mail messages. He also would like to further customize the Outlook window by creating his own Ribbon tab and changing defaults in the Outlook Options box.

SOFTWARE ORIENTATION

This lesson helps you to work efficiently and effectively with email using Microsoft Outlook 2013.

Figure 2-1

Microsoft Outlook provides comprehensive tools for composing and managing email.

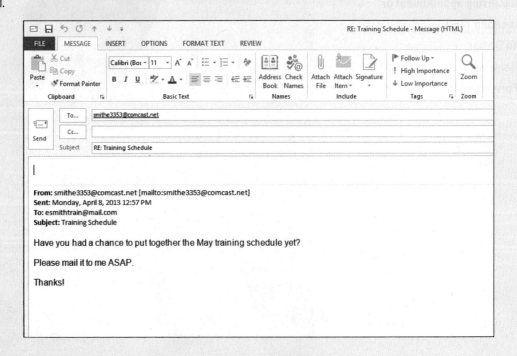

STARTING UP

You will not need to work with any files for this lesson.

OUTLOOK VIEWS

Microsoft Outlook is a communication, scheduling, and information management system. As you've already seen, Outlook contains four different main views:

- **Mail:** for viewing and receiving e-mail messages.

- **People:** for managing contact information.

- **Calendar:** for scheduling appointments and activities.

- **Tasks:** for managing personal tasks and for managing assignments for others.

Since Mail view is the default view you enter when opening Outlook, the program lets users modify the window to include different aspects of each of these four views from the Mail view.

The activities presented in this lesson focus on the Mail and Calendar views of Microsoft Outlook. Many of the activities like printing items, customizing the Outlook window, and turning on and off of different task panes can be accomplished in either the same way or very similar ways in all of Outlook's different views.

PRINTING IN OUTLOOK VIEWS

There will be times when you'll need to print items from any or all of the different views. For example, you might need to print e-mails from the Mail view, calendars from the Calendar view, and so on.

Printing in the Mail view

Workplace **Ready**

After you've established your Outlook calendar and entered many of your appointments and meetings into, you can print calendars showing your appointments and meetings in Daily, Weekly, and Monthly Styled Calendars.

When you are in the Mail view, you can choose to print your e-mails in a Memo Style or a Table Style. The Memo Style prints just the e-mail item you select from the Inbox. The Table Style prints the entire Inbox list.

STEP BY STEP	Printing from the Mail view

1 From your Inbox, select an e-mail message.

2 From the Mail view, click the File tab. Then, in the Backstage view, click **Print**.

The Print window opens. It is a combined view that shows the Print box on the left side and the Print Preview window on the right.

From the Print box, you can select the printer to print to, printer options, and whether to print in a Table Style or a Memo Style.

3   Select the Table Style. The entire Inbox list is printed.

4   Select the Memo Style. The e-mail item you selected in Step 1 is printed.

Take Note   To close Print without printing anything, press Esc or click the left-facing arrow at the top of the Print screen and Backstage view to return to the Mail view.

Figure 2-2

Print preview of an e-mail item.

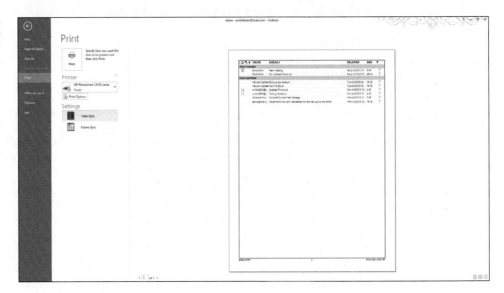

5   To close the Print section, click Exit.

Printing in the Calendar view

Workplace Ready: After you've established your Outlook calendar and entered many of your appointments and meetings into, you can print calendars showing your appointments and meetings in Daily, Weekly, and Monthly Styled Calendars.

Another common view to print from in Outlook is the Calendar. When printing in the Calendar view, you can print different time intervals, such as month, week, day, or even an individual appointment. Any appointments and meetings scheduled on given days will also appear on the printout.

STEP BY STEP   **Printing from the Calendar view**

1   From the bottom-left corner, click the Calendar button to switch to the Calendar view. Notice that the default period shown is Month.

2   Click the File tab, and click Print.

The Print box appears, and it's very similar to the one in the Mail view: the Print box is on the left side and the Print Preview is on the right side. The Print box contains options such as the printer to print from; print options that allow you to adjust settings on your printer; and settings that allow you to pick the date interval that will print. Notice that the period that's selected in your Calendar view is the one that's automatically selected to print. (In this case, the period that's selected is Month, since the Calendar view is showing a Month period.)

3   Under Settings, click Weekly Calendar Style. Notice that the Print Preview updates to display a week rather than the month. Click different settings to see what they look like in Print Preview.

Figure 2-3

Print Preview of Calendar view.

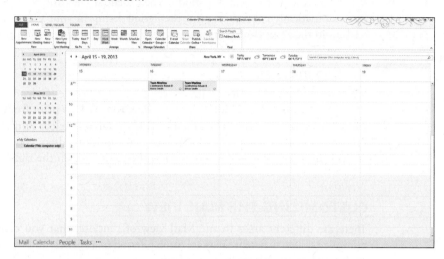

4   Press Esc to close the Print box without actually printing anything.

Adjusting views in Calendar

If you don't want Month to be your default period in the Calendar View, you can adjust it to the period you need. This is done on the Home tab in the Arrange group, which contains the following buttons: Next 7 days, Work Week, Week, Month, and Schedule View..

STEP BY STEP   Adjusting views in the Calendar

1   In the Calendar view, click Work Week from the Arrange group of the Home tab. The view adjusts to only show Monday through Friday in the middle screen.

Figure 2-4

The Work Week calendar view only displays Monday through Friday.

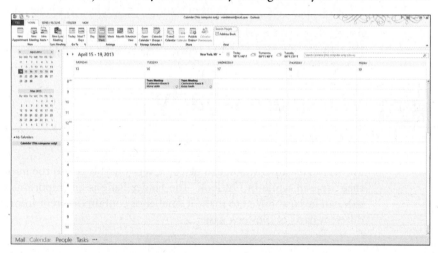

2   Click some of the other buttons in the Arrange group and notice what the views look like.

3   Click the **Mail** button in the bottom left area of the Outlook window to return to the Mail view.

Take Note   When you change the default period in the Calendar view and then print from this view, the Print Box automatically chooses to print the period set up in your Calendar view. You can change the settings in the Print Box to print a different period as explained in the previous exercise.

Printing in other views

Printing in Outlook's other main views, Tasks and People (Calendar), is very similar to print in the Calendar and Mail views. Select the view you wish to print from. Select the individual item, you wish to print and then click the File Ribbon tab and select Print. Remember, you will go into Print Preview after selecting Print. You can customize the item you are printing from the left side of the Print Preview window and preview the print item on the right.

CUSTOMIZING THE MAIL VIEW

There are different areas in the Mail view of Outlook that you can turned on or off and also minimize. These different areas are often referred to as panes, and the buttons for controlling them are located on the View tab, in the Layout group.

About the Folder pane

The first of these panes is the Folder pane. The Folder pane is always open by default in any view of Outlook. Depending on Outlook View you have displayed on the screen, the button in the Folder pane change as follows:

- **Mail view**: displays the personal folders and mail folders necessary to organize your e-mail.

- **Calendar view**: displays calendars for reference.

- **People view**: shows the location of different sources for contacts available on your computer.

- **Tasks view**: shows locations of sources for task lists available on your computer.

Customizing the Folders pane for the Mail view

 Workplace **Ready**

The Mail view of Outlook can be come very busy. It is also the most common view people spend their time in while in Outlook. The Folder Pane is an important part of the Outlook window that can be customized to make it smaller or contain different information to make navigating to different parts of Outlook easier.

The most common view to use the Folder pane from is the Mail view, because you can use the Folder pane for organizing, reading, deleting, and moving e-mail messages into folders. As already mentioned, the Folder pane is always open by default, but you can keep it minimized or closed.

STEP BY STEP   **Minimizing the Folders pane**

1   Click the View tab. In the Layout group, click the Folder pane and select Minimized from the drop-down menu that appears.

The Folder pane folds into the side of the screen, leaving only a thin bar with small links to the Inbox, Sent, Trash, and All Folders. You can click these links to open a side bar to the right of the minimized Folder pane. This side bar shows the items contained within the link you selected.

Figure 2-5

Minimize the Folder pane.

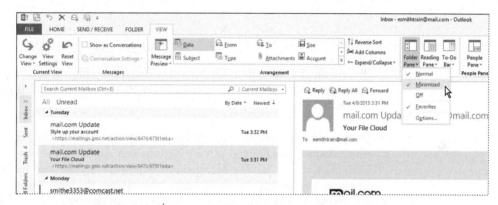

2   To restore the Folder pane, click the small arrow located on the top-right corner of the minimized Folder pane. The entire Folder pane becomes visible again.

The top section of the Folders pane contains an area called Favorites. You can select your top folders and add them to the Favorites area by dragging them up into the Favorites area from the Folder list below. You can also turn the Favorites area of the Folder pane on and off.

You will now turn off the Favorites area from the Folder pane.

3   In the View tab, click the Folder pane button. From the drop-down menu that appears, click Favorite to remove the check mark next to it. The Favorites section at the top of the Folder pane is no longer shown.

Figure 2-6

Turn off the Favorites area.

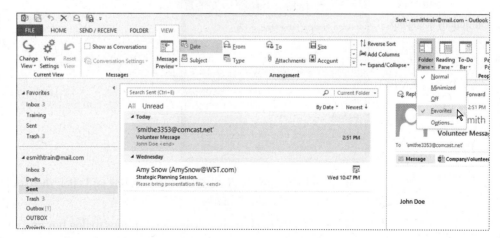

4   To turn the Favorites back on, click the Folder pane button and select Favorites from the drop-down menu to re-display the check mark. The Favorites reappears at the top of the Folder pane.

Folder pane navigation options

The area at the bottom of the Folder pane is called the Navigation Options. In here, you find the buttons that allow you to switch amongst the different Outlook views:

- Mail

- Calendar

- People

- Tasks

- Notes

- Folders

- Shortcuts

By default, the Navigation Options area shows only four of these views, but you can get to the other view buttons by clicking the ellipses button (...) located directly to the right of the last button.

From the Layout group in the View pane, you can access the Navigation Options dialog box, which controls the number of view buttons that appear in the Navigation Options area, and the order they appear in. The Navigation Options dialog box also has an option at the top called Compact Navigation. When you select this option, the view buttons in the Navigation Options area change from listing the button names, to just showing a picture representing the button.

STEP BY STEP   **Turning on Compact Navigation**

1   In the View tab, click the **Folder pane** button. From the drop-down menu that appears, click **Options**. The Navigation Options dialog box appears.

2   At the top-left corner of the box, select the **Compact Navigation** check box, and then click **OK** to close. The area at the bottom of the Folder pane (the Navigation Options area) now displays pictures representing the views, instead of their names.

Figure 2-7

Navigation Options dialog box.

3   Go back into the Navigation Options box and click the **Compact Navigation** check box to clear the check mark.

4   Click **OK** to close the Navigation Options dialog box and commit the change.

Customizing the Reading pane

The Reading pane is the area where you can see the specifics of any of the Outlook items that you have currently selected. For example, in the Mail view, the Reading pane displays the content of the e-mail message you have clicked. In the Calendar view, it displays the current calendar.

By default, the Reading pane appears on the right side of the Outlook window. However, you can relocate it to the bottom of the window, or turn it off.

You will move the Reading pane to appear at the bottom of the screen, and then turn it off and back on again.

STEP BY STEP   **Customizing the Reading Pane**

1   In the Layout group of the View tab, click **Reading pane**. From the drop-down menu that appears, click **Bottom**. The Reading pane changes its location to appear at the bottom of the Outlook window.

Figure 2-8

Reading pane appears at the bottom of the Outlook Window.

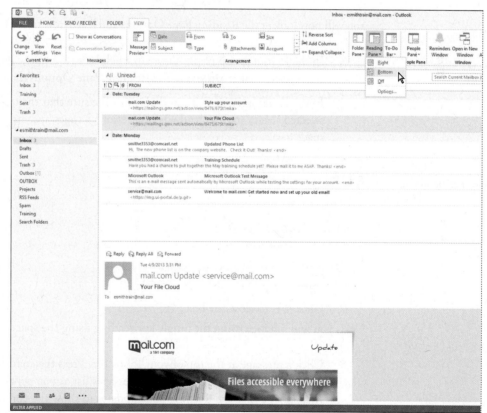

Photo used with permission of Microsoft

2   Click an e-mail message in your Inbox to see how the message's content now appears at the bottom of the screen.

3   To turn off the Reading pane, click **Reading pane** in the Layout group of the View tab, and then choose **Off** from the drop-down menu that appears. The Reading pane turns off from the bottom of your screen.

4   To turn the Reading pane back on, click **Reading pane** in the Layout group of the View tab, and then choose **Right** from the drop-down menu that appears. The Reading pane now appears in its original position at the right side of the Outlook window.

From the Layout group in the View pane, you can access the Reading Pane Options dialog box, which contains check boxes to control how items are dealt with when they are viewed in the Reading pane. These options include:

- **Marking items as read when viewed in the Reading pane**: this option is turned off by default. When you select this option, you can set the number of seconds Outlook should wait before marking the item as read.

Take Note   New items appear in a different color when they come into your Inbox. Once you open these new items and view them, Outlook marks the items as having been read and changes their color so you can visually identify the items you have already read

- **Mark item as read when selection changes**: when you move your focus to another item, Outlook marks the original item as read. This option is on by default.

- **Single key reading using the space bar**: this option allows you to move down from message to message in your Inbox or other views by pressing the spacebar. As you press the spacebar and move down in the item list, your Reading pane updates to the item you have selected. This option is automatically on by default.

You will now look at the Reading Pane Options and learn how to use them when reviewing e-mail.

5   In the Layout group of the View tab, click Reading pane. From the drop-down menu that appears, click Options. The Reading Pane Options dialog box appears.

6   In the Reading Pane Options dialog box, be sure that the last two check boxes are selected (Mark item as read when selection changes and Single key reading using the space bar).

Figure 2-9

Reading Pane Options dialog box open.

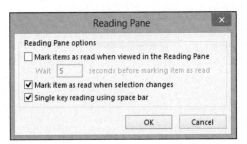

7   Click OK to close the box.

Next, you will practice using the Single key reading using the space bar option.

8   Click a message at the top of your Inbox list. Press the spacebar. Watch as the selection in your Inbox list moves down the messages list as you continue to press the spacebar. Also, notice that the Reading pane updates to show the content of the selected message. You can use this method of reviewing your messages to browse through your e-mail list in a quick and convenient manner.

Customizing the To-Do bar

The **To-Do bar** shows the Outlook items that you currently need to perform or review. The To-Do bar appears on the far right side of the Outlook window, and it can display up to three different items, individually or together. These items are:

- **Current calendar**: when you click a specific date on the calendar, Outlook will switch to the Calendar view to show that date. Also, any appointments or meetings that you have scheduled in Outlook appear directly below the calendar.

• **People:** this is Search box where you can type a contact's name to try to locate the contact (or contacts with similar names) from the People view. When you type a contact's name in the Search box and press Enter, Outlook displays a list of possible matches. Click any of the names from search results to access the name and e-mail the contact.

• **Tasks:** a list of the current tasks that you have flagged for priority completion in Outlook.

You will turn the To-Do bar and add the calendar, people search, and task list to it, and then turn it off.

STEP BY STEP   **Customizing the To-Do bar**

   1   In the Layout group of the View tab, click **To-Do bar**. From the drop-down menu that appears, click **Calendar**.

   2   Repeat Step 1 to choose **People and Tasks** from the drop-down menu. Notice that the far right side of the Outlook window now displays a current calendar (that you can adjust to display different months), a people search box, and a task list.

Figure 2-10

The To-Do bar open and displaying a calendar, people search tool, and task list.

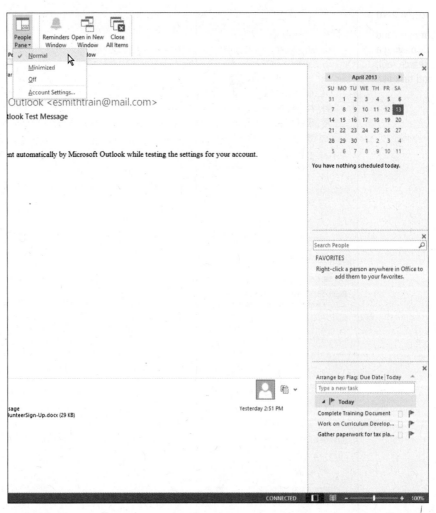

3 In the Layout group of the View tab, click To-Do bar. From the drop-down menu that appears, click **Off**. The To-Do bar closes.

Customizing the People pane

The People pane provides you with information about the individuals who send you e-mail. It's also called the Outlook Social Connector and it's normally minimized when you read e-mail. You can drag it up to display more information in a normal view. If you use Outlook and SharePoint at work, you can see your work contacts in the People pane. If you maintain social media accounts on sites such as LinkedIn or Facebook, you can also use the Outlook Social Connector to show you updates from those sites without leaving Outlook.

STEP BY STEP   **Adjusting the People pane**

1 From the Layout group in the View tab, click the **People** pane. Click **Normal**. The People pane appears at the bottom of your Outlook window.

2 Click the **People** pane, and on it, click **Minimized**. Drag up the thin gray bar at the top of the minimized People pane, to view it again.

Figure 2-11

People pane open in Normal view.

3 Click the **People** pane, and on it, click **Off**. The People pane turns off.

To connect your People pane to social media websites for which you have accounts, click the People pane and select Account Setting at the bottom of the box. Select the appropriate social networking sites to view their information from within Outlook and make sure the Reading pane is turned on.

Customizing the Ribbons

In Microsoft Outlook 2013, you can customize the Ribbons by turning Ribbon tabs on and off, moving Ribbon groups within the same Ribbon tab, and creating your own Ribbon tabs. You cannot delete any of the buttons or Ribbon tabs created by Microsoft.

You will customize the Outlook Ribbon tabs and create your own custom Ribbon tab with buttons that you select.

STEP BY STEP   **Customizing the Ribbons**

---

1   Click the File tab, and then click **Options** in the Backstage view. The Outlook Options dialog box opens.

2   In the Outlook Options box, click **Customize Ribbon** from the menu pane.

The Customize the Ribbon tab appears. The left side shows popular commands that you can add to a personal Ribbon tab and group. The right side shows the current Outlook Ribbon tabs with expand and collapse buttons and a check box appearing next to each tab. When you clear the checkmark from any of those check boxes, the corresponding Ribbon closes and is not visible in Outlook.

3   Select the check box next to the Send/Receive Ribbon. Click **OK**. Notice that the Send/Receive Ribbon tab is turned off in the Mail view of Outlook.

4   Return to the Customize Ribbon tab of the Outlook Options box. At the bottom of the box and on the right side, click **New Tab**. The New Tab appears in the list on the right, along with the other Ribbon tabs in Outlook. It also has a New Group listed under it. You can change the location of your new ribbon tab in the vertical list by dragging it up or down.

Figure 2-12

Customize the Ribbon tab, adding a new Ribbon tab

5   To rename the Ribbon, click the New Tab in the Ribbon list to select it, and then click the Rename button at the bottom of the list. Type Training. Click OK.

6   To add buttons to your new Ribbon tab, click the plus sign button next to your new Ribbon tab. It opens to display your New Group. Use the Rename button to rename your new group.

7   Take buttons from the left side of the Customize the Ribbon box and drag them to your New Group on the right side.

You can also find other buttons by clicking the drop-down arrow next to Popular Commands at the top left side of the box, and selecting a different ribbon or category of buttons.

8   Click OK and view your new Ribbon tab at the top of the Outlook window. Click it and look at your customized group of Ribbon commands.

If you don't need your customized Ribbon and want to delete it and return Ribbons to their original positions, you can reset them in the Customize the Ribbon tab of the Outlook Options box.

You will now reset your Ribbon tabs and delete your customized Ribbon tab.

9   Return to the Outlook Options box and the Customize the Ribbon tab. On the right side of the box, click Reset. Click Reset all customizations.

10   A Microsoft Office box opens with a question to Delete all Ribbon and Quick Access Toolbar Customizations for this program. Click Yes. The custom Ribbon tab is removed.

If you don't want to reset your Quick Access Toolbar, you can right-click your custom Ribbon tab on the right side of the Customize the Ribbon box, and select Remove from the list. This removes the customized Ribbon, but not any other customizations, such as shortcuts.

Bottom Line

Bottom Line Summary: Users are able to print different items in each of the Outlook views. They can use the Print Preview window and printer setting to customize what is printed. Users can also customize the different views in Outlook by utilizing tools on the View Ribbon tab and also changing options for the different panes of Outlook like the Folder Pane, Reading Pane, and To Do Bar.

FORWARDING AND REPLYING TO E-MAIL

After you receive e-mail, you might need to respond to it or forward the message to another person. **Replying** is the term used when you respond to a message you have received by sending a message back. **Forwarding** a message is when you send the message you received on to another recipient.

Take Note   You can forward a selected e-mail message by pressing Ctrl+F . Ctrl+R will open a reply message for a selected e-mail.

Replying to an e-mail message

You will now practice replying to an e-mail message from your Outlook Inbox.

STEP BY STEP **Replying to an e-mail**

1. Select a message from your Inbox that you can appropriately reply to. Double-click the message.

2. In the message box, click **Reply** in the Respond group.

Take Note When there are multiple recipients on the e-mail message, you can click the Reply All button to simultaneously reply to everyone addressed in the e-mail.

Figure 2-13

Reply E-mail message box open.

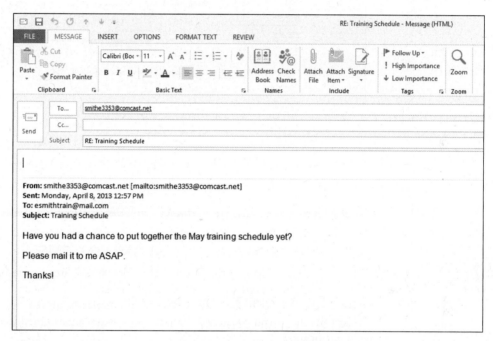

Another e-mail box opens with the letters RE (which mean Reply) at the top of the message box. The original e-mail message box opens behind the new message box. The new message is addressed to the person who sent the original e-mail, and the original message appears at the bottom of the new message box. A cursor is blinking in the area where you can begin typing your reply.

3. Type a reply in the body section of the e-mail, and then click **Send** at the top left of the box.

4. To close the original message box, click the **X** in the top-right corner.

Forwarding an e-mail message

You will now practice forwarding an e-mail message from your Outlook Inbox.

STEP BY STEP **Forwarding an e-mail**

1. Select a message from your Inbox that you can appropriately forward to someone else. Click the message in your Inbox list to select it.

2   On the Home tab in the Respond group, click Forward. You can also double-click the message in the Inbox; the message box opens, and a Forward button appears on the Respond group in the Message tab. Click the Forward button.

A new message box opens in the Reading pane. The original message appears at the bottom of the message, and the cursor blinks in the To field, ready for you to address the message.

3   In the To field, enter the e-mail address of the person to whom you're forwarding the message.

4   Enter a message in the body section of the e-mail. Click Send.

Figure 2-14

Forward E-Mail message open in the Reading pane.

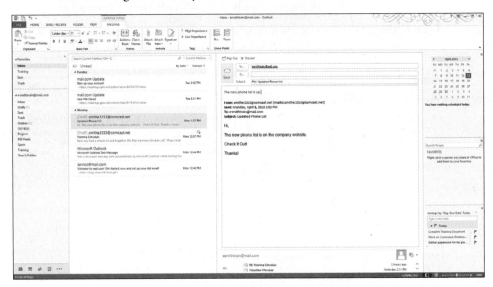

USING RULES TO MANAGE INCOMING ITEMS

Rules help to cut down on the physical filing of Outlook items or repetitive actions. Usually, rules are set-up to run automatically. For example, when you receive an e-mail message with a specific word in the Subject line, you can have it automatically moved into a certain folder. There is a wizard that helps you create and manage rules. Rules are assigned to two categories, organization and notification.

Creating a Rule to manage e-mail

STEP BY STEP   Creating a Rule

1   From the Move group in the Home tab, click Rules. Then click Create Rule.

2   Select the check box next to Subject contains. Enter Phone Lists. Whenever a message is receive with a Subject containing the text Phone Lists, the Rule will run.

3   Under Do the Following, click Move the Item to Folder. Click the Select Folder Button. A list of all your Outlook folders appears. Click Training, and then click OK.

Figure 2-15

Create Rule dialog box.

4   A Success box opens with a message that your Phone Lists rule has been created. The box also contains a check box asking whether to Run this rule now on messages already in the current folder. Don't select this check box; but click OK.

5   In the Home tab, click New E-mail. In the new e-mail message box, address the e-mail to the current e-mail address you are using in Outlook on your current computer. Enter Phone Lists in the Subject line. Type a message in the body, and then click Send.

6   On the Home tab, click the Send/Receive All Folders button. This ensures that your e-mail is received quickly.

Take Note   You can also press F9 key to Send and Receive for all folders in Outlook.

7   Check the Training folder; you should see the e-mail you just sent.

Managing a Rule

Once you've created a rule, you can manage it, edit it, or delete it using Manage Rules & Alerts. Along with editing rules, you can also copy rules or run rules directly from the Manage Rules & Alerts Box.

STEP BY STEP   **Turning off a Rule**

1   From the Move group in the Home tab, click Rules. Click Manage Rules & Alerts. The Rules and Alerts dialog box opens.

The top of the Rules and Alerts box contains the following buttons for managing rules: New Rule, Change Rule, Copy (copying rules), Delete (delete rules), Run Rules Now (run a selected rule from the box), and Options. The middle section of the Rules and Alerts box is a list of all the current rules running or available in Outlook. The Phone List rule should appear with a check mark next to it. The bottom of the box shows a description of the currently selected rule and contains hyperlinks to sections of the rule that can you can click and edit.

Figure 2-16

Rules and Alerts box open.

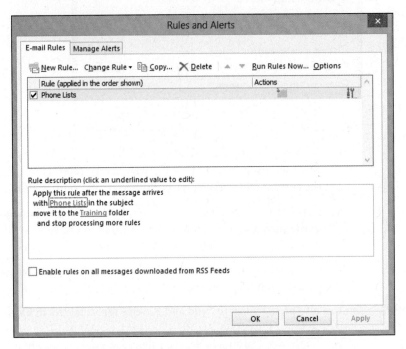

2   Click to clear the check box next to the Phone List rule to turn it off.

3   Click the Phone List rule to select it. Click Delete at the top of the Rules and Alerts to delete the rule. The Delete Rule box opens. Click OK.

RECURRING APPOINTMENTS AND MEETINGS

It's not uncommon for meetings and appointments set in Outlook to be recurring events. For example, a team project meeting could be a recurring meeting; a recurring appointment could be a dentist or doctor appointment, and so on. Remember, appointments are set just for you. Meetings involve multiple people and can be e-mailed to the people you want to invite to the meeting. Meetings and appointments can be created from any view in Outlook.

Creating a recurring appointment

STEP BY STEP   **Create a recurring appointment**

1   From the Mail view, click New Items in the Home tab. Click Appointment; a new appointment box opens.

2   In the Subject box, enter Realtor Meeting.

3   In the Location box, enter 1234 Main St.

4   In the Options group on the Message tab, click Recurrence (the button looks like a circle with two arrows). The Appointment Recurrence dialog box opens.

Figure 2-17

Creating a recurring appointment.

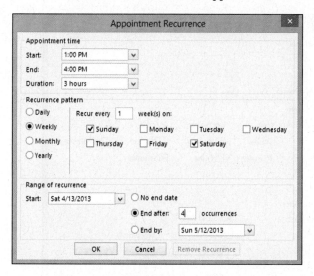

5   Select Start Time to be 1:00PM and an End Time to be 4:00PM. The Duration automatically indicates 3 hours.

6   Under the Recurrence pattern, select Weekly and Recur every 1 week on. Check off Sunday and Saturday. Under Range of recurrence, select a Start date of the following Saturday and select to End after 4 occurrences. Click OK.

The recurring appointment is saved in your calendar. Go to the Calendar view and click the Start date you set for your appointment; you'll see it displayed for the current week, and recurring for the following 4 weeks.

Creating a recurring meeting

A **recurring meeting** is similar to a recurring appointment; however, you can e-mail meetings, and they can be accepted or declined by invitees.

STEP BY STEP   Create a recurring meeting

1   From the Mail view, click New Items and select Meeting. A new meeting box opens. Notice that it is addressed from your current e-mail address.

2   On the Meeting tab, in the Options group, Click Recurrence. The Appointment Recurrence box opens.

Figure 2-18

Creating a recurring meeting.

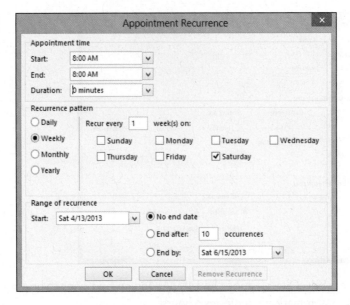

3   Set the Start to 8:00AM and the End to 9:00AM.

4   Set the Recurrence pattern to be Weekly and select Tuesday.

5   Set the Start to be the current end with no end date. Click OK

6   Back in the Meeting box, click the To and enter your e-mail address. In the Subject field, enter Team Meeting. In Location, enter Conference Room B.

7   Click Send. The Meeting is e-mailed to the invitee.

When meeting requests are received in the Inbox, they have a small calendar symbol next to them. This is an indicator that the message is a meeting request and not just a normal e-mail message.

JUNK E-MAIL OPTIONS

Receiving e-mail from unwanted parties is a very common occurrence today. Unwanted e-mail is often called Junk Mail or Spam. Outlook has a built-in system to help you manage the **Junk mail** that you might receive. The Junk mail menu allows you to block e-mail from specific senders and domains, and it allows you to unblock and receive content from senders and domains that you select as safe content. There are also junk mail options that will manage how Outlook deals with junk mail.

You will manage the junk e-mail options in Outlook.

STEP BY STEP   **Managing Junk e-mail**

1   Select an e-mail message in your Inbox. From the Delete group in the Home tab, click Junk. The Junk menu appears with several options.

Figure 2-19

Junk E-mail Menu.

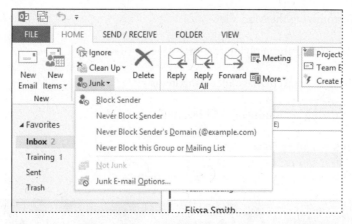

• **Block Sender**: when a message is selected, this option blocks all incoming mail from that sender.

• **Never Block Sender**: adds a selected message's sender to a safe list.

• **Never Block Sender's Domain (@example)**: allows any e-mail from a selected domain to always be accepted into Outlook.

• **Never block this group or Mailing list**: allows all e-mail from a specific mailing group or list.

• **Not Junk**: this option is grayed out because this option is only used to remove items from the Spam folder when they are placed there mistakenly.

• **Junk E-Mail Options**: contains options for managing Outlook's junk e-mail settings, such as where junk e-mail is sent, a safe senders list, a safe recipients list, a Blocked Senders list, and an International area.

2   Click Never Block Sender. A Microsoft Outlook Information box opens stating that The Sender of the Selected Message has been added to your Safe Senders List. Click OK.

Bottom Line

To take this e-mail off your Safe Senders list, you can go into the Junk Email Options box, into the Safe Senders tab, and delete the e-mail address from that list.

Bottom line Summary: Users respond and reply to e-mail messages. They also set Rules to place incoming e-mail messages into specific folder. Users also set junk e-mail options to manage spam.

What you learned in this lesson:

- Outlook Views

- Printing in Outlook Views

- Customizing the Mail View

- Forwarding and replying to e-mail

- Using Rules to manage incoming items

- Recurring appointments and meetings

- Junk e-mail options

Knowledge Assessment

True/ False

Circle T if the statement is true or F it the statement is false.

T F 1. The four main views of Outlook are Mail, People, Calendar, and Tasks.

T F 2. To print any Outlook item, you must click on Print, located on the Home Ribbon tab.

T F 3. When printing calendar items, the Print Options box near print settings will allow you to pick the calendar dates you want your printed items to cover.

T F 4. The Reading Pane is made to display specifics of Outlook items in the area of Outlook you are viewing. In the Mail view, it shows specifics of the e-mail item selected in the Inbox.

T F 5. The Folder Pane shows specific Outlook activities that need to be completed or reviewed.

T F 6. In Outlook 2013, you can customize the Ribbon tabs by creating a customized Ribbon tab and group, but you can't delete any of the default Ribbon tabs that are part of the software.

T F 7. When you reply to a message, you send an e-mail message you've received on to another e-mail recipient.

T F 8. To create a Rule to move e-mail into specific folders, you click Move button in the Move group on the Home Ribbon tab.

T F 9. A reoccurring meeting or appointment is one that happens only once.

T F 10. The Junk Mail options all you to block e-mail from specific senders and domains.

Multiple Choice

Select the best response for the following statements.

1. Which view in Outlook is the default view?
   a. Mail
   b. Calendar
   c. People
   d. Contacts

2. From the Mail view, you can choose to print mail items in two different views, which are?
   a. Image Style and Table Style
   b. Memo style and Table Style
   c. Clip Style and Paste Style
   d. Signature Style and Stationary Style

3. The Reading Pane can be viewed in different parts of the Outlook window. These areas are:
   a. Top and Bottom
   b. Left and Right
   c. Top Only
   d. Right, Bottom, and turned off

4. How can the Folder Pane in Outlook be customized?
   a. It can be turned off or minimized.
   b. It can be turned off, minimized, or the order of items in its list can be adjusted.
   c. It can be added to the Ribbon tabs.
   d. None B
   e. The Folder Pane can be minimized, turned off, or the order of items in the list can be adjusted.

5. The People Pane is also sometimes called the:
   a. Contact Pane
   b. Outlook Bar
   c. Outlook Social Connector
   d. Folder Pane

6. The recurrence pattern on a reoccurring appointment or meeting can be:
   a. Daily, Weekly, Monthly, or Yearly
   b. Weekly Only
   c. Monthly and Daily
   d. Yearly Only

7. Under the Junk Mail options, if a sender is blocked it means:
   a. Only messages with certain subjects from the sender are blocked.
   b. All messages from the sender are blocked.
   c. Only messages sent between 12AM and 5AM are blocked.
   d. None of the Above

8. From the Reading Pane options, you can set options on how the Reading Pane deals with Outlook items that have been:
   a. Deleted
   b. Printed
   c. Selected or opened
   d. Edited

9. When replying to an e-mail message, the box where the reply message is typed will have the abbreviation of what at the top:

   a. NM for new message

   b. CC for carbon copy

   c. FU for follow up

   d. RE for reply

10. When there are multiple individuals need to be replied to within an e-mail message, which button will accomplish this task?

   a. Underline button

   b. Bold button

   c. Forward button

   d. Reply All button

Competency Assessment

Project 2-1: Adding appointments to Outlook

You will add two new Outlook appointments to your calendar and then prepare to print a week's view of them.

1. From the Calendar view, click New Appointment on the Home Ribbon tab.

2. Schedule a new appointment for the current week at a location and time of your choice and Save and Close the appointment.

3. Repeat the process and create a second New Appointment for the same week and Save and Close the second new appointment as well.

4. On the Home Ribbon tab in the Calendar view, in the Arrange group, Click Work Week to view the appointment in a 5-day work week view.

5. In the same, Arrange group, click Month and view the appointments in a month view.

6. Click the File Ribbon tab to enter the Backstage view.

7. Click Print to enter the Print Preview and print settings box.

8. On the left side of the Print Preview box, select different settings to see how the two appointments will print.

9. Click Weekly Agenda style.

10. Hit the ESC button on your keyboard to exit the Print Preview screen.

Project 2-2: Customizing the Mail view

In the Mail view of Outlook, you will customize the view with the Folder Pane and Reading Pane. You will also customize the view of items in your Inbox.

1. Click the View Ribbon tab in the Mail view of Outlook.

2. In the Arrange group, click the From option. (Items in the Inbox list will be sorted based on the From field).

3. Click Date in the Arrange group, to change the setting back to their default.

4. In the Layout group of the View Ribbon tab, click the Folder Pane.

5. Select Minimized.

6. Click the Folder Pane button again and select Normal to open it back up.

7. Click the Reading Pane button in the Layout group, select Right. The Reading Pane will move to right hand side of the screen.

8. In the Layout group, Click To Do Bar.

9. Select Calendar. (A current calendar should open on the right side of your screen).

10. Go through the Folder Pane, Reading Pane, and To Do Bar and change their locations and options to fit your personal preferences.

Proficiency Assessment

Project 2-3: Customizing the Ribbon

You will create a customized Ribbon tab.

1. Click File to enter the Backstage view and select Options.

2. Click Customize Ribbon on the left hand side of the box.

3. Click the New Tab button (located on the bottom right hand side of the box)

4. Your New Tab will appear with a New Group under it in the current Ribbon list. Click the New Tab and then click Rename.

5. In the Rename box, type a name of your choice for the new Ribbon tab.

6. Under your new Ribbon tab, click the New Group and also rename it.

7. From the left side of the Customize Ribbon box, select different categories of Ribbon button and drag them under your new Ribbon on the right. Add at least three new buttons to your Ribbon.

8. Click OK to view your new Ribbon tab.

9. To remove your new Ribbon tab, go back into the Customize Ribbon tab and either uncheck the new Ribbon to turn it off or click Remove to delete it. Remember, you can't delete Ribbons tabs that are defaults in Outlook. You can only delete and change Ribbon tabs that you create.

Project 2-4: Forwarding and replying to e-mails

You will forward and reply to e-mail messages. You will also set Junk Mail setting for e-mail messages.

1. Select an appropriate e-mail message and click the Forward button.

2. Type a new e-mail address and forward the message to a new e-mail recipient.

3. Select an appropriate e-mail message and click the Reply button.

4. Type a reply to the e-mail message and send it back to the original sender.

5. Back in your Inbox, select another e-mail message (don't open it up).

6. On the Home Ribbon tab, in the Delete group, click Junk.

7. From the Junk list, click Junk E-mail Options.

8. Preview the setting in the Junk E-Mail Options box and close it.

Mastery Assessment

Project 2-5: Setting up appointment

You need to create some recurring appointments and also reoccurring meetings for a new business project.

1. From the Calendar area, create a new reoccurring appointment that reoccurs at a set time and location on a weekly basis for at least three months. Set a reminder for 30 minutes before the appointment is scheduled to occur.

2. Create a new recurring meeting that occurs once a week for two months and e-mail it to at least three other individuals.

3. Select one appointment in your calendar and delete it.

Project 2-6: Customizing Outlook views

You will customize different Outlook views and view Outlook items in the Print Preview window.

1. From the Inbox, customize the Reading Pane, so you can preview new incoming messages from the Bottom portion of the Mail window. Select one e-mail message and preview it in the Table Style.

2. From the People view, select an existing contact, and Print Preview the contact in the Memo Style.

3. From the Inbox, create a New Rule to move incoming e-mail into the folder.

Microsoft OneNote 2013

Microsoft OneNote 2013 Jumpstart

LESSON SKILL MATRIX

In this lesson, you will learn the following skills:

Discovering OneNote	Creating a new Notebook section
Exploring the OneNote environment	Customizing OneNote
Working in Backstage view	Getting help
OneNote Searching	Ending a OneNote session

KEY TERMS

- **Pages**
- **Section**
- **Notebook**
- **Pages pane**
- **Content pane**

 Tina works for an interior design firm and wants a better place to keep track of her client projects that offers flexibility and lots of room for creativity. Tina needs to learn the basics of the OneNote interface, so she can begin creating Notebooks and inserting her project data into them.

SOFTWARE ORIENTATION

This lesson gets you started with the essential capabilities of Microsoft OneNote 2013.

Figure 1-1

A. Quick Access Toolbar.
B. Ribbon. C. Section tabs.
D. Content pane. E. Pages
pane.

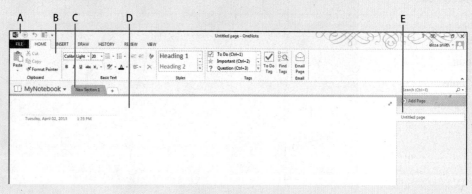

STARTING UP

In this lesson, you'll work with several files from the OneNote01lessons folder. Make sure that you have loaded the OfficeLessons folder onto your computer.

Discovering OneNote

OneNote is one of the least known products in the Microsoft Office Suite. However, OneNote is a powerful organization tool very much like an electronic **notebook** or three-ring binder. OneNote is a data collection and organization tool that allows you to take a variety of data types and combine them into an electronic notebook. The different data types that can be organized from within OneNote include:

- Text

- Images

- Audio

- Video

- Hyperlinks & web pages

- Freehand sketches

OneNote is organized very similarly to a physical notebook, such as a three-ring binder that students use in a school setting. For example, OneNote Notebooks contain **Sections**, which in turn contain **Pages** that you can use to store your content. Just as is the case with three-ring binders, you can rearrange OneNote Notebook Sections and Pages as needed. OneNote has a user friendly design and is easy to customize to your personal needs.

OneNote can help you manage notes in situations where you would normally use a physical notebook. Here are some examples:

- Vacation planning: maps, things to see, pictures, videos

- Musician planner: songs, videos, pictures, gig calendar, band bios

- Student notebook: Science, Algebra, Music, English

- Event planning: venue locations, pictures, vendors, schedules

EXPLORING THE ONENOTE ENVIRONMENT

There are two main views in OneNote: Normal View (Notebook View) and Backstage View. The Notebook View appears when you open OneNote.

Opening OneNote

Open OneNote by doing one of the following:

- Click Start > All Programs > Microsoft Office > Microsoft OneNote.

- Click Start, type OneNote in the Search text box, and then click Microsoft OneNote 2013.

- If there is a desktop shortcut for OneNote on your screen, double-click it.

OneNote opens in the Normal view, ready for you to begin creating Notebooks.

About the Send to OneNote command

When you open OneNote 2013, a side command called Send to OneNote also opens; it appears next to the OneNote icon in the task bar at the bottom of your screen.

Figure 1-2

OneNote and Send to OneNote programs launched on the task pane.

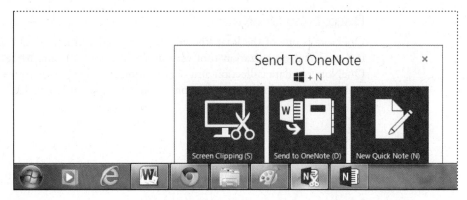

The *Send to OneNote* command has the following three commands:

- **Screen Clipping**: use it for creating a screen clipping of the current window and sending it directly to OneNote.

- **Send to OneNote**: use to take the current information on your screen and insert it into OneNote.

- **New Quick Note**: use it to type quick notes and add them to the QuickNotes section of OneNote.

You will use some of the functions on the Send to OneNote command in the next lesson.

Opening a new blank Notebook

Creating a new Notebook is similar to creating a database. You need to name the Notebook and save it before it can be opened, viewed, and edited.

STEP BY STEP   **Opening a new blank Notebook**

1   From the Ribbon tabs, select File, and from the Backstage view, select New.

2   In New, select Computer and in the Notebook Name type text field type Las Vegas Trip.

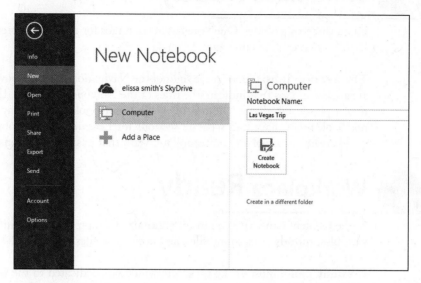

3   Click the text *Create in a different folder*, navigate to the OneNote01lessons folder, and click Create.

Normal (Notebook) view

Let's take a closer look at the OneNote user interface and its components, and learn how to navigate in OneNote.

OneNote opens in the Normal view, displaying a page in a Notebook. The mouse cursor appears above a text placeholder that shows the current date and time. With the mouse cursor in this position, you can begin typing a title above the date.

The following components appear in the OneNote window:

- **Ribbon:** if you have used other Microsoft Office 2013 programs, you will be familiar with the Ribbon tabs. Remember that you can minimize the Ribbon tabs and only see the tabbed headings. To open the Ribbon tabs again, double-click any of the tabbed headings. The Ribbon in OneNote contains the following headings:

- **Home:** contains the most commonly used buttons for editing text in the Normal view.

- **Insert:** for inserting other types of files and information into OneNote Notebooks, such as tables, images, audio, video, and images.

- **Draw:** for creating and editing both hand and computer drawn images.

- **History:** for organizing Shared Notebooks and different versions of Notebook files.

- **Review:** contains the spell checker, thesaurus, and other tools for preparing a Notebook for printing, viewing, and sharing with others.

- **View:** for viewing, zooming, and controlling the basic layout of the Notebook.

- **Notebook** tab: located directly under the File and Home Ribbon tab commands, it is a drop-down list that shows all your open notebooks.

Workplace **Ready**

Like a three-ring binder, OneNote has Section tabs for creating deferent partitions in a notebook. Each Section can contain pages.

The Section tabs: found to the right of the Navigation bar and above the Notebook pane, these are a series of tabs that indicate the titles of the Notebook Sections. These Sections are analogous to the plastic tab dividers found in physical notebooks. For example, your high school Math notebook might have had separate sections for Lecture Notes, Problems, and Homework. You could create one OneNote Notebook for Math that has these Sections.

Workplace **Ready**

In the Content pane, you can insert all kinds of data to be viewed in your notebook like images, wordfiles, spreadsheets, sound files, and even video files.

Content pane: most of the OneNote window is dedicated to the **Content pane**. This is the active page of the Notebook, in which you can add and view different types of content. The title of the active page appears at the top. For pages that you create, the date and time of the most recent update also appears.

Pages pane: located to the right of the Content pane, the Pages pane displays Pages and Subpages for the active Notebook.

Take Note You can adjust the width of the Page pane by resting your mouse pointer on the left border. Your mouse pointer will turn into a double-headed arrow pointing left and right. You can drag it in either direction to make the Pages pane narrower or wider.

Figure 1-4

The OneNote window in Normal view with the Notebook tab open.

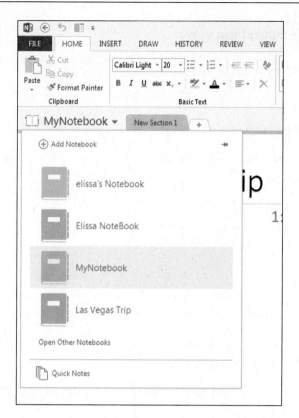

Take Note   The Pages pane will look different on each computer because they will have different Notebooks that were created on it.

Quick Access Toolbar: found in the upper-left corner of every Microsoft Office 2013 program interface, the Quick Access Toolbar contains buttons for selecting frequently used functions. By default, the OneNote Quick Access Toolbar contains the following buttons:

• OneNote Logo: displays a drop-down menu with Window sizing options and the option to close OneNote.

• Back: returns you to a previous Notebook or section.

• Undo: it reverses the action you recently performed in OneNote.

• Dock to Desktop: docks your current OneNote view to your computer's Desktop.

• Customize Quick Access Toolbar drop-down arrow: adds shortcut buttons to the toolbar.

Figure 1-5

The Quick Access Toolbar.

WORKING IN BACKSTAGE VIEW

While Normal (Notebook) view is where you do most of your work in OneNote, Backstage View is also important. The Backstage view is the place where you can manage a notebook by printing, saving, or even adjusting your personal Office account setting.

Take Note   The File tab, which displays Backstage view when clicked, always has a colored background, even when it is not the active tab. You can identify the active tab by the borders that appear on the left, right, and top of the active tab.

STEP BY STEP   **Viewing the Backstage view**

1   To display Backstage View, click the File tab.

Figure 1-6

Backstage View appears, with
the Info command active.

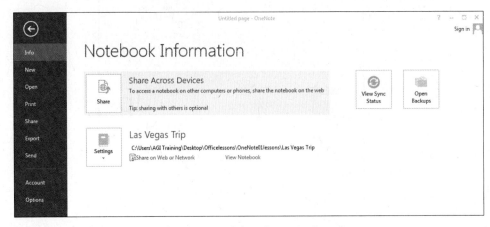

The following list gives a brief overview of the tabs in Backstage view:

* **Info:** manage and view Notebook properties; share and view synchronization status (if applicable); and open backup Notebook copies.

* **New:** name and create a Notebook to be stored on the Web in your SkyDrive account or on your own computer or network.

* **Open:** open a Notebook, either by browsing or selecting a recently closed Notebook.

* **Print:** print from the Print dialog box and Print Preview from a separate Print Preview dialog box.

* **Share:** share notebook by putting it on your SkyDrive or SharePoint location.

* **Export:** save notebook as another files type, including OneNote 2007, PDF, XPS, MS Word, or as a Single webpage. You can then open these files in other applications.

* **Send:** send the current Page as an e-mail, e-mail attachment, PDF, to MS Word, or to a web blog.

* **Account:** manage your user account information and the Microsoft Office version you're using.

* **Options:** open the OneNote Options box to customize the OneNote software, such as the display, proofing options, the Ribbon tabs, the Quick Access Toolbar, security settings, and more.

SEARCHING ONENOTE

One drawback of a physical notebook is that it can be difficult to find relevant information within it, despite the use of sections and tab dividers. Fortunately, OneNote has a powerful Search tool you can use to quickly find content.

The information stored in a notebook can be very varied. Using the Search box can save vast amounts of time when looking for content in a notebook.

STEP BY STEP   **Searching a Notebook**

1   With your cursor blinking in your new Notebook, type Day 1 - Itinerary Bus Trip just
     above the current date and time. Click outside of the text box.

2   In the Search text box located in the upper-right corner, directly above the Pages pane,
     click the drop-down menu and select This Notebook.

Take Note   The default Search Scope is All Notebooks. To limit it to the present Notebook, click the drop-
     down menu and click This Notebook. Then click the drop-down menu again and click Set This
     Scope as Default.

3   Type bus trip in the Search text box.

Figure 1-7

Pages that contain the text bus
appear as you type. The results
are highlighted in the search
results drop-down list.

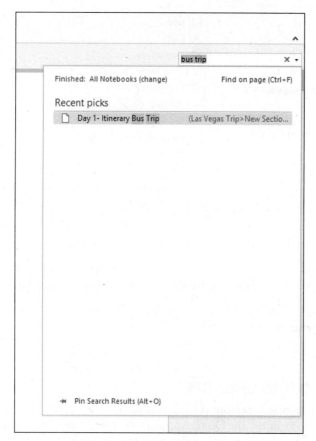

4   Click the search result to display the page that *bus trip* was found on with the query text
     highlighted.

5   To clear the search result list, click outside the list.

Bottom Line   The OneNote interface is explored and discussed including the Backstage view, Pages page,
     Contents pane, Section tabs, and Quick Access Toolbar. Searching for items in a notebook pages
     is also discussed.

Creating a new Notebook section

You can organize your data in OneNote Notebooks. One critical component of this is being able
to create new Sections in your Notebooks as needed.

In this part of the lesson, you will organize the data in the **Las Vegas Trip** Notebook by adding a
new Section. You can add a new Section by right-clicking existing Section tabs or by clicking the
Create a New Section plus tab button directly to the right of the other section tabs.

STEP BY STEP   **Adding a new Section**

> 1   Right-click the section tab called New Section 1. From the shortcut menu that appears, select New Section.

Figure 1-8

Right-click any existing Section tab to open the menu and add a new section by selecting the New Section option from the shortcut menu that appears.

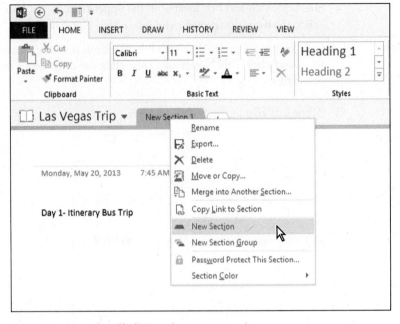

A new Section tab called New Section 2 appears.

> 2   In the highlighted title field, type Day 2 Travel.
>
> 3   Click the *Day 2 Travel Section* tab. The new Section opens and the mouse cursor appears above the date heading, ready for you to type a Heading for the new Section.
>
> 4   Type Airport. The new page title, *Airport*, appears in the Page pane to the right of the Contents pane.
>
> 5   Double-click the New Section 1 tab and type Day 1 Travel to rename this section.

CUSTOMIZING ONENOTE

You can customize OneNote components to suit your needs, just as you can with all Microsoft Office 2013 programs. The Quick Access Toolbar is a favorite customization area, because it allows you to place convenient one-click shortcuts to your favorite functions in OneNote.

Now you will customize the Quick Access Toolbar to include the Print and Format Painter buttons. If you have completed the Microsoft Word lessons, you will be familiar with this process.

STEP BY STEP   **Customizing the Quick Access Toolbar**

1 Click the Customize Quick Access Toolbar button, which is the black arrow located at the far right of the toolbar.

Figure 1-9

The default appearance of the Quick Access Toolbar, showing the Customize button list open at the far right.

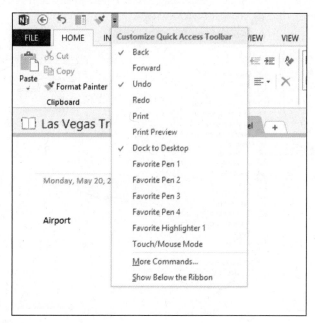

2 From the drop-down menu, select *Print*. The Print command appears in the Quick Access Toolbar.

3 Click the Customize Quick Access Toolbar button.

4 From the drop-down menu, select More Commands. The OneNote Options Quick Access Toolbar window opens and shows a lengthy list of popular commands.

5 Scroll down the list that's located on the left side of the box under the Choose Popular Commands From until you find the command Format Painter, and then select it.

6 Click the **Add** button located in the middle of the box. The Format Painter now appears on the right side of the list of Quick Access Toolbar commands, below the newly added Print command.

Figure 1-10

The OneNote Options, Customize the Quick Access Toolbar
box open and showing the two
newly added buttons on the
right side, under Customize
Quick Access Toolbar List.

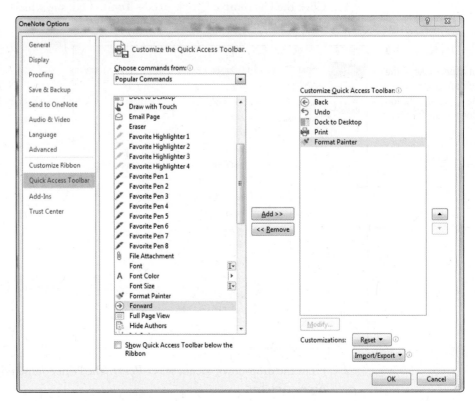

7 Click **OK** and notice the newly added commands on the Quick Access Toolbar.

Figure 1-11

The Quick Access Toolbar now
displays both
new commands.

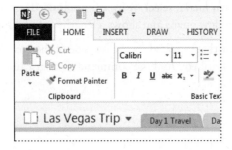

GETTING HELP

You can easily access the OneNote Help system when you need answers to a question or need help performing a task.

To access the Help system, press the F1 key or click the Help button. (The Help button is located in the top-right corner of the OneNote screen, directly to the left of the Ribbon Display Options button.)

ENDING A ONENOTE SESSION

To end a session, you can do one of the following:

STEP BY STEP	**Ending a OneNote session**

1 Click the OneNote logo button located in the top-left corner of the program.

Figure 1-12

Close the program using the
OneNote logo button located
in the top-left corner.

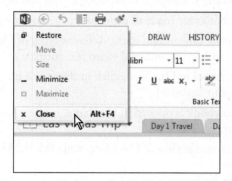

2 Click the Close button located in the upper-right corner of the program interface.

Take Note OneNote automatically saves the Notebook you are working in every time you edit content or design so you don't have to.

Bottom Line New OneNote notebooks are created, pages are customized, and other Section tabs are customized. Users also use the OneNote Help to look for assistance with the OneNote program.

What you learned in this lesson:

• Discovering OneNote

• Exploring the OneNote environment

• Working in Backstage view

• Searching OneNote

• Creating a new Notebook section

• Customizing OneNote

• Getting help

• Ending a OneNote session

Knowledge Assessment

True/ False

Circle T if the statement is true or F it the statement is false.

T F 1. Microsoft OneNote is designed to be like a digital notebook.

T F 2. OneNote notebooks are made of pages and pages are comprised of sections.

T F 3. The Contents pane can contain many different types of files including images, word processing, spreadsheet, sound, and video files formats.

T F 4. To use the search tool in OneNote, click in the search box, type a search topic, and press enter on your keyboard.

T F 5. When a new notebook is opened in OneNote, it opens with no sections or pages. You have to create them.

T F 6. To access the Backstage view of OneNote, you click the Home Ribbon tab.
     Answer: False
     To access the Backstage view in OneNote, you click the File Ribbon tab.

T F 7. The Send option in the Backstage view allows the current Page to be sent as an e-mail, e-mail attachment, PDF, to MS Word, or to a web blog.

T F 8. The width of the Pages pane can be adjusted by using the Page Adjustment button on the Home Ribbon tab.

T F 9. To create a new section tab, you need to click on the Create a New Section button located directly to the right hand side of the current section tabs.

T F 10 To customize the OneNote environment, you can add new buttons (shortcuts) of your choice to the Home Ribbon tab.

Multiple Choice

Select the best response for the following statements.

1. OneNote notebook can contain a wide variety of file formats from word processing files to video and sound files. Users can also add:
   a. free hand sketches
   b. database files
   c. macro codes
   d. new ribbon tabs

2. If someone were creating a OneNote notebook regarding a vacation, what are some of the possible Sections their notebook might contain?
   a. recipes, agenda, invitation ideas, and locations
   b. algebra, science, health, and math
   c. maps, things to see, pictures, and videos
   d. projects, team members, brain storming, and new developments

3. When OneNote opens, it opens in which view?
   a. the Backstage view
   b. the Print Preview
   c. the Inbox
   d. the Normal view

4. When OneNote opens, a side command also opens called Send to OneNote. It contains three options to send information into OneNote. These options are:
   a. Send images file, send word tables, and send Quick Notes
   b. Screen Clipping, Send to OneNote, New Quick Note
   c. Open Outlook, Paste to Word, and Move to OneNote
   d. None of the above

5. The Insert Ribbon tab in OneNote allows:
   a. drawing to be edited.
   b. a notebook's history to be tracked
   c. spell check and other document review tools to be applied to a notebooks
   d. content to be inserted into the notebook

6. Some methods for renaming a section tab are:
   a. Right-click and select Rename
   b. Double-click on the section tab
   c. Click Home and Rename
   d. Both A and B

7. If you want to further customize the OneNote software like create custom ribbon tabs, you need to open the:
   a. note book design box
   b. print preview
   c. OneNote options box
   d. New notebook box

8. The default search scope for search box is All Notebooks. To limit it to the present Notebook, click the dropdown menu and click:
   a. This Notebook
   b. This Spreadsheet
   c. This Video File
   d. This Web Meeting

9. When a new notebook is created, you must provide a:
   a. section name
   b. notebook name (file name)
   c. page name
   d. None of the Above

10. To Insert a new page into a notebook:
    a. Click the new page button on the Review Ribbon tab
    b. Click the Add Page button at the top of the Pages pane
    c. Click new page on the Insert Ribbon tab
    d. Click new page on the bottom right and corner of the window

Competency Assessment

Project 1-1: Creating a new Notebook

You will create a new blank notebook and rename section and pages within it.

1. Click **File** and from the Backstage view, click **New**.
2. From New, click **Computer** to save the New notebook on your own computer.
3. Under Notebook Name type **Vacation Planning**.
4. Click **Create Notebook**.
5. The new notebook will open in the OneNote normal view with a new section and new page ready for you to enter information into. Your cursor should be blinking in the Content pane above a date like, type **Sightseeing**. This will be become the name of your new page.
6. Double-click on the **New Section 1** tab above the content pane, type **Day 1**.
7. Click the **Create a New Section** (plus sign button) located to the right of the current Section tabs.
8. Where the New Section 1 tab is highlighted, type **Day 2**.

    In the Contents pane, click above the new date line and type the page title, **Museum Tours**.
9. Click on the **Day 1** section tab and anywhere in the Content pane, type **Top 5 Spots**.
10. Right click on the notebook heading, near the section tabs that says, Vacation Planning and click **Close This Notebook**.

Project 1-2: Creating and editing a Notebook

You will create a new Notebook and use the Backstage view to work with your new notebook.

1. Click **File** and then click **New** in the Backstage view.
2. Create the new notebook on your computer and call it **Client X Project**.
3. When the new notebook opens, Rename the section 1 to, **Client Preferences**.
4. Rename the new page **Client Expectations.**
5. From the Backstage view list, click **Share**.

    Notice the Share section allows you to Share your notebooks via the Microsoft SkyDrive or other network drives, if you connect them.
6. In Backstage view list, click **Print** to enter the print area.

    Notice the print preview area is empty, because you haven't yet typed anything into the Contents pane of the notebook.
6. From the Backstage view list, click **Export**. The Export area opens and displays a screen showing the Export options for a OneNote notebook.
7. Click the Backstage options, click **Send**. The Send area opens and displays a screen of different options for e-mailing notebooks.
8. Click the **Back** button at the top of the Backstage view list to return to your Notebook.
9. Close the notebook.

Proficiency Assessment

Project 1-3: **Opening and searching an existing Notebook**

You will open an existing notebook and search information within it.

1. Click File and Open in the Backstage view.
2. Navigate to the OneNote01lessons folder and open the OneNote Package file called **Las Vegas Trip.onepkg**. (You may need to change the File Types to All File in the Open Notebook box to see the Las Vegas Trip file.)
3. In the Specify File Properties box, type a new name for your copy of the notebook, **My New Las Vegas Trip**.
4. In the file path, browse to put the new copy of the notebook in your lesson folder or in a location on your local network that you choose. (Just remember, you can't save two notebook files with the same name in the same directory.) Press Create.
5. The My New Las Vegas Trip notebook opens. It should have three section headings called: Day 1 Travel, Day 2 Travel, and Day 3 Travel.
6. Perform a search in the current notebook for some specific information. Click on the drop down arrow at the right side of the search box and select This Notebook. This will make the search only search in the current notebook.
7. In the search field, type Hoover Dam.
8. Under the search field, click on the first Hoover Dam in the search results. OneNote will automatically take you to that piece of text or item in the notebook.

   If you've closed the My Las Vegas Trip notebook, open it again. You can find it in listed in the Recent Notebook list, located in the Open area of the Backstage view. In the My Las Vegas Trip notebook, you will customize the Quick Access Toolbar and other elements in the OneNote window.
9. Click on the Customize Quick Access Toolbar button.
10. Click on Print Preview to add the Print Preview button to the Quick Access Toolbar.
11. Click on the Customize Quick Access Toolbar button again and click More Commands towards the bottom of the list.
12. The OneNote options box opens with the Customize the Quick Access Toolbar tab open.
13. From the left side of the box under, Choose commands from select different categories of buttons to add to your current Quick Access Toolbar bar buttons listed on the right. Click the Add button in the middle of the box to take buttons from the left and add them to the list on the right. Select at least, three buttons of your choice and add them to your Quick Access Toolbar.
14. Click OK to close the OneNote options box.
15. On the Pages pane, left-drag the left side of the pane to make it narrower to allow a larger viewing area in the Contents pane.
16. Adjust the Pages pane back to its original width.
17. Close the notebook.

Mastery Assessment

Project 1-4: Creating and managing a Notebook

You need to create a new notebook with sections and pages.

1. Create a new notebook. Name the notebook **University Project** and save it on your computer.

2. In the new notebook, create four sections with the following section names
   - Project Images
   - Project Text
   - Project Due Dates
   - Project Research

3. For the following section tabs, create the following pages:
   - Project Images Page Titles Below:
   - Internet Images
   - Scanned Images
   - Project Text Page Titles Below:
   - Word documents
   - PDF Files
   - Project Due Dates Page Titles Below:
   - Weeks
   - Project Research Pages Titles Below:
   - Online Databases
   - University Library Sources

Project 1-5: Adding sections to a Notebook

You will open an existing Notebook and add some new sections to it and search for information within it.

1. From the OneNote01lessons folder open the Notebook, **Company Summer Party** and call it, My Summer Company Party. Add two more sections to the notebook: Flyer Information and Entertainment.

2. Customize the Quick Access Toolbar, so it has both the Print and Print Preview shortcut buttons on it.

3. Add two new pages to the Entertainment section and title them whatever you want.

LESSON SKILL MATRIX

In this lesson, you will learn the following skills:

Managing Notebooks

Saving a Notebook

Managing Sections

Managing Pages

Grouping Sections

Inserting content into Notebook Pages

KEY TERMS

- Direct text entry
- Section groups
- Web content

Xavier is a manager and has a basic working knowledge of OneNote. He has just started using OneNote to create notebooks for managing different projects that his team is working on. He wants to gain a better working knowledge of the different types of information that can be inserted into a OneNote notebook including images, sounds clips and video clips that will give his notebooks more depth.

SOFTWARE ORIENTATION

This lesson helps you to work more effectively with Notebooks, Pages, and Sections.

Figure 2-9

Export tab in the Backstage view.

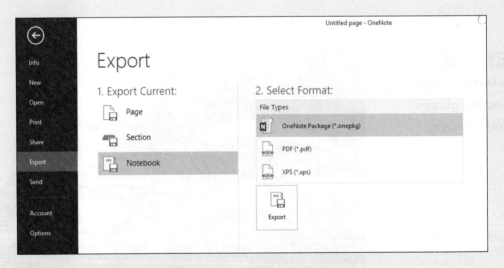

STARTING UP

In this lesson, you'll work with a file from the OneNote02lessons folder. Make sure that you have loaded the OfficeLessons folder onto your computer.

MANAGING NOTEBOOKS

Now that you're familiar with the OneNote working environment and have explored a Notebook, you will create one. Throughout this lesson, you will see how a OneNote Notebook can store and manage information in various formats, including web page text and graphics, document files, spreadsheets, and multimedia.

STEP BY STEP	Creating a new Notebook

1   Open the OneNote program by clicking Start > All Programs > Microsoft Office > Microsoft OneNote.

2   On the File Ribbon tab, click New. To store the Notebook locally, click Computer under New Notebook.

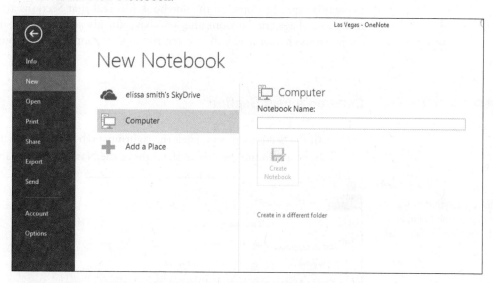

Figure 2-2

Creating a Notebook in Backstage view.

3   Type **My First Notebook** in the Notebook Name field. Click *Create in a different folder*, navigate to the OneNote02lessons folder, and click Create.

4   Click the Create Notebook button.

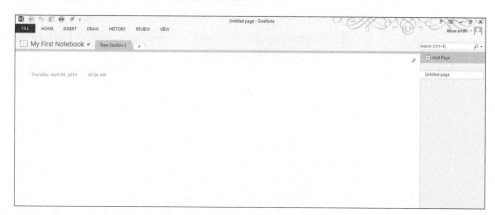

Figure 2-3

The new Notebook appears in the Normal (Notebook) view.

When the new Notebook opens, the Title bar at the top of the screen reads, Untitled page -

OneNote. Most Microsoft Office programs display the document filename in the Title bar. However, OneNote is focused on the Page, so the Page name appears in the title bar at the top of the OneNote window, not the Document name.

Take Note   Sometimes, previously used Notebooks are present in the Notebook pane. If you want to close a Notebook, open the Notebook pane, right-click the Notebook you want to close, and select Close This Notebook.

MANAGING SECTIONS

Once your new Notebook is created, you can add Sections and Pages to it. At this point, you should give the overall design of your new Notebook some thought and planning.

Workplace Ready

In some ways, Sections are like worksheet tabs in an Excel workbook. Sections can be named, groups, and the tabs can even be colored by right-clicking on the section tab and selecting Section Color.

As explained in the previous lesson, remember that Sections are created by the Notebook author to organize specific points in the notebook file, and that Sections are made up of pages. You can re-organize Page and Sections after you have already added them. Since you created a Section in the previous chapter, you will now create a new Section in a new notebook.

STEP BY STEP   **Creating a new Section**

1   In the Section tab row, click the rightmost tab that displays a small black plus sign. This button is found directly to the right of the New Section 1 tab.

Figure 2-4

Click the tab that displays a small plus sign found to the right of the New Section 1 tab.

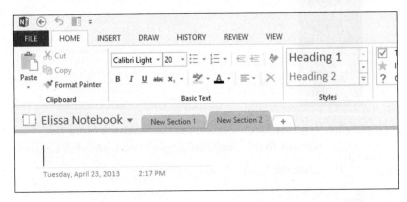

2   Repeat step 1 three times so the new Notebook has four Sections. Next, you'll change the names of these sections.

STEP BY STEP   **Renaming a Section**

1   Double-click the New Section 1 tab. It becomes highlighted.

2   Type Set List and press Enter to rename the tab.

3   Repeat these steps on the next three tabs and name them Song Ideas, Gigs, and Gear.

Figure 2-5

Each new Section contains a default Page, currently named Untitled Page.

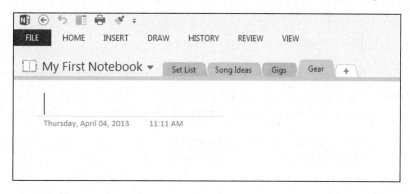

Take Note   If there are too many tabs across the Section row, some will be hidden. Click the down-arrow ( ) to show the rest of the sections.

GROUPING SECTIONS

Your Notebook might include several Sections that are related in some way. You can group those Sections to make them easier to manage into **Section Groups**. The value of Section grouping becomes more apparent as the number of Groups increases to fill the Section tab row.

STEP BY STEP   **Creating Section groups**

1   On the Section tab row, right-click the area to the right of the tabs and to the left of the Search text field.

Figure 2-6

Creating a new Section group.

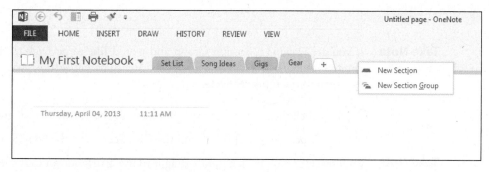

2   In the drop-down menu, click New Section Group. The New Section Group title appears highlighted.

3   Type Song Stuff and press Enter.

Figure 2-7

The new Section group appears.

Take Note   You can also rename a Section Group by right-clicking the Section Group, selecting Rename, typing the new name over the top of the old one, and pressing Enter

Once you have created a Section Group, you can add an existing Section tab to the Group by dragging it over the top of the Group.

STEP BY STEP   **Adding a Section to a group**

1   Click the Set List Section tab and drag it to the newly created Song Stuff group. The Set List Section disappears inside the Song Stuff Section Group.

2   Your view changes to show the Song Stuff Section Group in the Contents pane; the Set List Section appears in the Section tabs pane below the Ribbon buttons.

Figure 2-8

The new Section group appears with the Set List Section showing in it.

Take Note   If you are viewing a Section Group and would like to go back to the previous Section view or Parent Group, click the **arrow** (⑤). Navigate to parent section group button and click the **arrow** to return to the top level Section

3   Click the **back arrow** (⑤) to return to the parent section group.

4   Repeat steps 1 and 2 to add the Gigs Section to the Song Stuff group.

Take Note   To move a Section from a group, drag it to the arrow button to the left of the Section tabs, rest it over the arrow until the Parent Group appears, and drop it back with the existing Sections or in a different Section Group on the right side of Section tab area

SAVING A NOTEBOOK

OneNote doesn't have a Save button on the Ribbon like other Microsoft Office programs do. This is because OneNote automatically saves your work whenever you close a Section or Notebook, and constantly while you take notes.

Saving a copy of a Notebook

Although OneNote continually saves your work, you can always manually save a copy of your Notebook, Page, or Section to a different location. In this example, you will save a copy of your Notebook.

If you a copy of your entire notebook that will still work in the OneNote program, you need to be sure and pick the File Format: OneNote Package (.onepkg). This way the notebook will be exported into a format that can be reopened in OneNote again.

STEP BY STEP   **Saving a copy of a Notebook**

1   Choose the File and select Export in the Backstage view.

Figure 2-9

Export tab in the Backstage view.

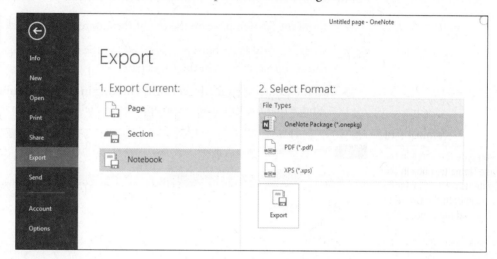

2   Under Number 1, Export Current, click Notebook.

3   Under Number 2, Select Format, click OneNote Package.

4   Click the Export button.

5   In the Save As dialog box, navigate to the OneNote02lessons folder.

6   In the File name box, type Music Project and click Save.

Don't close the file; you will use it in the next section.

Next, you'll learn to manage Pages, which will hold your content.

MANAGING PAGES

OneNote allows you to create multiple Pages within a Section to make it more versatile. If a Page becomes too large, you can break it up into Subpages.

Adding and renaming Pages

The easiest way to create a new Page is to press Ctrl+N. You can also create pages for the Section you are in by clicking Add Page at the top of the Pages pane on the right side of the screen. In the following exercise, you will learn how to add a new page by adding a page to the section labeled Gear.

STEP BY STEP   **Adding a Page**

1   From the Section pane on the top of the Contents page, click Gear.

2   Click the Add Page button (⊕ Add Page) at the top of the Pages pane on the right. A new untitled page appears in the Pages pane.

3   In the Contents pane, the cursor is blinking in the Page Name text box; type Bass Gear. Notice that the Page name also appears in the Page pane on the right side of the screen.

Figure 1-10

As you type the name in the Page Name text box in the Contents pane, it instantly appears in both the OneNote title bar and the Pages pane.

4   Create another page in the same Gear section, and call it Microphones.

Bottom Line   The beginning part of this lesson is all about notebook management. Notebooks are named and created. Next, users spend time learning how to manage Section tabs by creating, naming, renaming, moving, and grouping them. Users also create, name, and move pages as well.

STEP BY STEP   **Renaming a Page**

1   In the Pages pane, right-click the page named *Bass Gear*. A context menu appears.

2   In the context menu, choose Rename; in the Content pane where it currently says Bass Gear, type Extension Cords to replace the name. Press Enter to finish.

INSERTING CONTENT INTO NOTEBOOK PAGES

OneNote Notebooks have a very flexible structure that you can change as needed and use to collect and organize content of various types, in the following ways:

- **Direct text entry** (such as typing)

- Copying and pasting

- Creating a drawing using a mouse, touchpad, or electronic pen

- Adding audio and video notes

- Inserting web content

- The following sections explain how to add content in all of these different ways.

STEP BY STEP | **Inserting content by typing**

1   Click anywhere on the Microphone page and start typing Two Microphones & Two Jacks

Figure 2-11

Typed text appears inside a constantly expanding container.

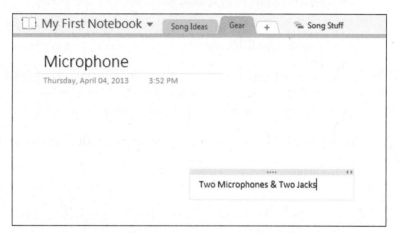

2   Select the text you just typed on the Microphone page, and from the Home Ribbon tab, choose Bold to apply a Bold font style to the text; using the Font Color button, select a dark purple color.

3   Click outside the note container when you have finished typing and formatting.

4   Move the container by clicking and dragging its border and moving it anywhere on the page.

STEP BY STEP | **Inserting content by copying and pasting**

1   Navigate to the OneNote02lessons folder, and open the Microsoft Word file titled **Music Schedule**.

2   Select all the text in the file by dragging or using the keyboard shortcut Ctrl+A. Copy the text to the clipboard either by pressing Ctrl+C on your keyboard, or by selecting the text with your mouse, right-clicking, and selecting Copy.

3   Paste the text onto the Microphone Page in OneNote by right-clicking to display the Paste options.

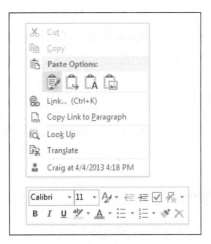

4   Select the first Paste option, Keep Source Formatting.

The Paste options available are:

- **Keep Source Formatting**: maintains the selected text's original font, size, and style.

- **Merge Formatting**: adopts the standard formatting used by OneNote.

- **Keep Text Only**: removes any non-text items, such as images, and pastes text only.

- **Picture:** inserts copied/cut image files.

Creating a drawing using a mouse, touchpad, or electronic pen

As with a paper-based Notebook, text isn't always sufficient to convey meaning, so drawing a map or figure may be necessary. You can use your computer's mouse, touchpad, or electronic pen to draw pictures and illustrations in OneNote.

STEP BY STEP   **Creating a drawing**

1   Choose the Song Ideas Section and the Untitled page, and then click the Draw tab, located in the middle of the Ribbon.

2   Click the drop-down arrow to the right of the drawing tools to view more options.

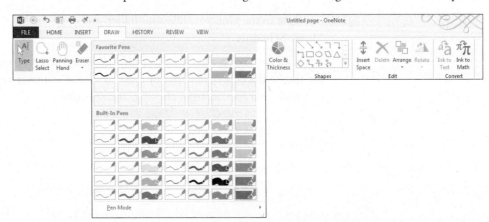

3   Select the Dark Blue Pen (1 mm) from the Built-In Pens section in the Tools group.

Figure 2-14

Dark Blue 1 mm drawing Pen selected from the Built-In Pens section of the Tools group.

4   Draw anywhere on the page by clicking and dragging the mouse to create a drawing.

5   On the far right of the Draw tab, click Select Objects or Type Text button (⬚). Click your graphic in the Contents pane, press and hold the mouse button, and drag the graphic around your entire graphic. Release your mouse pointer.

6   A dashed line borders your entire graphic. Drag your graphic to another location on the page.

Inserting audio and video notes

When you record audio, be sure your computer's microphone is on and working well. When you want to listen to audio in a notebook, be sure the sound on your computer is turned on.

You can add audio and video to Notebooks, along with text and graphics. OneNote also includes the ability to record audio, such as a melody, an odd pronunciation, or other sounds.:

STEP BY STEP	Recording audio

1   Choose the Set List Section located in the Song Stuff Section Group, and name the Untitled page, Melodies. Next, you will place an audio note on the Melodies page.

2   From the Recording group on the Insert tab, click Record Audio and begin humming or singing your favorite tune.

3   When you are finished, click the Stop button in the Playback group.

4   A Melodies text box appears with the time and date that the tune was recorded listed near the bottom.

Figure 2-15

After you click the Record Audio button, OneNote opens to the Audio & Video Playback Context Ribbon tab.

Take Note   It is not easy to tell when OneNote is recording. Look for the elapsed time on the Audio & Video Playback Context Ribbon tab in the middle of the Playback group. If it is changing, OneNote is recording.

5   Double-click the melodies icon to play it (or click Play in the Audio & Video Playback tab).

Another powerful tool available in OneNote is the ability to record and store video files. The process for recording video in OneNote is very similar to recording audio.

STEP BY STEP   **Recording a video**

1   Choose the Gigs section and name the Untitled page Movements. Next, you will place a video on the Movements page.

2   From the Recording Group on the Insert tab, click Record Video. An icon for the video file appears on the page.

You can see what your camera is recording. However, if you click Pause, it's not obvious that recording has stopped, since you continue to see the camera's video feed.

3   Click **Stop** in the Playback group to end the recording.

Figure 2-16

The Audio & Video Playback Context tab appears, displaying playback control.

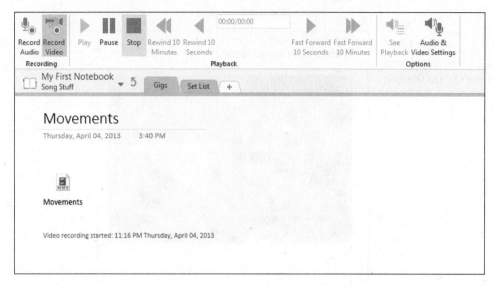

4   Double-click the icon on the Movements icon to play your video, or click **Play** in the Audio & Video Playback tab.

Inserting web content

You might want to add content from the Web into your OneNote Notebook. The procedure is straightforward, but you will need an internet connection and a web browser to get to your **web content.**

| STEP BY STEP | **Inserting a screenshot** |

1   From your web browser, open the web page **office.microsoft.com/en-us/images/** and type **band** in the Search text field. You will insert this image into the OneNote Notebook.

2   Return to OneNote and the current Notebook and click the **Microphone Page** located in the Gear section. You'll insert the clipping here.

3   Click anywhere on the page and type **important info about the band**.

Figure 2-17

Insert Screen Clipping button highlighted on the Insert Ribbon tab.

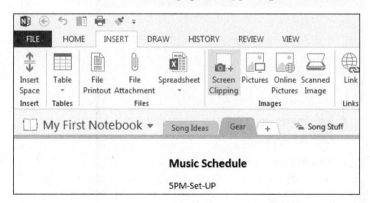

4   Click the **Insert Ribbon** tab and select **Screen Clipping** from the Images group. The screen shows the currently opened website with a faded screen.

5   In the browser window, click the top-left corner of the image you chose, drag to the bottom-right corner, and release the mouse button.

Figure 2-18

The screen clipping now appears in your OneNote Notebook.

Photo used with permission of Microsoft

Take Note   Notice that OneNote also inserts a date and timestamp under the inserted screen clipping

There might be times when you'd like to add an entire web page in your OneNote Notebook. This activity will only work using the browser Microsoft Internet Explorer.

STEP BY STEP   **Inserting a web page**

1   Toggle back to Internet Explorer where you still have *office.microsoft.com/en-us/images/* still open. Right-click close to the bottom of the menu and select **Send to OneNote**.

2   In the Select Location in OneNote window, click **My First Notebook**, **Song Stuff Section Group**, and then the **Gigs Section**. Click **OK**.

Figure 2-19

The Selection Location in OneNote dialog box appears in the Internet Explorer Window.

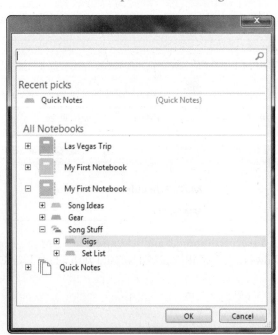

OneNote places the website on a new page in the Gigs Section of the Notebook.

Figure 2-20

The web page appears as a new Page in your OneNote Notebook. (Note that its appearance in OneNote and in Internet Explorer might differ slightly.)

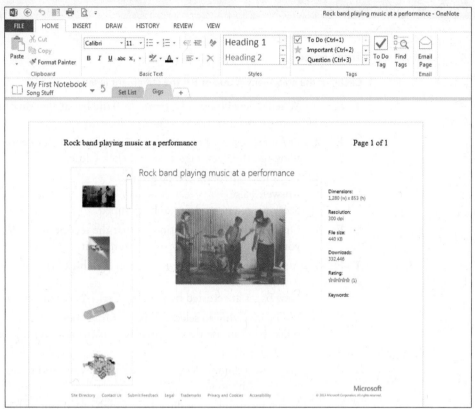

Photo and clip art used with permission of Microsoft

3 You don't need to save your file; OneNote automatically saves it.

Bottom Line

The second half of this lesson is all about inserting content into a notebook. Users insert content into a notebook through direct data entry. Next, they insert a drawing created in OneNote using the Draw Ribbon tab. Users also record and insert audio and video clips into a notebook. Finally, users insert web content, including an entire webpage into a notebook page.

What you learned in this lesson:

- Managing Notebooks

- Managing Sections

- Grouping Sections

- Saving a Notebook

- Managing Pages

- Inserting content into Notebook Pages

Knowledge Assessment

True/ False

Circle T if the statement is true or F it the statement is false.

T F 1. When a new Notebook opens, the Title bar at the top of the screen reads, Untitled page - OneNote.

T F 2. Previously opened notebooks will display in the Notebook pane, to close these notebooks go the Backstage view and click Close.

T F 3. Pages in a notebook can be groups.
Answer: False
Sections in a notebook can be grouped.

T F 4. One reason to group sections is that the section row tab can become too crowded if your notebook has too many sections in it.

T F 5. An easy way to create a new section is to hit Ctrl + N on your keyboard.
Answer: False
New pages are created by pressing Ctrl + N on the keyboard.

T F 6. If you are trying to select all the text in a document to copy and paste into a notebook, you can use the Select All keyboard short cut of, Ctrl + A, to get all the data selected.

T F 7. To create a digital mouse based drawing, you need to use the tools available on the History Ribbon tab.

T F 8. When recording an audio clip in OneNote, it can be hard to tell that OneNote is actually recording, you can look for elapsed time on the Video Playback context Ribbon tab.
Answer: True

T F 9. To record audio or video files in a notebook, you need to use the Recording group on the Insert Ribbon tab.

T F 10. If you want to insert an entire webpage into a notebook, you can use any web browser.
Answer: False
You can only insert an entire webpage into a notebook if you use Microsoft Internet Explorer.

Multiple Choice

Select the best response for the following statements.

1. To create a new section group, you:

    a. right-click anywhere in the section tab row and select New Group

    b. double-click on existing section tabs

    c. click the Home Ribbon tab and copy

    d. click the Insert Ribbon tab and section group

2. You can copy or move an existing section into another notebook, as long as the other notebook is:

    a. on your computer or network

    b. closed

    c. open

    d. saved as a PDF file format.

3. When viewing a Section group, you can move back to view the other section tabs outside of that section group by:

   a. closing the current notebook

   b. clicking the Navigate to parent group section arrow button

   c. clicking the back button in the Backstage view

   d. None of the Above

4. When you want to save a notebook, you go to:

   a. File Ribbon tab, Backstage view, and Account

   b. Home Ribbon tab and Email page button

   c. Insert Ribbon tab and Video Clipping button

   d. File Ribbon tab, Backstage view, and Export

5. When exporting (saving) a spreadsheet, your choices are to:

   a. export individual content in the notebook

   b. export the entire notebook, an individual section, or an individual page

   c. export the first page in the notebook

   d. export the first section in the notebook

6. When you create a new for a page in OneNote, where does it appear in the OneNote window?

   a. At bottom middle

   b. In the Quick Access Toolbar

   c. On the Home Ribbon tab

   d. At the top, in the title bar

7. What is an easy keyboard shortcut you can use to copy information that you want to paste into a OneNote notebook?

   a. Ctrl + P

   b. Ctrl + V

   c. Ctrl + C

   d. Ctrl + S.

8. What button on the Draw Ribbon tab will erase a drawing?

   A. Black Pen

   B. Lasso Select

   C. Planning Hand

   D. Eraser

9. If you are in the middle of recording an audio clip and need to take a break, how can you stop the recording without having to start over?

   a. Stop button

   b. Pause button

   c. Time elapsed button

   d. None of the Above

10. The Screen Clipping button on the Insert Ribbon tab, will insert a screen clipping from your computer of what?

    a. last window you had open

    b. your desktop

    c. Insert Ribbon tab

    d. notebook window

Competency Assessment

Project 2-1: Creating a new Notebook and adding sections and section groups

In this exercise, you will create a new blank notebook and add sections and section groups.

1. Click File and from the Backstage view, click New.
2. From New, click Computer to save the New notebook on your own computer.
3. Under Notebook Name, type Monthly Team Training.
4. Click Create Notebook.
5. The new notebook will open in the OneNote normal view with a new section and new page ready for you to enter information into. Your cursor should be blinking in the Content pane above a date like, type Training Goal. This will be become the name of your new page.
6. Double-click on the New Section 1 tab above the content pane, type Introduction.
7. Click the Create a New Section (plus sign button) located to the right of the current Section tabs.
8. Where the New Section 2 tab is highlighted, type Training Activity.
9. Right-click anywhere in the section tab row, select New Section Group, and name the new Section Group Training Area.
10. Left-drag the Training Activity section over the top of the Training Area section group to make it part of the section.
11. Close the notebook.

Project 2-2: Creating a Notebook and using the Management tools

You will create a new Notebook and use both page and notebook management tools.

1. Click File and then click New in the Backstage view.
2. Create the new notebook on your computer and call it Family Reunion Ideas.
3. When the new notebook opens, create two new sections in the notebook and name them Dinner Plans and Day Activities.
4. Click on the Dinner Plans section tab and create one new page called Jones Resort.
5. Click the Add Page button at the top of the Pages pane and add another new page called City Pool.
6. Left-drag the City Pool page, so it is listed above the Jones Resort page in the Pages pane.
7. Click the City Pool page, so it's showing in the Contents pane.
8. Click File to enter the Backstage view and click Export.
9. Under Export Current, select Page.
10. Under Select Format, select PDF and click Export.
11. Navigate to a location where you can save the file to your hard drive and name the export file City Pool. The City Pool page will be saved as a PDF file in that folder on your computer's hard drive.
12. Close the notebook.

Proficiency Assessment

Project 2-3: Creating a drawing

You will create a new notebook, create a free hand mouse drawing in the notebook, and also place a screen clipping in the notebook.

1. Click File and New. Name the notebook Project 2-3_new.
2. Click the Draw Ribbon tab, using some of the drawing tools, create your own mouse drawing in the Contents pane. Practice trying different thicknesses of lines and other tools on the Draw Ribbon tab.
3. Insert another new page and open it. Give the page a name of your own choice.
4. Launch your web browser and open your favorite web page. Find a graphic on the webpage that you can create a screen clipping of and place into your new notebook.
5. Return to your notebook (Make sure you don't click on any other windows before returning to your notebook in OneNote).
6. Click the Insert Ribbon tab and Screen Clipping.
7. Your screen will fade, open your web browser with the site you just visited showing, and your mouse cursor or will turn into a cross-hair (intersecting lines).
8. Left drag a rectangle around the graphic, you want to create a screen clipping of or of the section of the web page and left click.
9. You will go directly back to your notebook in OneNote with the screen clipping displayed in the Contents pane. Because it is a screen clipping, OneNote will also add a time stamp under the screen clipping.
10. Close the notebook.

Project 2-4: Adding content from Word and Excel into a Notebook

Create a new notebook and insert both a Microsoft Word document and Microsoft Excel Spreadsheet into the notebook.

1. Click File and New. Name the notebook Project 2-4_new.
2. Name your new section tab whatever you choose.
3. Name your new page whatever you choose.
4. Insert a second new page into your section and name it whatever you choose.
5. Click the Insert Ribbon tab, in the Files group click File Printout.
6. In the Choose a File or Set of Files to Insert box, navigate to the OneNote02lessons folder and click **The Travelling Musicians.docx**. The files get inserted back into the current notebook page.
7. Click on the first page in the new notebook and click the Spreadsheet button in the Files group and select Existing Spreadsheet.
8. In the Choose Document to Insert box, navigate to the OneNote02lessons folder and select **Fairy Tale List.xlsx**.
9. From the Insert File box, click Attach File. The spreadsheet appears as a linked icon on your notebook page.
10. Close the notebook.

Mastery Assessment

Project 2-5: Inserting a graphic file

Create a new notebook with sections and pages, insert a graphic file into the notebook, and a spreadsheet.

1. Create a new notebook. Name the notebook Project 2-5_new.

2. In the new notebook, create four sections with the following section names:
   Project Images
   Project Spreadsheets
   Project Text
   Project Slides

3. Create two pages in the Project Images folder called: Web Images and Hand Drawn Images.

4. In the Project Spreadsheets section, insert the file spreadsheet: **Northwind Traders Rep Sales**. Click Insert Spreadsheet.

Project 2-6: Inserting a screen clipping and recording a sound clipping

Create a new notebook and insert a screen clipping and record a sound clipping in the notebook.

1. Create a new notebook. Name the notebook Project 2-6_new. In the new notebook, add one more new page, so you have a total of two pages.

2. On the first new page, insert a screen clipping from your favorite website using the Screen Clipping button on the Insert Ribbon tab.

3. On the second page, create a sound recording of yourself singing Happy Birthday and insert it on the second page of the notebook using the Record Audio button on the Insert Ribbon tab.

Microsoft Access 2013

1 Introduction to Microsoft Access 2013

LESSON SKILL MATRIX

In this lesson, you will learn the following skills:

What is Access?	Getting Help
Ways to use Access	Ending An Access Session
Database basics	
Exploring a database	
Working with records	
Customizing the Quick Access Toolbar	

KEY TERMS

- **Database**
- **Relational database**
- **Table**
- **Query**
- **Form**
- **Report**
- **Field**
- **Record**

Tina owns a small boutique and would like to create a database of information regarding her customers. She wants to use Microsoft Access and have the database track information like customer addresses, favorite products, order dates, and products ordered. She needs to learn to use Microsoft Access and then create her database in the software.

SOFTWARE ORIENTATION

This lesson helps you understand database essentials and introduces you to Microsoft Access 2013.

Figure 1-1

Access is a database for storing and managing records.

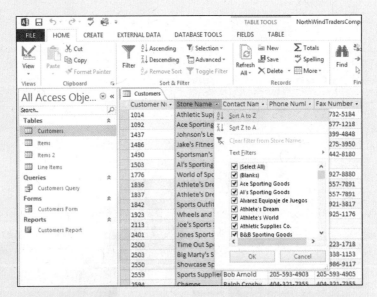

STARTING UP

In this lesson, you'll work with several files from the Access01lessons folder. Make sure that you have loaded the OfficeLessons folder onto your computer.

WHAT IS ACCESS?

Access is a **database** program that allows you to store and organize your data in useful ways through reports, forms, and webpages. It is available in certain editions of Microsoft Office, but you can also purchase it separately.

Access is a **relational database** program that uses related tables to store, organize, and retrieve data. You can use Access locally on your computer or through the Internet. Access is used by small and large companies throughout the world to store their data and make it accessible in useful ways.

WAYS TO USE ACCESS

You can use Access to create, modify, and manage databases through any of the following tasks:

* Creating a new database from scratch or based on a template.

* Establishing relationships between types of information.

* Adding data to a database through a table or through a form.

* Designing forms for data entry or viewing information.

* Importing data into Access from other programs or linking to external data sources.

* Running filters and queries on the database to extract relevant data.

* Generating reports to emphasize and present different portions of your data.

DATABASE BASICS

Access 2013 is a software database program that allows you to organize a collection of data. This includes the data's storage, query, retrieval, and maintenance of information. Databases are used to organize data from company customer addresses and phone numbers to company products and parts.

Databases and spreadsheets serve similar purposes; however, they are also different. If your data can be easily entered, stored, viewed, extracted, and managed within a spreadsheet, it is best to keep the information within Microsoft Excel. An example would be a small staff directory that includes items such as Last Name, First Name, Office, Phone Number, Department, and Start Date. However, when your data becomes more complicated, Access might be a better tool for managing the data.

Basic database terminology

The terms described in this section are frequently used when discussing databases, and it's useful to understand them before starting to work with an Access database.

Databases are made up of objects. With these objects, you can perform specific tasks. Below is a list of the main objects available in Access:

- **Table:** the most important and foundational object in an Access database. Tables store data in records and fields, which correspond to rows and columns, respectively. The data is usually about a particular category of things, such as employees or orders.

- **Query:** a question that you ask about the data stored in a table. Queries can also make a request of the data or perform an action such as a filter on the data. A query can bring data together from multiple tables to serve as the source of data for a form or report.

- **Form:** an object where you place controls for taking actions or for entering, displaying, and editing data in fields. Access objects resemble online forms. They are primarily used for viewing information from database tables and also for entering data into tables.

- **Report:** a printout of your database information that's formatted and organized according to your specifications. Examples of reports are sales summaries, phone lists, and mailing labels.

Tables are the most important object in your database because this where all the information in your database is stored. The other database objects access the tables to organize, report, and perform different actions to the information contained therein. This is why a solid understanding of tables is critical to using Access and understanding how the other database objects work in conjunction to the tables.

Below are two important terms you need to understand about database tables:

- **Field:** a table column or category. For example, a FirstName field would likely be found in an Employees table.

- **Record:** a set of fields containing data for a single entry and appearing in one row of a database table.

Database design tips

Database design can be complex and require a high degree of advanced designing skills and background that can take a great deal of time and training to obtain. However, for basic database design, you can start with the following tips:

- Plan, plan, plan! You should never rush into creating the components of a database. We highly recommend that you gather as much information as possible from individuals who will be using the database. Examples of important components to plan are: the types of tables that are needed, the table fields, how the tables are related, etc.

- Create a sketch of the database tables on a piece of paper, and use lines and arrows to show how they're related.

- Each table should have only one purpose; for example, one table will be used to keep track of orders, another to keep track of customers, yet another to keep track of employees, etc.

- Avoid duplication of data; for example, don't add Customer fields to the Orders table. Redundant data increases the size and complexity of your database, increases the likelihood of data entry or retrieval errors, and slows the speed of the database.

QUICK TOUR OF ACCESS 2013

Understanding the capabilities of Access helps you understand and use the program more effectively. Before you start using a database, you need to either open an existing one or create a new blank database. You will create a new blank database, so that you can overview database's user interface in the next section.

STEP BY STEP   **Opening an Access 2013 file**

1   To open Access, choose Start > Programs > Microsoft Office > Microsoft Access 2013.

Figure 1-2

Backstage view of Access 2013.

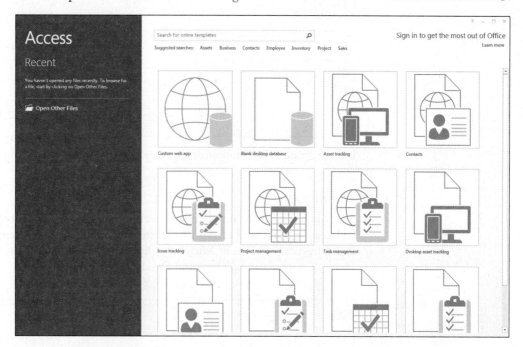

Access 2013 opens in Backstage view, where you can create a new database, open an existing database, and view featured content from *Office.com*. Backstage view is described in more detail in the next section.

You can always access Backstage view, even when working in a database, by clicking the File tab.

2   At the bottom left of the Access opening screen, click Open Other Files.

3   From the Open screen, click Computer > Browse to the Access01lesson folder, and Open **NorthWindTradersCompanyDatabase**.

Take Note   You can get out of the Backstage view by pressing ESC on your keyboard or by clicking the Back button (the circle button with the left facing arrow in it at the top of the Backstage menu.)

Access 2013 components

The Access 2013 interface has the following main components:

- **The Ribbon**: this bar across the top of the interface contains several tabs, which in turn contain groups of commands that are visible on all tabs, except File.

- **Backstage view**: this view appears by default when you launch Access 2013; it's comprised by the group of commands available on the Ribbon's File tab.

Take Note   The File tab always has a colored background, even when it is not the active tab. You can identify the active tab by the borders on either side of it.

- **The Navigation pane:** the area on the left side of the interface that displays lists of database objects when a database is open. You can use it to open and organize database objects.

Figure 1-3

NorthWindTradersCompany-Database, showing an open Navigation pane.

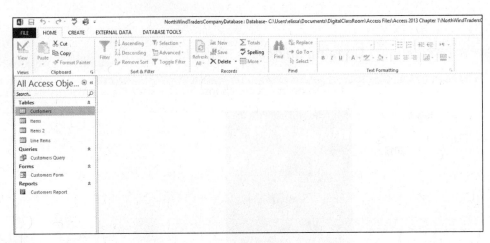

Let's examine these components in more detail.

The Ribbon

The Ribbon is divided into tabs, and within each tab there are groups of commands. The Ribbon replaces the traditional menus that existed across the top of the screen and the toolbars that were found in older versions of Microsoft Office. The primary Ribbon tabs for Access 2013 are File, Home, Create, External Data, and Database Tools.

Figure 1- 4

The Access 2013 ribbon is divided into tabs.

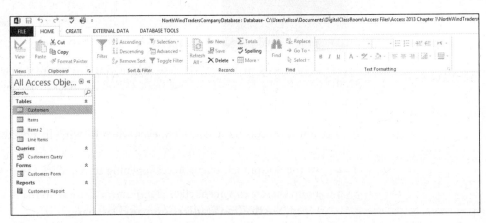

There are times when different Ribbons open in Access depending on your current task in the software. These are called Context Ribbon tabs. The Table Tools and Fields and Tables are Context Ribbon tabs that only open when you are adding or editing records in an Access table. When you close the Access table or switch to a different view, the Fields and Tables Ribbon tabs turn off.

You can also hide and show the Ribbon by double-clicking the active command tab, making it easy to maximize your workspace as needed.

STEP BY STEP   **Showing the Ribbon**

1   Notice the Ribbon and its tabs divided into groups of commands.

Figure 1-5

The Ribbon in full view,
showing groups of commands.

2   Hide the Ribbon by double-clicking the Home tab.

Figure 1- 6

The Ribbon with its command
groups hidden.

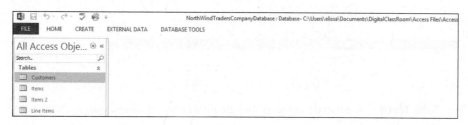

3   Show the Ribbon by clicking the Home tab again.

You have successfully toggled the Ribbon by clicking the active tab. You can also toggle the Ribbon by clicking the Minimize/Expand arrow button in the upper-right corner.

Backstage view

Backstage view is the first view you see after you launch Access 2013. It contains information and commands that affect an entire database, such as the following: opening and saving a database; a list of recently opened databases; tabs for database information, recent databases, and database creation. You can also launch the help system and manage options in Backstage view.

Navigation pane

The Navigation pane, which replaces the Database window of some older versions of Access, is located on the left side of the Access 2013 interface when a database is open.

Figure 1-7

The Navigation pane allows you to view and manage the database's objects, and is customizable.

Take Note   A database's objects include items such as tables, queries, forms, and reports.

You can toggle the Navigation pane just as you did with the Ribbon. Although the result is the same, the procedure is slightly different. You'll toggle and examine the Navigation pane in more detail after you've opened a database that contains some actual data.

Choose File > Close to close this file.

EXPLORING A DATABASE

Now that we've covered some introductory information, we'll examine a database and discover how it works.

Opening a sample template

1 Click the File tab to get back into Backstage view.

2 From Backstage view, select New, and then click the Contacts category located next to the Suggested Searches.

Figure 1-8

Choose the Desktop contacts template.

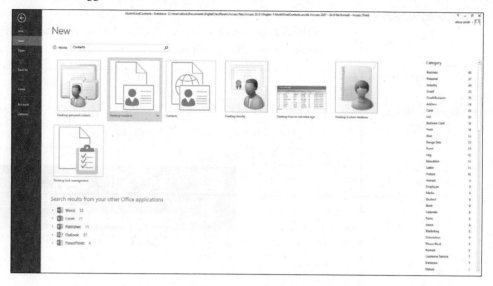

3 Select Desktop contacts. Then, in the Desktop contact box, type CustomerContacts for the File Name. Click the small folder icon, browse to the Access01lessons folder and click OK. (You need to save the new database with a file name before you can start using it.)

4 Click Create. If the tutorial box Getting Started with Contacts opens up, click the Close button in the top-right corner. The database opens and the Home Ribbon tab is currently open.

Take Note   You might see a Security Warning at the top of the screen. If so, click Enable Content.

Figure 1-9

The contacts database, showing a collapsed Navigation pane on the left side.

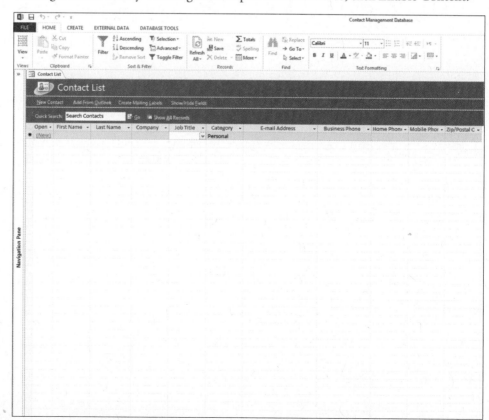

Let's explore the Navigation pane. Just as is the case with the Ribbon, you can show or hide the Navigation pane to get more or less room to view individual database objects.

Showing and hiding the Navigation pane

1   If the Navigation pane is closed, click the **Open/Close** button (⊠) in the upper-right corner to view the contents.

Figure 1-10

Click the Open/Close button to expand or collapse the Navigation pane.

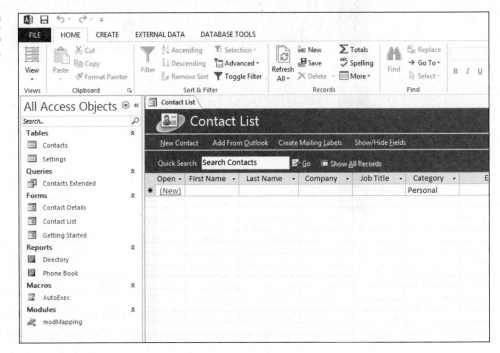

2 Click the Open/Close button a second time to close the Navigation pane. It doesn't quite disappear, but it collapses to show only the title bar of the pane.

3 Click the Open/Close button again to restore the Navigation pane.

Take Note You can alter the Navigation pane's width by clicking and dragging its right border.

The Navigation pane displays the database's objects. The default view shows all the main categories, which are Tables, Queries, Forms, Reports, Macros, and Modules. The database's different objects are listed under their appropriate headings. Your database can contain as many objects as necessary to manage your information.

You will use the Search text box at the top of the Navigation pane to search for a specific object.

STEP BY STEP **Searching for an object using the Navigation pane**

1 On each heading in the Navigation pane, click the **down-arrow** to show objects. You will need to scroll down to access all the headings.

2 Type **contact list** in the Search text box.

As you type, objects that contain this text begin to appear in the Navigation pane below, until only objects containing the exact same spelling remain.

Figure 1-11

The Search engine will instantly finds objects that match the text you type.

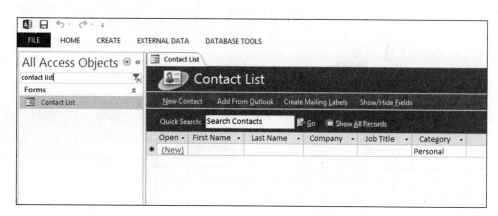

3 Delete the text in the Search text box, either by clicking the **Clear Search String** icon (🗙) to the right of the Search text box, or by pressing the **Delete** or **backspace** key on your keyboard. This will turn the Navigation pane back to showing all your database objects.

There may be times when you only want to change the view in the Navigation pane or only view one specific category of object to arrange the appearance of the objects in the Navigation pane.

STEP BY STEP   **Changing the view in the Navigation pane**

1   Click the **down-arrow** button in the upper-right corner of the Navigation pane.

The Navigation pane shows that the Object Type and All Access Objects are checked. This means that all the database's objects are currently showing in the Navigation pane.

Figure 1-12

Use the Navigation pane to choose how objects are displayed and organized.

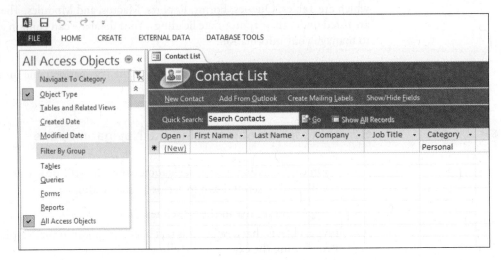

2   Change the Navigation pane to show tables by clicking **Tables** in this drop-down menu. Only Table database objects appear in the Navigation pane.

Figure 1-13

The Navigation pane configured to display only Tables.

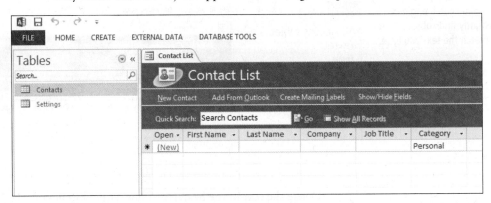

3   Click the **down-arrow** button again and change the display settings back to **All Access Objects**. The Navigation pane will again show all the categories of database objects.

Double-click an object to open it or access more options by right-clicking an object.

To manage objects in the Navigation pane follow these steps:

STEP BY STEP   **Managing objects in the Navigation pane**

1   Right-click an object, such as *Contacts*, to open a context menu.

The menu lists several options, depending on the object. For a table, these options include such items as Open, Design View, Import, and Export. (For more details about Importing, see Lesson 2, "Getting Started with Microsoft Access 2013.") The important thing to remember is that you can right-click objects to perform actions or to view information.

Figure 1-14

The context menu lists many options for managing items in the Navigation pane.

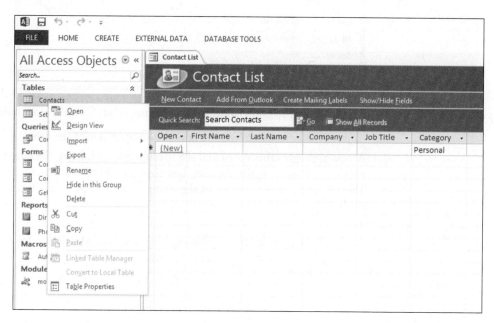

2   Choose **File > Close** to close this file.

Access is made up of database objects. The foundational object is the database table. All database objects can be viewed, opened, and even renamed from the Navigation Pane. The Ribbon tabs replace tool bars from past versions of Access and the Backstage view provides users with database management tools like saving, printing, and opening existing databases.

WORKING WITH RECORDS

Now that you've become familiar with basic database components, you can begin working with database tables. We'll use the Customers table in the **NorthwindTradersCompanyDatabase** database to search for, sort, add, and delete a record.

Searching for a record

There will be times when you need to locate a specific record in a table, and it can become especially critical if your table contains thousands of records.

STEP BY STEP   **Searching a table for a record**

1   Choose **File > Open** and navigate to the Access01lessons folder. Double-click **NorthwindTradersCompanyDatabase** to open the file.

2   Double-click the Customers table listed in Navigation pane, or right-click the Customers table and select **Open**. The Customers Table opens in the middle of your screen and looks like a table or spreadsheet with rows and columns.

3   With the Customer table opened, press **Ctrl+F** or click the **Find** button (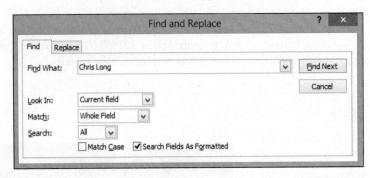) in the Home tab Ribbon (Editing group). The Find and Replace dialog box appears.

4   In the Find What text box, type **Chris Long**.

Figure 1-15

The Find and Replace window appears.

5   From the Look In drop-down menu, select **Current** document.

6   Click the **Find Next** button on the right side of the box.

Access highlights the record and the specific cell containing the name Chris Long. If you press the **Find Next** button again, a dialog box appears telling you that no more search items were found. There is only one occurrence of the name Chris Long in the Customers table. Click **OK** to close the box.

7   When you are finished using Find and Replace, click **Cancel** to close it.

Sorting records

Notice that the Customers table is sorted in order by the Customer Number field, which is the first field on the far left side of the table. You can choose to sort by other fields in the table.

STEP BY STEP   **Sorting records**

1   Click the drop-down arrow on the right side of the Store Name column heading.

2   From the drop-down list that appears, select **Sort A to Z**.

The records are now sorted by StoreName, not by ID.

Figure 1-16

Sort Records in Store Name column in Ascending Order.

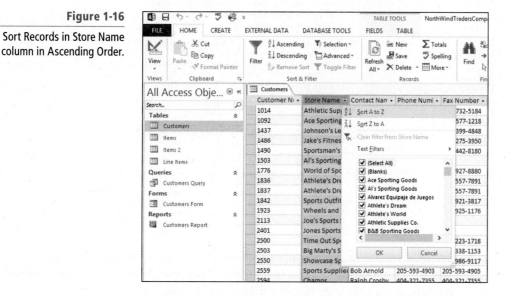

Adding and deleting records

There are times when you might need to add or delete records from a database table, and this section explains how.

Adding a record

There are a few different ways to add new records to a table. The first is to click in the very last row of the table, where there will be a star to indicate that the row is blank (note that you might need to scroll down to find it if your table has a lot of records). To add a new record, just start typing in this blank row.

If you don't want to scroll to the very bottom of the table, which might be particularly inconvenient if the table has numerous records, you can add a new record by right-clicking any row.

Adding a record by right-clicking

1 Right-click the Record Selector (the leftmost square) of any row.

Figure 1-17

Add a record regardless of your present location in a table.

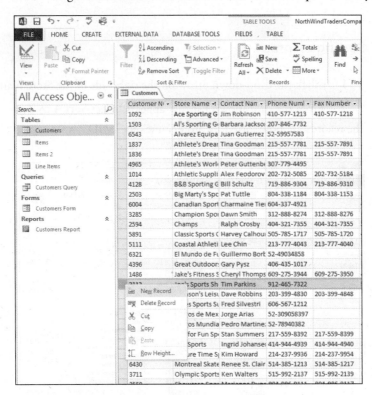

2 From the context menu that appears, choose New Record. This will automatically move your mouse cursor down to the bottom row of the table. Note that the mouse cursor is blinking in the Customer Number field of the last row.

Take Note You can move to the next field by clicking in it with your mouse, or pressing tab, enter, or the right arrow key on your keyboard.

3 Add three records with the following Customer Numbers:

7001

7002

7003

STEP BY STEP   **Deleting a record**

    1   Right-click the Record Selector (the leftmost square) of the record that you want to delete. (For practice, choose one of the records that you added in the previous exercise.)

    2   Click Delete Record. A Warning box appears asking whether you are sure you want to delete the record, since the activity can't be undone. (This means that you Undo button will not work after the record is deleted.) Click Yes to delete.

Take Note   When an Access table is open, records can be added, deleted, and edited in the table. When a record is deleted, it is a permanent deletion. Undo will not bring it back.

CUSTOMIZING THE QUICK ACCESS TOOLBAR

The Quick Access Toolbar provides convenient, one-click access to your favorite tools. Initially, the toolbar in the document displays the Save, Redo, and Undo options, and the Customize Quick Access Toolbar button.

You will customize the toolbar to include the Quick Print and Spell Check buttons. If you have completed some of our other Microsoft Office lessons, you will already be familiar with this process.

Figure 1-18

The Quick Access Toolbar.

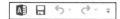

To customize the Quick Access Toolbar to include the Quick Print and Spelling commands:

STEP BY STEP   **Customizing the quick Access Toolbar**

    1   Click the Customize Quick Access Toolbar button and from the drop-down menu, choose Spelling.

The Quick Access Toolbar now contains the Quick Print and Spelling commands.

Figure 1-19

The new command is now added to the Quick Access Toolbar.

    2   To remove a command, right-click it, and then choose Remove from Quick Access Toolbar.

GETTING HELP

Microsoft Access contains a Help system designed to help you quickly get answers to questions regarding your Access database.

STEP BY STEP	Using the Help System

1   Press the F1 key or click the Help button (?) in the top-right corner of the Access screen. The Help System appears.

Figure 1-20

Get help by pressing F1 or clicking the Help button.

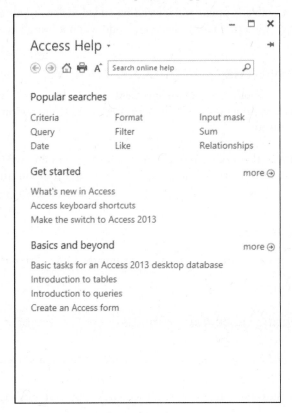

2   To close the Help box, click the X button (⊠) in the top-right corner.

ENDING AN ACCESS SESSION

You can quickly end a Microsoft Access session by following these steps.

STEP BY STEP	Ending a session

1   Click the File tab and then Save.

2   Click the Close button (⊠) located in the upper-right corner of the program.

What you learned in this lesson:

- What is Access?
- Ways to use Access
- Database basics
- Exploring a database
- Working with records
- Customizing the Quick Access Toolbar
- Getting Help
- Ending an Access Session

True False

Circle T if the statement is true or F it the statement is false.

T F 1. Microsoft Access allows you to store and organize your data through the use of graphics.

T F 2. Databases and spreadsheets have many similar functions.

T F 3. When data becomes too complicated to manage in a spreadsheet, a database is often a very useful tool for begin managing the data.

T F 4. Microsoft Access is made up objects.

T F 5. The most important object in an Access database is a Form.

T F 6. In an Access database a table column is called a Category.

T F 7. The Navigation Pane located on left hand side of the Access interface allows you to open, close, and organize database objects.

T F 8. If you hit Ctrl + F on the keyboard while in a Table, you will open the Spell Check.

T F 9. If you delete a record in an open Table, Undo will bring it back.

T F 10. One method for inserting a new record into an open Table is to right-click the Record Selector next to an existing record and then select New Record in the context menu.

Multiple Choice

Select the best response for the following statements.

1. Why are tables considered the most important object in an Access database:
   a. They allow users to print data in useful ways.
   b. They allow data to be filtered and categorized in new ways.
   c. They allow users to more easily enter data into the database.
   d. They allow data to be stored in rows and columns and manipulated in other database objects.

2. What is the main purpose of a data base Forms?
   a. Creating a pleasing print out of database information.
   b. To allow for easy filtering and sorting of large database tables.
   c. To allow for easy data-entry, editing, and display of data stored in Tables.
   d. To allow for easy viewing of data in an internet browser.

3. What are some important points to consider before creating database?
   a. Plan carefully, each table should have only one main purpose, and avoid duplication in your data.
   b. Planning isn't critical. You will need most of your time for data-entry.
   c. Ensure your forms have carefully planned out layouts to create excellent visual impact and clarity.
   d. Spent the bulk of your time considering what size paper your reports will need to print on to fit all the information.

4. What screen does Microsoft Access open when you first enter the program?
   a. The Save screen.
   b. The Backstage view.
   c. The Options box.
   d. The Navigation Pane.

5. What are the main (default) categories of the Navigation Pane?

    a. Tables, Queries, Forms, Reports, Macros, and Modules

    b. Forms only

    c. Reports and Queries

    d. The database by itself

6. To sort records in an Access table, you

    a. Click on the Create Ribbon tab. and select Sort

    b. Right-click on the field heading and select Sort A to Z or Sort Z to A

    c. Use the navigation area at the bottom of the table

    d. Go to the Backstage view

7. What two methods will open the Help in Access?

    a. Right-click anywhere on the screen and select Help or type Help in a table cell

    b. Hit the F1 key on the keyboard or click the Help button in the top right hand corner the Access window

    c. Select Help from the Backstage view or click the Help button on the bottom of the screen.

    d. Click the Help button on the Quick Access Toolbar or click the Help button on the Home Ribbon tab.

8. Why do different Ribbon tabs open in Access depending on what you are doing in your database?

    a. Depending on your task in the database, different Ribbon tabs called Context Ribbons may open to help you complete your task.

    b. If different Ribbon tabs open, it means you need to save your database.

    c. Different Ribbon tabs may open when a database table becomes too large.

    d. Different Ribbon tabs never open in Access.

9. What is the difference between a record and a field in a database?

    a. A record is can only be viewed in a form

    b. A field only allows for numerical information to be stored in it; while a record can hold any type of information

    c. There are no differences between fields and records, the two terms can be used interchangeably

    d. Records are rows in a database table and fields are columns.

10. Where can you add your favorite database shortcuts?

    a. Shortcut buttons can placed on the Quick Access Toolbar

    b. Add favorite shortcuts to any Ribbon tab by customizing it

    c. Add shortcuts to the bottom of the Access window

    d. Add shortcuts to the Navigation Pane

Competency Assessment

Project 1-1: Creating and editing a new database using a template

Create a new database based on a Microsoft Template and edit an existing table in the database to track information regarding your company's inventory.

1. Click File. From the Backstage view, click New.
2. In the New area, click Desktop asset tracking.
3. Browse to the Access01lessons folder.
4. In the File name box, type Northwind Traders Products and click Create.
5. The Navigation pane will open with many database objects already created. Expand and collapse the Navigation pane.
6. From the Navigation pane, double-click on the Assets table to open it.
7. Double-click the Contacts table and open it up.
8. Minimize the Ribbon tabs.
9. Enter a record of your choosing into the top row of the table.
10. Click the File Ribbon tab and in the Backstage view, click Close.

Project 1-2: Creating a new database

Create a new database from scratch.

1. Click File and from the Backstage view, click New.
2. Click Blank desktop database.
3. Type the File name: HR Management.
4. The new database will open with one table. The new table will be open and is called, Table 1.
5. Collapse the Navigation pane.
6. Click on the Customize Quick Access Toolbar arrow and add three new short-cut buttons to the Quick Access toolbar of your choosing.
7. Minimize the Ribbon tabs.
8. Maximize the Ribbon tabs.
9. With the Table1 open, notice the Context ribbon tabs that are open.
10. Click on the Table Tools, Field Ribbon tab and explore some of its buttons.
11. Click on the Table Tools, Table Ribbon tab and explore some of its buttons.
12. Click File and Close to close the database.

Proficiency Assessment

Project 1-3: Creating a customer database using a template

You are working for a company that has been tracking their customer contacts in an Excel spreadsheet. However, you need a more powerful contact management tool and want to see what Access has to offer. You will open a new database based on a contact management template available from Microsoft and explore it.

1. From New in Backstage view, click the Contacts category in the templates categories.
2. Click the Desktop contacts template.
3. Name the database, Customer Contacts and create the database.
4. If a tutorial box titled, Getting Started with Contacts opens, close the box.
5. From the Navigation pane, open the Contacts table.
6. Type three new records into the table using information of your choosing but applicable to the table. (Hint: Don't worry about typing anything in the ID field; Access will automatically fill in this field for you.)
7. Right-click on one of your records and delete.
8. Type a new record to replace the deleted one.
9. Save and then close the table.

Project 1-4: Creating a new database and adding tables

You need to create a new database to track information regarding a new project. The database will need to have three tables. It will be created from scratch because none of the Microsoft Access templates are applicable to your information.

1. From New in Backstage view, click Blank desktop database.
2. Name the database, Project X and click Create.
3. When the database opens, it will contain one blank table.
4. Click the Create Ribbon tab and click the Tables button in the Tables group. A second blank table called Table 2 will open.
5. Click the Create Ribbon tab again and create a third blank table. It will be called Table 3.
6. In the Navigation pane, filter the Navigation pane list to only display tables.
7. Return the Navigation pane to display all objects.
8. In the Search box, above the Navigation pane, type Table2 and hit enter.
9. Notice even though it is opened, it will become the active table in the middle of your screen.
10. Click File > Save and then File > close to close the database.

Project 1-5: Selecting the best template for a project

You have just started working for a small business that currently maintains all its HR data in a spreadsheet. The HR manager would like to begin managing this data in an Access database. After meeting with the HR manager, you decide to create your database based on an Access template.

1. Select the best Access template for managing HR data from the templates available with Microsoft Access.

2. Explore the tables that are created with the template and make note of which tables in the template will be most useful to your company's needs in regards to this project.

3. Select a table in your new database and enter 10 records into your new database using applicable company information (that you create). Then perform a **Find and Sort** on the new records to show your HR manager how the data can be managed from the database tables.

4. Save your file as **Project1-5_done**.

Project 1-6: Finding and editing data

You need to locate specific data in a database and make some changes to it.

1. Reopen the database used at the beginning of this lesson called **NorthWindTradersCompanyDatabase**. Save this database as **Project1-6_done**.

2. In the Customers table, delete three records with following Customer Numbers: 3711, 3285, and 3504.

3. Sort the Customers table by the Store Name field in ascending order.

4. In the Items2 table, sort the Product Description field by ascending order.

5. Close both the tables and the database.

LESSON SKILL MATRIX

In this lesson, you will learn the following skills:

Access 2013 database types

Tables, views, and data types

Importing data from a Microsoft Excel spreadsheet

Renaming a New Table from an Excel spreadsheet

KEY TERMS

- **Desktop (standard) Database**
- **Web app database**
- **Datasheet view**
- **Design view**
- **Primary Key**
- **Data type**

Javier owns a company that manufactures custom clocks. He has always kept track of his inventory and products in an Excel spreadsheet. However, he wants to be able to create reports and forms to make it easier to track his clock inventory using a database program like Microsoft Access. He has a basic understanding of Access, and he is now ready to create tables for an inventory database and also import some of the data from his Excel spreadsheets into his Access database.

SOFTWARE ORIENTATION

This lesson helps you to work with creating databases and importing data into a database using Microsoft Access 2013

Figure 2-1

Microsoft Access database interface

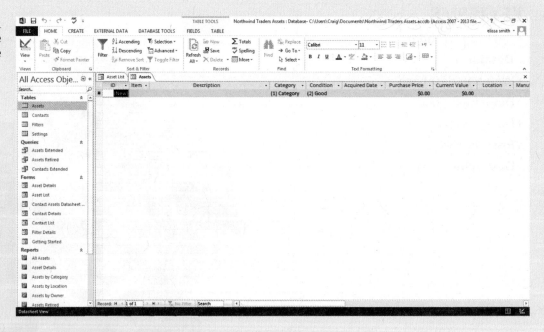

STARTING UP

In this lesson, you'll work with several files from the Access02lessons folder. Make sure that you have loaded the OfficeLessons folder onto your computer.

ACCESS 2013 DATABASE TYPES

Access 2013 has two types of databases:

Desktop (standard) database, which is stored on your computer, a network, or another computer storage location and run directly from the location on your computer. The exercises in this lesson involve the desktop database type.

An **Access web app**, which was introduced with Access 2013. This new type of database can be built from Access, and then used and shared with others as a SharePoint app in a web browser. You create the app by selecting the type of data you want to track (contacts, tasks, projects, and so on), and Access makes the database structure, complete with views that let you add and edit data.

Creating a simple database

In Lesson 1, you explored a database. Now you will create one. Access 2013 has two methods for creating a database.

The first method is to use the templates provided with Access 2013. A template is a database created for a specific type of task that contains several pre-made database objects. When using a template to create a database, all you need to do is add your own data to the tables, and customize the template as needed.

When you use templates to create databases, you're not limited to using the objects as they come with the templates; you can customize the objects and adapt them to fit your needs. For example, if you have a better design for a form, you need a different field name for a table, or you need a new table, you can customize these objects. You can also add your own database objects to the ones that already exist in the template.

The second option for creating a database is to create a new and empty database from scratch. Many people use this option when the database they need to create is too complicated and they cannot locate a suitable template.

 # Workplace **Ready**

It's also very common for Access users to work with existing databases. You will probably enter information into the database, create new database objects, and edit existing data.

Creating a database using a template

STEP BY STEP	**Creating a database using a template**

1   Open Access if it is not already opened and open the Backstage view. Select the New command.

The New area displays several categories of templates. In the Search for Online Templates box, you can search for online templates from the Office.com site. There are also suggested search topics listed under the search box, such as Assets, Business Contacts, Inventory, Project, Sales, and more.

Workplace Ready: Microsoft Access templates are created to fit the needs of many broad business uses. If you are needing to create a database, be sure to carefully look over the Access templates, one of them may fit your needs.

The next area includes different templates that appear as thumbnails. These templates are available for you to select directly from the New area of the Backstage view, and they are either Access apps or Desktop Access databases. Below is a list of these templates:

- Custom web app: Access app made for you to customize from scratch

- Blank desktop database: creates a new blank database

- Desktop contacts

- Asset Tracking

- Contacts

- Issue tracking

- Project management:

- Desktop asset tracking

- Desktop issue Tracking

- Desktop project management

- Desktop task management

Figure 2-2

The Backstage view appears with the New tab selected.

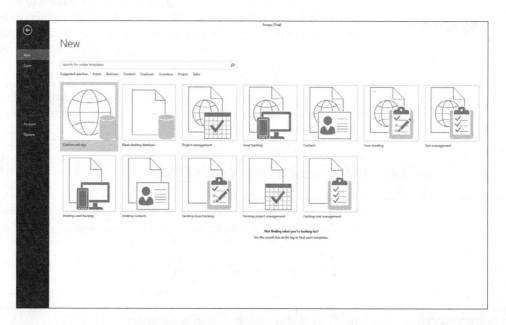

2   From the second row, select the *Desktop asset tracking* template. The Desktop asset tracking information box opens.

Figure 2-3

Desktop asset tracking information dialog box.

3   In the File Name box, type the File Name **NorthWind Traders Assets**. Click **browse**, navigate to the Access02lessons folder, and click **OK**. Now click **Create**.

When the database opens, you may see a warning about disabled content. Click **Enable Content**. You may then see a message box labeled *Getting Started with Assets*. You can close it by clicking the **Close** button in the top-right corner.

Look at the Navigation bar. Notice the different objects that are automatically created because your database is based on a template.

4   In the Navigation pane, under the Tables Object category, double-click the table called *Assets*.

When the table opens, notice that there are no records in it. However, all the fields (columns) are set up and prepared for you to enter information into the table.

5   Click the File Ribbon tab and select **Close**. This closes the database, but leaves Access running.

Take Note You can have multiple databases open simultaneously, but closing unused databases frees up your computer's resources and speeds up processes in the database that you are working with.

STEP BY STEP | **Creating a database from scratch**

1 Click **File** to enter the Backstage view, and then select **New**.

2 From the first row, select *Blank desktop database*. The Blank desktop database box opens.

3 In the File Name text box, type **SCRATCH**, browse to the Access02lessons folder, and click **OK**. Click **Create** and notice that only one object is created for this database: Table1.

Figure 2-4

The SCRATCH database opens with the Table1 object open and ready for data entry. It is the only object that is created when you make a new blank database.

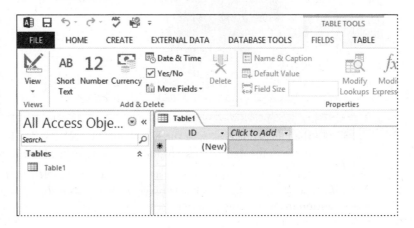

Saving a new table

Now that your new database is open, and you have one new table created, you need to give your table a name.

STEP BY STEP | **Saving a new table**

1 In the Quick Access Toolbar, click the **Save** icon (⊞) or choose **File > Save**. The Save As dialog box appears.

2 In the Table Name text box, type **Assets**. Press **Enter** or click **OK**.

TABLES, VIEWS, AND DATA TYPES

Tables are crucial to Access databases and form the framework of relational databases. Next, you will investigate various ways to view tables, and how to prepare them for the data they will hold.

• You can view tables in Access 2013 in one of two ways: Datasheet view and Design view.

• **Datasheet view** is designed for data entry and viewing records. You can add, delete, edit, sort, filter, and print records from this view. You can also insert, delete, categorize new fields, and change their order.

- **Design view** is where the table's design is the focus. It lists all the fields with their data types and descriptions. In this view, you do not see the actual records.

Creating a table in Datasheet view

Datasheet view allows you to add tables and fields to your database. It resembles a spreadsheet, such as you would find in Excel.

| STEP BY STEP | Creating a table in Datasheet view |

1 Using the **SCRATCH** database that you created in the previous section, click the Create tab.

2 From the Tables group (second group of commands from the left), select the Table command. *Table1* appears in Datasheet view.

3 To rename Table1, click the Save button in the Quick Access Toolbar. When the Save As dialog box appears, type Products in the text box, and then press Enter.

In Datasheet view, you can examine the table more closely and notice the following:

- The words Datasheet View are displayed in the lower-left corner of the Status Bar. (The status bar is located at the bottom of the Access window.)

- The Datasheet view icon ( ) is active in the lower-right corner of the Status Bar; the Design View icon ( ) is inactive.

In the Views group of Home tab, the Design View command appears in color. When you click the down-arrow, you can see in the menu that the Datasheet view option is active, but the Design view option is inactive. The Design View icon is the one that appears in the View group because it's the option that you can toggle to when you are in the Datasheet view.

Figure 2-5

Datasheet View button active on Home tab after clicking the Design View command.

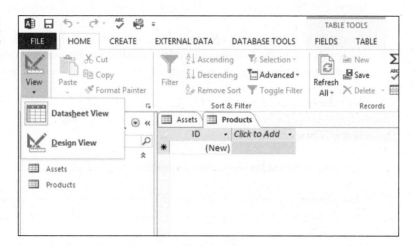

Take Note   Although the Design View command is in color in the Views group of the Home tab, Access is currently in Datasheet view.

Next, you'll spend some time examining the table's Datasheet view. When you create a new table, Access automatically creates a field (first column) in the new table. This field is called ID and Access assigns it to be a Primary Key. (A Primary Key is a unique record identifier for a table.)

The second column is ready for you to assign it a field data type.

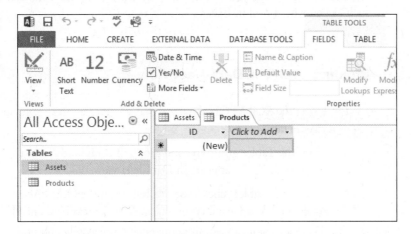

Adding fields to an Access table

There are multiple ways to add fields to a datasheet. One way is to assign the **data type** and then enter the name of the field. A field's data type determines the type of information that can be stored in that column of your table, and the type of information that *cannot* be stored in the column. For example, if you have a Funds field of data type Currency, you couldn't enter letters or characters such as A, B, C; you also could enter letters into a Birthday field with a Date/Time data type.

There are ten basic data types available in an Access table:

- **Short Text** (*formerly called* **Text**): alphanumeric data (names, titles, etc.). The maximum length allowed is 255 characters.

- **Long Text** (*formerly called* **Memo**): large amounts of alphanumeric data, for example, sentences and paragraphs. The maximum number of characters allowed is up to about 1 gigabyte (GB), but controls to display long text are limited to the first 64,000 characters.

- **Number:** numeric data.

- **Date/Time:** dates and times.

- **Currency:** monetary data, stored with four decimal places of precision.

- **AutoNumber:** unique value generated by Access for each new record; often a primary key field that Access automatically generates in new Access tables.

- **Yes/No:** Boolean (true/false) data. Access stores the numeric value zero (0) for false, and -1 for true.

- **OLE Object:** pictures, graphs, or other ActiveX objects from another Windows-based application.

- **Hyperlink:** a link address to a document or file on the Internet, on an intranet, on a local area network (LAN), or on your local computer.

- **Attachment:** files such as pictures, documents, spreadsheets, or charts that you can attach to a field. Each Attachment field can contain an unlimited number of attachments per record, up to the storage limit of the size of a database file.

- **Calculated:** an expression that uses data from one or more fields. You can designate different result data types from the expression. Dependent on the data type of the Result Type property. Short Text data type results can be up to 243 characters long. Long Text, Number, Yes/No, and Date/Time should match their respective data types.

- **Lookup Wizard:** the Lookup Wizard entry in the Data Type column in Design view is not actually a data type. When you choose this entry, a wizard starts to help you define either a simple or complex lookup field. A simple lookup field uses the contents of another table or a value list to validate the contents of a single value per row. A complex lookup field allows you to store multiple values of the same data type in each row. Dependent on the data type of the lookup field.

The most common data type is Short Text.

Data types can have some unexpected properties. For example, the Text field can contain numbers, and numbers can have a data type such as Text, Number, and Currency.

For this next exercise, you will add these three fields to the Products table you created in the previous exercise: Product Name, Product Number, and Order Date.

STEP BY STEP   **Adding fields to an Access table**

1. In the second column heading, click the **Click to Add** down-arrow, and then select *Short Text*. The words Click to Add are replaced with Field1.

2. Rename the heading Field1 by typing **Product Name**, and then press **Enter**.

3. Repeat steps 1 and 2 for the third column heading. Choose **Number** for the Data Type field and rename the heading to **Product Number**.

4. Repeat steps 1 and 2 for the fourth column heading. Choose **Date/Time** for the Data Type field and rename the heading to **Order Date**.

Figure 2-7

Creating a Date/Time field called Order Date in the Products Table.

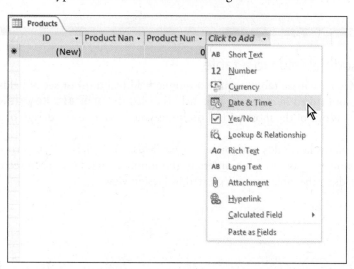

5. Save the Product table, but don't close it. You will use it in the next section.

Creating a table in Design view

You can use Design view to add tables and fields to your database. Design view offers more control over field structure and properties than Datasheet view. Design view is also well-suited for controlling field data types and descriptions.

When creating a table using Design view, you begin by creating the table structure in Design view; you then switch to Datasheet view to enter or import data.

STEP BY STEP   **Adding a table to a database using Design view**

1. Using the **SCRATCH** database you used in the previous exercises, click the Create tab, and then select the Table Design command from the Tables group.

The new table appears as a separate tab and is open in Design view. Look at the status bar at the bottom of the window. The words *Design View* appear on the left side of the status bar, and the Design View icon ( ) is active on the right side.

Figure 2-8

The Status bar shows the Design view icon. The new Table opens in Design View.

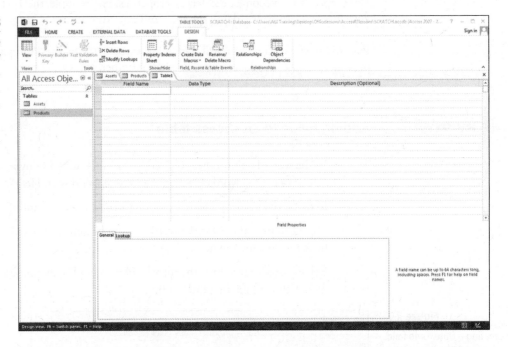

Adding fields to a table

Many database tables require a unique field (column) or set of fields that uniquely identify each record stored in the table. This field is called the **primary key field**. The selection of a primary key is one of the most critical decisions you'll make in the design of a new table.

Primary key fields cannot be memo fields, OLE fields. A primary key field is often a unique number or combination or letters and numbers that make each record unique. You will now add fields to the table you just created in Design view.

STEP BY STEP | **Adding fields to a table**

1   Add the following information in each of the columns:

FIELD NAME	DATA TYPE	DESCRIPTION
Vendor Number	Short Text	Vendor Identification Number
Vendor Address	Long Text	Vendor Address
Vendor Contact Name	Short Text	Contact Person's Phone Number
Current	Yes/No	Active Vendor

Figure 2-9

Creating a Yes/No field in Design View.

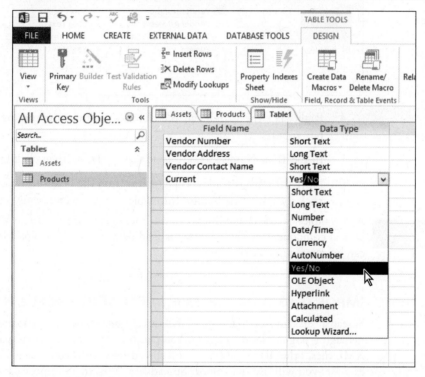

For many fields, a description might seem unnecessary, but you should enter a description for any field that might have an unclear name. The description appears in that table's status bar when the field is selected using Datasheet view; this is helpful to others when entering data.

2   From the Field Name column, select the Vendor Number cell.

3   From the Table Tools > Design context Ribbon tab, click the Primary Key button (). A small gold key appears to the left of the Vendor Number cell representing that this field has now become the primary key for this table. It will allow each row to be uniquely identified and assist in sorting, filtering, and table relationships.

Figure 2-10

Selecting the Primary Key.

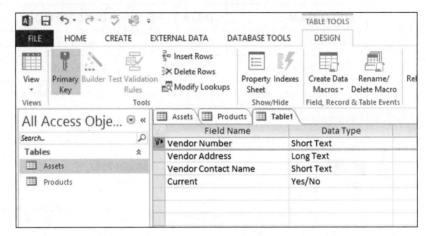

4   Right-click the Table1 tab and choose Save from the context menu. The Save As dialog box appears.

5   In the Table Name text box, type Vendor Info. Then click OK.

6   Now, the table is ready for data-entry from the Datasheet view. To change views, right-click the tab of the Vendor Info table and select Datasheet view from the context menu.

Bottom Line

Access tables can be create in two views. These views are the Table View and the Design View. A critical component in Table Design is field data types. Data types determine what types of data can be entered into Access tables.

IMPORTING DATA FROM A MICROSOFT EXCEL SPREADSHEET

Spreadsheets can store data, but databases are more powerful, expandable, and often easier when managing large amounts of data. You can import data from external sources, such as text files, XML files, other database types, and spreadsheets into your Access 2013 databases. In this next exercise, you will use the Import Spreadsheet Wizard to import data from an Excel spreadsheet into your table.

Workplace Ready

Many businesses utilize Microsoft Excel spreadsheets to track business information. As time passes, they realize they need more tools for reporting and tracking information and Access provides that tools. Importing Excel spreadsheet into Access is an easy process and allows Excel information to be made into an Access database.

STEP BY STEP   **Importing data from a Microsoft Excel spreadsheet**

1   Open the program Microsoft Excel and choose File > Open. Navigate to the Access02lessons folder and double-click Orders to open the spreadsheet.

When the Orders spreadsheet opens in Microsoft Excel, notice that each column has a column heading (name) and that each row underneath is continual with no blank rows between.

This spreadsheets looks very much like an Access table. When the spreadsheet is formatted like this, it makes it easy to import it into Access as table.

2   Switch back to Access where your **SCRATCH** database is still active by clicking the Access icon found on the Task bar along the bottom of your screen.

3   In Access, select the External Data tab. From the Import & Link group, click Excel.

4   In the Get External Data window, click Browse, navigate to the **Orders** Excel file in the Access02lessons folder, and select it. Click Open. The path and file name of the **Orders** Excel file appears in the File name text field.

5   The option Import the source data into a new table in the current database is selected by default. Don't change this selection.

6   Click OK. The Import Spreadsheet Wizard opens. Click Next; the first row of your Excel spreadsheet already contains column headings.

7   Click Finish, and then click Close.

8   In the Navigation pane, double-click the new table called **Sheet1** to open it and see the imported data.

Figure 2-11

The data has been imported from the Excel spreadsheet into your Access table.

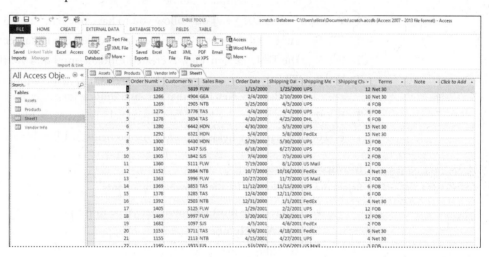

TO RENAME A NEW SHEET

STEP BY STEP	**Renaming a new sheet**

1   Right-click the Sheet1 table Tab, and select Close from the context menu.

2   In the Navigation pane, right-click the Sheet1 Table. A context menu appears.

3   From the context menu, choose Rename. The Sheet1 name appears highlighted.

4   Type Orders to replace the highlighted text, and then press Enter.

Take Note Data can be imported into Access from various program including Microsoft Excel. The Spreadsheet Import Wizard is a tool designed specifically for this purpose.

What you learned in this lesson:

• Access 2013 database types

• Tables, views, and data types

• Importing data from a Microsoft Excel spreadsheet

• Renaming a New Table from an Excel spreadsheet

Knowledge Assessment

True/ False

Circle T if the statement is true or F it the statement is false.

T F 1. Microsoft Access 2013 provides users with three types of databases: desktop, web app, and mobile.

T F 2. There are two methods for creating a new database: creating an empty database from scratch or creating a database based on a template.

T F 3. It is very common to Access users to work in existing databases by updating data, creating new objects, and entering new data into the existing database.

T F 4. When creating a database based on a template, it isn't necessary to provide a file name before the template can be used.

T F 5. Access 2013 will only allow you to have one database open at a time.

T F 6. Access tables have two views that are called the Datasheet View and the Design View.

T F 7. The Table Design View is created for data-entry and viewing records.

T F 8. When you create a new table in Access, the first column in the table is called ID and is a Primary Key field that acts as a unique identifier for information in the table.

T F 9. There are twelve basic data types (field types) available in Access tables.

T F 10. Primary key fields cannot be memo fields, OLE fields, or Memo fields.

Multiple Choice

Select the best response for the following statements.

1. What is the most common data type in Access?
   a. AutoNumber
   b. Short Text
   c. Date/Time
   d. Currency

2. Why is the data type of a field so critical to a table's design?
   a. Data type will determine the type of information that can be stored or not stored in that field (column) of your Access table.
   b. Data type's password protect specific table fields, and only those with the password can enter data into those columns.
   c. Data type is only critical if the table is being imported from another program like Excel.
   d. Data types determine how many records an Access table can hold.

3. An AutoNumber data type is created by Access and has what specific characteristics?
   a. AutoNumber fields can only hold text.
   b. AutoNumber fields must be blank.
   c. AutoNumber fields contain a unique value and often act as a primary key.
   d. AutoNumber fields allow users to link images to their Access tables.

4. When importing spreadsheet information from Excel into access, what tool is used?
   a. The Table Wizard
   b. The Query Wizard
   c. The Table Design Wizard
   d. The Import Spreadsheet Wizard

5. You can easily rename a table in Access by:
   a. Closing the table and opening it again in Design View
   b. Closing the table, right-clicking on it in the Navigation Pane, and selecting Rename
   c. Creating a query with the new table name
   d. Printing all the records in the table

6. What makes the web app database type different from the desktop database type?
   a. The Web app database can be used and shared with others as a SharePoint app in a web browser; while a desktop database will only work if the user has Access installed on their computer.
   b. The web app database will only run on a computer with an Apple operating system, and the desktop database will only run on a computer with a windows operating system.
   c. The web app will only run in Internet Explorer and the desktop database type will only open databases in Firefox.
   d. None of the Above.

7. From the Access Datasheet view, you can:
   a. Set specific properties on your table data types
   b. control how many records are entered into your table
   c. Create new data types
   d. add, delete, edit, sort, filter, and print table records

8. How many characters can a Short Text field hold?
   a. 105
   b. 255
   c. 305
   d. 105

9. If you need to create a field to hold monetary information, what should the data type be?
   a. Date/Time
   b. Yes/No
   c. Currency
   d. AutoNumber

10. When creating a table in Design view, you first focus on:
    a. Creating the table's design, data types, and properties
    b. Entering data
    c. Printing data
    d. Creating new database objects

Project 2-1: Creating a new table in Design view

You will open the Northwind Traders Tables database and create a new table in the Design view and set table properties in the table.

1. Click **File**. From the Backstage view, click Open and navigate to your student drive.
2. Open the file **Northwind Traders Tables**. Save the file as **Project2-1_done**.
3. Click the Create Ribbon tab. From the Tables group, click Table Design.
4. Your new blank table will open in the Table Design view.
5. Your cursor will be blinking in the Field Name column. Type Manager Name in the Field Name text field.
6. In the Data Type column, type Short Text.
7. In the Description column, type Full Manager Name.
8. From the following table, enter the following field names:

Field Name	Data Type	Description
Department	Short Text	Department Name
Department Description	Long Text	Department Description
Department Code	Number	Department Numeric Code

Right-click on the new table tab and choose Datasheet view.

9. Name the new table, Managers. Don't set a primary key, when it prompts to do this.
10. Close the database.

Project 2-2: Editing a table in Datasheet view

Edit an existing table in the Datasheet view by editing data types and also inserting some new columns into the table.

1. From Open in the Backstage view, navigate to the Acces02lessons folder and open the **Northwind Traders Tables** database. Save the file as **Project2-2_done**. From the Navigation pane, open the Customers table in the Datasheet view.
2. Right-click on the Customers table tab and click Design view.
3. In the Description field, for Customer Number, add the following, Each Number should contain the prefix CU#.
4. Scroll down in the field names list and under the last field, Contract Date, add an Email field.
5. Set the data type to Hyperlink.
6. Close the database.

Project 2-3: Creating a new database from a template

You will create a new database based on a template from the Business category of Microsoft Access templates.

1. From the File Ribbon tab, select New.
2. Under New, search the Business category of templates.
3. Select the Desktop customer service template.
4. Name the template, Northwind Traders Customer Service.
5. Make sure the Navigation pane is open and is sorted by Object Type.
6. Open the Customers table.
7. Enter three new records into the Customers table.
8. Switch and view the table in the Design View.
9. Close the database.

Project 2-4: Importing Excel data into a database

You need to open an existing database and import some data from an Excel spreadsheet into the database.

1. From the Access02lessons folder, open the file, **Northwind Traders Import**.
2. From the lesson folder, open the Excel file, **Northwind Traders Employee List**. Take a look at the information in this spreadsheet. It contains an employee list that you want to be part of your Northwind Traders Import database. You will import this spreadsheet into the Northwind Traders Import database. Close Excel.
3. Return to Access and click the External Data Ribbon tab.
4. In the Import & Link group, click Excel. The Get External Data dialog box will open.
5. Browse to the lesson folder and select the Northwind Traders Employee List. Keep the top option, Import the source data into a new table in the current database, selected. Click OK.
6. The Import Spreadsheet Wizard will open.
7. Click Finish and Close in the Import Spreadsheet Wizard.
8. Open the new table. It will be called Employees.
9. Close the database.

Project 2-5: Choosing an appropriate template for a project

Your company needs an inventory tracking database. You will find a template to create the database from and create a new table in the database with specific fields.

1. Create a new database based on the template, Desktop Product Inventory. Name the new database Northwind Traders Inventory.

2. Create a new table in the database with the following Fields and data types:

Field Name	Data Type
Inventory Number	Number
Inventory Category	Short Text
Inventory Description	Long Text
Date Established	Date/Time
Currently in Stock	Yes/No

3. Enter three records of your choice into the table.

Project 2-6: Importing and editing Excel data in a database

You need to import an Excel spreadsheet into an existing database and also edit the data once it is imported into Access.

1. From the Access02lessons folder, open the file, **Northwind Traders Fields**. Save the database as **Project2-6_done**.

2. Using the External Data Ribbon tab, import the spreadsheet titled, **Northwind Traders Quarterly Sales** into your database. You will need to import the data from the sheet titled, Qtr 1.

3. After the Qtr 1 sheet data is imported into Access, open the new table and delete the heading rows containing the spreadsheet's titles, rename the fields (columns), and set some data types where appropriate in the Access table.

4. Close the table and database.

Microsoft Publisher 2013

1 Introduction to Microsoft Publisher 2013

LESSON SKILL MATRIX

In this lesson, you will learn the following skills:

What is Publisher

Publisher Basics

Quick Tour of Publisher 2013

Customizing the Quick Access Toolbar

Getting Help

KEY TERMS

- **word processor**
- **template**
- **publication**

 Christoff works for a small non-profit company. His company has recently completed some very successful projects and wants to start sharing some of their new successes with customers. To do this, Christoff would like to create a monthly newsletter letter in Microsoft Publisher highlighting upcoming customer events and successful projects that the company has recently completed.

SOFTWARE ORIENTATION

This lesson provides an overview of the capabilities of Microsoft Publisher 2013.

Figure 1-1

Microsoft Publisher interface

Image used with permission of Microsoft

STARTING UP

In this lesson, you'll work with several files from the Pub01lessons folder. Make sure that you have loaded the OfficeLessons folder onto your computer.

WHAT IS PUBLISHER?

Publisher is an application that helps you create professional-looking publications quickly and easily. It is available in certain editions of Microsoft Office and can also be purchased separately.

 # Workplace **Ready**

Microsoft Publisher is a desktop publishing program that contains all the tools necessary to create professional publications like newsletters, flyers, invitations, certificates, brochures, and even full-length magazines.

Publisher combines the power of a **word processor** and the creativity of a graphics application into one flexible and easy-to-use tool for creating newsletters, brochures, letterheads, and business cards without having to study for a degree in graphic design.

Ways to use Publisher

You can use Publisher to create, design, and edit publications. You can use Publisher for tasks such as:

• Create **publications**, from your own designs or included templates

• Enter and edit text or import text from other documents such as Microsoft Word

• Add pictures, place them precisely, and crop them to the size you want

• Create and use Building Blocks, which are reusable pieces of content

• Print your document to a local printer, or prepare it for e-mail distribution

PUBLISHER BASICS

Publisher 2013 allows you to create a publication from a template or from scratch.

A **template** is a document with preset formatting and placeholder text that makes it easy to see what information to enter in the placeholder area. Publisher 2013 gives you access to 600 installed templates organized in different categories, including advertisements, greeting cards, labels, and invitations. After you select a template, you can modify the layout and select options in the right pane to help you customize the page.

If you can't find a suitable template among those provided, you can also download additional templates from *Office.com*. You can also create your own publications for specific jobs such as a flyer for a special event, a fundraiser, or even creating your own personal stationery. In addition to creating publications for print, you can also create them for use on the Web or in e-mail.

Quick tour of Publisher 2013

Understanding the components of Publisher helps you to use it more effectively. You'll start by taking a quick tour of the Publisher interface.

   Backstage view of Publisher 2013

1   Choose Start > Programs > Microsoft Office > Microsoft Publisher 2013.

Figure 1-2

Backstage view of Publisher 2013.

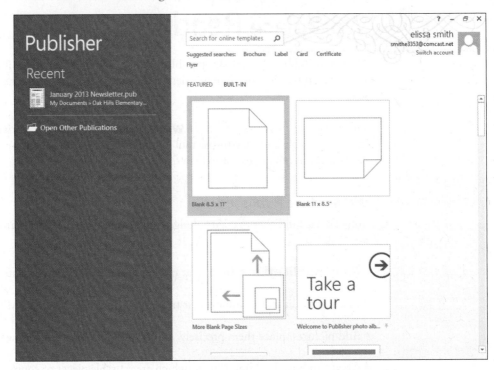

Publisher 2013 opens in Backstage view, where you can create a new publication, open an existing publication, and view featured content from *Office.com*. Backstage view is described in more detail in the next section.

You can always access Backstage view (Figure 1-2), even when working on a publication, by clicking the File tab.

Publisher 2013 components

To find your way around Publisher 2013, you'll want to understand these main components of its interface:

Like other Office products, the Ribbon tabs in Publisher can be minimized by double-clicking on their tabbed headings to allow for more room to see the actual file being worked on.

- **The Ribbon**: This bar across the top of the interface contains 7 default tabs. These tabs contain groups of commands, which are visible on all tabs except File.

- **Backstage view**: This view, which appears by default when you launch Publisher 2013, displays a group of vertically placed commands on the Ribbon's File tab.

Take Note   The File tab always has a colored background, even when it is not the active tab. You can identify the active tab by the borders on either side of it.

• **The Navigation pane**: The area on the left side of the interface, shown in Figure 1-3, displays pages when a publication is open, or vertical command options in Backstage view.

Figure 1-3

An open publication, showing the Navigation pane on the left side.

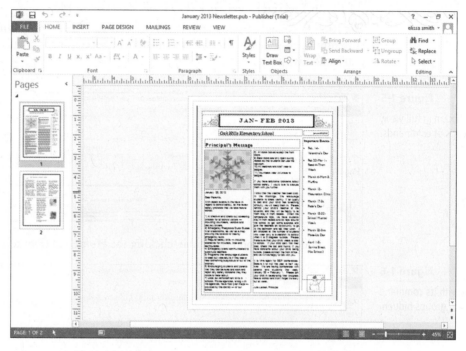

Image used with permission of Microsoft

Before you start working in Publisher, it's important you examine its components in more detail.

The Ribbon

The Ribbon is divided into tabs, and each tab contains groups of commands. The Ribbon replaces menus that exist across the top of the screen in many other apps, as well as toolbars as displayed in Figure 1-4. The primary tabs of Publisher 2013 are File, Home, Insert, Page Design, Mailings, Review, and View.

Figure 1-4

The Publisher 2013 Ribbon is divided into tabs.

The Ribbon's appearance changes depending on the task you are performing in your document. Some tabs, such as the Format tab, only appear in certain contexts. These are called Context Ribbon tabs. For example, when a publication is open in Publisher 2013 and a text box is drawn on the page, the Ribbon displays two new context tabs called Drawing Tools Format and Textbox Tool Format. Both these new ribbon tabs are made for formatting the text in the text box and formatting the text box itself. They will turn off as soon the text box is no longer selected.

You can hide the buttons on the Ribbon tabs and show them again by double-clicking the active command tab. This makes it easy to maximize your workspace as needed so you can see more of the document on which you are working.

STEP BY STEP   **Hiding and showing the Ribbon**

1   In Backstage view, click the Home tab (Figure 1-5).

The Ribbon changes from a simple row of tabs to a group of commands. If no documents are currently open or your document is blank, these commands will appear inactive because no publication is open.

Figure 1-5

The Ribbon in full view, showing groups of commands.

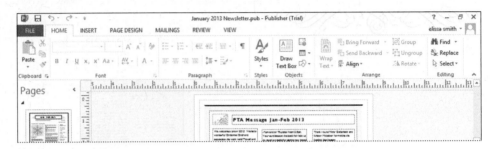

2   Hide the Ribbon by double-clicking the Home tab (Figure 1-6).

Figure 1-6

The Ribbon with its command groups hidden.

3   Show the Ribbon by clicking the Home tab again.

You have successfully toggled the Ribbon by clicking the active tab. You can also toggle the Ribbon by clicking the Minimize/Expand arrow button in the upper-right corner.

Backstage view

When you launch Publisher 2013 you are presented with the Backstage view, as shown in Figure 1-7. This contains information and commands that affect an entire publication. These commands include information about the document you have open:

• **New** for opening new blank documents and templates

• **Save** and **Save As** for saving files

• **Print** for printing files and viewing them in print preview

• **Share** for sharing files through e-mail

• **Export** for exporting publisher files in different formats

• **Close** for closing the current file open in publisher

• **Account** (new to 2013) for viewing information about the office user and version of Microsoft Office

• **Options** for changing defaults and settings in the software.

Figure 1-7

Publisher 2013 Backstage
view.

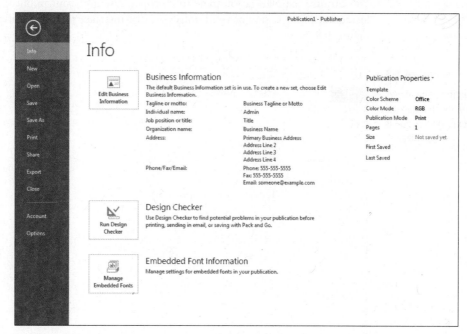

Publisher Options in Backstage view

You can use the Publisher Options command, located on the bottom of the Backstage view, to customize and make changes to the Publisher software. The tabs are located on the left side of the box and run down vertically. When a different tab is clicked, the middle of the box changes. The tabs include the following categories: General; Proofing; Save; Language; Customize Ribbon; Quick Access Toolbar; Add-Ins; and Trust Center.

Navigation pane

You can use the Navigation pane to view pages within your publication and manage them. It is located on the left side of the Publisher 2013 interface when a publication is open, as shown in Figure 1-8.

Figure 1-8

The Navigation pane allows you to view and manage the publication's pages, and is customizable.

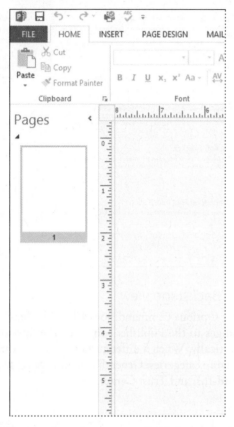

Bottom Line

Bottom Line Summaries: Publisher contains many of the same interface features as other Office products. These include the Ribbon tabs and updated Backstage view. Publisher's Navigation Pane allows for easy navigation between different pages in longer publications

Opening a publication

Now that you're more familiar with the interface, you'll examine a sample publication and perform some simple tasks in Publisher.

STEP BY STEP   **Opening a template**

1   If you are not already in the Backstage view, click the File tab. Click New.

2   Choose Flyer from the list of Suggested searches.

3   Click Event from the Category list (Figure 1-9) and then choose Event invitation flyer.

Figure 1-9

Open an existing publication using File > New.

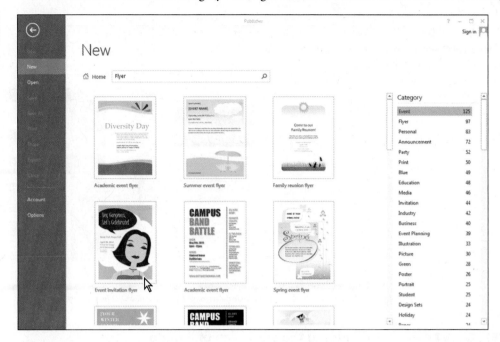

Image used with permission of Microsoft

4   An informational box about the selected template will appear. Click the Create button in the bottom middle of the box.

A new publisher document based on the selected template appears in the Publisher window.

5   Click File > Close to close this file. Do not save it.

STEP BY STEP   **Opening an existing publication**

1   In Backstage view, click Open.

2   Browse to the Pub01lessons folder and double-click **NorthWindNewsletter**.

Changing your view

You can view the pages in your publication in a one-page or a two-page spread, as long as the document is at least two pages in length. A two-page spread mimics the way a publication looks lying open in front of you, with two pages facing each other, such as the left and right pages in a magazine.

STEP BY STEP   **Viewing a publication in multiple views**

1   Click the View tab.

2   In the Layout group, click the Two-Page Spread button or the Single Page button.

The selected view displays (Figure 1-10), and the button you clicked is now selected.

Figure 1-10

Click the Single Page or Two-Page Spread button on the status bar.

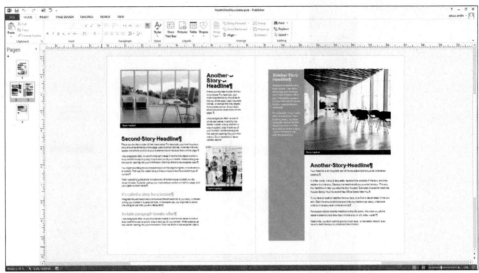

© Auris/iStockphoto; © Image Source/Getty Images; © Martin Barraud/OJO Images/Getty Images

STEP BY STEP   **Changing the view size of a page**

1   Click the View tab.

2   To select standard view sizes, in the Zoom group click any of the following buttons: 100%, Whole Page, Page Width, or Selected Objects.

Press F9 to toggle between current and 100% views.

3   To specify a custom view size, click the Zoom list arrow, and then select a view percentage (Figure 1-11).

Figure 1-11

Choose a custom view size from the Zoom list.

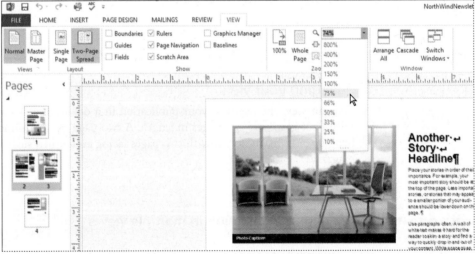

© Auris/iStockphoto

Click the Zoom In or Zoom Out button or drag the Zoom slider on the status bar to change the view magnification.

Saving a publication

By default, Publisher saves the files you create in a working folder. You can also specify a different location for saving files, like SkyDrive, so you can access them from any computer connected to the Internet.

STEP BY STEP   **Saving a publication**

1   Choose File > Save As.

2   Navigate to the Pub02lessons folder and name the file **NorthWindNewsletter_work**.

3   Click Save.

CUSTOMIZING THE QUICK ACCESS TOOLBAR

Use the Quick Access Toolbar for convenient, one-click access to your favorite tools. By default, the Quick Access Toolbar toolbar displays the Save, Redo, and Undo buttons, and the Customize Quick Access Toolbar button as shown in Figure 1-12.

Now you will customize the toolbar to include the Quick Print and Spell Check buttons. If you have completed previous lessons in this book, you will already be familiar with this process.

Figure 1-12

The Quick Access Toolbar.To customize the Quick Access Toolbar:

STEP BY STEP   **Customizing the Quick Access Toolbar**

1   Make sure you are not in the Backstage view; you can't see the Quick Access Toolbar from this view. Click the Customize Quick Access Toolbar button (■).

2   In the drop-down menu, click Quick Print.

3   Click the Customize Quick Access Toolbar button, again.

4   In the drop-down menu, click Spelling.

The Quick Access Toolbar as displayed in Figure 1-13, now contains the Quick Print and Print Preview buttons.

Figure 1-13

The new commands are now added to the Quick Access Toolbar.

5   To remove a button, right-click it, and click Remove from Quick Access Toolbar.

Getting help

If you run into a problem or aren't sure how to perform a certain task, you can easily get help in Publisher by doing one of the following:

STEP BY STEP   **Using the Help feature**

1   Press the F1 on the top of your computer's keyboard The Help window will appear (Figure 1-14).

2   Click the **Help** button, a small question mark located in the top right corner of the Publisher window.

Figure 1-14

Get help by pressing F1 or clicking the Help button located in the upper right corner of the window, next to the Minimize button.

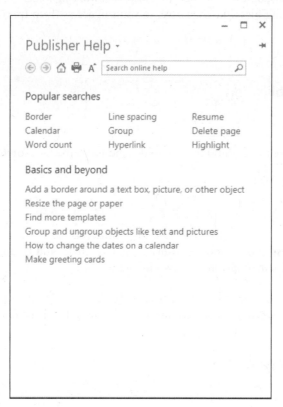

Closing a Publisher session

When you're finished exploring Publisher, save your file and close the program using these steps:

STEP BY STEP   **Closing a session**

1   Click **Save** (⊟) on the Quick Access Toolbar.

2   Click the **Close** button located in the upper-right corner of the Publisher window.

Bottom Line

Many important file management activities in Publisher are managed from the Backstage view. From Backstage view, publications can be saved, closed, and printed. For customizing the view of publications and also the Publisher window, users can utilize tools available on the View Ribbon tab.

What you learned in this lesson:

• What is Publisher

• Publisher Basics

• Quick Tour of Publisher 2013

• Customizing the Quick Access Toolbar

• Getting Help

Knowledge Assessment

True/ False

Circle T if the statement is true or F it the statement is false.

T F 1. Microsoft Publisher 2013 is a spreadsheet program.

T F 2. There are over 200 Publisher templates available from the Office.com website.

T F 3. Documents created in Publisher are often called Publications.

T F 4. When Publisher is first opened, users are taken the Backstage view of Publisher to open a new or existing publication.

T F 5. The Publisher Navigation Pane allows users to navigate between rows in a spreadsheet.

T F 6. If you want to view more than one page of your publication at a time in Publisher, you can use the Two-Page Spread button on the View Ribbon tab.

T F 7. When saving a publication, users need to use Save on the Home Ribbon tab.

T F 8. Publications contain place holders where video files can be entered into a publication.

T F 9. The Help system in Publisher is set-up to run like an internet browser.

T F 10. Users can only add ten different buttons to the Quick Access toolbar.

Multiple Choice

Select the best response for the following statements.

1. What is a word processing program?
   a. a spreadsheet program
   b. a database
   c. a program made for editing and entering text
   d. presentation program

2. Publisher is a desktop publishing program that allows for:
   a. text and graphics to be placed side by side in a publication
   b. data to be stored in a table format
   c. slides to be created for a presentation
   d. charts to be made

3. What are some of the templates categories available in Microsoft Publisher?
   a. Spreadsheets
   b. Slide shows and charts
   c. Queries and macros
   d. Flyers and brochures

4. To get to the Backstage view in Publisher, users click on the:
   a. View Ribbon
   b. File Ribbon
   c. Page Design Ribbon
   d. Review Ribbon

5. In publications with more than one page, what allows for easy movement between pages?
   a. The Quick Access Toolbar
   b. The Home Ribbon tab
   c. The Navigation Pane
   d. The Backstage View

6. To turn the Rulers in the Publisher window on and off, you must use:
   a. Uncheck the Rulers button in the Show group of the View Ribbon tab
   b. Copy on the Home Ribbon
   c. the Rulers under the Backstage view
   d. Hit the F1 key on the Keyboard

7. When you click on text in a Publisher document it is often surrounded by a dashed border. This is called:
   a. A graphic
   b. A place holder
   c. A print dialog box
   d. A text table

8. The Navigation Pane can be minimized by:
   a. Clicking on the Close button
   b. Clicking on the Home Ribbon
   c. Clicking on the Collapse Page Navigation Pane button
   d. All of the above

9. What are the three default buttons available on the Publisher Quick Access Toolbar?
   a. Save, Print, and Copy
   b. Save, Undo, and Redo
   c. Spell Check, Print, and Close
   d. Cut, Copy, Paste

10. If a Publisher publication isn't saved before it is closed, information in the publication will be:
   a. Saved anyway
   b. Saved in a Word document
   c. Lost
   d. None of the above

Competency Assessment

Project 1-1: Creating a document based on a template.

Create an Event Flyer based on one of the Microsoft Publisher templates.

1. Click File and select Open in the Backstage view.
2. Under the template categories, click Flyer.
3. Click the Event invitation flyer with tear-off tabs template and then click Create.
4. Click the View Ribbon tab.
5. In the Zoom group, click the 100% button to zoom in on the document.
6. Click in the Title Text place holder, Hey Gorgeous, Let's Celebrate.
7. Select the text by dragging over it.
8. Type: You're Invited!
9. Click the File Ribbon tab to enter the Backstage view.
10. Click Save.
11. Save the flyer in the lesson folder with the name, My Event.

Project 1-2: **Opening and editing an existing file.**

Open and edit an existing brochure in Publisher.

1. Click File and then click Open.
2. Under Open, select Computer and navigate to the Pub01lessons folder.
3. Open the file, **Northwind Traders Brochure**.
3. In the Navigation Pane, navigate to the fourth page of the brochure.
4. Click the Collapse Page Navigation Pane button and minimize the Navigation Pane.
5. Open the Navigation Pane up again.
6. Click the View Ribbon tab.
7. In the Layout group, select Two-Page Spread
8. Click File and Close to close the publication.

Proficiency Assessment

Project 1-3: **Creating a newsletter based on a template.**

Create a new newsletter based on one of the templates in Microsoft Publisher.

1. From the File Ribbon tab, select New.
2. In the template search box, type Newsletters.
3. Click the Business Newsletter and then click Create.
4. Click the File Ribbon tab and select Save.
5. Navigate to the Pub01lessons folder and save the Newsletter as, **Northwind Traders Business Newsletter**.
6. On Page 1 of the newsletter, click on the placeholder for the text, Trader News.
7. Select the Text and type in its place, Northwind Traders.
8. Close the Newsletter.

Project 1-4: **Creating a new publication.**

Create a new blank publication and enter text into it.

1. From the Backstage view, select New.
2. Click Blank, 8.5 X 11 and the new blank page will open.
3. Click File and then choose Save.
4. Navigate to the Pub01lessons folder and save the new blank document as **Standard Size**.
5. Click the Page Design Ribbon tab.
6. In the Page Set-Up group, click Margins.
7. Click Moderate under the Margin menu and change the margins to .5 inches on all four sides.
8. Close the document.

Project 1-5: Selecting and using an existing template.

Your company needs to create an event flyer for a summer company barbeque. Use a Publisher template to create the flyer.

1. Create a flyer for the company summer barbeque using one of the Publisher templates. You can select the flyer of your choice.
2. Save the flyer and name it Summer Company Party.
3. Enter text in the placeholders of your choice to complete the flyer.
4. Close the flyer.

Project 1-6: Editing an existing document.

Editing a Thank you note in Publisher.

1. From the Pub01lessons folder, open the file, **Northwind Traders Thank you**.
2. Enter your own address or an address of your choice on the second page.
3. Under the Backstage view, go into the Print Preview and view the document.
4. Close the Publication.

LESSON SKILL MATRIX

In this lesson, you will learn the following skills:

Creating a blank publication	Inserting a text box
Formatting text	Inserting and modifying images
Printing your publication	Using Pack and Go
Sending a publication using e-mail	

KEY TERMS

- **Thumbnails**
- **Page orientation**
- **Text box**
- **Images**

Muong works for a small marketing company and needs to develop a brochure regarding an upcoming conference her company is hosting for a client. The brochure needs to contain customized graphics and text. Muong only has a few days to complete the brochure and get it printed at a local shop.

SOFTWARE ORIENTATION

This lesson gets you started creating and distributing publications using Microsoft Publisher 2013.

Figure 2-1

Page Design
workspace.

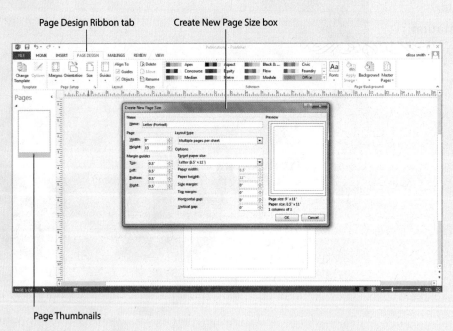

Page Design Ribbon tab   Create New Page Size box

Page Thumbnails

STARTING UP

In this lesson, you'll work with several files from the Pub02lessons folder. Make sure that you have loaded the OfficeLessons folder onto your computer.

CREATING A BLANK PUBLICATION

Bottom Line

In Lesson 1, you saw how Publisher's preset design templates can help you create a new publication. In this lesson, you'll explore how to create a new blank publication, for those times when the provided templates don't meet your needs.

STEP BY STEP	Creating a blank publication

1   Choose Start > Programs > Microsoft Office 2013 > Microsoft Publisher 2013.

2   Click the File tab, if you are not already in Backstage view, and then click New. If you are in the Recent section, choose Open Publications and then click New.

3   Click More Blank Page Sizes, and then Create New Page Size, under the Custom heading, to define a new size for your document.

Take Note   You can click Blank 8.5″ × 11″ or Blank 11″ × 8.5″ to quickly create a standard letter-sized blank publication, or choose from a selection of standard page sizes by clicking More Blank Page Sizes.

4   In the Create New Page Size dialog box, name your document Newsletter. Then set the width to 9 inches and height to 12 inches, respectively. Leave the margins at their defaults, and click OK.

Figure 2-2

Define a new publication size.

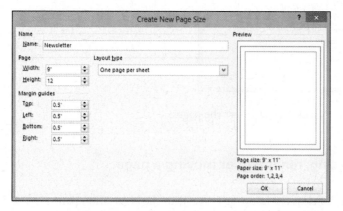

5   In the Customize section located on the right side of the screen, click the Color Scheme down arrow, and choose the Civic scheme. Then click the Font Scheme down arrow, and choose the Equity scheme.

6   Click the Create New down arrow under Business Information, select Create new.

7   Type your name, job position, and contact information in the provided fields. Click Save to attach this information to your file.

8   Click Create to accept the settings for your new blank publication.

9   On the Quick Access Toolbar, click the Save button (◼). In the dialog box that appears, navigate to the Pub02lessons folder, name the file Newsletter, and click Save.

Working with pages

The **thumbnails** in the Navigation pane correspond to pages in your publication. You just created a one-page document, but if you find it necessary to add or delete pages, you can do so one page or one spread at a time.

Take Note   If you're working on a publication with multiple pages, you'll want to display the page before or after the one you want to insert. You'll be choosing whether to add a page before or after the current page.

STEP BY STEP   **Inserting one or more pages**

1   Click the Insert tab, and then click the Page drop-down arrow in the Pages group, located on the far left side of the ribbon. Choose Insert Page from the menu that appears, third option down.

Take Note   To insert a single blank page, choose Insert Blank Page. To insert a duplicate page, choose Insert Duplicate Page.

2   In the Insert Page dialog box, change the settings so that you're inserting three new blank pages after the current page, as shown in Figure 2-3.

Figure 2-3

Insert new blank pages into your publication.

3   Click OK to insert the pages.

STEP BY STEP   **Deleting, renaming or moving a page**

1   Select the last page (page 4) in the Navigation pane.

2   Click the Page Design tab. On the Pages group, fourth group from the left, click the Delete button. This will remove page 4 from your publication. This may not be obvious because the current document only contains blank pages. However, the changes will show in the Navigation pane.

3   On the same Ribbon tab and in the same group, click the Move button. In the Move selected pages section of the Move Page dialog box, click the After option button. Choose Page 1, from the This page list, and click OK to move page 3 to a position after page 1.

Take Note   You can also drag a page icon in the Navigation pane to move it.

4   On the Page Design tab in the Pages group (Figure 2-4), click the Rename button, and in the Rename Page dialog box, rename Page Title to Page 2. Click OK.

Figure 2-4

Use the Page Design tab to delete, rename, or move pages.

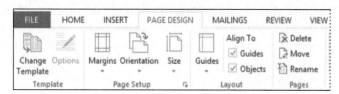

You won't see the new name for this page listed anywhere visibly in the Publisher window. However, renaming a page can be important, especially if you deleted a page and replaced it with a new page or an existing page. The replacement page will not rename automatically. You have to click the rename button and rename it yourself.

STEP BY STEP   **Setting page margins**

The blue rectangle that appears within the boundaries of your page represents the page's margins. Publisher automatically sets the margins to one-half inch when you create a new document, but if you need to adjust the margin size, you can choose from several options in the Margins area of the Page Design tab.

To quickly adjust the margins of the document:

1   On the Page Design tab in the Page Setup group, click the Margins button drop-down arrow, as displayed in Figure 2-5.

Figure 2-5

Use page margins to guide you.

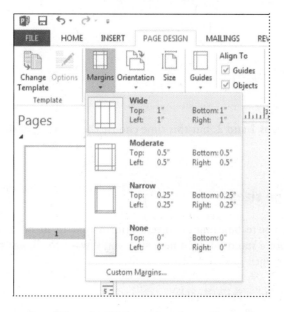

2   Select the Wide option that will set all margins (top, bottom, left, and right) to one inch.

Take Note   The margins are only for guidance. It is possible to place text, graphics, and other objects outside the document margins in Publisher.

STEP BY STEP   **Changing page orientation**

There are times when the **page orientation** of a document needs to be changed. you may want to switch the page orientation. So far, this blank document has been in a portrait format, but you can easily switch to landscape format and then back to portrait, if needed.

1   Click the Page Design tab.

2   Click the Orientation button in the Page Setup group to reveal the options.

3   Choose the Landscape option to change the layout.

Figure 2-6

Change your page orientation to Landscape.

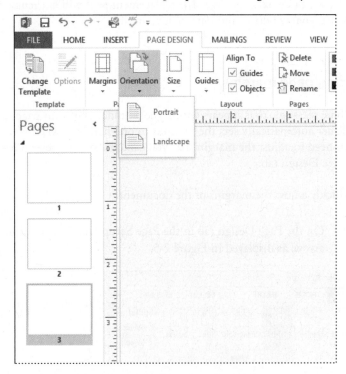

4   Repeat steps 1 and 2, but this time choose the Portrait option to return to the portrait orientation.

STEP BY STEP   **Changing page sizes**

The publication you're building is currently formatted to fit on a 9 x 12-inch sheet of paper. Because this is not a standard document size, you'll want to change the size to Letter before you begin adding content.

1   Click the Page Design tab.

2   Click the Size button, found in the Page Setup group (Figure 2-7).

3   Choose Letter (Portrait) from the Size menu to change the size of the current publication to that of a standard Letter. Choose Wide from the Margins button drop-down menu to set the margins back to 1".

Figure 2-7

Change your page size to Letter.

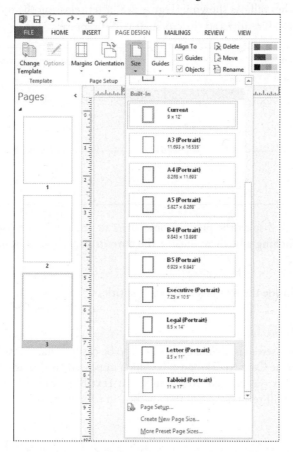

Take Note   Publisher does not allow you to mix page sizes and orientations within a single document. If you must use multiple page sizes or orientations, you will have to create separate documents.

Now that you have set up your publication's pages, margins, orientation, and size, you'll begin to add content to it.

INSERTING A TEXT BOX

Bottom Line   Any text that you add to a Publisher document must be contained in a **text box**. To add a title to your newsletter, you'll first insert a text box and then enter your text inside the box.

If your text doesn't fit inside a text box, you can do one of the following:

• Make the text box bigger

• Reduce the size of the text

• Continue the text in another text box on the same page or on another page

STEP BY STEP   Inserting a text box

1   Select the first page from the Navigation pane on the left of the screen. Click the Insert tab on the Ribbon, and in the Text group located third group in from the right, click the Draw Text Box button.

2 The mouse pointer turned into a set of intersecting black lines called a crosshair. In your publication, move your cursor over the intersection of the left and top margins, and click and drag diagonally until you have a text box that stretches to the right margin and is 2½ inches tall. As shown in Figure 2-8, after releasing the mouse button, the mouse pointer will return and the crosshair will disappear.

Figure 2-8

Draw a text box to hold your newsletter's title.

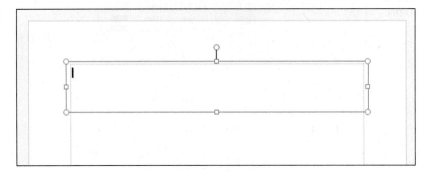

Take Note   You may have to display the publication's rulers to accurately measure the text box's height. Do this by right-clicking anywhere outside the current page, and choosing Rulers from the context menu that appears.

3 Click inside the text box and type the title, Bike Hikes.

Bottom Line

FORMATTING TEXT

The text you've inserted is obviously too small to be easily seen. This will be fixed by using the Text Box Tools Format Context Ribbon tab, which appeared to the right of the existing ribbon tabs when the text box was created. Remember, the Text Box Tools tab will disappear if you deselect the text box. It will reappear when the text box in selected again.

STEP BY STEP   **Formatting text**

1 Select the title by clicking and dragging over it inside the text box.

2 Click the Text Box Tools Format tab, and in the Font section, choose Franklin Gothic Book from the Font drop-down menu.

3 Also in the Font section, use the Font Size drop-down menu to change the size to 72 points.

4 Click the Bold button to make the title more visible, and the Italic button to give it more style.

5 Add some color to the title by clicking the Font Color drop-down menu, and selecting Accent 3 from the scheme colors chosen earlier in this lesson (Figure 2-9). Click outside the text box to de-select the title.

Figure 2-9

Format your text using options in the Font section of the toolbar.

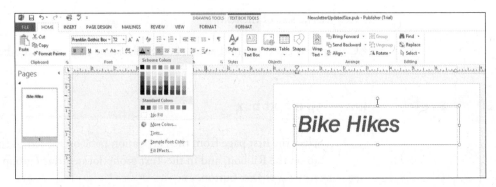

6   Choose **File** > **Save As** and in the dialog box that appears, locate the Newsletter file you saved earlier, and click **Save** to replace it with your new file.

Next you'll insert some body copy into the publication, and learn how to thread it from text box to text box.

STEP BY STEP   **Flowing text**

You've created a single text box, and added a small amount of text to it. However, if you want to continue a story from one part of a page to another, or even between pages, you can flow text between two or more connected text boxes. Publisher allows you to do this with the click of a button.

Take Note   You can also connect text boxes prior to adding text to them. When you add your text, it will automatically flow from one text box to the next.

1   Open Microsoft Word, choose **File** > **Open** and navigate to the Pub02lessons folder. Double click to open the file called **BikeHikeLocations**.

2   Highlight the text found in this document. This can be done by pressing **Ctrl+A**. Press **Ctrl+C** to copy. Switch back over to the Publisher document.

3   Draw a text box on each of your three pages. Click the **Draw Text Box** button each time a text box is drawn. Use creativity to mix and match box shapes and sizes and make the layout more interesting.

4   Click in the first text box, and press **Ctrl+V** to paste your text.

5   Click the **Text In Overflow** button (➥) that appears to the right of the text box. It looks like an ellipse or three black dots. The cursor changes to a pitcher icon after its clicked, which means that the text is ready to pour into the next frame.

6   Click in the next frame on the second page, and the text flows into it automatically. If the Text In Overflow button appears again, continue clicking and pouring into additional text boxes, until all the text is placed in the created text boxes on the subsequent pages.

Figure 2-10

When you see the pitcher icon, you can flow text into the next frame.

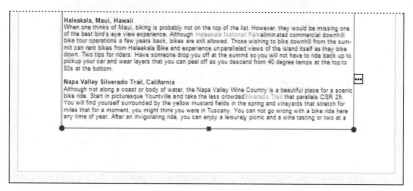

Take Note   You can use the Previous and Next tools in the Linking group of the Text Box Tools Format Context Ribbon tab to view all the connected text boxes in your publication. Use the Break tool if you want to break a link from one text box to the next.

Continue inserting and formatting text in your Newsletter publication to fill the available space on all three pages. When you're satisfied with the look and feel of the text, you're ready to start inserting and modifying images.

INSERTING AND MODIFYING IMAGES

Text-heavy publications lack visual appeal when compared to those that also incorporate images. Luckily, Publisher 2013 includes useful features for not only inserting, but also modifying those **images** in your publications. These tools enable you to adjust brightness and contrast, add various artistic effects, rotate an image, and even crop an image without having to leave the program.

STEP BY STEP   **Inserting an image**

1   Return to the first page of your publication, using the Navigation pane on the left.

2   On the Insert tab, in the Illustrations group, click the Picture button.

3   In the left pane of the Insert Picture dialog box, navigate to the Pub02lessons folder, inside the OfficeLessons folder you loaded onto your hard drive earlier.

4   Select the image named **biker.jpg**, and then click the Insert button.

Figure 2-11

Insert a picture into your publication.

© George Doyle/Stockbyte/Getty Images

As shown in Figure 2-11, the image is imported into a picture box in your publication.

5   If the image is too large or small, click and drag on the corners of the image to adjust its size. To adjust the location of the image on the page, drag on the center of the image to position it where it should go the page. Notice that the text within the text boxes shifts to accommodate the image. Play with the placement and size of the image on the first page of the publication.

Take Note   You can't click and drag an image to another page in your publication. Use the Copy and Paste feature to move images between pages.

STEP BY STEP   **Modifying an image**

1   Select the picture, and click the Picture Tools Format Context Ribbon tab (Figure 2-12).

Figure 2-12

Use the Picture Tools Format
tab to modify placed images.

2   Open the Picture Styles Gallery on the left side of the ribbon. It will drop down and display different formatting options for your graphic. Roll your cursor over each of styles in the Picture Styles gallery to preview their effects. Click Soft Edge Rectangle style.

3   In the Adjust group of the toolbar, click the Corrections drop-down menu, and choose Brightness: 50%, Contrast: 50%.

4   Directly to the right of the Corrections button, click the Recolor drop-down menu, and choose Cyanotype.

5   In the Arrange group of the toolbar, click the Rotate drop-down menu, and choose Free Rotate to allow rotating of the graphic by dragging it in the direction you want to rotate it. To do this, click the image and then click one of the small green circle buttons found on each of the four corners of the picture box and drag to the left a quarter of an inch.

6   Click the Crop drop-down menu on the Crop group of the tab, and choose Crop to Shape. Select Oval from the Basic Shapes section. Use the handles that appear to drag and reshape the selection until the image shows only the portion you want to keep. Click anywhere outside of the image to de-select it and accept the crop.

7   Resize your final image and place it in the top-right corner of Page 1. Resize the text box so text flows to the left of the image.

8   Click Save in the Quick Access Toolbar to save your work.

PRINTING YOUR PUBLICATION

Bottom Line   The ultimate goal of using of Publisher 2013 is to produce high-quality print publications. You can print these on a desktop printer, or send them out to a commercial print shop using a convenient packaging feature.

STEP BY STEP   **Printing to a desktop printer**

1   Click the File tab, and then click Print.

2   In the Print section, enter the number of copies to print in the Copies of print job text box.

3   In the Printer section, make sure that the correct printer is selected. The properties for your default printer appear automatically.

4   In the Settings section, do the following:
   • Confirm that the range of pages is correct.
   • Choose the format for imposing (or arranging) your pages on the printed sheet.

Take Note   Ask your printer if it's necessary for you to impose your pages for printing.
   • Choose the paper size.
   • Choose whether to print on one side of the sheet of paper or both.
   • If your printer is capable of printing in color, choose color or grayscale printing.

5   When you're ready to print, click the Print button in the top left hand corner.

USING PACK AND GO

Publisher's Pack and Go Wizard packages your publication and its linked files into a single file that you can send to a commercial printer. You can also take the packed file to another computer to be edited. Using the Pack and Go Wizard ensures that you have all the files necessary to hand off the completed publication to someone who can work with or view it.

STEP BY STEP   Saving for a commercial printer

1   Click the File tab.

2   Choose Export (new in Publisher 2013) from the Backstage commands, and then select Save for a Commercial Printer (Figure 2-13).

Figure 2-13

Use the Pack and Go Wizard to package your files for commercial printing.

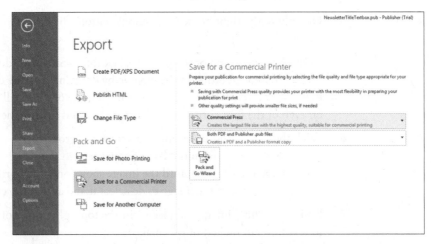

3   Under Save for a Commercial Printer, you have the following options:

Commercial Press with options to create different qualities and customized print qualities.

Both PDF and Publisher .pub files with options that will save files as a PDF and/or Publisher files: You can save to both formats, and either, depending on your printer's requirements.

4   Click the Pack and Go Wizard button.

5   If you are prompted to save your publication, click OK. Locate the previous version and replace it with your new version.

6   In the next window, browse to select the Desktop as the location for saving your (packaged) files. Click Next and then OK to finish packaging the publication into a single file.

Take Note   In the Export area, you can also save your publication as an HTML file, a Microsoft Publisher 2013 template, an older version of Microsoft Publisher, or save the entire document as a graphic like a JPEG.

SENDING A PUBLICATION USING E-MAIL

In addition to saving your publication, you can send it as either an e-mail message or an attachment.

In order to send a publication using e-mail, you must have one of the following programs installed on your computer:

• Microsoft Office Outlook

• Outlook Express (version 5.0 or later)

• Windows Mail

Sending your publication using e-mail

1 Click the **File** tab.

2 Choose **Share** > **Email**, as shown in Figure 2-14.

Figure 2-14

Use Share to send your publication using e-mail.

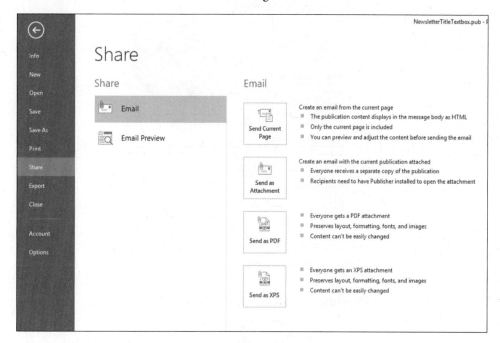

3 Choose one of the following four options:

• **Send Current Page**: This sends the currently selected page from your publication as an HTML e-mail message, so the recipients do not need to have Publisher to view the publication. You can preview the e-mail in your default web browser, and adjust or cancel the message before you send it.

• **Send as Attachment**: Every recipient receives their own copy of the publication, and each recipient must have Publisher installed in order to open the attachment.

• **Send as PDF**: This option preserves fonts, formatting, and images, but the recipients must have a PDF reader installed on their computer, such as Adobe Reader (available from Adobe Systems).

• **Send as XPS**: This option preserves fonts, formatting, and images, but cannot be easily modified.

4 When your e-mail program launches, enter the recipients' addresses, a subject line, and any other options, and click **Send**.

E-mail preview

This feature allows you to see what your publication will look like in an e-mail message by opening it as an HTML version in your default web browser (Figure 2-15).

Figure 2-15

Preview your e-mail publication in a web browser.

© George Doyle/Stockbyte/Getty Images

STEP BY STEP   **Previewing an e-mail**

1   Click the File tab.

2   Choose Share > Email Preview, and then click the Email Preview button to the right.

3   Close out of the internet browser and then choose File > Close to close the current document.

Congratulations! You have finished this lesson, and you now have the basic skill set to create publications from scratch in Microsoft Publisher 2013.

What you learned in this lesson:

- Creating a blank publication

- Inserting a text box

- Formatting text

- Inserting and modifying images

- Printing your publication

- Using Pack and Go

- Sending a publication using e-mail

Knowledge Assessment

True/False

Circle T if the statement is true or F it the statement is false.

T   F   1. Microsoft Publisher 2013 not only creates printable documents but online publications like email newsletters.

T   F   2. If you create a new publication with only one page in it, you cannot add additional pages.

T   F   3. Publisher automatically sets the margins of a new standard blank document to ½ inch on all four sides of the page.

T   F   4. To change the size of a document, click the Page Design Ribbon tab and click Size in the Page Set up group.

T   F   5. Text inserted into a Publisher document must be contained in a graphic holder

T   F   6. If a text box isn't big enough to hold the text, you can left drag the sides and corners of the textbox to increase or decrease its size.

T   F   7. If you enter text into a textbox on one page, you can flow the text onto another page and a different textbox using the paste tool.

T   F   8. Graphics help to add visual appeal to documents and break up text heavy portions of a publication.

T   F   9. Graphics can be inserted and edited in Publisher publications.

T   F   10. The crop tool allows the color contrast of graphics to be edited.

Multiple Choice

Select the best response for the following statements.

1. Publisher publications can be saved in a variety of formats including PDF's and other file formats like:
   a. HTML and graphic formats like JPEG, PNG, and GIFF.
   b. Access databases
   c. Excel and PowerPoint files
   d. None of the above

2. When preparing a publication for commercial printing, what tool helps to package a publication and all its linking files together for printing:
   a. The graphic import wizard
   b. The spreadsheet import wizard
   c. The Pack and Go Wizard
   d. The Table Import Wizard

3. To move graphics between pages in a publication, you must:
   a. Drag and drop the graphic onto the new page
   b. Copy/cut and paste the graphic onto the new page
   c. Delete the graphic and insert it again on a new page
   d. Use the import wizard

4. The E-mail Preview feature allows you to view your publication as an email message by:
   a. Opening it as an HTML version in your default web browser
   b. Saving the publication as a PDF
   c. Print previewing an e-mail version of the publication
   d. Cutting the text into a new publication

5. If you want to insert an exact copy of the current page, into a publication:
   a. Open a new publication
   b. Print Preview the document
   c. From the Home Ribbon tab, paste in a new page
   d. From the Insert Ribbon tab, click Page, and Insert Duplicate Page

6. The Picture Styles Gallery is available on what Ribbon tab when an image is selected:
   a. The Picture Tools, Format, context Ribbon tab
   b. The Home Ribbon tab, Clipboard group
   c. The Insert Ribbon tab
   d. The View Ribbon tab.

7. The Print Preview in Publisher 2013 combines both a Print Preview window and a:
   a. graphic editing area
   b. printer settings area
   c. copy and paste area
   d. insert objects area.

8. To access the e-mail tools available in Publisher, you need to go to File and click:
   a. Accounts
   b. Print
   c. Info
   d. Share

9. If two blank text boxes are created, you can flow text between them before text is entered into them by clicking on the first empty text box and then clicking on the:
   a. Copy and paste on the Home Ribbon tab
   b. Online pictures in the Insert Ribbon tab
   c. Text Box Tools, Format contextual Ribbon, Create Link button
   d. View Ribbon tab, Show group

10. Publisher allows for easy copying/cutting of text from what types of programs into Publisher publications:
    a. Word processing programs like Microsoft Word
    b. Spreadsheet programs like Microsoft Excel
    c. Presentation programs like Microsoft PowerPoint
    d. Database programs like Microsoft Access.

Competency Assessment

Project 2-1: Creating a publication

Create a blank one page publication, edit its size, and other page properties.

1. Click **File** and **New** in the Backstage view.
2. Click **Blank, 8.5 X 11"** from the new publication choices.
3. After the new blank publication opens, click the **Page Design** Ribbon tab.
4. In the Page Setup group, click **Size**.
5. Towards the bottom of the available sizes, click **Legal(Portrait) 8.5 X 14"**.
6. After the document resizes, click **Margin** in the Page Setup group.

7. In the Margins list, click Wide and set the margins to 1" on all four sides of the publication.
8. In the Page Setup group, click Orientation.
9. Click Landscape to change the publication's orientation.
10. Click File and Save As.
11. Save the File in the Pub02lessons folder as Legal Landscape.
12. Click File and Close in Backstage view to close the publication.

Project 2-2: Editing a publication

Open and edit a publication created in the last activity by adding text boxes and additional pages to the document.

1. Click File and Open in the Backstage view.
2. From the Pub02lessons folder, select the **Legal Landscape** file, created in the last activity.
3. After the publication opens, click the Insert Ribbon tab.
4. In the Page group, click Page.
5. Click Insert Blank Page, a new blank page will be added to the publication.
6. Click on the Page 2 thumbnail (the new blank page) in the Navigation pane.
7. Click back on the Page 1 thumbnail.
8. Click on the Insert Ribbon tab.
9. In the Draw group, click Draw Text Box. Your mouse pointer will burn into a cross-hair (two intersecting lines).
10. On Page 1 of your publication, left-drag the cross hair and create a text box approximately 2 inches by 2inches.
11. Click inside the new text box and type some text of your choice.
12. Click File and Close in Backstage view to close the publication. Don't save changes to the file.

Proficiency Assessment

Project 2-3: Inserting a Microsoft Word document

You will edit an existing newsletter and insert text from a Microsoft Word document into the publication.

1. From the File Ribbon tab, click Open and navigate to the Pub02lessons folder. Open **Northwind Traders Summer Newsletter**. Save the file as Northwind Traders Summer Newsletter with Updates.
2. Click on each of the page thumbnails and explore the newsletter.
3. Go back to Page 1.
4. From the Pub02lesson`s folder, open the Microsoft Word file, **Great Summer Party Ideas**. Select all the text and copy (Ctrl+C) it to your Office Clipboard.
5. Return to your Publisher publication, on Page 1, select the text on page 1, Enter Story Here.
6. Paste the copied text from Microsoft Word (Ctrl+V) into the text box on page 1.
7. Click File and Save to save changes to the document.

Project 2-4: Inserting an image

You will continue to edit the same publication from the previous activity by inserting an image into the newsletter.

1. If you have already closed the Northwind Traders Summer Newsletter or have not completed the previous Proficiency activity, open the file, **Northwind Traders Summer Newsletter with Updates** before beginning.

2. Click the Page 1 thumbnail.

3. You will insert a picnic graphic from the online pictures gallery available through Office.com. Click Insert, on the Illustrations group, click Online Pictures.

4. In the search field at the top right of the Office.com Clip Art box, type Picnic and press Enter to begin looking for images.

5. Double-click an image of your choice in the box.

6. The image will download and appear on Page 1 of your publication. It will probably be too big.

7. Click on the image to select it.

8. Use your mouse cursor to size the corners of the image and adjust its size, so it fits appropriately on the bottom of page 1 in your publication. Use your mouse cursor to drag the image, so the image is placed appropriately at the bottom of Page 1.

9. Close the publication.

Mastery Assessment

Project 2-5: Customizing a publication

Create a new blank publication, customize its page design, and then create empty text boxes and connect them for flowing text between them.

1. Create a new blank publication based on the standard size, 8.5 X 11". After the document is created add three additional pages to the document, so it contains four pages.

2. Customize the margins on each page and set them to 1" inch on all four sides of the page.

3. On each page, create a large text box that takes up the entire page. Link the text box on page 1 to page 2 and continue linking the text boxes, so text can flow from Page 1 all the way to the textbox on Page 4. (Hint: Don't forget to use the Text Box Tool, Format contextual Ribbon tab and the Create Link button in the Linking group.)

4. Save the document in the Pub02lessons folder as Reflow.

Project 2-6: Printing and emailing a document

Prepare a document for printing and also for e-mail.

1. From the Pub02lessons folder, open the file, **Northwind Traders Email Newsletter**. Print preview the file and change the print setting, so the e-mail newsletter will print on one page, also adjust the publication to print in gray scale and view it, and then change it back.

2. In the Page Design Ribbon tab, apply different Schemes to the publication until you find one that suits you needs and save the file.

3. Under Share in the Backstage view, use the E-mail Preview to preview the e-mail in your web browser. Close the Publication.

A

absolute cell reference   Refers to a cell, and the reference does not change when copied/pasted. For instance, $B$9 refers to cell B9, and when the cell containing the reference is used to AutoFill other cells, they will all refer to B9 rather than to analogous cells in their own row.

absolute placement   Locating a float in a "physical" location relative to the page, rather than positioning it relative to the text around it.

Accept Changes   Tool to incorporate an edit into the "baseline" version of a document with Track Changes on.

access control   Features to regulate which users get access to which parts of a document. Word can provide access control by user, file, document region, and type of edit.

Account picture   A picture which represents your user account. By default, Windows 8 uses a generic icon, although you can use a personal photo or take a picture using your device's camera (if your current device has an available camera or webcam).

accounting format   Number format – displays currency symbol, aligns decimal points, encloses negative values in parentheses.

Action Center   An icon that contains a message, which appears when you need to take an action.

address block   A complex field whose output is a formatted address. Combines multiple merge fields – e.g., Name, Street 1, Street 2, City, (optionally) Title.

alignment   Location of an object or text piece – left, right, center (radiating out from center, ragged right and left edges), or justified (aligned with both right and left margins). See also justification.

alignment guides   Reactive guidelines that appear to help user place slide elements symmetrically, proportionately, etc.

All Markup   Displays the actual content of inline edits to a document when Track Changes is enabled: deleted text struck through, new text underlined, etc.

animation   Visual effect in which one or more slide element is transformed, or moved. PowerPoint includes four animation types: Entrace, Exit, Emphasis, and Motion Paths (custom movement).

App control menu   contains commands that help you control the size and appearance of the app window as well as close the window

Appointment   An individual calendar event scheduled for the individual Outlook user.

Archive   A method for saving old e-mail messages in a different location on a computer, so the Inbox doesn't become so cluttered with information.

arguments   The variables passed to a function, on which the function will operate. The PMT(rate,nper,pv,[fv],[type]) function takes five arguments, the last two of which are optional.

Attachment   Attachment A file attached to an e-mail message that a recipient can open.

Auditing (tools)   Set of tools in Formulas tab to analyze the syntax and dependencies of formulas – e.g., can visually highlight which data a formula takes as arguments.

AutoFill   Tool to populate cell range based on selected cell data – e.g., if top three cells in a column fill with 1, 2, 3, then AutoFill can extrapolate to fill subsequent cells with 4, 5, 6, etc.

AutoFit   A method to adjust the size or spacing of a page element to fit its contents or surroundings. Enabling AutoFit contents for a table cell will expand the cell to fit its widest content; Fixed column width will wrap (or simply hide) its contents based on the selected cell size.

AutoSum   Populates cell automatically with summary function (SUM by default) applied to adjacent cell range.

Average   Commonly-used function to generate the arithmetic mean of a group of numbers. Takes one or more values or ranges as arguments.

B

Backstage Area   Replaces the File menu in recent versions of Office. Houses Save, Open, Print, Export, File Info, and other commands, as well as application options and user account settings. Accessed with Alt+F or by selecting the File tab.

bitmap   Defines the individual pixels of an image. As opposed to a vector image, which is built from geometric shapes and so can be scaled up without losing quality, bitmaps degrade in quality as they scale up.

blog   (Also "weblog") A website displaying posts (articles, essays, photo galleries, etc.), usually in reverse chronological order. Word can edit posts and upload directly to most popular blog hosting providers.

blog post   A single entry on a blog, containing text, images, and/or links to other online resources. When editing a blog in Word, equivalent to a single .docx file.

Border Painter   Applies formatting to a table cell border, much like the Format Painter for text, but does not create cell borders (which is the job of Draw Table tool).

C

caption   Text "tag" displayed along with an image, optionally including label, number, description (e.g., "Figure 4: Annual Revenues").

category   Blog posts are tagged with one or more categories, which help readers browse and search collections of posts more easily.

cell   Intersection of a single row and column -- can contain numeric or text data, an image or other media object, or a formula which generates dynamic output.

cell address   Location of a cell rather than its contents (e.g., C15). Also known as cell reference.

cell reference   A pointer to the contents of another cell. The formula =A4+C4 contains two cell references, to the contents of A4 and C4. If the contents of those cells change, formulas referring to those cells will update automatically.

cell style   Fill, font, border parameters bundled together, analogous to a text style in Word.

Change Case   Command set to transform capitalization of selected text to all uppercase, lowercase, Title Case, etc.

character   A single letter, number, symbol, punctuation mark, or space.

Charms bar   A menu launched on the Start screen used to connect hardware and display settings menus

chart area   Contains all chart elements – the outermost border of the chart object.

chart title   Chart element identifying the chart for the reader (not an internal identifier for Excel).

codec   Often used to mean "media format," though it strictly refers to a program that encodes and decodes streaming media

color scheme   Collection of text/fill/accent colors chosen to work well together, available from Page Layout > Colors dropdown.

column   Vertical array of table cells. In a database or list, columns correspond to fields – a list of students might have columns for First Name, Last Name, and Date of Birth.

column   Vertical stack of cells.

columnar form   Broken into columns, e.g., a set of names in the form Firstname Lastname could be split into two columns, one for each name, using each name's blank space as the delimiter.

Combine Documents   Shows two different versions of the same document, highlighting tracked changes in each version; user can accept or reject those edits one by one (e.g., reviewing two collaborators' different edits to the same baseline document).

Compare Documents   Shows two documents, each with tracked changes accepted, highlighting differences; where they differ, user can choose either document.

comparison formula   Compares two numbers and returns 1 (true) or 0 (false). Common comparison operators include <, >, and =. Often used to form IF/THEN statements, e.g., IF(A6>5,"Bigger","Smaller").

compress   W/r/t embedded media, compression simply means downsizing media files by sacrificing some image/ sound quality. PowerPoint includes a Compress Media command that will attempt to downsize embedded media files in a presentation.

Compressed file   A single file that contains one or more files that were compressed to save space

conditional field   A field code which bases its output on whether a specific condition has been met. For instance: IF recipient is a donor THEN add "Thank you," ELSE add "Good day."

conditional formatting   Altering cell contents/formatting when certain conditions are met (e.g., highlighting a cell if its value > 50).

Configuration process   The process of organizing a computer to access e-mail servers and download and upload e-mail messages to that server.

Contacts An individual or entity entered into the People area of Outlook. The information tracked generally incluzqdes e-mail addresses, phone numbers, street addresses, and other important contact information.

Content Pane The main area of a notebook where information is entered and saved.

contextual tab Appears in the Ribbon, at the far right, when specific objects (e.g., images or tables) are selected, offering tools applicable only to those objects.

Control Panel A collection of settings controlling the appearance and behavior of your local computer.

copy Command to duplicate (but not alter) selected data and add to clipboard for pasting.

COUNTIF Takes a cell range and a criterion (which comes back true or false), and provides a count of cells in the range that meet the criterion.

cover page Specially-formatted page at front of document, usually including title, subtitle, author(s), and other document information. Generated with the Insert > Cover Page command. Each document theme includes built-in cover page options.

criteria range Cell range used by Advanced Sort to filter multiple columns. Can provide a filter criterion for each field in a database.

crop Cut away all but a portion of an image.

cross-reference Dynamically updated reference to an object within the document – a cross-reference to Figure 3, for instance, will update to refer to Figure 6 if the referent figure moves to later in the document.

Custom Slide Show A named subset of a slide show, allowing multiple tailored presentations using a single slide deck.

custom sort Complex reordering of a list based on one or more criteria, e.g., sorting a phone book first by phone number, then city, then first name.

custom template Template created by the user. By default Excel stores these in a local folder separate from Microsoft's online template library.

cut Command to remove selected data to clipboard for pasting.

D

data marker Visual representation of a single data point, corresponding to a single cell.

data series Related data points plotted in a chart, each uniquely visually identified in some way (e.g., with a different color).

data source An external file from which Word draws the data for a mail merge. For, a database, the data source references information specifying a database and how to connect to it – e.g., name/location and login credentials.

data table Combines a single formula and a range of data values for one or two variables in the formula, allowing the user to generate a range of possible outputs for the formula given reasonable inputs in the table.

Data type A field's data type determines the type of information that can be stored in that column of your table, and the type of information that cannot be stored in the column.

Data Validation Controls what kind of data can be entered into a cell range -- for instance, Phone Number and Age entry fields may only accept numeric strings.

database A collection of records, each containing values corresponding to different fields, e.g., a list of user records, each of which contains a Username, Real Name, Phone Number, and Last Login field. Can be presented in tabular format, though this is not always optimal.

Datasheet view Table view designed for data entry and viewing records. You can add, delete, edit, sort, filter, and print records from this view. You can also insert, delete, categorize new fields, and change their order

Date/Time field When updated, displays current time. User can specify formatting, e.g., 4/25/03 or 25 April 2003, etc.

delimiter Character(s) used to divide a text string, e.g., "Bill-Simmons-Jr" could be split into three parts (Bill, Simmons, and Jr) using the hypen (-) as the delimiter.

Design Tab Houses document-level formatting/style tools: Theme and Style Set galleries, Color/Font Set dropdowns, text effects, etc. Individual text pieces are styled with tools in the Home tab.

Design view This table view is where the table's design is the focus. It lists all the fields with their data types and descriptions. In this view, you do not see the actual records.

Desktop (standard) database is a database which is stored on your computer, a network, or another computer storage location and run directly from the location on your computer.

Desktop app Used to launch other Windows 8 apps.

desktop shortcut An icon that appears on the desktop, enabling you to open the program that is represented.

Direct text entry Typing something directly into the program.

Document Properties   A collection of "metadata" fields, edited through the Document Properties pane or Backstage, which can be inserted into the document – e.g., Author, Title, etc.

E

effects (text effects?)   Visual effects applied to cells within a worksheet, selected from gallery in Page Layout tab

embedded object   An image, table, or other page element which has been added to a Word file, and saved as part of its .docx file.

endnote   Citation or explanatory note laid out at end of section or document. Edited and formatted with commands in References > Footnotes.

Eraser tool   Tool to erase cell borders within a table, thereby merging those cells.

error alert   Warns user when invalid data has been entered in a cell using Data Validation.

exit animation   PowerPoint animation in which an element exits the slide rather than appearing on click.

F

Field   Code (instructions) for Word to automatically insert content. To insert the current date into a document, for instance, add a Date field, which will automatically update to reflect the date.

field   A single element of a database record, mapping to a column in Excel (where a record is a row).

Field   a table column or category. For example, a FirstName field would likely be found in an Employees table.

field code   Instructions (code) to generate content for display. Inserting a field into a document tells Word to display the contents of that field, rather than its identifier; e.g., an Author field will output the author's name, edited in Document Properties.

File Explorer   A program you use to work with files on your computer, viewing them, organizing them by creating folders for them, moving or copying them, renaming them, and deleting them

File History   Microsoft's included backup utility (if you are using Windows 8 Pro or higher), which takes hourly snapshots of all the files and backs them up to an external hard drive, a second hard drive, or a network hard drive.

File Ribbon tab   Always a different shade, takes users to the Backstage view and important file management tools.

fill   The background color of a table cell.

fill color   Background color of a cell.

filter   Tool to show only some entries in a list, based on filtering criteria (e.g., only phonebook entries whose last name is Smith).

Flash Fill   Tool to evaluate cell range for patterns in data, then automatically fill remainder of data according to pattern.

Float   A page element such as an image or text box, which "floats" above the paper/background, and can be moved around and absolutely or relatively positioned without changing its contents.

Folder Pane   A task pane that appears on the left side of the Outlook window that allows for quick navigation within different areas of Outlook.

Folders   A repository in which you can place related files on your hard drive

font set   Heading/body fonts paired together, chosen from Page Layout > Fonts dropdown.

Footer   Printable area below the main text of a page. Often contains file/author info, date, page number, or running document/chapter titles.

footer   Running page-bottom information (e.g., page number, current date, filename, etc.).

footnote   Citation or explanatory note printed at bottom of a page. Edited and formatted w/commands in References > Footnotes group.

Form   an object where you place controls for taking actions or for entering, displaying and editing data in fields. Access objects resemble online forms. They are primarily used for viewing information from database tables and also for entering data into tables.

form letter   A single letter structure, into which data from an external source is inserted to generate individual "personalized" letters.

format   Display mode of numeric data – e.g., the same number might display as 5, 5.0, 5e0, or $5 based on the number format used.

Format Painter   Tool to copy formatting info, rather than text, and "paint" it into other text in a document. To use, select some text, click the Format Painter, then select the text you wish to "paint."

Format Painter   Tool to copy the formatting info from one cell onto another cell/range.

Format Pane   Task pane from which all of a slide element's visual style parameters can be altered.

formula   A mathematical equation that calculates a value. Identified by a leading equals sign (=), e.g., =A9^3.

Formula bar Input area for cell text, located below the Ribbon. Displays contents of selected cell. When a cell contains a formula, the cell itself displays its output, but the Formula bar shows the formula itself.

Forwarding When you send a message you have received to another message recipient.

freeze (row or column) Keep a row or column visible as you scroll through a spreadsheet.

function Prewritten formula to transform one or more inputs (variables) to return one or more values.

Function Library A searchable, browsable, categorized collection of mathematical/textual operations available for use in Excel formulas.

Gallery Visual menu of options. The Style Set gallery, for instance, shows a small preview of each available Style Set. Mouse over a gallery to preview the effect of a selection on a document.

G

Goal Seek Tool to tweak the value of a variable in a formula in order to generate a desired output (i.e., an equation solver).

gradient A gradual blend of colors; e.g., a background that slowly fades from green to white as the eye moves from right to left.

grand total Extra row (not an additional record) added to a list with a summary function (sum, average, count, etc.) for all rows.

gridlines Provide charts with a background grid, for easier reading. Can be toggled in the Chart Elements pane.

Grouping Grouped objects (for instance, two images and a small arrow connecting them) can be manipulated all at once for ease of use. Grouping commands reside in the Page Layout > Arrange group.

H

handle Draggable box at corner of cell/range; different handles indicate different behaviors when dragging.

Handout Master Editing view for laying out audience handout (including slide thumbnails or outline).

Header Printable area above the main text on a page. Often contains file/author info, date, page number, or running document/chapter titles.

header Running page-top information (see footer).

Heading Piece of text formatted with a Heading style. Word uses Heading styles as document divisions and to generate outlines, and headings can be collapsed to reduce screen clutter.

heading In tables, the cell that identifies the contents of a column or (less commonly) row. Word and Excel can usually detect the presence of a header row, or prompt the user to identify header.

Heading style Text styles for section headings, e.g., Heading 1 for top-level section titles and Heading 2 for subsections. Word's built-in heading styles automatically generate a document outline, and allow automatic text folding

Help button Fast access to Publisher's built-in Help system.

Hibernate mode A power saving state in which your open programs and settings are stored in memory and your computer is then powered off. When power is turned on, the computer can quickly resume operation with the same programs running when you wake it from this mode.

hidden characters Non-printing characters like tabs, paragraph markers, and spaces. Optionally viewed with the Home > Show Hidden Characters command.

horizontal axis Also known as x-axis. Generally identifies data points (by name, time, etc.) while y-axis generally measures magnitude.

Hot spots Regions of the screen or display that activate other functionality, such as menus or bars that you can enter information into or change settings with.

Hotspots a corner of the screen that aids mouse and touch users, and can be used to launch a command or menu.

hyperlink Clickable text within a document – usually HTML or PDF – which causes an online resource to open, generally in a web browser. Hyperlinks are indicated by underlined, emphasized, or colored text, and often have a Tooltip-like popup indicating destination or further explanation.

I

If Function that takes three arguments: a test that returns true/false, and values to return depending on the test's outcome. IF(A5>0,"Bigger","Smaller") returns (outputs) "Bigger" if A5>0, otherwise returns "Smaller."

Images Another name for graphics.

In Line with Text (object layout) The opposite of absolute placement – inline objects sit in a line of text, and are laid out by Word much like characters or words; they move as the surrounding text moves.

infographic Visual representation of data – chart, graph, map, etc.

ink annotations   Scribbled annotations added during presentation with presenter pen tool – can be saved and included in .pptx file.

input message   Prompts user when entering data in a cell using Data Validation.

Internet Explorer   Windows 8 contains a legacy version of the Microsoft web browser, in addition to an updated native app version.

invisible field   Non-printing field code.

J

Junk E-mail or Spam   Unwanted e-mail often sent by businesses promoting their services and products.

justification   Word's term for "full justified" text, with line beginnings and ends both flush against the left and right margins. In typesetting. Word's default alignment is "flush left, ragged right"; fully justified text will squash or stretch to fill an entire line

K

Keep Source Formatting   When using paste options, this choice maintains the selected text's original font, size, and style.

Keep Text Only   When using paste options, removes any non-text items, such as images, and pastes text only.

Keyboard Shortcuts   Sequences or combinations of keystrokes to carry out application commands – e.g., Ctrl+N for New Document, or Alt,F,A,1 for the Save As command in the active directory.

kiosk   Self-running presentation allowing minimal interaction; in Kiosk Mode a presentation loops automatically and ignores most keyboard input.

L

Landscape Orientation   Horizontal page layout (i.e., longest side horizontal).

laser pointer   Presenter View pen tool for drawing attention to slide elements; leaves no annotations.

Launch Screen   Displays when you launch Word 2013, with recent documents and template gallery.

legend   Indicates which color/pattern corresponds to which data series in a chart.

Libraries   are virtual folders. Libraries don't actually store your fi les; instead, they are shortcuts to the folders that store your fi les.

linked data   Source data for a chart. When a chart is created, it refers to the source data rather than "containing" its own data; when data updates, chart can refresh to reflect new values.

linked object   A copy of an image, table, or other page element whose source data comes from an external file; changes to that file are reflected in the linked copy until the source and linked copy are unlinked.

list   Sortable, searchable collection of records, each made up of one or more fields. Also known as a database.

Live tiles   Tiles on the Start Screen that contain information from the app that the tile represents. For example, the Flickr tile shows current and updated images from your Flickr account.

Local accounts   A local login using a username and password that is used to login to a single device or computer.

Lock screen   The Lock screen appears the first time you start Windows 8 and each time you restart your computer (or manually lock your computer if you're stepping away from your desk).

locked cell   A locked cell's contents can't be changed. By default, all cells in a protected sheet are locked. Locking can be toggled for cell ranges whether or not worksheet is protected.

M

mail merge   MS Word tool to generate form letters from a Word document and database. The same tool can in fact be used to generate other document types (e.g., flash cards, labels,ement marking a major interval on the chart's axis – analogous to the numbers on a clock, which mark 5-minute intervals, while less prominent hash marks (minor gridlines) mark one minute each.

Margins   The top/bottom, right/left, and inside/outside spaces around the main content area of a page in Word. In common use, refers to either the area around the printable part of a page or printed matter outside the text block, like header and footer area.

Max   Returns the largest value in a range

Median   Returns the median value in a range.

Meeting   A calendar event scheduled for multiple Outlook users.

merge (cells)   Combine several cells into one large one.

Merge Cells   Combine one or more adjacent cells into a single large cell, which occupies a region of the table rather than a single cell address.

Merge Formatting   When using paste options, adopts the standard formatting used by OneNote.

Microsoft account   a new type of log in account that you can use when you start your computer.

Min   Returns the smallest value in a range.

Minimize button   Used to reduce the app window to a button on the taskbar

Motion Path   Custom animation trajectory; the user draws a path which the object will follow when the animation is triggered.

N

Name Manager   Tool for specifying and organizing names assigned to ranges in a workbook. Can analyze regions of a worksheet and automatically assign names to cell ranges based on headers.

narration   Spoken audio which can be added during rehearsal runs and played during presentation. Can be saved as part of .pptx file.

Navigation pane   displays common locations on your computer that you might need to review

Navigation Pane   A task pane housing the Find feature and other tools for quickly scanning a document based on logical structure (e.g., a searchable mini-outline). In long publications the Navigation Pane is used for fast and easy navigation between pages in a long publication.

nested table   A table embedded into one cell of another table. Unlike split cells, nested tables don't inherit the formatting/style of the surrounding (outer) table.

Network access indicator   An icon that displays representing the type of network connection you are currently using: wired, or wireless.

No Markup   Displays edited document without indicating Tracked Changes (the most "up to date" document version), but continues to store those changes.

Notebook   A OneNote document is called a Notebook.

Notes Master   Editing view for laying out presenter notes page.

Notes Page   Printable notes meant to be distributed to presentation audience rather than read by presenter. Can be formatted with Notes Master.

Notes Page   Presenter-facing printed page with slide and written notes, prompts, or script. Formatted in the Notes Master view.

Notification Area   displays messages pertinent at the time they appear

Notifications   Pop-up messages informing you of important information or application updates (such as new e-mails in the Mail app).

NOW   Returns the current date and time, utilizing current cell formatting.

O

operator   Symbol indicating basic function – e.g., + indicates addition, & connects two pieces of text, : indicates range.

P

page break   Analogous to a carriage return, moves cursor to top of next page.

Page Layout mode   Viewing mode that shows how spreadsheet will be laid out on printed pages.

Page orientation   is the way in which a rectangular page is oriented for normal viewing. The two most common types of orientation are portrait and landscape. Landscape provides a short and wide orientation, while portrait provides a tall and thin orientation for printed page.

Pages   Sections in a Notebook are organized into pages.

Pages Pane   located to the right of the Content pane, the Pages pane displays Pages and Subpages for the active Notebook.

pagination   How a document's content is distributed across individual pages.

Pane   Dockable window that collects tools relating to one task – an image's Formatting Pane, for instance, includes several tabs housing a wide variety of image/formatting layout commands.

Panning   Scroll horizontally in an application or on a web page.

password protection   Requires a password before changes can be made. Files, workbooks, worksheets, and cell ranges can be password protected.

paste   Insert clipboard contents at cursor (without clearing clipboard).

Paste Options   A popup button with which you can specify the behavior of the Paste command after pasting in content; also a dropdown menu in the Home > Clipboard group. Options include preserving and discarding source formatting, linking to source, merging formatting, and more.

Picture   When using paste options, inserts copied/cut image files.

Pinning   adding a tile to the Start Screen or Desktop task bar.

PivotTable   Tool to summarize table data by mapping database fields to the rows, columns, filters, and values of a table.

PivotTable field   Columns in a database map to the rows, columns, filters, and values (the fields) of a PivotTable.

Placeholder Text   Dummy text to fill space on a layout, giving a sense of how text areas, images and other page elements will fit together. Can be locked to prevent accidentally collapsing the structure of a complex layout. In PowerPoint, placeholder text appears in text area during slide editing but does not display during slide show.

plot   Graphical representation of relationships between data points – the area of the chart bounded by x- and y-axis.

plot area   Region of a chart object containing the data points, bounded by horizontal/vertical axes.

PMT   Calculates loan payments. Takes three arguments: interest rate, number of payments, and principal. Also takes two additional optional arguments: future value (defaults to 0 for a loan) and payment type (i.e., end/beginning of payment period).

points   1/72 of an inch; 12pt type is set with each character in a box roughly 1/6 of an inch high. Distinct from bullet point.

Portrait Orientation   Vertical page layout (i.e., longest side up and down).

Presenter View   Full-featured presenter-facing screen, including pen tools, next slide preview, and notes pane.

Preview pane   Part of the File Explorer that shows a larger view of the file. For example, image files will display a thumbnail view in the Preview pane.

Primary Key   A primary key field is often a unique number or combination or letters and numbers that make each record unique.

Print Area   Section of worksheet that will be printed or outputted to PDF.

Print Layout   Displays print/PDF output of a document in true "What You See Is What You Get" mode,including images, borders, effects, and full text formatting.

protected mode   In protected mode (Protected View) editing commands are unavailable. The user can enable editing commands by unlocking the file or declaring to Excel that the file is trusted.

Q

Query   a question that you ask about the data stored in a table. Queries can also make a request of the data or perform an action such as a filter on the data. A query can bring data together from multiple tables to serve as the source of data for a form or report.

Quick Access Toolbar   A toolbar with a set of commonly used commands from the Ribbon interface, including Undo and Quick Print. It can be customized to contain shortcuts.

Quick Analysis tool   Conditionally formats cell ranges based on analysis of cell contents.

Quick Link menu   Enables you to open useful desktop apps, such as the Device Manager, Control Panel, Disk Manager, Computer Management Console, Task Manager, File Explorer, and more.

R

range   Group/block of selected cells. Excel indicates selected range visually with a border. To specify a range, use the colon operator – A6:A8 indicates cells A6, A7, and A8.

range name   Uniquely identifies a range of cells for use in formulas. Assigned and managed in the Name Manager.

Read Mode   Displays content of an article with no editing interface, one screenful at a time, for quick document review independent of fine-grained layout concerns. Takes full advantage of touch gestures for navigation.

Recipient   The receiver of an e-mail message.

record   One item in a list or database, uniquely identified, containing one or more fields.

Record   a set of fields containing data for a single entry and appearing in one row of a database table.

Recurring appointment or meeting   A meeting or appointment that recurs at a regular interval.

Recycle Bin   A temporary holding area for things you intend to delete.

Refresh   A less drastic approach to system recovery which clears all the legacy settings and apps and anything not within Windows users folders. It then reinstalls Windows and places a list of what was eliminated on the Desktop for you to review.

Reject Changes   Tool to dismiss a change and delete its record from the Tracked Changes list.

Relational Database   relational database program that uses related tables to store, organize, and retrieve data.

relative cell reference   Refers to a cell relative to itself, rather than by absolute location in the worksheet. When a reference to B9 in cell C9 is copied to C10, the reference will change to B10.

Replying   When you respond to an e-mail message you have received by sending a message back.

Report   a printout of your database information that's formatted and organized according to your specifications. Examples of reports are sales summaries, phone lists, and mailing labels.

Reset   The most drastic system recovery tool available; it wipes your hard drive and reinstalls Windows. You will lose all your personal data, all your settings, and programs you installed, including their settings, product keys, and passwords.

Restart command   Closes all open programs then powers off the machine and immediately powers it on again. This process clears your computer's memory and does not attempt to save your computer's state to your hard drive.

Restore button   appears when an app window is maximized to fill the entire computer screen.

revert   Replace a document with an earlier version. Word 2013 doesn't support full version control, but does allow the user to "take back" tracked changes and revert to a baseline document version.

Reviewing Pane   Analogous to Navigation Pane, provides list of document edits and which user contributed them.

Ribbon   A menu bar that contains commands pertaining, for the most part, to the app you're viewing.

rotation handle   Appears on a text box or image when selected. Click and drag in a circle to rotate the float

row   Horizontal array of cells in a table. When table acts as a database or list, a row contains a single record.

S

Save   Saves current state of the active file to disk, either locally or in the cloud. If the document has already been saved, the Save command overwrites the old copy.

Save As   Saves current state of the active file to disk with a new name – i.e., it doesn't overwrite other saved copies of the file. The new version remains the active file.

scale (i.e. chart scale – along axis)   Maps the length of a chart axis to the range of values it represents.

Scenario   A named set of values for the variables in a formula, e.g., several budget Scenarios could be saved in a single .xlsx file, each with a different balance of spending/ saving, letting the user compare budget approaches

section break   Marks division between two document sections, which can be independently formatted and laid out. Optionally includes page break.

Section Group   A related group of sections that have been put together in a group.

Sections   Segments of a OneNote notebook.

Select Table handle   Appears when table is selected. Clicking the handle selects, not the data within the table, but the entire object for placement on the page.

Selection Pane   Task pane for selecting objects and reordering them in the "stack" of slide elements.

separator   Character inserted into a large number to aid readability, most commonly the comma to mark off thousands (as in 2,330 or 3,888,102).

Set Up Show (dialog box)   For customizing presentation mode and monitor setup.

Shape Style   Bundled visual effects for slide elements. Sets line, fill, gradient, effects, and text formatting properties with one click.

SharePoint   A suite of web apps for collaboration, content management, and team communications.Office-like interface, and extensive integration with Office (especially its online version, Office 365).

Shut Down command   Turns off your computer entirely so it does not use any electricity. All user sessions are closed, and any running files are copied to RAM (the operating system) before shutting down, so they can be resumed when you turn on the computer again. This functionality is similar to Hibernate mode.

Sign in screen   Where you enter your password and sign into the operating system.

Simple Markup   Notes the presence of edits in a document with Track Changes on, but doesn't display full edits inline.

SkyDrive   Microsoft's remote storage service, allowing syncing of remote/local data and sharing (through skydrive.com) of folders and files. Fully integrated into Office 2013 and Windows 8.

Sleep mode   A power saving state in which power is withheld from non-essential components, but the computer can quickly resume operation with the same programs running when you wake it from this mode.

slicer   Interactive tool to filter out data series in a chart or graph.

slicer   A button to filter the data in a given table column; slicers helpfully illustrate the current filter state of a table, improving readability and allowing quick interactive experimentation

slide layout   Visual layout for a specific kind of slide, which can be reused throughout a presentation; e.g., Title Slide, Image with Caption. Custom slide layouts work the same as the built-in layouts.

Slide Master   The basic slide meta-layout from which all of a slide deck's individual slide layouts inherit visual features; e.g., an image on the Slide Master will appear on all individual slide layouts, but the reverse is not true.

Slide Show view   Simple presentation view duplicating audience screen for presenter.

Slide Sorter   PowerPoint view in which entire presentation is visible as grouped mini-slides which can be reordered or zoomed into.

SmartArt   Tool to turn structured text like bulleted lists into charts, graphs, and other infographics.

sort   To present the records in a database in order based on one or more keys. An ascending alphabetical sort by Last Name would present a name list such that the last names run A-Z, with "ties" broken by a secondary key (e.g., first name)..

sparkline   Miniature line/bar chart, contained in a single cell, summarizing data relationship rather than indicating specific data values.

speaker notes   Text pieces attached to PowerPoint slides, to be consulted by presenter during a talk. Speaker notes are not shown to the audience.

SQL   Structured Query Language, a standard language for accessing and managing the contents of databases. MS Access uses SQL, though most users won't need to write SQL code directly to use Access.

Start Screen   A screen that contains tiles representing programs installed on your operating system.

Status bar   Customizable display area at the bottom of the screen, with space for word/page count, zoom slider, etc.

Subfolders   A folder that is inside a parent folder.

subheading   A lower-level heading (e.g. Heading 2) indicating a subpart of a top-level heading. Word automatically maps subheading text styles onto heading levels in Outline View

subtotal   Inner row added to a list (not an additional record) to show summary function (sum, average, count, etc.) of a subset of records -- e.g., the total population of the ten most populous states, then the total for the next ten, etc.

Sum   Returns unweighted sum of a range of cells. This is the default action of the AutoSum tool.

Synchronous Scrolling   Split-screen scrolling, where two different views of a document scroll at the same time when either view receives a scroll command.

synoptic   The synoptic version of a document contains edits and comments from all contributors across all versions.

syntax   Rules for structure in a language, e.g., Word will not be able to use a field code unless it's written with the proper syntax.

System Tray   An area of the desktop app that contains a Notification Area, Action Center, network access indicator, speaker volume control, and access to a calendar and clock.

T

tab bar   Line of clickable tabs (e.g., File, Design) above the Ribbon; click each to reveal its associated command groups.

tab stop   The destination of the cursor each time Tab is pressed – if none are manually inserted, Word defaults to left-justified tab stops every 0.5".

Table   the most important and foundational object in an Access database. Tables store data in records and fields, which correspond to rows and columns, respectively. The data is usually about a particular category of things, such as employees or orders.

Table of Figures   List of images in a document, analogous to Table of Content. Generated with References > Insert Table of Figures.

Table Style   Bundled border/fill/font settings, selected from the Table Tools > Design > Table Styles gallery. Table Styles alter slightly when Table Style settings are changed.

Table Style options   Settings that tie the Style of a table to its format/purpose –for instance, enabling the Total Row option for a table would highlight the last horizontal line of cells, indicating its use as an aggregation of data rather than a single record.

tabular data   Information presented in the form of a matrix or table.

Task Manager   A system utility which displays all the running applications and processes, as well as displays a list of CPU and memory usage for each app and background process.

Taskbar   Upsed to display buttons that represent apps that can be opened and apps that are already running.

Tasks   An activity that needs to be completed with a specific start date and due date but no location.

template   Pre-built Office file with space for user data and customization. Ctrl+S creates a new file based on the template, rather than saving over the template itself.

template library   Microsoft's online collection of templates, accessible from the Backstage area

Term   Definition

text attributes   Formatting parameters for text, e.g., boldface, underline, etc.

text box   A type of object containing formatted text, which "floats" above, below, or in line with the text layer. Allows the user to input text information to be used by the program

Text Pane (SmartArt)   The Text Pane attached to a piece of SmartArt holds the structured text (bulleted list) that provides the SmartArt's raw data. Updating the Text Pane automatically updates the SmartArt.

Text Style   Set of text characteristics (font, color, alignment, top/bottom spacing, etc.) bundled together for reuse throughout a document. To create consistent headings, for instance, define a Heading 1 style once, then apply it to every top-level heading in the document.

Theme   A predefined set of background images, colors, sounds, and screen savers used to personalize your user desktop. Bundles together fonts, colors, visual effects into a coherent visual aesthetic.

Theme Colors   Also known as color scheme. A set of colors chosen to work pleasingly together, used as default colors for visual elements in the document.

Thumbnails   reduced-size versions of pictures, used to help in recognizing and organizing them, serving the same role for images as a normal text.

Tiles   Squares or rectangles on the Start Screen that represent the apps that you can run on your computer.

Title bar   The bar at the top of a window, that usually displays the app's name and the name of the document that is currently open

title slide   Standard first slide layout, included with each of PowerPoint's built-in themes.

To Do bar   A task bar containing links to current Outlook items and events that need to be dealt with.

Tooltip   Informational popup that appears, by default, when the mouse pointer hovers over Ribbon commands and other interface elements. Useful for discovering keyboard

Track Changes   When enabled, Word stores a "baseline" document version and highlights edits to the baseline, allowing the user to accept or reject those edits, and to compare/combine versions of the document.

transition   Full-slide animation that transforms one PowerPoint slide into the next.

U

Unpinning   removing a tile from the Start screen or Desktop task bar.

V

values   Numbers used in calculations.

variant   Alternate version of document theme with different color scheme but same structure/layout.

vertical axis   Also known as y-axis. Generally indicates magnitude (vs. categories/items on x-axis).

W

Web app database   was introduced with Access 2013. This new type of database can be built from Access, and then used and shared with others as a SharePoint app in a web browser. You create the app by selecting the type of data you want to track (contacts, tasks, projects, and so on), and Access makes the database structure, complete with views that let you add and edit data.

Web Content   Information that is viewed in a web browser

What–If Analysis   Set of tools for changing cell values to see their effect on formula outputs.

widescreen   Movie-style slide aspect ratio, with 16:9 proportions (width:height) rather than the standard 4:3.

Windows legacy apps   apps associated with earlier versions of windows that run on the Desktop app such as Wordpad, Calculator, Notepad, and Paint.

Windows Update   Microsoft's update utility which comes with Windows 8 and allows you to automatically download and install important updates for Windows 8 and other Microsoft programs, such as Microsoft Office.

WinKey   The Windows logo key on your keyboard, used for shortcuts.

Wizard   Guided, step-by-step approach to complex tasks in Office; essentially a user-friendly front end. User answers questions to provide Office necessary information to carry out a task, e.g., a mail merge.

Word Wrap   Text wraps around to a new line when it's too long to display in the given space; a "paragraph" is actually a single long line, wrapped one or more times.

WordArt   Tool to apply visual effects and styling to text in Office documents. WordArt styles are distinct from normal font/style options.

workbook   A regular Excel file, consisting of one or more worksheets.

workbook protection   Locks the structure of a workbook, with or without password protection.

worksheet   A "spreadsheet" -- rows and columns of data in tabular form.

wrap   Break a long text line into multiple shorter lines, preserving them as a single paragraph object.

WYSIWYG   "What You See Is What You Get": describes applications in which the user works directly with an approximation of final print output. As opposed to working with raw text (code) to generate styled output. Office apps are WYSIWYG.

Index

Photo Credits for Lesson Opener Images

Unit 1: Microsoft Windows 8
Lesson 1, pages 3 and 4: ©webphotographeer/iStockPhoto
Lesson 2, pages 25 and 26: ©Livingpix/iStockPhoto
Lesson 3, pages 57 and 58: ©sasimoto/iStockPhoto
Lesson 4, pages 93 and 94: ©TommL/iStockPhoto
Lesson 5, pages 137 and 138: ©Blend_Images/iStockPhoto

Unit 2: Internet Explorer & the Web
Lesson 1, pages 175 and 176: ©iPandastudio/iStockPhoto
Lesson 2, pages 211 and 212: ©Mutlu Kurtbas/iStockPhoto

Unit 3: Microsoft Word 2013
Lesson 1, pages 253 and 254: ©jldeines/iStockPhoto
Lesson 2, pages 271 and 272: ©a-wrangler/iStockPhoto
Lesson 3, pages 287 and 288: ©studiocasper/iStockPhoto
Lesson 4, pages 303 and 304: ©mbrowe/iStockPhoto
Lesson 5, pages 327 and 328: ©Juanmonino/iStockPhoto
Lesson 6, pages 349 and 350: ©SunforRise/iStockPhoto
Lesson 7, pages 367 and 368: ©Pgiam/iStockPhoto
Lesson 8, pages 381 and 382: ©GlobalStock/iStockPhoto

Unit 4: Microsoft Excel 2013
Lesson 1, pages 393 and 394: ©catenarymedia/iStockPhoto
Lesson 2, pages 413 and 414: ©LawrenceSawyer/iStockPhoto
Lesson 3, pages 445 and 446: ©Vasko/iStockPhoto
Lesson 4, pages 479 and 480: ©MorePixels/iStockPhoto
Lesson 5, pages 509 and 510: ©RBFried/iStockPhoto
Lesson 6, pages 539 and 540: ©cmcderm1/iStockPhoto
Lesson 7, pages 565 and 566: ©Devonyu/iStockPhoto
Lesson 8, pages 583 and 584: ©miflippo/iStockPhoto

Unit 5: Microsoft PowerPoint 2013
Lesson 1, pages 625 and 626: ©kzenon/iStockPhoto
Lesson 2, pages 645 and 646: ©MichaelDeLeon/iStockPhoto
Lesson 3, pages 663 and 664: ©Anna Bryukhanova/iStockPhoto
Lesson 4, pages 681 and 682: ©mstay/iStockPhoto
Lesson 5, pages 701 and 702: _human ©/iStockPhoto
Lesson 6, pages 721 and 722: ©sturti/iStockPhoto

Unit 6: Microsoft Outlook 2013
Lesson 1, pages 745 and 746: ©mediaphotos/iStockPhoto
Lesson 2, pages 769 and 770: ©mediaphotos/iStockPhoto